Portrait of

America

PORTRAIT OF AMERICA

SEVENTH EDITION

VOLUME II

*From Reconstruction
to the Present*

STEPHEN B. OATES

University of Massachusetts, Amherst

HOUGHTON MIFFLIN COMPANY   BOSTON   NEW YORK

Again, for Greg and Stephanie with my love

Sponsoring editor   Jeffrey Greene
Senior project editor   Rosemary Winfield
Production/design coordinator   Jennifer Waddell
Senior manufacturing coordinator   Sally Culler
Marketing manager   Sandra McGuire

Printed in the U.S.A.
Library of Congress Catalog Card Number: 98-72072
ISBN: 0-395-90078-6
    6789-DH-02 01 00

CONTENTS

The traditional view of Reconstruction, popularized in *Gone with the Wind* and *The Birth of a Nation,* portrayed the period as a "blackout of honest" government in which treacherous Radicals tried to put black people on top in Dixie and turned the region over to hordes of carpetbaggers, scalawags, and "ignorant" Negroes who "stole the South blind." The foremost Reconstruction scholar of our time describes how the new view of Reconstruction, which emerged full force in the 1960s, exposed the racist assumptions of the old interpretation and made President Andrew Johnson and unrepentant southern whites the real villains. Instead of being a misguided experiment in extremism, Reconstruction accomplished many positive things, but ultimately failed because it was not radical enough.

An eminent and prolific historian of the Civil War and Reconstruction era challenges the traditional view of the carpetbaggers as a bunch of Yankee rogues who came South to form coalitions with the Negroes and scalawags (southern Republicans) in order to make money from political corruption. Current argues that the most numerous and most significant carpetbaggers were ambitious, energetic men who "brought their saving or their borrowings to invest, who eventually got into politics for idealistic as well as selfish reasons, and who in office behaved no better and no worse than most of their contemporaries."

A knowledgeable and insightful portrait of the great holy man and warrior of the buffalo-hunting Lakota. Sitting Bull's life serves as a window to what happened to the Plains Indians when they collided with a rapacious, acquisitive invader with superior military power.

Thanks to the efforts of irrepressible Esther McQuigg Morris, the first woman in the world to hold the office of justice of the peace,

and the U.S. bid for empire. They also draw significant parallels between the Filipino war and the war in Vietnam six decades later.

revolutionized American technology. His mass-produced cars not only made Americans more mobile but also created a culture of leisure. According to Nash, the key to Ford himself was his ambivalence: he looked forward and backward at the same time, defending his technology while extolling the values of the era it supplanted.

The Nineteenth Amendment gave women the right to vote, but they still faced insurmountable prejudice and discrimination against them in American politics. Perry argues that a "new office-seeking female leadership" should have emerged in the twenties, but none did so because men were determined to keep women in separate and subordinate political roles. Accommodating themselves to "a reality they could not control," veteran female leaders accepted the idea of operating politically within their own "gender sphere." Perry examines how that affected the careers of four famous suffragists, including Anna Eleanor Roosevelt.

Eight months after President Hoover proclaimed that poverty in America was almost eliminated, the country plunged into the worst depression in its history. Textbooks explain in detail the economic reasons for the crash of 1929 and the ensuing Depression, but none captures the human suffering and the failure of early relief efforts better than Watkins's prize-winning *The Great Depression,* a companion to the popular PBS television series, from which this selection is excerpted.

Hamby offers a convincing reassessment of Franklin Roosevelt and the New Deal. Although FDR was strongly influenced by the Progressive tradition, Hamby says, progressivism provided no guidelines for dealing with economic disaster. Therefore the flexible Roosevelt opted for a strategy of action that borrowed from Progressive doctrines, added some experimentation, threw in some Keynesian economics, and produced a New Deal reform program that created "a political economy of countervailing powers." FDR's "final legacy," Hamby believes, was his creation of a new political tradition that defined American politics as pluralistic, liberal, and international.

through the fireball of destruction. The personal details that inform this sensitive account make the unbelievable imaginable.

PREFACE

Like its predecessors, the Seventh Edition of this anthology stresses the human side of history, suggesting how the interaction of people and events shaped the course of the American past. I chose selections for *Portrait of America* that make history live and that were written for students, not for professional historians. The essays, narratives, and biographical portraits gathered here humanize American history, portraying it as a story of real people who actually lived, who struggled, enjoyed triumphs, suffered failures and anxieties, just like people in our own time. I hope that the anthology is an example of humanistic history at its best, the kind that combines scrupulous and engaging scholarship with a compelling narrative style. Since college survey audiences are not professional ones, they might enjoy reading history if it is presented in an exciting and readable form.

There is another reason why students find *Portrait of America* edifying: it showcases the writings of some of America's most eminent historians. The prizes their work has won testify to their important places in the galaxy of American letters. Eric Foner's outstanding new study of Reconstruction received the Bancroft Prize and the Francis Parkman Prize of the Society of American Historians. Richard N. Current has garnered the Bancroft Prize, the O. Max Gardner Prize, and the George Bante Award. Arthur M. Schlesinger Jr. has won two Pulitzer Prizes, two National Book Awards, the Gold Medal Award of the American Institute of Arts and Letters, the Francis Parkman Prize, and the Bancroft Prize. James Mac-Gregor Burns has received the Pulitzer Prize, plus the National Book Award and the Francis Parkman Prize. David McCullough has won the National Book Award and the Pulitzer Prize. Paul Fussell has received the National Book Award, the National

Book Critics Circle Award, and the Ralph Waldo Emerson Award. T. H. Watkins has won the National Book Award, the Los Angeles Times Book Award, and the Robert Marshall Award; and Elisabeth Perry has been a Senior Fellow of the National Endowment for the Humanities. Many of the other contributors have also received significant literary and scholarly awards. Thus *Portrait of America* offers readers a unique opportunity to learn from a lineup of nationally recognized historians and writers.

The Seventh Edition of Volume II has been extensively revised and features eleven new selections:

- Eric Foner's brilliant essay on the new view of Reconstruction;
- Richard N. Current's trenchant reassessment of the carpetbaggers of the Reconstruction era;
- Dee Brown's account of how women first won the right to vote in Wyoming Territory and later in several Western states;
- Sean Dennis Cashman's account of "the Negro protest movement" and the great debate between Booker T. Washington and W.E.B. Du Bois;
- Paul Fussell's unforgettable description of the horrors of trench warfare in the Great War of 1914–1918;
- Elisabeth Perry's discussion of why suffrage for women did not make them equal partners with men in American political life;
- T. H. Watkins's haunting account of the human suffering and the failure of relief efforts in the early years of the Great Depression;
- Charles Cawthon's cogent and highly original discussion of how the Normandy landing in 1944 marked "the final, pivotal point" in America's march to global power;
- Robert James Maddox's provocative argument

that the U.S. had to drop the atomic bomb in order to end the war with Japan;

• David McCullough's sparkling portrait of Harry Truman, the tough little man from Missouri;

• Otto Friedrich's judicious and even-handed account of the triumphs and failures of Richard Nixon;

• Peter Schweizer's analysis of how the Reagan administration contributed to the fall of the Soviet Union and the end of the Cold War.

The Seventh Edition retains the best and most popular selections of the previous editions. Even so, I have revised the introductions to several of them. I hope that *Portrait of America* remains as balanced as ever, for it offers samplings of virtually every kind of history—men's and women's, black and white, social and cultural, political and military, urban and economic, national and local—so that students can appreciate the rich diversity of the American experience.

Portrait of America contains several important features that help students learn from its contents. Each selection is preceded by a glossary that identifies important individuals, events, and concepts that appear in the reading. Introductions set the selections in proper context and suggest ways to approach studying them. They also tie all the selections together so that they can be read more or less as connected episodes. Study questions following the selections raise significant issues and encourage students to make comparisons and contrasts between the selections. The questions also help students review the readings and suggest points for class discussion.

The anthology is intended for use largely in college survey courses. It could be utilized as a supplement to a textbook or to a list of paperback readings. Or it could serve as the basic text. The book is organized into fifteen parts according to periods or themes; each part contains two or three related selections. This organization allows readers to make comparisons and contrasts between different events or viewpoints.

The Seventh Edition could not have been assembled without the help of others. My talented assistant, Karl Anderson, not only helped me choose the new selections, but helped me write the glossaries and the study questions for the new pieces and the synopses of the selections for the Table of Contents. Since he is an undergraduate history major, he proved to be invaluable in assessing whether a potential selection was suitable for students in college survey courses. My former assistants, Anne-Marie Taylor and Professor Karen Smith of the University of Emporia, and Professor Betty L. Mitchell of the University of Massachusetts, Dartmouth, wrote the study questions for other selections. I want to thank the following professors for reviewing one or both volumes:

John Duke, Alvin Community College
Jan S. Weaver, Texas A & M University–
  Kingsville
Andrew D. May, Emory University
Brian Lister, University of Maine at Farmington

S. B. O.

Portrait of

America

RECONSTRUCTION:
"A SPLENDID FAILURE"

1

The New View of Reconstruction

ERIC FONER

"Whatever you were taught or thought you knew about the post–Civil War era is probably wrong in the light of recent study." So went the editorial comment in the issue of American Heritage *in which "The New View of Reconstruction" originally appeared. If you think that Reconstruction was a tragic time when fanatical Radicals like Old Thad Stevens and Charles Sumner took control of Reconstruction away from a moderate Andrew Johnson, sought to "put the colored people on top" in the conquered South, and turned it over to hordes of roguish carpetbaggers, traitorous scalawags, and ignorant and uppity Negroes who "stole the south blind," you will be in for a surprise. The new interpretation of Reconstruction, which broke full force in the 1960s, cast President Andrew Johnson and unrepentant southern whites as the real villains of the drama. It argues that Reconstruction, instead of being a misguided experiment in extremism, was in fact not nearly radical enough. The new view of the postwar years, and the story of how it replaced the traditional interpretation, is the subject of this selection by Eric Foner, today's foremost historian of the Reconstruction era.*

To place his essay in historical context, it would be well to review the attitudes of southern blacks and whites as the war drew to a close, and to describe Johnson's reconstruction policy. For the deeply religious slaves, the Civil War had had profound religious meaning. Hundreds of thousands of them, writes historian Vincent Harding, "believed unswervingly that their God moved in history to deliver his people, and they had been looking eagerly, praying hourly, waiting desperately for the glory of the coming of the Lord. For them, all the raucous, roaring guns of Charleston Harbor and Bull Run, and Antietam and Fort Pillow, of Shiloh and Murfreesboro and Richmond were the certain voice of God, announcing his judgment across the bloody stretches of the South."

During the course of the war, African Americans believed, God did deliver them. With the Confederacy's collapse, as one song went, "slavery chain done broke at last."

> *Slavery chain done broke at last!*
> *Broke at last! Broke at last!*
> *Slavery chain done broke at last!*
> *Gonna praise God till I die!*

Some reacted to their liberation with cautious elation. When a young Virginia woman heard her former masters weeping over the capture of Jefferson Davis, she went down to a spring alone and cried out, "Glory, glory, hallelujah to Jesus! I's free! I's free!" Suddenly afraid, she looked about. What if the white folks had heard her? But seeing no one, she fell to the ground and kissed it, thanking "Master Jesus" over and over. For her, freedom meant hope — hope that she could find her husband and four children who had been sold to a slave trader.

Others celebrated their liberation in public. In Athens, Georgia, they danced around a liberty pole; in Charleston, they paraded through the streets. Many African Americans, however, were wary and uncertain. "You're joking me," one man said when the master told him he was free. He asked some neighbors if they were free also. "I couldn't believe we was all free alike," he said. Some African Americans, out of feelings of obligation or compassion, remained on the home place to help their former masters. But others were hostile. When a woman named Cady heard that the war was over, she decided to protest the cruel treatment she had suffered as a slave. She threw down her hoe, marched up to the big house, found the mistress, and flipped her dress up. She told the white woman, "Kiss my ass!"

For Cady, for the young black woman of Virginia, for hosts of other African Americans, freedom meant an end to the manifold evils of slavery; it meant the right to say what they felt and go where they wanted. But what else did freedom mean to them? As black leaders of Charleston said, it meant that blacks should enjoy full citizenship, have the right to vote, and run for political office. It meant federal protection from their former masters lest they attempt to revive slavery. And it meant economic security in the form of land, so that the blacks could exercise self-help and be economically independent of their former masters.

If the end of the war was a time of profound hope for black Americans, it was a monumental calamity for most southern whites. By turns, they were angry, helpless, vindictive, resigned, and heartsick. Their cherished South was not just defeated; it was annihilated. The South's major cities were in ruins, railroads and industry desolated, commerce paralyzed, and two-thirds of the assessed wealth, including billions of dollars in slaves, destroyed. As one historian says, "Many [white southerners] were already grieving over sons, plantations, and fortunes taken by war; losing their blacks was the final blow." Some masters shot or hanged African Americans who proclaimed their freedom. That was a harbinger of the years of Reconstruction, for most white southerners were certain that their cause had been just and were entirely unrepentant about fighting against the Union. A popular ballad captured the mood in postwar Dixie:

> Oh, I'm a good ole Rebel, now that's just what I am
> For this fair land of freedom I do not care a damn.
> I'm glad I fit against it, I only wish't we'd won
> And I don't want no pardon for nothin' what I done. . . .

> I hates the Yankee nation and everything they do
> I hates the Declaration of Independence too
> I hates the glorious Union, 'tis dripping with our blood
> And I hate the striped banner, I fit it all I could. . . .

> I can't take up my musket and fight 'em now no mo'
> But I ain't gonna love 'em and that is certain sho'
> And I don't want no pardon for what I was and am
> And I won't be reconstructed and I don't care a damn.

In Washington, Republican leaders were jubilant in victory and determined to deal firmly with southern whites in order to preserve the fruits of the war. But what about the new president, Andrew Johnson? A profane, hard-drinking Tennessee Democrat who bragged about his plebeian origins, Johnson had been the only southern senator to oppose secession openly. He had sided with the Union, served as war governor of Tennessee, and became Lincoln's running mate in 1864, on a Union ticket comprising both Republicans and War Democrats. As a result of the assassination of Lincoln, Johnson was now president, and he faced one of the most difficult tasks ever to confront an American chief executive: how to bind the nation's wounds, preserve African American freedom, and restore the southern states to their proper places in the Union.

Lincoln had contemplated an army of occupation for the South, thinking that military force might be necessary to protect the former slaves and prevent the old southern leadership from returning to power. Now there was such an army in the South: some 200,000 Union troops had moved in to restore order there and to perform whatever reconstruction duties Johnson might ask of them.

Initially, Republican leaders were hopeful about Johnson, for in talking about his native region he seemed tough, even uncompromising. But as he set about restoring defeated Dixie, Johnson alarmed and then enraged congressional Republicans by adopting

4

a soft, conciliatory reconstruction policy. The president not only opposed granting blacks the right to vote but allowed former Confederates to return to power in the southern states. He stood by as they adopted black codes that reduced blacks to a virtual condition of peonage, and he hotly opposed congressional interference in the reconstruction process. He even urged southern states to reject the Fourteenth Amendment, pushed through Congress by the Republicans, which would protect southern blacks. The amendment would prevent the states from enacting laws that abridged "the privileges or immunities of citizens of the United States." I would also bar the states from depriving "any person of life, liberty, or property, without due process of law," or from denying any person the "equal protection of the law." Johnson did more than just oppose the amendment; he damned Republican leaders like Charles Sumner of Massachusetts and Thaddeus Stevens of Pennsylvania, calling them tyrants and traitors. He even campaigned against the Republican party in the 1866 off-year elections. As a consequence, he alienated moderate as well as radical Republicans, who soon united against him. When the 1866 elections gave the Republicans huge majorities in both houses of Congress, they took control of Reconstruction and set about reforming the South themselves, enfranchising the freedmen and giving them the right to vote and hold office.

This gives you the proper historical background for Foner's lucid and judicious essay on the new view of Reconstruction and its leading participants. Foner concludes that Reconstruction was "a splendid failure," in that it did not resolve "the debate over the meaning of freedom in American life" and did not provide African Americans with the economic security they needed to be truly free in a capitalist country. Alas, that failure was to plague black Americans for generations to come. But for Foner, the "animating vision" of Reconstruction — an America in which all would enjoy "the right to rise," to go as far as their talent and toil would take them unimpeded by "inherited caste distinctions" — is profoundly relevant to a country "still grappling with the unresolved legacy of emancipation."

GLOSSARY

CARPETBAGGERS   Northerners, most of them former soldiers, who migrated to the South in search of economic opportunities.

DU BOIS, W. E. B.   Great black scholar and author of a seminal work, *Black Reconstruction in America* (1935), which offered "a monumental" reassessment of Reconstruction and damned the historical profession for adhering to the traditional racist interpretation of the era.

FREEDMEN'S BUREAU   Established by congressional statute in March 1865, the Bureau of Freedmen, Refugees, and Abandoned Lands was supposed to provide food and schools for the former slaves, help them secure jobs, and make certain they received fair wages.

FIFTEENTH AMENDMENT Adopted in 1870, it asserted that "the right of citizens of the United States to vote shall not be denied or abridged by the United States or by any State on account of race, color, or previous condition of servitude."

JOHNSON, ANDREW United States president, 1865–1869. Because he defied and obstructed congressional reconstruction measures, the Republican-controlled House of Representatives voted to impeach him, but the Senate failed to convict him by just one vote; it was the first and last attempt to impeach an American president for political reasons.

KU KLUX KLAN Southern white supremacist group organized in response to the Fifteenth Amendment; dressed in white sheets and hoods, Klansmen tried to prevent African Americans from voting by mob violence and other means of intimidation.

LAND DISTRIBUTION Proposal championed by a few Radical Republicans to confiscate the estates of ex-Confederates and distribute the land among the former slaves. Had that been done, Foner writes elsewhere, it "would have had profound consequences for Southern society, weakening the land-based economic and political power of the old ruling class, offering blacks a measure of choice as to whether, when, and under what circumstances to enter the labor market, and affecting the former slaves' conception of themselves." Land confiscation never happened because most Republicans thought it too bold a step and shrank from violating southern whites' property rights.

REDEEMERS Southern whites who overthrew Republican rule in the southern states, thus "redeeming" them.

SCALAWAGS Southern whites who became Republicans; they were "old line Whig Unionists who had opposed secession in the first place" or poor whites who had long resented the planters' rule.

STEVENS, THADDEUS Leading Radical Republican in the national House of Representatives, he was an idealistic reformer who demanded that blacks enjoy full rights as citizens and that former rebel lands be confiscated and distributed among the former slaves. He promoted the Fourteenth Amendment and was the major instigator of the 1867 Reconstruction Acts, which subjected the former Confederate states to military rule and granted universal male suffrage, which gave the freedmen the right to vote. He was also a major force in the impeachment trial of Andrew Johnson.

SUMNER, CHARLES One of the leading Radical Republicans in the U.S. Senate, he too was a committed idealist who advocated complete civil and political equality for African Americans. "More than any of his political contemporaries," writes his biographer, David Herbert Donald, "Sumner realized that the future of American democracy depended upon the ability of the white and black races to live together in peace and equity."

I n the past twenty years, no period of American history has been the subject of a more thoroughgoing reevaluation than Reconstruction — the violent, dramatic, and still controversial era following the Civil War. Race relations, politics, social life, and economic change during Reconstruction have all been reinterpreted in the light of changed attitudes toward the place of blacks within American society. If historians have not yet forged a fully satisfying portrait of Reconstruction as a whole, the traditional interpretation that dominated historical writing for much of this century has irrevocably been laid to rest.

Anyone who attended high school before 1960 learned that Reconstruction was an era of unrelieved sordidness in American political and social life. The martyred Lincoln, according to this view, had planned a quick and painless readmission of the Southern states as equal members of the national family. President Andrew Johnson, his successor, attempted to carry out Lincoln's policies but was foiled by the Radical Republicans (also known as Vindictives or Jacobins). Motivated by an irrational hatred of Rebels or by ties with Northern capitalists out to plunder the South, the Radicals swept aside Johnson's lenient program and fastened black supremacy upon the defeated Confederacy. An orgy of corruption followed, presided over by unscrupulous Carpetbaggers (Northerners who ventured south to reap the spoils of office), traitorous scalawags (Southern whites who cooperated with the new governments for personal gain), and the ignorant and childlike freedmen, who were incapable of properly exercising the political power that had been thrust upon them. After much needless suffering, the white community of the South banded together to overthrow

these "black" governments and restore home rule (their euphemism for white supremacy). All told, Reconstruction was just about the darkest page in the American saga.

Originating in anti-Reconstruction propaganda of Southern Democrats during the 1870s, this traditional interpretation achieved scholarly legitimacy around the turn of the century through the work of William Dunning and his students at Columbia University. It reached the larger public through films like *Birth of a Nation* and *Gone With the Wind* and that best-selling work of mythmaking masquerading as history, *The Tragic Era* by Claude G. Bowers. In language as exaggerated as it was colorful, Bowers told how Andrew Johnson "fought the bravest battle for constitutional liberty and for the preservation of our institutions ever waged by an Executive" but was overwhelmed by the "poisonous propaganda" of the Radicals. Southern whites, as a result, "literally were put to the torture" by "emissaries of hate" who manipulated the "simple-minded" freedmen, inflaming the Negroes' "egotism" and even inspiring "lustful assaults" by blacks upon white womanhood.

In a discipline that sometimes seems to pride itself on the rapid rise and fall of historical interpretations, this traditional portrait of Reconstruction enjoyed remarkable staying power. The long reign of the old interpretation is not difficult to explain. It presented a set of easily identifiable heroes and villains. It enjoyed the imprimatur of the nation's leading scholars. And it accorded with the political and social realities of the first half of this century. This image of Reconstruction helped freeze the mind of the white South in unalterable opposition to any movement for breaching the ascendancy of the Democratic party, eliminating segregation, or readmitting disfranchised blacks to the vote.

Nevertheless, the demise of the traditional interpretation was inevitable, for it ignored the testimony of the central participant in the drama of Reconstruction — the black freedman. Furthermore, it was

From Eric Foner, "The New View of Reconstruction," American Heritage, vol. 34, no. 6 (October/November, 1983), pp. 1–15. Reprinted by permission of *American Heritage* magazine, a division of Forbes, Inc. Copyright © Forbes, Inc., 1983.

grounded in the conviction that blacks were unfit to share in political power. As Dunning's Columbia colleague John W. Burgess put it, "A black skin means membership in a race of men which has never of itself succeeded in subjecting passion to reason, has never, therefore, created any civilization of any kind." Once objective scholarship and modern experience rendered that assumption untenable, the entire edifice was bound to fall.

The work of "revising" the history of Reconstruction began with the writings of a handful of survivors of the era, such as John R. Lynch, who had served as a black congressman from Mississippi after the Civil War. In the 1930s white scholars like Francis Simkins and Robert Woody carried the task forward. Then, in 1935, the black historian and activist W. E. B. Du Bois produced *Black Reconstruction in America*, a monumental reevaluation that closed with an irrefutable indictment of a historical profession that had sacrificed scholarly objectivity on the altar of racial bias. "One fact and one alone," he wrote, "explains the attitude of most recent writers toward Reconstruction; they cannot conceive of Negroes as men." Du Bois's work, however, was ignored by most historians.

It was not until the 1960s that the full force of the revisionist wave broke over the field. Then, in rapid succession, virtually every assumption of the traditional viewpoint was systematically dismantled. A drastically different portrait emerged to take its place. President Lincoln did not have a coherent "plan" for Reconstruction, but at the time of his assassination he had been cautiously contemplating black suffrage. Andrew Johnson was a stubborn, racist politician who lacked the ability to compromise. By isolating himself from the broad currents of public opinion that had nourished Lincoln's career, Johnson created an impasse with Congress that Lincoln would certainly have avoided, thus throwing away his political power and destroying his own plans for reconstructing the South.

The Radicals in Congress were acquitted of both vindictive motives and the charge of serving as the stalking-horses of Northern capitalism. They emerged instead as idealists in the best nineteenth-century reform tradition. Radical leaders like Charles Sumner and Thaddeus Stevens had worked for the rights of blacks long before any conceivable political advantage flowed from such a commitment. Stevens refused to sign the Pennsylvania Constitution of 1838 because it disfranchised the state's black citizens; Sumner led a fight in the 1850s to integrate Boston's public schools. Their Reconstruction policies were based on principle, not petty political advantage, for the central issue dividing Johnson and these Radical Republicans was the civil rights of freedmen. Studies of congressional policy-making, such as Eric L. McKitrick's *Andrew Johnson and Reconstruction*, also revealed that Reconstruction legislation, ranging from the Civil Rights Act of 1866 to the Fourteenth and Fifteenth Amendments, enjoyed broad support from moderate and conservative Republicans. It was not simply the work of a narrow radical faction.

Even more startling was the revised portrait of Reconstruction in the South itself. Imbued with the spirit of the civil rights movement and rejecting entirely the racial assumptions that had underpinned the traditional interpretation, these historians evaluated Reconstruction from the black point of view. Works like Joel Williamson's *After Slavery* portrayed the period as a time of extraordinary political, social, and economic progress for blacks. The establishment of public school systems, the granting of equal citizenship to blacks, the effort to restore the devastated Southern economy, the attempt to construct an interracial political democracy from the ashes of slavery, all these were commendable achievements, not the elements of Bowers's "tragic era."

Unlike earlier writers, the revisionists stressed the active role of the freedmen in shaping Reconstruction. Black initiative established as many schools as did Northern religious societies and the Freedmen's Bureau. The right to vote was not simply thrust upon them by meddling outsiders, since blacks began agitating for the suffrage as soon as they were freed. In 1865 black conventions throughout the South issued eloquent, though unheeded, appeals for equal civil and political rights.

With the advent of Radical Reconstruction in 1867, the freedmen did enjoy a real measure of political power. But black supremacy never existed. In most states blacks held only a small fraction of political offices, and even in South Carolina, where they comprised a majority of the state legislature's lower house, effective power remained in white hands. As for corruption, moral standards in both government and private enterprise were at low ebb throughout the nation in postwar years — the era of Boss Tweed, the Credit Mobilier scandal, and the Whiskey Ring. Southern corruption could hardly be blamed on former slaves.

Other actors in the Reconstruction drama also came in for reevaluation. Most carpetbaggers were former Union soldiers seeking economic opportunity in the postwar South, not unscrupulous adventurers. Their motives, a typically American amalgam of humanitarianism and the pursuit of profit, were no more insidious than those of Western pioneers. Scalawags, previously seen as traitors to the white race, now emerged as "Old Line" Whig Unionists who had opposed secession in the first place or as poor whites who had long resented planters' domination of Southern life and who saw in Reconstruction a chance to recast Southern society along more democratic lines. Strongholds of Southern white Republicanism like east Tennessee and western North Carolina had been the scene of resistance to Confederate rule throughout the Civil War; now, as one scalawag newspaper put it, the choice was "between salvation at the hand of the Negro or destruction at the hand of the rebels."

At the same time, the Ku Klux Klan and kindred groups, whose campaign of violence against black and white Republicans had been minimized or excused in older writings, were portrayed as they really were. Earlier scholars had conveyed the impression that the Klan intimidated blacks mainly by dressing as ghosts and playing on the freedmen's superstitions. In fact, black fears were all too real: the Klan was a terrorist organization that beat and killed its political opponents to deprive blacks of their newly won rights. The complicity of the Democratic party and the silence of prominent whites in the face of such outrages stood as an indictment of the moral code the South had inherited from the days of slavery.

By the end of the 1960s, then, the old interpretation had been completely reversed. Southern freedmen were the heroes, the "Redeemers" who overthrew Reconstruction were the villains, and if the era was "tragic," it was because change did not go far enough. Reconstruction had been a time of real progress and its failure a lost opportunity for the South and the nation. But the legacy of Reconstruction — the Fourteenth and Fifteenth Amendments — endured to inspire future efforts for civil rights. As Kenneth Stampp wrote in *The Era of Reconstruction*, a superb summary of revisionist findings published in 1965, "If it was worth four years of civil war to save the Union, it was worth a few years of radical reconstruction to give the American Negro the ultimate promise of equal civil and political rights."

As Stampp's statement suggests, the reevaluation of the first Reconstruction was inspired in large measure by the impact of the second — the modern civil rights movement. And with the waning of that movement in recent years, writing on Reconstruction has undergone still another transformation. Instead of seeing the Civil War and its aftermath as a second American Revolution (as Charles Beard had), a regression into barbarism (as Bowers argued), or a golden opportunity squandered (as the revisionists saw it), recent writers argue that Radical Recon-

Black legislators in the South Carolina House of Representatives are voting on an appropriation bill in 1873. African Americans had a majority in the lower house, yet "effective power," as Eric Foner writes, remained in white hands." (North Wind Picture Archives)

struction was not really very radical. Since land was not distributed to the former slaves, they remained economically dependent upon their former owners. The planter class survived both the war and Reconstruction with its property (apart from slaves) and prestige more or less intact.

Not only changing times but also the changing concerns of historians have contributed to this latest reassessment of Reconstruction. The hallmark of the past decade's historical writing has been an emphasis upon "social history" — the evocation of the past lives of ordinary Americans — and the downplaying of strictly political events. When applied to Recon-struction, this concern with the "social" suggested that black suffrage and officeholding, once seen as the most radical departures of the Reconstruction era, were relatively insignificant.

Recent historians have focused their investigations not upon the politics of Reconstruction but upon the social and economic aspects of the transition from slavery to freedom. Herbert Gutman's influential study of the black family during and after slavery found little change in family structure or relations between men and women resulting from emancipation. Under slavery most blacks had lived in nuclear

In 1871, members of the North Carolina Ku Klux Klan discuss the murder of another victim. As Foner points out, the Klan was a terrorist organization that beat and killed its political opponents to deprive blacks of their newly won rights." (North Wind Picture Archives)

thority and control over their own day-to-day lives shaped the black response to emancipation.

In the post–Civil War South the surest guarantee of economic autonomy, blacks believed, was land. To the freedmen the justice of a claim to land based on their years of unrequited labor appeared self-evident. As an Alabama black convention put it, "The property which they [the planters] hold was nearly all earned by the sweat of *our* brows." As Leon Litwack showed in *Been in the Storm So Long*, a Pulitzer Prize–winning account of the black response to emancipation, many freedmen in 1865 and 1866 refused to sign labor contracts, expecting the federal government to give them land. In some localities, as one Alabama overseer reported, they "set up claims to the plantation and all on it."

In the end, of course, the vast majority of Southern blacks remained propertyless and poor. But exactly why the South, and especially its black population, suffered from dire poverty and economic retardation in the decades following the Civil War is a matter of much dispute. In *One Kind of Freedom*, economists Roger Ransom and Richard Sutch indicted country merchants for monopolizing credit and charging usurious interest rates, forcing black tenants into debt and locking the South into a dependence on cotton production that impoverished the entire region. But Jonathan Wiener, in his study of postwar Alabama, argued that planters used their political power to compel blacks to remain on the plantations. Planters succeeded in stabilizing the plantation system, but only by blocking the growth of alternative enterprises, like factories, that might draw off black laborers, thus locking the region into a pattern of economic backwardness.

family units, although they faced the constant threat of separation from loved ones by sale. Reconstruction provided the opportunity for blacks to solidify their preexisting family ties. Conflicts over whether black women should work in the cotton fields (planters said yes, many black families said no) and over white attempts to "apprentice" black children revealed that the autonomy of family life was a major preoccupation of the freedmen. Indeed, whether manifested in their withdrawal from churches controlled by whites, in the blossoming black fraternal, benevolent, and self-improvement organizations, or in the demise of the slave quarters and their replacement by small tenant farms occupied by individual families, the quest for independence from white au-

If the thrust of recent writing has emphasized the social and economic aspects of Reconstruction, politics has not been entirely neglected. But political studies have also reflected the postrevisionist mood summarized by C. Vann Woodward when he observed "how essentially nonrevolutionary and conservative Reconstruction really was." Recent writers, unlike their revisionist predecessors, have found little to praise in federal policy toward the emancipated blacks.

A new sensitivity to the strength of prejudice and laissez-faire ideas in the nineteenth-century North has led many historians to doubt whether the Republican party ever made a genuine commitment to racial justice in the South. The granting of black suffrage was an alternative to a long-term federal responsibility for protecting the rights of the former slaves. Once enfranchised, blacks could be left to fend for themselves. With the exception of a few Radicals like Thaddeus Stevens, nearly all Northern policy-makers and educators are criticized today for assuming that, so long as the unfettered operations of the marketplace afforded blacks the opportunity to advance through diligent labor, federal efforts to assist them in acquiring land were unnecessary.

Probably the most innovative recent writing on Reconstruction politics has centered on a broad reassessment of black Republicanism, largely undertaken by a new generation of black historians. Scholars like Thomas Holt and Nell Painter insist that Reconstruction was not simply a matter of black and white. Conflicts within the black community, no less than divisions among whites, shaped Reconstruction politics. Where revisionist scholars, both black and white, had celebrated the accomplishments of black political leaders, Holt, Painter, and others charge that they failed to address the economic plight of the black masses. Painter criticized "representative colored men," as national black leaders were called, for failing to provide ordinary freedmen with effective political leadership. Holt found that black officeholders in South Carolina mostly emerged from the old free mulatto class of Charleston, which shared many assumptions with prominent whites. "Basically bourgeois in their origins and orientation," he wrote, they "failed to act in the interest of black peasants."

In emphasizing the persistence from slavery of divisions between free blacks and slaves, these writers reflect the increasing concern with continuity and conservatism in Reconstruction. Their work reflects a startling extension of revisionist premises. If, as has been argued for the past twenty years, blacks were active agents rather than mere victims of manipulation, then they could not be absolved of blame for the ultimate failure of Reconstruction.

Despite the excellence of recent writing and the continual expansion of our knowledge of the period, historians of Reconstruction today face a unique dilemma. An old interpretation has been overthrown, but a coherent new synthesis has yet to take its place. The revisionists of the 1960s effectively established a series of negative points: the Reconstruction governments were not as bad as had been portrayed, black supremacy was a myth, the Radicals were not cynical manipulators of the freedmen. Yet no convincing overall portrait of the quality of political and social life emerged from their writings. More recent historians have rightly pointed to elements of continuity that spanned the nineteenth-century Southern experience, especially the survival, in modified form, of the plantation system. Nevertheless, by denying the real changes that did occur, they have failed to provide a convincing portrait of an era characterized above all by drama, turmoil, and social change.

Building upon the findings of the past twenty years of scholarship, a new portrait of Reconstruction ought to begin by viewing it not as a specific time period, bounded by the years 1865 and 1877, but as an episode in a prolonged historical process — American society's adjustment to the consequences of the Civil War and emancipation. The Civil War, of course, raised the decisive questions of America's national existence: the relations between local and national authority, the definition of citizenship, and the balance between force and consent in generating obedience to authority. The war and Reconstruction, as Allan Nevins observed over fifty years ago, marked the "emergence of modern America." This was the era of the completion of the national railroad network, the creation of the modern steel industry, the conquest of the West and final subduing of the Indians, and the expansion of the mining frontier. Lincoln's America — the world of the small farm and artisan shop — gave way to a rapidly industrializing economy. The issues that galvanized postwar Northern politics — from the question of the greenback currency to the mode of paying holders of the national debt — arose from the economic changes unleashed by the Civil War.

Above all, the war irrevocably abolished slavery. Since 1619, when "twenty negars" disembarked from a Dutch ship in Virginia, racial injustice had haunted American life, mocking its professed ideals even as tobacco and cotton, the products of slave labor, helped finance the nation's economic development. Now the implications of the black presence could no longer be ignored. The Civil War resolved the problem of slavery but, as the Philadelphia diarist Sydney George Fisher observed in June 1865, it opened an even more intractable problem: "What shall we do with the Negro?" Indeed, he went on, this was a problem "*incapable* of any solution that will satisfy both North and South."

As Fisher realized, the focal point of Reconstruction was the social revolution known as emancipation. Plantation slavery was simultaneously a system of labor, a form of racial domination, and the foundation upon which arose a distinctive ruling class within the South. Its demise threw open the most fundamental questions of economy, society, and politics. A new system of labor, social, racial, and political relations had to be created to replace slavery.

The United States was not the only nation to experience emancipation in the nineteenth century. Neither plantation slavery nor abolition were unique to the United States. But Reconstruction was. In a comparative perspective Radical Reconstruction

stands as a remarkable experiment, the only effort of a society experiencing abolition to bring the former slaves within the umbrella of equal citizenship. Because the Radicals did not achieve everything they wanted, historians have lately tended to play down the stunning departure represented by black suffrage and officeholding. Former slaves, most fewer than two years removed from bondage, debated the fundamental questions of the polity: What is a republican form of government? Should the state provide equal education for all? How could political equality be reconciled with a society in which property was so unequally distributed? There was something inspiring in the way such men met the challenge of Reconstruction. "I knew nothing more than to obey my master," James K. Greene, an Alabama black politician, later recalled. "But the tocsin of freedom sounded and knocked at the door and we walked out like free men and we met the exigencies as they grew up, and shouldered the responsibilities."

"You never saw a people more excited on the subject of politics than are the negroes of the south," one planter observed in 1867. And there were more than a few Southern whites as well who in these years shook off the prejudices of the past to embrace the vision of a new South dedicated to the principles of equal citizenship and social justice. One ordinary South Carolinian expressed the new sense of possibility in 1868 to the Republican governor of the state: "I am sorry that I cannot write an elegant stiled letter to your excellency. But I rejoice to think that God almighty has given to the poor of S.C. a Gov. to hear to feel to protect the humble poor without distinction to race or color. . . . I am a native borned S.C. a poor man never owned a Negro in my life nor my father before me. . . . Remember the true and loyal are the poor of the whites and blacks, outside of these you can find none loyal."

Few modern scholars believe the Reconstruction governments established in the south in 1867 and

1868 fulfilled the aspirations of their humble constituents. While their achievements in such realms as education, civil rights, and the economic rebuilding of the South are now widely appreciated, historians today believe they failed to affect either the economic plight of the emancipated slave or the ongoing transformation of independent white farmers into cotton tenants. Yet their opponents did perceive the Reconstruction governments in precisely this way — as representatives of a revolution that had put the bottom rail, both racial and economic, on top. This perception helps explain the ferocity of the attacks leveled against them and the pervasiveness of violence in the postemancipation South.

The spectacle of black men voting and holding office was anathema to large numbers of Southern whites. Even more disturbing, at least in the view of those who still controlled the plantation regions of the South, was the emergence of local officials, black and white, who sympathized with the plight of the black laborer. Alabama's vagrancy law was a "dead letter" in 1870, "because those who are charged with its enforcement are indebted to the vagrant vote for their offices and emoluments." Political debates over the level and incidence of taxation, the control of crops, and the resolution of contract disputes revealed that a primary issue on Reconstruction was the role of government in a plantation society. During presidential Reconstruction, and after "Redemption," with planters and their allies in control of politics, the law emerged as a means of stabilizing and promoting the plantation system. If Radical Reconstruction failed to redistribute the land of the South, the ouster of the planter class from control of politics at least ensured that the sanctions of the criminal law would not be employed to discipline the black labor force.

An understanding of this fundamental conflict over the relation between government and society helps explain the pervasive complaints concerning corruption and "extravagance" during Radical Reconstruction. Corruption there was aplenty; tax rates did rise sharply. More significant than the rate of taxation, however, was the change in its incidence. For the first time, planters and white farmers had to pay a significant portion of their income to the government, while propertyless blacks often escaped scot-free. Several states, moreover, enacted heavy taxes on uncultivated land to discourage land speculation and force land onto the market, benefiting, it was hoped, the freedmen.

As time passed, complaints about the "extravagance" and corruption of Southern governments found a sympathetic audience among influential Northerners. The Democratic charge that universal suffrage in the South was responsible for high taxes and governmental extravagance coincided with a rising conviction among the urban middle classes of the North that city government had to be taken out of the hands of the immigrant poor and returned to the "best men" — the educated, professional, financially independent citizens unable to exert much political influence at a time of mass parties and machine politics. Increasingly the "respectable" middle classes began to retreat from the very notion of universal suffrage. The poor were no longer perceived as honest producers, the backbone of the social order; now they became the "dangerous classes," the "mob." As the historian Francis Parkman put it, too much power rested with "masses of imported ignorance and hereditary ineptitude." To Parkman the Irish of the Northern cities and the blacks of the South were equally incapable of utilizing the ballot: "Witness the municipal corruptions of New York, and the monstrosities of negro rule in South Carolina." Such attitudes helped to justify Northern inaction as, one by one, the Reconstruction regimes of the South were overthrown by political violence.

In the end, then, neither the abolition of slavery nor Reconstruction succeeded in resolving the debate over the meaning of freedom in American life. Twenty years before the American Civil War, writing about the prospect of abolition in France's colonies, Alexis de Tocqueville had written, "If the Negroes have the right to become free, the [planters] have the incontestable right not to be ruined by the Negroes' freedom." And in the United States, as in nearly every plantation society that experienced the end of slavery, a rigid social and political dichotomy between former master and former slave, an ideology of racism, and a dependent labor force with limited economic opportunities all survived abolition. Unless one means by freedom the simple fact of not being a slave, emancipation thrust blacks into a kind of no-man's land, a partial freedom that made a mockery of the American ideal of equal citizenship.

Yet by the same token the ultimate outcome underscores the uniqueness of Reconstruction itself. Alone among the societies that abolished slavery in the nineteenth century, the United States, for a moment, offered the freedmen a measure of political control over their own destinies. However brief its sway, Reconstruction allowed scope for a remarkable political and social mobilization of the black community. It opened doors of opportunity that could never be completely closed. Reconstruction transformed the lives of Southern blacks in ways unmeasurable by statistics and unreachable by law. It raised their expectations and aspirations, redefined their status in relation to the larger society, and allowed space for the creation of institutions that enabled them to survive the repression that followed. And it established constitutional principles of civil and political equality that, while flagrantly violated after Redemption, planted the seeds of future struggle.

Certainly, in terms of the sense of possibility with which it opened, Reconstruction failed. But as Du Bois observed, it was a "splendid failure." For its animating vision — a society in which social advancement would be open to all on the basis of individual merit, not inherited caste distinctions — is as old as America itself and remains relevant to a nation still grappling with the unresolved legacy of emancipation.

QUESTIONS TO CONSIDER

1   What was the traditional view of Reconstruction? On what racial and political assumptions was it based? When and why did this view end?

2   What is the new view of Reconstruction? Who are the heroes and the villains in the new scenario? What activities, in the new view, shaped the black response to emancipation? Explain why more recent writers have faulted federal policy toward the liberated blacks. How was their criticism of federal policy different from the criticism of that policy by the traditional Reconstruction historians? Why do some recent writers argue that Radical Reconstruction was not nearly radical enough?

3   What social forces spawned white terrorist groups like the Ku Klux Klan during Reconstruction? What was the purpose of such groups? Why would a white person want to join them?

4   What did historian Alan Nevins mean when he declared that the Civil War and Reconstruction marked "the emergence of modern America"?

5   How does Foner define the plantation-slavery system? Did emancipation and the war destroy all facets of the system?

6   At the end of his essay, Foner quotes W. E. B. Du Bois that Reconstruction was "a splendid failure." How was it splendid? How was it a failure?

2

A New Look at the Carpetbaggers

RICHARD N. CURRENT

The carpetbagger — a northerner who moved to the South after the Civil War — is one of the most maligned and misunderstood players in the drama of Reconstruction. The traditional view portrays the carpetbagger as corrupt and dishonest Yankee who went south after Congress's Reconstruction Acts of 1867 divided the region into military districts and granted political rights to the freedmen. The carpetbaggers, in the old view, entered southern politics, formed coalitions with Negroes and scalawags ("traitorous" southerners who became Republicans), and proceeded to "steal the South blind."

While admitting that there were scoundrels and political tramps among the carpetbaggers, Richard N. Current, an eminent and prolific historian of the Civil War and Reconstruction era, challenges the old view that the whole class of carpetbaggers was evil and predatory. A revisionist like Eric Foner, the author of the preceding selection, Current finds that most carpetbaggers were "men of substance" — civilians and former Union soldiers who went south before 1867, intending to settle in the region, not steal it blind. For them, the South was a new frontier, like the West, where dreams of a prosperous and pleasant new life could be realized. The carpetbaggers became southern businessmen and planters as well as politicians. While some of the last named were guilty of misgovernment and corruption, many others were honest and capable. Because they "disturbed the relations between the races" by favoring Negro political rights, the carpetbaggers earned the undying hatred of native southern whites. Current concludes that the most numerous and most significant carpetbaggers were ambitious, energetic men who "brought their savings or their borrowings to invest, who eventually got into politics for idealistic as well as selfish reasons, and who in office behaved no better and no worse than most of their contemporaries.

GLOSSARY

CLAYTON, POWELL Carpetbag governor of Arkansas who had owned a plantation there since the end of the Civil War.

FREEDMEN Former slaves who, instead of being passive recipients of freedom, agitated from the start of Reconstruction for full citizenship and the right to vote.

MORGAN, ALBERT T. AND CHARLES Brothers who moved from Wisconsin to Mississippi, where they invested about $50,000 in lumbering and planting enterprises.

RED SHIRTS Military clubs of southern white Democrats who, armed with rifles and revolvers, sought to intimidate African Americans and break up Republican meetings.

TOURGÉE, ALBION W. Ohio man who moved to North Carolina and invested $5,000 in a nursery business.

UNION LEAGUES Organized by agents of the Freedmen's Bureau and by Federal soldiers, these organizations sought to win the allegiance of the freedmen to the Republican party.

WARNER, WILLARD Ohio legislator who moved to Alabama in 1868, was elected to the national senate from that state, and bought land with the idea of making an economic career in the South, which he eventually did.

WHITE LEAGUES Organized in 1874 in Louisiana, they were "Ku Klux without the disguise and secrecy," as one historian described them. They claimed to have formed to preserve the white race and to protect themselves against the "Republican alliances" in the state. In New Orleans, they were "organized, drilled and militant bodies."

The story of the postbellum South is often told as if it were a morality play or a television melodrama. The characters personify Good or Evil, and they are so clearly identified that there is no mistaking the "good guys" and the "bad guys." One of the villains, who deserves the boos and hisses he is sure to get, is the carpetbagger. As usually portrayed, this contemptible Yankee possesses as little honor or intelligence as he does property, and he possesses so little property that he can, quite literally, carry all of it with him in a carpetbag. He is attracted southward by the chance for power and plunder that he sees when the vote is given to southern Negroes and taken from some of the southern whites by the Reconstruction Acts of 1867. Going south in 1867 or after, he meddles in the politics of places where, as a mere roving adventurer, he has no true interest. For a time he and his kind run the southern states. At last, when the drama ends, Good has triumphed over Evil, and the carpetbagger has got his comeuppance. But he leaves behind him a trail of corruption, misgovernment, and lastingly disturbed race relations.

That picture may seem an exaggeration, a caricature. If so, it nevertheless has passed for a long time as a true, historical likeness, and it continues to pass as such. A standard dictionary defines *carpetbagger* as a term of contempt for northern men who went south "to seek private gain under the often corrupt reconstruction governments." Another dictionary, based on "historical principles," contains this definition: "One of the poor northern adventurers who, carrying all their belongings in carpetbags, went south to profit from the social and political upheaval after the Civil War." A recent textbook refers to "the Radical carpetbaggers who had poured into the

Reprinted by permission of Louisiana State University Press, from Richard N. Current, "Carpetbaggers Reconsidered," in Kenneth M. Stampp and Leon F. Litwack (eds.), *Reconstruction: An Anthology of Revisionist Writings*. Copyright © 1969 by Louisiana State University Press.

The old view of Reconstruction, as Richard N. Current says, portrayed the carpetbagger as "a contemptible Yankee" who "possesses as little honor or intelligence as he does property, and he possesses so little property that he can, quite literally, carry all of it with him in a carpetbag. He is attracted southward by the chance for power and plunder." Current's essay disputes this traditional view. (Corbis-Bettmann)

defeated section after the passage of the First Reconstruction Act of March, 1867." The prevailing conception, then, is that these men were late arrivals who waited till the Negro was given the suffrage and who then went off with their carpetbags, cynically, to take advantage of the colored vote.

Even those who hold that view concede that "a few were men of substance, bent on settling in the South," and that some of them took up residence there before the passage of the Reconstruction Acts. With respect to men of this kind, however, the question has been raised whether they should be considered carpetbaggers at all. Many of the northerners active in Mississippi politics after 1867, the historian of Reconstruction in that state observes, had arrived as would-be planters before 1867. "It is

incorrect, therefore to call them 'carpet baggers,'" this historian remarks. "They did not go South to get offices, for there were no offices for them to fill. The causes which led them to settle there were purely economic, and not political." Thus the brothers Albert T. and Charles Morgan, when they moved from Wisconsin to Mississippi, "came not as carpetbaggers," for they brought with them some $50,000, which they invested in planting and lumbering enterprises (and lost). And the much better-known figure Albion W. Tourgée, who moved from Ohio to North Carolina, was perhaps no carpetbagger, either, for he took with him $5,000 which he put into a nursery business (and also lost).

Now, suppose it could be demonstrated that, among the northern politicians in the South during Reconstruction, men essentially like the Morgans and Tourgée were not the few but the many, not exceptional but fairly typical. Suppose that the majority moved to the South before 1867, before the establishment of the "corrupt reconstruction governments," and hence for reasons other than to seek private gain or political power under such governments. One of two conclusions must follow. Either we must say that true carpetbaggers were much fewer and less significant than has been commonly supposed, or we must seek a new definition of the word.

In redefining it, we should consider the actual usage on the part of southerners during the Reconstruction period. We may learn something of its denotation as well as its connotation if we look at the way they applied it to a specific person: the one-time Union army officer Willard Warner, of Ohio and Alabama.

Warner might seem, at first glance, to exemplify the latecomer rising immediately in southern politics, for he completed his term in the Ohio legislature and was elected to the United States Senate from Alabama in the same year, 1868. But he was not really a new arrival. He had visited Alabama and, with a partner, had leased a plantation there in the fall of 1865. He bought land in the state the next year, and he spent most of the spring and summer of

1866 and most of the autumn and winter of 1867–68 on his Alabama land. He intended to make an economic career in the South (and indeed he was eventually to do so).

At first, Warner had no trouble with his Alabama neighbors. "A Northern man, who is not a fool, or foolish fanatic," he wrote from his plantation in the spring of 1866, "may live pleasantly in Alabama, without abating one jot of his self-respect, or independence." At one time or another, as he was to testify later, the leading Democrats of the state, among them ex-Confederate General James H. Clanton, came to him and said: "General, when we talk about carpetbaggers we want you to understand that we don't mean you; you have come here and invested what means you had in property here, and you have the same interest there that we have."

The Alabamans changed their attitude toward Warner when he was elected to office with Negro support. Afterwards (1871) General Clanton himself explained:

If a man should come here and invest $100,000, and in the next year seek the highest offices, by appealing to the basest prejudices of an ignorant race, we would call him a political carpet-bagger. But if he followed his legitimate business, took his chances with the rest, behaved himself, and did not stir up strife, we would call him a gentleman. General Warner bought land; I fixed some titles for him, and I assured him that when men came there to take their chances with us for life, we would take them by the hand. But we found out his designs. Before his seat in Ohio got cold, he was running the negro machine among us to put himself in office.

Another Alabama Democrat, from Huntsville, in the area where Warner had bought land, elaborated further upon the same theme in testifying before a congressional committee, as follows:

Question: You have used the epithets "carpet-bagger" and "scalawag" repeatedly . . . give us an accurate definition.

Answer: Well, sir, the term carpet-bagger is not applied to northern men who came here to settle in the South, but a carpet-bagger is generally understood to be a man who comes here for office sake, of an ignorant or bad character, and who seeks to array the negroes against the whites; who is a kind of political dry-nurse for the negro population, in order to get office through them.

Question: Then it does not necessary suppose that he should be a northern man?

Answer: Yes, sir; it does suppose that he is to be a northern man, but it does not apply to all northern men that come here.

Question: If he is an intelligent, educated man, and comes here for office, then he is not a carpet-bagger, I understand?

Answer: No, sir; we do not generally call them carpet-baggers.

Question: If he is a northern man possessed of good character and seeks office he is not a carpet-bagger?

Answer: Mr. Chairman, there are so few northern men who come here of intelligence and character, that join the republican party and look for office alone to the negroes, that we have never made a class for them. . . . They stand *sui generis*. . . . But the term "carpet-bagger" was applied to the office-seeker from the North who comes here seeking office by the negroes, by arraying their political passions and prejudices against the white people of the community.

Question: The man in addition to that, under your definition, must be an ignorant man and of bad character?

Answer: Yes, sir; he is generally of that description. We regard any man as a man of bad character who seeks to create hostility between the races. . . .

Question: Having given the definition of the carpet-bagger, you may now define scalawag.

Answer: A scalawag is his subservient tool and accomplice, who is a native of the country.

So far as these two Alabamans were concerned, it obviously made no difference whether a northerner came before 1867 or after, whether he brought with him and invested thousands of dollars or was penniless, whether he was well educated or illiterate, or whether he was of good or bad character in the ordinary sense. He was, by definition, a carpetbagger and a man of ignorant and bad character if he, at any time, encouraged political activity on the part of the Negroes and thus arrayed the blacks against the whites, that is, the Republicans against the Democrats. He was not a carpetbagger if he steered entirely clear of politics or if he consistently talked and voted as a Democrat or Conservative.

This usage was not confined to Alabama; it prevailed throughout the South. To speak of "economic carpetbaggers," as historians sometimes do, is therefore rather hard to justify on a historical basis. Politics — Republican politics — was the distinguishing mark of the man whom the Democrats and Conservatives after 1867 dubbed a carpetbagger, and they called him by that name whether or not he had gone South originally for economic rather than political reasons. To speak of "Negro carpetbaggers" is also something of an anachronism. Colored men from the North did go south and enter politics, of course, but in the Reconstruction lexicon (with its distinction among carpetbaggers, scalawags, and Negroes) they were put in a category of their own. Northern-born or southern-born, the Negro was a Negro to the southern Conservatives, and they did not ordinarily refer to him as a carpetbagger. From contemporary usage, then, we derive the following as a non-valuational definition: the men called carpetbaggers were *white northerners who went south after the beginning of the Civil War and, sooner or later, became active in politics as Republicans.*

With this definition at hand, we can proceed to make at least a rudimentary survey of the so-called carpetbaggers as a group, in order to find out how well they fit the traditional concept with respect to their background. Let us consider first the state and local officeholders. There were hundreds of these people, and many of them left too few traces for us now to track them down. Studies have touched upon the subject in some of the states, and though fragmentary, these studies at least suggest that most of the men

under consideration do not conform to the stereotype.

In Arkansas the carpetbag governor (1868–72) Powell Clayton had owned and lived on a plantation since 1865. Many years later he was to gather data showing that the overwhelming majority of the so-called carpetbaggers, who were in office when he was, had arrived in Arkansas before 1867, and that the small minority who came as late as 1867 "did so when the Democrats were in full power, and before the officers to be elected or appointed, together with their salaries and emoluments, had been fixed by the [reconstructed] State Constitution." Clayton adds:

With a very few exceptions, the Northern men who settled in Arkansas came there with the Federal Army, and . . . were so much impressed with its genial climate and great natural resources as to cause them . . . to make it their future home. A number, like myself and my brother William, had contracted matrimonial ties. Many of them had been away from home so long as practically to have lost their identity in the States [from which they had come]. . . . These were the reasons that influenced their settlement in Arkansas rather than the existence of any political expectations.

That, of course, is *ex parte* testimony, from one of the carpetbaggers himself. Still, he supports his conclusion with ample and specific evidence.

And, with respect to some of the other states, southern historians have tended toward similar conclusions. In Alabama, says one of these historians, "many of the carpet-bag politicians were northern men who had failed at cotton planting." In Florida, says another, about a third of the forty-six delegates elected in 1867 to the state constitutional convention were white Republicans from the North. "Most of the Northerners had been in the state for a year or more and were *bona fide* citizens of the commonwealth." "As a class," they were "intellectually the best men among the delegates." In Mississippi, says a third, "the genuine 'carpet baggers' who came after the adoption of the reconstruction policy were comparatively few in number." The vast majority of the so-called carpet-baggers in Mississippi were men who had arrived earlier as planters.

Information is not available regarding all the carpet-bag officeholders in all the reconstructed states. What is needed, then, is information about a representative sample of such officeholders. A sample could be made of the carpetbag governors, of whom the total was nine. Eight of the nine arrived in the South before 1867. Two were officers of the Freedmen's Bureau, two were civilian officials of the federal government, and four were private enterprisers — two of them planters, one lawyer, and the other a minister of the gospel. The single late-comer, Adelbert Ames of Massachusetts and Mississippi, first appeared in Mississippi as a regular army officer and as a military governor, not as an adventurer in search of a political job.

A larger sample consists of the entire body of white northerners who during the Reconstruction period were elected as Republicans to represent southern constituencies in either branch of Congress. Altogether, there were about sixty-two of these men, seventeen in the Senate and forty-five in the House of Representatives. It is impossible to be absolutely precise in listing these congressional carpetbaggers. There were a few borderline cases where, for example, a man was born in the South but raised or educated in the North, and it is hard to know whether he should be classified as a northerner or not.

Of the sixty-two senators and congressmen, practically all were veterans of the Union army. That is not surprising, and it does not alter the accepted stereotype. More surprising, in view of the carpetbagger's reputation for "ignorant or bad character," is the fact that a large proportion were well educated. About two-thirds of the group (forty-three of the sixty-two) had studied law, medicine, or engineering enough to practice the profession, or had attended one or more years of college, or had been school teachers. Of the senators alone, approximately half were college graduates. Seemingly the academic and intellectual attainments of the carpetbaggers in

Congress were, on the whole, at least as high as those of the other members of Congress, whether from the North or from the South.

Still more significant is the fact that nearly five-sixths of the entire carpetbag group — fifty of the sixty-two — had arrived in the South before 1867, before the passage of the Reconstruction Acts, before the granting of political rights to the Negro. Of the fifty early arrivals, only fifteen appeared on the southern scene as Treasury Department employees, Freedmen's Bureau officials, or members of the post-war occupation forces (and at least a few of these fifteen soon left the government service and went into private enterprise). Thirty-five of the fifty were engaged in farming or business or the professions from the time of their arrival or soon after.

As for those other twelve of the sixty-two — the twelve who did not begin to live in the South until 1867 or later — more than half (at least seven) took up some private occupation before getting public office. Their comparatively late arrival does not, in itself, signify that they moved south merely for "office sake."

If, then, the sixty-two carpetbag congressmen and senators make up a representative sample, we must conclude that a majority of the carpetbaggers, taken as a whole, do not conform to the traditional view, at least so far as their backgrounds are concerned. With comparatively few exceptions, the so-called carpetbaggers had moved South for reasons other than a lust for offices newly made available by the passage of the Reconstruction Acts. These men were, in fact, a part of the multitude of Union officers and soldiers who, during or soon after the war, chose to remain in or return to the land they had helped to conquer.

To thousands of the young men in blue, at and after the war's end, the South beckoned as a land of wondrous charm, a place of almost magical opportunity. "Northern men are going to do well in every part of the South. The Southern men are too indolent to work and the Yankees are bound to win."

So, for example, a cavalry sergeant wrote from Texas to his sister back home in Ohio in 1866. "I have some idea that I will not remain in Ohio long, and maybe I will locate in the sunny South," he continued. "What think you of roses blooming in open air in November, and the gardens glorious with flowers."

Here, in the South, was a new frontier, another and a better West. Some men compared the two frontiers before choosing the southern one, as did the Morgan brothers, who first looked over Kansas and then decided upon Mississippi. Albert T. Morgan afterwards wrote that the former cry, "Go West, young man,: had been changed to "Go South, young man," and in 1865 the change was "already quite apparent, in the purpose of those of the North who were seeking new homes." Many years later Albion W. Tourgée recalled the hopes and dreams with which, in the fall of 1865, he had settled as a badly wounded veteran in Greensboro, North Carolina:

He expected the future to be as bright and busy within the conquered territory as it had been along the ever-advancing frontier of the West. . . . He expected the whole region to be transformed by the power of commerce, manufactures, and the incursion of Northern life, thought, capital, industry, and enterprise. . . . Because he thought he bore a shattered life he sought a milder clime. He took his young wife with him, and they builded their first home-nest almost before the smoke of battle disappeared. . . . His first object was restored health; his next desire, to share the general prosperity.

Once they had been released from the army, thousands of other Union soldiers and officers returned to the South with similar dreams of prosperity and a pleasant life. For the moment, land was cheap and cotton dear. Labor was abundant, and the Negroes were expected to work more willingly for their liberators than for their late masters. So the veterans turned South. At the end of 1865 a newsman from the North learned that, in Alabama alone, there were already five thousand of them "engaged in planting and trading." Even more than the uplands of Alabama, Tennessee, and Georgia, the Mississippi Valley was proving an "attraction to adventurous capital," this traveling reporter found. "Men from the Middle States and the great West were everywhere, buying and leasing plantations, hiring freedmen, and setting thousands of ploughs in motion." No impecunious wanderers were these, but bringers of "adventurous capital." They paid cash for lands or leases, for wages, for supplies. At a time when the South was languishing for money, these newcomers provided it, put it into circulation, and thus gave the economy a lift.

Most of those who thus adventured with their capital were to lose it. They failed for several reasons. At cotton planting the Yankees were novices, unused to local conditions and deluded in their expectations of the Negro as a free worker, or so the southerners said. Actually the southerners as well as the Yankees ran into economic difficulties during the first few years after the war. "Various causes have arisen to prostrate the people, leaving them nearly ruined," a contemporary observed early in 1867, "among which I may more especially mention the following, which could not have been foreseen or provided against: The too great drouth at one season, which destroyed and blasted their corn; too much rain at another season, which injured their cotton; and then the army worm, which came out of the ground in vast numbers, destroyed what was left." There was, besides, the federal cotton tax, which both northern and southern planters denounced as ruinous.

Often, whether as planters or as businessmen, the northerners faced a special disadvantage — the hostility of the people around them. "The rebels will not buy from a Galvanized Yankee, or Loyal Unionist, nor from a Yankee either," a Unionist Virginian complained late in 1865, "the result being that loyal or Northern merchants are failing all over the South." In many places the Yankees were boycotted if they sympathized with or voted for Republicans. "Only one hundred and one men were found base enough to vote for the Radical ticket," a Memphis newspaper reported in April, 1866. "We have held up the names of a portion of these men and written small pox over their doors in order that our people might shun them."

Discouraged and disillusioned after a year or two in their new homes, large numbers of the Yankees abandoned them and returned to the North. Others, of whom some were successful and some were not, remained in the South. Of those who remained, many turned to state and local politics as Republicans in 1867 or after. These comprised the majority of that class of men who eventually came to be known as carpetbaggers.

Before 1867 the northerners in the South possessed only limited opportunities in politics. As Republicans, they could not hope to be elected to office. As newcomers, they often found it difficult even to vote, because of the residence requirements. The Georgia constitution, as remade after the war, extended the residence requirement in that state from six months to two years. "Now it is generally admitted," a northern settler in Georgia protested, "that this change . . . has been effected to prevent loyal men who were obliged to leave here during the war and those who have come here since the war from having any voice in choosing the officers of the State and representatives to Congress." Of course, the newcomers could seek federal jobs, and many of them did so, but again they faced something of a handicap, for they understood that President Johnson preferred "Southern citizens" when "suitable persons" among them could be found.

To the northern settlers remaining in the South the congressional acts of 1867 suddenly brought political opportunity and also, as some of them saw it, political responsibility. Tourgée, for one, sought election to the new constitutional convention in North Carolina because, having failed in business and lost the savings he had brought, he needed the

money he would be paid as a delegate. But he sought election also because he was concerned about Negro rights and wished to do what he could to protect them. A more prosperous settler, a planter of Carroll Parish, Louisiana, who once had been an Ohio school superintendent, took an active interest in southern politics for reasons that he explained, in April, 1867, to Senator John Sherman:

On the closing of my services as a Soldier, I became a member of the firm of Lynch, Ruggles & Co., which was organized in Circleville, Ohio, for the purpose of buying lands in the South and planting. We have located at this point, which is 40 miles above Vicksburg, have purchased lands, have organized most efficient labor forces, & our investment now is on a scale which makes us on *that* account deeply interested in every effort made to bring peace to the South. . . .

I . . . respectfully ask your advice as to the proper course to be pursued by Northern men in the South who sympathize with Congress in the present crisis. . . . I have never held a civil office and never intended to, if I can avoid it; but we have a large force at work, have their confidence, and now as they are voters, they look to our advice, and I want to give it as wisely as possible. Other Northern men are similarly situated. . . .

The position of some of these other northern men was later recalled by C. M. Hamilton, a Pennsylvanian who had gone to Florida in 1864, as a Freedmen's Bureau agent, and had become after 1867 one of the most prominent carpetbaggers of that state. In 1871 he told a congressional committee investigating the Ku Klux Klan:

. . . when the reconstruction acts first passed Congress, the Yankees, as we are called, most of us soldiers who were in the South, rather stood back, did not really feel at that time that they [we] had any particular right to interfere in politics, or to take part in them. But the reconstruction laws were passed; reconstruction was necessary; . . . the democratic party of the South adopted the policy of masterly inactivity . . . ; there was a new element here that had been enfranchised who were without leaders. The northern men in the South, and there were but a handful of them in this State, who had been in the Army, took hold of this matter of reconstruction, and they have perfected it so far as it has been accomplished.

These northerners, already in the South in 1867, felt they had a right and a duty to be where they were and to do what they did. They were Americans. They had fought a war to keep the nation one. South as well as North, it was *their* country. They had chosen to live in the southern part of it. This was now their home, and they had a stake in its future as well as the future of the country as a whole. Their attitude should be quite understandable — as understandable as the feeling of the majority of southern whites.

Naturally, the native Conservatives and Democrats resented the northern Republicans and reviled them with such epithets as "aliens," "birds of passage," and "carpetbaggers." As applied to most of the men, however, these were not objective and descriptive terms. The Union veterans who settled in the South were impelled by a variety and a mixture of motives: restlessness, patriotic idealism, the desire to get ahead, and what not. But so were the pioneers at other times and places in the United States. So were the southerners themselves who moved westward or northward during the Reconstruction period. At that time the newer states of the Southwest (such as Alabama, Mississippi, and especially Arkansas) were filled with fairly recent arrivals from the older states of the Southeast. And at that time there were more southerners residing in the North than northerners in the South. The latter were no more "birds of passage" than the former. Perhaps the frontiersman has been too much idealized for his propensity to rove. Certainly the carpetbagger has been too much condemned for the mere act of moving from one part of the country to another.

Even if all this be conceded, there remain of course the other elements of the carpetbagger stereo-type — the charges of misgovernment, corruption, and racial disturbance.

With regard to the charge of misgovernment and corruption, it is hard to generalize about the carpetbaggers as a class. Nevertheless, a few tentative observations may be made. First, the extent and duration of "carpetbag rule" has been exaggerated. In six of the eleven ex-Confederate states (Texas, Tennessee, Alabama, Georgia, Virginia, North Carolina) there was never a carpetbag governor; there was never a majority of carpetbaggers among the Republicans in or out of office; certainly there was never anything approaching carpetbagger domination of state politics. In all those states the Republicans held power only briefly if at all, and they held it, to the extent that they did so, by means of their strength among Negroes and scalawags. In the other five states (Arkansas, Mississippi, Louisiana, Florida, South Carolina) there were carpetbag governors part of the time, but even in these states the carpetbaggers could maintain themselves only with Negro and native white support. Second, the extent of illegal and illegitimate spending by the carpetbag governments has been exaggerated — if spending for schools, transportation, and other social and economic services be considered legitimate. Third, the improper spending, the private use of public funds, was by no means the work of carpetbaggers alone, nor were they the only beneficiaries: heavily involved also were native whites, including Conservatives and Democrats as well as scalawags. Fourth, probably the great majority of the carpetbaggers were no more corrupt than the great majority of contemporary officeholders throughout the United States.

Consider the carpetbag governors, who are generally mentioned as the most conspicuous examples of dishonesty. One of them, Joseph Brooks of Arkansas, did not succeed in exercising uncontested power, for either good or evil, and was soon ousted. Two of the governors, R. K. Scott of South Carolina and W. P. Kellogg of Louisiana, are rather difficult to defend. Four others — Powell Clayton of Arkansas, Harrison

Reed and M. L. Stearns of Florida, and H. C. Warmoth of Louisiana — were loudly accused but never really proved guilty of misusing their offices for private profit. Only one of the four, Warmoth, seems actually to have made much money while in Reconstruction politics, and he made a fortune. While governor, he admitted that there was "a frightful amount of corruption" in Louisiana. He explained, however, that the temptation came from the business interests who offered bribes, and he insisted that the Republicans, black as well as white, had resisted bribery as well as had the Democrats. It might be more true to say that Louisiana corrupted Warmoth (if indeed he was corrupted) than to say that Warmoth corrupted Louisiana. The other two carpetbag governors, Adelbert Ames of Mississippi and D. H. Chamberlain of South Carolina, were economy-minded and strictly honest.

There remains the charge that the carpetbaggers disturbed the relations between the races in the South. Of course, the carpetbaggers did so. Their doing so was the basic cause of the animus against them. This is the reason why the honest ones among them, the men likes Ames and Chamberlain and Warner, were as thoroughly hated and as strongly opposed as were any of the Yankee scoundrels. Most of the southern whites opposed the granting of political rights to the former slaves. The carpetbaggers encouraged the Negroes to exercise such rights. Thus the carpetbaggers upset the pattern of race relationships, the pattern of Negro passivity, which most white southerners considered ideal.

The party struggle in the postwar South amounted to something more than ordinary politics. In some of its aspects it was equivalent to a continuation, or a renewal, of the Civil War.

On the one hand, southern Conservatives thought of themselves as still fighting for home rule and white supremacy — in essence much the same war aims as the Confederacy had pursued. Carpetbaggers, on the other hand, saw their own basic objective as the reunification of the country, which had been in-

completely won at Appomattox, and as the emancipation of the Negroes, who had been partially freed by the adoption of the Thirteenth Amendment.

On both sides the methods frequently were those of actual, though irregular, warfare. The Ku Klux Klan, the White League, the Red Shirts, and the various kinds of rifle companies were military or semi-military organizations. So, too, were the state militias, the Union Leagues and Loyal Leagues, and the other partisan institutions of the carpetbaggers and their Negro allies. The carpetbaggers served, so to speak, as officers of frontline troops, deep in enemy territory, "on the picket line of freedom in the South." The embattled Republicans undoubtedly suffered much heavier casualties than did their foes.

True, the Republicans had the advantage of support by the regular United States Army, but often that support was more a potentiality than a fact, and at critical moments it failed to materialize. As for the warriors of white supremacy, they had the backing of northern sympathizers in strength and numbers that would have gladdened the heart of Jefferson Davis in that earlier war time when he was angling for the aid of the Knights of the Golden Circle. The carpetbaggers were divided and weakened by the Republican party schism of 1872, by personal rivalries among themselves, and by jealousies between them and their Negro and scalawag associates. Finally, as some of the carpetbaggers saw it, they were stabbed in the back — abandoned by the government and the people at the North.

The history of this losing campaign has been written almost exclusively from the southern, or Democratic, or disillusioned Republican point of view: the story of the carpetbaggers has been told mainly by their enemies. Historical scholarship has given its sanction to the propaganda of the victorious side in the Reconstruction War. That propaganda, like most, has its elements of truth, and like most, its elements of distortion and downright falsehood. Not that the carpetbaggers were invariably the apostles of righteousness and truth. We would make little progress toward historical understanding if we merely took the same old morality play and switched the labels of Evil and Good. But surely the time has long since passed when we can, uncritically, accept the "carpetbagger" stereotype.

No doubt men can be found who fit it. No doubt there were political tramps who went South to make cynical use of the Negro vote and who contrived to win both office and illicit gain. But such men were few and comparatively unimportant. Far more numerous and more significant were those energetic and ambitious men who, with or without carpetbags, brought their savings or their borrowings to invest, who eventually got into politics for idealistic as well as selfish reasons, and who in office behaved no better and no worse then most of their contemporaries. Some of these men, like some others of their time, proved corrupt. It would be interesting to know whether, as peculators, the carpetbaggers took out more than a small fraction of the money that, as speculators, they had brought in.

QUESTIONS TO CONSIDER

1   What was the main cause of southern white animosity toward the carpetbaggers? Does this animosity explain why the carpetbaggers were so maligned in early histories of Reconstruction?

2   Does Current make a persuasive case in his reconsideration of the carpetbaggers? What evidence does he use to demonstrate that they were not, as a whole, the Yankee rogues that southern whites made them out to be?

3   Current observes that "the party struggle in the postwar South amounted to something more than ordinary politics. In some of its aspects it was equivalent to a continuation, or a renewal, of the Civil War." Do you agree with this statement? What was the outcome of this postwar struggle? How did these events affect U. S. history? Is this struggle over?

4   How do you think the term *carpetbagger* ought to be defined? Is a *carpetbagger* necessarily bad?

5   From what you have read in Foner's and Current's essays, do you think that Reconstruction was at all successful? In what ways did it succeed? In what ways did it fail? What is the legacy of Reconstruction for modern America?

CONQUEST OF THE WEST

3

Sitting Bull and the Sioux Resistance

ROBERT M. UTLEY

In the forty years after the Civil War, American pioneers conquered and exploited an immense inner frontier that lay between California and the Mississippi River. It was an area as diverse as it was expansive, a region of windy prairies, towering mountains, painted deserts, and awesome canyons. Heading east out of California or west from the Mississippi, Americans by the thousands poured into this great heartland, laying out cattle ranches and farms, building towns and mining camps, and creating a variety of local and state governments. People moved to the frontier for various reasons: to start a new life, seek glory and adventure, strike it rich in a single, fabulous windfall, and prevail over the West's challenging environment.

Still, the winning of the West was not all romance. Driven by the aggressive, exploitive imperatives of their culture, American pioneers — especially whites — infiltrated Indian lands and hunting grounds, and conflicts between settlers and Indians broke out all across the frontier line, thus opening a gruesome chapter in the westward movement after the Civil War. The fact was that white-dominated America tended to regard the Indians as savages who deserved violent treatment. If these "ignorant nomads" blocked the advance of Christian civilization across the West, they should be "removed." And so, terrible fights erupted whenever whites and Indians came into contact. Trying to reduce the violence, the government sent out additional federal troops, including several African American regiments; instead of enforcing existing treaties, the soldiers usually defended whites who violated the pacts, which only provoked the Indians all the more.

In 1867, the federal government decided to confine the Indians to small, remote reservations in areas of the West spurned by United States settlers. Herein lies a paradox, for the whites' handling of the Indians in the late 1860s contrasted sharply with the way they treated southern blacks. The Congress that approved the small reservation policy, with its philosophy of strict segregation and inequality for western Indians, was the same Congress that attempted to give African American men in the South political rights equal to those of white men.

But many Indian bands refused to surrender their ancient hunting grounds, refused to be herded onto reservations and made to "walk the white man's road," and they fought back tenaciously. None did so with more resolve than the warrior elements of the proud, buffalo-hunting Lakota (or Sioux) of the northern Plains, who united behind Sitting Bull and vowed to throw the white invaders out of Lakota country. Sitting Bull, the great holy man and war chief of the Hunkpapa Lakota, is the subject of the selection by Robert M. Utley, a distinguished historian and biographer of the American West. Based on his newly published biography, The Lance and the Shield: The Life and Times of Sitting Bull *(1993), Utley's essay affords rare insight into Lakota culture and what happened to it when it collided with a rapacious, acquisitive invader whose superior military power, forked tongue, and deadly diseases brought doom to Native Americans everywhere.*

As Utley points out, the government's small-reservation policy, which was implemented by treaties in 1868, split the Lakota into two camps. The agency Indians, under the leadership of Red Cloud of the Oglala Sioux, accepted reservation life and tried to adapt to it. The nonreservation Indians, headed by Sitting Bull, elected to fight the United States Army in a desperate attempt to save "the free life of old." Indeed, rising to the unprecedented position of head chief of all the Lakota, Sitting Bull assembled the most formidable Indian force in the West, one that on a hot June day in 1876 massacred George Armstrong Custer and 262 men of the United States Seventh Cavalry in the Battle of the Little Bighorn in Montana. But it was a Pyrrhic victory for the Lakota and their Cheyenne allies: in the fall, the army trapped them and compelled them to surrender. Sitting Bull escaped to Canada, and his followers ended up in out-of-the-way reservations in the Dakota Territory.

The other western tribes met the same fate. Overwhelmed by superior firepower and faced with starvation, because whites were exterminating the buffalo, the Indians' "commissary," the Native Americans had no choice but to abandon their way of life and submit to segregation on small reservations in the Dakotas, Oklahoma, New Mexico, Oregon, Idaho, and Montana. The federal government systematically obliterated Indian culture and tribal organization, placed the Indians on individual plots of land, and ordered them to become farmers and accept the culture of their conquerors. By 1890, thanks to generations of bloodletting and sickness, scarcely 200,000 Indians remained in the United States, compared with the 2 million Indians in North America at the time of the European discovery.

Meanwhile, Sitting Bull himself returned from Canada and surrendered to the military, which placed him on the Standing Rock Reservation as a prisoner of war. Here, as

Utley says, the Indian agent — a petty tyrant — attempted to destroy Sitting Bull's reputation among his incarcerated people. Yet the great Lakota war chief and holy man remained indomitable: he accepted schooling for his offspring but rejected all other government efforts to make Indians into "imitation whites."

Defeated and broken in spirit, many reservation Indians turned to religion for comfort in a hostile world. First the Indians of Nevada, then the Lakota and other Plains Indians took up the Ghost Dance, a sacred ritual that reaffirmed tribal unity and prophesied the return of the old days, when the buffalo would be plentiful again and the Indians would be free of the white invaders. Intimidated by such a "frightful conglomeration of rituals and customs," as one white put it, the United States government outlawed the Ghost Dance. But Sitting Bull and his people kept on dancing. Indeed, Sitting Bull became "the high priest of the religion at Standing Rock," which put him on a collision course with the Indian agent and his Lakota police. Utley recounts the violent, ironic climax to Sitting Bull's life and goes on to observe that he lost his struggle with white Americans, not because of any personal failing but because of "impersonal forces beyond his control or even his understanding." As you study Sitting Bull's life, the evolution of his three distinct personalities, and his tragic end, you might want to consider this question: Which do you think was the better way for the Indians to deal with the white invaders — the appeasement of Red Cloud, or the uncompromising resistance of Sitting Bull?

GLOSSARY

ARROW CREEK (Battle, August 13, 1872) Here Sitting Bull performed a feat of bravery that awed his followers: he seated himself and calmly smoked his pipe within range of the soldiers' guns.

BLACK HILLS (SOUTH DAKOTA) Sacred Lakota domain called Paha Sapa; goldminers invading the Black Hills helped ignite the Great Sioux War of 1876.

BROTHERTON, MAJOR DAVID H. Accepted Sitting Bull's surrender in 1881.

CRAZY HORSE An Oglala Lakota and the greatest of all the Sioux war chiefs, he also fought to drive the white invaders away and save the old ways.

CROW FOOT Sitting Bull's favorite son who died with him in the confrontation with Indian police in 1890.

CROWS Plains Indian tribe and traditional enemy of the Lakota.

FORT LARAMIE TREATY (1868) Set aside all of present-day South Dakota west of the Missouri River as the Great Sioux Reservation.

FOUR HORNS Sitting Bull's uncle who was wounded in the Battle of Killdeer Mountain.

GHOST DANCE RELIGION Begun by a Paiute messiah named Wovoca, the Ghost Dance movement swept the Plains Indians incarcerated on reservations; it prophesied the end of the white invaders and the return of the buffalo and all previous generations of Indians.

HUNKPAPA   Sitting Bull's division of the Lakota; the other six divisions were Miniconjou, Sans Arc, Two Kettle, Bruele, Oglala, and Blackfeet Sioux (not to be confused with the Blackfeet tribe that lived and hunted northwest of the Lakota).

KILLDEER MOUNTAIN (battle, July 28, 1864)   A "calamitous" defeat for the Lakota that pointed up the futility of the Indians' fighting an open battle with well-armed soldiers.

LONG KNIVES   Indian name for white soldiers armed with rifles and bayonets.

McLAUGHLIN, JAMES   Agent of the Standing Rock Lakota Reservation who tried to shape the Indians into "imitation whites" and to destroy Sitting Bull's reputation.

SULLY, GENERAL ALFRED   Commanded United States Army forces in the Battle of Killdeer Mountain.

SUN DANCE   The central ceremony in the sacred life of the Lakota; in it the dancers engaged in self-sacrifice and self-torture in order to gain the favor of the Great Mysterious and ensure a successful buffalo hunt.

WAKANTANKA   Lakota word for the Great Mysterious.

WICHASHA WAKAN   Lakota term for a holy man such as Sitting Bull.

Sitting Bull's fighting days ended on July 20, 1881, when he led his little band of faithful headmen into the cramped office of the commanding officer at Fort Buford, Dakota Territory. All were shabbily dressed and gaunt from the hunger of their Canadian exile. Sitting Bull, once the mightiest chief of the Lakota Sioux, wore a threadbare calico shirt and black leggings; a tattered, dirty blanket was loosely draped around his waist. Suffering a severe eye infection, he had tied a kerchief turbanlike around his head and drawn it partly across his eyes. Beneath, his dark seamed face with jutting nose and chin and perpetually downturned mouth registered both resignation and despair.

His men grouped behind him, the Sioux chief sat next to the blue-clad soldier chief. Placing his Winchester rifle beneath the chair, Sitting Bull drew to him his five-year-old son Crow Foot. Major David H. Brotherton opened the council by setting forth the terms on which the surrender would be received. In fact, they were no terms at all, since the U.S. government's adamant insistence on unconditional surrender had put off this day until starvation left no other recourse.

After the officer ceased speaking, Sitting Bull slumped in his chair, silent and glum. Brotherton invited him to speak. He sat motionless for five minutes — as if in a trance, thought one witness. He said a few words to his men, then gestured to Crow Foot, who picked up his father's rifle and handed it to the army officer. Then Sitting Bull spoke in words that the interpreter translated:

I surrender this rifle to you through my young son, whom I now desire to teach in this manner that he has become a friend of the Americans. I wish him to learn the habits of the whites and to be educated as their sons are educated. I

From Robert M. Utley, "Sitting Bull and the Sioux Resistance," *MHQ: The Quarterly Journal of Military History,* 5(4) (summer 1993), 48–53, 56–59. Reprinted by permission.

wish it to be remembered that I was the last man of my tribe to surrender my rifle. This boy has given it to you, and he now wants to know how he is going to make a living.

The ceremony at Fort Buford marked the end, at age fifty, of Sitting Bull's career as a warrior, war leader, and tribal war chief, a career that had begun at the age of fourteen, when he counted his first coup on a Crow Indian. He had achieved power and distinction in other fields, too — as a *wichasha wakan,* a holy man; as a band chief; and finally, a post unique in Sioux history, as supreme chief of all the Lakota tribes. His war honors and trophies, however, provided his greatest satisfaction. That he understood the tragic symbolism of giving up his rifle he betrayed in a song composed to connect what had been to what would be: A warrior / I have been / Now / It is all over / A hard time / I have.

What "had been" began in 1831 with Sitting Bull's birth into a distinguished family of the Hunkpapa tribe, one of the seven tribes of Teton or Lakota Sioux. A nomadic people, the Lakotas occupied the high plains between the Missouri River and the Bighorn Mountains while ranging north to the British possessions and south as far as the Platte and Republican rivers. Together, they numbered between 15,000 and 20,000 people. Other Sioux lived to the east — Yanktons and Yanktonais east of the Missouri River, and Dakotas, or Santees, in Minnesota.

At the age of fourteen, his name was not yet Sitting Bull but Jumping Badger, although his deliberate and willful ways had earned him the nickname Hunkesni, or "Slow." Much against his parents' counsel, Slow insisted on accompanying a war party of ten men striking westward from the Powder River in search of horses and scalps of the enemy Crow tribe. Unproven lads often tagged along on such expeditions as errand boys. They learned the ways of war without actually fighting.

On the third day out, crossing a divide, the party spotted a dozen mounted Crows gathered in conference beside a creek. Whooping and shouting, the Lakotas raced down the slope in a headlong charge. Startled, the Crows spread out to receive the attack. But one Crow spurred his horse to escape. Slow, mounted on a sturdy gray horse his father had given him, his naked body painted yellow from head to foot and hung with colorful strands of beads, shrieked a war cry and galloped in pursuit. The powerful gray swiftly overtook the quarry. Pulling abreast, Slow smashed his adversary with a tomahawk and knocked him from his mount. Another warrior hurried in to finish the act and count second coup. In fierce fighting, the Sioux killed all but four of the Crows, who fled the field.

In a jubilant ceremony at the home village, Slow donned his first white eagle feather, emblem of a first coup, and entered one of the world's most highly developed warrior societies. His mother presented him with the beaded, feathered lance that became his favorite offensive weapon. His father presented a shield bearing a sacred design that appeared to him in a dream. From his father also came his own name, to replace Slow and resonate in the history of not only the Sioux but their enemies as well: Tatanka-Iyotanka, Sitting Bull.

As Sitting Bull's adolescent years fell behind in the 1840s, he took on his adult build. With a heavy, muscular frame, a big chest, and a large head, he impressed people as short and stocky, although he stood five feet ten inches tall. His dark hair reached to his shoulders, often braided with otter fur on one side, hanging loose on the other. A severe part at the center of the scalp glistened with a heavy streak of crimson paint. A low forehead surmounted piercing eyes, a broad nose, and thin lips. Although dexterous afoot and superbly agile mounted, he was thought by some to be awkward and even clumsy.

In adulthood Sitting Bull developed into the Hunkpapa incarnate, the admired epitome of the four cardinal virtues of the Lakotas: bravery, fortitude, generosity, and wisdom. "There was something in Sitting Bull that everybody liked," one of his tribesmen recalled. "Children liked him because he was kind, the women because he was kind to the family and liked to settle family troubles. Men liked him because he was brave. Medicine men liked him because they knew he was a man they could consider a leader."

Sitting Bull evolved three distinct personalities. One was the superlative warrior and huntsman, adept at all the techniques of war and the hunt, boastful of his deeds, laden with honors and ambitious for more, celebrated and rewarded with high rank by his people. Another personality was the holy man, suffused with reverence and mysticism, communing constantly with Wakantanka, the Great Mysterious, dreaming sacred dreams and carrying out the rites and ceremonies they mandated, entreating for the welfare of his people, offering sacrifices ranging from a buffalo carcass to his own flesh. A third was the good tribesman, a man of kindness, generosity, and humility, unostentatious in dress and bearing, composer and singer of songs, a friend of children and old people, peacemaker, sportsman, gentle humorist, wise counselor, and leader. That he excelled in all three realms testified to uncommon merit.

The Lakota culture was hardly a generation old at the time of Sitting Bull's birth. Only around the beginning of the nineteenth century did the Lakotas become fully mounted on horses and begin to acquire guns. Horses and guns enabled them to seize and defend their rich hunting grounds, to follow the great migrating herds of buffalo that shaped their distinctive way of life, and by the middle of the nineteenth century to evolve into the proud and powerful monarchs of the northern Great Plains. Ironically, by furnishing the horses and guns, white people made possible the Lakota way of life; then, in less than a century, they destroyed it.

In the years of Sitting Bull's youth, the Hunkpapas had little conception of the white world. The only whites they knew were traders based at posts along the Missouri River. From them, or other tribes acting as intermediaries, came the horses and guns, along with other useful manufactures. Whites in substantial numbers lived 500 miles to the southeast; the Hunkpapas sensed no threat from them. Their hostility was reserved for enemy tribes such as the Crows, Flatheads, Assiniboines, and Arikaras.

By Sitting Bull's thirtieth birthday, however, the white world had begun to intrude alarmingly on the Hunkpapas. Treaty makers, government agents, and soldiers had begun to appear along the upper Missouri in the 1850s, and by the 1860s the menace had grown distressingly clear. Settlers fingered up the river valleys to the south. Emigrants bound for the gold mines of western Montana killed the buffalo and grazed their livestock on the choice grasses. The voracious boilers of the steamboats consumed the timber stands in the river valleys. The Hunkpapas began to add the whites to their list of enemies.

By this time Sitting Bull had participated in many war expeditions. These were usually limited both in objectives and in scale, though large-scale expeditions and pitched battles sometimes occurred. He had performed many feats of bravery that won the applause of his people and membership in the men's societies that played a major part in Lakota life. He became a war chief of the Hunkpapa tribe. His very name struck terror in the hearts of enemy warriors. Observing this effect, his comrades sometimes disconcerted an opponent by shouting, "Tatanka-Iyotanka tahoksila!" — "We are Sitting Bull's boys!"

Sitting Bull and his "boys" fought for a variety of motives. Where their range overlapped with that of others, they fought for control of hunting grounds. They fought in defense against the aggressions of others; for plunder, chiefly the horses that constituted the prime measure of wealth; for revenge of injuries real and fancied; for glory and the strictly

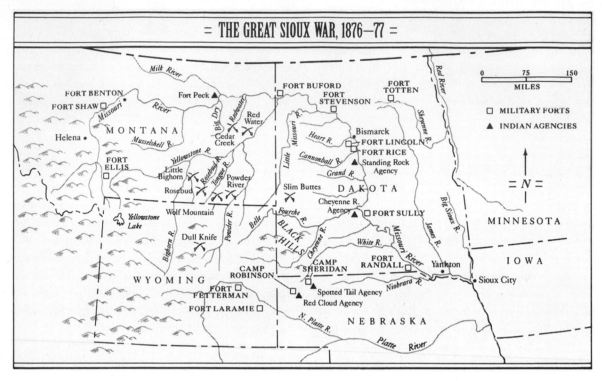

(From The Lance and the Shield *by Robert M. Utley. Maps by Jeffrey L. Ward. Copyright © 1993 by Jeffrey L. Ward. Re-* *printed by permission of Henry Holt and Company, Inc.)*

prescribed war honors that determined prestige and leadership.

In any battle, whatever the scale, the Hunkpapas, like all Plains Indians, fought in time-honored fashion. Singly and in knots they galloped back and forth, firing arrows or musket balls at the enemy. Sometimes they gathered in bunches for a thrust aimed at overrunning their foes. Each man indulged in a variety of flashy escapades to display bravery; he followed a leader only when it suited his convenience or inclination. In any such encounter, Sitting Bull's role was chiefly, through exhortation and example, to inspire men to exhibit ever greater personal daring and to join with him in whatever tactical move circumstances seemed to dictate. Neither he nor any other chief "commanded," as whites used the term.

Typifying this mode of combat and Sitting Bull's part in it was the Lakotas' most memorable fight with an enemy tribe. This occurred in the winter of 1869–70, and they remembered it as the Thirty-Crows-Killed battle.

Sitting Bull's band wintered that year in Montana, along the Missouri River and Big Dry Creek. In the middle of the winter, amid bitter cold and deep snow, two Hunkpapa boys were returning from a day of hunting when a party of thirty Crows cut their trail in the snow. Except for two men mounted on one pony, the Crows were afoot. The two hurried to overtake the boys and succeeded in killing one. Wounded, the other escaped to carry word to the Hunkpapa village.

At once Sitting Bull organized a revenge expedition of about 100 warriors. Guided by the surviving boy, the men found their enemies posted behind rock breastworks at the head of Big Dry Creek. As dawn broke, the Hunkpapas attacked. A few on each side had firearms, but most had only bow and arrows. The Hunkpapas fought in the usual fashion, each man for himself, each striving for deeds of bravery and the coups that added to war honors. Although outnumbered more than three to one, the Crows enjoyed the advantages of defense from a fortified position. Steady in their own bravery, they sold their lives dearly. But as the morning hours slipped by, the Hunkpapas gradually took their toll on the Crows.

Like his warriors, Sitting Bull charged as chance presented and retreated when the fire grew too hot. Once he darted to the breastworks and reached across with his bow to count three coups. Finally, as noon approached, he and his comrades surged forward, leaped the walls, and in desperate hand-to-hand fighting killed the last of the Crows. Hunkpapa casualties were much lighter: Thirteen died and seventeen limped off with serious wounds.

This style of combat worked well enough against an enemy practicing the same style, as Crows, Assiniboines, and other Plains tribes did. Pursued in battles with white people, especially white soldiers, it had severe drawbacks.

Sitting Bull's Hunkpapas and other Lakotas of the upper Missouri had their first combat with United States troops in 1863–64. In two summer campaigns, Generals Henry H. Sibley and Alfred Sully led formidable expeditions to the Dakota plains, at first to round up Santee Sioux fugitives from the Minnesota uprising of 1862, then to punish Lakotas who had interfered with the migration to the newly discovered Montana mines.

Almost certainly, Sitting Bull fought in the battles of Dead Buffalo Lake and Stony Lake, July 26 and 28, 1863. He may have been at Whitestone Hill on September 3, 1863. He unquestionably played a leading part in the battles of Killdeer Mountain and the Badlands, July 28 and August 7–9, 1864. In all

these fights, the Indians relied on their traditional techniques, and in all they suffered severe to calamitous defeats.

Killdeer Mountain should have shown the Sioux the perils of trying to take on the soldiers in open battle. As many as 1,400 lodges representing four Lakota tribes traced the southern edge of a low range of rugged, wooded mountains falling away on the north to the Little Missouri badlands. A series of buttes and ridges, separated by deep gorges, rose stairlike to the dominating mountain mass. In this natural fortress, emboldened by a force exceeding 2,000 warriors, the Sioux felt confident of routing the approaching army of General Sully.

With 2,200 cavalry and artillery, Sully advanced across the parched plains from the south. Judging the terrain too broken for mounted action, he dismounted and pushed forward on a broad front of skirmishers. Horseholders, then wagons and artillery, brought up the rear.

The Indians came out to meet him. Resplendent in paint and war costume, they sat their ponies in little clusters on every hill and ridge facing the blue lines and curling around their flanks. When within range, the two forces opened fire.

For five miles the fighting roiled northward toward the village at the foot of Killdeer Mountain, the Lakotas attacking in typical fashion. Despite their numbers, however, they could not slow the steady advance of the soldiers.

Mounted on a fast sorrel and armed with musket and bow and arrows, Sitting Bull fought with his usual bravery. As the soldiers launched a final assault aimed at the village itself, he saw a bullet slam into the back of his revered uncle, Chief Four Horns. "I am shot," yelled Four Horns, clinging grimly to his mount.

Sitting Bull dashed to the rescue, seized the horse's bridle, and, as his young nephew White Bull steadied the injured man, led the way into a sheltering thicket. There Sitting Bull gave Four Horns water to drink, applied medicine to the wound, and bandaged it. The bullet remained inside, Four Horns said; he could feel it and it hurt. (Later he recovered and explained that the bullet had dropped into his stomach and never bothered him again.)

While Sitting Bull doctored his uncle, the soldiers won final victory, scattering men, women, and children into the mountains and seizing the village. The next day they methodically destroyed everything that could benefit the Indians. Lodges, meat, robes, utensils — all went up in flames. The troops counted more than a hundred Sioux bodies left on the battlefield; how many dead and wounded were carried away is not known. By contrast, Sully reported casualties of two killed and ten wounded.

The Sibley-Sully campaigns, especially Killdeer Mountain, gave Sitting Bull his first taste of battle with the Long Knives. They did not, he discovered, fight like Indians. Instead they fought in organized formations, obedient to commands of their officers, and brought overwhelming firepower to bear. Their rifled muskets claimed greater range, accuracy, and hitting force than the feeble smoothbore trade muskets of the Indians. The soldiers' cannon in particular were frightening and deadly.

The lessons were clear: Acquire better firearms, and avoid open battle with the Long Knives, relying instead on the hit-and-run tactics at which the Sioux excelled. Sitting Bull's record suggests that he fully grasped the first lesson, only partly the second. Not surprisingly in view of the dictates of culture, neither he nor any other chief ever thought to fight in disciplined formations maneuvered by a hierarchy of command.

The Battle of Killdeer Mountain heralded two decades of conflict with the Long Knives. As whites edged onto the northern Great Plains, soldiers came to protect them. Their "war houses" on the Missouri River, along with the steamboats that carried people and merchandise to the Montana mines, infuriated the Sioux. No chief took a more uncomplicated or inflexible view of this invasion than Sitting Bull. Ex-

cept for traders, he held, the whites must all get out of Lakota domain and quit traveling through it. If they would not go peaceably, they would be driven out.

It now fell to Sitting Bull to embody the spirit of Lakota resistance to the white threat. Throughout the late 1860s he led the Hunkpapa offensive against the whites. In this aggressive war, he wielded his favorite attack weapon, the lance, which symbolized his role as the offensive arm of the Hunkpapa tribe.

Principal objectives of the offensive were the military posts of the upper Missouri: Forts Rice, Stevenson, Totten, and Buford. Permanent abodes of the detested Long Knives, the forts stood for the resolve of the whites to possess Lakota territory. The campaign took the form mainly of raids near the forts. Logging details, stock herders, mail riders, and travelers bound for the mines periodically ran afoul of nearby war parties.

Sioux usually regarded direct assaults as risks not worth the prospective gain, but twice they launched such attacks, in each instance with Sitting Bull in the lead. The first occurred at Fort Rice on July 28, 1865. In four hours of desperate fighting, the garrison of "Galvanized Yankees" — Confederate prisoners enlisted for Indian duty — held the defenses and drove off the assailants with well-directed rifle and artillery fire. The second clash occurred on December 24, 1866, when Sitting Bull and his warriors seized the outbuildings of Fort Buford and battled their foes until routed by artillery and charging infantry.

Sitting Bull's offensive on the upper Missouri paralleled an even more determined one to the west, in the Powder River country, over the same issues. Spearheaded by Red Cloud's Oglala tribe, Lakotas fought to close the Bozeman Trail to the Montana mines and get rid of the three forts the army had built to guard travelers. Unlike Sitting Bull, Red Cloud won his war. In the Fort Laramie Treaty of 1868, the United States yielded the three forts and agreed to regard the Powder River country as "unceded Indian country." There the Sioux could live so long as the buffalo sustained their way of life.

The Treaty of 1868 profoundly shaped the destiny of both Red Cloud and Sitting Bull. Besides the unceded territory, it defined a Great Sioux Reservation — all the present state of South Dakota west of the Missouri — and bound all Sioux to settle there eventually. Within a few years Red Cloud and many of his followers had settled there, launching him on a career as mediator between his people and government authorities.

For his part, Sitting Bull scorned the treaty, the reservation, and everything else associated with the whites (except trade goods, especially arms and ammunition). He had not signed this or any other treaty, and never would. He intended to live as always, following the buffalo, raiding Crows and Assiniboines, and defending his homeland. "You are fools," he had lectured some agency Indians, "to make yourselves slaves to a piece of fat bacon, some hard-tack, and a little sugar and coffee."

In Red Cloud and Sitting Bull, the Treaty of 1868 personalized two powerful magnetic poles of leadership. Red Cloud emerged as the principal chief of the agency Lakotas, those who chose to live within the Great Sioux Reservation and accept government dole. Sitting Bull emerged as the principal chief of the nonreservation Lakotas, who ranged the plains country in the free life of old. Indeed, he had his followers proclaim him supreme chief of all the Lakotas. Such a post had never existed, but his force of personality gave it substance.

The Sitting Bull bands, the "northern Indians," the "hunting bands," or simply the "hostiles," in the white lexicon, numbered about 450 lodges, about 4,000 people including about 800 fighting men. Ranging the valleys of the Yellowstone River and its southern tributaries, many bands came together in the summer for the annual sun dance and perhaps a communal buffalo hunt and a big war expedition against an enemy tribe. In the winter they scattered

Sitting Bull in 1885, four years after his surrender. The great Lakota was both a holy man and a war chief who embodied the four cardinal virtues of his people: bravery, fortitude, generosity, and wisdom. The crucifix he wears in this photograph was supposedly presented to him by a Jesuit missionary in 1868. (Library of Congress)

to remote valleys to sit out the cold, hungry months. In the warm season their numbers swelled with reservation kin out for a summer's lark. In the frigid season their numbers dwindled as rations at the agencies beckoned.

In the aftermath of the Treaty of 1868, with the Lakotas increasingly divided into reservation and nonreservation factions, Sitting Bull called off his offensive against the Missouri River forts. From now on he would fight the white people only in defense of his homeland — the Powder and Yellowstone country that roughly coincided with the unceded territory of the treaty. Sitting Bull's last raid on Fort Buford occurred in September 1870. Now the shield instead of the lance symbolized his role among Lakotas.

Staunchly backing Sitting Bull in his new defense posture was the greatest of all Lakota war leaders — Crazy Horse of the Oglalas. He shared Sitting Bull's aversion to the reservation and the ways of the white people. To the hunting bands, he was a chief second in stature only to Sitting Bull.

Of more ambiguous conviction was another war chief, Gall of the Hunkpapas. Close to Sitting Bull since childhood, Gall tended to take counsel in expediency. Sometimes he even slipped into the Hunkpapa agency at Grand River to sample government rations.

The defensive policy expressed itself most forcibly in the opposition of the hunting bands to the Northern Pacific Railroad. In the summers of 1872 and 1873, they fought army units escorting company surveyors marking out a rail route in the Yellowstone Valley. This was the heart of Lakota hunting grounds and the more valuable to them because only recently wrested from the Crows at great cost in blood.

At the Battle of Arrow Creek on August 13, 1872, Sitting Bull performed one of his most memorable feats of bravery. Urged on by Sitting Bull and Crazy Horse, Lakota and Cheyenne warriors struck engineers and their cavalry guardians in the bend of a dry streambed in the upper Yellowstone Valley.

As the sun rose on the battlefield, all eyes turned in wonder to Sitting Bull, who staged a spectacle of bravery so imaginative that it surpassed all others that day. Getting his pipe and tobacco pouch from his horse, he walked from the bluffs out into the open valley to within enemy range. Seating himself on

the ground, he shouted, "Who other Indians wish to smoke with me come." As Sitting Bull calmly and with studied deliberation filled the bowl with tobacco, his nephew White Bull, Gets-the-Best-Of, and two Cheyennes ventured into the open and seated themselves beside the chief.

The "smoking party," as White Bull termed it, was a terrifying experience. After kindling the tobacco, Sitting Bull puffed placidly, then passed the pipe to his companions. With pounding hearts, each puffed vigorously and passed it quickly down the line. Throughout he said nothing, just looked around and smoked quietly as bullets kicked up dirt and sang through the air. When all the tobacco had burned, Sitting Bull picked up a stick, thoroughly cleaned the bowl, and stowed the pipe in its pouch. He rose and slowly walked back to the admiring knots of fellow tribesmen. The other smokers ran back.

This ingenious exhibition, so captivating to people who placed great emphasis on daring, added to Sitting Bull's long list of valorous deeds. It reinforced his reputation for bravery and answered those who, in the worsening factionalism of the early 1870s, mocked his pretensions. It was, White Bull remembered, "the bravest deed possible."

After 1873 the Northern Pacific faded from the Lakotas' list of grievances. In four inconclusive battles and a few skirmishes, they had expressed their violent opposition, but they had not stopped the railroad. The Panic of 1873 did that, and the railhead rested at Bismarck, on the Missouri, until after other events had neutralized the Sioux.

Although furious, the Sitting Bull bands offered no violent opposition to a far more blatant assault on their territory. Blazing the "Thieves' Road" into the Black Hills, the Custer Expedition of 1874 saw only a few Lakotas and fought none. But the discovery of gold set off a rush that doomed the Indians' possession of the hills.

It also confronted the administration of President Ulysses S. Grant with a hard dilemma. The Black

Hills lay within the Great Sioux Reservation, inarguably guaranteed the Indians by the Treaty of 1868. Yet miners flocked to the hills, and the electorate demanded that the government legalize the invasion. In part because of intimidation by the Sitting Bull bands, however, the reservation chiefs refused to sell. Not until the independent bands yielded to government control, federal officials concluded, could they buy the Black Hills.

A rationale was necessary to force the hunting bands onto the Great Sioux Reservation. They had not interfered with the gold rush, and although they had not signed the Treaty of 1868, it sanctioned their residence in the unceded territory. The defensive policy of Sitting Bull and Crazy Horse, furthermore, left only the thinnest pretext for military force. But their young men had raided Crows, Assiniboines, and Arikaras, as they had always done. They had also terrorized whites on the upper Yellowstone, more in fear of what might happen than of what had happened. In these treaty violations by people who had never subscribed to a treaty, the government found its excuse to order the Sitting Bull bands to the reservation or face military action. Such were the origins of the Great Sioux War of 1876.

Even when confronted with the government's ultimatum in their winter villages, Sitting Bull and his fellow chiefs did not understand that a war was brewing. They were minding their own business and had no plans to fight the white soldiers. Then, on March 17, 1876, cavalry stormed through a village on Powder River, killing two and wounding several others; now the hunting bands knew the Long Knives had declared war.

Sitting Bull drew the winter camps together for self-defense. As spring gave way to summer, reservation Indians began to make their way westward, to join in the defense. By late June his village had swollen from 3,000 to 7,000 people, from 800 to 1,800 warriors.

Now forty-five, Sitting Bull no longer took the lead on the battlefield. He was the "old man chief" and holy man whose judgment and counsel guided the policies and decisions of the allied tribes. Crazy Horse, Gall, and other fighters set the example in combat.

At a sun dance early in June, in supplication to Wakantanka, Sitting Bull gave 100 pieces of flesh from his arms. He also fasted and danced while gazing at the sun. Just below the sun he saw soldiers and horses bearing down on an Indian village. They rode upside down, their feet to the sky, their heads to the earth with hats falling off. A voice proclaimed: "These soldiers do not possess ears. They are to die." The vision and prophecy thrilled his people.

Soldiers were coming — three armies from three directions. They were led by General Alfred H. Terry, Colonel John Gibbon, and "Three Stars," George Crook. With Terry rode "Long Hair," George Armstrong Custer. On June 17, 1876, Sitting Bull's warriors confronted General Crook on the upper reaches of Rosebud Creek. Shoshone and Crow auxiliaries broke the Sioux charge and saved Crook's force from being overrun. Sitting Bull, his arms cut and useless from the sun-dance sacrifice, ranged the lines, exhorting the warriors. Crook limped back to his supply base.

The Battle of the Rosebud did not fulfill Sitting Bull's prophecy. Crook's soldiers had not fallen into the Sioux camp and died. But a week later, Long Hair Custer and his cavalrymen fell into the Sioux camp. It sprawled sleepily in the Little Bighorn Valley on that hot Sunday of June 25, 1876. As depicted in the sun-dance vision, many soldiers died.

A stunned white world gave Sitting Bull all the credit. The "Napoleon of the Sioux," the *New York Herald* labeled him two weeks later, and in subsequent issues self-appointed experts explained how such a catastrophe had happened. One of them declared that the famed Jesuit missionary Father Pierre-Jean De Smet had taught Sitting Bull to speak and read French; the chief had then studied French histories of the Napoleonic Wars and "modeled his generalship after the little Corsican corporal." An army officer, who should have known better, wrote, "The tactics of Sitting Bull seem to have been those pursued by the great Napoleon in his famous campaign of 1814, and were the same practiced by General Lee at Richmond in 1864–65." Soon the nation would be told that Sitting Bull, in a youthful guise, had attended West Point.

In such fantasies a dazed public and a mortified army sought explanations for the disaster that had befallen a supposedly elite regiment and its valiant commander. They wanted to believe that Custer's 7th Cavalry had been overwhelmed by superior numbers commanded by a military genius, the Napoleon of the Sioux.

The truth, of course, was that, as at Killdeer Mountain and all other encounters with Plains tribes, there had been no Indian general at the Little Bighorn. As one of his followers pointed out, "The chief might give orders to fight but he does not direct how to proceed."

The Indians did not win the battle because of generalship or even leadership. They won because they outnumbered the enemy three to one, because they were united, confident, and angry, and above all because the threat to their women and children fired every man with determination to save his family. The Indians won, too, because their foes let themselves be beaten in fragments. Both in the valley and on the battle ridge where the "last stand" occurred, command and control collapsed, discipline evaporated, and men panicked, which left the initiative to the Indians.

If whites ascribed Napoleonic genius to Sitting Bull in 1876, in less than a decade they had produced another interpretation. On the reservation, abetted by Indians currying favor with the Great Father, white officials now said Sitting Bull had not participated in the battle at all; he had remained in his teepee making medicine, or fled to the hills in

terror, even abandoning his family, or skulked somewhere else safely out of danger.

In truth, at the Battle of the Little Bighorn, Sitting Bull was a chief several times over whose bravery no one questioned. He was far more valuable as a counselor than as a fighting man. Leave that to the young warriors striving for glory. Chiefs were expected to fight only to protect noncombatants, and that is what he did when soldiers led by Major Marcus Reno threatened the women and children at the upper end of the village.

After that threat receded, he could have withdrawn with honor. Instead he continued to fire at the soldiers and shout encouragement to the warriors, hovering on the edge of the fighting until everyone left to confront Custer downstream. Then he posted himself at the village's northern end, where many women and children had collected. More than enough men swarmed on the battle ridge to wipe out Long Hair, which they did in less than an hour.

Sitting Bull's significance at the Little Bighorn lay not in flaunting bravery, or directing the movements of warriors, or even inspiring them to fight. It lay instead in leadership so wise and powerful that it drew together and held together a muscular coalition of tribes, one so infused with his defiant cast of mind that it could rout Three Stars Crook at the Rosebud and rub out Long Hair Custer at the Little Bighorn. Never had the Sioux triumphed so spectacularly — and they never would again. For that triumph, more than any other chief they could thank Sitting Bull.

But the triumph contained the seeds of defeat. A stunned nation lashed back, and the Sioux country swarmed with regiments of "Custer avengers." By the spring of 1877, most of the hunting bands had surrendered and gone to the reservation, setting the stage for the government to seize the Black Hills and legalize the invasion.

Sitting Bull could not stomach such humiliation. With a die-hard following he crossed the "medicine road" into the land of the Grandmother. There he got along famously with the queen's redcoats, the North-West Mounted Police, and formed his first close ties to white men. But the buffalo were disappearing in Canada as they were in the United States, and "Bear Coat" — General Nelson A. Miles — watched the boundary like a hawk. After four years of hardship, starvation overcame humiliation, and young Crow Foot handed his father's rifle to Major Brotherton.

The final decade was one of despair. After nearly two years as a prisoner of war, Sitting Bull went to the reservation. At Standing Rock Agency, Agent James McLaughlin's goal was to transform his charges into imitation whites. He sought to make them into tillers of the soil embracing Christianity, Americanism, and the customs and values of the white people. Sitting Bull refused to be made over. He accepted what he thought would be beneficial, such as schooling for his children and grandchildren, and rejected the rest. Finding him unpliable, McLaughlin launched the campaign of ridicule and derision that included the imputation of cowardice at the Little Bighorn.

Hunger, disease, a decade of cultural breakdown, and another land grab made the Sioux reservations fertile ground for the Ghost Dance religion that took root in 1890. It promised a new world, without whites, peopled by all the generations of Indians that had gone before, and stocked with an abundance of buffalo and other game. Whether Sitting Bull truly believed, he functioned as the high priest of the religion at Standing Rock. The government decided to remove him to a distant military post.

Irony and tragedy stalked Sitting Bull's final days. Not the Long Knives of old, but *ceska maza,* "metal breasts" (for their police badges) of his own tribe, closed in on their former leader. At dawn on December 15, 1890, a platoon of Indian policemen forced their way into his cabin on Grand River and placed him under arrest. Excited Ghost Dancers crowded around the cabin, and his own son Crow Foot, now fourteen, taunted him for giving up. The volatile confrontation blew up in a paroxysm of gunfire and hand-to-hand fighting. Sitting Bull went down, shot at close range in the chest and the back of the head by *ceska maza.* Crow Foot died too, beaten and shot by enraged policemen.

The Hunkpapas, even those who had forsaken the old ways, knew McLaughlin's portrait of Sitting Bull to be grotesquely flawed. They well remembered he had been a magnificent warrior, an inspiring war chief, a statesman and political leader of vast wisdom, a holy man of marvelous power, and to his last day a leader of compelling force.

The world remembers Sitting Bull not for what he achieved in his own culture but for his battle against the westward movement of the American people. It is this battle that gives him nearly universal name recognition beyond his own culture. In this struggle, as both lance and shield, his inflexibility served him well. He acted on faultless reasoning: The land of the Lakotas belonged to the Lakotas, and no whites had any right to be there. He fought to keep them out, and when that failed, he fought to defend his people and his territory from invasion. He lost not because of failings of leadership or, given his cultural outlook, failings of judgment, but because of impersonal forces beyond his control or even his understanding.

QUESTIONS TO CONSIDER

1   How did Lakota culture change during the nineteenth century? What effect did white settlers have on that culture throughout the century?

2   What was the traditional Lakota manner of fighting, and what were the values that it highlighted? Why did this style of warfare not work against white troops, and what lessons does Robert Utley think Sitting Bull should have learned from this?

3   Describe Sitting Bull and his three "personalities." Discuss the stance he took toward whites and compare it with that taken by Red Cloud. Which one of them do you think was right and why?

4   What were the principal interests of Americans in Sioux territory, and how did Americans generally react to Sitting Bull's effort at resistance? How did the United States government deal with the Lakota Sioux? How and on what pretext did they finally break the resistance of Sitting Bull's people?

5   Describe life on the reservation. What was the principal purpose of the reservation from the American point of view? What is the significance of the Ghost Dance religion and of Sitting Bull's tragic death? How do you feel about Utley's conclusion that Sitting Bull lost, not because of any personal or cultural failings but because of forces beyond his control?

4

Women First Won the Right to Vote in the American West

DEE BROWN

With the Indians out of the way, Americans were free at last to conquer the vast Great Plains that reached from Texas to the Canadian border in the center of the country. Westering farmers had stopped at the edge of this enormous grassland because its arid climate and shallow topsoil seemed unsuited to agricultural techniques devised in the East. But after the Civil War came the development of new farming techniques and new machinery such as the windmill, the chilled-iron plow, and the combine, all of which made agriculture feasible on the windy prairies. As a consequence, farmers from east of the Mississippi swarmed there during the postwar years, some claiming 160 acres free under the 1862 Homestead Act, most buying their land from speculators or the railroads. In the 1880s alone, more than 1 million people poured onto the Great Plains from the Great Lakes states. Meanwhile, after the failure of Reconstruction, African Americans headed west as well; they were sodbusters, cowboys, speculators, miners, lawmen, desperadoes, and cavalrymen. Asian and Mexican Americans were present, too, all contributing to the drama of frontier conquest. The pioneers lived in all manner of homes — from dugouts to sod houses — battling tornadoes, hail, dust storms, blizzards, prairie fires, and grasshopper plagues in an endless struggle to make new lives for themselves on the nation's last frontier.

The westering experience tended to break down traditional male and female "spheres," which stripped women of all political and legal rights and restricted them to the home while their husbands had jobs and careers in the outside world and ran political *affairs. As modern scholarship has demonstrated, frontier women were not chained to the home but were close to equal partners with their menfolk: in addition to their household chores, the women helped their husbands hunt, gather water and fuel, and plant and harvest.*

It's not surprising that, in the more egalitarian atmosphere of the frontier, women first won the right to vote, doing so just fourteen years after the Civil War. The movement for women's suffrage, of course, did not begin in the West. It started in the East, many years before the Civil War, when American women first organized to break the shackles of strict domesticity and to expand their rights and opportunities. Led by eloquent and energetic Elizabeth Cady Stanton, the early feminists rejected the notion of female inferiority and advocated full sexual equality with men. They demanded equal access to education, the trades, and the professions and an end to the sexual double standard. They wanted the right to vote, too, not as an end in itself but as a means of achieving their broader aim — to make women self-sufficient, equal partners in all areas of human enterprise.

After the Civil War, American feminists organized the Equal Rights Association, but the movement soon split over the timing of women's suffrage demands. The debate focused on the proposed Fifteenth Amendment, discussed in an earlier selection, which sought to protect the former slaves by enfranchising African American men. The amendment did not include women, black or white. One women's rights group, led by Julia Ward Howe, author of "The Battle Hymn of the Republic," endorsed the amendment, agreeing with its Republican framers that African American suffrage was already controversial enough and would go down to defeat if women's suffrage were linked to it. Better, they believed, to get African American men enfranchised first. Another feminist group, led by Stanton and Susan B. Anthony, opposed the amendment as "an open, deliberate insult to American womanhood." Anthony and Stanton considered it extremely unfair that uneducated black men should gain the elective franchise while educated women were denied it. The struggle between the two women's groups reached a turning point at the 1869 convention of the Equal Rights Association, where Anthony and Stanton tried but failed to unite the delegates behind a projected Sixteenth Amendment to the Constitution that would enfranchise women. After that, the Anthony-Stanton faction formed one national suffrage organization while their rivals formed another.

That was in the East. Out in Wyoming Territory, in the same year that eastern feminists failed to unite behind the enfranchisement of women, irrepressible Esther McQuigg Morris, the first woman in the world to hold the office of justice of the peace, launched a campaign to pressure the territorial legislature to grant Wyoming women the right to vote and to hold office. Dee Brown, a prolific historian of the American West, tells the story of how Morris and her colleagues overcame a wall of opposition to get the "Female Suffrage Act" passed by the all-male legislature and the male governor a full

44

fifty years before the adoption of the Nineteenth Amendment. But the fight for women's political rights in Wyoming did not end there, for Morris and her colleagues had to overcome a strong male backlash in order to preserve their newly won right to participate in the democratic process. Their victory opened the way for women to vote in Colorado, Idaho, and Utah, all of which gave hope and inspiration to embattled suffragists in the East. That story will resume in selection 15.

GLOSSARY

ANTHONY, SUSAN B.   She and her lifetime associate, Elizabeth Cady Stanton, were two of the great leaders of the women's suffrage movement after the Civil War. In 1869, they established the National Woman Suffrage Association.

CAMPBELL, JOHN   Republican governor of Wyoming who on December 10, 1869, signed the "Female Suffrage Act" — the first such measure in America — which enfranchised women of the territory.

MORRIS, ESTHER MCQUIGG   The first woman in the world to hold the office of justice of the peace, she was chiefly responsible for persuading the Wyoming territorial government to pass the "Female Suffrage Act."

NICHOLS, CLARINA   A fiery leader in the women's rights movement in Kansas. Despite her efforts, women did not win the right to vote until 1912.

RANKIN, JEANNETTE   First woman elected to the U S Congress, in 1917; she represented Montana.

ROSS, NELLIE TAYLOR   Elected governor of Wyoming in 1925, she was the first female in the United States to hold such an office.

STANTON, ELIZABETH CADY   See *Anthony, Susan B.*

I

On the evening of September 2, 1869, in a small shack in South Pass City, Wyoming Territory, occurred an event that has since become known as "the Esther Morris tea party." This Wyoming tea party had as much significance in the fight for women's rights as the Boston Tea Party had in the American struggle for independence.

At the time she gave her tea party Esther Mc-Quigg Morris was fifty-five years old, a self-reliant lady of great charm, who enjoyed fierce battles and was accustomed to winning most of them. Orphaned at eleven, she supported herself as a milliner in Oswego, New York, until she married John Slack. Then in her later years she followed her second husband, John Morris, to Wyoming to keep house for him while he tried to make a fortune in the gold diggings.

Because of Esther Morris' air of quiet reserve and her strong personality, South Pass City elected her justice of the peace — the first woman to hold that office anywhere in the world. In the late 1860's, South Pass City was the largest city in Wyoming, a row of miners' shacks stretching along a ledge of the

Dee Brown, "Women First Won the Right to Vote in the American West," chapter originally titled, "Wyoming Tea Party," in Brown, *The Gentle Tamers: Women of the Old Wild West* (Lincoln: University of Nebraska Press, 1968), pp. 238–251. Reprinted by permission of Sterling Lord Literistic, Inc. Copyright © 1968 by Dee Brown.

Nellie Taylor Ross was elected governor of Wyoming in 1925, the first woman in America to hold such an office. (American Heritage Center/University of Wyoming)

Wind River Mountains, with a population of three thousand, mostly males seeking gold. Soon after her election the rowdies of the place undertook to intimidate her, but of the forty cases she tried during her term of office not one was appealed, and the more respectable males of the community testified that she conducted her office with greater credit than most men, "administering justice with a vigorous and impartial hand."

Esther Morris' unique office naturally attracted considerable publicity around the country. Some of the eastern sporting papers, notably the *Police Gazette* and *Day's Doings,* printed cartoons of Esther Morris, J.P., representing her as being a formidable female

who sat with her feet propped on the magistrate's desk, conducting her court with a cigar between her lips and whittling a heap of shavings with a huge jackknife.

These disparaging caricatures barely amused Mrs. Morris, but she wasted no time being annoyed by them. She was too busy with such important matters as seeing that laws were passed giving women the right to vote. On the eve of Wyoming's first territorial elections, September 2, 1869, she invited twenty of the most influential citizens of South Pass City to a tea party in her tidy little miner's shack. Among the guests were Colonel William H. Bright, Democratic candidate for the legislature, and Captain Herman G. Nickerson, Republican candidate. At the proper moment during the convivial evening, Esther Morris dropped what she thought would be a bombshell into the conversation. With quiet seriousness, she suddenly asked each candidate if he would introduce a bill in the new legislature that would give the women of Wyoming the right to vote. At that time, no woman in the world had such a legal right.

If the gentlemen thought Mrs. Morris was joking, she soon made it plain that she was not. Colonel Bright knew her well enough to recognize her sincerity. He had a high regard for her learning, her abilities, and above all her skill as a nurse. Esther Morris had probably saved the life of his wife Betty, nursing her through a difficult childbirth. Colonel Bright replied that he would introduce a women's suffrage bill. And then not to be outdone, the Republican candidate, Herman Nickerson, said he would do the same if elected.

Very likely, neither candidate had any expectation that such a bill would ever reach a vote. In those days, women's suffrage in the United States was considered by males as a subject for humorous remarks or bitter condemnation, depending upon the temperament of the discussant. But they reckoned without Esther Morris' determination.

As soon as the election was over and Colonel

William Bright had won, Mrs. Morris took her campaign to Betty Bright. The new legislator's wife was an intelligent woman, and she put up a convincing case for women's suffrage. Her husband has been quoted as saying before going down to Cheyenne for the convening of the legislature: "Betty, it's a shame that I should be a member of the Legislature and make laws for such a woman as you. You are a great deal better than I am; you know a great deal more and you would make a better member of the Assembly than I. I have made up my mind that I will do everything in my power to give you the ballot."

On October 1, 1869, the Wyoming territorial legislature assembled for the first time. It was a body composed entirely of Democrats but with a Republican holding the office of governor and possessing the power of veto. A few days later, William Bright was elected president of the Senate, a position of authority that readily enabled him to sound out opinions of the men who composed the two houses of the legislature. Bright brought up the idea of a women's suffrage bill, arguing that it would give the Democrats a chance to show the Republicans they were a more advanced party, and that it also would advertise Wyoming Territory as nothing else could. None of his fellow members seemed to consider the bill seriously, but only a few spoke out in opposition. Undoubtedly some of those in favor foresaw an opportunity to embarrass the Republican governor, John Campbell, who would be placed in the position of having to veto it.

Bright drew up his bill, "An Act to Grant to the Women of Wyoming Territory the Right of Suffrage and to Hold Office," and introduced it November 9, 1869. The text was brief and to the point:

Be it enacted by the Council and the House of Representatives of the Territory of Wyoming:

Sec. 1.   That every woman of the age of eighteen years, residing in this Territory, may, at every election to be holden under the laws thereof, cast her vote. And her rights to the elective franchise and to hold office shall be the same under the elective laws of the territory, as those of electors.

Sec. 2.   This act shall take effect and be in force from and after its passage.

A vote was taken, and the result startled all Wyoming — six in favor, two opposed, one absent.

The bill now went to the House, and as the news spread about the Territory males and females alike wondered if Colonel Bright's "Female Suffrage Act" was not some sort of huge practical joke. But Esther Morris and a number of other women saw it as a golden opportunity; they wrote letters and made personal calls upon members of the legislature and the Governor. Sensing a drift in the winds of public opinion, Cheyenne's two newspapers came out heartily in support of the bill.

Bill Nye of the *Laramie Boomerang,* however, quoted a mythical railroad man's remarks on the proposed law: "Gentlemen, this is a pretty important move. It's a kind of a wild train on a single track, and we've got to keep our eye peeled or we'll get into the ditch. It's a new conductor making his first run. He don't know the stations yet, and he feels just as if there were a spotter in every coach besides. Female suffrage changes the management of the whole line, and may put the entire outfit in the hands of a receiver in two years. We can't tell when Wyoming Territory may be sidetracked with a lot of female conductors and superintendents and a posse of giddy girls at the brakes."

When the bill finally was introduced in the House, a formidable opposition group was set to kill it with amendments. Ben Sheek, the principal opponent, moved that the age requirement be changed to thirty years in place of eighteen, on the theory that no woman would vote because none would admit to being thirty. When this failed to pass, he offered a substitute, requiring that the word "woman" be stricken out and the phrase "all colored women and squaws" be inserted. Another legislator proposed that a vote on the bill be postponed until July 4, 1870 — a holiday and a year when the legislature ordinarily would not be in session.

Debate was acrimonious, but all amendments failed except one, a change in the age requirement from eighteen to twenty-one being accepted. The vote on the bill was six in favor, four opposed, one absent.

Now the fate of the "Female Suffrage Act" lay in the hands of Governor John Campbell. Several of the Democrats who had voted for the bill were certain the Republican Governor would veto it. But there was something in Campbell's background the legislators were unaware of; as a young man he had lived in Salem, Ohio, one of the first towns to hold a women's suffrage convention. A lover of oratory, he had attended the convention in order to hear Susan B. Anthony speak, and he had been impressed by her arguments in favor of the vote for women. Although caught now in a bitter crossfire of opinion for and against the territorial suffrage bill, Campbell signed it, on December 10, 1869. And for the first time anywhere on earth, women had won the legal right to vote.

According to a prominent Wyoming male citizen, the most amazed inhabitants of the territory were the women themselves. "If a troop of angels had come down with flaming swords for their vindication," he recalled, "they would not have been much more astounded than they were when that bill became a law." One Wyoming woman, however, probably was not so surprised. She was Esther Morris, whose tea party had set the miracle in motion, a lady who enjoyed a good fight and was accustomed to winning most of the time.

2

Even before they had an opportunity to vote in an election, a few Wyoming females found themselves involved in the second provision of the suffrage act —

the right to hold office. During late 1869 and early 1870, thousands of idle railroad laborers collected in Laramie following completion of the Union Pacific, and lawlessness almost got out of hand. Male juries brought in so few convictions that when the grand jury was empaneled in March 1870, someone had the brilliant idea of recognizing the new Wyoming law and naming women to jury duty.

Six women and six men were summoned to sit on the grand jury, the first notice going to Eliza Stewart, Laramie school-teacher. And for the first time in criminal court history, the presiding justice brought the assembly to order with the words: "Ladies and gentlemen of the Grand Jury."

The justice, John H. Howe, realizing the significance of the event, told the women that "the eyes of the world were upon them as pioneers serving in a movement that was to test the power of being able to protect and defend themselves from the evils of which women were victims . . . You shall not be driven by the sneers, jeers and insults of a laughing crowd from the temple of justice, as your sisters have from some of the medical colleges of the land. The strong hand of the law shall protect you . . . it will be a sorry day for any man who shall so far forget the courtesies due and paid by every American gentleman to every American lady as to even by act of word endeavor to deter you from the exercise of those rights with which the law has invested you."

As soon as news reached the eastern states that a female grand jury had been empaneled in wild Wyoming, a number of illustrated weeklies dispatched reporters, photographers, and artists to record this phenomenal event. Asked to sit for photographs, the women jurors refused, and when they discovered newspaper artists in the courtroom sketching their portraits, they donned heavy veils. The artists resorted to caricature, as in the case of Esther Morris when she was justice of the peace. Some eastern publications printed illustrations showing the women holding babies in their laps while doing jury service, captioned with such couplets as:

Baby, baby, don't get in a fury;
Your mamma's gone to sit on the jury.

There were many sly jokes made about locking the two sexes up in one room until they could reach decisions on cases, but the sheriff solved the problem by locking the women in one room with a female bailiff on the door, the men in another room with a male bailiff.

This first mixed grand jury was in session for three weeks, hearing bills brought for consideration for murder cases, cattle and horse stealing, and illegal branding. The women took their duties seriously, indicting almost all the businessmen in Laramie for keeping their places open on Sunday contrary to law. Even Judge Howe was embarrassed. If he convicted all, practically every influential businessman in town would be in jail. He solved that dilemma by paroling the gentlemen on their individual written promises to keep the law thereafter.

3

The first election in which Wyoming's women voted was held September 6, 1870. Early on the morning of that historic day, Louisa Ann Swain, age seventy, of Laramie, Wyoming, fastened a fresh clean apron over her housedress and walked to the polls. She was carrying an empty pail for yeast to be purchased at a bakeshop on her return home. Louisa Swain was the first woman in the world to cast a vote in a public election.

Over in Cheyenne, the *Daily Leader* reported in its evening edition: "At noon today the election was progressing quietly in this city. Many ladies have voted and without molestation or interference . . . The first lady voting in Cheyenne was Mrs. Howe, the wife of the U. S. Marshal. Hers was a straight Republican ticket."

Margaret Thomson Hunter, a Scotch-born housewife, said that on that first election day her neighbor, a Mr. Hellman, stopped by and asked her to go and vote for him. "I was busy making pies and hadn't intended voting, but after all Mr. Hellman was a neighbor, and also a very good friend of my husband's. So I pushed my pies aside, removed my apron, and tidied myself up a bit. Then I got into the buggy with Mr. Hellman and he drove me to the polls. Well, I voted and as we turned to leave we came face to face with my husband. When I explained to him that I had just voted for Mr. Hellman, I thought he would have a fit. You see, my husband was a staunch Democrat, and one of the leaders in his party, and there I had just voted for a Republican. He was never so humiliated in all his life, he told me. Then I said he should have explained those things to me if they were so important, for he knew I had never done any voting in Scotland."

Bill Nye's account of the first election in Laramie was favorable: "No rum was sold, women rode to the polls in carriages furnished by the two parties, and every man was straining himself to be a gentleman because there were votes at stake."

4

Late in the following year, 1871, the women's suffrage law ran into rough weather, mainly because the Democrats lost several seats in the legislative elections. The Democrats blamed these defeats on the very voters they had enfranchised in 1869 — the ungrateful women.

Legislators Ben Sheek, C. K. Nuckolls, and W. R. Steele — all Democrats — opened fiery attacks upon the female suffrage law, and a bill was introduced to repeal it. "I think women were made to obey," declared Nuckolls. "They generally promise to obey, at any rate, and I think you had better abolish this female suffrage act or get up a new marriage ceremony to fit it."

His colleague, W. R. Steele, made a strong seconding speech, which has been preserved in this recording: "Women got so degraded as to go to the polls and vote and ask other women to go to the polls. This woman suffrage business will sap the foundations of society. Woman can't engage in politics without losin' her virtue. No woman ain't got no right to sit on a jury, nohow, unless she is a man and every lawyer knows it. They watch the face of the judge too much when the lawyer is addressin' 'em. I don't believe she's fit for it, nohow. If those hev it tuck from 'em now can at least prevent any more of them from gitten it, and thus save the unborn babe and the girl of sixteen."

Although Democrats still controlled the legislature, the prosuffrage members could not stem the opposition tide. The repeal bill passed both houses and went to Governor Campbell. Campbell vetoed it immediately, and thus a Republican saved a law that was created originally by Democrats and then was repudiated by them. The score was even, and both parties thenceforth could claim credit for infranchising the female voters of Wyoming.

Again, some eighteen years later, the women's suffrage law was thrust suddenly into a state of jeopardy. In 1889, when Wyoming applied for statehood, opposition developed in the U. S. House of Representatives because of the suffrage article in the territory's constitution. James Carey, who was in Washington, D. C., representing Wyoming's case for statehood, became concerned over the mounting attack, and he telegraphed back to Cheyenne for instructions. Local newspapers published a report of the situation, and rumors spread that Wyoming would not be admitted to the Union as a state unless the suffrage law was abolished. A group of Cheyenne women telegraphed Carey: DROP US IF YOU MUST. WE CAN TRUST THE MEN OF WYOMING TO ENFRANCHISE US AFTER OUR TERRITORY BECOMES A STATE. But the legislature meanwhile had also sent a telegram to the Washington delegate: WE MAY STAY OUT OF THE UNION A HUNDRED YEARS, BUT WE WILL COME IN WITH OUR WOMEN.

Wyoming's bill of admission to statehood barely squeezed through the House committee and then was passed into law by the narrow margins of 139 to 127 in the House, 29 to 18 in the Senate.

From that time forward few male politicians in Wyoming were so bold or so foolish as to make public statements against female suffrage. "It has been weighed and not found wanting," the new state's Chief Justice declared. "It has made our elections quiet and orderly. No rudeness, brawling or disorder appears or would be tolerated at the polling booths. There is no more difficulty or indelicacy in depositing a ballot in the urn than in dropping a letter in the postoffice."

When a Boston newspaper ran a story on the new state, the editor included an interview with "a gentleman from Wyoming" traveling in the East. At that safe distance from Wyoming, the reckless male uttered some disparaging remarks about women's suffrage, not suspecting that he would be quoted in the Cheyenne press a short time later. The mayor of Cheyenne promptly wired the Boston newspaper that the "prominent gentleman was a horse thief convicted by a jury half of whom were women," and that his remarks therefore were biased.

Thus defended by their males, Wyoming's women peacefully cast their ballots for several years, then audaciously began running for office. In 1910, Mary G. Bellamy won the distinction of being the first woman elected to a state legislature. Seven years later, the all-male United States Congress was startled to find a woman in its membership for the first time in history — Jeannette Rankin, Representative from Montana. And on January 5, 1925, the first female state governor in the nation, Nellie Taylor Ross, was installed at Cheyenne.

Because Wyoming was the first place — and for a long time the only place — in the world where women could vote, professional suffragettes of the late nineteenth century journeyed there like Moslems to Mecca. Susan B. Anthony, Dr. Mary Walker, Ann Eliza Young, and Sarah Lippincott were among those making pilgrimages. Mrs. Lippincott, who wrote under the pseudonym Grace Greenwood, was sadly disappointed in Cheyenne of the 1870's. "As the capital of the Territory that has taken the first bold practical step in the matter of woman's civil rights, the place commends itself to my heart, certainly I should rejoice to find it a very Eden, a vale of Cashmere, — which it isn't."

Outside of Wyoming, the fine-mannered eastern suffragettes had a hard time of it in the West. Travel conditions were arduous; the suffragettes found few people of either sex willing to listen to them and often met with active opposition. When Susan B. Anthony and Anna Shaw were making an early western tour, they arrived in a small Dakota town one Sunday morning to discover that the local clergymen had persuaded all the women of the town to stay away from their suffrage meeting. The reason given for the ban was that the meeting was scheduled to be held in a church on a Sabbath day. The two women immediately rented the local theater, roused a printer out of bed, and hired him to run off some handbills which they distributed personally to each dwelling in town. "We had a glorious meeting," said Anna Shaw. "Both Miss Anthony and I were in excellent fighting trim."

Another time, Miss Shaw was snowbound in a western train, the only woman among a crowd of cowboys and cattlemen. "They were an odoriferous lot," she recalled, "who smoked diligently, and played cards without ceasing, but in deference to my presence they swore only mildly, and under their breath. At last they wearied of their game, and one of them rose, and came to me. 'I heard you lecture the other night,' he said awkwardly, 'and I've bin tellin' the fellers about it. We'd like to have a lecture now.'"

Anna Shaw consented to say a few words, and the men went through the snowbound train to bring in the remaining passengers. The meeting began with the singing of a Moody and Sankey hymn, followed by "Where Is My Wandering Boy Tonight?" in which all joined with special zest. Then Anna Shaw delivered one of her lectures on women's suffrage. The men listened politely, and after the meeting ended they made the speaker a bed by taking the bottoms out of two seats, arranging them crosswise, and donating their overcoats for bedding. Anna Shaw crept in between the overcoats and slept peacefully until she was aroused the next morning by the rumble of a snowplow.

Much as it had been a skirmishing ground in the early struggles over Negro slavery, Kansas became a western battlefield in the fight for women's suffrage. Even before the Civil War, advocates of women's rights in Kansas had linked their cause with that of slaves and unenfranchised free Negroes. Kansas diarists of the 1850's indicate that local debating societies frequently argued the question, "Resolved that Women Should Execute the Election Franchise." The negative side usually won.

Clarina Nichols was the most articulate of Kansas' pioneer lecturers on women's rights. In 1859, the Fort Scott *Democrat* reported she had delivered a fiery speech in the local hospital. "Of course the room was crowded, and although the weather was very warm, there was a large number of ladies in attendance. She said if the men didn't give them their rights, they would revolt — wouldn't marry. What a row that would make. They wanted to vote but didn't care about holding office if the men only behaved themselves. Haven't heard of any converts in this region."

When Kansas became a state in 1861, Clarina Nichols fought so hard for women's suffrage that the lawmakers saw fit to compromise and allow Kansas women the small privilege of voting in district school elections. That is why some Kansans claim that their women were voting eight years before the women of Wyoming won that right.

In 1867, professional suffragettes decided the time was ripe to take more ground in Kansas. They invaded the state in force, Elizabeth Stanton, Lucy Stone, Olympia Brown, and Susan B. Anthony combining their efforts for a grand tour. "We had a low, easy carriage, drawn by two mules," said Elizabeth Stanton, "in which we stored about a bushel of tracts, two valises, a pail for watering the mules, a basket of apples, crackers, and other such refreshments as we could purchase on the way. Some things were suspended underneath the carriage, some packed on behind, and some under the seat and at our feet . . . We spoke in log cabins, in depots, unfinished schoolhouses, churches, hotels, barns, and in the open air."

The *Topeka Weekly Leader*'s editor wrote most irreverently of this tour and its participants. Female suffrage, he declared, was "a pernicious doctrine." He described Elizabeth Stanton as "a buxom gray haired matron of about fifty" whose speech "was elegant and eloquent — everything but convincing." Susan B. Anthony "seemed only desirous to sell some pamphlet speeches of Parker Pillsbury and other ancient ladies, at the small price of twenty-five cents each. As preliminary thereto, however, she entered into a discursory argument of the right of suffrage for females. She insisted that as men and women were of the same physical formation (with a slight variation), their political rights were the same."

Through the next three decades the suffrage war raged in Kansas, but it was all to no avail. Kansas women did not win the franchise until 1912.

Other western women were victorious, however, long before that date. The women of Colorado, Idaho, and Utah were voting before 1900; indeed, the first dozen states to pass women's suffrage acts were all western states, far to the west of the Mississippi River. The pioneers in petticoats were casting off their shackles in preparation for a final taming of the masculine Wild West.

QUESTIONS TO CONSIDER

1 Why was it that in Wyoming, a frontier territory, women were considered worthy of voting and holding political office when they were deemed wholly unfit to exercise such rights in the East? Since Esther McQuigg Morris and her female colleagues initially had no political power in Wyoming, how were they able to win the right to vote?

2 Dee Brown says that in 1871 the Female Suffrage Act "ran into rough weather." Who wanted to repeal the measure? Why? How were women able to retain the elective franchise?

3 Why was Kansas "a western battlefield in the fight for women's suffrage"? What did the suffragists do to win the vote there? Why did they fail to achieve that goal until 1912?

4 In the two selections on Reconstruction, we saw that the federal government was willing to enfranchise black men, including former slaves, in the postwar years. Why did the government refuse to grant women, including well-educated women like Elizabeth Cady Stanton and Susan B. Anthony, the same right?

III

THE NEW INDUSTRIAL ORDER

5

The Master of Steel: Andrew Carnegie

ROBERT L. HEILBRONER

From the 1820s on, the United States industrialized at an impressive rate. But the real boost came during the Civil War, when the United States Congress created a national currency and banking system, enacted homestead legislation, and appropriated federal aid for a transcontinental railroad. Such measures, argues historian James M. McPherson, provided "the blueprint for modern America." From the crucible of civil war emerged a new America of big business, heavy industry, and commercial farming that became by 1880 "the foremost industrial nation" in the world. The federal government played a crucial role in the postwar boom. One Republican administration after another not only maintained a protective tariff to minimize foreign competition but gave away millions of dollars' worth of public land to railroad companies, adopted a hard-money policy that pleased big business, and — except for the Interstate Commerce and Sherman Anti-trust Acts, both adopted because of popular unrest — cheerfully refused to regulate or restrict the consolidation of America's new industrial order.

It was during the Gilded Age (as Mark Twain called it), an era between Robert E. Lee's surrender at Appomattox and the turn of the century, that American capitalism, growing for decades now, produced mighty combinations that controlled most of the nation's wealth. The leaders of the new industrial order comprised a complex gallery of individuals popularly known as the robber barons. There had, of course, been many rich Americans before the Gilded Age, people who made fortunes from traffic in lands and goods. But the post–Civil War robber barons were a different breed, for they controlled the essential tools of the booming industrial economy itself: railroads (the nation's basic transportation system), banking, and manufacturing. They eliminated competition, set prices, exploited workers, and commanded the awe or fear of an entire generation. Enough of them were rags-to-riches individuals, the kind celebrated in the novels of Horatio Alger, to encourage the notion of the American dream at work, a dream that in the United States all who were capable could rise to the top. Some of the tycoons were gaudy vulgarians such as one H. A. W. Tabor. Finding a portrait of Shakespeare hanging in a Denver opera house that he had built, Tabor demanded that the portrait be replaced with his own, storming, "What the hell has Shakespeare done for Denver?" Others were industrial pirates such as Jay Gould, a consumptive rascal who made his money by various nefarious means.

But other entrepreneurs fit a different pattern: like the rapacious capitalist played by Michael Douglas in the movie Wall Street, they were obsessed with the power that wealth brought them. An example was Cornelius "Commodore" Vanderbilt, who began his career as a ferryboatman, rose to ownership of riverboats (hence his nickname), and went on to become a railroad magnate who owned a transportation empire worth $80 million and lived in splendor in a Manhattan mansion. This rowdy, profane man loved to win in any way he could, once proclaiming, "Law? What do I care about the law. H'ain't I got the power?"

Then there was John D. Rockefeller, a quiet, penny-pinching millionaire whose Standard Oil Company became one of the nation's most powerful monopolies. Indeed, Rockefeller's business methods, stressing the virtues of order, organization, and planning, set the example of modern business organization. Unlike other Gilded Age entrepreneurs, however, Rockefeller had little interest in money for money's sake. At the end of his life, through foundations named after him, he donated millions of dollars to religious activities, medical research, and higher education.

And then there was steel magnate Andrew Carnegie, the subject of the insightful portrait that follows. Another self-made man, Carnegie was at one time the richest person in the world. Perhaps more than any other tycoon, he embodied the spirit of the age, a man who not only created but advocated and celebrated industrial power. He defended democracy, capitalism, and the Anglo-Saxon race, and he even argued that evolution produced millionaires such as he, ignoring the fact that such folk enjoyed generous government benefits, not to mention the help of federal troops serving as strikebreakers. Yet Carnegie also acted on his own self-proclaimed sense of duty: having amassed a prodigious fortune, he proceeded to give almost all of it away during his lifetime. In him, Robert L. Heilbroner sees both the failures and the integrity of Gilded Age America.

GLOSSARY

ALGER, HORATIO   Gilded Age author whose heroes rose from poverty to greatness and thus fulfilled the "American Dream."

AMERICAN FEDERATION OF LABOR   Organized in 1886 with Samuel Gompers as president, the AFL was an association of trade unions whose membership consisted exclusively of skilled workers.

CARNEGIE CORPORATION OF NEW YORK   After making his fortune, Andrew Carnegie established this "first great modern" philanthropic foundation.

CARNEGIE, McCANDLESS & COMPANY   Andrew Carnegie's British-American steel company and the nucleus of his steel empire.

FRICK, HENRY   Self-made millionaire who amalgamated his coke empire and Andrew Carnegie's steelworks and assumed "the active management of the whole." Frick, Captain William Jones, and Charles Schwab constituted "the vital energy" of the Carnegie empire.

GOSPEL OF WEALTH   Andrew Carnegie's philosophy (in a book of that title) that the millionaire had a duty to distribute wealth while still alive.

JONES, CAPTAIN WILLIAM   One of a "brilliant assemblage" of men around Andrew Carnegie, "a kind of Paul Bunyan of steel," who was inventive in handling machinery and talented at dealing with people.

KNIGHTS OF LABOR   America's first major labor union, founded in 1869. By 1886, its membership numbered more than 700,000.

MORGAN, J. P.   Wealthy banker who purchased the Carnegie steel empire in 1901 for $492 million; it became the core of the United States Steel Company.

PULLMAN, GEORGE   Developed the Pullman railroad sleeping car and joined forces with Andrew Carnegie to form the Pullman Palace Car Company.

SCHWAB, CHARLES   Assistant manager of Andrew Carnegie's Braddock plant and another of the brilliant men surrounding Carnegie.

SCOTT, THOMAS A.   Superintendent of the Pennsylvania Railroad and Andrew Carnegie's boss who first encouraged him to invest in stock.

UNITED STATES STEEL COMPANY   J. P. Morgan merged the Carnegie empire with other interests to create this huge corporation, which controlled more than 60 percent of America's steel production.

WOODRUFF, T. T.   When Andrew Carnegie bought a one-eighth interest in Woodruff's company, Woodruff began production of the first sleeping car for trains.

Toward the end of his days, at the close of World War I, Andrew Carnegie was already a kind of national legend. His meteoric rise, the scandals and successes of his industrial generalship —all this was blurred into nostalgic memory. What was left was a small, rather feeble man with a white beard and pale, penetrating eyes, who could occasionally be seen puttering around his mansion on upper Fifth Avenue, a benevolent old gentleman who still rated an annual birthday interview but was even then a venerable relic of a fast-disappearing era. Carnegie himself looked back on his career with a certain savored incredulity. "How much did you say I had given away, Poynton?" he would inquire of his private secretary; "$324,657,399" was the answer. "Good Heaven!" Carnegie would exclaim. "Where did I ever get all that money?"

Where he *had* got all that money was indeed a legendary story, for even in an age known for its acquisitive triumphs, Carnegie's touch had been an extraordinary one. He had begun, in true Horatio Alger fashion, at the bottom; he had ended, in a manner that put the wildest of Alger's novels to shame, at the very pinnacle of success. At the close of his great deal with J. P. Morgan in 1901, when the Carnegie steel empire was sold to form the core of the new United States Steel Company, the banker had extended his hand and delivered the ultimate encomium of the times: "Mr. Carnegie," he said, "I want to congratulate you on being the richest man in the world."

It was certainly as "the richest man in the world" that Carnegie attracted the attention of his contemporaries. Yet this is hardly why we look back on him with interest today. As an enormous money-maker Carnegie was a flashy, but hardly a profound, hero of the times; and the attitudes of Earnestness and Self-

Reprinted from *American Heritage,* August 1960, pp. 4–9, 107–111, by permission of the author.

Assurance, so engaging in the young immigrant, become irritating when they are congealed in the millionaire. But what lifts Carnegie's life above the rut of a one-dimensional success story is an aspect of which his contemporaries were relatively unaware.

Going through his papers after his death, Carnegie's executors came across a memorandum that he had written to himself fifty years before, carefully preserved in a little yellow box of keepsakes and mementos. It brings us back to December, 1868, when Carnegie, a young man flushed with the first taste of great success, retired to his suite in the opulent Hotel St. Nicholas in New York, to total up his profits for the year. It had been a tremendous year and the calculation must have been extremely pleasurable. Yet this is what he wrote as he reflected on the figures:

Thirty-three and an income of $50,000 per annum! By this time two in years I can so arrange all my business as to secure at least $50,000 per annum. Beyond this never earn —make no effort to increase fortune, but spend the surplus each year for benevolent purposes. Cast aside business forever, except for others.

Settle in Oxford and get a thorough education, making the acquaintance of literary men—this will take three years of active work—pay especial attention to speaking in public. Settle then in London and purchase a controlling interest in some newspaper or live review and give the general management of it attention, taking part in public matters, especially those connected with education and improvement of the poorer classes.

Man must have an idol—the amassing of wealth is one of the worst species of idolatry—no idol more debasing than the worship of money. Whatever I engage in I must push inordinately; therefore should I be careful to choose that life which will be the most elevating in its character. To continue much longer overwhelmed by business cares and with most of my thoughts wholly upon the way to make more money in the shortest time, must degrade me beyond hope of permanent recovery. I will resign business at thirty-five, but during the ensuing two years I wish to spend the afternoons in receiving instruction and in reading systematically.

It is a document which in more ways than one is Carnegie to the very life: brash, incredibly self-confident, chockablock with self-conscious virtue — and more than a little hypocritical. For the program so nobly outlined went largely unrealized. Instead of retiring in two years, Carnegie went on for thirty-three more; even then it was with considerable difficulty that he was persuaded to quit. Far from shunning further money-making, he proceeded to roll up his fortune with an uninhibited drive that led one unfriendly biographer to characterize him as "the greediest little gentleman ever created." Certainly he was one of the most aggressive profit seekers of his time. Typically, when an associate jubilantly cabled: "No. 8 furnace broke all records today," Carnegie coldly replied, "What were the other furnaces doing?"

It is this contrast between his hopes and his performance that makes Carnegie interesting. For when we review his life, what we see is more than the career of another nineteenth-century acquisitor. We see the unequal struggle between a man who loved money — loved making it, having it, spending it — and a man who, at bottom, was ashamed of himself for his acquisitive desires. All during his lifetime, the moneymaker seemed to win. But what lifts Carnegie's story out of the ordinary is that the other Carnegie ultimately triumphed. At his death public speculation placed the size of his estate at about five hundred million dollars. In fact it came to $22,881,575. Carnegie *had* become the richest man in the world — but something had also driven him to give away ninety per cent of his wealth.

Actually, his contemporaries knew of Carnegie's inquietude about money. In 1889, before he was world-famous, he had written an article for the *North American Review* entitled "The Gospel of Wealth" —

Andrew Carnegie, in his mid-twenties when photographed here in 1861, was the son of Scottish working-class radicals and the product of a stern religious upbringing. In his younger days, he thought that the amassing of wealth was "one of the worst species of idolatry." However, he abandoned his plans to retire at thirty-five in order to devote his energies to self-improvement and benevolent enterprises. Instead, he became one of the richest men the world had ever known. (Courtesy, Carnegie Corporation of New York)

an article that contained the startling phrase: "The man who dies thus rich dies disgraced." It was hardly surprising, however, if the world took these sentiments at a liberal discount: homiletic millionaires who preached the virtues of austerity were no novelty; Carnegie himself, returning in 1879 from a trip to the miseries of India, had been able to write with perfect sincerity, "How very little the millionaire has beyond the peasant, and how very often his addi-tions tend not to happiness but to misery."

What the world may well have underestimated, however, was a concern more deeply rooted than these pieties revealed. For, unlike so many of his self-made peers, who also rose from poverty, Carnegie was the product of a *radical* environment. The village of Dunfermline, Scotland, when he was born there in 1835, was renowned as a center of rev-olutionary ferment, and Carnegie's family was itself caught up in the radical movement of the times. His father was a regular speaker at the Chartist rallies, which were an almost daily occurrence in Dun-fermline in the 1840's, and his uncle was an impas-sioned orator for the rights of the working class to vote and strike. All this made an indelible impression on Carnegie's childhood.

"I remember as if it were yesterday," he wrote seventy years later, "being awakened during the night by a tap at the back window by men who had come to inform my parents that my uncle, Bailie Morrison, had been thrown in jail because he dared to hold a meeting which had been forbidden . . . It is not to be wondered at that, nursed amid such sur-roundings, I developed into a violent young Repub-lican whose motto was 'death to privilege.'"

From another uncle, George Lauder, Carnegie ab-sorbed a second passion that was also to reveal itself in his later career. This was his love of poetry, first that of the poet Burns, with its overtones of romantic egalitar-ianism, and then later, of Shakespeare. Immense quan-tities of both were not only committed to memory, but made into an integral — indeed, sometimes an embar-rassingly evident — part of his life: on first visiting the Doge's palace in Venice he thrust a companion in the ducal throne and held him pinioned there while he orated the appropriate speeches from *Othello*. Once, seeing Vanderbilt walking on Fifth Avenue, Carnegie smugly remarked, "I would not exchange his millions for my knowledge of Shakespeare."

But it was more than just a love of poetry that re-mained with Carnegie. Virtually alone among his fellow acquisitors, he was driven by a genuine re-spect for the power of thought to seek answers for questions that never even occurred to them. Later, when he "discovered" Herbert Spencer, the English sociologist, Carnegie wrote to him, addressing him as "Master," and it was as "Master" that Spencer re-mained, even after Carnegie's lavishness had left Spencer very much in his debt.

But Carnegie's early life was shaped by currents more material than intellectual. The grinding process of industrial change had begun slowly but in-eluctably to undermine the cottage weaving that was the traditional means of employment in Dun-fermline. The Industrial Revolution, in the shape of new steam mills, was forcing out the hand weavers, and one by one the looms which constituted the en-tire capital of the Carnegie family had to be sold. Carnegie never forgot the shock of his father return-ing home to tell him, in despair, "Andra, I can get nae mair work."

A family council of war was held, and it was de-cided that there was only one possible course — they must try their luck in America, to which two sisters of Carnegie's mother, Margaret, had already emi-grated. With the aid of a few friends the money for the crossing was scraped together, and at thirteen Andrew found himself transported to the only coun-try in which his career would have been possible.

It hardly got off to an auspicious start, however. The family made their way to Allegheny, Pennsylva-nia, a raw and bustling town where Carnegie's father again sought work as an independent weaver. But it was as hopeless to compete against the great mills in America as in Scotland, and soon father and son were forced to seek work in the local cotton mills. There Andrew worked from six in the morning until six at night, making $1.20 as a bobbin boy.

After a while his father quit — factory work was impossible for the traditional small enterpriser — and Andrew got a "better" job with a new firm, tending an engine deep in a dungeon cellar and dipping newly made cotton spools in a vat of oil. Even the raise to $3 a week . . . could not overcome the horrors of that lonely and foul-smelling basement. It was perhaps the only time in Carnegie's life when his self-assurance deserted him: to the end of his days the merest whiff of oil could make him deathly sick.

Yet he was certain, as he wrote home at sixteen, that "anyone could get along in this Country," and the rags-to-riches saga shortly began. The telegraph had just come to Pittsburgh, and one evening over a game of checkers, the manager of the local office informed Andrew's uncle that he was looking for a messenger. Andy got the job and, in true Alger fashion, set out to excel in it. Within a few weeks he had carefully memorized the names and the locations, not only of the main streets in Pittsburgh, but of the main firms, so that he was the quickest of all the messenger boys.

He came early and stayed late, watched the telegraphers at work, and at home at night learned the Morse code. As a result he was soon the head of the growing messenger service, and a skilled telegrapher himself. One day he dazzled the office by taking a message "by ear" instead of by the commonly used tape printer, and since he was then only the third operator in the country able to turn the trick, citizens used to drop into the office to watch Andy take down the words "hot from the wire."

One such citizen who was especially impressed with young Carnegie's determination was Thomas A. Scott, in time to become one of the colorful railway magnates of the West, but then the local superintendent of the Pennsylvania Railroad. Soon thereafter Carnegie became "Scott's Andy" — telegrapher, secretary, and general factotum — at thirty-five dollars a month. In his *Autobiography* Carnegie recalls an instance which enabled him to begin the next stage of his career.

One morning I reached the office and found that a serious accident on the Eastern Division had delayed the express passenger train westward, and that the passenger train eastward was proceeding with a flagman in advance at every curve. The freight trains in both directions were standing on the sidings. Mr. Scott was not to be found. Finally I could not resist the temptation to plunge in, take the responsibility, give "train orders" and set matters going. "Death or Westminster Abbey" flashed across my mind. I knew it was dismissal, disgrace, perhaps criminal punishment for me if I erred. On the other hand, I could bring in the wearied freight train men who had lain out all night. I knew I could. I knew just what to do, and so I began.

Signing Scott's name to the orders, Carnegie flashed out the necessary instructions to bring order out of the tangle. The trains moved; there were no mishaps. When Scott reached the office Carnegie told him what he had done. Scott said not a word but looked carefully over all that had taken place. After a little he moved away from Carnegie's desk to his own, and that was the end of it. "But I noticed," Carnegie concluded good-humoredly, "that he came in very regularly and in good time for some mornings after that."

It is hardly to be wondered at that Carnegie became Scott's favorite, his "white-haired Scotch devil." Impetuous but not rash, full of enthusiasm and good-natured charm, the small lad with his blunt, open features and his slight Scottish burr was every executive's dream of an assistant. Soon Scott repaid Andy for his services by introducing him to a new and very different kind of opportunity. He gave Carnegie the chance to subscribe to five hundred dollars' worth of Adams Express stock, a company which Scott assured Andy would prosper mightily.

Carnegie had not fifty dollars saved, much less five hundred, but it was a chance he could ill afford to miss. He reported the offer to his mother, and that pillar of the family unhesitatingly mortgaged their home to raise the necessary money. When the first dividend check came in, with its ornate Spencerian flourishes, Carnegie had something like a revelation. "I shall remember that check as long as I live," he subsequently wrote. "It gave me the first penny of revenue from capital — something that I had not worked for with the sweat of my brow. 'Eureka!' I cried, 'Here's the goose that lays the golden eggs.'" He was right; within a few years his investment in the Adams Express Company was paying annual dividends of $1,400.

It was not long thereafter that an even more propitious chance presented itself. Carnegie was riding on the Pennsylvania line one day when he was approached by a "farmer-looking" man carrying a small green bag in his hand. The other introduced himself as T. T. Woodruff and quite frankly said that he wanted a chance to talk with someone connected with the railroad. Whereupon he opened his bag and took out a small model of the first sleeping car.

Carnegie was immediately impressed with its possibilities, and he quickly arranged for Woodruff to meet Scott. When the latter agreed to give the cars a trial, Woodruff in appreciation offered Carnegie a chance to subscribe to a one-eighth interest in the new company. A local banker agreed to lend Andy the few hundred dollars needed for the initial payment — the rest being financed from dividends. Once again Andy had made a shrewd investment: within two years the Woodruff Palace Car Company was paying him a return of more than $5,000 a year.

Investments now began to play an increasingly important role in Carnegie's career. Through his railroad contacts he came to recognize the possibilities in manufacturing the heavy equipment needed by the rapidly expanding lines, and soon he was instrumental in organizing companies to meet these needs. One of them, the Keystone Bridge Company, was the first successful manufacturer of iron railway bridges. Another, the Pittsburgh Locomotive Works, made engines. And most important of all, an interest in a local iron works run by an irascible German named Andrew Kloman brought Carnegie into actual contact with the manufacture of iron itself.

None of these new ventures required any substantial outlay of cash. His interest in the Keystone Bridge Company, for instance, which was to earn him $15,000 in 1868, came to him "in return for services rendered in its promotion" — services which Carnegie, as a young railroad executive, was then in a highly strategic position to deliver. Similarly the interest in the Kloman works reflected no contribution on Carnegie's part except that of being the human catalyst and buffer between some highly excitable participants.

By 1865 his "side" activities had become so important that he decided to leave the Pennsylvania Railroad. He was by then superintendent, Scott having moved up to a vice presidency, but his salary of $2,400 was already vastly overshadowed by his income from various ventures. One purchase alone — the Storey farm in Pennsylvania oil country, which Carnegie and a few associates picked up for $40,000 — was eventually to pay the group a million dollars in dividends in *one* year. About this time a friend dropped in on Carnegie and asked him how he was doing. "Oh, I'm rich, I'm rich!" he exclaimed.

He was indeed embarked on the road to riches, and determined, as he later wrote in his *Autobiography,* that "nothing could be allowed to interfere for a moment with my business career." Hence it comes as a surprise to note that it was at this very point that Carnegie retired to his suite to write his curiously introspective and troubled thoughts about the pursuit of wealth. But the momentum of events was to prove far too strong for these moralistic doubts. Moving his headquarters to New York to promote his various interests, he soon found himself swept along by a succession of irresistible opportunities for money-making.

One of these took place quite by chance. Carnegie was trying to sell the Woodruff sleeping car at the same time that a formidable rival named George Pullman was also seeking to land contracts for his sleeping car, and the railroads were naturally taking advantage of the competitive situation. One summer evening in 1869 Carnegie found himself mounting the resplendent marble stairway of the St. Nicholas Hotel side by side with his competitor.

"Good evening, Mr. Pullman," said Carnegie in his ebullient manner. Pullman was barely cordial.

"How strange we should meet here," Carnegie went on, to which the other replied nothing at all.

"Mr. Pullman," said Carnegie, after an embarrassing pause, "don't you think we are making nice fools of ourselves?" At this Pullman evinced a glimmer of interest: "What do you mean?" he inquired. Carnegie quickly pointed out that competition between the two companies was helping no one but the railroads. "Well," said Pullman, "what do you suggest we do?"

"Unite!" said Carnegie. "Let's make a joint proposition to the Union Pacific, your company and mine. Why not organize a new company to do it?" "What would you call it?" asked Pullman suspiciously. "The Pullman Palace Car Company," said Carnegie and with this shrewd psychological stroke won his point. A new company was formed, and in time Carnegie became its largest stockholder.

Meanwhile, events pushed Carnegie into yet another lucrative field. To finance the proliferating railway systems of America, British capital was badly needed, and with his Scottish ancestry, his verve, and his excellent railroad connections Carnegie was the natural choice for a go-between. His brief case stuffed with bonds and prospectuses, Carnegie became a transatlantic commuter, soon developing intimate relations both with great bankers like Junius Morgan (the father of J. P. Morgan), and with the heads of most of the great American roads. These trips earned him not only large commissions — exceeding on occasion $100,000 for a single turn — but even more important, established connections that were later to be of immense value. He himself later testified candidly on their benefits before a group of respectfully awed senators:

For instance, I want a great contract for rails. Sidney Dillon of the Union Pacific was a personal friend of mine. Huntington was a friend. Dear Butler Duncan, that called

on me the other day, was a friend. Those and other men were presidents of railroads ... Take Huntington; you know C. P. Huntington. He was hard up very often. He was a great man, but he had a great deal of paper out. I knew his things were good. When he wanted credit I gave it to him. If you help a man that way, what chance has any paid agent going to these men? It was absurd.

But his trips to England brought Carnegie something still more valuable. They gave him steel. It is fair to say that as late as 1872 Carnegie did not see the future that awaited him as the Steel King of the world. The still modest conglomeration of foundries and mills he was gradually assembling in the Allegheny and Monongahela valleys was but one of many business interests, and not one for which he envisioned any extraordinary future. Indeed, to repeated pleas that he lead the way in developing a steel industry for America by substituting steel for iron rails, his reply was succinct: "Pioneering don't pay."

What made him change his mind? The story goes that he was awe-struck by the volcanic, spectacular eruption of a Bessemer converter, which he saw for the first time during a visit to a British mill. It was precisely the sort of display that would have appealed to Carnegie's mind — a wild, demonic, physical process miraculously contained and controlled by the dwarfed figures of the steel men themselves. At any rate, overnight Carnegie became the perfervid prophet of steel. Jumping on the first available steamer, he rushed home with the cry, "The day of iron has passed!" To the consternation of his colleagues, the hitherto reluctant pioneer became an advocate of the most daring technological and business expansion; he joined them enthusiastically in forming Carnegie, McCandless & Company, which was the nucleus of the empire that the next thirty years would bring forth.

The actual process of growth involved every aspect of successful business enterprise of the times: acquisition and merger, pools and commercial piracy, and even, on one occasion, an outright fraud in selling the United States government overpriced and underdone steel armor plate. But it would be as foolish to maintain that the Carnegie empire grew by trickery as to deny that sharp practice had its place. Essentially what lay behind the spectacular expansion were three facts.

The first of these was the sheer economic expansion of the industry in the first days of burgeoning steel use. Everywhere steel replaced iron or found new uses — and not only in railroads but in ships, buildings, bridges, machinery of all sorts. As Henry Frick himself once remarked, if the Carnegie group had not filled the need for steel another would have. But it must be admitted that Carnegie's company did its job superlatively well. In 1885 Great Britain led the world in the production of steel. Fourteen years later her total output was 695,000 tons less than the output of the Carnegie Steel Company alone.

Second was the brilliant assemblage of personal talent with which Carnegie surrounded himself. Among them, three in particular stood out. One was Captain William Jones, a Homeric figure who lumbered through the glowing fires and clanging machinery of the works like a kind of Paul Bunyan of steel, skilled at handling men, inventive in handling equipment, and enough of a natural artist to produce papers for the British Iron and Steel Institute that earned him a literary as well as a technical reputation. Then there was Henry Frick, himself a self-made millionaire, whose coke empire naturally complemented Carnegie's steelworks. When the two were amalgamated, Frick took over the active management of the whole, and under his forceful hand the annual output of the Carnegie works rose tenfold. Yet another was Charles Schwab, who came out of the tiny monastic town of Loretto, Pennsylvania, to take a job as a stake driver. Six months later he had been promoted by Jones into the assistant managership of the Braddock plant.

These men, and a score like them, constituted the vital energy of the Carnegie works. As Carnegie himself said, "Take away all our money, our great works, ore mines and coke ovens, but leave our organization, and in four years I shall have re-established myself."

But the third factor in the growth of the empire was Carnegie himself. A master salesman and a skilled diplomat of business at its highest levels, Carnegie was also a ruthless driver of his men. He pitted his associates and subordinates in competition with one another until a feverish atmosphere pervaded the whole organization. "You cannot imagine the abounding sense of freedom and relief I experience as soon as I get on board a steamer and sail past Sandy Hook," he once said to Captain Jones. "My God!" replied Jones. "Think of the relief to us!"

But Carnegie could win loyalties as well. All his promising young men were given gratis ownership participations — minuscule fractions of one per cent, which were enough, however, to make them millionaires in their own right. Deeply grateful to Jones, Carnegie once offered him a similar participation. Jones hemmed and hawed and finally refused; he would be unable to work effectively with the men, he said, once he was a partner. Carnegie insisted that his contribution be recognized and asked Jones what he wanted. "Well," said the latter, "you might pay me a hell of a big salary." "We'll do it!" said Carnegie. "From this time forth you shall receive the same salary as the President of the United States." "Ah, Andy, that's the kind of talk," said Captain Bill.

Within three decades, on the flood tide of economic expansion, propelled by brilliant executive work and relentless pressure from Carnegie, the company made immense strides. "Such a magnificent aggregation of industrial power has never before been under the domination of a single man," reported a biographer in 1902, describing the Gargantuan structure of steel and coke and ore and transport. Had the writer known of the profits earned by this aggregation he might have been even more impressed: three and a half million dollars in 1889, seven million in 1897, twenty-one million in 1899, and an immense forty million in 1900. "Where is there such a business!" Carnegie had exulted, and no wonder — the majority share of all these earnings, without hindrance of income tax, went directly into his pockets.

Nevertheless, with enormous success came problems. One of these was the restiveness of certain partners, under the "Iron-Clad" agreement, which prevented any of them from selling their shares to anyone but the company itself — an arrangement which meant, of course, that the far higher valuation of an outside purchaser could not be realized. Particularly chagrined was Frick, when, as the culmination of other disagreements between them, Carnegie sought to buy him out "at the value appearing on the books." Another problem was a looming competitive struggle in the steel industry itself that presaged a period of bitter industrial warfare ahead. And last was Carnegie's own growing desire to "get out."

Already he was spending half of each year abroad, first traveling, and then, after his late marriage, in residence in the great Skibo Castle he built for his wife on Dornoch Firth, Scotland. There he ran his business enterprises with one hand while he courted the literary and creative world with the other, entertaining Kipling and Matthew Arnold, Paderewski and Lloyd George, Woodrow Wilson and Theodore Roosevelt, Gladstone, and of course, Herbert Spencer, the Master. But even his career as "Laird" of Skibo could not remove him from the worries — and triumphs — of his business: a steady flow of cables and correspondence intruded on the "serious" side of life.

In his late years, Carnegie turned again toward the idealism of his youth. Declaring that his riches had come to him as a "sacred trust" to administer for the good of humanity, he endowed numerous philanthropies and managed to give away 90 percent of his wealth before he died. (Carnegie Corporation of New York)

It was Schwab who cut the knot. Having risen to the very summit of the Carnegie concern he was invited in December, 1900, to give a speech on the future of the steel industry at the University Club in New York. There, before eighty of the nation's top business leaders he painted a glowing picture of what could be done if a super-company of steel were formed, integrated from top to bottom, self-sufficient with regard to its raw materials, balanced in its array of final products. One of the guests was the imperious J. P. Morgan, and as the speech progressed it was noticed that his concentration grew more and more intense. After dinner Morgan rose and took the young steel man by the elbow and engaged him in private conversation for half an hour while he plied him with rapid and penetrating questions; then a few weeks later he invited him to a private meeting in the great library of his home. They talked from nine o'clock in the evening until dawn. As the sun began to stream in through the library windows, the banker finally rose. "Well," he said to Schwab, "if Andy wants to sell, I'll buy. Go and find his price."

Carnegie at first did not wish to sell. Faced with the actual prospect of a withdrawal from the business he had built into the mightiest single industrial empire in the world, he was frightened and dismayed. He sat silent before Schwab's report, brooding, loath to inquire into details. But soon his enthusiasm returned. No such opportunity was likely to present itself again. In short order a figure of $492,000,000 was agreed on for the entire enterprise, of which Carnegie himself was to receive $300,000,000 in five per cent gold bonds and preferred stock. Carnegie jotted down the terms of the transaction on a slip of paper and told Schwab to bring it to Morgan. The banker glanced only briefly at the paper. "I accept," he said.

After the formalities were in due course completed, Carnegie was in a euphoric mood. "Now, Pierpont, I am the happiest man in the world," he said. Morgan was by no means unhappy himself: his own banking company had made a direct profit of $12,500,000 in the underwriting transaction, and this was but a prelude to a stream of lucrative financings under Morgan's aegis, by which the total capitalization was rapidly raised to $1,400,000,000. A few years later, Morgan and Carnegie found themselves aboard the same steamer en route to Europe. They fell into talk and Carnegie confessed, "I made one mistake, Pierpont, when I sold out to you."

"What was that?" asked the banker.

"I should have asked you for $100,000,000 more than I did."

Morgan grinned. "Well," he said, "you would have got it if you had."

Thus was written *finis* to one stage of Carnegie's career. Now it would be seen to what extent his "radical pronouncements" were serious. For in the *Gospel of Wealth* — the famous article combined with others in book form — Carnegie had proclaimed the duty of the millionaire to administer and distribute his wealth *during his lifetime*. Though he might have "proved" his worth by his fortune, his heirs had shown no such evidence of their fitness. Carnegie

bluntly concluded: "By taxing estates heavily at his death, the State marks its condemnation of the selfish millionaire's unworthy life."

Coming from the leading millionaire of the day, these had been startling sentiments. So also were his views on the "labor question" which, if patronizing, were nonetheless humane and advanced for their day. The trouble was, of course, that the sentiments were somewhat difficult to credit. As one commentator of the day remarked, "His vision of what might be done with wealth had beauty and breadth and thus serenely overlooked the means by which wealth had been acquired."

For example, the novelist Hamlin Garland visited the steel towns from which the Carnegie millions came and bore away a description of work that was ugly, brutal, and exhausting: he contrasted the lavish care expended on the plants with the callous disregard of the pigsty homes: "the streets were horrible; the buildings poor; the sidewalks sunken and full of holes.... Everywhere the yellow mud of the streets lay kneaded into sticky masses through which groups of pale, lean men slouched in faded garments...." When the famous Homestead strike erupted in 1892, with its private army of Pinkerton detectives virtually at war with the workers, the Carnegie benevolence seemed revealed as shabby fakery. At Skibo Carnegie stood firmly behind the company's iron determination to break the strike. As a result, public sentiment swung sharply and suddenly against him; the St. Louis *Post-Dispatch* wrote: "Three months ago Andrew Carnegie was a man to be envied. Today he is an object of mingled pity and contempt. In the estimation of nine-tenths of the thinking people on both sides of the ocean he has ... confessed himself a moral coward."

In an important sense the newspaper was right. For though Carnegie continued to fight against "privilege," he saw privilege only in its fading aristocratic vestments and not in the new hierarchies of wealth and power to which he himself belonged. In

Skibo Castle he now played the role of the benign autocrat, awakening to the skirling of his private bagpiper and proceeding to breakfast to the sonorous accompaniment of the castle organ.

Meanwhile there had also come fame and honors in which Carnegie wallowed unashamedly. He counted the "freedoms" bestowed on him by grateful or hopeful cities and crowed, "I have fifty-two and Gladstone has only seventeen." He entertained the King of England and told him that democracy was better than monarchy, and met the German Kaiser: "Oh, yes, yes," said the latter worthy on being introduced. "I have read your books. You do not like kings." But Mark Twain, on hearing of this, was not fooled. "He says he is a scorner of kings and emperors and dukes," he wrote, "whereas he is like the rest of the human race: a slight attention from one of these can make him drunk for a week. . . ."

And yet it is not enough to conclude that Carnegie was in fact a smaller man than he conceived himself. For this judgment overlooks one immense and irrefutable fact. He did, in the end, abide by his self-imposed duty. He did give nearly all of his gigantic fortune away.

As one would suspect, the quality of the philanthropy reflected the man himself. There was, for example, a huge and sentimentally administered private pension fund to which access was to be had on the most trivial as well as the most worthy grounds: if it included a number of writers, statesmen, scientists, it also made room for two maiden ladies with whom Carnegie had once danced as a young man, a boyhood acquaintance who had once held Carnegie's books while he ran a race, a merchant to whom he had once delivered a telegram and who had subsequently fallen on hard times. And then, as one would expect, there was a benevolent autocracy in the administration of the larger philanthropies as well. "Now everybody vote Aye," was the way Carnegie typically determined the policies of the philanthropic "foundations" he established.

Yet if these flaws bore the stamp of one side of Carnegie's personality, there was also the other side — the side that, however crudely, asked important questions and however piously, concerned itself with great ideals. Of this the range and purpose of the main philanthropies gave unimpeachable testimony. There were the famous libraries — three thousand of them costing nearly sixty million dollars; there were the Carnegie institutes in Pittsburgh and Washington, Carnegie Hall in New York, the Hague Peace Palace, the Carnegie Endowment for International Peace, and the precedent-making Carnegie Corporation of New York, with its original enormous endowment of $125,000,000. In his instructions to the trustees of this first great modern foundation, couched in the simplified spelling of which he was an ardent advocate, we see Carnegie at his very best:

Conditions on erth [sic] inevitably change; hence, no wise man will bind Trustees forever to certain paths, causes, or institutions. I disclaim any intention of doing so . . . My chief happiness, as I write these lines lies in the thot [sic] that, even after I pass away, the welth [sic] that came to me to administer as a sacred trust for the good of my fellow men is to continue to benefit humanity . . .

If these sentiments move us — if Carnegie himself in retrospect moves us at last to grudging respect — it is not because his was the triumph of a saint or a philosopher. It is because it was the much more difficult triumph of a very human and fallible man struggling to retain his convictions in an age, and in the face of a career, which subjected them to impossible temptations. Carnegie is something of America writ large; his is the story of the Horatio Alger hero *after* he has made his million dollars. In the failures of Andrew Carnegie we see many of the failures of America itself. In his curious triumph, we see what we hope is our own steadfast core of integrity.

QUESTIONS TO CONSIDER

1   Robert L. Heilbroner suggests that Andrew Carnegie was interesting because of the contrasts in his character: the conflict between his Calvinist simplicity and his overpowering urge to accumulate wealth. What are the sources of Carnegie's contradictory character?

2   Describe Carnegie's personal "gospel of wealth." Did he live up to his own ideals? Why do you think he was attracted to the teachings of his "master," evolutionist Herbert Spencer?

3   All his life, Carnegie insisted upon his hatred of aristocratic privilege, yet he lived a life of magnificence in his Scottish castle, and he courted the acquaintance of famous politicians, scholars, and royal personages. How did he justify his actions? Did he see himself as a different sort of aristocrat? Why did he go back to Britain to live?

4   Carnegie left a rich legacy of philanthropies, most notably the vast network of libraries that has developed into our present public library system. How was the money to fund these philanthropies obtained in the first place? Why do you think Carnegie — and many others — failed to see the contrast between the good money could do and the way it was made? How might wealthy people in the Gilded Age have viewed the lives of the working poor?

5   How does what Heilbroner calls the "failure" of Andrew Carnegie reflect the failure of America in the Gilded Age? What were the social and economic consequences of the *Gospel of Wealth* and of huge concentrations of capital in late nineteenth-century America?

6

How the Other Side Lived

PAGE SMITH

Since the colonial era, a shortage of labor in America had kept wage levels higher here than overseas. Even so, the American worker had a miserable time of it in the grim industrial age. The expansion and mechanization of the factory system, which took place at an incredible rate after the Civil War, forced workers to make painful adjustments that reduced their status and independence.

Before industrialization, as C. Vann Woodward has said, skilled artisans who owned their own tools were likely to take pride in their craft and enjoy a strong bargaining position. The new factory system, Woodward points out, lowered the workers' status, forcing them to surrender their tools, a good deal of their bargaining power, and almost all the pride they took in their product. Under the employ of people they never knew and probably never saw, they operated a machine that made their craftsmanship insignificant, because their place at the machine could be taken by an unskilled worker. Their relationship to their work and to the boss became increasingly impersonal. With the factory growing ever larger, workers felt a dispiriting loss of identity, security, and meaning in the value of labor.

To make matters worse, the mass of statutes that protects factory workers today had not been enacted in the Gilded Age. This meant that laborers, including women and children, were at the mercy of the industrial bosses. In "company towns," employers owned all the houses, stores, and services and often bossed and harassed workers to the point of tyranny. With little to restrain them beyond their own consciences and the weak protest of labor, employers were likely to cut costs by slashing wages. Throughout the 1890s, wages remained at an average of $9 a week; farm workers received far less than that.

Despite how bad things were, workers in industrial America were slow to organize. Part of the problem was the bitter opposition of the industrial leaders, who broke strikes with

*hired thugs and associated organized labor with socialism and anarchy. But another diffi-
culty was the fragmentation of the work force, which was divided by color and race, sex and
age, as well as by national origin, geography, philosophy, and styles of protest. The
utopian Knights of Labor, founded in 1869, did attempt to unite the disparate working
population, appealing to both skilled and unskilled workers regardless of race, color, or nationality. The Knights understood clearly that the consolidation of industry made the consolidation of labor imperative. Rejecting strikes as a useful weapon, the organization sought
political as well as economic objectives, demanding equal pay for both sexes, an eight-hour
workday, and the abolition of child labor. But the union was only marginally successful: at
its peak, the Knights of Labor could claim little more than 700,000 members. When labor
conditions became intolerable, workers in specific areas ignored the Knights of Labor and resorted to spontaneous strikes to protest their lot, only to meet with adamant hostility on the
part of police, business and government leaders, and the public itself.*

*The other major union of the period was the conservative American Federation of
Labor (AFL), a loose coalition of craft unions founded under Samuel Gompers in
1881. From the outset, the AFL shunned government intervention in management-
labor relations and rejected political goals in favor of specific economic benefits for skilled
workers alone. It had little quarrel with industrial consolidation, and it ignored the mass
of unskilled laborers across the land.*

*Let us accompany historian Page Smith on a journey through the plants, railroads,
steel mills, oil fields, and coal mines of the Gilded Age and examine the lives and
working conditions of the men, women, and children employed by industrial captains
such as Andrew Carnegie. As Smith makes clear, American workers in the iron age of
industry toiled in conditions almost inconceivable to us today. Smith's account reminds
us that, necessary though industrialization was for the United States, it came at a terrible human cost.*

GLOSSARY

JONES, MARY "MOTHER"   Legendary
champion of the rights of miners and the author of a
graphic "account of a miner's life."

MARX, ELEANOR, AND EDWARD AVELING
The daughter of Karl Marx and her husband toured
the United States in 1886, surveying labor
conditions there and talking with socialists and labor
leaders; the Avelings concluded that the condition of
working men and women in America was as bad as
that of Britain's laboring class.

PHILLIPS, WENDELL   Former abolitionist who
raised his voice on behalf of the American worker;
he demanded higher wages and shorter working
hours and urged organization and group efforts to
challenge "the organization of capital."

THE SHANTY BOY   A kind of documentary
story about the brutal and dangerous conditions in
American lumber camps.

In 1886 Karl Marx's daughter Eleanor Marx Aveling and her husband, Edward, visited the United States to make a general survey of labor conditions and to talk with socialists and labor leaders around the country. They were struck by the activity in the labor movement generally, both in unionization and in radical political action on the part of various socialist and anarchist groups. In their opinion, the condition of workingmen and women in the United States was in every important respect as bad as that of the British working class. In addition, unionization in America was twenty or thirty years behind that in Britain. On the other hand, there were far more labor newspapers and journals in the United States than in Britain. The Avelings counted ninety-seven, including one entitled the *Woman's World* and excluding most of the foreign-language socialist and labor journals. Wherever the Avelings went they addressed large crowds of working-class people with a substantial admixture of middle- and upper-class reformers. In a twelve-week tour they visited thirty-five cities and towns as far west as Kansas. The meetings were, the Avelings wrote, "with the very rarest exceptions, largely attended. In many places hundreds of people were unable to gain admission.... We have never spoken to any audiences like the American audiences for patience, fairness, anxiety to get at the meaning of the speaker," they added. The Avelings found an enormous curiosity about the doctrines of socialism, which heretofore had been preached largely by Germans for German immigrants. "And in every town we met, both in private and in public, the leading men and women in the various working-class organizations."

In the view of the Avelings, British laborers still believed that "there is a community of interests between them and their employers.... But in America this mutual deception is nearly at an end. The workingmen and the capitalists in the majority of cases quite understand that each, as a class, is the deadly and inexorable foe of the other...." The capitalists believed the struggle must end "in the subjugation of the working class," while the workingmen were equally convinced it would end "in the abolition of all classes."

... The Avelings were also struck by the degree to which the labor commissioners of the various states in their statistical reports revealed a profound sympathy for the workingmen and women of their states. The report of the Massachusetts commissioners on conditions in Fall River, for example, noted that "every mill in the city is making money ... but the operatives travel in the same old path — sickness, suffering, and small pay.... There is a state of things that should make men blush for shame."

In state after state the testimony of workers in different industrial crafts was monotonously the same. Things were getting worse with each passing year. "Times are harder now than I ever knew them before," a laborer in Kansas declared, while another said, "The condition of the laboring classes is too bad for utterance, and is rapidly growing worse." The testimony was also uniformly to the effect that "the rich and poor are further apart than ever before." A coal miner reported that he had had to move five times during the year to find employment. In Michigan a worker in a shoe factory testified: "Labor to-day is poorer paid than ever before; more discontent exists, more men in despair, and if a change is not soon devised, trouble must come...."

The Avelings were convinced by their reading of the reports of the state labor commissioners and their own observations that, hours and wages aside, the physical demands placed by American employers on their workers were much more severe than those prevailing in Britain. American laborers started to work at an earlier age than their British counterparts, worked more strenuously, and died, on the average,

From *A People's History of the Past, Reconstruction Era, Vol. VI, The Rise of Industrial America* by Page Smith, McGraw-Hill. Reprinted by permission of the author.

almost a decade earlier. Thus the life expectancy of a British iron molder was fifty years and eleven months, while "the American moulder dies before he reaches the age of forty. . . ."

Employers and foremen practiced innumerable small deceits: short measures in the cloth mills; short weights in the mines; fines for the mildest infractions of innumerable restrictive rules governing every action of the worker. Blacklists and intimidation were common. Many workers reported to the Avelings that they were afraid to be seen talking to them for fear of losing their jobs and being thereafter black-listed as troublemakers, radicals, or union sympathizers. Workers were threatened with loss of their jobs simply for voting for political candidates antithetical to their employers. It was common practice for newly employed workers to be required to take an "ironclad oath" to belong to no working-class organization. Even subscription to a labor journal or newspaper could be cause for dismissal. Western Union, for example, required an oath which read, "I,— — —, . . . hereby promise and agree . . . that I will forthwith abandon any and all membership, connection, or affiliation with any organization or society, whether secret or open, which in any wise attempts to regulate the conditions of my services or the payment therefor. . . ." The Knights of Labor, which became the first major union in the country, was often specifically proscribed. The employees of the Warren Foundry were required immediately to "free [themselves] from a combination in hostility to the company. . . . If they are not willing to do so, we request them to leave our premises. . . ."

Employers often required their workers to accept in whole or in part company script in lieu of money, which script, needless to say, could be redeemed only at the company store. Companies commonly deducted from their employees' pay — in addition to advances from the company store — money for the salary of a doctor or nurse, rent for a company house, and coal given out by the company on credit. Thus it was not unusual for workers at the end of the year to find themselves actually in debt to the company that employed them. The reports of the New Jersey labor commissioners in 1884 contained numerous instances of workers who ended a year of labor in debt to the company. A worker in Paterson reported, "My actual earnings last year were but 100 dollars, while the cost of living was 400." A silk worker in the same town reported a 50 percent reduction in wages over a three-year period. A railroad employee told the Kansas commissioners: "A man . . . has to wait 50 days before he receives a cent of wages, and then only gets paid for 30 days, leaving the proceeds of 20 days' labor in the company's hands until he quits their employ."

Of a sample of 520 Michigan workers, 146 were paid weekly, 32 biweekly, 177 monthly, and 28 on demand, while 137 had no regular payday. Of the 137 with no regular payday, a number reported waiting 60 to 90 days for their pay. Only two-fifths of Michigan's factory employees were paid weekly, while two-fifths were paid monthly. As for hours, of 65,627 mill and factory "hands" in the state, 76 percent worked 60 hours a week or more. Moreover, 12 percent of the men, 22 percent of the women, and 34 percent of the children worked more than 10 hours daily.

Ironically, the men, better organized, worked on the average fewer hours than the women and children (the last worked longest of all). Tram drivers in Fall River, Massachusetts, worked an average of 15 hours a day, while for streetcar conductors in Kansas, 16 and 17 were standard. In New York bakers averaged 16 hours, six days a week. In the Pennsylvania coal mines 14 to 18 hours a day were typical, and one witness before the labor commissioners reported, "I know that some [men] go into the mines on Sunday, trying to make a living and cannot, while their employers own Sunday-schools, churches, preachers, Government bonds . . . with yachts, steamboats, orange plantations, and are very rich."

Along with low pay and long, long hours, workers in most trades and industries had to contend with extended periods of unemployment. In Topeka, Kansas, in 1885, of 660 skilled workmen, 156 worked part-time and 108 had no work at all. During the year 1 out of 5 skilled and unskilled workers was unemployed.

A constant complaint voiced to the Avelings on their tour in 1886 was that hundreds of thousands of men had been displaced by machines, a fact confirmed by one Philadelphia manufacturer, who told the Avelings that in a thirty-year period "machinery has displaced 6 times the amount of hand labor formerly required." In carpets, weaving, spinning ten to twenty times fewer workers were required; in spinning alone seventy-five times fewer. In the milling of flour one person did the work done by four a few decades earlier, while in machine tooling "one boy can produce as much as was formerly produced by 10 skilled men." In mining the story was similar. In the Hocking Valley of Ohio, improved machines enabled 160 men to do the work of 500.

The housing conditions of working-class men and women had deteriorated to an alarming degree. In New York City in 1883 there were 25,000 tenement buildings containing 1,000,000 inhabitants. Some 19,000 tenements accommodated 50 or more persons each, and families of 6 to 8 people living in a single room were not uncommon. The New York labor commissioners noted that the tenants "cook, eat, and sleep in the same room, men, women, and children together. Refuse of every description makes the floors damp and slimy, and the puny, half-naked children crawl or slide about it."

At Fall River sixteen houses occupied by more than 500 human beings used the same privy, and the odor was hardly to be endured in summer. In Lowell "the tenants of a single block had to carry their refuse of all kinds, and human excrements ... into Austin Avenue for deposit." In another block in Lowell, commissioners counted thirty-six tenements containing thirty-six families and 396 persons. Such "excessively filthy," "unsanitary," "foul," wretched, and dirty lodgings were the property of the mill-owners, whose workers were often required to live in them as a condition of employment.

In cigarmaking operations, often carried on at home, "I see women," one witness reported to the New York labor commissioners, "surrounded by filth with children waddling in it, and having sores on their hands and faces and various parts of the body.... They are all the time handling this tobacco they make into cigars." Every industry had its own peculiar health hazards. "Sewing machine girls are subject to diseases of the womb," a report noted, "and when married mostly have miscarriages. In tobacco factories women are mostly affected with nervous and hysterical complaints, consumption and chest ailments...."

"We have lived in English factory towns," the Avelings wrote, "and know something of English factory hands; but we may fairly say we have never in the English Manchester seen women so worn out and degraded, such famine in their cheeks, such need and oppression, starving in their eyes, as in the women we saw trudging to their work in the New Hampshire Manchester. What must the children born of such women be?" A consequence of the starvation wages paid women workers and the uncertainty of their employment was that many of them were driven to part-time prostitution or, as the New York labor commissioners' report put it, "*quasi* prostitution.... When out of work they cohabit with one or two men, but when work was obtained dropped such associations." In addition, many women complained to the commissioners that they were taken advantage of sexually by their bosses or employers. In Kansas City and Indianapolis two clergymen told the Avelings "of the fearful state of women forced to choose between starvation and prostitution" in those "flourishing towns."

It was also evident to the Avelings that wherever possible men were replaced as factory operatives by women and children, who were paid far lower wages. The criterion in replacing a man with a woman or child was simply whether the latter had the strength to operate a particular machine.

The New Jersey labor commissioners noted: "Woman and child labor is much lower priced than that of men . . . the hours of labor are longer and the rate of wages less, women never agitate, they merely 'toil and scrimp, and bear.'" However, those women who joined the Knights of Labor received the same wages as the men. Tens of thousands of women worked in what later came to be called sweatshops as seamstresses paid by piecework. The New York labor bureau report for 1885 noted that an expert at crocheting shawls could make no more than 12 to 15 cents a day. Seamstresses, in addition, were required to pay for the machine and for the thread they used. A sewer earned $1.50 per dozen for trousers. Vests were 15 cents apiece; gloves, 90 cents a dozen. An experienced "tailoress" earned no more than $3 or $4 a week. Less skilled millinery workers made 12 cents a day and were paid every two weeks. While the law required that chairs be provided for women workers, they were frequently not allowed to sit down. Of 1,322 women studied in a survey of the New York clothing industry, 27 earned $6 per week and 534 earned $1 a week. Fines were exacted, such as 25 cents for being five minutes late (two days' wages for a millinery worker); $1 for eating at the loom; 25 cents for washing hands; for imperfect work, for sitting down, for taking a drink of water, and so on.

The rooms in which women worked were foul, poorly ventilated, dirty, and badly lighted. It was a common practice to lock the workers in their rooms, thereby risking lives in case of fire. "One hundred women and small girls work in a cellar without ventilation, and electric light burning all day," the New York commissioners reported. Workers often suffered crippling injuries and sometimes incurable diseases. A woman who made artificial flowers found that her hands had been "poisoned" by the coloring she used. When she could not work, she was discharged, and the labor commissioners had to bring suit against her employer to collect 50 cents in back wages.

Mill "girls" came in all ages; many were married, and many were immigrants and the daughters of immigrants. All of them received lower wages than their male coworkers. Before the advent of protective legislation, most worked longer hours than men, too. Although wretchedly paid, these textile workers may have been better off than their sisters in city sweatshops, who were paid by piecework and frequently earned no more than $1 a week. Despite their hard lives and soiled clothing, the women seem proud to be photographed on the job. (Museum of American Textile History)

Increasingly child labor competed with schooling. A report of the New Jersey labor commissioners of 1885 noted that of an estimated 343,897 children of school age in the state, 89,254 attended no school, and of these, the majority worked in factories or in mines. In New York, out of 1,685,000 children and young people between the ages of five and twenty-one, only 1,041,089 were listed as enrolled in the "common schools," and average daily attendance was 583,142. In other words, on any given day an average of 1,101,958 children were *absent from school.*

Fully a third of these Massillon, Ohio, iron-mill workers were children. On the average, children in nineteenth-century mines and factories worked ten hours a day, often in dangerous conditions, and were paid at the bottom of the wage scale. Frequently, child labor competed with schooling. In one city alone, on any given day, two-thirds of the school-age children were absent from school. Labor commissioners feared that the country was raising "an army of uneducated and undisciplined children." (Massillon Museum)

Even allowing for a number educated in private schools, the figure seemed to the commissioners "almost incredible." They declared: "An army of uneducated and undisciplined children is growing up among us."

Each year saw an increase in the numbers of children laboring. In Michigan statistics indicated that seventy-one "establishments" — factories and businesses — in forty-six towns and cities employed 350 boys and girls between eight and fourteen years of age. In New Jersey there were twice as many children employed in factories in 1880 as there had been ten years earlier, while the increase of women was 142 percent in the same time. In Detroit in 1885, ninety-two businesses employed 372 boys and girls at 50 cents a day for the boys and 31 cents for the girls. In Connecticut, out of a factory labor force of 70,000, 5,000 were children under fifteen.

In the mills of Yorkville, in New York City, children under fourteen worked an eleven-hour day, while in the cigar factories, which employed many children, the workday was ten hours. "In the smaller bakeries," the Avelings reported, "children of from 9 to 13 start work at eleven at night and go on until 4 in the morning."

The Pennsylvania mines were dangerous places for boys. Thousands were killed or maimed each year without compensation or aid of any kind except that which might be provided by some local charitable group. The *Luzerne Union* reported in January, 1876: "During the past week nearly one boy a day has been killed, and the public has become so familiar with these calamities, that no attention is given them after the first announcement through a newspaper or a neighbor." A Sunday school convention that met in Scranton in 1874 was taken on a tour of the nearby mines, where they saw the "bare-footed, black-faced urchins ... picking slate from the dusty diamonds" and then heard a lecture on the "wonders of the Great Creator" — that was to say, on fossils.

A Fall River textile worker named Thomas O'Donnell told a Senate Committee on Labor-Capital Relations in 1883: "I have a brother who has four children besides his wife and himself. All he earns is $1.50 a day. He works in the iron works at Fall River. He only works nine months out of twelve. There is generally three months of stoppage ... and his wife and family all have to be supported for a year out of the wages of nine months — $1.50 a day for nine months to support six of them. It does not stand to reason that those children and he himself can have natural food and be naturally dressed. His children are often sick, and he has to call in doctors." O'Donnell himself earned $133 a year with which to feed a family of four. He dug clams and scavenged wood and coal.

Two seven-story factory buildings in Rochester, New York, one employing 150 and the other about 270 women, had only one stairway each. An Ohio fire inspector, describing similar conditions, wrote that "it is somewhat difficult to speak with calmness

of men who, while liberally insuring their property against fire, so that in case of such a visitation — a danger always imminent — their pockets shall not suffer, will not spend a dollar for the security of the lives of those by whose labor they profit."

A Massachusetts labor commissioner sounded more like a reformer than a bureaucrat when he wrote at the end of a report describing the conditions of child labor in that state: "I plead for the little ones.... In these days of legislative interference, when the shield of the State protects the dumb beast from the merciless blows of his driver; when the over-worked horse is remembered and released from his work ... it would seem pitiable if childhood's want of leisure for rest of body and education should be denied them. Massachusetts ... goes on regardless of the consequences, protecting the strong, forgetting the weak and poor ... under the false plea of non-interference with the liberty of the people. The children have rights that the State is bound to respect. Their right is to play and make merry; to be at school, to be players not workers."

Quite by accident the Avelings discovered one of the most exploited groups in the United States: cowboys. Taken by their hosts in Kansas City to a Wild West show, they got into conversation with a handsome, blue-eyed cowboy named Broncho John, who, with encouragement from the Avelings, described vividly the manner in which ranchers exploited their hands. "To our great astonishment," the Avelings wrote, "he plunged at once into a denunciation of capitalists in general and of ranchowners in particular. Broncho John estimated that there were at least 10,000 cowboys" — the Avelings believed there were many more — and "no class is harder worked ... none so poorly paid for their services" because "they have no organization in back of them" while their employers had "one of the strongest and most systematic and, at the same time, despotic unions that was ever formed to awe and dictate to labor." Listening to Broncho John, the

Avelings, confident that "a Cowboy Assembly of the Knights of Labor or a Cowboy Union is sure to be started in the near future," devoted a whole chapter in their study *The Working-Class Movement in America* to the hardships of the cowboy.

Mary ("Mother") Jones, whose labors on behalf of miners made her a legendary figure among those who labored in the earth, wrote a vivid account of a coal miner's life: "Mining at best is wretched work, and the life and surroundings of the miner are hard and ugly. His work is down in the black depths of the earth. He works alone in a drift. There can be little friendly companionship as there is in the factory; as there is among men who build bridges and houses, working together in groups. The work is dirty. Coal dust grinds itself into the skin, never to be removed. The miner must stoop as he works in the drift. He becomes bent like a gnome. His work is utterly fatiguing. Muscles and bones ache. His lungs breathe coal dust and the strange, damp air of places that are never filled with sunlight. His house is a poor makeshift and there is little to encourage him to make it attractive. . . . Around his house is mud and slush. Great mounds of culm, black and sullen, surround him. His children are perpetually grimy from play on the culm mounds. The wife struggles with dirt, with inadequate water supply, with small wages, with overcrowded shacks."

The breaker boys, who picked flint and rocks out of the coal, Mary Jones wrote, "did men's work and they had men's ways, men's vices and men's pleasures. They fought and spit tobacco and told stories out on the culm piles of a Sunday. They joined the breaker boys union and beat up scabs." Mother Jones lamented to her death that there was "still too little joy and beauty in the miner's life"; the end of the "long, long struggle" was not yet.

Lumbering was akin to mining in the type of man it attracted and the arduous and highly hazardous nature of the work involved. John W. Fitzmaurice, who worked in lumber camps, told the story of them in *The Shanty Boy,* a kind of documentary which painted a vivid picture of the cruelly hard and dangerous conditions. He quoted the foreman of one such camp as declaring, "It's saw-logs we're after out here," and Fitzmaurice added, "it is saw logs men are after in the woods, and in the rush, push and crush to get them, God help the sick or wounded!" The men were pitted against each other in merciless competition for the number of logs cut in a day. At the end of each day the tally was made. "As each speaks the others listen nervously, and with ill-concealed jealousy, to the men with the big figures. . . . This hurry and rush brings to the surface the 'survival of the fittest,' and the weakling or debauched fall out by the way. Consequently, the hospital business never lags." The larger camps had bars and prostitutes as standard adjuncts.

In every industry the story was monotonously the same: paupers' wages; the constant fear of dismissal; wretched and unsanitary working conditions; ten-, twelve-, and even fourteen-hour days (sixteen for bakers); six- and sometimes seven-day weeks; erratic pay; little or no compensation for injuries or fatalities; a constant increase in the number of women and children employed under such conditions; and, worst of all, the widespread conviction that workingmen and women (not to mention children) had been losing ground ever since the end of the Civil War.

Under such circumstances it is hardly surprising that the number of strikes increased year by year following the Great Strikes of 1877. In 1881 there were 471 strikes affecting 2,928 companies and 129,521 employees. Five years later the number of strikes had risen to 1,411, involving 9,861 companies and almost half a million employees. Roughly half (46 percent) of the struck companies acquiesced in the principal demands of the strikers. Over 3,000 more strikes were partially successful, and 40 percent of the strikes, involving 50 percent of the strikers, were judged "failures."

But the formation of unions was dishearteningly slow. The fierce competition between mine operators was one factor impeding effective unions. Marginal operators, struggling, especially in depression years, to stay solvent or at least existent, saw unions as dangerous enemies. Even more significant was the constant turnover of workers themselves. In such circumstances it was difficult for able leadership to emerge and to develop loyalty among a transient population. Every mining village had a nucleus of professional men, storekeepers, mine officials, and a few "old families," but the workers themselves came and went through the middle years of the century with bewildering rapidity. Rather than endure the rigors of long strikes, miners would simply decamp. The mineowners suffered from this phenomenon almost as much as the workers themselves. One deplored the fact that "the best men have of course gone," while the least enterprising and capable remained. In the Pennsylvania coal fields the widely varying national origins of the workers were another deterrent to common action. Welsh, Irish, English, and Germans had provided the initial cadres. During and more dramatically after the Civil War, Italians, Poles, and Slovaks began to come in increasing numbers. Italians were especially in demand as strikebreakers in the bituminous coal fields of Pennsylvania. Race wars were common. Particular traits were attributed by employers to each ethnic group. The Welsh, for example, were described by one mineowner as "a little tricky, & [apt] to lie a little more or less gently, as it suited their purposes," and as "bearing malice, and . . . being clannish." The larger towns where different ethnic groups lived were divided into sections or neighborhoods called by such names as "Scotch Hill, Welshtown, Shanty Mill or Cork Lane or Paddy's Land, Nigger Hill, Dutch Hollow, . . . Little Italy, Hungarian Hill, Polander Street." Each ethnic group had its own social customs, from the exuberant Polish wedding to the Welsh eisteddfod and the German *Turnverein* or *Sängerfest*. The different nationalities often could not even converse with each other, let alone work together to improve conditions.

When the Sage Foundation put out a report on the conditions in the Carnegie steel mills, it emphasized the role of immigrant labor. Slavs and Italians were given preference in employment, the report stated, "because of their docility, their habit of silent submission . . . and their willingness to work long hours and overtime without a murmur. Foreigners as a rule earn the lowest wages and work the full stint of hours. . . .

"Many work in intense heat, the din of machinery and the noise of escaping steam. The congested conditions of most of the plants in Pittsburgh add to the physical discomfort . . . while their ignorance of the language and of modern machinery increases the risk. How many of the Slavs, Lithuanians and Italians are injured in Pittsburgh in one year is unknown. No reliable statistics are compiled. . . . When I mentioned a plant that had a bad reputation to a priest he said: 'Oh, that is the slaughter-house; they kill them there every day.' . . . It is undoubtedly true, that exaggerated though the reports may be, the waste in life and limb is great, and if it all fell upon the native-born a cry would long since have gone up which would have stayed the slaughter."

With the slaves freed, [former abolitionist] Wendell Phillips . . . devoted a portion of his reformist energies to the plight of the Indian, but he had more than enough left for the workingman. He had watched the postwar business and financial interests, the growth of the railroads, and the first stirrings of modern industrialism with growing alarm. In October, 1871, at the Boston Music Hall, he expressed his indignation with the "capitalists." A few months later, addressing the International Grand Lodge of the Knights of St. Crispin, Phillips urged his listeners to "get hold of the great question of labor, and having hold of it, grapple with it, rip it open, invest it with light, gathering the facts, piercing the brains about them . . . then I know, sure as fate, though I may not live to see it, that *they will certainly conquer this nation in twenty years*. It is impossible that they should not." Phillips stressed the importance of organization. "I welcome organization," he declared. "I do not care whether it calls itself trades-union, Crispin, international, or commune; any thing that masses up a unit in order that they may put in a united force to face the organization of capital; anything that does that, I say amen to it. One hundred thousand men [the number of members claimed by the Knights of St. Crispin]. It is an immense army. I do not care whether it considers chiefly the industrial or the political question; it can control the land if it is in earnest." The abolitionists had been only a handful, but they "knew what they wanted, and were determined to have it. Therefore they got it." It was the same with the struggle of workingmen for decent conditions and decent wages.

Phillips offered his listeners a larger vision than simply higher pay and shorter hours. When he looked "out upon Christendom, with its 300,000,000 of people," he saw that a third of them did not have enough to eat. "Now, I say," he declared, "that the social civilization which condemns every third man in it to be below the average in the nourishment God prepared for them" was ordained from below, by greedy and sinful men, rather than from above. "Now I say that the civilization that has produced this state of things in nearly the hundredth year of the American Revolution did not come from above." Long hours, poor food, and hard work brutalized a man and crowded him "down to mere animal life, . . . eclipsed his aspirations, dulled his senses, stunted his intellect, and made him a mere tool to work. . . . That is why I say, lift a man; give him life; let him work eight hours a day; give him the school; develop his taste for music; give him a garden; give him beautiful things to see and good books to read. . . . Unless there is power in your movement, industrially and politically, the last knell of democratic liberty in this Union is struck; for, as I said, there is no power in the State to resist such a giant as the Pennsylvania road. . . . From Boston to New Orleans, from Mobile to Rochester, from Baltimore to St. Louis, we have now but one purpose, and that is, having driven all other political questions out of the arena, the only question left is labor — the relations of capital and labor."

Those relations, however, became increasingly strained. In 1886, labor militancy reached a climax when the rhetoric of solidarity resulted in spontaneous strikes, sympathetic work stoppages, and even boycotts and political demonstrations nationwide. In Chicago's Haymarket Square, labor militancy turned violent. During an anarchist demonstration against police brutality, someone hurled a bomb that killed a police officer and fatally injured five other people. Although the bomb thrower was never identified, a jury convicted eight anarchists, four of whom died on the gallows. The episode was a terrible reversal for the incipient labor movement, as courts and police clamped down and unions became associated in the public mind with disorder and violence. The Knights of Labor suffered an irreversible decline in membership; by 1893, it was dead.

That left only the American Federation of Labor, the conservative union of exclusively skilled workers, which by 1905 had a membership of more than 1.5 million. As America entered the twentieth century, the vast majority of American workers — 30 million men and 8 million women — remained unorganized, underpaid, and overworked. In 1909, for example, a laborer in a manufacturing plant toiled fifty-nine hours a week for less than $10. Not until Woodrow Wilson's presidency did the federal government abolish child labor and grant railroad workers an eight-hour workday.

QUESTIONS TO CONSIDER

1   Who were Eleanor and Edward Aveling, and what was their political bias? What were they looking for in America? What useful comparisons could the Avelings supply to highlight their picture of working-class America? Why does Page Smith use the Avelings' journey around working America to structure his article?

2   What effect did the arrival of ever-increasing waves of immigrants have on America's workingclass populations? How did the owners of industry use immigrant labor? What problems did the isolation of individual ethnic groups present for labor organizers? What was the effect of mechanization on workers?

3   Drawing on what you have read here, describe a typical American industrial town in the late nineteenth century. Where would people live in the town? How would they live? Describe a typical working day for a man, a woman, a child. What would a mining town look like? What was the significance of the company store?

4   Where was the United States government in relation to all the misery and squalor of the urban and industrial working classes? What was the role of the state labor commissions and private foundations such as the Sage Foundation? Was there any sympathy for the plight of laboring people? What essential philosophies associated with democracy and capitalism made government slow to pass protective legislation? Why might the workers themselves have resented some aspects of protective legislation?

5   "The formation of unions was dishearteningly slow," says Page Smith. The Avelings found labor organization in America twenty or thirty years behind that in England. Discuss the obstacles that stood in the way of American labor organization, particularly among miners and unskilled laborers.

7

A Little Milk, a Little Honey: Jewish Immigrants in America

DAVID BOROFF

The Gilded Age witnessed an enormous surge of immigration from Europe, as the romantic lure of America seemed to draw more people than ever. For Europeans, as one historian has noted, "America was rich, America was good, America was hope, America was the future." They came over by the millions, crowding into American cities and swelling the bottom ranks of American labor. Between 1850 and 1910, some 22,800,000 immigrants arrived in the United States, more than three-fourths of them after 1881. There was also a significant shift in the source of immigration. The "old" immigrants were from western and northern Europe — Britain, Ireland, Germany, and the Scandinavian countries. But in the 1890s, most immigrants were from eastern and southern Europe — Russia, Serbia, Austria-Hungary, and Italy — and most were Jewish or Catholic. When these people arrived in America's northeastern cities, they invariably antagonized native-born Protestants, who unfairly blamed them for America's growing urban problems.

The major gateway of the new immigration was New York City, where the population swelled from 1.5 million in 1870 to a spectacular 5 million by 1915. The constant stream of new arrivals made New York the largest and most ethnically diverse city in America. In fact, by 1900, more than three-fourths of New York's citizenry was foreign born. Among them were several hundred thousand eastern European Jews, most of whom settled in the crowded and tumultuous Lower East Side, where they lived in conditions that contrasted sharply with the dream of America that had brought them here.

David Boroff provides a vivid picture of the Jewish immigrants, who first began arriving in New Amsterdam (later New York) in 1654. His focus, however, is on the period after 1880, when Jewish immigration was, as he puts it, "in flood tide." Boroff's lively narrative not only captures the immigrant experience but points out the influence of the Jewish immigrants on the United States and America's influence on them.

In significant ways, the Jewish immigrant experience mirrored that of other ethnic groups newly arrived in America. Italians, Poles, Slovaks, Greeks, and Irish also congregated in "immigrant ghettos" in which they tended to recreate the features of the Old World societies they had left behind. While the ghetto had its bleak side, it nevertheless afforded ethnic groups "a sense of belonging," of "cultural cohesiveness" that assuaged the pain of leaving their homelands and starting over in a strange, often overwhelming new land.

GLOSSARY

AUSWANDERERHALLEN   Emigrant buildings in Hamburg.

CANTOR   In a synagogue's religious service, this officer performs the liturgy and sings or chants the prayers.

CASTLE GARDEN   Huge building, situated at the foot of Manhattan, where immigrants were cleaned and interrogated after their arrival.

CHEDERS   Hebrew schools.

COFFEE HOUSE   The most popular cultural institution in the Jewish ghetto.

GEHENNA   Hell.

GENTILE   People who are not Jewish.

GREENHORN, OR GREENER   Pejorative term for newly arrived immigrants.

JEWISH DAILY FORWARD   Socialistic Yiddish newspaper, edited by Abraham Cahan.

LANDSLEIT   Jewish term for fellow townsmen.

MAX HOCHSTIM ASSOCIATION   Energetically recruited girls to work as prostitutes.

NEW YORK INDEPENDENT BENEVOLENT ASSOCIATION   An organization of pimps.

ORTHODOX JEW   One who adheres faithfully to traditional Judaism, who is devoted to the study of the Torah, attends synagogue daily, and takes care to observe the Sabbath, Jewish holy days, dietary laws, and religious festivals.

"PIG MARKET"   Functioned as the labor exchange on the Lower East Side.

POGROM   Organized massacre of Jews.

SHTETL   Typical small Jewish town in Europe.

WHITE PLAGUE   Immigrants' term for tuberculosis.

YIDDISH   The Hebrew-German dialect and the main vehicle for a Jewish cultural renaissance between 1890 and World War I.

ZHID   Yiddish word for "leave."

It started with a trickle and ended in a flood. The first to come were twenty-three Jews from Brazil who landed in New Amsterdam in 1654, in flight from a country no longer hospitable to them. They were, in origin, Spanish and Portuguese Jews (many with grandiloquent Iberian names) whose families had been wandering for a century and a half. New Amsterdam provided a chilly reception. Governor Peter Stuyvesant at first asked them to leave, but kinder hearts in the Dutch West India Company granted them the right to stay, "provided the poor among them . . . be supported by their own nation." By the end of the century, there were perhaps one hundred Jews; by the middle of the eighteenth century, there were about three hundred in New York, and smaller communities in Newport, Philadelphia, and Charleston.

Because of their literacy, zeal, and overseas connections, colonial Jews prospered as merchants, though there were artisans and laborers among them. The Jewish community was tightly knit, but there was a serious shortage of trained religious functionaries. There wasn't a single American rabbi, for example, until the nineteenth century. Jews were well regarded, particularly in New England. Puritan culture leaned heavily on the Old Testament, and Harvard students learned Hebrew; indeed, during the American Revolution, the suggestion was advanced that Hebrew replace English as the official language of the new country. The absence of an established national religion made it possible for Judaism to be regarded as merely another religion in a pluralistic society. The early days of the new republic were thus a happy time for Jews. Prosperous and productive, they were admitted to American communal life with few restrictions. It is little wonder that a Jewish spokesman asked rhetorically in 1820: "On what spot in this habitable Globe does an Israelite enjoy more blessings, more privileges?"

The second wave of immigration during the nineteenth century is often described as German, but that is misleading. Actually, there were many East European Jews among the immigrants who came in the half century before 1870. However, the German influence was strong, and there was a powerful undercurrent of Western enlightenment at work. These Jews came because economic depression and the Industrial Revolution had made their lot as artisans and small merchants intolerable. For some there was also the threatening backwash of the failure of the Revolution of 1848. Moreover, in Germany at this time Jews were largely disfranchised and discriminated against. During this period, between 200,000 and 400,000 Jews emigrated to this country, and the Jewish population had risen to about half a million by 1870.

This was the colorful era of the peddler and his pack. Peddling was an easy way to get started — it required little capital — and it often rewarded enterprise and daring. Jewish peddlers fanned out through the young country into farmland and mining camp, frontier and Indian territory. The more successful peddlers ultimately settled in one place as storekeepers. (Some proud businesses . . . made their start this way.) Feeling somewhat alienated from the older, settled Jews, who had a reputation for declining piety, the new immigrants organized their own synagogues and community facilities, such as cemeteries and hospitals. In general, these immigrants were amiably received by native Americans, who, unsophisticated about differences that were crucial to the immigrants themselves, regarded all Central Europeans as "Germans."

Essentially, the emigration route was the same between 1820 and 1870 as it would be in the post-1880 exodus. The travellers stayed in emigration inns while awaiting their ship, and since they had all their resources with them, they were in danger of

From David Boroff, "A Little Milk, a Little Honey," *American Heritage,* October/November 1966, Vol. 17, No. 6. Reprinted by permission of *American Heritage* magazine, a division of Forbes, Inc. Copyright © Forbes, Inc., 1966.

being robbed. The journey itself was hazardous and, in the days of the sailing vessels when a good wind was indispensable, almost interminable. Nor were the appointments very comfortable even for the relatively well to do. A German Jew who made the journey in 1856 reported that his cabin, little more than six feet by six feet, housed six passengers in triple-decker bunks. When a storm raged, the passengers had to retire to their cabins lest they be washed off the deck by waves. "Deprived of air," he wrote, "it soon became unbearable in the cabins in which six sea-sick persons breathed." On this particular journey, sea water began to trickle into the cabins, and the planks had to be retarred.

Still, the emigration experience was a good deal easier than it would be later. For one thing, the immigrants were better educated and better acquainted with modern political and social attitudes than the oppressed and bewildered East European multitudes who came after 1880. Fewer in number, they were treated courteously by ships' captains. (On a journey in 1839, described by David Mayer, the ship's captain turned over his own cabin to the Jewish passengers for their prayers and regularly visited those Jews who were ill.) Moreover, there was still the bloom of adventure about the overseas voyage. Ships left Europe amid the booming of cannon, while on shore ladies enthusiastically waved their handkerchiefs. On the way over, there was a holiday atmosphere despite the hazards, and there was great jubilation when land was sighted.

There were, however, rude shocks when the voyagers arrived in this country. The anguish of Castle Garden and Ellis Island was well in the future when immigration first began to swell. But New York seemed inhospitable, its pace frantic, the outlook not entirely hopeful. Isaac M. Wise, a distinguished rabbi who made the journey in 1846, was appalled. "The whole city appeared to me like a large shop," he wrote, "where everyone buys or sells, cheats or is cheated. I had never before seen a city so bare of all art and of every trace of good taste; likewise I had

never witnessed anywhere such rushing, hurrying, chasing, running. . . . Everything seemed so pitifully small and paltry; and I had had so exalted an idea of the land of freedom." Moreover, he no sooner landed in New York than he was abused by a German drayman whose services he had declined. "Aha! thought I," he later wrote, "you have left home and kindred in order to get away from the disgusting Judaeo-phobia and here the first German greeting that sounds in your ears is hep! hep!" (The expletive was a Central European equivalent of "Kike.") Another German Jew who worked as a clothing salesman was affronted by the way customers were to be "lured" into buying ("I did not think this occupation corresponded in any way to my views of a merchant's dignity").

After 1880, Jewish immigration into the United States was in flood tide. And the source was principally East Europe, where by 1880 three-quarters of the world's 7.7 million Jews were living. In all, over two million Jews came to these shores in little more than three decades — about one-third of Europe's Jewry. Some of them came, as their predecessors had come, because of shrinking economic opportunities. In Russia and in the Austro-Hungarian empire, the growth of large-scale agriculture squeezed out Jewish middlemen as it destroyed the independent peasantry, while in the cities the development of manufacturing reduced the need for Jewish artisans. Vast numbers of Jews became petty tradesmen or even *luftmenschen* (men without visible means of support who drifted from one thing to another). In Galicia, around 1900, there was a Jewish trader for every ten peasants, and the average value of his stock came to only twenty dollars.

Savage discrimination and pogroms also incited Jews to emigrate. The Barefoot Brigades — bands of marauding Russian peasants — brought devastation and bloodshed to Jewish towns and cities. On a higher social level, there was the "cold pogrom," a government policy calculated to destroy Jewish life. The official hope was that one third of Russia's Jews would die out, one third would emigrate, and one third would be converted to the Orthodox Church. Crushing restrictions were imposed. Jews were required to live within the Pale of Settlement in western Russia, they could not Russify their names, and they were subjected to rigorous quotas for schooling and professional training. Nor could general studies be included in the curriculum of Jewish religious schools. It was a life of poverty and fear.

Nevertheless, the *shtetl,* the typical small Jewish town, was a triumph of endurance and spiritual integrity. It was a place where degradation and squalor could not wipe out dignity, where learning flourished in the face of hopelessness, and where a tough, sardonic humor provided catharsis for the tribulations of an existence that was barely endurable. The abrasions and humiliations of everyday life were healed by a rich heritage of custom and ceremony. And there was always Sabbath — "The Bride of the Sabbath," as the Jews called the day of rest — to bring repose and exaltation to a life always sorely tried.

To be sure, even this world showed signs of disintegration. Secular learning, long resisted by East European Jews and officially denied to them, began to make inroads. Piety gave way to revolutionary fervor, and Jews began to play a heroic role in Czarist Russia's bloody history of insurrection and suppression.

This was the bleak, airless milieu from which the emigrants came. A typical expression of the Jewish attitude towards emigration from Russia — both its hopefulness and the absence of remorse — was provided by Dr. George Price, who had come to this country in one of the waves of East European emigration:

Should this Jewish emigrant regret his leave-taking of his native land which fails to appreciate him? No! A thousand times no! He must not regret fleeing the clutches of the blood-thirsty crocodile. Sympathy for this country? How ironical it sounds! Am I not despised? Am I not urged to leave? Do I not hear the word *Zhid* constantly? . . . Be thou cursed forever my wicked homeland, because you remind me of the Inquisition. . . . May you rue the day when you exiled the people who worked for your welfare.

After 1880, going to America — no other country really lured — became the great drama of redemption for the masses of East European Jews. (For some, of course, Palestine had that role even in the late nineteenth century, but these were an undaunted Zionist cadre prepared to endure the severest hardships.) The assassination of Czar Alexander II in 1881, and the subsequent pogrom, marked the beginning of the new influx. By the end of the century, 700,000 Jews had arrived, about one quarter of them totally illiterate, almost all of them impoverished. Throughout East Europe, Jews talked longingly about America as the "goldene medinah" (the golden province), and biblical imagery — "the land of milk and honey" — came easily to their lips. Those who could write were kept busy composing letters to distant kin — or even to husbands — in America. (Much of the time, the husband went first, and by abstemious living saved enough to fetch wife and children from the old country.) Children played at "emigrating games," and for the entire *shtetl* it was an exciting moment when the mail-carrier announced how many letters had arrived from America.

German steamship companies assiduously advertised the glories of the new land and provided a one-price rate from *shtetl* to New York. Emigration inns were established in Brody (in the Ukraine) and in the port cities of Bremen and Hamburg, where emigrants would gather for the trip. There were rumors that groups of prosperous German Jews would underwrite their migration to America; and in fact such people often did help their co-religionists when they were stranded without funds in the port cities of Germany. Within Russia itself, the government after 1880 more or less acquiesced in the emigration of Jews, and connived in the vast business of "stealing the border" (smuggling emigrants across). After 1892, emigration was legal — except for those of draft age — but large numbers left with forged papers, because that proved to be far easier than getting tangled in the red tape of the Tzarist bureaucracy. Forged documents, to be sure, were expensive — they cost twenty-five rubles, for many Jews the equivalent of five weeks' wages. Nor was the departure from home entirely a happy event. There were the uncertainties of the new life, the fear that in America "one became a gentile." Given the Jewish aptitude for lugubriousness, a family's departure was often like a funeral, lachrymose and anguished, with the neighbors carting off the furniture that would no longer be needed.

For people who had rarely ventured beyond the boundaries of their own village, going to America was an epic adventure. They travelled with pitifully little money; the average immigrant arrived in New York with only about twenty dollars. With their domestic impedimenta — bedding, brass candlesticks, samovars — they would proceed to the port cities by rail, cart, and even on foot. At the emigration inns, they had to wait their turn. Thousands milled around, entreating officials for departure cards. There were scenes of near chaos — mothers shrieking, children crying; battered wicker trunks, bedding, utensils in wild disarray. At Hamburg, arriving emigrants were put in the "unclean" section of the *Auswandererhallen* until examined by physicians who decided whether their clothing and baggage had to be disinfected. After examination, Jews could not leave the center; other emigrants could.

The ocean voyage provided little respite. (Some elected to sail by way of Liverpool at a reduction of nine dollars from the usual rate of thirty-four dollars.) Immigrants long remembered the "smell of ship," a distillation of many putrescences. Those who went in steerage slept on mattresses filled with straw and kept their clothes on to keep warm. The berth itself was generally six feet long, two feet wide, and two and a half feet high, and it had to accommodate the passenger's luggage. Food was another problem. Many Orthodox Jews subsisted on herring, black bread, and tea which they brought because they did not trust the dietary purity of the ship's food. Some ships actually maintained a separate galley for kosher food, which was coveted by non-Jewish passengers because it was allegedly better.

Unsophisticated about travel and faced by genuine dangers, Jewish emigrants found the overseas trip a long and terrifying experience. But when land was finally sighted, the passengers often began to cheer and shout. "I looked up at the sky," an immigrant wrote years later. "It seemed much bluer and the sun much brighter than in the old country. It reminded me on [*sic*] the Garden of Eden."

Unhappily, the friendly reception that most immigrants envisioned in the new land rarely materialized. Castle Garden in the Battery, at the foot of Manhattan — and later Ellis Island in New York Harbor — proved to be almost as traumatic as the journey itself. "Castle Garden," an immigrant wrote, "is a large building, a Gehenna, through which all Jewish arrivals must pass to be cleansed before they are considered worthy of breathing freely the air of the land of the almighty dollar. . . . If in Brody, thousands crowded about, here tens of thousands thronged about; if there they were starving, here they were dying; if there they were crushed, here they were simply beaten."

One must make allowances for the impassioned hyperbole of the suffering immigrant, but there is little doubt that the immigration officials were harassed, overworked, and often unsympathetic. Authorized to pass on the admissibility of the newcomers, immigration officers struck terror into their hearts by asking questions designed to reveal their literacy and social attitudes. "How much is six times six?" an inspector asked a woman in the grip of nervousness, then casually asked the next man, "Have you ever been in jail?"

There were, of course, representatives of Jewish defense groups present, especially from the Hebrew

Immigrant Aid Society. But by this time, the immigrants, out of patience and exhausted, tended to view them somewhat balefully. The Jewish officials tended to be highhanded, and the temporary barracks which they administered on Ward's Island for those not yet settled soon became notorious. Discontent culminated in a riot over food; one day the director — called The Father — had to swim ashore for his life, and the police were hastily summoned.

Most immigrants went directly from Castle Garden or Ellis Island to the teeming streets of Manhattan, where they sought relatives or *landsleit* (fellow townsmen) who had gone before them. Easy marks for hucksters and swindlers, they were overcharged by draymen for carrying their paltry possessions, engaged as strikebreakers, or hired at shamelessly low wages.

"Greenhorn" or "greener" was their common name. A term of vilification, the source of a thousand cruel jokes, it was their shame and their destiny. On top of everything else, the immigrants had to abide the contempt of their co-religionists who had preceded them to America by forty or fifty years. By the time the heavy East European immigration set in, German Jews had achieved high mercantile status and an uneasy integration into American society. They did not want to be reminded of their kinship with these uncouth and impoverished Jews who were regarded vaguely as a kind of Oriental influx. There was a good deal of sentiment against "aiding such paupers to emigrate to these shores." One charitable organization declared: "Organized immigration from Russia, Roumania, and other semi-barbarous countries is a mistake and has proved to be a failure. It is no relief to the Jews of Russia, Poland, etc., and it jeopardizes the well-being of the American Jews."

A genuine uptown-downtown split soon developed, with condescension on one side and resentment on the other. The German Jews objected as bitterly to the rigid, old-world Orthodoxy of the immigrants as they did to their new involvement in trade unions. They were fearful, too, of the competition they would offer in the needle trades. (Indeed, the East Europeans ultimately forced the uptown Jews out of the industry.) On the other side of the barricades, Russian Jews complained that at the hands of their uptown brethren, "every man is questioned like a criminal, is looked down upon . . . just as if he were standing before a Russian official." Nevertheless, many German Jews responded to the call of conscience by providing funds for needy immigrants and setting up preparatory schools for immigrant children for whom no room was yet available in the hopelessly overcrowded public schools.

Many comfortably settled German Jews saw dispersion as the answer to the problem. Efforts were made to divert immigrants to small towns in other parts of the country, but these were largely ineffective. There were also some gallant adventures with farming in such remote places as South Dakota, Oregon, and Louisiana. Though the Jewish pioneers were brave and idealistic, drought, disease, and ineptitude conspired against them. (In Oregon, for example, they tried to raise corn in cattle country, while in Louisiana they found themselves in malarial terrain.) Only chicken farming in New Jersey proved to be successful to any great degree. Farm jobs for Jews were available, but as one immigrant said: "I have no desire to be a farm hand to an ignorant Yankee at the end of the world. I would rather work here at half the price in a factory; for then I would at least be able to spend my free evenings with my friends."

It was in New York, then, that the bulk of the immigrants settled — in the swarming, tumultuous Lower East Side — with smaller concentrations in Boston, Philadelphia, and Chicago. Far less adaptable than the German Jews who were now lording it over them, disoriented and frightened, the East European immigrants constituted a vast and exploited proletariat. According to a survey in 1890, sixty per cent of all immigrant Jews worked in the needle trades. This industry had gone through a process of decentralization in which contractors carried out the bulk of production, receiving merely the cut goods from the manufacturer. Contracting establishments were everywhere in the Lower East Side, including the contractors' homes, where pressers warmed their irons on the very stove on which the boss's wife was preparing supper. The contractors also gave out "section" work to families and *landsleit* who would struggle to meet the quotas at home. The bondage of the sewing machine was therefore extended into the tenements, with entire families enslaved by the machine's voracious demands. The Hester Street "pig market," where one could buy anything, became the labor exchange; there tailors, operators, finishers, basters, and pressers would congregate on Saturday in the hope of being hired by contractors.

Life in the sweatshops of the Lower East Side was hard, but it made immigrants employable from the start, and a weekly wage of five dollars — the equivalent of ten rubles — looked good in immigrant eyes. Moreover they were among their own kin and kind, and the sweatshops, noisome as they were, were still the scene of lively political and even literary discussions. (In some cigar-making shops, in fact, the bosses hired "readers" to keep the minds of the workers occupied with classic and Yiddish literature as they performed their repetitive chores.) East European Jews, near the end of the century, made up a large part of the skilled labor force in New York, ranking first in twenty-six out of forty-seven trades, and serving, for example, as bakers, building-trade workers, painters, furriers, jewellers, and tinsmiths.

Almost one quarter of all the immigrants tried their hands as tradesmen — largely as peddlers or as pushcart vendors in the madhouse bazaar of the Lower East Side. For some it was an apprenticeship in low-toned commerce that would lead to more elegant careers. For others it was merely a martyrdom that enabled them to subsist. It was a modest enough investment — five dollars for a license, one dollar for a basket, and four dollars for wares. They stocked up on pins and needles, shoe laces, polish, and handker-

chiefs, learned some basic expressions ("You wanna buy somethin'?"), and were on their hapless way.

It was the professions, of course, that exerted the keenest attraction to Jews, with their reverence for learning. For most of them it was too late; they had to reconcile themselves to more humble callings. But it was not too late for their children, and between 1897 and 1907, the number of Jewish physicians in Manhattan rose from 450 to 1,000. Of all the professions it was medicine that excited the greatest veneration. (Some of this veneration spilled over into pharmacy, and "druggists" were highly respected figures who were called upon to prescribe for minor — and even major — ills, and to serve as scribes for the letters that the immigrants were unable to read and write themselves.) There were Jewish lawyers on the Lower East Side and by 1901 over 140 Jewish policemen, recruited in part by Theodore Roosevelt, who, as police commissioner, had issued a call for "the Maccabee or fighting Jewish type."

The Lower East Side was the American counterpart of the ghetto for Jewish immigrants, as well as their glittering capital. At its peak, around 1910, it packed over 350,000 people into a comparatively small area — roughly from Canal Street to Fourteenth Street — with as many as 523 people per acre, so that Arnold Bennett was moved to remark that "the architecture seemed to sweat humanity at every window and door." The most densely populated part of the city, it held one sixth of Manhattan's population and most of New York's office buildings and factories. "Uptowners" used to delight in visiting it (as a later generation would visit Harlem) to taste its exotic flavor. But the great mass of Jews lived there because the living was cheap, and there was a vital Jewish community that gave solace to the lonely and comfort to the pious.

A single man could find lodgings of a sort, including coffee morning and night, for three dollars a month. For a family, rent was about ten dollars a month, milk was four cents a quart, kosher meat twelve cents a pound, herring a penny or two. A kitchen table could be bought for a dollar, chairs at thirty-five cents each. One managed, but the life was oppressive. Most families lived in the notorious "dumbbell" flats of old-law tenements (built prior to 1901). Congested, often dirty and unsanitary, these tenements were six or seven stories high and had four apartments on each floor. Only one room in each three or four room apartment received direct air and sunlight, and the families on each floor shared a toilet in the hall.

Many families not only used their flats as workshops but also took in boarders to make ends meet. [Journalist and reformer] Jacob Riis tells of a two-room apartment on Allen Street which housed parents, six children, and six boarders. "Two daughters sewed clothes at home. The elevated railway passed by the window. The cantor rehearses, a train passes, the shoemaker bangs, ten brats run around like goats, the wife putters. . . . At night we all try to get some sleep in the stifling, roach-infested two rooms." In the summer, the tenants spilled out into fire escapes and rooftops, which were converted into bedrooms.

Nevertheless, life on the Lower East Side had surprising vitality. Despite the highest population density in the city, the Tenth Ward had one of the lowest death rates. In part, this was because of the strenuous personal cleanliness of Jews, dictated by their religion. Though only eight per cent of the East European Jews had baths, bathhouses and steam rooms on the Lower East Side did a booming business. There was, of course, a heavy incidence of tuberculosis — "the white plague." Those who were afflicted could be heard crying out, *Luft! Gib mir luft!* ("Air! Give me air!"). It was, in fact, this terror of "consumption" that impelled some East Side Jews to become farmers in the Catskills at the turn of the century, thus forerunning the gaudy career of the Catskill Borscht Belt resort hotels. The same fear impelled Jews on the Lower East Side to move to Washington Heights and the Bronx, where the altitude was higher, the air presumably purer.

Alcoholism, a prime affliction of most immigrant groups, was almost unknown among Jews. They drank ritualistically on holidays but almost never to excess. They were, instead, addicted to seltzer or soda water . . . which they viewed as "the worker's champagne." The suicide rate was relatively low, though higher than in the *shtetl,* and there was always a shudder of sympathy when the Yiddish press announced that someone had *genumen di ges* (taken gas).

The Lower East Side was from the start the scene of considerable crime. But its inhabitants became concerned when the crime rate among the young people seemed to rise steeply around 1910. There was a good deal of prostitution. The dancing academies, which achieved popularity early in this century, became recruiting centers for prostitutes. In 1908–9, of 581 foreign women arrested for prostitution, 225 were Jewish. There was the notorious Max Hochstim Association, which actively recruited girls, while the New York Independent Benevolent Association — an organization of pimps — provided sick benefits, burial privileges, bail, and protection money for prostitutes. The membership was even summoned to funerals with a two-dollar fine imposed on those who did not attend. Prostitution was so taken for granted that Canal Street had stores on one side featuring sacerdotal articles, while brothels were housed on the other.

Family life on the Lower East Side was cohesive and warm, though there was an edge of shrillness and hysteria to it. Marriages were not always happy, but if wives were viewed as an affliction, children were regarded as a blessing. The kitchen was the center of the household, and food was almost always being served to either family or visitors. No matter how poor they were, Jewish families ate well — even to excess — and mothers considered their children woefully underweight unless they were well cushioned with fat.

It was a life with few conventional graces. Handkerchiefs were barely known, and the Yiddish newspapers had to propagandize for their use. Old men smelled of snuff, and in spite of bathing, children often had lice in their hair and were sent home from school by the visiting nurse for a kerosene bath. Bedbugs were considered an inevitability, and pajamas were viewed as an upper-class affectation. Parents quarrelled bitterly — with passionate and resourceful invective — in the presence of their children. Telephones were virtually unknown, and a telegram surely meant disaster from afar.

The zeal of the immigrants on behalf of their children was no less than awe-inspiring. Parents yearned for lofty careers for their offspring, with medicine at the pinnacle. In better-off homes, there was always a piano ("solid mahogany"), and parents often spent their precious reserves to arrange a "concert" for their precocious youngsters, often followed by a ball in one of the Lower East Side's many halls.

To be sure, the children inspired a full measure of anxiety in their parents. "Amerikane kinder" was the rueful plaint of the elders, who could not fathom the baffling new ways of the young. Parents were nervous about their daughters' chastity, and younger brothers — often six or seven years old — would be dispatched as chaperones when the girls met their boy friends. There was uneasiness about Jewish street gangs and the growing problem of delinquency. The old folks were vexed by the new tides of secularism and political radicalism that were weaning their children from traditional pieties. But most of all, they feared that their sons would not achieve the success that would redeem their own efforts, humiliations, and failures in the harsh new land. Pressure on their children was relentless. But on the whole the children did well, astonishingly well. "The ease and rapidity with which they learn," Jacob Riis wrote, "is equalled only by their good behavior and close attention while in school. There is no whispering and no rioting at these desks." Samuel Chotzinoff, the music critic, tells a story which reveals the attitude of the Jewish schoolboy. When an altercation threatened between Chotzinoff and a classmate, his antag-

onist's reaction was to challenge him to spell "combustible."

The Lower East Side was a striking demonstration that financial want does not necessarily mean cultural poverty. The immigrant Jews were nearly always poor and often illiterate, but they were not culturally deprived. In fact, between 1890 and World War I, the Jewish community provides a remarkable chapter in American cultural history. Liberated from the constrictions of European captivity, immigrant Jews experienced a great surge of intellectual vitality. Yiddish, the Hebrew-German dialect which some people had casually dismissed as a barbarous "jargon," became the vehicle of this cultural renascence. Between 1885 and 1914, over 150 publications of all kinds made their appearance. But the new Yiddish journalism reached its apogee with the *Jewish Daily Forward* under the long editorial reign of Abraham Cahan. The *Forward* was humanitarian, pro-labor, and socialistic. But it was also an instrument for acclimatizing immigrants in the new environment. It provided practical hints on how to deal with the new world, letters from the troubled (*Bintel Brief*), and even, at one time, a primer on baseball ("explained to non-sports"). The *Forward* also published and fostered an enormous amount of literature in Yiddish — both original works by writers of considerable talent, and translations of classic writers.

In this cultural ferment, immigrants studied English in dozens of night schools and ransacked the resources of the Aguilar Free Library on East Broadway. "When I had [a] book in my hand," an immigrant wrote, "I pressed it to my heart and wanted to kiss it." The Educational Alliance, also on East Broadway, had a rich program designed to make immigrant Jews more American and their sons more Jewish. And there were scores of settlement houses, debating clubs, ethical societies, and literary circles which attracted the young. In fact, courtships were carried on in a rarefied atmosphere full of lofty talk about art, politics, and philosophy. And though there was much venturesome palaver about sexual

Yiddish sheet music from 1912. The song celebrates Ellis Island, which had replaced Castle Garden in 1892 as the point of entry for immigrants. A culture within a culture, Jewish New York had its own schools, newspapers, publishing houses, literary and musical circles, and a thriving Yiddish theater. (Sheet Music Collection, The John Hay Library, Brown University)

freedom, actual behavior tended to be quite strait-laced.

But the most popular cultural institution was the café or coffee house, which served as the Jewish saloon. There were about 250 of them, each with its own following. Here the litterateurs sat for hours over steaming glasses of tea; revolutionaries and Bohemians gathered to make their pronouncements or raise money for causes; actors and playwrights came to hold court. For immigrant Jews, talk was the breath of life itself. The passion for music and theater knew no bounds. When Beethoven's Ninth Sym-

phony was performed one summer night in 1915, mounted police had to be summoned to keep order outside Lewisohn Stadium, so heavy was the press of crowds eager for the twenty-five-cent stone seats. Theater (in Yiddish) was to the Jewish immigrants what Shakespeare and Marlowe had been to the groundlings in Elizabethan England. Tickets were cheap — twenty-five cents to one dollar — and theatergoing was universal. It was a raucous, robust, and communal experience. Mothers brought their babies (except in some of the "swellest" theaters, which forbade it), and peddlers hawked their wares between the acts. There were theater parties for trade unions and *landsmanschaften* (societies of fellow townsmen), and the audience milled around and renewed old friendships or argued the merits of the play. The stage curtain had bold advertisements of stores or blown-up portraits of stars.

There was an intense cult of personality in the Yiddish theater and a system of claques not unlike that which exists in grand opera today. The undisputed monarch was Boris Thomashefsky, and a theater program of his day offered this panegyric:

> Tomashefsky! Artist great!
> No praise is good enough for you!
> Of all the stars you remain the king
> You seek no tricks, no false quibbles;
> One sees truth itself playing.
> Your appearance is godly to us
> Every movement is full of grace
> Pleasing is your every gesture
> Sugar sweet your every turn
> You remain the king of the stage
> Everything falls to your feet.

Many of the plays were sentimental trash — heroic "operas" on historical themes, "greenhorn" melodramas full of cruel abandonments and tearful reunions, romantic musicals, and even topical dramas dealing with such immediate events as the Homestead Strike, the Johnstown Flood, and the Kishinev

Pogrom of 1903. Adaptability and a talent for facile plagiarism were the essence of the playwright's art in those days, and "Professor" Moses Horwitz wrote 167 plays, most of them adaptations of old operas and melodramas. The plays were so predictable that an actor once admitted he didn't even have to learn his lines; he merely had to have a sense of the general situation and then adapt lines from other plays.

There was, of course, a serious Yiddish drama, introduced principally by Jacob Gordin, who adapted classical and modernist drama to the Yiddish stage. Jewish intellectuals were jubilant at this development. But the process of acculturation had its amusing and grotesque aspects. Shakespeare was a great favorite but *verbessert und vergrossert"* (improved and enlarged). There was the Jewish *King Lear* in which Cordelia becomes Goldele. (The theme of filial ingratitude was a "natural" on the Lower East Side, where parents constantly made heroic sacrifices.) *Hamlet* was also given a Jewish coloration, the prince becoming a rabbinical student who returns from the seminary to discover treachery at home. And *A Doll's House* by Ibsen was transformed into *Minna,* in which a sensitive and intelligent young woman, married to an ignorant laborer, falls in love with her boarder and ultimately commits suicide.

Related to the Jewish love of theater was the immigrant's adoration of the cantor, a profession which evoked as much flamboyance and egotistical preening as acting did. (In fact, actors would sometimes grow beards before the high holydays and find jobs as cantors.) Synagogues vied with each other for celebrated cantors, sometimes as a way of getting out of debt, since tickets were sold for the high-holyday services.

The Lower East Side was a vibrant community, full of color and gusto, in which the Jewish immigrant felt marvelously at home, safe from the terrors of the alien city. But it was a setting too for fierce conflict and enervating strain. There were three major influences at work, each pulling in a separate direction: Jewish Orthodoxy, assimilationism, and the new socialist gospel. The immigrants were Orthodox, but their children tended to break away. *Cheders* (Hebrew schools) were everywhere, in basements and stores and tenements, and the old custom of giving a child a taste of honey when he was beginning to learn to read — as symbolic of the sweetness of study — persisted. But the young, eager to be accepted into American society, despised the old ways and their "greenhorn" teachers. Fathers began to view their sons as "free-thinkers," a term that was anathema to them. Observance of the Law declined, and the Saturday Sabbath was ignored by many Jews. A virulent antireligious tendency developed among many "enlightened" Jews, who would hold profane balls on the most sacred evening of the year — Yom Kippur — at which they would dance and eat nonkosher food. (Yom Kippur is a fast day.) And the trade-union movement also generated uneasiness among the pious elders of the Lower East Side. "Do you want us to bow down to your archaic God?" a radical newspaper asked. "Each era has its new Torah. Ours is one of freedom and justice."

But for many immigrants the basic discontent was with their American experience itself. The golden province turned out to be a place of tenements and sweatshops. A familiar cry was *"a klug of Columbus!"* ("a curse on Columbus") or, "Who ever asked him, Columbus, to discover America?" Ellis Island was called *Trernindzl* (Island of Tears), and Abraham Cahan, in his initial reaction to the horrors of immigration, thundered: "Be cursed, immigration! Cursed by those conditions which have brought you into being. How many souls have you broken, how many courageous and mighty souls have you shattered." The fact remains that most Jewish immigrants, in the long run, made a happy adjustment to their new land.

After 1910, the Lower East Side went into a decline. Its strange glory was over. New areas of Jewish settlement opened up in Brooklyn, the Bronx, and in upper Manhattan. By the mid-twenties, less than ten per cent of New York's Jews lived on the Lower East Side, although it still remained the heartland to which one returned to shop, to see Yiddish theater, and to renew old ties. By 1924 Jewish immigration into the United States was severely reduced by new immigration laws, and the saga of mass immigration was done. But the intensities of the Jewish immigrant experience had already made an indelible mark on American culture and history that would endure for many years.

QUESTIONS TO CONSIDER

1   Compare the migration experience of Jewish immigrants to America in the periods before and after 1880. In what ways did the experience become easier or more difficult? How did the immigrants themselves change?

2   For some Jewish immigrants, America was "the land of milk and honey," whereas others cursed Columbus and called Ellis Island the "Island of Tears." Discuss the reality of the Jewish immigrant experience hidden behind both images of America.

3   Analyze the reasons for the ambivalent feelings and divisions that developed between newer eastern European Jewish immigrants and those Jews, usually of German origin, who had been settled in the United States for several generations.

4   The lure of land in the New World brought generations of Europeans to America. Why did the bulk of eastern European Jewish immigrants choose to remain in urban industrial centers such as New York City? Was there anything about their *shtetl* experience that made Jews more adaptable to city life?

5   Boroff says, "The immigrant Jews were nearly always poor and often illiterate, but they were not culturally deprived." What evidence is there to support this statement?

REFORM AND EXPANSION

8

The Populist Protest

In the Gilded Age, politics became a big business, too, as the big industrialists poured money into government circles at an unprecedented rate. Men now entered politics for the same reason they went into business: to make their fortunes. The new politics even derived much of its vocabulary from the world of industry. "A political party," contended American statesman William H. Seward, "is in one sense a joint stock company in which those who contribute the most direct the action and management of the concern." The United States Senate became known as the Millionaires' Club, because only the rich and powerful seemed able to get in. A sizable portion of both major parties not only vigorously defended the industrial barons but were as eager to accept their campaign contributions as the barons were ready to give them. A number of politicians shamelessly took bribes as well.

In the 1880s, the two national parties — the Republicans and Democrats — had a monopoly on American politics, and neither was responsive to the grassroots of America. The industrial consolidation had left many victims in its wake — workers, farmers, consumers, and small or aspiring business and professional people who wanted their share of opportunity and wealth. Among the most devastated victims of the new industrial order were one-crop family farmers in the South, Texas, and the states of the Great Plains. By the 1880s, faced with ruinous farm prices and the advent of mechanized, diversified, commercial agriculture, southern and midwestern small farmers and southern sharecroppers, black and white alike, were in desperate straits and yet had no place to turn for help. American agrarians, it seemed, had no choice but to organize cooperative action among themselves. They had tried this in the Grange movement of the previous decade, but that movement had faded when prosperity returned in the late 1870s. But by the mid-1880s, as Bernard Weisberger has written, farmers everywhere suffered "from a long, deflationary squeeze between falling agricultural prices, on the one hand, and, on the other, rising interest rates, freight charges, and production costs that they argued were artificially boosted by the trusts and the tariff." To make matters worse, the farmers saw big business — the "money power" — buying off politicians in exchange for favorable legislation. As a consequence, first in Texas and then across the South and the Plains, American farmers organized alliances to protect themselves against the rich and powerful who ran America. The Alliance movement was an effort at cooperative agriculture to free farmers from "the furnishing merchants," banks, trusts, and railroads. The alliances, in turn, led to political organization, first in the People's Party of Kansas (which drew men and women alike to its banners) and ultimately in the national People's party, or the Populist party, which was formed in Omaha, Nebraska, in 1892. According to Lawrence Goodwyn, author of Democratic Promise (1976) and The Populist Moment (1978), the agrarian revolt that culminated in the Populist crusade constituted "the largest democratic mass movement in American history." And the objective of that mass movement was to restore government to the people.

In the selection that follows, James MacGregor Burns recounts the story of the Populist crusade, pointing out how it broke down racial barriers in the South and attracted a cadre of talented women orators and activists in Kansas. Burns stresses that "the idea of liberty" was populism's energizing force. The word liberty meant different things to different Americans in that period, but to the Populists it meant more than individual freedom, more than freedom from interference and exploitation. To Populist farmers and their middle-class leaders, liberty meant self-fulfillment through cooperative action. Thus, as Burns concludes, the Populists moved closer than any other American group to the third of the great concepts of the Enlightenment. The first two were liberty and equality. The third was "fraternity, or comradeship."

GLOSSARY

CROP LIEN SYSTEM   A system of agricultural credit in the South, by which black and white farmers obtained from local country stores the seed and equipment they needed in exchange for liens or claims against their crops.

DIGGS, ANNIE   Journalist and lay preacher in the Unitarian church who wrote for the Populist cause and became associate editor of the Populist newspaper, the Topeka *Advocate*.

FARMERS' ALLIANCE OF TEXAS   "Built firmly on a network of suballiances," or neighborhood chapters, this organization was the prototype for farmers' alliances in other states.

GREENBACKERS   Pressed Washington to issue inflationary paper money — greenbacks — that would make it easier for debtors to pay what they owed.

JUTE BAGGING   Jute is a strong, rough fiber used to make gunny and burlap bagging.

LAMB, WILLIAM   First state lecturer for the Texas Alliance and one of its most creative and radical leaders.

LEASE, MARY   One of the first woman lawyers in Kansas and an indefatigable activist in numerous causes. Lease was a stemwinding lecturer for the Kansas Populists.

LEWELLING, LORENZO   First Populist governor of Kansas who headed the "first People's party government on earth" in that prairie state.

MACUNE, CHARLES   Texas Alliance leader who envisioned a national network of state Alliance Exchanges, which would collectively buy equipment and supplies and market cotton; he became the first president of the National Farmers' Alliance and Cooperative Union.

McCORMICK, FANNY   Assistant state lecturer and noted leader of the Kansas Populists.

SIMPSON, "SOCKLESS JERRY"   Kansas Populist who won a seat in Congress in 1890 and promoted the Alliance program there.

SINGLE-TAX MOVEMENT   Contending that monopolists grew rich because of rising land values, the proponents of the movement advocated a single tax on land in place of all other taxes; such a tax, they believed, would destroy monopolies, lead to a more equitable distribution of wealth, and end poverty.

SUBTREASURY PLAN   Charles Macune's plan for "providing treasury notes to farmers, as a means of financing cooperatives with public rather than private credit and thus enlisting the government in the struggle to raise agricultural prices."

WATSON, TOM   Southern reformer who helped promote the Alliance platform in Congress and forged a biracial Populist coalition in Georgia.

WEAVER, JAMES B.   Populist party candidate for president in 1892.

*S*omewhere in central Texas, sometime in the late eighties: In the twilight splendor of the Plains, men and women march along dusty trails toward the glow of a campfire in the distance. Some walk; some ride horses or burros; some — whole families — jolt along on covered wagons or buckboards. With their creased, careworn faces, their poor gingham clothes, they might seem to be one more trek in the great western movement of American homesteaders. But not so. These people walk with hope and pride — even with exhilaration as they reach a hillcrest and see stretching for miles ahead and behind thousands of people marching with them, hundreds of wagons emblazoned with crude signs and banners. Soon they reach their encampment, not to settle down for the night but, in company with five or ten thousand comrades, to hear fiery speeches late into the evening.

These people will be part of an arresting venture in popular grass-roots democracy, part of the "flowering of the largest democratic mass movement in American history," in Lawrence Goodwyn's judgment. Ultimately they will fail — but not until they have given the nation an experiment in democratic ideas, creative leadership and followership, and comradely cooperation.

At first on the Texas frontier but soon in the South and Midwest, farmers in the mid-1880s collectively sensed that something was terribly wrong. In the South, farmers white and black were shackled by the crop lien system and the plummeting price of cotton. In the West, homesteaders were losing their mortgaged homes. Grain prices fell so low that Kansas farm families burned corn for heat. Everywhere farmers suffered from a contracting currency, heavy taxation, and gouging by railroads and other

From James MacGregor Burns, *The American Experiment,* Vol. 2: *The Workshop of Democracy,* 180–191. Copyright © 1985 by James MacGregor Burns. Reprinted by permission of Alfred A. Knopf, Inc.

monopolies. As farmers perceived the "money power" buying elections and public officials in order to pass class legislation, some agrarian leaders and editors wondered if the farm areas trembled on the brink of revolution.

The crop lien system, tight money, and the rest of the farmers' ills — these seemed remote and impersonal to many an eastern city dweller. But for countless Southern cotton farmers "crop lien" set the conditions of their existence.

It meant walking into the store of the "furnishing merchant," approaching the counter with head down and perhaps hat in hand, and murmuring a list of needs. It meant paying "the man" no money but watching him list items and figures in a big ledger. It meant returning month after month for these mumbled exchanges, as the list of debts grew longer. It meant . . . that the farmer brought in the produce from his long year's hard labor, watched his cotton weighed and sold, and then learned that the figures in the ledger, often with enormously inflated interest, added up to more than his crop was worth — but that the merchant would carry him into the next year if he signed a note mortgaging his next year's crop to the merchant. It meant returning home for another year's toil, knowing that he might lose his spread and join the army of landless tenant farmers. From start to finish it meant fear, self-abasing deference, hatred of self and others.

Above all, the system meant loss of liberty, as the farmer became shackled to one crop and one merchant — loss of liberty for men and women raised in the Jeffersonian tradition of individual freedom in a decentralized agrarian republic, in the Jacksonian tradition of equality of opportunity in a land free of usurious banks and grasping monopolies. Their forefathers had fought for independence; was a second American revolution needed to overthrow a new, an economic, monarchy? "Laboring men of America," proclaimed a tract, the voices of 1776 "ring down through the corridors of time and tell you to strike" against the "monopolies and combinations that are

eating out the heart of the Nation." But strike how? "Not with glittering musket, flaming sword and deadly cannon," the pamphlet exhorted, "but with the silent, potent and all-powerful ballot, the only vestige of liberty left."

One course seemed clear — people must organize themselves as powerfully against the trusts as the trusts were organized against them. But organize how? Economically or politically? Experience did not make for easy answers. Farmers had plunged into politics with Greenbackers and laborites and ended up on the short end of the ballot counts. The answer of the recently founded Farmers' Alliance in Texas was to try both economic and political structures, but more intensively and comprehensively than ever before. Built firmly on a network of "suballiances" — neighborhood chapters of several dozen members meeting once or twice a month to pray, sing, conduct rituals, debate issues, and do organizational business — the state Alliance experimented with several types of grass-roots cooperatives, including stores, county trade committees to bargain with merchants, and county-wide "bulking" of cotton.

The key to Alliance power was not organization, though, but leadership — and not the leadership merely of a few persons at the top but of dozens, then hundreds, of men and women who were specially hired and trained to journey across the state visiting suballiances, helping to form new ones, and above all teaching members graphically and in detail about the complex political and economic issues of the day, both national issues like money and finance and local ones like the building and expanding of co-ops. These were the famed "lecturers," who in turn were responsible to a state lecturer. The Alliance's first state lecturer was William Lamb, a rugged, red-haired, thirty-four-year-old farmer. Born in Tennessee, he had traveled alone at sixteen to the Texas frontier, where he lived in a log hut until he could build a house, raise children with his wife, and learn to read and write at night.

Lamb soon emerged as one of the most creative and radical of Alliance leaders. When the Great Southwest Strike erupted against Jay Gould's railroad early in 1886, Lamb defied the more conservative Alliance leaders by demanding that the Alliance back a Knights of Labor boycott. Though suballiances gave food and money to striking railroad workers, the strike collapsed. The Knights continued on their downward slide, but the Texas Alliance continued its phenomenal growth, with perhaps 2,000 suballiances and 100,000 members by the summer of that year.

Lamb and other lecturers also took leadership on another critical issue facing the Alliance. Wracked by scorching drought, crop failures, and increasing tenantry, Texas farmers by 1886 were meeting in schoolhouses and clamoring for a new strategy — *political* action. They were impatient with the old shibboleth that the Alliance must steer clear of politics because politics would kill it. The decisive turning point in the agrarian revolt came at the Alliance state convention in Cleburne in early August 1886. A majority of the disgruntled, rustic-looking delegates from eighty-four counties "demanded" of the state and federal governments "such legislation as shall secure to our people freedom from the onerous and shameful abuses that the industrial classes are now suffering at the hands of arrogant capitalists and arrogant corporations" — legislation including an interstate commerce law and land reform measures. A conservative minority, opposing a proposal for greenbacks that defied the Democratic party, rejected the demands, absconded with the treasury, and formed a strictly "nonpartisan" Alliance.

At this critical moment Charles Macune, another leader fresh from the grass roots, stepped into the fray. Settled on the Texas frontier at nineteen after early years of poverty and wanderings, Macune had married, studied law and medicine, and practiced both. Developing into a skillful writer, compelling speaker, and innovative thinker, Macune had become well versed in farming matters and active in his county Alliance. And now this tall, magnetic physician-lawyer-farmer, buoyed by the rising militance of the delegates, proposed an ingenious compromise that was also a creative act of leadership.

Persuading the conservatives to give up their rival Alliance and the radicals to tone down their drive toward partisan politics, he proposed an expansion that was both geographic and functional. In his dazzling vision, a national network of state Alliance "Exchanges," starting in Texas, would collectively market cotton and buy supplies and farm equipment. This giant farmers' cooperative would not only achieve higher, more stable prices, but would provide the credit to free all farmers from the furnishing merchant and mortgage company. Thus, he proclaimed, mortgage-burdened farmers could "assert their freedom from the tyranny of organized capital." At a statewide meeting at Waco in January 1887 the farmer delegates enthusiastically adopted Macune's grand strategy, decided on merger with the Louisiana Farmers' Union, and chose Macune as first president of the National Farmers' Alliance and Cooperative Union. The state Alliance built a huge headquarters in Dallas even while doubling its membership and preparing a small army of lecturers to proselytize the South during mid-1887.

Even that army of enthusiasts seemed astonished by the response. "The farmers seemed like unto ripe fruit," one reported from North Carolina. "You can garner them by a gentle shake of the bush." He had held twenty-seven meetings in one county and left twenty-seven suballiances in his wake. With cotton down to eight cents a pound, farmers were desperate for relief. Together they and the lecturers set up trade committees, cotton yards, and warehouses in hundreds of counties, along with state exchanges. Georgia, with its big state exchange and its cooperative stores, gins, and warehouses, was the most successful. When manufacturers of the commonly used jute bagging organized a trust and doubled the price, the Georgia Alliance — and later other state groups — successfully boycotted the "jute trust," using cotton or pine straw instead, while protesting farmers donned cotton bagging and even witnessed a double wedding in which both brides and both grooms were decked out in that finery.

The idea of farm cooperation swept into the Midwest. The Alliance came to be most deeply rooted in the corn and wheat fields of Kansas, where a great boom had busted in 1887 amid mounting debts and foreclosures. When political efforts failed the next year, farm leaders visited Texas and returned full of missionary zeal. The formation of suballiances and the building of cooperatives proceeded feverishly until the entire state boasted of over 3,000 local units. When the "twine trust" hiked by 50 percent the price of the twine used to bind wheat, the Alliance staged a boycott. The trust lowered its price.

As early as 1889, however, Alliance leaders in Kansas were concluding that education and cooperation were not enough, that electoral political action was necessary too. The question was not whether to engage in politics but how — independent political action versus third-party efforts versus working through a major party; lobbying and pressuring established parties versus direct action to take power. The existing political landscape was barren. The Republican and Democratic parties both were sectional entities, appealing to lingering Civil War hatreds to win elections. Farmers who actually shared common conditions and needs were polarized by politicians who waved the bloody shirt. Though most farm leaders in Kansas spurned "partisan politics" at every turn, what they actually rejected was the familiar brand of party politics animated by sectionalism and penetrated by railroad and other monopolies. Many envisioned not just an alternative party, but an alternative *kind* of party that would overcome racial and sectional hatred and respond to grass-roots needs.

A county "people's convention" that nominated — and elected — a "people's ticket" for county offices against the trusts inspired Alliance leaders in Kansas to raise their sights to state action. A convention of industrial organizations in Topeka, with delegates from the Knights of Labor and the "single tax" movement as well as from Alliance groups, assembled in Representative Hall in the statehouse, formally set up the People's Party of Kansas, and called a state convention to choose statewide candidates and adopt the first People's Party platform.

Once again new leaders emerged out of this agitation and conflict. In the "Big Seventh" congressional district in southwest Kansas, a Medicine Lodge rancher and town marshal named Jerry Simpson quickly emerged as the most noted Kansas Populist. A sailor on the Great Lakes and later an Illinois soldier in the Civil War, Simpson had run a farm and sawmill in northeastern Kansas before turning to cattle-raising. After the harsh winter of 1887 killed his cattle and destroyed his life's savings, he turned to the Alliance and the new political insurgency.

Simpson won his imperishable title as "Sockless Jerry" during his campaign in 1890 against Colonel James Hallowell. "I tried to get hold of the crowd," Simpson recalled. "I referred to the fact that my opponent was known as a 'Prince.' Princes, I said, wear silk socks. I don't wear any." Hallowell, he went on, boasted that he had been to Topeka and had made laws. Picking up a book, Simpson recalled, he tapped on a page with his finger. "I said, here is one of Hal's laws. I find that it is a law to tax dogs, but I see that Hal proposes to charge two dollars for a bitch and only one dollar for a son of a bitch. Now the party I belong to believes in equal and exact justice to all."

Women leaders in Kansas attracted even more attention than the men. "Women who never dreamed of becoming public speakers," wrote Annie Diggs, "grew eloquent in their zeal and fervor. Josh Billings' saying that 'wimmin is everywhere,' was literally true in that wonderful picknicking, speech-making Alliance summer of 1890." While most Alliance women did rather mundane tasks, a good number of them emerged as compelling leaders and stump speakers. Diggs herself had worked actively in the Women's Christian Temperance Union in

The Populist movement in Kansas attracted a number of talented professional women. "Women who never dreamed of becoming public speakers," said Annie Diggs, "grew eloquent in their zeal and fervor." Diggs, Fanny McCormick, Sarah Emery — all became noted women leaders. But it was Mary Lease, shown above, who attracted the most attention. One of the first female lawyers in the country, Lease was a mesmerizing lecturer for the People's Party of Kansas. "What you farmers need to do," she told agrarian audiences, "is to raise less corn and more Hell!" (Kansas State Historical Society)

Kansas and as a lay preacher in the Unitarian Church when, in the mid-eighties, she journeyed east to become Boston correspondent for several Kansas papers. She returned to Kansas, worked with the Alliance, wrote on suffrage and temperance and Alliance issues despite a public disavowal by her Republican editor, and then joined Stephen McLallin, a leading Populist editor, as associate editor of the Topeka *Advocate*. Together they shaped it into the leading reform paper in the state.

There were other noted women leaders: Fanny McCormick, assistant state lecturer who ran for state superintendent of public instruction; Sarah Emery, author of the widely read *Seven Financial Conspiracies* and a spellbinding orator; Kansas-born Fanny Vickrey, another gifted orator. But attracting most attention of all was the indomitable Mary Lease.

Lease was born in Pennsylvania of parents who were Irish political exiles and grew up in a family devastated by the Civil War; her two brothers died in the fighting, her father in Andersonville prison. She moved to Kansas in the early 1870s, taught parochial school, raised a family, tried and failed at farming, studied law — "pinning sheets of notes above her wash tub" — became one of the first woman lawyers of Kansas, and began a tempestuous career as a speaker for Irish nationalism, temperance, woman's suffrage, union labor, and the Alliance. A tall, stately woman, she had "a golden voice," in [journalist] William Allen White's recollection, "a deep, rich contralto, a singing voice that had hypnotic qualities." But she could also hurl "sentences like Jove hurled thunderbolts," Diggs said, as she gave scores of speeches, some over two hours long, throughout Kansas. Pointing to the starving families of Chicago and the wasted corn piled along the railroad tracks or burned for heat, she exclaimed, "What you farmers need to do is to raise less corn and more Hell!"

Led by such women and men champions, propelled by acute needs and high hopes, the Kansas Populists roared to a sensational victory in 1890. They carried 96 of the 125 seats in the state's lower house and swept five out of seven congressional districts, sending Sockless Jerry along with the four others to Washington.

"THE PEOPLE ON TOP!" headlined the *Nonconformist*. But were they? The Populists elected only one statewide official, their candidate for attorney general. The Republicans still controlled the state administration, the holdover Senate, and the judiciary.

The House passed a woman's suffrage bill but the Senate axed it. The Populists' one victory was to oust a conservative United States senator and send Populist editor William Peffer to Washington in his place. And now they had a crucial issue — Republican subversion of the will of the people. The Kansas Populists conducted a repeat crusade in 1892 with massive parades and encampments. This time they elected the entire state ticket and most of their congressional candidates again, including Simpson, and gained control of the Senate — but lost their majority in the House, amid accusations of wholesale Republican fraud.

The "first People's party government on earth" was inaugurated in Topeka at the start of 1893. After a spectacular parade through downtown Topeka the new governor, Lorenzo Lewelling, gave a stirring address — his "incendiary Haymarket inaugural," a GOP editor called it — followed by Lease and Simpson. But the gala was shortlived. When the new legislature convened, the Populists organized the state Senate, but they and the Republicans each claimed a majority in the House. There followed a tug-of-war that would have been comic opera if the stakes had not been so high: each "majority" organized its own "House" with speaker and officers; neither side would vacate the hall, so they stayed put all night, with the two speakers sleeping, gavels in hand, facing each other behind the podium; finally Lewelling called up the militia — including a Gatling gun minus its firing pin — while the Republicans mobilized an army of deputy sheriffs, college students, and railroad workers. The GOP legislators smashed their way into the hall with a sledgehammer; and the militia commander, a loyal Republican like most of his troops, refused the governor's order to expel the invaders.

Bloodshed was narrowly averted when the Populists agreed to let the Republican-dominated Kansas Supreme Court rule on the issue, and predictably the court ruled against them. The Populists then paid the price. Their legislators fared worse than in 1891,

passing two election reform measures and putting suffrage on the ballot, but not accomplishing much else. Their chief priority, railroad regulation with teeth, was a direct casualty of the conflict. Clearly, under the American and Kansan systems of checks and balances, a movement could win elections but still not win power.

Alliance cooperation and Populist politics spread through other Northern states, moving west into the mountain states toward the Pacific, north into Minnesota and the Dakotas, east into the big corn spreads. Everywhere the new movement mobilized people and encountered Republican party power and entrenched elites. Thus "in sundry ways, at different speeds, at varied levels of intensity, and at diverse stages of political consciousness, the farmers brought the People's Party of the United States into being," in Goodwyn's summarization. "In so doing, they placed on the nation's political stage the first multi-sectional democratic mass movement since the American Revolution."

It was in the South, however, that the Alliance continued to expand most dramatically and yet to encounter the biggest obstacles. The first of these obstacles was the Southern Democracy [or Democratic Party], which continued to live off its role as defender of the Lost Cause. The second, closely connected, was race — not *simply* race, as C. Vann Woodward has explained, but "the complexities of the class economy growing out of race, the heritage of manumitted slave psychology, and the demagogic uses to which the politician was able to put race prejudice." Southern Populists reluctantly concluded that they could not achieve the subtreasury plan for credit and currency and other reforms unless they forged a biracial coalition of small landowners, tenant farmers, and sharecroppers. This meant war with the Southern Democracy and potential division within Populism.

Georgia was an even more tumultuous battleground than Kansas. There one man, backed by the mass of poor farmers, personified the entire movement: Tom Watson. Descended from prosperous slaveholders, he had seen his father lose his forty-five slaves and 1,400 acres after Appomattox and end up as a tavern owner in Augusta. Young Watson managed to spend two years at Mercer University before running out of money. After years of poverty he turned to law, prospered, and won election to the Georgia lower house at twenty-six, but quit before his term ended.

"I did not lead the Alliance," Watson recalled. "I followed the Alliance, and I am proud that I did." After taking leadership in the "jute fight," he decided to run for Congress as a Democrat with Alliance backing. The white Georgia Alliance sought to field its own candidates within the Democratic Party and back non-Alliance candidates only if they endorsed the Alliance program — the "Alliance yardstick," they called it. Alliance leaders took over the Democratic party state convention, wrote the party platform, won control of both houses of the "farmers' legislature," elected the governor and six of ten members of Congress. Watson trounced his Republican opponent almost ten to one in a fight as "hot as Nebuchadnezzar's furnace."

Coalitions embody conflicts. The lines were now drawn between Alliance members who were mainly Democrats and Democrats who were mainly Alliancers. The national Alliance had urged that its members of Congress not join any party caucus that did not endorse the Alliance platform. The whole Southern delegation but one stayed with the majority Democratic caucus and elected a Georgian, Charles Crisp, to the speakership. The exception was Watson. He and Sockless Jerry Simpson introduced the Alliance platform into Congress, fighting especially hard for the subtreasury proposal. Virtually none of the platform was even reported out of committee except the subtreasury item, which finally came to the floor after Watson used every maneuver to pry it out of committee; by then it was too late for action.

Beaten in Washington, Watson flourished politically at home. This was a time when many black tenants and sharecroppers were becoming alienated from the GOP and were turning to the new party. Watson called on blacks as well as whites to overthrow the plutocracy that had used race hatred to bolster its rule. "You are kept apart," he told black and white Georgians, "that you may be separately fleeced of your earnings." Campaigning for reelection in 1892, now as leader of the Georgia People's Party, Watson championed political equality for blacks, economic equality to a lesser extent — and social equality or "mixing" not at all. But despite both white and black Populist support, Watson was beaten for reelection in a campaign marked by massive election fraud and the killing of a score of Populists, most of them black.

Texas was having its own problems with the entrenched white Democracy and entrenched capital. The Texas Alliance Exchange, the linchpin of cooperative efforts, had gotten off to a flying start by selling vast amounts of cotton to eastern mills and abroad and buying supplies and equipment. Still, it could not break the enslavement of tenants and sharecroppers to the crop lien system, and increasingly it suffered from lack of capital. Banks in Dallas and elsewhere turned a cold face to requests for loans. Desperately the leadership turned to the suballiances themselves for money. In a remarkable popular mobilization, thousands of farmers marched to county courthouses to pledge help. It was not enough; a year later the Texas Exchange closed its doors for good.

The ever-resourceful Charles Macune now presented his subtreasury plan, providing treasury notes to farmers, as a means of financing cooperatives with public rather than private credit and thus enlisting the government in the struggle to raise agricultural prices. The indefatigable William Lamb fashioned this economic reform into a weapon of political revolt as he launched a full-scale lecturing campaign in each congressional district. The Texas Alliance won a stunning victory through the Democratic Party in 1890, electing a governor and a legislature committed to most Alliance demands, but a host of Democratic "loyalists" opposed the subtreasury and bolted from the Alliance. Spurred by Lamb and other leaders, Alliance members decided to create the People's Party of Texas. At the founding convention in August 1891 white and black delegates forged a remarkable coalition, with a commitment to political and economic equality for blacks.

As the presidential election year of 1892 approached, Alliance leaders were concluding that a *national* People's Party was needed to consolidate the grand coalition of farmers and workers, strengthen the state parties, and seize control of the federal government. Plans were carefully laid. The Alliance organized a massive lecturing campaign, distributed vast quantities of books and pamphlets, including [Edward] Bellamy's *Looking Backward,* and formed a National Reform Press Association to coordinate the propaganda efforts of the one-hundred-strong Populist newspapers. A St. Louis conference of farm, labor, and women delegates drew up a platform and heard the Minnesota Populist orator and novelist Ignatius Donnelly give an unforgettable speech in which he charged: "Corruption dominates the ballot box, the legislatures, the Congress, and touches even the ermine of the bench. . . . The fruits of the toil of millions are boldly stolen to build up colossal fortunes, unprecedented in the history of the world, while their possessors despise the republic and endanger liberty. From the same prolific womb of governmental injustice we breed two great classes — paupers and millionaires."

Then came the national founding convention of the People's Party, Omaha, July 4, 1892. The delegates adopted a platform that harked back to the "Cleburne demands" six years earlier and indeed to decades of labor, farm, and socialist manifestos: a flexible "national currency" to be distributed by means of the subtreasury plan; free and unlimited coinage of silver and gold; a graduated income tax; government ownership and operation of the railroads, telegraph, and telephone; barring of alien land ownership and return of land held by railroads and other corporations "in excess of their actual needs"; political reforms such as the direct election of United States senators. But the platform ignored labor's most urgent needs and omitted mention of woman's suffrage. The convention also took a moderate course in nominating for president James B. Weaver of Iowa, the reform editor and ex-Union general who had led the Greenbackers in 1880, balancing him with an ex-Confederate general as his running mate.

Plunging into the election campaign, the Populists unsheathed their thousands of lecturers, their orators such as Lease and Donnelly, their tactics in some states of opportunistic coalition-building with Republicans in the South and especially with Democrats in the West. Weaver and his wife were rotten-egged in the South — Mrs. Weaver to the point that, according to Lease, she "was made a regular walking omelet by the southern chivalry of Georgia." The results were promising for a fledgling third party: Weaver polled over one million votes, actually carrying Kansas and four western states with twenty-two electoral votes. Populist governors were elected in Kansas, Colorado, and North Dakota. But in the Northeast, parts of the Midwest, and the South the party fared poorly. In Texas the Populists lost badly to the Democrats. It was with mingled hopes and an exhilarating sense of momentum that the Populists turned to the economic and political struggles ahead.

The idea of liberty had been the animating impulse behind the Alliance. But during the century soon to come to an end that idea had also guided organized capital and labor. Each group of course meant something different by "liberty" — businessmen meant freedom from interference with property, labor meant freedom from boss control of its working life, farmers meant freedom from furnishing merchants, banks, railroads, trusts. More than the other groups, however, the Alliance had made liberty into a positive idea — realizing and fulfilling oneself by gaining broader control of one's working environment through participation in Alliance cooperatives. Along with industrial workers, Populist farmers had also preached the idea of equality — a real equality of opportunity. But the cooperators, with their denunciations of "selfish individualism," had moved even more than labor toward the third great concept in the Enlightenment trinity — *fraternity*, or *comradeship*. The idea of cooperation had grown out of, and had sustained, the practices of sisterhood and brotherhood.

And if the Populists had realized all three values to a greater extent than any other large group, it was mainly because of a conscious effort toward the intensive use of massive numbers of second-cadre activists — 35,000 or more "lecturers" — in rousing farmers to political self-consciousness. As in all deeply felt democratic movements, the great leaders were educators, and the great teachers were leaders.

Populism was short-lived as a third-party movement. In the South, Tom Watson's interracial coalition collapsed when conservative whites accused it of undermining white supremacy. On the national level, the Democrats stole much of the Populists' appeal when they nominated William Jennings Bryan, a reformer and a westerner, for president in the campaign of 1896. Amid bickering and grumbling, the Populists "fused" with the Democrats that year, and both organizations went down to defeat in an election that brought Republican William McKinley to power. For the Populists, the election was a disaster from which the party never recovered. "Never again," writes one historian, "would American farmers unite so militantly to demand economic reform. And never again would so large a group of Americans raise so forceful a protest against the nature of the industrial economy."

Even so, populism had a lasting effect on American poli-

tics. It helped usher in a new era of reform in the United States, the Progressive era, which will be treated in subsequent selections. During the Progressive era, many Populist demands became politically respectable and were enacted into law. Among these were a graduated income tax, a managed currency, a lower tariff, and the direct election of United States senators. The New Deal of the 1930s, moreover, adopted and modified Populist proposals for a crop storage system and agricultural credit.

Many historians contend that populism influenced later political movements, such as Huey Long's in the 1930s and George Wallace's in the 1960s. Even today there are politicians who call themselves populists, or who are so labeled. David Duke, Louisiana politico and former head of the Ku Klux Klan, has been called a populist. So have Jesse Jackson and Ronald Reagan. But in "The Party of the People" (American Heritage, May/June 1992), historian Bernard Weisberger warns that the term is misused when applied indiscriminately to modern politicians and modern political attitudes. Stressing "the importance of historical context" and accuracy, Weisberger insists that the term populism be confined to the insurgent farmers of the 1890s, who gave the word its original meaning.

QUESTIONS TO CONSIDER

1 What problems plagued American farmers in the late nineteenth century? How did this situation contrast with the traditional ideal of the farmer's role in the American republic? How did it compare with the conditions of American labor that you saw in selection 6?

2 Discuss the early farmers' alliances. How did they work and spread their message? What did they hope to accomplish? Where were they most successful?

3 When the farmers decided to organize politically on the state level, why did they choose to form a third party rather than join one of the two major parties? How were they treated by the Republicans and Democrats? What particular obstacles did they

face in the South? How did Tom Watson appeal to southern farmers? How did he fare politically and why?

4 What were the basic principles of the national People's party? What issues did it not address? How did the party fare in its first election in 1892?

5 What were the different conceptions of liberty held by capital, labor, and farmers? What does Burns mean when he says that more than anything else the farmers' alliance "had made liberty into a positive idea"? How does the populist movement compare with the development of the labor movement you read about in selection 6? Why do you think they were so different?

9

America's First Southeast Asian War: The Philippine Insurrection

DAVID R. KOHLER AND JAMES W. WENSYEL

The last quarter of the nineteenth century marked the second age of imperialism, a time when the industrial nations of Europe — Britain, Germany, France, Holland, and Russia — claimed colonies in Africa and spheres of influence in distant China. The United States, flexing its imperial muscles in the 1890s, was also alive with "aggressive, expansionistic, and jingoistic" sentiments. In 1893, with the help of 150 marines from a United States cruiser, American residents in Hawaii deposed the queen of the islands, set up a provisional government, and clamored for annexation. In 1898, the United States formally annexed Hawaii, thus expanding American territory and interests in the Pacific. In 1898–1899, the United States gained additional Pacific possessions in a controversial war with Spain, by then a second-rate power whose old empire in the Americas had all but disintegrated.

American expansionists, cheered on by a truculent yellow press, did not cause the war with Spain. But American policymakers and business leaders did use it as a means to extend American economic and political power. The war itself grew out of deplorable conditions in Cuba, caused by decades of Spanish misrule. A series of Cuban revolts and Spanish atrocities, which the American press exaggerated, aroused Americans' sympathy for the Cubans, whose cause seemed identical to that of the American patriots in 1776. In February 1898, American sentiment turned to outrage when the United States battleship Maine *blew up in Havana harbor, killing 260 American sailors. The cause of the explosion was never established, but American expansionists — among them, Assistant Secre-*

tary of the Navy Theodore Roosevelt — blamed Spain and demanded war. Overnight a slogan caught the imagination of the country: "Remember the Maine! To hell with Spain!"

In March, President William McKinley demanded that Spain agree to negotiations that would grant independence to Cuba. Faced with the possibility of a disastrous war in a distant hemisphere, Spain tried to maneuver, declaring an armistice with Cuban insurgents but hedging on Cuban independence. By then, both President McKinley and Congress were prepared for war. When Congress adopted a resolution recognizing Cuban independence, Spain retaliated by declaring war on the United States; the next day, Congress responded in kind.

Less than a week later, the American Asiatic Squadron under Commodore George Dewey won a dazzling victory in Manila Bay in the Spanish-held Philippines. As it turned out, the navy's Roosevelt had secured the command for Dewey and had directed him to prepare for action two months before official hostilities commenced. The United States also invaded Cuba, where Teddy Roosevelt gained national fame as colonel of the Rough Riders. After ten weeks of fighting, Spain capitulated, giving up control of Cuba and surrendering Puerto Rico, Guam, and the Philippines to the United States. For Secretary of State John Hay, it had been "a splendid little war."

Much has been written about the Spanish-American War and the United States empire that emerged from it. Much less is known about an important offshoot of that war — an American military campaign against Philippine insurgents that lasted three years, involved 126,000 United States troops, and resulted in 7,000 American and some 216,000 Filipino casualties. The United States learned a number of hard lessons about fighting against nationalist insurgents in distant Asian jungles, but sixty years later another generation of Americans forgot those lessons when plunging into a similar conflict in Vietnam. In the selection that follows, David R. Kohler, a naval special warfare officer, and James W. Wensyel, a retired army officer and the author of several books, narrate American involvement in the Filipino insurrection of 1898–1902, showing how it grew out of the Spanish-American War and the American bid for empire. The authors point out the influence of the Indian wars on American tactics in the Philippines, and they draw several significant parallels between the Philippine conflict and America's involvement in Vietnam. It was the Philippine conflict that generated strategic hamlets, free-fire zones, and search-and-destroy missions — terms that were later seared into the history of American involvement in Vietnam. You will find it instructive to read and discuss this selection in connection with George C. Herring's account of Vietnam (selection 25). In what ways were the two conflicts alike and in what ways did they differ? As experienced military men, Kohler and Wensyel contend that future American leaders should ponder the lessons of the Philippine and Vietnamese conflicts before embarking on similar adventures.

GLOSSARY

AGUINALDO Y FAMY, GENERALISSIMO EMILIO   Commander of the Filipino nationalists who fought the Spaniards and then the Americans in an effort to achieve Philippine independence.

BOLO KNIFE   This sharp-edged instrument was the Filipino revolutionary's main weapon.

DEWEY, COMMODORE GEORGE   Commander of the American Asiatic Squadron, which sank the Spanish fleet in the Battle of Manila Bay, May 1, 1898.

GRAYSON, WILLIAM "WILLIE" WALTER   The Philippine insurrection began when he and his fellow soldiers seized Filipino nationalists within their picket line and firing broke out between the American and Filipino camps.

GUERRILLA WARFARE   Like the Vietcong and North Vietnamese sixty years later, the Filipinos eschewed conventional, Western-style warfare of pitched battles and dispersed throughout the countryside conducting "hit-and-run operations by small bands."

MACABEBES   Filipino mercenaries from the central Luzon province of Pampanga province who fought for Spain and the United States against their own countrymen.

MacARTHUR, GENERAL ARTHUR   Assuming command of United States forces in 1900, he initiated new tactics designed to isolate the Filipino guerrillas from the villages that supported them; his tactics gave rise to strategic hamlets, free-fire zones, and search-and-destroy operations.

MAHAN, ADMIRAL ALFRED THAYER   United States naval strategist who contended that sea power and overseas colonies were the keys to national power; his writings greatly influenced American imperialists such as Teddy Roosevelt and Henry Cabot Lodge.

MERRITT, MAJOR GENERAL WESLEY   Commanded the United States Philippine Expeditionary Force, sent to oust the Spaniards from the islands.

SANTAYANA, GEORGE   Spanish-born philosopher, poet, and educator who observed that those who do not learn from the mistakes of the past are doomed to repeat them.

SMITH, BRIGADIER GENERAL JACOB W. "HELL ROARING JAKE"   Veteran of the Wounded Knee Sioux massacre of 1890; when the insurgents on Samar Island massacred fifty-nine American soldiers, "Hell Roaring" Smith ordered his men to burn and kill their way across the island in retaliation.

TAFT, WILLIAM HOWARD   Headed a United States civilian commission that took over the Philippine colonial government in 1901.

USS MAINE   The mysterious sinking of this American battleship was the catalyst of the Spanish-American War.

"WATER CURE"   American method of torture devised in retaliation for Filipino acts of terrorism (booby traps and assassination); a bamboo reed was placed in an insurgent's mouth, and water, often salted or dirty, was poured down his throat until he was so painfully bloated that he talked.

"WHITE MAN'S BURDEN"   Racist concept, popular among American imperialists, that whites had a "moral responsibility" to uplift and civilize supposedly inferior dark-skinned people such as the Filipinos.

Guerrilla warfare ... jungle terrain ... search and destroy missions ... benevolent pacification ... strategic hamlets ... terrorism ... ambushes ... free-fire zones ... booby traps ... waning support from civilians at home. These words call forth from the national consciousness uncomfortable images of a war Americans fought and died in not long ago in Southeast Asia. But while the phrases may first bring to mind America's painful experience in Vietnam during the 1960s and '70s, they also aptly describe a much earlier conflict — the Philippine Insurrection — that foreshadowed this and other insurgent wars in Asia.

The Philippine-American War of 1898–1902 is one of our nation's most obscure and least-understood campaigns. Sometimes called the "Bolo War" because of the Filipino insurgents' lethally effective use of razor-sharp bolo knives or machetes against the American expeditionary force occupying the islands, it is often viewed as a mere appendage of the one-hundred-day Spanish-American War. But suppressing the guerrilla warfare waged by Philippine nationalists seeking self-rule proved far more difficult, protracted, and costly for American forces than the conventional war with Spain that had preceded it.

America's campaign to smash the Philippine Insurrection was, ironically, a direct consequence of U.S. efforts to secure independence for other *insurrectos* halfway around the world in Cuba. On May 1, 1898, less than a week after Congress declared war against Spain, a naval squadron commanded by Commodore George Dewey steamed into Manila Bay to engage the Spanish warships defending that nation's Pacific possession. In a brief action Dewey

achieved a stunning victory, sinking all of the enemy vessels with no significant American losses. Destroying the Spanish fleet, however, did not ensure U.S. possession of the Philippines. An estimated 15,000 Spanish soldiers still occupied Manila and the surrounding region. Those forces would have to be rooted out by infantry.

President William McKinley had already ordered a Philippine Expeditionary Force of volunteer and regular army infantry, artillery, and cavalry units (nearly seven thousand men), under the command of Major General Wesley Merritt, to "reduce Spanish power in that quarter [Philippine Islands] and give order and security to the islands while in the possession of the United States."

Sent to the Philippines in the summer of 1898, this limited force was committed without fully considering the operation's potential length and cost. American military and government leaders also failed to anticipate the consequences of ignoring the Filipino rebels who, under Generalissimo Don Emilio Aguinaldo y Famy, had been waging a war for independence against Spain for the past two years. And when American insensitivity toward Aguinaldo eventually led to open warfare with the rebels, the American leaders grossly underestimated the determination of the seemingly ill-trained and poorly armed insurgents. They additionally failed to perceive the difficulties involved in conducting military operations in a tropical environment and among a hostile native population, and they did not recognize the burden of fighting at the end of a seven-thousand-mile-long logistics trail.

Asian engagements, the Americans learned for the first time, are costly. The enterprise, so modestly begun, eventually saw more than 126,000 American officers and men deployed to the Philippines. Four times as many soldiers served in this undeclared war in the Pacific as had been sent to the Caribbean during the Spanish-American War. During the three-year conflict, American troops and Filipino insur-

From David R. Kohler and James W. Wensyel, "Our First Southeast Asian War," *American History Illustrated* (January/February 1990), 19–30. Reprinted through the courtesy of Cowles Magazines, publisher of *American History Illustrated*.

gents fought in more than 2,800 engagements. American casualties ultimately totaled 4,234 killed and 2,818 wounded, and the insurgents lost about 16,000 men. The civilian population suffered even more; as many as 200,000 Filipinos died from famine, pestilence, or the unfortunate happenstance of being too close to the fighting. The Philippine war cost the United States $600 million before the insurgents were subdued.

The costly experience offered valuable and timeless lessons about guerrilla warfare in Asia; unfortunately, those lessons had to be relearned sixty years later in another war that, despite the modern technology involved, bore surprising parallels to America's first Southeast Asian campaign.

☆

ORIGINS

America's war with Spain, formally declared by the United States on April 25, 1898, had been several years in the making. During that time the American "yellow press," led by Joseph Pulitzer's *New York World* and William Randolph Hearst's *New York Journal,* trumpeted reports of heroic Cuban *insurrectos* revolting against their cruel Spanish rulers. Journalists vividly described harsh measures taken by Spanish officials to quell the Cuban revolution. The sensational accounts, often exaggerated, reminded Americans of their own uphill fight for independence and nourished the feeling that America was destined to intervene so that the Cuban people might also taste freedom.

Furthermore, expansionists suggested that the revolt against a European power, taking place less than one hundred miles from American shores, offered a splendid opportunity to turn the Caribbean into an American sea. Businessmen pointed out that $50 million in American capital was invested in the Cuban sugar and mining industries. Revolutions resulting in burned cane fields jeopardized that invest-

ment. As 1898 opened, American relations with Spain quickly declined.

In January 1898 the U.S. battleship *Maine* was sent to Cuba, ostensibly on a courtesy visit. On February 15 the warship was destroyed by a mysterious explosion while at anchor in Havana harbor, killing 262 of her 350-man crew. The navy's formal inquiry, completed on March 28, suggested that the explosion was due to an external force — a mine.

On March 29, the Spanish government received an ultimatum from Washington, D.C.: Spain's army in Cuba was to lay down its arms while the United States negotiated between the rebels and the Spaniards. The Spanish forces were also told to abolish all *reconcentrado* camps (tightly controlled areas, similar to the strategic hamlets later tried in Vietnam, where peasants were regrouped to deny food and intelligence to insurgents and to promote tighter security). Spain initially rejected the humiliation of surrendering its arms in the field but then capitulated on all points. The Americans were not satisfied.

On April 11, declaring that Spanish responses were inadequate, President McKinley told a joint session of Congress that "I have exhausted every effort to relieve the intolerable condition . . . at our doors. I now ask the Congress to empower the president to take measures to secure a full and final termination of hostilities in Cuba, to secure . . . the establishment of a stable government, and to use the military and naval forces of the United States . . . for these purposes. . . ."

Congress adopted the proposed resolution on April 19. Learning this, Spain declared war on the 24th. The following day, the United States responded with its own declaration of war.

The bulk of the American navy quickly gathered on the Atlantic coast. McKinley called for 125,000 volunteers to bolster the less than eighty-thousand-man regular army. His call was quickly oversubscribed; volunteers fought to be the first to land on Cuba's beaches.

The first major battle of the war, however, was fought not in Cuba but seven thousand miles to the west — in Manila Bay. Dewey's victory over Spanish Admiral Patricio Montojo y Pasarón (a rather hollow victory as Montojo's fleet consisted of seven unarmored ships, three of which had wooden hulls and one that had to be towed to the battle area) was wildly acclaimed in America.

American leaders, believing that the Philippines would now fall into America's grasp like a ripe plum, had to decide what to do with their prize. They could not return the islands to Spain, nor could they allow them to pass to France or Germany, America's commercial rivals in the Orient. The American press rejected the idea of a British protectorate. And, after four hundred years of despotic Spanish rule in which Filipinos had little or no chance to practice self-government, native leaders seemed unlikely candidates for managing their own affairs. McKinley faced a grand opportunity for imperialistic expansion that could not be ignored.

The debate sharply divided his cabinet — and the country. American public opinion over acquisition of the Philippines divided into two basic factions: imperialists versus anti-imperialists.

The imperialists, mostly Republicans, included such figures as Theodore Roosevelt (then assistant secretary of the navy), Henry Cabot Lodge (Massachusetts senator), and Albert Beveridge (Indiana senator). These individuals were, for the most part, disciples of Alfred Thayer Mahan, a naval strategist who touted theories of national power and prestige through sea power and acquisition of overseas colonies for trade purposes and naval coaling stations.

The anti-imperialists, staunchly against American annexation of the Philippines, were mainly Democrats. Such men as former presidents Grover Cleveland and Rutherford B. Hayes, steel magnate Andrew Carnegie, William Jennings Bryan, union leader Samuel Gompers, and Mark Twain warned

that by taking the Philippines the United States would march the road to ruin earlier traveled by the Roman Empire. Furthermore, they argued, America would be denying Filipinos the right of self-determination guaranteed by our own Constitution. The more practical-minded also pointed out that imperialistic policy would require maintaining an expensive army and navy there.

Racism, though demonstrated in different ways, pervaded the arguments of both sides. Imperialists spoke of the "white man's burden" and moral responsibility to "uplift the child races everywhere" and to provide "orderly development for the unfortunate and less able races." They spoke of America's "civilizing mission" of pacifying Filipinos by "benevolent assimilation" and saw the opening of the overseas frontier much as their forefathers had viewed the western frontier. The "subjugation of the Injun" (wherever he might be found) was a concept grasped by American youth — the war's most enthusiastic supporters (in contrast to young America's opposition to the war in Vietnam many years later).

The anti-imperialists extolled the sacredness of independence and self-determination for the Filipinos. Racism, however, also crept into their argument, for they believed that "protection against race mingling" was a historic American policy that would be reversed by imperialism. To them, annexation of the Philippines would admit "alien, inferior, and mongrel races to our nationality."

As the debate raged, Dewey continued to hold Manila Bay, and the Philippines seemed to await America's pleasure. President McKinley would ultimately cast the deciding vote in determining America's role in that country. McKinley, a genial, rather laid-back, former congressman from Ohio and one-time major in the Union army, remains a rather ambiguous figure during this period. In his Inaugural Address he had affirmed that "We want no wars of conquest; we must avoid the temptation of territorial aggression." Thereafter, however, he made few comments on pacifism, and, fourteen weeks after becoming president, signed the bill annexing Hawaii.

Speaking of Cuba in December 1897, McKinley said, "I speak not of forcible annexation, for that cannot be thought of. That, by our code of morality, would be criminal aggression." Nevertheless, he constantly pressured Madrid to end Spanish rule in Cuba, leading four months later to America's war with Spain.

McKinley described experiencing extreme turmoil, soul-searching, and prayer over the Philippine annexation issue until, he declared, one night in a dream the Lord revealed to him that "there was nothing left for us to do but to take them all [the Philippine Islands] and to educate the Filipinos, and uplift, and civilize, and Christianize them." He apparently didn't realize that the Philippines had been staunchly Roman Catholic for more than 350 years under Spanish colonialism. Nor could he anticipate the difficulties that, having cast its fortune with the expansionists, America would now face in the Philippines.

☆

PROSECUTING THE WAR

Meanwhile, in the Philippine Islands, Major General Wesley Merritt's Philippine Expeditionary Force went about its job. In late June, General Thomas Anderson led an advance party ashore at Cavite. He then established Camp Merritt, visited General Aguinaldo's rebel forces entrenched around Manila, and made plans for seizing that city once Merritt arrived with the main body of armed forces.

Anderson quickly learned that military operations in the Philippines could be difficult. His soldiers, hastily assembled and dispatched with limited prior training, were poorly disciplined and inadequately equipped. Many still wore woolen uniforms despite the tropical climate. A staff officer described the army's baptism at Manila: ". . . the heat was oppressive and the rain kept falling. At times the trenches were filled with two feet of water, and soon the men's shoes were ruined. Their heavy khaki uniforms were a nuisance; they perspired constantly, the loss of body salts inducing chronic fatigue. Prickly heat broke out, inflamed by scratching and rubbing. Within a week the first cases of dysentery, malaria, cholera, and dengue fever showed up at sick call."

During his first meeting with Dewey, Anderson remarked that some American leaders were considering annexation of the Philippines. "If the United States intends to hold the Philippine Islands," Dewey responded, "it will make things awkward, because just a week ago Aguinaldo proclaimed the independence of the Philippine Islands from Spain and seems intent on establishing his own government."

A Filipino independence movement led by Aguinaldo had been active in the islands since 1896 and, within weeks of Dewey's victory, Aguinaldo's revolutionaries controlled most of the archipelago.

Aguinaldo, twenty-nine years old in 1898, had taken over his father's position as mayor of his hometown of Kawit before becoming a revolutionary. In a minor skirmish with Spanish soldiers, he had rallied the Filipinos to victory. Thereafter, his popularity grew as did his ragtag but determined army. Aguinaldo was slight of build, shy, and soft-spoken, but a strict disciplinarian.

As his rebel force besieged Manila, Aguinaldo declared a formal government for the Philippines with himself as president and generalissimo. He proclaimed his "nation's" independence and called for Filipinos to rally to his army and to the Americans, declaring that "the Americans . . . extend their protecting mantle to our beloved country . . . When you see the American flag flying, assemble in numbers: they are our redeemers!" But his enthusiasm for the United States later waned.

Merritt put off Aguinaldo's increasingly strident demands that America recognize his government and guarantee the Filipinos' independence. Aguinaldo perceived the American general's attitude as condescending and demeaning.

United States troops sent to the Philippines found the tropical climate and terrain "almost as deadly as combat." The first contingent of soldiers arrived wearing woolen uniforms. Thousands of *Americans fell victim to dysentery and malaria. (Keystone-Mast Collection, California Museum of Photography, University of California, Riverside)*

On August 13, Merritt's forces occupied Manila almost without firing a shot; in a face-saving maneuver the Spanish defenders had agreed to surrender to the Americans to avoid being captured — and perhaps massacred — by the Filipino insurgents. Merritt's troops physically blocked Aguinaldo's rebels, who had spent weeks in the trenches around the city, from participating in the assault. The Filipino general and his followers felt betrayed at being denied a share in the victory.

Further disenchanted, Aguinaldo would later find his revolutionary government unrepresented at the Paris peace talks determining his country's fate. He would learn that Spain had ceded the Philippines to the United States for $20 million.

Officers at Merritt's headquarters had little faith in the Filipinos' ability to govern themselves. "Should our power ... be withdrawn," an early report declared, "the Philippines would speedily lapse into anarchy, which would excuse ... the intervention of other powers and the division of the islands among them."

Meanwhile, friction between American soldiers and the Filipinos increased. Much of the Americans' conduct betrayed their racial bias. Soldiers referred to the natives as "niggers" and "gugus," epithets whose meanings were clear to the Filipinos. In retaliation, the island inhabitants refused to give way on sidewalks and muscled American officers into the streets. Men of the expeditionary force in turn escalated tensions by stopping Filipinos at gun point, searching them without cause, "confiscating" shopkeepers' goods, and beating those who resisted.

On the night of February 4, 1899, the simmering pot finally boiled over. Private William "Willie" Walter Grayson and several other soldiers of Company D, 1st Nebraska Volunteer Infantry, apprehended a group of armed insurgents within their regimental picket line. Shots were exchanged, and three Filipino *insurrectos* fell dead. Heavy firing erupted between the two camps.

In the bloody battle that followed, the Filipinos suffered tremendous casualties (an estimated two thousand to five thousand dead, contrasted with fifty-nine Americans killed) and were forced to withdraw. The Philippine Insurrection had begun.

☆

GUERRILLA WARFARE

The Americans, hampered by a shortage of troops and the oncoming rainy season, could initially do little more than extend their defensive perimeter beyond Manila and establish a toehold on several islands to the south. By the end of March, however, American forces seized Malolos, the seat of Aguinaldo's revolutionary government. But Aguinaldo escaped, simply melting into the jungle. In the fall, using conventional methods of warfare, the Americans first struck south, then north of Manila across the central Luzon plain. After hard marching and tough fighting, the expeditionary force occupied northern Luzon, dispersed the rebel army, and barely missed capturing Aguinaldo.

Believing that occupying the remainder of the Philippines would be easy, the Americans wrongly concluded that the war was virtually ended. But when the troops attempted to control the territory they had seized, they found that the Filipino revolutionaries were not defeated but had merely changed strategies. Abandoning western-style conventional warfare, Aguinaldo had decided to adopt guerrilla tactics.

Aguinaldo moved to a secret mountain headquarters at Palanan in northern Luzon, ordering his troops to disperse and avoid pitched battles in favor of hit-and-run operations by small bands. Ambushing parties of Americans and applying terror to coerce support from other Filipinos, the insurrectionists now blended into the countryside, where they enjoyed superior intelligence information, ample supplies, and tight security. The guerrillas moved freely between the scattered American units, cutting telegraph lines, attacking supply trains, and assaulting straggling infantrymen. When the Americans pursued their tormentors, they fell into well planned ambushes. The insurgents' barbarity and ruthlessness during these attacks were notorious.

The guerrilla tactics helped to offset the inequities that existed between the two armies. The American troops were far better armed, for example, carrying .45-caliber Springfield single-shot rifles, Mausers, and then-modern .30-caliber repeating Krag-Jorgensen rifles. They also had field artillery and machine guns. The revolutionaries, on the other hand, were limited to a miscellaneous assortment of handguns, a few Mauser repeating rifles taken from the Spanish, and antique muzzle-loaders. The sharp-edged bolo knife was the revolutionary's primary weapon, and he used it well. Probably more American soldiers were hacked to death by bolos than were killed by Mauser bullets.

As would later be the case in Vietnam, the guerrillas had some clear advantages. They knew the terrain, were inured to the climate, and could generally count on a friendly population. As in Vietnam, villages controlled by the insurgents provided havens from which the guerrillas could attack, then fade back into hiding.

Americans soon began to feel that they were under siege in a land of enemies, and their fears were heightened because they never could be sure who among the population was hostile. A seemingly friendly peasant might actually be a murderer. Lieutenant Colonel J. T. Wickham, commanding the 26th Infantry Regiment, recorded that "a large flag of truce enticed officers into ambushes . . . Privates Dugan, Hayes, and Tracy were murdered by town authorities . . . Private Nolan [was] tied up by ladies while in a stupor; the insurgents cut his throat . . . The body of Corporal Doneley was dug up, burned, and mutilated . . . Private O'Hearn, captured by apparently friendly people was tied to a tree, burned over a slow fire, and slashed up . . . Lieutenant Max Wagner was assassinated by insurgents disguised in American uniforms."

As in later guerrilla movements, such terrorism became a standard tactic for the insurgents. Both Filipinos and Americans were their victims. In preying on their countrymen, the guerrillas had a dual purpose: to discourage any Filipinos disposed to cooperate with the Americans, and to demonstrate to people in a particular region that they ruled that area and could destroy inhabitants and villages not supporting the revolution. The most favored terroristic weapon was assassination of local leaders, who were usually executed in a manner (such as beheading or burying alive) calculated to horrify everyone.

By the spring of 1900 the war was going badly for the Americans. Their task forces, sent out to search and destroy, found little and destroyed less.

The monsoon rains, jungle terrain, hostile native population, and a determined guerrilla force made the American soldiers' marches long and miserable. One described a five-week-long infantry operation: ". . . our troops had been on half rations for two weeks. Wallowing through hip-deep muck, lugging a ten-pound rifle and a belt . . . with 200 rounds of

ammunition, drenched to the skin and with their feet becoming heavier with mud at every step, the infantry became discouraged. Some men simply cried, others slipped down in the mud and refused to rise. Threats and appeals by the officers were of no avail. Only a promise of food in the next town and the threat that if they remained behind they would be butchered by marauding bands of insurgents forced some to their feet to struggle on."

News reports of the army's difficulties began to erode the American public's support for the war. "To chase barefooted insurgents with water buffalo carts as a wagon train may be simply ridiculous," charged one correspondent, "but to load volunteers down with 200 rounds of ammunition and one day's rations, and to put on their heads felt hats used by no other army in the tropics . . . to trot these same soldiers in the boiling sun over a country without roads, is positively criminal. . . . There are over five thousand men in the general hospital."

Another reported that the American outlook "is blacker now than it has been since the beginning of the war . . . the whole population . . . sympathizes with the insurgents. The insurgents came to Pasig [a local area whose government cooperated with the Americans] and their first act was to hang the 'Presidente' for treason in surrendering to Americans. 'Presidentes' do not surrender to us anymore."

☆

NEW STRATEGIES

Early in the war U.S. military commanders had realized that, unlike the American Indians who had been herded onto reservations, eight million Filipinos (many of them hostile) would have to be governed in place. The Americans chose to emphasize pacification through good works rather than by harsh measures, hoping to convince Filipinos that the

American colonial government had a sincere interest in their welfare and could be trusted.

As the army expanded its control across the islands, it reorganized local municipal governments and trained Filipinos to take over civil functions in the democratic political structure the Americans planned to establish. American soldiers performed police duties, distributed food, established and taught at schools, and built roads and telegraph lines.

As the war progressed, however, the U.S. commanders saw that the terrorism practiced by Aguinaldo's guerrillas was far more effective in controlling the populace than was their own benevolent approach. Although the Americans did not abandon pacification through good works, it was thereafter subordinated to the "civilize 'em with a Krag" (Krag-Jorgensen rifle) philosophy. From December 1900 onward, captured revolutionaries faced deportation, imprisonment, or execution.

The American army also changed its combat strategy to counter that of its enemy. As in the insurgents' army, the new tactics emphasized mobility and surprise. Breaking into small units — the battalion became the largest maneuver force — the Americans gradually spread over the islands until each of the larger towns was occupied by one or two rifle companies. From these bases American troops began platoon- and company-size operations to pressure local guerrilla bands.

Because of the difficult terrain, limited visibility, and requirement for mobility, artillery now saw limited use except as a defensive weapon. The infantry became the main offensive arm, with mounted riflemen used to pursue the fleeing enemy. Cavalry patrols were so valued for their mobility that American military leaders hired trusted Filipinos as mounted scouts and cavalrymen.

The Americans made other efforts to "Filipinize" the war — letting Asians fight Asians. (A similar tactic had been used in the American Indian campaigns twenty years before; it would resurface in Vietnam sixty years later as "Vietnamization.") In the Philippines the Americans recruited five thousand Macabebes, mercenaries from the central Luzon province of Pampanga, to form the American officered Philippine Scouts. The Macabebes had for centuries fought in native battalions under the Spanish flag — even against their own countrymen when the revolution began in 1896.

Just as a later generation of American soldiers would react to the guerrilla war in Vietnam, American soldiers in the Philippines responded to insurgent terrorism in kind, matching cruelty with cruelty. Such actions vented their frustration at being unable to find and destroy the enemy. An increasing number of Americans viewed all Filipinos as enemies.

"We make everyone get into his house by 7 P.M. and we only tell a man once," Corporal Sam Gillis of the 1st California Volunteer Regiment wrote to his family. "If he refuses, we shoot him. We killed over 300 natives the first night. . . . If they fire a shot from a house, we burn the house and every house near it."

Another infantryman frankly admitted that "with an enemy like this to fight, it is not surprising that the boys should soon adopt 'no quarter' as a motto and fill the blacks full of lead before finding out whether they are friends or enemies."

That attitude should not have been too surprising. The army's campaigns against the Plains Indians were reference points for the generation of Americans that took the Philippines. Many of the senior officers and noncommissioned officers — often veterans of the Indian wars — considered Filipinos to be "as full of treachery as our Arizona Apache." "The country won't be pacified," one soldier told a reporter, "until the niggers are killed off like the Indians." A popular soldiers' refrain, sung to the tune of "Tramp, tramp, tramp, the boys are marching," began, "Damn, damn, damn the Filipinos," and again spoke of "civilizing 'em with a Krag."

Reprisals against civilians by Americans as well

as insurgents became common. General Lloyd Wheaton, leading a U.S. offensive southeast of Manila, found his men impaled on the bamboo prongs of booby traps and with throats slit while they slept. After two of his companies were ambushed, Wheaton ordered that every town and village within twelve miles be burned.

The Americans developed their own terrorist methods, many of which would be used in later Southeast Asian wars. One was torturing suspected guerrillas or insurgent sympathizers to force them to reveal locations of other guerrillas and their supplies. An often-utilized form of persuasion was the "water cure," placing a bamboo reed in the victim's mouth and pouring water (some used salt water or dirty water) down his throat, thus painfully distending the victim's stomach. The subject, allowed to void this, would, under threat of repetition, usually talk freely. Another method of torture, the "rope cure," consisted of wrapping a rope around the victim's neck and torso until it formed a sort of girdle. A stick (or Krag rifle), placed between the ropes and twisted, then effectively created a combination of smothering and garroting.

The anti-imperialist press reported such American brutality in lurid detail. As a result, a number of officers and soldiers were court-martialed for torturing and other cruelties. Their punishments, however, seemed remarkably lenient. Of ten officers tried for "looting, torture, and murder," three were acquitted; of the seven convicted, five were reprimanded, one was reprimanded and fined $300, and one lost thirty-five places in the army's seniority list and forfeited half his pay for nine months.

Officers and soldiers, fighting a cruel, determined, and dangerous enemy, could not understand public condemnation of the brutality they felt was necessary to win. They had not experienced such criticism during the Indian wars, where total extermination of the enemy was condoned by the press and the American public, and they failed to grasp the difference now. Press reports, loss of public support, and the soldiers' feeling of betrayal — features of an insurgent war — would resurface decades later during the Vietnam conflict.

☆

SUCCESS

Although U.S. military leaders were frustrated by the guerrillas' determination on the one hand and by eroding American support for the war on the other, most believed that the insurgents could be subdued. Especially optimistic was General Arthur MacArthur, who in 1900 assumed command of the seventy thousand American troops in the Philippines. MacArthur adopted a strategy like that successfully used by General Zachary Taylor in the Second Seminole War in 1835; he believed that success depended upon the Americans' ability to isolate the guerrillas from their support in the villages. Thus were born "strategic hamlets," "free-fire zones," and "search and destroy" missions, concepts the American army would revive decades later in Vietnam.

MacArthur strengthened the more than five hundred small strong points held by Americans throughout the Philippine Islands. Each post was garrisoned by at least one company of American infantrymen. The natives around each base were driven from their homes, which were then destroyed. Soldiers herded the displaced natives into *reconcentrado* camps, where they could be "protected" by the nearby garrisons. Crops, food stores, and houses outside the camps were destroyed to deny them to the guerrillas. Surrounding each camp was a "dead line," within which anyone appearing would be shot on sight.

Operating from these small garrisons, the Americans pressured the guerrillas, allowing them no rest. Kept off balance, short of supplies, and constantly pursued by the American army, the Filipino guerrillas, suffering from sickness, hunger, and dwindling popular support, began to lose their will to fight. Many insurgent leaders surrendered, signaling that the tide at last had turned in the Americans' favor.

In March 1901, a group of Macabebe Scouts, commanded by American Colonel Frederick "Fighting Fred" Funston, captured Aguinaldo. Aguinaldo's subsequent proclamation that he would fight no more, and his pledge of loyalty to the United States, sped the collapse of the insurrection.

As in the past, and as would happen again during the Vietnam conflict of the 1960s and '70s, American optimism was premature. Although a civilian commission headed by William H. Taft took control of the colonial government from the American army in July 1901, the army faced more bitter fighting in its "pacification" of the islands.

As the war sputtered, the insurgents' massacre of fifty-nine American soldiers at Balangiga on the island of Samar caused Brigadier General Jacob W. "Hell-Roaring Jake" Smith, veteran of the Wounded Knee massacre of the Sioux in 1890, to order his officers to turn Samar into a "howling wilderness." His orders to a battalion of three hundred Marines headed for Samar were precise: "I want no prisoners. I wish you to kill and burn, the more you kill and burn the better it will please me. I want all persons killed who are capable of bearing arms against the United States." Fortunately, the Marines did not take Smith's orders literally and, later, Smith would be court-martialed.

On July 4, 1902, the Philippine Insurrection officially ended. Although it took the American army another eleven years to crush the fierce Moros of the southern Philippines, the civil government's security force (the Philippine Constabulary), aided by the army's Philippine Scouts, maintained a fitful peace throughout the islands. The army's campaign to secure the Philippines as an American colony had succeeded.

American commanders would have experienced vastly greater difficulties except for two distinct advantages: 1) the enemy had to operate in a restricted area, in isolated islands, and was prevented by the U.S. Navy from importing weapons and other needed supplies; and 2) though the insurgents attempted to enlist help from Japan, no outside power intervened. These conditions would not prevail in some subsequent guerrilla conflicts in Asia.

In addition to the many tactical lessons the army learned from fighting a guerrilla war in a tropical climate, other problems experienced during this campaign validated the need for several military reforms that were subsequently carried out, including improved logistics, tropical medicine, and communications.

The combination of harsh and unrelenting military force against the guerrillas, complemented by the exercise of fair and equitable civil government and civic action toward those who cooperated, proved to be the Americans' most effective tactic for dealing with the insurgency. This probably was the most significant lesson to be learned from the Philippine Insurrection.

☆

LESSONS FOR THE FUTURE

Vietnam veterans reading this account might nod in recollection of a personal, perhaps painful experience from their own war.

Many similarities exist between America's three-year struggle with the Filipino *insurrectos* and the decade-long campaign against the Communists in Vietnam. Both wars, modestly begun, went far beyond what anyone had foreseen in time, money, equipment, manpower, casualties, and suffering.

Both wars featured small-unit infantry actions. Young infantrymen, if they had any initial enthusiasm, usually lost it once they saw the war's true nature; they nevertheless learned to endure their allotted time while adopting personal self-survival measures as months "in-country" lengthened and casualty lists grew.

Both wars were harsh, brutal, cruel. Both had

their Samar Islands and their My Lais. Human nature being what it is, both conflicts also included acts of great heroism, kindness, compassion, and self-sacrifice.

Both wars saw an increasingly disenchanted American public withdrawing its support (and even disavowing its servicemen) as the campaigns dragged on, casualties mounted, and news accounts vividly described the horror of the battlefields.

Some useful lessons might be gleaned from a comparison of the two conflicts. Human nature really does not change — war will bring out the best and the worst in the tired, wet, hungry, and fearful men who are doing the fighting. Guerrilla campaigns — particularly where local military and civic reforms cannot be effected to separate the guerrilla from his base of popular support — will be long and difficult, and will demand tremendous commitments in resources and national will. Finally, before America commits its armed forces to similar ventures in the future, it would do well to recall the lessons learned from previous campaigns. For, as the Spanish-born American educator, poet, and philosopher George Santayana reminded us, those who do not learn from the past are doomed to repeat it.

QUESTIONS TO CONSIDER

1   How and why did the United States initially become involved in the Philippines? What, according to the authors, were the fundamental mistakes committed by the Americans in making that decision?

2   Why did the Americans decide to take over the Philippines? What were the different categories of American public opinion in reaction to this development? How were they different, and what attitudes did they share?

3   What military advantages did the Philippine insurgents have? What were American military tactics and goals, and how did they change in response to the conditions of the Philippine conflict?

4   How does the conflict in the Philippines compare with the Indian wars that preceded it and with the later war in Vietnam? In particular, how did the American public and American soldiers differ in comparing the Philippine conflict with the Indian wars, and what were the results and significance of this difference?

5   What, according to the authors, are the lessons to be learned from our involvement in the Philippines? Have they been learned?

Currents of the Progressive Era

IO

Theodore Roosevelt, President

EDMUND MORRIS

Despite a long, enervating depression, American industry continued to expand and consolidate throughout the 1890s, and the rate of expansion was even faster in the first decade of the twentieth century. By then, economic concentration had resulted in a handful of giant combinations that were dominating each area of industrial activity. In 1909, 1 percent of American business enterprises produced 44 percent of the nation's manufactured goods. Money and property were so maldistributed that 1 percent of the United States population — the corporate magnates and their families — owned seven-eighths of the country's wealth. Middle-class families were getting by, although precariously. And the rest — industrial workers in America's teeming, dilapidated cities and debtor farmers in the South and West — lived in poverty.

The Populist movement, as we have seen, posed the first serious challenge to the new industrial order and the corporate bosses who controlled it. The Populist insurgents made thousands aware of the need for reform — the need to correct the abuses of industrial monopolies and to protect the mass of the nation's people. So did liberal intellectuals and crusading journalists — the celebrated muckrakers who exposed glaring malpractices in business and in municipal governments. Thanks to these men and women, thanks to tensions caused by rapid and unmanaged industrial growth, and thanks to a genuine desire to revive humanitarian democracy, there emerged the complex Progressive movement, which lasted from the late 1890s through the First World War. For the most part, those who joined the ranks of progressivism were victims of monopolies and were anxious to dismantle the biggest of them and control the rest.

Progressivism transcended party labels, as Democrats and Republicans alike took up the banners of reform. In the Democratic party, William Jennings Bryan crusaded against the conservative Republican–big business alliance that ran the country; later Bryan passed the leadership of Democratic progressivism to Woodrow Wilson, the subject of a subsequent selection. In the Republican party, "Fighting Bob" La Follette, governor of Wisconsin, made his state a model of progressivism. But the best-known Progressive Republican was the man who found himself elevated to the White House when an assassin murdered William McKinley in 1901. "Now look!" exclaimed a horrified Republican. "That damned cowboy is president of the United States."

That damned cowboy, of course, was Theodore Roosevelt, a whirlwind of a man whose motto was "Get action, do things; be sane, don't fritter away your time; create, act, take a place wherever you are and be somebody: get action." Get action he did, as he hunted big game on three continents, sparred with prizefighters, rode with cowboys, dashed off voluminous histories, knocked down a tough in a western saloon, led the celebrated Rough Riders during the Spanish-American War, terrorized a police force, ran the Empire State as governor, and rose to the nation's highest office. Never mind that he was an accidental president. Once in the presidency, he put on a performance — for surely that is the word for it — that held the nation spellbound

What president since the Civil War had had such uninhibited gusto, such a sense of the dramatic? He conducted a vigorous foreign policy that made the United States a major presence in the world. He dispatched a fleet of white battleships around the globe and won a Nobel Peace Prize for mediating the Russo-Japanese War. In this hemisphere, he rattled the Monroe Doctrine, ordered American troops to Santo Domingo, stationed marines in Cuba, encouraged a revolution against the Republic of Colombia that established the new nation of Panama, and then acquired the rights to build a canal there that would furnish America with a lifeline to the Pacific. Roosevelt's actions in Panama were provocative, even unethical, but he didn't care. As he said later, "If I had followed traditional conservative methods I would have submitted a dignified state paper of probably two hundred pages to the Congress and the debate would be going on yet, but I took the Canal Zone and let the Congress debate, and while the debate goes on, the canal does also."

He was just as vigorous in his domestic policy. He trumpeted the cause of conservation, sent troops to protect strikers in the Pennsylvania coal mines, and thundered so violently against "the malefactors of great wealth" and "the criminal rich" that conservative Republicans were appalled. The first post–Civil War president to recognize the threat of monopolies and trusts to America's economic life, TR shook his fist in the face of banker J. Pierpont Morgan, and his attorney general initiated more antitrust suits than all previous attorneys general combined. As a result, TR won a reputation as a crusading "trust buster." In point of fact, he accepted business consolidation as an economic reality in America and, instead of crushing all business combinations, established a policy of government scrutiny and control. Thus, he attacked only "bad" or "evil" trusts and left the "good" ones alone. Indeed, as one scholar put it, "the first great wave of business consolidation" actually came to a climax during Roosevelt's presidency.

Behind Roosevelt's actions was a volatile personality that kept his legions of followers enthralled. And that personality, full of contradiction, of great charm and physical exuberance, of egotistical moralizing and militarism, fairly explodes off the pages that follow. In them, TR's Pulitzer Prize–winning biographer, Edmund Morris, makes us aware of the importance of personal qualities in shaping the conduct and careers of historical figures. As you read this spirited portrait, you may not always like Theodore Roosevelt, but you will never find him boring.

GLOSSARY

HANNA, MARK   Chairman of the Republican National Committee who aspired to take over the White House after TR had finished his "caretaker" term.

LIVINGSTONE, ROBERT   Journalist who praised TR's great "gift of personal magnetism."

ROOSEVELT, ALICE LEE   TR's first wife, who died of Bright's disease (kidney inflammation) on the same day that TR's mother died of typhoid fever.

ROOSEVELT, MARTHA BULLOCH "MITTIE"   TR's mother.

TEEDIE   TR's boyhood nickname.

WASHINGTON, BOOKER T.   The Head of Alabama's all-black Tuskegee Institute whom TR invited to dine at the White House; "it was the first time that a president had ever entertained a black man in the first house of the land," and it enraged southern white supremacists.

Let us dispose, in short order, with Theodore Roosevelt's faults. He was an incorrigible preacher of platitudes. . . . He significantly reduced the wildlife population of some three continents. He piled his dessert plate with so many peaches that the cream spilled over the sides. And he used to make rude faces out of the presidential carriage at small boys in the streets of Washington.

Now those last two faults are forgivable if we accept British diplomat Cecil Spring-Rice's advice, "You must always remember the President is about six." The first fault — his preachiness — is excused by the fact that the American electorate dearly loves a moralist. As to the second and most significant fault — Theodore Roosevelt's genuine blood-lust and desire to destroy his adversaries, whether they be rhinoceroses or members of the United States Senate — it is paradoxically so much a part of his virtues, both as a man and a politician, that I will come back to it in more detail later.

From Edmund Morris, "Theodore Roosevelt, President," *American Heritage,* June/July 1981, Vol. 32, No. 4. Reprinted by permission of *American Heritage* magazine, a division of Forbes Inc. Copyright © Forbes, Inc., 1981.

One of the minor irritations I have to contend with as a biographer is that whenever I go to the library to look for books about Roosevelt, Theodore, they infallibly are mixed up with books about Roosevelt, Franklin — and I guess FDR scholars have the same problem in reverse. Time was when the single word "Roosevelt" meant only Theodore; FDR himself frequently had to insist, in the early thirties, that he was not TR's son. He was merely a fifth cousin, and what was even more distant, a Democrat to boot. In time, of course, Franklin succeeded in preempting the early meaning of the word "Roosevelt," to the point that TR's public image, which once loomed as large as Washington's and Lincoln's, began to fade like a Cheshire cat from popular memory. By the time of FDR's own death in 1945, little was left but the ghost of a toothy grin.

Only a few veterans of the earlier Roosevelt era survived to testify that if Franklin was the greater politician, it was only by a hairsbreadth, and as far as sheer personality was concerned, Theodore's superiority could be measured in spades. They pointed out that FDR himself declared, late in life, that his "cousin Ted" was the greatest man he ever knew.

Presently the veterans too died. But that ghostly grin continued to float in the national consciousness, as if to indicate that its owner was meditating a reappearance. I first became aware of the power behind the grin in Washington, in February of 1976. The National Theater was trying out an ill-fated musical by Alan Lerner and Leonard Bernstein, *1600 Pennsylvania Avenue.* For two and a half hours Ken Howard worked his way through a chronological series of impersonations of historic Presidents. The audience sat on its hands, stiff with boredom, until the very end, when Mr. Howard clamped on a pair of pince-nez and a false mustache, and bared all his teeth in a grin. The entire theater burst into delighted applause.

What intrigued me was the fact that few people there could have known much about TR beyond the obvious clichés of San Juan Hill and the Big Stick. Yet somehow, subconsciously, they realized that here for once was a positive President, warm and tough and authoritative and funny, who believed in America and who, to quote Owen Wister, "grasped his optimism tight lest it escape him."

In [recent times] Theodore Roosevelt has made his long-promised comeback. He has been the subject of a *Newsweek* cover story on American heroes; Russell Baker has called him a cinch to carry all fifty states if he were running for the White House today; he's starring on Broadway in *Tintypes,* on television in *Bully,* and you'll . . . see him on the big screen in *Ragtime.* Every season brings a new crop of reassessments in the university presses, and as for the pulp mills, he figures largely in the latest installment of John Jakes's Kent Chronicles. No time like the present, therefore, to study that giant personality in color and fine detail.

When referring to Theodore Roosevelt I do not use the word "giant" loosely. "Every inch of him," said William Allen White, "was overengined." Lyman Gage likened him, mentally and physically, to two strong men combined; Gifford Pinchot said that his normal appetite was enough for four people, Charles J. Bonaparte estimated that his mind moved ten times faster than average, and TR himself, not wanting to get into double figures, modestly remarked, "I have enjoyed as much of life as any nine men I know." John Morley made a famous comparison in 1904 between Theodore Roosevelt and the Niagara Falls, "both great wonders of nature." John Burroughs wrote that TR's mere proximity made him nervous. "There was always something imminent about him, like an avalanche that the sound of your voice might loosen." Ida Tarbell, sitting next to him at a musicale, had a sudden hallucination that the President was about to burst. "I felt his clothes might not contain him, he was so steamed up, so ready to go, to attack anything, anywhere."

Reading all these remarks it comes as a surprise to discover that TR's chest measured a normal forty-two inches, and that he stood only five feet nine in his size seven shoes. Yet unquestionably his initial impact was physical, and it was overwhelming. I have amused myself over the years with collecting the metaphors that contemporaries used to describe this Rooseveltian "presence." Here's a random selection. [Novelist] Edith Wharton thought him radioactive; Archie Butt and others used phrases to do with electricity, high-voltage wires, generators, and dynamos; Lawrence Abbott compared him to an electromagnetic nimbus; John Burroughs to "a kind of electric bombshell, if there can be such a thing"; James E. Watson was reminded of TNT; and Senator Joseph Foraker, in an excess of imagination, called TR "a steam-engine in trousers." There are countless other steam-engine metaphors, from Henry Adams' "swift and awful Chicago express" to Henry James's "verily, a wonderful little machine: destined to be overstrained, perhaps, but not as yet, truly, betraying the least creak." Lastly we have [western writer] Owen Wister comparing TR to a solar conflagration that cast no shadow, only radiance.

These metaphors sound fulsome, but they refer only to TR's physical effect, which was felt with equal power by friends and enemies. People actually tingled in his company; there was something sensually stimulating about it. They came out of the presidential office flushed, short-breathed, energized, as if they had been treated to a sniff of white powder. He had, as Oscar Straus once said, "the quality of vitalizing things." His youthfulness (he was not yet forty-three at the beginning of his first term, and barely fifty at the end of his second), his air of glossy good health, his powerful handshake — all these things combined to give an impression of irresistible force and personal impetus.

But TR was not just a physical phenomenon. In many ways the quality of his personality was more remarkable than its quantity. Here again, I have discovered recurrences of the same words in contemporary descriptions. One of the more frequent images is that of sweetness. "He was as sweet a man," wrote Henry Watterson, "as ever scuttled a ship or cut a throat." But most comments are kinder than that. "There is a sweetness about him that is very compelling," sighed Woodrow Wilson. "You can't resist the man." Robert Livingstone, a journalist, wrote after TR's death: "He had the double gifts of a sweet nature that came out in every handtouch and tone . . . and a sincerely powerful personality that left the uneffaceable impression that whatever he said was right. Such a combination was simply irresistible." Livingstone's final verdict was that Theodore Roosevelt had "unquestionably the greatest gift of personal magnetism ever possessed by an American."

That may or may not be true, but certainly there are very few recorded examples of anybody, even TR's bitterest political critics, being able to resist him in person. Brand Whitlock, Mark Twain, John Jay Chapman, William Jennings Bryan, and Henry James were all seduced by his charm, if only temporarily. Peevish little Henry Adams spent much of the period from 1901 to 1909 penning a series of magnificent insults to the President's reputation. But this did not prevent him from accepting frequent invitations to dine at the White House and basking gloomily in TR's effulgence. By the time the Roosevelt era came to an end, Adams was inconsolable. "My last vision of fun and gaiety will vanish when my Theodore goes . . . never can we replace him."

It's a pity that the two men never had a public slanging match over the table, because when it came to personal invective, TR could give as good as he got. There was the rather slow British ambassador whom he accused of having "a mind that functions at six guinea-pig power." There was the State Supreme Court Justice he called "an amiable old fuzzy-wuzzy with sweetbread brains." There was that "unspeakable villainous little monkey," President Castro of Venezuela, and President Marroquin of Colombia, whom he described in one word as a "Pithecanthropoid." Woodrow Wilson was "a Byzantine logothete" (even Wilson had to go to the dictionary for that one); [retail magnate] John Wanamaker was "an ill-constitutioned creature, oily, with bristles sticking up through the oil," and poor Senator Warren Pfeffer never quite recovered from being called "a pin-headed anarchistic crank, of hirsute and slabsided aspect." TR did not use bad language — the nearest to it I've found is his description of [jurist and statesman] Charles Evans Hughes as "a psalm-singing son of a bitch," but then Charles Evans Hughes tended to invite such descriptions. Moreover, TR usually took the sting out of his insults by collapsing into laughter as he uttered them. Booth Tarkington detected "an undertone of Homeric chuckling" even when Roosevelt seemed to be seriously castigating someone — "as if, after all, he loved the fun of hating, rather than the hating itself."

Humor, indeed, was always TR's saving grace. A reporter who spent a week with him in the White House calculated that he laughed, on average, a hundred times a day — and what was more, laughed heartily. "He laughs like an irresponsible schoolboy on a lark, his face flushing ruddy, his eyes nearly closed, his utterance choked with merriment, his speech abandoned for a weird falsetto. . . . The President is a joker, and (what many jokers are not) a humorist as well."

If there were nothing more to Theodore Roosevelt's personality than physical exuberance, humor, and charm, he would indeed have been what he sometimes is misperceived to be: a simple-minded, amiable bully. Actually he was an exceedingly complex man, a polygon (to use Brander Matthews' word) of so many political, intellectual, and social facets that the closer one gets to him, the less one is able to see him in the round. Consider merely this random list of attributes and achievements:

He graduated *magna cum laude* from Harvard University. He was the author of a four-volume history of the winning of the West which was considered definitive in his lifetime, and a history of the naval war of 1812 which remains definitive to this day. He also wrote biographies of Thomas Hart Benton, Gouverneur Morris, and Oliver Cromwell, and some fourteen other volumes of history, natural history, literary criticism, autobiography, political philosophy, and military memoirs, not to mention countless articles and approximately seventy-five thousand letters. He spent nearly three years of his life in Europe and the Levant, and had a wide circle of intellectual correspondents on both sides of the Atlantic. He habitually read one to three books a day, on subjects ranging from architecture to zoology, averaging two or three pages a minute and effortlessly memorizing the paragraphs that interested him. He could recite poetry by the hour in English, German, and French. He married two women and fathered six children. He was a boxing championship finalist, a Fifth Avenue socialite, a New York State Assemblyman, a Dakota cowboy, a deputy sheriff, a president of the Little Missouri Stockmen's Association, United States Civil Service Commissioner, Police Commissioner of New York City, Assistant Secretary of the Navy, Colonel of the Rough Riders, Governor of New York, Vice-President, and finally President of the United States. He was a founding member of the National Institute of Arts and Letters and a fellow of the American Historical Society. He was accepted by Washington's scientific community as a skilled ornithologist, paleontologist, and taxidermist (during the White House years, specimens that confused experts at the Smithsonian were occasionally sent to TR for identification), and he was recognized as the world authority on the big-game mammals of North America.

Now all these achievements *predate* his assumption of the Presidency — in other words, he packed them into his first forty-three years. I will spare you another list of the things he packed into his last ten, after leaving the White House in 1909, except to say that the total of books rose to thirty-eight, the total of letters to 150,000, and the catalogue of careers expanded to include world statesman, big game collector for the Smithsonian, magazine columnist, and South American explorer.

127

If it were possible to take a cross section of TR's personality, as geologists, say, ponder a chunk of continent, you would be presented with a picture of seismic richness and confusion. The most order I have been able to make of it is to isolate four major character seams. They might be traced back to childhood. Each seam stood out bright and clear in youth and early middle age, but they began to merge about the time he was forty. Indeed the white heat of the Presidency soon fused them all into solid metal. But so long as they were distinct they may be identified as aggression, righteousness, pride, and militarism. Before suggesting how they affected his performance as President, I'd like to explain how they originated.

The most fundamental characteristic of Theodore Roosevelt was his aggression — conquest being, to him, synonymous with growth. From the moment he first dragged breath into his asthmatic lungs, the sickly little boy fought for a larger share of the world. He could never get enough air; disease had to be destroyed; he had to fight his way through big, heavy books to gain a man's knowledge. Just as the struggle for wind made him stretch his chest, so did the difficulty of relating to abnormally contrasting parents extend his imagination. Theodore Senior was the epitome of hard, thrusting Northern manhood; Mittie Roosevelt was the quintessence of soft, yielding Southern femininity. The Civil War — the first political phenomenon little Teedie was ever aware of — symbolically opposed one to the other. There was no question as to which side, and which parent, the child preferred. He naughtily prayed God, in Mittie's presence, to "grind the Southern troops to powder," and the victory of Union arms reinforced his belief in the superiority of Strength over Weakness, Right over Wrong, Realism over Romance.

Teedie's youthful "ofserv-a-tions" in natural history gave him further proof of the laws of natural selection, long before he fully understood [Charles] Darwin and Herbert Spencer. For weeks he watched in fascination while a tiny shrew successively devoured a mass of beetles, then a mouse twice her size, then a snake so large it whipped her from side to side of the cage as she was gnawing through its neck. From then on the rule of tooth and claw, aided by superior intelligence, was a persistent theme in Theodore Roosevelt's writings.

Blood sports, which he took up as a result of his shooting for specimens, enabled him to feel the "strong eager pleasure" of the shrew in vanquishing ever larger foes; his exuberant dancing and whooping after killing a particularly dangerous animal struck more than one observer as macabre. From among his own kind, at college, he selected the fairest and most unobtainable mate — "See that girl? I'm going to marry her. She won't have me, but I am going to have *her!*" — and he ferociously hunted her down. That was Alice Lee Roosevelt, mother of the late Alice Longworth.

During his first years in politics, in the New York State Assembly, he won power through constant attack. The death of Alice Lee, coming as it did just after the birth of his first child — at the moment of fruition of his manhood — only intensified his will to fight. He hurried West, to where the battle for life was fiercest. The West did not welcome him; it had to be won, like everything else he lusted for. Win it he did, by dint of the greatest physical and mental stretchings-out he had yet made. In doing so he built up the magnificent body that became such an inspiration to the American people (one frail little boy who vowed to follow the President's example was the future world heavyweight champion, Gene Tunney). And by living on equal terms with the likes of Hashknife Simpson, Bat Masterson, Modesty Carter, Bronco Charlie Miller, and Hell-Roaring Bill Jones, he added another mental frontier to those he already had inherited at birth. Theodore Roosevelt, Eastern son of a Northern father and a Southern mother, could now call himself a Westerner also.

TR's second governing impulse was his personal righteousness. As one reviewer of his books remarked, "He seems to have been born with his mind made up." No violent shocks disturbed his tranquil, prosperous childhood in New York City. Privately educated, he suffered none of the traumas of school. Thanks to the security of his home, the strong leadership of his father, and the adoration of his brother and sisters, Teedie entered adolescence with no sexual or psychological doubts whatsoever. Or if he had any, he simply reasoned them out, according to the Judeo-Christian principles Theodore Senior had taught him, reached the proper moral decision, and that was that. "Thank heaven!" he wrote in his diary after falling in love with Alice Lee, "I am perfectly pure."

His three great bereavements (the death of his father in 1878, and the deaths of his mother and wife in the same house and on the same day in 1884) came too late in his development to do him any permanent emotional damage. They only served to convince him more that he must be strong, honest, clean-living, and industrious. "At least I can live," he wrote, "so as not to dishonor the memory of the dead whom I so loved," and never was a cliché more heartfelt. Experiment after experiment proved the correctness of his instincts — in graduating *magna cum laude* from Harvard, in marrying successfully, in defying the doctors who ordered him to live a sedentary life, in winning international acclaim as writer and politician long before he was thirty. (He received his first nomination for the Presidency, by the Baltimore *American,* when he was only twenty-eight; it had to be pointed out to the newspaper's editor that he was constitutionally debarred from that honor for the next seven years.)

In wild Dakota Territory, he proceeded to knock down insolent cowboys, establish the foundations of federal government, pursue boat thieves in the name of the law, and preach the gospel of responsible citizenship. One of the first things he did after Benjamin Harrison appointed him Civil Service Commissioner was call for the prosecution of Postmaster General William Wallace of Indianapolis — who just hap-

pened to be the President's best friend. "That young man," Harrison growled, "wants to put the whole world right between sunrise and sunset."

TR's egotistic moralizing as a reform Police Commissioner of New York City was so insufferable that the *Herald* published a transcript of one of his speeches with the personal pronoun emphasized in heavy type. The effect, in a column of gray newsprint, was of buckshot at close range. This did not stop TR from using the personal pronoun thirteen times in the first four sentences of his account of the Spanish-American War. In fact, a story went around that halfway through the typesetting, Scribner's had to send for an extra supply of capital *I's.*

The third characteristic of Theodore Roosevelt's personality was his sense of pride, both as an aristocrat and as an American. From birth, servants and tradespeople deferred to him. Men and women of high quality came to visit his parents and treated him as one of their number. He accepted his status without question, as he did the charitable responsibilities it entailed. At a very early age he was required to accompany his father on Sunday excursions to a lodging house for Irish newsboys and a night school for little Italians. It cannot have escaped his attention that certain immigrant groups lacked the intellectual and social graces of others. Extended tours of Europe and the Levant as a child, teen-ager, and young man soon taught him that this was not due to ethnic inferiority so much as to centuries of economic and political deprivation. Prosperous, independent countries like England and Germany were relatively free of slums and disease; but in Italy women and children scrabbled like chickens for scraps of his cake, and in Ireland people lay down in the road from sheer hunger. From what he read, things were no better in the Slavic countries.

Only in America, with its limitless economic opportunities and freedom from political bondage, might these peasants begin to improve their stock. And only in America could they revitalize their racial characteristics. His own extremely mixed ancestry proved that a generation or two of life in the New World was enough to blend all kinds of European blood into a new, dynamic American breed. (As President, he had a habit when shaking hands with ethnic groups of saying, "Congratulations, I'm German too!" and "Dee-lighted! I'm also Scotch-Irish, you know!" Newspapermen privately referred to him as "Old Fifty-seven Varieties.")

TR knew the value of an ethnic vote as well as the next man. There is a famous — alas, probably apocryphal — story of his appointment of Oscar Straus as the first Jewish Cabinet officer in American history. At a banquet to celebrate the appointment, TR made a passionate speech full of phrases like "regardless of race, color, or creed" and then turned to Jacob Schiff, the New York Jewish leader, and said, "Isn't that so, Mr. Schiff?" But Schiff, who was very deaf and had heard little of the speech, replied, "Dot's right, Mr. President, you came to me and said, 'Chake, who is der best Choo I can put in de Cabinet?'"

TR realized, of course, that the gap between himself and Joe Murray — the Irish ward-heeler who got him into the New York Assembly — was unbridgeable outside of politics. But in America a low-born man had the opportunity — the *duty* — to fight his way up from the gutter, as Joe had done. He might then merit an invitation to lunch at Sagamore Hill, or at least tea, assuming he wore a clean shirt and observed decent proprieties.

Here I must emphasize that TR was not a snob in the trivial sense. He had nothing but contempt for the [aristocratic] Newport set and the more languid members of the Four Hundred. When he said, at twenty-one, that he wanted to be a member of "the governing class," he was aware that it was socially beneath his own. At Albany, and in the [Dakota] Bad Lands, and as Colonel of the Rough Riders, he preferred to work with men who were coarse but efficient, rather than those who were polished and weak. He believed, he said, in "the aristocracy of worth," and cherished the revolution that had al-

lowed such an elite to rise to the top in government. On the other hand (to use his favorite phrase) the historian John Blum has noted that he rarely appointed impoverished or unlettered men to responsible positions. He made great political capital, as President, of the fact that his sons attended the village school at Oyster Bay, along with the sons of his servants, of whom at least one was black; but as soon as the boys reached puberty he whisked them off to Groton.

Only the very young or very old dared call him "Teddy" to his face. Roosevelt was a patrician to the tips of his tapering fingers, yet he maintained till death what one correspondent called an "almost unnatural" identity with the masses. "I don't see how you understand the common people so well, Theodore," complained Henry Cabot Lodge. "No, Cabot, you never will," said TR, grinning triumphantly, "because I am one of them, and you are not." TR deluded himself. His plebeian strength was due to understanding, not empathy.

The fourth and final major trait of Theodore Roosevelt's character was his militarism. I will not deal with it in much detail because it is a familiar aspect of him, and in any case did not manifest itself much during his Presidency. There is no doubt that in youth, and again in old age, he was in love with war; but oddly enough, of all our great Presidents, he remains the only one not primarily associated with war (indeed, he won the Nobel Peace Prize in 1906).

He did not lack for military influences as a child; four of his Georgian ancestors had been military men, and stories of their exploits were told him by his mother. Two of his uncles served with distinction in the Confederate navy — a fact of which he proudly boasts in his *Autobiography,* while making no reference to his father's civilian status. . . .

When TR learned to read, he reveled in stories "about the soldiers of Valley Forge, and Morgan's riflemen," and confessed, "I had a great desire to be like them." In his senior year at Harvard, he suddenly developed an interest in strategy and tactics and began to write *The Naval War of 1812;* within eighteen months he was the world expert on that subject. As soon as he left college he joined the National Guard and quickly became a captain, which stood him in good stead when he was called upon to lead a cavalry regiment in 1898. Throughout his literary years he made a study of classical and modern campaigns, and he would wage the great battles of history with knives and forks and spoons on his tablecloth. No doubt much of this fascination with things military related to his natural aggression, but there was an intellectual attraction too: he read abstract tomes on armaments, navigation, ballistics, strategy, and service administration as greedily as swashbuckling memoirs. Nothing is more remarkable about *The Naval War of 1812* than its cold impartiality, its use of figures and diagrams to destroy patriotic myths. Roosevelt understood that great battles are fought by thinking men, that mental courage is superior to physical bravado. Nobody thrilled more to the tramp of marching boots than he, but he believed that men must march for honorable reasons, in obedience to the written orders of a democratically elected Commander in Chief. In that respect, at least, the pen was mightier than the sword.

Now how much did these four character traits — aggression, righteousness, pride, and militarism — affect TR's performance as President of the United States? The answer is, strongly, as befits a strong character and a strong Chief Executive. The way he arrived at this "personal equation" is interesting, because he was actually in a weak position at the beginning of his first administration.

When TR took the oath of office on September 14, 1901, he was the youngest man ever to do so — a Vice President, elevated by assassination, confronted by a nervous Cabinet and a hostile Senate. Yet from the moment he raised his hand in that little parlor in Buffalo, it was apparent that he intended to translate his personal power into presidential power. The hand did not stop at the shoulder; he raised it high above his head, and held it there, "steady as if carved out of marble." His right foot pawed the floor. *Aggression.* He repeated the words of the oath confidently, adding an extra phrase, not called for in the Constitution, at the end: "And so I swear." *Righteousness.* His two senior Cabinet officers, [Secretary of State] John Hay and [Secretary of the Treasury] Lyman Gage, were not present at the ceremony, but TR announced that they had telegraphed promises of loyalty to him. Actually they had not; they were both considering resignation, but TR knew any such resignations would be construed as votes of no confidence in him, and he was determined to forestall them. By announcing that Hay and Gage would stay, out of loyalty to the memory of the dead President, he made it morally impossible for them to quit. *Pride.*

As for *militarism,* TR was seen much in the company of the New York State Adjutant General the next few days, and an armed escort of cavalrymen accompanied him wherever he went. This was perhaps understandable, in view of the fact that a President had just been assassinated, but it is a matter of record that more and more uniforms were seen glittering around TR as the months and years went on. Toward the end of his second administration, *Harper's Weekly* complained that "there has been witnessed under President Roosevelt an exclusiveness, a rigor of etiquette, and a display of swords and gold braid such as none of his predecessors ever dreamed of."

As the theatrical gestures at TR's Inauguration make plain, he was one of the most flagrant showmen ever to tread the Washington boards. He had a genius for dramatic entrances — and always was sure the spotlight was trained his way before he made one. The first thing he asked at Buffalo was, "Where are all the newspapermen?" Only three reporters were present. His secretary explained that there was no room for more. Ignoring him, TR sent out for the rest of the press corps. Two dozen scribes came joyfully crowding in, and the subsequent proceedings were reported to the nation with a wealth of detail.

Here again we see a pattern of presidential performance developing. The exaggerated concern for the rights of reporters, the carefully staged gestures (so easy to write up, such fun to read about!) — it was as if he sensed right away that a tame press, and an infatuated public, were his surest guarantees of political security. To win election in his own right in 1904 — his overriding ambition for the next three years — he would have to awake these two sleeping giants and enlist their aid in moral warfare against his political opponents, notably Senator Mark Hanna. (Hanna was chairman of the Republican National Committee and the obvious choice to take over McKinley's government after "that damned cowboy," as he called TR, had filled in as interim caretaker.)

The new President accordingly took his case straight to the press and the public. Both instantly fell in love with him. Neither seemed to notice that administratively and legislatively he accomplished virtually nothing in his first year in office. As David S. Barry of the *Sun* wrote, "Roosevelt's personality was so fascinating, so appealing to the popular fancy, so overpowering, so alive, and altogether so unique that . . . it overshadowed his public acts; that is, the public was more interested in him, and the way he did things . . . than they were about what he did."

This does not mean that TR managed, or even tried, to please all the people all the time. He was quite ready to antagonize a large minority in order to win the approval of a small majority. The swords had hardly stopped rattling on the top of McKinley's coffin when the following press release was issued: "Mr. Booker T. Washington of Tuskegee, Alabama, dined with the President last evening." Now this release, arguably the shortest and most explosive ever put out by the White House, has always been assumed to be a reluctant confirmation of the discovery of a reporter combing TR's guest book. Actually the President himself issued it, at two o'clock in the morning — that

This famous photograph of Teddy Roosevelt was taken in 1912. The mustache and toothy grin, the laughing eyes crinkled shut behind wire-rimmed glasses, have become caricature symbols of TR that we recognize easily in our own day. Yet they are equally evidence of the personal charm and self-confidence that were the key to TR's enormous popularity, a popularity that, when combined with his aggression, his pride, and his patriotism, made him a successful president. (Brown Brothers)

is, just in time for maximum exposure in the first edition of the newspapers. By breakfast time white supremacists all over the South were gagging over their grits at such headlines as ROOSEVELT DINES A NIGGER, and PRESIDENT PROPOSES TO CODDLE THE SONS OF HAM. This was the first time that a President had ever entertained a black man in the first house of the land. The public outcry was deafening — horror in the South, acclamation in the North — but overnight 9,000,000 Negroes, hitherto loyal to Senator Hanna, trooped into the Rooseveltian camp. TR never felt the need to dine a black man again.

Although we may have no doubt he had the re-distribution of Southern patronage in mind when he sent his invitation to Washington, another motive was simply to stamp a bright, clear, first impression of himself upon the public imagination. "I," he seemed to be saying, "am a man *aggressive* enough to challenge a hundred-year prejudice, *righteous* enough to do so for moral reasons, and *proud* enough to ad-vertise the fact."

Again and again during the next seven years, he reinforced these perceptions of his personality. He aggressively prosecuted J. P. Morgan, Edward H. Harriman, and John D. Rockefeller (the holy trinity of American capitalism) in the Northern Securities antitrust case, threw the Monroe Doctrine at Kaiser Wilhelm's feet like a token of war in the Caribbean, rooted out corruption in his own administration, and crushed Hanna's 1904 presidential challenge by pub-licly humiliating the Senator when he was running for reelection in 1903. He righteously took the side of the American worker and the American consumer against big business in the great anthracite [coal] strike [in Pennsylvania], proclaimed the vanity of muckrake journalists, forced higher ethical standards upon the food and drug industry, ordered the dis-honorable discharge of 160 Negro soldiers [charged with rioting and shooting in "the Brownsville Af-fair" in Texas], and to quote Mark Twain, "dug so many tunnels under the Constitution that the trans-portation facilities enjoyed by that document are ri-valled only by the City of New York."

For example, when the anthracite strike began to drag into the freezing fall of 1902, TR's obvious sympathy for the miners, and for millions of Ameri-cans who could not afford the rise in fuel prices, began to worry conservative members of Congress.

One day Representative James E. Watson was horri-fied to hear that the President had decided to send federal troops in to reopen the anthracite mines on grounds of general hardship. Watson rushed round to the White House. "What about the Constitution of the United States?" he pleaded. "What about seiz-ing private property for public purposes without the due processes of law?"

TR wheeled around, shook Watson by the shoul-der, and roared, "*To hell with the Constitution when the people want coal!*" Remarks like that caused old Joe Cannon to sigh, "Roosevelt's got no more respect for the Constitution than a tomcat has for a marriage license."

Pride, both in himself and his office, was particu-larly noticeable in TR's second term, the so-called imperial years, when Henry James complained, "Theodore Rex is distinctly tending — or trying to make a court." But this accusation was not true. Al-though the Roosevelts entertained much more elabo-rately than any of their predecessors, they confined their pomp and protocol to occasions of state. At times, indeed, they were remarkable for the all-Amer-ican variety of their guests. On any given day one might find a Rough Rider, a poet, a British viscount, a wolf hunter, and a Roman Catholic cardinal at the White House table, each being treated with the gen-tlemanly naturalness which was one of TR's most en-dearing traits. His pride manifested itself in things like his refusal to address foreign monarchs as "Your Majesty," in his offer to mediate the Russo-Japanese War (no American President had yet had such global presumptions), and, when he won the Nobel Peace Prize for successfully bringing the war to a conclusion, in refusing to keep a penny of the forty-thousand-dol-lar prize money. This was by no means an easy deci-sion, because TR could have used the funds: he spent all his presidential salary on official functions and was not himself a wealthy man. He confessed he was tempted to put the Nobel money into a trust for his children, but decided it belonged to the United States.

Pride and patriotism were inseparable in Theodore Roosevelt's character; indeed, if we accept Lord Morely's axiom that he "was" America, they may be considered as complementary characteristics. And neither of them was false. Just as he was always willing to lose a political battle in order to win a political war, so in diplomatic negotiations was he sedulous to allow his opponents the chance to save face — take all the glory of settlement if need be — as long as the essential victory was his.

As I have noted earlier, TR's militarism did not loom large during his Presidency. The organizational structure of the U.S. Army was revamped in such a way as to strengthen the powers of the Commander in Chief, but Secretary of war Elihu Root takes credit for that. TR can certainly take the credit for expanding the American Navy from fifth to second place in the world during his seven and a half years of power — an amazing achievement, but quite in keeping with his policy, inherited from Washington, that "to be prepared for war is the most effectual means to promote peace." The gunboat TR sent to Panama in 1903 was the only example of him shaking a naked mailed fist in the face of a weaker power; for the rest of the time he kept that fist sheathed in a velvet glove. The metaphor of velvet on iron, incidentally, was TR's own; it makes a refreshing change from the Big Stick.

If I may be permitted a final metaphor of my own, I would like to quote one from *The Rise of Theodore Roosevelt* in an attempt to explain why, on the whole, TR's character shows to better advantage as President than in his years out of power. "The man's personality was cyclonic, in that he tended to become unstable in times of low pressure." The slightest rise in the barometer outside, and his turbulence smoothed into a whir of coordinated activity, while a core of stillness developed within. Under maximum pressure Roosevelt was sunny, calm, and unnaturally clear. This explains why the first Roosevelt era was a period of fair weather. Power became Theodore Roosevelt, and absolute power became him best of all. He loved being President and was so good at his job that the American people loved him for loving it. TR genuinely dreaded having to leave the White House, and let us remember that a third term was his for the asking in 1908. But his knowledge that power corrupts even the man who most deserves it, his reverence for the Washingtonian principle that power must punctually revert to those whose gift it is, persuaded him to make this supreme sacrifice in his prime. The time would come, not many years hence, when fatal insolence tempted him to renege on his decision. That is another story. But the self denial that he exercised in 1908 gives us one more reason to admire Old Fifty-seven Varieties.

QUESTIONS TO CONSIDER

1 How would you describe Theodore Roosevelt's character and personality? To what extent was he shaped by the era in which he lived? What is your impression of his intellectual capabilities?

2 Morris suggests that TR's presidency was stamped by his four most salient character traits or governing impulses: aggression, self-righteousness, pride, and militarism. What does Morris see as the sources of each of these characteristics? How did each characteristic affect TR's presidency? How much did TR's charm influence his presidency and his effect on Americans?

3 What does Morris mean when he says that Theodore Roosevelt's presidency was a performance? Do you think it was a successful or unsuccessful show, by and large? Was TR any the less sincere for all his showmanship?

4 In what ways do you think TR's was a potentially dangerous or risky personality for a president?

How, for example, did he regard the Constitution when it got in the way of things he thought were important?

5   Can you think of any presidents to compare with Theodore Roosevelt? Could a Theodore Roosevelt be elected in the political climate of the late twentieth century? How would a modern-day electorate feel about a president with such an impenetrable ego or one who behaved with such highhandedness as Roosevelt exhibited in his gunboat diplomacy off Colombia? You may want to keep Teddy Roosevelt in mind when you read about Ronald Reagan in selection 30.

11

African Americans and the Quest for Civil Rights

SEAN DENNIS CASHMAN

During the Progressive era, African Americans launched a protest movement against legally enforced segregation and the whole philosophy of white supremacy and black inferiority that underlay it. Segregation was worse in the South, because that was where most African Americans lived. Indeed, by the beginning of the twentieth century, southern whites had turned their region into a bastion of white supremacy and racial discrimination. A farrago of state constitutional amendments, Jim Crow laws, and local ordinances shackled African Americans to the bottom of the South's racist social order. African Americans could not vote or run for political office; they had to attend separate and inferior "colored" schools, sit in segregated waiting rooms in southern depots, ride in segregated trains and streetcars, drink from separate water fountains, relieve themselves in separate restrooms, lodge only in "colored" hotels, and face humiliating "Whites Only" signs at public swimming pools, golf courses, and libraries. In Jackson, Mississippi, they were buried in a separate cemetery. Woe to African Americans who tried to cross the color line: they could expect a gunshot, incineration, or a lynching. Indeed, lynchings multiplied at an alarming rate in the Deep South. Meanwhile, in Plessy v. Ferguson (1896) the United States Supreme Court upheld "separate but equal" accommodations in Dixie. Never mind that facilities for African Americans were almost never equal to those for whites; the Court ruled that no discrimination was involved. Justice John Marshall Harlan, however, issued a ringing dissent, arguing that "our Constitution is colorblind, and neither knows nor tolerates classes among citizens."

Initially, especially in the South, African Americans submitted to living as third-class citizens in a white dominated country. In that period of reaction, there was little else they could do. Most followed the advice of Booker T. Washington, the head of all-black

Tuskegee Institute in Alabama, who had been born a slave. In 1895, in Atlanta, Washington urged African Americans to forget about political and social equality for now and to learn skills and trades to support themselves. By imitating white standards and values, perhaps they could earn white people's friendship and preserve racial peace. But as Martin Luther King Jr. noted later, it was "an obnoxious negative peace" in which "the Negro's mind and soul were enslaved."

In the following selection, historian Sean Dennis Cashman describes in lucid and eloquent detail what black Americans faced in this period of racial reaction. He offers trenchant insights, based on the best of modern scholarship, into the origins of segregation, and explains the two very different reactions to it by Booker T. Washington, a southern black, and W. E. B. Du Bois, a northern African-American, who became Washington's ideological adversary. Du Bois exhorted the blacks' "Talented Tenth" to take the lead and find solutions to the misery of the black masses. In 1905, against a backdrop of spiraling racial violence, Du Bois met with a small band of well-educated, bold, and unhappy African American professionals and businessmen in the city of Niagara Falls, Canada (the blacks could not stay in a hotel on the American side of the falls). They drafted a blazing manifesto demanding justice and equality for African Americans. The Niagara platform became the blueprint for the National Association for the Advancement of Colored People (NAACP), established in 1909 in the centennial of Abraham Lincoln's birth. Du Bois and seven other Niagara leaders joined nineteen white racial progressives on the NAACP's original board (the racial imbalance reflected the paternalistic attitudes of the white founders). The first nationwide organization dedicated to gaining African Americans their rights as citizens, the NAACP concentrated on legal action and court battles. It won its first victory in 1915 — the same year the twentieth-century Ku Klux Klan was founded on Stone Mountain in Georgia — when the United States Supreme Court outlawed the grandfather clause to the state constitutions of Oklahoma and Maryland. Those clauses had prohibited African Americans from voting unless their grandfathers had voted in 1860.

In Cashman's stirring pages, you will meet Du Bois and other significant figures who launched the "Negro rebellion" in Progressive America.

GLOSSARY

ACCOMMODATION   Doctrine preached by Booker T. Washington calling for southern blacks to forget about racial equality, to accommodate themselves to the South's racist social order, and to learn skills and trades to support themselves.

ATLANTA COMPROMISE   Speaking in Atlanta in 1895, Washington propounded the doctrine of accommodation, which later became known as the "Atlanta Compromise."

BROWN, HENRY BILLINGS   Justice of the Supreme Court in the case of *Plessy v. Ferguson* (1896), who spoke for the majority in ruling that "If one race be inferior to the other socially, the Constitution of the United States cannot put them upon the same plane."

BROWNSVILLE "RIOT"   Three companies of the black Twenty-Fifth Regiment of the U.S. Army allegedly rioted in Brownsville, Texas, in 1906 after some of the soldiers had retaliated against whites for racial insults. The charges were unproved, but President Theodore Roosevelt "arbitrarily" discharged the three companies in question.

BUCHANAN V. WARLEY (1917)   The United States Supreme Court unanimously held that "all citizens of the United States shall have the same right in every state and territory, as is enjoyed by white citizens thereof, to inherit, purchase, lease, sell, hold and convey real and personal property." See also *Corrigan V. Buckley.*

CORRIGAN V. BUCKLEY (1926)   The *Buchanan v. Warley* decision resulted in "a spate of private restrictive covenants under which residents agreed to sell or rent their property to individuals of one race only." The court upheld the practice in *Corrigan v. Buckley.*

DU BOIS, W. E. B.   Reclusive professor of economics and sociology at Atlanta University who emerged as the leader of the African American elite, created the "myth of the Talented Tenth," helped found the NAACP, and served as first editor of the NAACP's official publication, *Crisis*; by his own reckoning, he was "the main factor in revolutionizing the attitude of the American Negro toward caste" between 1910 and 1930.

GRADUALISM   Another name for Booker T. Washington's doctrine of accommodation to the racial status quo; it stressed "patience, proposed submission, and emphasized material progress."

GREAT MIGRATION   During the 1910s and 1920s, blacks by the tens of thousands migrated from the South to the North. "The exodus," writes Cashman, "was mainly spontaneous and largely unorganized; whatever the personal motives for individual moves, the collective motive was bad treatment in the South."

HARLAN, JOHN MARSHALL   Justice of the United States Supreme Court who dissented from the majority decision in *Plessy v. Ferguson,* arguing that "our constitution is color-blind, and neither knows nor tolerates classes among citizens."

JEFFERIES, JAMES J.   When black boxer Jack Johnson won the heavy weight title in 1908, white racists persuaded former world champion James J. Jefferies to unretire and fight Johnson for the title. Johnson whipped this "great white hope" in Reno, Nevada, in 1912.

JIM CROW LAWS   Southern state and local laws that enforced segregation and discrimination against African Americans. They were called Jim Crow laws from the name of a song sung by Thomas Rice in a black minstrel show before the Civil War.

JOHNSON, JACK   An African American from Galveston, Texas, who won the heavyweight boxing title in 1908 and by doing so "aroused deep consternation throughout the white community." An excellent film about his life, *The Great White Hope* (1970) stars James Earl Jones as the legendary black boxer who was "the greatest heavyweight of his time."

NIAGARA MOVEMENT   In 1905, Du Bois and a cadre of other angry and unhappy black leaders met on the Canadian side of Niagara Falls and drafted a searing manifesto demanding justice and equality for black Americans. The Niagara platform became a blueprint for the National Association for the Advancement of Colored People (NAACP), established in 1909. It was the first nationwide organization dedicated to gaining African Americans their rights as citizens.

PLESSY V. FERGUSON (1896)   Decision of the United States Supreme Court that upheld "separate but equal" accommodations for whites and African Americans in the South.

POLL TAX   A southern state tax on the right to vote, aimed at proscribing the poorer Negroes.

THE SOULS OF BLACK FOLK (1903)   Du Bois's brilliant collection of essays that summoned African Americans to resist Booker T. Washington's doctrine of accommodation.

TILLMAN, BEN "PITCHFORK"   Rabidly white supremacist governor of South Carolina and U. S. Senator.

TROTTER, WILLIAM   African American real-estate broker who in 1901 founded the *Boston Guardian* and devoted himself to destroying the teachings of Booker T. Washington.

VILLARD, OSWALD GARRISON   Grandson of William Lloyd Garrison, the great nineteenth-century abolitionist, Villard was a white journalist and pacifist who helped found the NAACP and served as chairman of its board.

WASHINGTON, BOOKER T.   Between 1903 and 1915, the champion of accommodation, who had once dined with President Theodore Roosevelt, found himself under a zealous ideological attack by Du Bois, Trotter, and other members of the radical African American elite.

WILLARD, JESS   The "great white hope" to defeat black heavyweight champion Jack Johnson, Willard was a former cowboy known for his strength. In a title fight in Havana, Cuba, in 1915, Willard knocked out a poorly conditioned Johnson, winning the title for the white race.

WILSON, WOODROW   President of the United States (1913–1921); his was "the most racist administration since the Civil War." Encouraged by his first wife and his postmaster general, Wilson "allowed systematic segregation in government offices, shops, restrooms, and lunchrooms. African Americans were even removed from appointments they had previously held."

The story of African-Americans and their quest for civil rights in the twentieth century ... is a story with deep resonances. It is about nothing less than the transformation of African-American citizens' place in American society — constitutional, social and cultural — and it tells us something of the transformations white society had to ask of itself.

In a century where one of the primary themes of art has been the relationship of the individual and society, the continuously shifting fortunes of African-American citizens in American society have proved fertile subjects for argument and discussion. Moreover, the experience of African-Americans makes a stark comment on a central paradox of American history — how a nation composed of such diverse ethnic groups and beliefs could endure and survive. Thus novelist James Baldwin declared, "The story of the Negro in America is the story of America, or, more precisely, it is the story of Americans." His most fundamental point seems to have been that, as the African-American experience moved from slavery to incarceration to freedom and citizenship, African-Americans were, ironically enough, especially privileged to articulate the problems and preoccupations of men and women in modern society. . . .

The original circumstances for the development of a civil rights movement to restore their due dignity to African-American citizens had not been promising at the turn of the century and for several decades thereafter. Of the total American population of 76,094,000 in 1900, 8,833,000 were African-Americans — about 11.5 percent of the whole. Over 85 percent of them lived in the South — the eleven states of the old Confederacy and five others, Oklahoma and Kentucky to the west and Delaware,

Sean Dennis Cashman, "African Americans and the Quest for Civil Rights," *African Americans and the Quest for Civil Rights, 1900–1990* (New York: New York University Press, 1991). Reprinted by permission of the New York University Press.

Maryland, West Virginia, and the District of Columbia to the north. Of the total population of 24,524,000 of this "Census South," 7,923,000 were African-Americans. Thus, whereas the ratio of African-Americans to whites across the country as a whole was, approximately, one in nine, in the South it was one in three. In two states, Mississippi and South Carolina, they predominated.

The abolition of slavery and the destruction of the rebel Confederacy in the Civil War (1861–1865) had led to the granting of equal social and political rights to African-Americans in the period of Reconstruction (1865–1877). The Thirteenth Amendment (1865) proscribed slavery. The first section of the Fourteenth Amendment (1866) defined American citizens as all those born or naturalized in the United States. It enjoined states from abridging their rights to life, liberty, property, and process of law. The second section of the amendment threatened to reduce proportionately the representation in Congress of any state denying the suffrage to adult males. Congress determined to protect African-American suffrage in the South by the Fifteenth Amendment (1869–1870), according to which the right to vote was not to be denied "on account of race, color, or previous condition of servitude." Yet forty years later these rights had been assailed or eroded by white racists. The abject position of African-Americans was such that historian Rayford Logan in *The Betrayal of the Negro* (1954; 1969) described the turn of the century as "the nadir" of African-American history, notwithstanding the existence of slavery up to 1865.

☆

THE TYRANT CUSTOM — RACE RELATIONS AT THEIR NADIR

The regular intimacy of contact under slavery was being superseded by a caste system with next to no sustained contact, which resulted in an inexorable gulf between African-Americans and whites. Although African-Americans were the largest of America's ethnic minorities, they were segregated in schooling, housing, and places of public accommodation, such as parks, theaters, hospitals, schools, libraries, courts, and even cemeteries. The variety and fluidity of access of the late nineteenth century were abandoned as state after state adopted rigid segregation in a series of so-called Jim Crow laws. ("Jim Crow" was the title of a minstrel song in 1830 that presented African-Americans as childlike and inferior.)

In *The Strange Career of Jim Crow* (1955) historian C. Vann Woodward argues that cast-iron segregation was a product of the late nineteenth and early twentieth centuries and that the avalanche of Jim Crow laws began when poor white farmers came to power. Moreover, a new generation of African-Americans had grown up who had never known slavery. Previously, aristocratic southerners had shown a paternalistic attitude to African-Americans, protecting them from some overt racist attacks by poor whites. They knew that they did not need segregation laws to confirm their own privileged social position. Nevertheless, none of the states passed a single comprehensive segregation law. Instead, they proceeded piecemeal over a period of thirty to fifty years. Thus South Carolina segregated the races in successive stages, beginning with trains (1898) and moving to streetcars (1905), train depots and restaurants (1906), textile plants (1915 and 1916), circuses (1917), pool halls (1924), and beaches and recreation centers (1934). Georgia began with railroads and prisons (1891) and moved to sleeping cars (1899) and, finally, pool halls (1925), but refused to segregate places of public accommodation until 1954.

Another factor in turning the tide of white resentment was the move of African-Americans to new mining and industrial communities where, for the first time, white hillbillies were not only thrown into daily contact with them but also into competition for the same low-caste jobs at rockbottom wages. For low-class whites, social segregation was a means of asserting their superiority. As C. Vann Woodward puts it in his *The Origins of the New South* (1951), "It took a lot of ritual and Jim Crow to bolster the creed of white supremacy in the bosom of a white man working for a black man's wages." The South had made sure that African-Americans were socially and academically inferior by denying them a decent education. Southern legislatures starved African-American schools of adequate funds, thereby making it impossible for them to approach anywhere near the same standards. In 1910 the eleven southern states spent an average of $9.45 on each white pupil but only $2.90 on each African-American pupil.

The South reacted against the natural tide of resentment by African-Americans to its new restrictive policies with more repression. Mississippi was the first state effectively to disfranchise African-American citizens by a constitutional convention in 1890. It was followed by South Carolina in 1895, Louisiana in 1898, North Carolina (by an amendment) in 1900, Alabama in 1901, Virginia in 1901 and 1902, Georgia (by amendment) in 1908, and the new state of Oklahoma in 1910. Four more states achieved the same ends without amending their constitutions: Tennessee, Florida, Arkansas, and Texas. Three pernicious and sophistical arguments were advanced by the proponents of disfranchisement. The removal of the African-American vote, they said, would end corruption at elections. It would prevent African-Americans from holding the balance of power in contests between rival factions of whites. Moreover, it would oblige African-Americans to abandon their false hopes of betterment and, instead, make them accept their true social place. As a result, race relations would steadily improve.

The Mississippi Constitution of 1890 set the pattern. It required a poll tax of two dollars from prospective voters at registration. Those who intended to vote at elections had to present their receipt at the polls. Thus anyone who mislaid his receipt forfeited his vote. More insidious was the requirement that, in order to register, prospective voters had to be "able to read the Constitution, or to understand the Constitution when read." It also excluded those convicted of bribery, burglary, theft, and bigamy. Racist officials used the various ordinances to discriminate in favor of poor, illiterate whites and against African-Americans.

The ruling elites in other states approved of the new Mississippi plan and several states borrowed from one another. In so doing they improved on previous attempts to disfranchise African-Americans. For example, Louisiana believed that the understanding clause was so obviously suspect that it could be invalidated in a court case. Thus it hit on the grandfather clause as being, legally, more secure. Only those who had had a grandfather on the electoral roll of 1867 could vote.

These devices were nothing if not effective. In Louisiana, 130,344 African-Americans were registered to vote in 1890; in 1900 there were 5,320. In 1909 there were only 1,342. In Alabama there were 181,000 African-American voters in 1890; in 1900 there were three thousand. In the South as a whole African-American participation fell by 62 percent. In 1900 Ben ("Pitchfork") Tillman of South Carolina boasted on the floor of the Senate, "We have done our best. We have scratched our heads to find out how we could eliminate the last one of them. We stuffed ballot boxes. We shot them. We are not ashamed of it." Despite concessions to poor whites, white participation in elections also declined — by 26 percent. Thus while, on average, 73 percent of men voted in the 1890s, only 30 percent did so in the early 1900s. Opposition parties dwindled away and the Democrats were left undisputed champions of the South.

Social segregation was also upheld by the Supreme Court. Its most notorious decision came in *Plessy v. Ferguson* in 1896. Louisiana state law required "separate but equal" accommodations for African-American and white passengers on public carriers and provided a penalty for passengers sitting in the wrong car. Homer Plessy was an octoroon so pale that he usually passed for white, but when he sat in a white car he was arrested. He argued that the state law of Louisiana violated the Fourteenth and Fifteenth Amendments. Justice John Marshall Harlan of Kentucky agreed with him, maintaining. "Our constitution is color-blind and neither knows nor tolerates classes among citizens." Moreover, "What can more certainly arouse race hate, what more certainly create and perpetuate a feeling of distrust between these races, than state enactments which in fact proceed on the ground that colored citizens are so inferior and degraded that they cannot be allowed to sit in public coaches occupied by white citizens?" However, he was overruled by the other eight justices, who approved of the doctrine of "separate but equal." Justice Henry Billings Brown of Michigan, speaking for the majority on May 18, 1896, ruled with corrosive racial candor, "If one race be inferior to the other socially, the Constitution of the United States cannot put them upon the same plane." In *Williams v. Mississippi* on April 25, 1898, the Court went further and approved the Mississippi plan for disfranchising African-Americans. The Court unanimously upheld the opinion of Justice Joseph McKenna that "a state does not violate the equal protection clause of the fourteenth amendment when it requires eligible voters to be able to read, write, interpret, or understand any part of the Constitution."

Edgar Gardner Murphy, a humanitarian journalist, reported in *The Basis of Ascendancy* (1909) how extremists had moved "from an undiscriminating attack upon the Negro's ballot to a like attack upon his schools, his labor, his life — from the contention that no Negro shall vote to the contention that no Negro shall learn, that no Negro shall labor, and [by implication] that no Negro shall live." The result was an "all-absorbing autocracy of race," an "absolute identification of the stronger race with the very being of the state." In 1903 analyst Charles W. Chestnutt said that "the rights of the Negroes are at a lower ebb than at any time during the thirty-five years of their freedom, and the race prejudice more intense and uncompromising."

Racist scientists tried to prove that African-Americans were inferior to whites. In 1929 Lawrence Fick in the *South African Journal of Science* declared that Africans showed "a marked inferiority" to European whites and that the number who could benefit from education was limited. Americans measured intelligence on the basis of a test first developed by Frenchman Alfred Binet in 1905 and based on the skills expected of, and acquired by, educated children from the middle class. Not surprisingly, such a test found undereducated children, whether poor white, immigrant, or African-American, less intelligent. The final, conclusive "proof" of the inferiority of African-Americans came when African-American soldiers scored worse than whites in intelligence tests given in World War I. Subsequent investigation showed that African-Americans from the North scored higher than southern whites. Here was disturbing proof of the inferiority of southern education as a whole....

☆

BOOKER T. WASHINGTON AND W. E. B. DU BOIS

Since African-Americans were being displaced from their traditional trades and confined to menial jobs in the towns, those who did succeed in entering the worlds of business and the professions were obliged by white society to adopt its attitudes in order to retain their hard-won position. Their undeclared leader was Booker T. Washington, head of Tuskegee Industrial Institute, Alabama.

Booker Taliaferro Washington was born at Hale's Ford, Franklin County, Virginia, in 1856, the son of a white father and an African-American mother who was enslaved. At the end of the Civil War he worked in a coal mine and salt furnace at Malden, West Virginia, while he attended school. From 1872 to 1875 he studied at Hampton Institute, the Negro vocational school in Virginia, where he earned his keep by working as a janitor. He also taught school at Malden (1875–1877) and subsequently studied at Wayland Seminary, Washington, D.C. In 1879 he returned to Hampton Institute, where he was in charge of the Indian dormitory and night school. In 1881 he was selected to organize an African-American normal school at Tuskegee chartered by the Alabama legislature.

Thereafter, his name was practically synonymous with African-American education. In fact, Booker T. Washington created three major institutions: the Normal and Industrial Institute for Negroes, the college in rural Alabama devoted primarily to agricultural and technical education; the Tuskegee Machine, a lobby of African-American intellectuals, politicos, and educators and white philanthropists who supposed Washington's political and economic aims; and the National Negro Business League, committed to establishing and consolidating a system of African-American entrepreneurs within the existing framework of white capitalism. Washington believed that the optimum strategy for the rural masses of African-Americans was to concentrate as much as possible on economic independence by thrift and the acquisition of property. For the time being they were to disregard disfranchisement and Jim Crow social segregation. The encouragement Washington and his school of thought gave to a new generation of African-American entrepreneurs and their clients to "buy black" and to think in terms of black nationalism allowed them to rise commercially at the expense of a different group of artisans, caterers, and porters who were essentially integrationists and who had had the lion's share of the market among African-Americans in the 1870s and 1880s.

Washington was as well known as a propagandist and polemicist as he was as an educational leader. He was invited to speak at the opening of the Cotton States and International Exposition in Atlanta on September 18, 1895, by businessmen who recognized his remarkable powers of expression. His address was one of the most effective political speeches of the Gilded Age, a model fusion of substance and style.

In what was later called the Atlanta Compromise he abandoned the postwar ideal of racial equality in favor of increased economic opportunity for African-Americans. "The wisest among my race understand that the agitation of questions of social equality is the extremist folly and that progress in the enjoyment of all the privileges that will come to us must be the result of severe and constant struggle rather than of artificial forcing." He preached patience, proposed submission, and emphasized material progress. Those African-Americans who rejected the Atlanta Compromise, such as rising activist W. E. B. Du Bois, considered his stance a capitulation to blatant racism. But Washington was telling white society exactly what it wanted to hear — that African-Americans accepted the Protestant work ethic. His most widely reported remark was a subtle metaphor about racial harmony: "In all things social we can be as separate as the fingers, yet one as the hand in all things essential to mutual progress."

Washington's emphasis on racial pride, economic progress, and industrial education encouraged white politicians and businessmen, such as steel tycoon Andrew Carnegie, to subsidize the institutions for African-Americans that he recommended. Through his close connections with business he was able to raise the funds necessary to create the National Negro Business League in 1900. Moreover, he used money not to advance acquiescence by African-Americans but to fight segregation. Others sought a more open insistence on racial pride. In 1890 T. Thomas Fortune, a journalist of New York, persuaded forty African-American protection leagues in cities across the country to join in a national body, the Afro-American League. Historian C. Vann Woodward assesses Washington's work thus: "Washington's life mission was to find a pragmatic compromise that would resolve the antagonisms, suspicions, and aspirations of 'all three classes directly concerned — the Southern white man, the northern white man, and the Negro.' It proved, he admitted 'a difficult and at times a puzzling task.' But he moved with consummate diplomacy, trading renunciation for concession and playing sentiment against interest."

Five weeks into his presidency (1901–1909), Theodore Roosevelt invited Booker T. Washington to the White House on October 18, 1901. Roosevelt was also committed to trying to reconcile the South to the Republican party. His invitation was intended as a symbolic gesture to African-Americans and was widely interpreted as such. There was terrible logic in the subsequent outrage of racist southerners when the story broke. The New Orleans *Times-Democrat* thought Roosevelt's action mischievous: "When Mr. Roosevelt sits down to dinner with a negro, he declares that the negro is the social equal of the White Man." Senator Benjamin ("Pitchfork") Tillman, declared, "The action of President Roosevelt in entertaining that nigger will necessitate our killing a thousand niggers in the South before they will learn their place again."

Despite Washington's insistence on patience, some African-Americans began to agitate for desegregation on trains, a prime target of the protest movement that was the forerunner of civil rights. They reckoned that railroads would realize that it was more expensive to have segregated seating and would thus yield, it only for the sake of economy. In 1898 the Afro-American League called for a boycott of trains in protest of Jim Crow laws. In 1904 the Maryland Suffrage League began campaigning against the new Jim Crow law there and financed a successful lawsuit against segregated travel in 1905. Also in 1905, the Georgia Equal Rights League declared that African-Americans should be able "to travel in comfort and decency and receive a just equivalent for our money, and yet we are the victims of the most unreasonable sort of caste legislation." In 1909 the National Negro Conference denounced segregation and the oppression of African-Americans. Whites were taken aback by the effectiveness of boycotts when African-Americans either simply stopped using white-owned transport or established small companies of their own. While streetcar companies either ended segregation or went out of business, such as the streetcar company in Richmond, Virginia. However, the wave of protests was short lived.

Washington's approach of so-called gradualism could be justified as a necessary complement to the fearful atmosphere of prejudice and violence in the South. However, African-American intellectuals in the North grew impatient with his time-serving and ambiguity. William Trotter, son of Cleveland's recorder of deeds and a graduate of Harvard, founded the most vehemently critical paper, the *Boston Guardian,* in 1901, and roundly abused Washington for his association with Roosevelt, calling him a "self seeker" and a "skulking coward." Trotter criticized Washington at the 1903 annual convention of the Afro-American Council and created uproar at a meeting of the Boston Business League later the same year when he heckled Washington as he tried to speak. The uproar resulted in "the Boston riot" that ended with the imprisonment of Trotter for thirty days for having disturbed the peace. Nevertheless, Trotter and his creations were radical, vocal forces in the struggle for civil rights.

The publication of *The Souls of Black Folk* by W. E. B. Du Bois in 1903 solidified protest around a new spokesman. William Edward Burghardt Du Bois was born in Great Barrington, Massachusetts, in 1868, graduated from Fisk and Harvard, and attended the University of Berlin. After returning to America in 1894, he taught at Wilberforce University, Ohio, and Pennsylvania University before becoming professor of sociology at Atlanta. A handsome and invariably immaculately dressed man, Du Bois was also a creative writer who produced two novels, *The Quest of the Silver Fleece* (1911) and *The Dark Princess* (1928), and two volumes of essays and poems, *Dark Water* (1920) and *The Gift of Black Folk* (1924). One of Du Bois's early supporter, James

Weldon Johnson, said of *The Souls of Black Folk* that "it had a greater effect upon and within the Negro race than any single book published in the country since *Uncle Tom's Cabin.*" One of the essays was a withering attack on what Du Bois considered Washington's acceptance of the heinous doctrine of racial inferiority. Du Bois insisted on an end to accommodation: "By every civilized and peaceful method we must strive for the rights which the world accords to men."

Deeply angered by Washington's counterrevolutionary tactics and intensely hostile to the strategy of accommodation, Du Bois invited like-minded activist to a national conference at Fort Erie in July 1905 that established the Niagara Movement. This was an elite cadre of about four hundred college-educated professional people. The Niagara Movement committed itself to continuing vocal protest against "the abridgment of political and civil rights and against inequality of educational opportunity." Du Bois and others published the *Moon* and, later, the *Horizon* as unofficial journals of the movement. Nevertheless, the Niagara Movement failed to establish itself as a distinctive national voice.

Moreover, it was becoming obvious to increasing numbers of African-Americans and sympathetic whites that a policy of accommodation was futile in the face of outright racist hostility. Despite Washington's supposed influence with Roosevelt, the president arbitrarily discharged three companies of African-Americans of the Twenty-fifth Regiment on an unproven charge of rioting in Brownsville, Texas, on August 14, 1906, after some soldiers had retaliated against racial insults. For their part, Roosevelt and his successor, William Howard Taft, (1909–1913), had to hold together a diverse coalition of Republicans that included a section of gross racial bigots, the lily-whites, who wanted to establish an all-white Republican party in the South. To appease this faction both presidents limited the number of federal appointments of African-Americans, thereby contributing to racial prejudice.

W. E. B. Du Bois was the foremost member of a gifted group of African American leaders during the early years of the twentieth century. A "child of the black elite" and highly educated, with a bachelor's degree from Fisk and a Ph.D. from Harvard, he played a major role in the founding of the National Association for the Advancement of Colored People and raised the "black protest movement" to a new level of effectiveness. (Schomburg Center for Research in Black Culture, The New York Public Library; Astor, Lenox and Tilden Foundations)

☆

JACK JOHNSON AND THE GREAT WHITE HOPE

White southerners came to accept without question the racist orthodoxy of such men as educator Thomas Pearce Bailey, as expressed in his article

145

"Race Orthodoxy in the South" for *Neale's Monthly Magazine* (1903). He set forth a creed of fifteen points, including such statements as "the white race must dominate"; "The Teutonic peoples stand for race purity"; "The Negro is inferior and will remain so"; "Let there be such industrial education of the Negro as will best fit him to serve the white man"; and "Let the lowest white man count for more than the highest Negro." Even environmentalists who argued that nurture, rather than nature, determined human behavior were reluctant to challenge popular stereotypes. Progressive intellectual John R. Commons expressed the dominant reformist view in 1907. He claimed that African-Americans had opportunities "not only on equal terms, but actually on terms of preference over the whites." Their failure to rise "is recognized even by their partisans as something that was inevitable in the nature of the race at that stage of its development."

However, arguments about genetic inferiority were silenced when boxer Jack Johnson, an African-American and former stevedore from Galveston, Texas, won the world heavyweight boxing title from Canadian Tommy Burns in Sydney, Australia, on Boxing Day, December 26, 1908. Johnson's victory aroused deep consternation throughout the white community. Racists in Congress were so disturbed by the defeat of a white man by an African-American that they proposed, and had passed, a law forbidding the interstate transportation of motion picture films showing prize fights. Immediately after Johnson's sensational victory, former world champion James J. Jefferies, then living in retirement on a farm in California, was urged to come out of retirement to regain the title for the white race. He was eventually persuaded to do so and was defeated in a fifteen-round match at Reno, Nevada, on July 4, 1912.

Johnson was the greatest heavyweight of his time, standing over six feet tall and weighing over two hundred pounds. He moved with the swiftness and grace of a panther. He was widely known for his good nature, his "golden smile," which revealed numerous crowned teeth, and his badinage while in the ring. During the bout with Jefferies, Johnson stopped briefly to lean on the shoulders of his weary opponent and jeered at another, former fighter, Jim Corbett, at the ringside, saying, "Jim this big bum can't fight any better than you could." However, when a blow reached Johnson that really told, his veneer of good nature vanished and his killer instinct surfaced. He gloried in adulation and enjoyed provoking his numerous white critics. Johnson's prowess was a symbol of strength to African-Americans and his success could make him a rallying point for solidarity among them. In fact, he was inaugurating a mighty tradition of powerful African-American heavyweight champions extending through Joe Louis in the 1930s to Muhammad Ali in the 1960s and 1970s and then to Mike Tyson in the 1980s.

In the 1910s Jack Johnson's numerous white enemies determined to find a white challenger who could defeat him and restore the myth of white supremacy. The great white hope turned out to be Jess Willard of Kansas, a former cowpuncher who was known for feats of strength such as bending a silver dollar between his fingers. However, he was a mediocre fighter. Eventually Johnson, sated with European night life and adulation, became homesick and was keen to accept the suggestion of promoters that he should return and fight Willard. The venue would be Havana, Cuba. When Johnson arrived in poor condition, he disappointed his backers by doing next to no training and spending his days driving about the city with his white wife. The fight was held on April 5, 1915, with soldiers surrounding the stadium in order to prevent racial violence. The first twenty-two rounds were dull but in the twenty-third Johnson sank to the floor — though whether from a blow by Willard or from sunstroke, opinions differ. Thus fell the first of the great African-American stars of the worlds of entertainment and sports. Johnson returned to Chicago, attended subsequent boxing contests in which champions won millions, and in the 1930s became conductor of his own jazz orchestra.

☆

The NAACP and the Early Civil Rights Movement

Not surprisingly, given the prevailing atmosphere of hysteria stroked by institutional racism and the pseudoscientific jargon of prejudiced scientists, African-Americans became helpless victims of race riots instigated by malicious, scared whites, such as the one in Atlanta, Georgia, in 1906, in which ten African-Americans were killed before martial law restored order. In 1908, after a white women claimed she had been raped, whites invaded the African-American section of Springfield, Illinois, lynched two African-Americans, and flogged several others. The white assailants escaped without punishment. However, on this occasion the North was influenced by an article denouncing the outrage, "Race War in the North," written by a southern socialist, William English Walling. Together with settlement workers Mary White Ovington and Dr. Henry Moskowitz, Walling persuaded Oswald Garrison Villard, editor of the *New York Evening Post* and grandson of the abolitionist leader [William Lloyd Garrison], to call a conference on race in 1909, the centenary of the birth of Abraham Lincoln.

At a meeting in New York on May 31 and June 1, 1909, African-American and white American radicals proposed a new national organization to protect the rights of African-Americans and a similar conference in 1910 established the National Association for the Advancement of Colored People (NAACP), with its declared goal of "equal rights and opportunities for all." Under its first president, Moorfield Storey, the NAACP formed several hundred branches. Under the editorship of W. E. B. Du Bois, The NAACP journal, the *Crisis,* reached a circulation of one hundred thousand. Du Bois's own column, "As the Crow Flies," attacked white racism. Together with the *Chicago Defender,* the *Pittsburgh Courier,* and the *Baltimore African-American,* the *Crisis*

made an ever-increasing spectrum of literate African-Americans aware of their national responsibilities and what the nation owed them.

The NAACP's distinctive strategy was litigation to challenge racist laws. For example, in 1917 the NAACP challenged a statute of Louisville, Kentucky, requiring "the use of separate blocks for residence, places of abode, and places of assembly by white and colored people respectively." Moorfield Storey took the case to the Supreme Court at a time when it was, in the terms of analyst Richard Kluger, peopled by men of Paleolithic perspective, notable Justices Willis van Devanter and James Clark McReynolds. Nevertheless, in the case of *Buchanan v. Warley* the Court unanimously, and surprisingly, decided on November 5, 1917, that "all citizens of the United States shall have the same right in every state and territory, as is enjoyed by white citizens thereof, to inherit, purchase, lease, sell, hold and convey real and personal property." However, the *Buchanan* decision resulted in a spate of private restrictive covenants under which residents agreed to sell or rent their property to individuals of one race only. The Court subsequently upheld this pernicious practice in *Corrigan v. Buckley* in 1926, maintaining that civil rights were not protected against discrimination by individuals.

Another sequence of NAACP cases tested the constitutionality of disfranchisement. In 1910 Oklahoma introduced its own grandfather clause to prevent African-Americans from voting. Two of its election officials, Guinn and Beal, were prosecuted by the NAACP for carrying out the new state law. When the officials were found guilty of violating the Fifteenth Amendment by a district court, they appealed to the Supreme Court. However, in the case of *Guinn v. United States* (1915), the Court unanimously declared that the grandfather clause was "an unconstitutional evasion of the 15th Amendment guarantee that states would not deny citizens the right to vote because of their race." On the same day the Court ruled by seven votes to one in the case of

United States v. Mosely that it "upheld congressional power to relegate elections tainted with fraud and corruption." It seemed the law was on the side of civil rights for African-Americans.

Oklahoma reacted quickly. It passed a new election law, providing permanent registration for those entitled to vote according to the unconstitutional law and allowing African-Americans only twelve days to register or to be disqualified from voting for life. The new law was not contested in the Supreme Court for another twenty-two years. . . .

☆

THE GREAT MIGRATION

The way racist whites openly flouted the basic rights of African-American citizens was now so flagrant as to be scarcely credible in a society moving through a phase of self-styled progressivism. For African-Americans, the notion of progressive reform was a joke in very bad taste. Ironically, the African-American community, like the white, was stronger economically than ever. In 1913 African-Americans owned 550,000 houses, worked 937 farms, ran forty thousand businesses, and attended forty thousand African-American churches. There were thirty-five thousand African-American teachers, and 1.7 million African-American students attended public schools.

The accession of Woodrow Wilson to the presidency (1913–1921) resulted in the most racist administration since the Civil War. Southern Democrats were dominant in Congress, the White House, and the Supreme Court. African-American needs were peripheral to Wilson's interests. Inasmuch as he had views on the subject, they were in the tradition of southern paternalism. As a result, and spurred on by his first wife, Ellen Axson Wilson, he acquiesced in the unrest of segregation. His postmaster general, Albert S. Burleson, introduced the subject of segregation at an early cabinet meeting, suggesting separation to reduce friction between white and African-American railway clerks. Convinced by this argument, Wilson and the cabinet allowed systematic segregation in government offices, shops, rest rooms, and lunchrooms. African-Americans were even removed from appointments they had previously held. The sum total of the Wilson policies was that only eight African-Americans out of thirty working in the federal government in Washington retained their appointments.

Emboldened, racists began to demand that Congress legislate for segregation throughout the civil service, forbid interracial marriages, and even repeal the Fourteenth and Fifteenth Amendments. The South extended its segregation to public transport. Thus, African-Americans were prevented from using taxis reserved for whites in the state of Mississippi in 1922 and in the cities of Jacksonville in 1929 and Birmingham in 1930.

Such discrimination, important in itself, had more momentous consequences because of the contemporary exodus of African-Americans [to the North from the South, where 85 percent of African-Americans lived]. For the 1910s and 1920s were also years of the Great Migration. The immediate reason for the exodus was the industrial requirements of World War I. Whites were being drawn increasingly into the armed services and newly created war industries. However, the war prevented European immigrants from coming to America and taking their place as laborers. Thus, in 1915 agents for northern employers began recruiting African-American labor from the South. However, at least four times as many African-Americans went north on word of mouth than did so at the prompting of labor agents. The exodus was mainly spontaneous and largely unorganized; whatever the personal motives for individual moves, the collective motive was bad treatment in the South. The Great Migration was facilitated by railroad transportation and continued after the war was over. In sum, the South lost 323,000 African-Americans in the 1910s and 615,000 in the 1920s — about 8.2 percent of its African-American population. At the outset white attitudes in both the North and the South to the migration were somewhat ambivalent. As time went on, they became alarmist: northerners resented another ethnic disruption following in the wake of the new immigration; southerners did not want to lose their ready supply of cheap labor. Some southern communities passed laws to prevent African-Americans from leaving. This happened in Montgomery, Savannah, Greenville, and elsewhere. Charleston editor William Watts Ball commented ruefully in 1925, "We have plenty of Southerners whose disposition is identical with that of the ancient Egyptians — they would chase the Negroes to the Red Sea to bring them back." However, nothing could reverse the tide.

Whereas the Great Migration is often interpreted as part of the inevitable progress of African-Americans to full citizenship because they were less likely to encounter political disfranchisement in the North than the South, some, such as playwright August Wilson, believe that is represented an incorrect cultural choice for African-Americans intent on capturing their legacy. In April 1990 he told the *New York Times,* "We were land-based agrarian people from Africa. We were uprooted from Africa, and we spend over 200 years developing our culture as Black Americans. Then we left the South. We uprooted ourselves and attempted to transplant this culture to the pavements of the industrialized North. And it was a transplant that did not take. I think if we had stayed in the South, we would have been a stronger people. And because the connection between the South of the '20s, '30s and '40s has been broken, it's very difficult to understand who we are."

Southern blacks who migrated North found to their dismay that the North was hardly the promised land, and migrants found themselves herded into city ghettos and kept there by a host of real estate and municipal codes. Thereafter when African-Americans went north, as James Baldwin observed,

they did not go to New York City, they went to Harlem; they did not go to Chicago, they went to the South Side; they did not go to Los Angeles, they went to Watts. As historian Leronne Bennett Jr. wrote, "Real estate became the principal dynamic in the ensemble of northern race relations," and the walls of segregation erected across the urban North in turn produced a new anger and militancy, indeed "a new and different black world." Black Moslem leaders Malcolm X and Louis Farrakhan (Louis X), among others, would be furious products of the northern black ghetto.

QUESTIONS TO CONSIDER

1   What were the basic principles and ideals of W. E. B. Du Bois and how did they contrast with the program called for by Booker T. Washington? To which segments of the black and white population did each of them direct his concern and to whom did it appeal?

2   What were the fundamental goals of the Niagara movement? What did the movement accomplish, and what undermined it?

3   Why was Jack Johnson an important figure for black Americans? Why did he cause great consternation among white supremacists?

4   What is the NAACP? Who were its founders and what were their intentions? What methods did the NAACP use to gain advances for African-Americans?

5   What was the Great Migration? Do you think it was beneficial for black Americans to move North? What is the legacy of the Great Migration for the northern cities?

6   Consider America's social problems concerning race. What positive changes have there been since the Progressive Era? What problems remain? Why do you think the issue of race continues to be a major problem in America? Can the problem be solved?

VI

GRIM REALITIES
OF THE GREAT WAR
(1914–1918)

12

"Hell Cannot Be So Terrible": Trench Warfare on the Western Front

PAUL FUSSELL

What you are about to read is a vivid description of the trench warfare of the Great War, the most savage conflict ever fought up to that time. It was called the Great War then because nobody knew that an even more monstrous war lay in the future. The Great War began in 1914 when Austria-Hungary declared war on a small Balkan country named Serbia, whose staunch ally was Russia. Because of entangling alliances among Europe's great powers, the war quickly spread until it engulfed much of Europe, with the Central Powers (Austria-Hungary, Germany, and Turkey) fighting the Allied Powers (Russia, France, Britain, and Italy). It was the world's first "total war," in which whole societies battled one another. Before it was over, Russia had suffered almost 2 million casualties and collapsed in a Communist takeover; Germany had lost 2 million soldiers, France 1.5 million, and Britain almost 1 million.

The United States officially entered the war in April 1917, on the side of the Allies. The United States did so, in part, because the Germans had resorted to submarine war, torpedoing Allied warships without warning; to Americans, this seemed barbaric. The Allied blockade of the German coast, calculated to starve Germany into submission, did not strike most Americans the same way, because of their anti-German sentiment and sympathies for the Allies. When a German U-boat sank a British passenger ship, the Lusitania, *with 128 Americans on board, the United States was enraged. President Woodrow Wilson warned the Germans that if they continued to commit such outrages, the United States would take the necessary action to protect its citizens traveling on nonmilitary vessels. At first the Germans agreed not to sink any more enemy ships with Americans on board, but later withdrew the pledge on the grounds that Germany was already fighting American economic might — the United States was selling war materiel to the Allies — and had nothing to lose by attacking American merchant ships taking war supplies to Britain. "This means war," said Wilson. "The break that we have tried to prevent now seems inevitable." When the United States intercepted a secret telegram in which Germany invited Mexico to join the Central Powers, Wilson asked Congress to delcare war, and Congress did so with thunderous applause and cheering. "My message today," said Wilson, "was a message of death for our young men. How strange it seems to applaud that."*

The United States army, that spring of 1917, was pitifully small and weak to fight a war. A sickly Theodore Roosevelt, despite his loathing of Wilson, offered to raise a regiment to fight in Europe, but to no avail. At Wilson's urging, Congress enacted a conscription act to draft 3 million men into the armed services; another 2 million volunteered. It was not until the spring of 1918 that the American Expeditionary Force under General John J. Pershing arrived in western Europe in force. What they found at the front were horrors beyond their imagination. Since 1916, the opposing armies had committed themselves to deadly trench warfare in northern France and southeastern Belgium, which featured the deadly machine gun, barbed wire, and the most powerful artillery yet devised. The result was military stalemate and horrendous casualties. When ordered to attack, soldiers poured forth from trenches fronted by barbed wire, dashed across a shell-torn lunarscape called "no-man's land," and charged the rival trenches. Enemy machine guns mowed them down; chlorine gas poisoned them. In parts of France, the poison gas was to cling to the tops of caves for twenty years. And yet almost nothing was gained. In the Battle of Verdun in 1916, French and German forces suffered 700,000 combined casualties as they battered one another back and forth for ten hellish months, leaving a miasmic wasteland of smashed weapons, shattered helmets, shreds of clothing, rotting corpses, and twisted skeletons. "Humanity must be mad to do what it is doing," a French lieutenant wrote at Verdun. "Hell cannot be so terrible."

In the following selection, Paul Fussell, a veteran of the Second World War and a military historian, describes "the trench scene" in graphic and unforgettable prose. In his view, one cannot understand human conflict like the Great War simply by studying the decisions of leaders and the flow of great events. One must also get into the trenches with the common soldiers and sense the misery and chaos they suffered. That way one might gain melancholy insight into what warfare was really like.

When the Americans reached the front, they took their places in the Allied trenches and soon suffered the same miseries described by Fussell. Even though the selection focuses on the British, French, and Germans, what it says applies equally to the Americans. Fortunately for them, their role in the Great War was brief but critical. Their addition to the Allied forces ensured an Allied victory. Eight months after the Americans had arrived in force, Germany surrendered.

GLOSSARY

"BULLY"   British soldier's slang for tinned corned beef.

CHIROPODIST   One who treated foot ailments like corns, bunions, and trench foot.

CHLORINE GAS   Poison chlorine gas used in the great war; it was often called mustard gas because of its yellow-green color. Those who inhaled it choked to death.

BARBED WIRE   Heavy-duty metal wire with sharp barbs extruding from it every two inches or so. Its function in trench warfare was to prevent enemy forces from charging swiftly into entrenched positions.

HAIG, SIR DOUGLAS   Field marshal and commander in chief of the British army in the trench war.

MAXIM GUN   Named after Hiram Maxim, its American inventor, this rapid-fire machine gun was one of the most deadly weapons in the Great War; rapid-fire the machine gun was so effective that it made trenches almost unassailable.

NO MAN'S LAND   Shell-torn wasteland lying between opposing trenches, so called because no man could safely traverse it by day for fear of being shot by a sniper or blown to pieces by an artillery shell.

STAND-TO   Morning ritual in the British trenches; everyone in them would mount the fire-step, weapon at the ready, and watch the German lines in anticipation of an attack.

TRENCH (MILITARY)   A long, deep ditch used as a defensive position for troops. Trenches zigzagged in nearly continuous lines across most of the battlefront in France and Belgium; by some estimates, almost 25,000 miles of trenches were dug during the war.

"WASTAGE"   Term used by the British to describe the seven thousand British soldiers who died daily in the trenches.

YPRES SALIENT   One of the two main sectors in the British line, so narrow that it often induced claustrophobia among the troops.

The idea of "the trenches" has been assimilated so successfully by metaphor and myth ("Georgian complacency died in the trenches") that it is not easy now to recover a feeling for the actualities. *Entrenched,* in an expression like *entrenched power,* has been a dead metaphor so long that we must bestir ourselves to recover its literal sense. It is time to take a tour.

From the winter of 1914 until the spring of 1918 the trench system was fixed, moving here and there a few hundred yards, moving on great occasions as much as a few miles. London stationers purveying maps felt secure in stocking "sheets of 'The Western Front' with a thick wavy black line drawn from North to South alongside which was printed 'British Line.'" If one could have gotten high enough to look down at the whole line at once, one would have seen a series of multiple parallel excavations running for 400 miles down through Belgium and France, roughly in the shape of an *S* flattened at the sides and tipped to the left. From the North Sea coast of Belgium the line wandered southward, bulging out to contain Ypres, then dropping down to protect Béthune, Arras, and Albert. It continued south in front of Montidier, Compiègne, Soissons, Reims, Verdun, St. Mihiel, and Nancy, and finally attached its southernmost end to the Swiss border at Beurnevisin, in Alsace. The top forty miles — the part north of Ypres — was held by the Belgians; the next ninety miles, down to the river Ancre, were British; the French held the rest, to the south.

Henri Barbusse estimates that the French front alone contained about 6250 miles of trenches. Since the French occupied a little more than half the line,

the total length of the numerous trenches occupied by the British must come to about 6000 miles. We thus find over 12,000 miles of trenches on the Allied side alone. When we add the trenches of the Central Powers, we arrive at a figure of about 25,000 miles, equal to a trench sufficient to circle the earth. Theoretically it would have been possible to walk from Belgium to Switzerland entirely below ground, but although the lines were "continuous," they were not entirely seamless: occasionally mere shell holes or fortified strong-points would serve as a connecting link. Not a few survivors have performed the heady imaginative exercise of envisioning the whole line at once. Stanley Casson is one who, imagining the whole line from his position on the ground, implicitly submits the whole preposterous conception to the criterion of the "normally" rational and intelligible. As he remembers, looking back from 1935,

Our trenches stood on a faint slope, just overlooking German ground, with a vista of vague plainland below. Away to right and left stretched the great lines of defense as far as eye and imagination could stretch them. I used to wonder how long it would take for me to walk from the beaches of the North Sea to that curious end of all fighting against the Swiss boundary; to try to guess what each end looked like; to imagine what would happen if I passed a verbal message, in the manner of the parlor game, along to the next man on my right to be delivered to the end man of all up against the Alps. Would anything intelligible at all emerge?

Another imagination has contemplated a similar absurd transmission of sound all the way from north to south. Alexander Aitken remembers the Germans opposite him celebrating some happy public event in early June, 1916, presumably either the (ambiguous) German success at the naval battle of Jutland (May 31–June 1) or the drowning of Lord Kitchener, lost on June 5 when the cruiser *Hampshire* struck a mine and sank off the Orkney Islands. Aitken writes,

Paul Fussell, "'Hell Cannot Be So Terrible': Trench Warfare on the Western Front," chapter originally titled, "The Troglodyte World," in Fussell, *The Great War and Modern Memory* (New York: Oxford University Press, 1975), pp. 36–51. Copyright © 1975 by Oxford University Press, Inc. Used by permission of Oxford University Press, Inc.

A scene in an Allied trench in France. Such trenches were "wet, cold, smelly, and thoroughly squalid." When the Americans arrived toward the end of the Great War, they joined the British and French in "the troglodyte world" of trenches on the Western front. (Culver Pictures)

"There had been a morning in early June when a tremendous tin-canning and beating of shell-gongs had begun in the north and run south down their lines to end, without doubt, at Belfort and Mulhausen on the Swiss frontier." Impossible to believe, really, but in this mad setting, somehow plausible.

The British part of the line was normally populated by about 800 battalions of 1000 men each. They were concentrated in the two main sectors of the British effort: the Ypres Salient in Flanders and the Somme area in Picardy. Memory has given these two sectors the appearance of two distinguishable worlds. The Salient, at its largest point about nine miles wide and projecting some four miles into the

German line, was notable for its terrors of concentrated, accurate artillery fire. Every part of it could be covered from three sides, and at night one saw oneself almost surrounded by the circle of white and colored Very lights sent up by the Germans to illuminate the ground in front of their trenches or to signal to the artillery behind them. The "rear area" at Ypres was the battered city itself, where the troops harbored in cellars or in the old fortifications built by Vauban in the seventeenth century. It was eminently available to the German guns, and by the end of the war Ypres was flattened to the ground, its name a byword for a city totally destroyed. Another war later, in 1940, Colin Perry — who was not born

A photograph of No Man's land, the miasmic, shelltorn space between the rival trenches. This picture reveals the foundation of a house and a helmet with a skull in it. (Culver Pictures)

until four years after the Great War — could look at the ruins of London and speak of "the Ypres effect of Holborn." If the character of the Ypres sector was concentration and enclosure, inducing claustrophobia even above ground, the Somme was known — at least until July 1, 1916 — for its greater amplitude and security. German fire came generally from only one direction; and troops at rest could move further back. But then there was the Somme mud; although the argument about whether the mud wasn't really worse at Ypres was never settled.

Each of these two sectors had its symbolic piece of ruined public architecture. At Ypres it was the famous Cloth Hall, once a masterpiece of medieval

Flemish civic building. Its gradual destruction by artillery and its pathetic final dissolution were witnessed by hundreds of thousands, who never forgot this eloquent emblem of what happens when war collides with art. In the Somme the memorable ruined work of architecture, connoting this time the collision of the war with religion and the old pietics, was the battered Basilica in the town of Albert, or "Bert," as the troops called it. The grand if rather vulgar red and white brick edifice had been built a few years before the war, the result of a local ecclesiastic's enthusiasm. Together with his townsmen he hoped that Albert might become another Lourdes. Before the war 80,000 used to come on pilgrimages to Albert every year. The object of veneration inside the church was a statue of the Virgin, said to have been found in the Middle Ages by a local shepherd. But the statue of the Virgin never forgotten by the hordes of soldiers who passed through Albert was the colossal gilded one on top of the battered tall tower of the Basilica. This figure, called Notre Dame des Brebières, originally held the infant Christ in outstretched arms above her; but now the whole statue was bent down below the horizontal, giving the effect of a mother about to throw her child — in disgust? in sacrifice? — into the debris-littered street below. To Colonel Sir Maurice Hankey, Secretary of the War Committee, it was "a most pathetic sight." Some said that the statue had been bent down by French engineers to prevent the Germans from using it to aim at. But most — John Masefield among them — preferred to think it a victim of German artillery. Its obvious symbolic potential (which I will deal with later) impressed itself even on men who found they could refer to it only facetiously, as "The Lady of the Limp."

The two main British sectors duplicated each other also in their almost symbolic road systems. Each had a staging town behind: for Ypres it was Poperinghe (to the men, "Pop"); for the Somme, Amiens. From these towns troops proceeded with augmenting but usually well-concealed terror up a sinister road to the town of operations, either Ypres itself or Albert. And running into the enemy lines out of Ypres and Albert were the most sinister roads of all, one leading to Menin, the other to Bapaume, both in enemy territory. These roads defined the direction of ultimate attack and the hoped-for breakout. They were the goals of the bizarre inverse quest on which the soldiers were ironically embarked.

But most of the time they were not questing. They were sitting or lying or squatting in place below the level of the ground. "When all is said and done," Sassoon notes, "the war was mainly a matter of holes and ditches." And in these holes and ditches extending for ninety miles, continually, even in the

quietest times, some 7000 British men and officers were killed and wounded daily, just as a matter of course. "Wastage," the Staff called it.

There were normally three lines of trenches. The front-line trench was anywhere from fifty yards or so to a mile from its enemy counterpart. Several hundred yards behind it was the support trench line. And several hundred yards behind that was the reserve line. There were three kinds of trenches: firing trenches, like these; communication trenches, running roughly perpendicular to the line and connecting the three lines; and "saps," shallower ditches thrust out into No Man's Land, providing access to forward observation posts, listening posts, grenade-throwing posts, and machine gun positions. The end of a sap was usually not manned all the time: night was the favorite time for going out. Coming up from the rear, one reached the trenches by following a communication trench sometimes a mile or more long. It often began in a town and gradually deepened. By the time pedestrians reached the reserve line, they were well below ground level.

A firing trench was supposed to be six to eight feet deep and four or five feet wide. On the enemy side a parapet of earth or sandbags rose about two or three feet above the ground. A corresponding "parados" a foot or so high was often found on top of the friendly side. Into the sides of trenches were dug one- or two-man holes ("funk-holes"), and there were deeper dugouts, reached by dirt stairs, for use as command posts and officers' quarters. On the enemy side of a trench was a fire-step two feet high on which the defenders were supposed to stand, firing and throwing grenades, when repelling attack. A well-built trench did not run straight for any distance: that would have been to invite enfilade fire. Every few yards a good trench zig-zagged. It had frequent traverses designed to contain damage within a limited space. Moving along a trench thus involved a great deal of weaving and turning. The floor of a proper trench was covered with wooden duckboards, beneath which were sumps a few feet deep designed to collect water. The walls, perpetually crumbling, were supported by sandbags, corrugated iron, or bundles of sticks or rushes. Except at night and in half-light, there was of course no looking over the top except through periscopes, which could be purchased in the "Trench Requisites" section of the main London department stores. The few snipers on duty during the day observed No Man's Land through loopholes cut in sheets of armor plate.

The entanglements of barbed wire had to be positioned far enough out in front of the trench to keep the enemy from sneaking up to grenade-throwing distance. Interestingly, the two novelties that contributed most to the personal menace of the war could be said to be American inventions. Barbed wire had first appeared on the American frontier in the late nineteenth century for use in restraining animals. And the machine gun was the brainchild of Hiram Stevens Maxim (1840–1916), an American who, disillusioned with native patent law, established his Maxim Gun Company in England and began manufacturing his guns in 1889. He was finally knighted for his efforts. At first the British regard for barbed wire was on a par with Sir Douglas Haig's understanding of the machine gun. In the autumn of 1914, the first wire Private Frank Richards saw emplaced before the British positions was a single strand of agricultural wire found in the vicinity. Only later did the manufactured article begin to arrive from England in sufficient quantity to create the thickets of mock-organic rusty brown that helped give a look of eternal autumn to the front.

The whole British line was numbered by sections, neatly, from right to left. A section, normally occupied by a company, was roughly 300 yards wide. One might be occupying front-line trench section 51; or support trench S 51, behind it; or reserve trench SS 51, behind both. But a less formal way of identifying sections of trench was by place or street names with a distinctly London flavor. *Piccadilly* was a favorite; popular also were *Regent Street* and *Strand;* junctions were *Hyde Park Corner* and *Marble Arch.*

Greater wit — and deeper homesickness — sometimes surfaced in the naming of the German trenches opposite. Sassoon remembers "Durley" 's account of the attack at Delville Wood in September, 1916: "Our objective was Pint Trench, taking Bitter and Beer and clearing Ale and Vat, and also Pilsen Lane." Directional and traffic control signs were everywhere in the trenches, giving the whole system the air of a parody modern city, although one literally "underground."

The trenches I have described are more or less ideal, although not so ideal as the famous exhibition trenches dug in Kensington Gardens for the edification of the home front. These were clean, dry, and well furnished, with straight sides and sandbags neatly aligned. R. E. Vernède writes his wife from the real trenches that a friend of his has just returned from viewing the set of ideal ones. He "found he had never seen anything at all like it before." And Wilfred Owen calls the Kensington Gardens trenches "the laughing stock of the army." Explaining military routines to civilian readers, Ian Hay labors to give the impression that the real trenches are identical to the exhibition ones and that they are properly described in the language of normal domesticity a bit archly deployed:

The firing-trench is our place of business — our office in the city, so to speak. The supporting trench is our suburban residence, whither the weary toiler may betake himself periodically (or, more correctly, in relays) for purposes of refreshment and repose.

The reality was different. The British trenches were wet, cold, smelly, and thoroughly squalid. Compared with the precise and thorough German works, they were decidedly amateur, reflecting a complacency about the British genius for improvisation. Since defense offered little opportunity for the display of pluck or swank, it was by implication derogated in the officers' *Field Service Pocket Book.* One reason the British trench system was so haphazard and ramshackle was that it had originally taken form in accord with the official injunction: "The choice of a [defensive] position and its preparation must be made with a view to economizing the power expended on defense in order that the power of offense may be increased." And it was considered really useless to build solid fortifications anyway: "An occasional shell may strike and penetrate the parapet, but in the case of shrapnel the damage to the parapet will be trifling, while in the case of a shell filled with high explosive, the effect will be no worse on a thin parapet than on a thick one. It is, therefore, useless to spend time and labor on making a thick parapet simply to keep out shell." The repeatedly revived hopes for a general breakout and pursuit were another reason why the British trenches were so shabby. A typical soldier's view is George Coppard's:

The whole conduct of our trench warfare seemed to be based on the concept that we, the British, were not stopping in the trenches for long, but were tarrying awhile on the way to Berlin and that very soon we would be chasing Jerry across country. The result, in the long term, meant that we lived a mean and impoverished sort of existence in lousy scratch holes.

In contrast, the German trenches, as the British discovered during the attack on the Somme, were deep, clean, elaborate, and sometimes even comfortable. As Coppard found on the Somme, "Some of the [German] dugouts were thirty feet deep, with as many as sixteen bunk-beds, as well as door bells, water tanks with taps, and cupboards and mirrors." They also had boarded walls, floors, and ceilings; finished wooden staircases; electric light; real kitchens; and wallpaper and overstuffed furniture, the whole protected by steel outer doors. Foreign to the British style was a German dugout of the sort recalled by Ernst Jünger:

At Monchy . . . I was master of an underground dwelling approached by forty steps hewn in the solid chalk, so that even the heaviest shells at this depth made no more than a

pleasant rumble when we sat there over an interminable game of cards. In one wall I had a bed hewn out. . . . At its head hung an electric light so that I could read in comfort till I was sleepy. . . . The whole was shut off from the outer world by a dark-red curtain with rod and rings. . . .

As these examples suggest, there were "national styles" in trenches as in other things. The French trenches were nasty, cynical, efficient, and temporary. Kipling remembered the smell of delicious cooking emanating from some in Alsace. The English were amateur, vague, *ad hoc*, and temporary. The German were efficient, clean, pedantic, and permanent. Their occupants proposed to stay where they were.

Normally the British troops rotated trench duty. After a week of "rest" behind the lines, a unit would move up — at night — to relieve a unit in the front-line trench. After three days to a week or more in that position, the unit would move back for a similar length of time to the support trench, and finally back to the reserve. Then it was time for a week of rest again. In the three lines of trenches the main business of the soldier was to exercise self-control while being shelled. As the poet Louis Simpson has accurately remembered:

Being shelled is the main work of an infantry soldier, which no one talks about. Everyone has his own way of going about it. In general, it means lying face down and contracting your body into as small a space as possible. In novels [*The Naked and the Dead* is an example] you read about soldiers, at such moments, fouling themselves. The opposite is true. As all your parts are contracting, you are more likely to be constipated.

Simpson is recalling the Second War, but he might be recalling the First. While being shelled, the soldier either harbored in a dugout and hoped for something other than a direct hit or made himself as small as possible in a funk-hole. An unlucky sentry or two was supposed to be out in the open trench in all but the worst bombardments, watching through a periscope or loophole for signs of an attack. When only light shelling was in progress, people moved about the trenches freely, and we can get an idea of what life there was like if we posit a typical twenty-four hours in a front-line trench.

The day began about an hour before first light, which often meant at about 4:30. This was the moment for the invariable ritual of morning stand-to (short for the archaic formal command for repelling attack, "Stand to Arms"). Since dawn was the favorite time for launching attacks, at the order to stand-to everyone, officers, men, forward artillery observers, visitors, mounted the fire-step, weapon ready, and peered toward the German line. When it was almost full light and clear that the Germans were not going to attack that morning, everyone "stood down" and began preparing breakfast in small groups. The rations of tea, bread, and bacon, brought up in sandbags during the night, were broken out. The bacon was fried in mess-tin lids over small, and if possible smokeless, fires. If the men were lucky enough to be in a division whose commanding general permitted the issue of the dark and strong government rum, it was doled out from a jar with the traditional iron spoon, each man receiving about two tablespoonsful. Some put it into their tea, but most swallowed it straight. It was a precious thing, and serving it out was almost like a religious ceremonial, as David Jones recalls in *In Parenthesis*, where a corporal is performing the rite:

O have a care — don't spill the precious
O don't jog his hand — ministering;
do take care.
    O please — give the poor bugger elbow room.

Larger quantities might be issued to stimulate troops for an assault, and one soldier remembers what the air smelled like during a British attack: "Pervading the air was the smell of rum and blood." In 1922 one medical officer deposed before a parliamentary committee investigating the phenomenon of "shell shock": "Had it not been for the rum ration I do not think we should have won the war."

During the day the men cleaned weapons and repaired those parts of the trench damaged during the night. Or they wrote letters, deloused themselves, or slept. The officers inspected, encouraged, and strolled about looking nonchalant to inspirit the men. They censored the men's letters and dealt with the quantities of official inquiries brought them daily by runner. How many pipe-fitters had they in their company? Reply immediately. How many hairdressers, chiropodists, bicycle repairmen? Daily "returns" of the amount of ammunition and the quantity of trench stores had to be made. Reports of the nightly casualties had to be sent back. And letters of condolence, which as the war went on became form-letters of condolence, had to be written to the relatives of the killed and wounded. Men went to and fro on sentry duty or working parties, but no one showed himself above the trench. After evening stand-to, the real work began.

Most of it was above ground. Wiring parties repaired the wire in front of the position. Digging parties extended saps toward the enemy. Carrying parties brought up not just rations and mail but the heavy engineering materials needed for the constant repair and improvement of the trenches: timbers, A-frames, duckboards, stakes and wire, corrugated iron, sandbags, tarpaulins, pumping equipment. Bombs and ammunition and flares were carried forward. All this ant-work was illuminated brightly from time to time by German flares and interrupted very frequently by machine gun or artillery fire. Meanwhile night patrols and raiding parties were busy in No Man's Land. As morning approached, there was a nervous bustle to get the jobs done in time, to finish fitting the timbers, filling the sandbags, pounding in the stakes, and then returning mauls and picks and shovels to the Quartermaster Sergeant. By the time of stand-to, nothing human was visible above ground anywhere, but every day each side

161

scrutinized the look of the other's line for significant changes wrought by night.

Flanders and Picardy have always been notorious for dampness. It is not the least of the ironies of the war for the British that their trenches should have been dug where the water-table was the highest and the annual rainfall the most copious. Their trenches were always wet and often flooded several feet deep. Thigh-boots or waders were issued as standard articles of uniform. Wilfred Owen writes his mother from the Somme at the beginning of 1917: "The waders are of course indispensable. In 2½ miles of trench which I waded yesterday there was not one inch of dry ground. There is a mean depth of two feet of water." Pumps worked day and night but to little effect. Rumor held the Germans not only could make it rain when they wanted it to — that is, all the time — but had contrived some shrewd technical method for conducting the water in their lines into the British positions — perhaps piping it underground. Ultimately there was no defense against the water but humor. "Water knee deep and up to the waist in places," one soldier notes in his diary, "Rumors of being relieved by the Grand Fleet." One doesn't want to dwell excessively on such discomforts, but here it will do no harm to try to imagine what, in these conditions, going to the latrine was like.

The men were not the only live things in the line. They were accompanied everywhere by their lice, which the professional delousers in repositions behind the lines, with their steam vats for clothes and hot baths for troops, could do little to eliminate. The entry *lousy* in Eric Partridge's *Dictionary of Slang and Unconventional English* speaks volumes: "Contemptible; mean; filthy.... Standard English till 20th C, when, especially after the Great War, colloquial and used as a mere pejorative." *Lousy* with meaning *full of*, was "originally military" and entered the colloquial word-hoard around 1915: "That ridge is lousy with Fritz."

The famous rats also gave constant trouble. They were big and black, with wet, muddy hair. They fed largely on the flesh of cadavers and on dead horses. One shot them with revolvers or coshed them to death with pick-handles. Their hunger, vigor, intelligence, and courage are recalled in numerous anecdotes. One officer notes from the Ypres Salient: "We are fairly plagued with rats. They have eaten nearly everything in the mess, including the tablecloth and the operations orders! We borrowed a large cat and shut it up at night to exterminate them, and found the place empty next morning. The rats must have eaten it up, bones, fur, and all, and dragged it to their holes."

One can understand rats eating heartily there. It is harder to understand men doing so. The stench of rotten flesh was over everything, hardly repressed by the chloride of lime sprinkled on particularly offensive sites. Dead horses and dead men — and parts of both — were sometimes not buried for months and often simply became an element of parapets and trench walls. You could smell the front line miles before you could see it. Lingering pockets of gas added to the unappetizing atmosphere. Yet men ate three times a day, although what they ate reflected the usual gulf between the ideal and the actual. The propagandist George Adam announced with satisfaction that "the food of the army is based upon the conclusions of a committee, upon which sat several eminent scientists." The result, he asserted, is that the troops are "better fed than they are at home." Officially, each man got daily:

1¼ pounds fresh meat (or 1 pound preserved meat),

1¼ pounds bread,

4 ounces bacon,

3 ounces cheese,

½ pound fresh vegetables (or 2 ounces dried),

together with small amounts of tea, sugar, and jam. But in the trenches there was very seldom fresh meat, not for eating, anyway; instead there was "Bully" (tinned corned-beef) or "Maconochie" (ma-con'-ochie), a tinned meat-and-vegetable stew named after its manufacturer. If they did tend to grow tedious in the long run, both products were surprisingly good. The troops seemed to like the Maconochie best, but the Germans favored the British corned beef, seldom returning from a raid on the British lines without taking back as much as they could carry. On trench duty the British had as little fresh bread as fresh meat. "Pearl Biscuits" were the substitute. They reminded the men of dog biscuits, although, together with the Bully beef, they were popular with the French and Belgian urchins, who ran (or more often strolled) alongside the railway trains bringing troops up to the front, soliciting gifts by shouting, "Tommee! Bull-ee! Bee-skee!" When a company was out of the line, it fed better. It was then serviced by its company cookers — stoves on wheels — and often got something approaching the official ration, as it might also in a particularly somnolent part of the line, when hot food might come up at night in the large covered containers known as Dixies.

Clothing and equipment improved as the war went on, although at the outset there was a terrible dearth and improvisation. During the retreat from Mons, as Frank Richards testifies, "A lot of us had no caps: I was wearing a handkerchief knotted at the four corners — the only headgear I was to wear for some time." Crucial supplies had been omitted: "We had plenty of small-arm ammunition but no rifle-oil or rifle-rag to clean our rifles with. We used to cut pieces off our shirts ... and some of us who had bought small tins of vaseline ... for use on sore heels or chafed legs, used to grease our rifles with that." At the beginning line officers dressed very differently from the men. They wore riding-boots or leather puttees; melodramatically cut riding breeches; and flare-skirted tunics with Sam Browne belts. Discovering that this costume made them special targets in attacks (German gunners were instructed to fire first at the people with the thin knees), by the end they were dressing like the troops, wearing wrap puttees; straight trousers bloused below the knee; Other

Ranks' tunics with inconspicuous insignia, no longer on the cuffs but on the shoulders; and Other Ranks' web belts and haversacks. In 1914 both officers and men wore peaked caps, and it was rakish for officers to remove the grommet for a "Gorblimey" effect. Steel helmets were introduced at the end of 1915, giving the troops, as Sassoon observed, "a Chinese look." Herbert Read found the helmets "the only poetic thing in the British Army, for they are primeval in design and effect, like iron mushrooms." A perceptive observer could date corpses and skeletons lying on disused battlefields by their evolving dress. A month before the end of the war, Major P. H. Pilditch recalls, he

spent some time in the old No Man's Land of four years' duration.... It was a morbid but intensely interesting occupation tracing the various battles amongst the hundreds of skulls, bones and remains scattered thickly about. The progress of our successive attacks could be clearly seen from the types of equipment on the skeletons, soft cloth caps denoting the 1914 and early 1915 fighting, then respirators, then steel helmets marking attack in 1916. Also Australian slouch hats, used in the costly and abortive attack in 1916.

To be in the trenches was to experience an unreal, unforgettable enclosure and constraint, as well as a sense of being unoriented and lost. One saw two things only: the walls of an unlocalized, undifferentiated earth and the sky above. Fourteen years after the war J. R. Ackerley was wandering through an unfrequented part of a town in India. "The streets became narrower and narrower as I turned and turned," he writes, "until I felt I was back in the trenches, the houses upon either side being so much of the same color and substance as the rough ground between." That lost feeling is what struck Major Frank Isherwood, who writes his wife in December, 1914: "The trenches are a labyrinth, I have already lost myself repeatedly.... you can't get out of them and walk about the country or see anything at all but two muddy walls on each side of you." What a survivor of the Salient remembers fifty years later are the walls of dirt and the ceiling of sky, and his eloquent optative cry rises as if he were still imprisoned there: "To be out of this present, ever-present, eternally present misery, this stinking world of sticky, trickling earth ceilinged by a strip of threatening sky." As the only visible theater of variety, the sky becomes all-important. It was the sight of the sky, almost alone, that had the power to persuade a man that he was not already lost in a common grave.

QUESTIONS TO CONSIDER

1   What innovations in weapons and tactics in the Great War made the cavalry and infantry charges of nineteenth century obsolete? What made these innovations so costly in terms of human lives?

2   How were the trench systems of Britain, France, and Germany different? What were the reasons for such differences? Describe the trench philosophy of the British.

3   What was the rum ration? What purpose did it serve in the war? Do you think it played a vital role? Describe the soldiers' life in the trenches — the daily routine, rations, and misery they suffered.

4   Why was the Ypres Salient such a deadly place to be stationed? Describe some of the geographical features of this sector of the British line. Describe no man's land and explain why it was a deadly place to cross.

5   According to the author, what was the experience of being in the trenches? Describe what a soldier saw and felt in them. Did they have a lasting psychological effect on men who served in them?

13

Woodrow Wilson Wouldn't Yield

Thomas A. Bailey

Woodrow Wilson had a horror of violence and war. Why, then, would he lead the United States into a savage conflict like the Great War? The answer lies in Wilson's complex and contradictory character. A former college professor and president of Princeton with a Ph.D. in political economy, Wilson was a conservative Democrat before he won the presidency. Once in office, however, he became a Progressive reformer who embraced women's political rights (to be treated in a subsequent selection) and engineered the most sweeping legislative program since the days of Alexander Hamilton. Despite his spectacular achievements, Wilson was a sensitive, lonely man who wanted "the people to love me." And yet he felt a powerful need, he said, to guard his emotions "from painful overflow." Although his intellectual tradition was British (he extolled the British system of parliamentary government and extolled English conservatives such as Edmund Burke and William Gladstone), his politics were rooted in his southern heritage. A learned, eloquent champion of democracy, he nevertheless shared the racial prejudice that prevailed among white Americans of his generation, and as president he began a policy of discrimination against African Americans in federal employment.

In many ways, Wilson's foreign policy was even more paradoxical. He abhorred violence, yet he was inclined to use moralistic, gunboat diplomacy in dealing with Latin America: he transformed Nicaragua into a veritable United States protectorate, twice sent American forces into Mexico, and ordered full-scale military occupation of Haiti and the Dominican Republic. Although Wilson convinced himself that high moral purpose justified such intervention, it left a legacy of bitterness and distrust in Latin America.

Finally, despite the pacific liberalism he had learned from British intellectuals, Wilson led the United States into the Great War on a messianic crusade to make that conflict "a war to end all wars." To achieve that goal, he devised the League of Nations, a kind of world parliament, which was the sanest blueprint for world peace anyone had yet contrived. But Wilson's noble dream ended in a crushing defeat when the United States Senate rejected the League of Nations and America turned away from the idealism that had produced it. In this selection, diplomatic historian Thomas A. Bailey deftly describes how the clash of Wilson and his adversaries, combined with the sentiment of the times, brought about America's rejection of the League. In the end, Americans were not prepared for the responsibilities of world leadership that Wilson had thrust upon them.

GLOSSARY

BORAH, SENATOR WILLIAM E.   An isolationist Republican from Idaho who vowed to kill Wilson's treaty in the Senate.

CLEMENCEAU, GEORGES   The "French realist" at the Versailles peace conference; like David Lloyd George and Vittorio Orlando, he was "more interested in imperialism" than in Wilsonian idealism.

FOURTEEN POINTS   Wilson's blueprint for world peace and "the noblest expression" of his idealism; the last and most important point called for a league of nations, a kind of parliament of humankind, to resolve conflicts among nations and avoid future wars.

JINGOISM   Bellicose patriotism.

JOHNSON, SENATOR HIRAM W.   An isolationist Republican from California who joined the Senate opposition to Wilson's treaty.

LLOYD GEORGE, DAVID   British delegate to the Versailles peace conference.

LODGE, SENATOR HENRY CABOT   Republican and Boston Brahmin who "broke the back" of Wilson's treaty by getting a series of crippling reservations added to it in the Senate.

MONROE DOCTRINE   Promulgated by President James Monroe in 1823, it warned that the Western Hemisphere was closed to colonization by European powers and stated that America would stay out of Europe's wars.

ORLANDO, VITTORIO   Italian delegate to the Versailles peace conference (Italy had fought on the side of France and Great Britain in the First World War).

TREATY OF VERSAILLES (1919)   Formally ended the First World War; only about four of the Fourteen Points found their way into the treaty, as "the iron hand of circumstance had forced Wilson to compromise away many of his points in order to salvage his fourteenth point, the League of Nations."

The story of America's rejection of the League of Nations revolves largely around the personality and character of Thomas Woodrow Wilson, the twenty-eighth President of the United States. Born in Virginia and reared in Yankee-gutted Georgia and the Carolinas, Wilson early developed a burning hatred of war and a passionate attachment to the Confederate-embraced principle of self-determination for minority peoples. From the writings of Thomas Jefferson he derived much of his democratic idealism and his invincible faith in the judgment of the masses, if properly informed. From his stiff-backed Scotch Presbyterian forebears, he inherited a high degree of inflexibility; from his father, a dedicated Presbyterian minister, he learned a stern moral code that would tolerate no compromise with wrong, as defined by Woodrow Wilson.

As a leading academician who had first failed at law, he betrayed a contempt for "money-grubbing" lawyers, many of whom sat in the Senate, and an arrogance toward lesser intellects, including those of the "pygmy-minded" senators. As a devout Christian keenly aware of the wickedness of this world, he emerged as a fighting reformer, whether as president of Princeton, governor of New Jersey, or President of the United States.

As a war leader, Wilson was superb. Holding aloft the torch of idealism in one hand and the flaming sword of righteousness in the other, he aroused the masses to a holy crusade. We would fight a war to end wars; we would make the world safe for democracy. The phrase was not a mockery then. The American people, with an amazing display of self-sacrifice, supported the war effort unswervingly.

The noblest expression of Wilson's idealism was his Fourteen Points address to Congress in January,

From T. A. Bailey, "Wilson and the League," *American Heritage,* June/July 1957, Vol. 8, No. 4. Reprinted by permission of *American Heritage* magazine, a division of Forbes Inc. Copyright © Forbes, Inc., 1957.

1918. It compressed his war aims into punchy, placard-like paragraphs, expressly designed for propaganda purposes. It appealed tremendously to oppressed peoples everywhere by promising such goals as the end of secret treaties, freedom of the seas, the removal of economic barriers, a reduction of arms burdens, a fair adjustment of colonial claims, and self-determination for oppressed minorities. In Poland university men would meet on the streets of Warsaw, clasp hands, and soulfully utter one word, "Wilson." In remote regions of Italy peasants burned candles before poster portraits of the mighty new prophet arisen in the West.

The fourteenth and capstone point was a league of nations, designed to avert future wars. The basic idea was not original with Wilson; numerous thinkers, including Frenchmen and Britons, had been working on the concept long before he embraced it. Even Henry Cabot Lodge, the Republican senator from Massachusetts, had already spoken publicly in favor of *a* league of nations. But the more he heard about the Wilsonian League of Nations, the more critical of it he became.

A knowledge of the Wilson-Lodge feud is basic to an understanding of the tragedy that unfolded. Tall, slender, aristocratically bewhiskered, Dr. Henry Cabot Lodge (Ph.D., Harvard), had published a number of books and had been known as the scholar in politics before the appearance of Dr. Woodrow Wilson (Ph.D., Johns Hopkins). The Presbyterian professor had gone further in both scholarship and politics than the Boston Brahmin, whose mind was once described as resembling the soil of his native New England: "naturally barren but highly cultivated." Wilson and Lodge, two icy men, developed a mutual antipathy, which soon turned into freezing hatred.

The German armies, reeling under the blows of the Allies, were ready to give in by November, 1918. The formal armistice terms stipulated that Germany was to be guaranteed a peace based on the Fourteen Points, with two reservations concerning freedom of the seas and reparations.

Meanwhile the American people had keyed themselves up to the long-awaited march on Berlin; eager voices clamored to hang the Kaiser. Thus the sudden end of the shooting left inflamed patriots with a sense of frustration and letdown that boded ill for Wilson's policies. The red-faced Theodore Roosevelt, Lodge's intimate of long standing, cried that peace should be dictated by the chatter of machine guns and not the clicking of typewriters.

Wilson now towered at the dizzy pinnacle of his popularity and power. He had emerged as the moral arbiter of the world and the hope of all peoples for a better tomorrow. But regrettably his wartime sureness of touch began to desert him, and he made a series of costly fumbles. He was so preoccupied with reordering the world, someone has said, that he reminded one of the baseball player who knocks the ball into the bleachers and then forgets to touch home plate.

First came his brutally direct appeal for a Democratic Congress in October, 1918. The voters trooped to the polls the next month and, by a narrow margin, returned a Republican Congress. Wilson had not only goaded his partisan foes to fresh outbursts of fury, but he had unnecessarily staked his prestige on the outcome — and lost. When the Allied leaders met at the Paris peace table, he was the only one not entitled to be there, at least on the European basis of a parliamentary majority.

Wilson next announced that he was sailing for France, presumably to use his still enormous prestige to fashion an enduring peace. At this time no President had ever gone abroad, and Republicans condemned the decision as evidence of a dangerous Messiah complex — of a desire, as former President Taft put it, "to hog the whole show."

The naming of the remaining five men to the peace delegation caused partisans further anguish. Only one, Henry White, was a Republican, and he was a minor figure at that. The Republicans, now the majority party, complained that they had been good enough to die on the battlefield; they ought to have at least an equal voice at the peace table. Nor were any United States senators included, even though they would have a final whack at the treaty. Wilson did not have much respect for the "bungalow-minded" senators, and if he took one, the logical choice would be Henry Cabot Lodge. There were already enough feuds brewing at Paris without taking one along.

Doubtless some of the Big Business Republicans were out to "get" the President who had been responsible for the hated reformist legislation of 1913–14. If he managed to put over the League of Nations, his prestige would soar to new heights. He might even arrange — unspeakable thought! — to be elected again and again and again. Much of the partisan smog that finally suffocated the League would have been cleared away if Wilson had publicly declared, as he was urged to do, that in no circumstances would he run again. But he spurned such counsel, partly because he was actually receptive to the idea of a third term.

The American President, hysterically hailed by European crowds as "Voovro Veelson," came to the Paris peace table in January, 1919, to meet with Lloyd George of Britain, Clemenceau of France, and Orlando of Italy. To his dismay, he soon discovered that they were far more interested in imperialism than in idealism. When they sought to carve up the territorial booty without regard for the colonials, contrary to the Fourteen Points, the stern-jawed Presbyterian moralist interposed a ringing veto. The end result was the mandate system — a compromise between idealism and imperialism that turned out to be more imperialistic than idealistic.

Wilson's overriding concern was the League of Nations. He feared that if he did not get it completed and embedded in the treaty, the imperialistic powers might sidetrack it. Working at an incredible pace after hours, Wilson headed the commission that drafted the League Covenant in ten meetings and some thirty hours. He then persuaded the conference not only to approve the hastily constructed

Covenant but to incorporate it bodily in the peace treaty. In support of his adopted brain child he spoke so movingly on one occasion that even the hard-boiled reporters forgot to take notes.

Wilson now had to return hurriedly to the United States to sign bills and take care of other pressing business. Shortly after his arrival the mounting Republican opposition in the Senate flared up angrily. On March 4, 1919, 39 senators or senators-elect — more than enough to defeat the treaty — published a round robin to the effect that they would not approve the League in its existing form. This meant that Wilson had to return to Paris, hat in hand, and there weaken his position by having to seek modifications.

Stung to the quick, he struck back at his senatorial foes in an indiscreet speech in New York just before his departure. He boasted that when he brought the treaty back from Paris, the League Covenant would not only be tied in but so thoroughly tied in that it could not be cut out without killing the entire pact. The Senate, he assumed, would not dare to kill the treaty of peace outright.

At Paris the battle was now joined in deadly earnest. Clemenceau, the French realist, had little use for Wilson, the American idealist. "God gave us the ten commandments and we broke them," he reportedly sneered. "Wilson gave us the Fourteen Points — we shall see." Clemenceau's most disruptive demand was for the German Rhineland; but Wilson, the champion of self-determination, would never consent to handing several million Germans over to the tender mercies of the French. After a furious struggle, during which Wilson was stricken with influenza, Clemenceau was finally persuaded to yield the Rhineland and other demands in return for a security treaty. Under it, Britain and America agreed to come to the aid of France in the event of another unprovoked aggression. The United States Senate short-sightedly pigeonholed the pact, and France was left with neither the Rhineland nor security.

Two other deadlocks almost broke up the conference. Italy claimed the Adriatic port of Fiume, an area inhabited chiefly by Yugoslavs. In his battle for self-determination, Wilson dramatically appealed over the head of the Italian delegation to the Italian people, whereupon the delegates went home in a huff to receive popular endorsement. The final adjustment was a hollow victory for self-determination.

The politely bowing Japanese now stepped forward to press their economic claims to China's Shantung [province], which they had captured from the Germans early in the war. But to submit 30,000,000 Chinese to the influence of the Japanese would be another glaring violation of self-determination. The Japanese threatened to bolt the conference, as the Italians had already done, with consequent jeopardy to the League. In the end, Wilson reluctantly consented to a compromise that left the Japanese temporarily in possession of Shantung.

The Treaty of Versailles, as finally signed in June, 1919, included only about four of the original Fourteen Points. The Germans, with considerable justification, gave vent to loud cries of betrayal. But the iron hand of circumstance had forced Wilson to compromise away many of his points in order to salvage his fourteenth point, the League of Nations, which he hoped would iron out the injustices that had crept into the treaty. He was like the mother who throws her younger children to the pursuing wolves in order to save her sturdy first-born son.

Bitter opposition to the completed treaty had already begun to form in America. Tens of thousands of homesick and disillusioned soldiers were pouring home, determined to let Europe "stew in its own juice." The wartime idealism, inevitably doomed to slump, was now plunging to alarming depths. The beloved Allies had apparently turned out to be greedy imperialists. The war to make the world safe for democracy had obviously fallen dismally short of the goal. And at the end of the war to end wars there were about twenty conflicts of varying intensity being waged all over the globe.

The critics increased their clamor. Various foreign groups, including the Irish-Americans and the

This contemporary cartoon suggests that President Wilson's cherished hopes for a world League of Nations were as fragile and ephemeral as a soap bubble. In the end, a weak League of Nations took shape in Europe without the membership of the United States, whose people and their elected representatives, clinging to isolationism and suffering from postwar disillusionment, could not agree to adopt the charter. (Stock Montage, Inc.)

Italian-Americans, were complaining that the interests of the old country had been neglected. Professional liberals, for example the editors of the *New Republic,* were denouncing the treaty as too harsh. The illiberals, far more numerous, were denouncing it as not harsh enough. The Britain-haters, like the buzz-saw Senator James Reed of Missouri and the acid-penned [journalist] William R. Hearst, were proclaiming that England had emerged with undue influence. Such ultranationalists as the isolationist Senator William E. Borah of Idaho were insisting that the flag of no superstate should be hoisted above the glorious Stars and Stripes.

When the treaty came back from Paris, with the league firmly riveted in, Senator Lodge despaired of stopping it.

"What are you going to do? It's hopeless," he complained to Borah. "All the newspapers in my state are for it." The best that he could hope for was to add a few reservations. The Republicans had been given little opportunity to help write the treaty in Paris; they now felt that they were entitled to do a little rewriting in Washington.

Lodge deliberately adopted the technique of delay. As chairman of the powerful Senate Committee on Foreign Relations, he consumed two weeks by reading aloud the entire pact of 264 pages, even though it had already been printed. He then held time-consuming public hearings, during which persons with unpronounceable foreign names aired their grievances against the pact.

Lodge finally adopted the strategy of tacking reservations onto the treaty, and he was able to achieve his goal because of the peculiar composition of the Senate. There were 49 Republicans and 47 Democrats. The Republicans consisted of about twenty "strong reservationists" like Lodge, about twelve "mild reservationists" like future Secretary of State Kellogg, and about a dozen "irreconcilables." This last group was headed by Senator Borah and the no less isolationist Senator Hiram Johnson of California, a fiery spellbinder.

The Lodge reservations finally broke the back of the treaty. They were all added by a simple majority vote, even though the entire pact would have to be approved by a two-thirds vote. The dozen or so Republican mild reservationists were not happy over the strong Lodge reservations, and if Wilson had deferred sufficiently to these men, he might have persuaded them to vote with the Democrats. Had they done so, the Lodge reservations could have all been voted down, and a milder version, perhaps acceptable to Wilson, could have been substituted.

As the hot summer of 1919 wore on, Wilson became increasingly impatient with the deadlock in the Senate. Finally he decided to take his case to the country, as he had so often done in response to his ingrained "appeal habit." He had never been robust, and his friends urged him not to risk breaking himself down in a strenuous barnstorming campaign. But Wilson, having made up his mind, was unyielding. He had sent American boys into battle in a war to end wars; why should he not risk his life in battle for a League to end wars?

Wilson's spectacular tour met with limited enthusiasm in the Middle West, the home of several million German-Americans. After him, like baying bloodhounds, trailed Senators Borah and Johnson, sometimes speaking in the same halls a day or so later, to the accompaniment of cries of "Impeach him, impeach him!" But on the Pacific Coast and in the Rocky Mountain area the enthusiasm for Wilson and the League was overwhelming. The high point —and the breaking point—of the trip came at Pueblo, Colorado, where Wilson, with tears streaming down his cheeks, pleaded for his beloved League of Nations.

That night Wilson's weary body rebelled. He was whisked back to Washington, where he suffered a stroke that paralyzed the left side of his body. For weeks he lay in bed, a desperately sick man. The Democrats, who had no first-rate leader in the Senate, were left rudderless. With the wisdom of hindsight, we may say that Wilson might better have stayed in Washington, providing the necessary leadership and compromising with the opposition, insofar as compromise was possible. A good deal of compromise had already gone into the treaty, and a little more might have saved it.

Senator Lodge, cold and decisive, was now in the driver's seat. His Fourteen Reservations, a sardonic parallel to Wilson's Fourteen Points, had been whipped into shape. Most of them now seem either irrelevant, inconsequential, or unnecessary; some of them merely reaffirmed principles and policies, including the Monroe Doctrine, already guaranteed by the treaty or by the Constitution.

But Wilson, who hated the sound of Lodge's

name, would have no part of the Lodge reservations. They would, he insisted, emasculate the entire treaty. Yet the curious fact is that he had privately worked out his own set of reservations with the Democratic leader in the Senate, Gilbert M. Hitchcock, and these differed only in slight degree from those of Senator Lodge.

As the hour approached for the crucial vote in the Senate, it appeared that public opinion had veered a little. Although confused by the angry debate, it still favored the treaty—but with some safeguarding reservations. A stubborn Wilson was unwilling to accept this disheartening fact, or perhaps he was not made aware of it. Mrs. Wilson, backed by the President's personal physician, Dr. Cary Grayson, kept vigil at his bedside to warn the few visitors that disagreeable news might shock the invalid into a relapse.

In this highly unfavorable atmosphere, Senator Hitchcock had two conferences with Wilson on the eve of the Senate voting. He suggested compromise on a certain point, but Wilson shot back, "Let Lodge compromise!" Hitchcock conceded that the Senator would have to give ground but suggested that the White House might also hold out the olive branch. "Let Lodge hold out the olive branch," came the stern reply. On this inflexible note, and with Mrs. Wilson's anxiety mounting, the interview ended.

The Senate was ready for final action on November 19, 1919. At the critical moment Wilson sent a fateful letter to the Democratic minority in the Senate, urging them to vote down the treaty with the hated Lodge reservations so that a true ratification could be achieved. The Democrats, with more than the necessary one-third veto, heeded the voice of their crippled leader and rejected the treaty with reservations. The Republicans, with more than the necessary one-third veto, rejected the treaty without reservations.

The country was shocked by this exhibition of legislative paralysis. About four fifths of the senators professed to favor the treaty in some form, yet they were unable to agree on anything. An aroused public opinion forced the Senate to reconsider, and Lodge secretly entered into negotiations with the Democrats in an effort to work out acceptable reservations. He was making promising progress when Senator Borah got wind of his maneuvers through an anonymous telephone call. The leading irreconcilables hastily summoned a council of war, hauled Lodge before them, and bluntly accused him of treachery. Deeply disturbed, the Massachusetts Senator said: "Well, I suppose I'll have to resign as majority leader."

"No, by God!" burst out Borah. "You won't have a chance to resign! On Monday, I'll move for the election of a new majority leader and give the reasons for my action." Faced with an upheaval within his party such as had insured Wilson's election in 1912, Lodge agreed to drop his backstage negotiations.

The second-chance vote in the Senate came on March 19, 1920. Wilson again directed his loyal Democratic following to reject the treaty, disfigured as it was by the hateful Lodge reservations. But by this time there was no other form in which the pact could possibly be ratified. Twenty-one realistic Democrats turned their backs on Wilson and voted Yea; 23 loyal Democrats, mostly from the rock-ribbed South, joined with the irreconcilables to do the bidding of the White House. The treaty, though commanding a simple majority this time of 49 Yeas to 35 Nays, failed of the necessary two-thirds vote.

Wilson, struggling desperately against the Lodge reservation trap, had already summoned the nation in "solemn referendum" to give him a vote in favor of the League in the forthcoming presidential election of 1920. His hope was that he could then get the treaty approved without reservations. But this course was plainly futile. Even if all the anti-League senators up for re-election in 1920 had been replaced by the pro-League senators, Wilson would still have lacked the necessary two-thirds majority for an unreserved treaty.

The American people were never given a chance to express their views directly on the League of Nations. All they could do was vote either for the weak Democratic candidate, [James M.] Cox, who stood for the League, and the stuffed-shirt Republican candidate, [Warren G.] Harding, who wobbled all over the map of the League arguments. If the electorate had been given an opportunity to express itself, a powerful majority probably would have favored the world organization, with at least some reservations. But wearied of Wilsonism, idealism, and self-denial, and confused by the wordy fight over the treaty, the voters rose up and swept Harding into the White House. The winner had been more anti-League than pro-League, and his prodigious plurality of 7,000,000 votes condemned the League to death in America.

What caused this costly failure of American statesmanship?

Wilson's physical collapse intensifed his native stubbornness. A judicious compromise here and there no doubt would have secured Senate approval of the treaty, though of course with modifications. Wilson believed that in any event the Allies would reject the Lodge reservations. The probabilities are that the Allies would have worked out some kind of acceptance, so dire was their need of America's economic support, but Wilson never gave them a chance to act.

Senator Lodge was also inflexible, but prior to the second rejection he was evidently trying to get the treaty through — on his own terms. As majority leader of the Republicans, his primary task was to avoid another fatal split in his party. Wilson's primary task was to get the pact approved. From a purely political point of view, the Republicans had little to gain by engineering ratification of a Democratic treaty.

The two-thirds rule in the Senate, often singled out as the culprit, is of little relevance. Wilson almost certainly would have pigeonholed the treaty if it had passed with the Lodge reservations appended.

Wilson's insistence that the League be wedded to the treaty actually contributed to the final defeat of both. Either would have had a better chance if it had not been burdened by the enemies of the other. The United Nations, one should note, was set up in 1945 independently of any peace treaty.

Finally, American public opinion in 1919–20 was not yet ready for the onerous new world responsibilities that had suddenly been forced upon it. The isolationist tradition was still potent, and it was fortified by postwar disillusionment. If the sovereign voters had spoken out for the League with one voice, they almost certainly would have had their way. A treaty without reservations, or with a few reservations acceptable to Wilson, doubtless would have slipped through the Senate. But the American people were one war short of accepting leadership in a world organization for peace.

QUESTIONS TO CONSIDER

1   Woodrow Wilson's personal popularity was at an all-time high when he went to Paris in 1919. How had he achieved his vast international prestige? What happened to diminish it?

2   What prevailing sentiment did Wilson, the idealist, find among the representatives of European countries at the negotiating table in Versailles? What had happened to the "war to end all wars," the goal of which was to "make the world safe for democracy"? How did the Allied powers eventually compromise between imperialism and idealism?

3   Outline the process by which partisan politics, petty squabbles, and back-room maneuvering eventually led Congress to vote down the 1919 peace treaty and with it the League of Nations. What role did Henry Cabot Lodge play in the American rejection of the League? What does historian Thomas A. Bailey think Wilson's illness, coupled with his poor judgment on several occasions, contributed to the debacle in Congress over the treaty?

4   What does Bailey think would have happened if the American people had been given a chance to vote for the League? What specific conclusions does he reach about the collapse of the treaty and the failure of Wilsonian idealism in America and Europe?

5   Discuss the ambivalence of Americans in regard to the world leadership role that became available to them just after the First World War. What became of the vociferous jingoistic spirit that had brought about the Spanish-American War and the annexation of territories in the Pacific? What does Bailey mean when he says that "the American people were one war short of accepting leadership in a world organization for peace"? Imagine a world in which the young and powerful United States had joined the League of Nations in 1921. How might twentieth-century history have been rewritten?

THE TWENTIES

14

Henry Ford: Symbol of an Age

RODERICK NASH

The election of Warren G. Harding as president reflected a massive popular reaction against the missionary idealism of Woodrow Wilson and the reformist zeal of the Progressive era. Harding would take the country back to "normalcy," so that Americans might continue their "normal, onward way." Essentially, this meant that federal regulation of industry would be reduced to a minimum, that the business of government, as Calvin Coolidge put it, would be big business.

The popular stereotype of the 1920s is that it was a decade of political corruption, speculative orgies, violence, and the last happy fling before the Great Depression crushed American innocence. But in reality this decade of "normalcy" was a good deal more complex than that. True, business consolidation under Republican rule continued throughout the decade. True, excessive and irresponsible speculation on the New York Stock Exchange culminated in the crash of 1929. True, organized crime was widespread, and gang wars rocked Chicago and New York. And true, a revolution in manners and morals challenged traditional standards and profoundly upset Americans who clung to the old morality.

Yet for many contemporaries, the 1920s were a time of exhilarating hope and high expectation for the United States. In fact, a number of intellectuals found much in American life to celebrate. Most optimistic of all were the businesspeople, who believed they were living in a new era — a time not only of conservative Republican leadership in Washington but of striking innovation and change in business itself. As industrial officials happily observed, corporate managers were bringing scientific procedures and efficient techniques to industry. This change, they contended, would raise production so high that poverty would soon be eliminated and the American dream of abundance for all would be attained at last. Their expectations, alas, perished in the crash of 1929 and the ensuing Depression, the worst the country had ever known.

During the 1920s, however, the United States seemed enormously prosperous, and the American businessperson enjoyed new preeminence in American life. One businessman became a leading figure of the decade. Indeed, his technological genius, love of country, and old-fashioned Americanism made him a folk hero to a large segment of American society. This was car maker Henry Ford, who introduced the first car built for the common person — the Model T — and whose technique of assembly-line production revolutionized American technology. What Ford wrought, as David Halberstam has said, also profoundly altered the way Americans lived: it made them far more mobile than they had been in the railroad age, and it created a culture of leisure in which people thought as much about recreation as they did about their jobs. As we shall see in a subsequent selection, the automobile dramatically changed American customs of courtship.

Ironically, Ford himself despised most of the social changes he helped bring about. A champion of the Protestant work ethic, he abhorred the very idea of leisure. "Work," he contended, "is the salvation of the race, morally, physically, socially. Work does more than get us our living; it gets us our life." He could be remarkably contradictory and unpredictable. He introduced the $5 wage for an eight-hour day (which revolutionized labor policy in industrial America) and yet opposed the union movement. He owned a fifty-six-room mansion and built the Ford Motor Company into what one author described as the biggest "family-owned industrial empire in the world," accumulating a total of $1 billion in profits, and yet he claimed to care little for material things and pleasures. "I have never known," he said, "what to do with money after my expenses were paid." In the end, he donated $40 million to philanthropic enterprises. He considered himself a pacifist, so much so that in 1915 he dispatched a "peace ship" to Europe in a futile if honorable attempt to stop the First World War. Yet this same man had what Roderick Nash calls a rural, "Bible-belt morality." He expatiated on the evils of jazz (it was all "monkey talk" and "jungle squeals") and blamed it and the new dances on a Jewish conspiracy. In fact, he published anti-Semitic diatribes in his Dearborn, Michigan, newspaper (he did retract his anti-Semitic statements in 1927).

The key to Ford's contradictory mind, as Nash says in the next selection, was ambivalence. He was both "old and new." He looked backward and forward at the same time, defending technology while extolling the old rural values and attitudes of a bygone era. In this respect, he symbolized the America of his age — a changing, industrial America that longed for the security of the old days as it struggled with the complexities of the new.

GLOSSARY

ALGER, HORATIO   Gilded Age author whose heroes rose from poverty to greatness and thus fulfilled the "American dream."

FORDISMUS   German word for Ford's "revolutionary mass-production techniques."

McGUFFEY READER   Its "moral-coated language lessons" in such stories as "The Hare and the Tortoise" were the staple of Ford's academic diet.

MODEL T   Ford's first automobile, built for the masses.

Few names were better known to Americans from 1917 to 1930 than that of Henry Ford. Whether one read his publications,[1] or followed his headline-making public life, or merely drove the car his company manufactured, Ford was inescapable in the twenties. Indeed it is possible to think of these years as the automobile age and Henry Ford as its czar. The flivver, along with the flask and the flapper, seemed to represent the 1920s in the minds of its people as well as its historians.

Cars symbolized change. They upset familiar patterns of living, working, recreating, even thinking. Much of the roar of the twenties came from the internal combustion engine. While providing portable bedrooms in which to enjoy the decade's alleged sexual freedom, cars also assisted gangsters and bootleggers in getting away. The image of two of them in every garage helped elect a President in 1928. The rise of widespread use of the automobile, in a word, contributed significantly to setting the twenties apart. And Henry Ford, calling machinery the "new Messiah" (as he did in 1929), seemed to herald the new era.

Beneath the surface, however, such generalizations ring hollow. Neither Ford nor the twenties merited the clichés with which each has been so frequently discussed. In the case of the man, both old and new mingled in his mind. On the one hand Ford was a builder and bulwark of the modern, mechanized nation; on the other he devoted a remarkable amount of effort and expense to sustaining

---

From pp. 154–163 of *The Nervous Generation: American Thought, 1917–1930* by Roderick Nash. Published by Rand-McNally Publishing Company, Chicago. © 1970 by Roderick Nash. Reprinted by permission of Roderick Nash.

[1]In all probability Henry Ford did not actually write the numerous books, pamphlets, and articles associated with his name and attributed to him in this chapter. He was not a literary man; his critics even alleged he could not read! But Ford could pay people to express his opinions for him, and there is no reason to think that the ideas these writers recorded were not those of their employer.

Henry Ford at the peak of his power, about 1914. As Nash observed, Henry Ford was a "plain, honest, old-fashioned billionaire" and "technological genius" who fretted about the new morality of the Jazz Age, ridiculing jazz itself as "monkey talk" and "jungle squeals" and blaming illicit liquor on a Jewish conspiracy. Still, despite his rural outlook and biblical virtues, Ford was one of the most popular Americans of the Roaring Twenties. (Collection of Greenfield Village and Henry Ford Museum, Dearborn, Michigan)

old-fashioned America. In fact, the nostalgic, backward-looking Henry Ford repeatedly deplored the very conditions that Ford the revolutionary industrialist did so much to bring about. This ambivalence did not signify a lack of values so much as a superfluity. His faith was strong if bigoted and contradictory. His prescriptions for America were clear if

simple-minded. He seemed to the masses to demonstrate that there could be change without disruption, and in so doing he eased the twenties' tensions. "The average citizen," editorialized the *New Republic* in 1923, "sees Ford as a sort of enlarged crayon portrait of himself; the man able to fulfill his own suppressed desires, who has achieved enormous riches, fame and power without departing from the pioneer-and-homespun tradition." In this nervous clinging to old values even while undermining them Ford was indeed a "crayon portrait" of his age.

But was Ford typical of the twenties? Can he really be said to symbolize the age? He was, after all, in his middle fifties when the decade began. However, a great many Americans were also middle-aged in the 1920s, far more in fact than the twenty-year-old collegians who have hitherto characterized these years. And at one point even a group of college students ranked Ford as the third greatest figure of all time, behind Napoleon and Jesus Christ.

The Dearborn, Michigan, into which Henry Ford was born in 1863 was a small farming community only a generation removed from the frontier. Both sides of the Ford family had agrarian backgrounds, and the children grew up on the farm. Henry's formal education began and ended in the Scotch Settlement School which he attended for eight years. The staple of his academic diet was the McGuffey reader with its moral-coated language lessons. When Ford left school to become an apprentice mechanic in Detroit, he also left the farm. But the farm never left Henry. Agrarian ideas and values shaped his thought even as he became an industrial king.

The 1880s for Ford were a time of aimlessness, his only real interest being in tinkering with watches and other engines. In 1892 he joined the Edison Company in Detroit as an engineer. During his spare time he struggled with the problem of building a gasoline engine compact enough to power a moving vehicle. By 1896 Ford had his automobile. Soon he had it doing ninety miles per hour! It required seven years more, however, for him to secure the necessary financial and administrative backing to launch the Ford Motor Company. The rest was pure Horatio Alger.

The first Model T appeared in 1908, and it soon made good Ford's boast that he could build a car for the masses. Six thousand sold the first year. Six years later, after the introduction of assembly line production, the figure was 248,000. From May to December 1920 almost 700,000 Model Ts rolled out of the Ford plants. The total for 1921 was one million. In 1923, 57 percent of all cars manufactured in the United States were Fords. Three years later the Ford Motor Company produced its thirteen millionth car. From the perspective of efficient production the Ford organization was also something of a miracle. In 1913 it required twelve hours to make a car. The following year, after the introduction of the assembly line techniques, the figure dropped to ninety-three minutes. In 1920 Ford achieved his long-time dream of building one car for every minute of the working day. And still he was unsatisfied. On October 31, 1925, the Ford Motor Company manufactured 9,109 Model Ts, one every ten seconds. This was the high point, and competition was rising to challenge Ford's preeminence, but by the end of the twenties Henry Ford was a legend, a folk hero, and reputedly the richest man who ever lived. Transcending the role of automobile manufacturer, he had become an international symbol of the new industrialism. The Germans coined a word to describe the revolutionary mass production techniques: *Fordismus.* At home Ford's popularity reached the point where he could be seriously considered a presidential possibility for the election of 1924.

Fortunately for the historian of his thought, if not always for himself, Henry Ford had a propensity for forthrightly stating his opinions on a wide variety of subjects outside his field of competence. He also had the money to publish and otherwise implement his ideas. The resulting intellectual portrait was that of a mind steeped in traditional Americanism. For Ford agrarian simplicity, McGuffey morality, and Algerian determination were sacred objects. Nationalism was writ large over all Ford did, and America was great because of its heritage of freedom, fairness, and hard, honest work. Ford's confidence in the beneficence of old-fashioned virtues verged on the fanatical. The "spirit of '76," equal opportunity democracy, rugged individualism, the home, and motherhood were Ford's touchstones of reality. He deified pioneer ethics and values. "More men are beaten than fail," he declared in 1928. "It is not wisdom they need, or money, or brilliance, or pull, but just plain gristle and bone." A decade earlier "Mr. Ford's Page" in the *Dearborn Independent* stated that "one of the great things about the American people is that they are pioneers." This idea led easily to American messianism. "No one can contemplate the nation to which we belong," the editorial continued, "without realizing the distinctive prophetic character of its obvious mission to the world. We are pioneers. We are pathfinders. We are the roadbuilders. We are the guides, the vanguards of Humanity." Theodore Roosevelt and Woodrow Wilson had said as much, but Ford was writing *after* the war that allegedly ended the nation's innocence and mocked its mission.

Ford's intense commitment to the traditional American faith led him to suspect and ultimately to detest whatever was un-American. The same loyalties compelled him to search for explanations for the unpleasant aspects of the American 1920s that exonerated the old-time, "native" citizen. The immigrant, and particularly the Jew, were primary targets of Ford's fire. In editorial after editorial in the *Dearborn Independent* and in several books Ford argued that aliens who had no knowledge of "the principles which have made our civilization" were responsible for its "marked deterioration" in the 1920s. They were, moreover, determined to take over the country if not the world. Spurred by such fears, Ford became a subscriber to the tired legend of an international Jewish conspiracy. When he couldn't find sufficient evidence for such a plot, Ford dispatched a number of special detectives to probe the affairs of prominent Jews and collect documentation. The search resulted in the "discovery" of the so-called "Protocols of the Learned Elders of Zion," an alleged exposition of the scheme by which the Jews planned to overthrow Gentile domination. Although the "Protocols" was exposed as a forgery in 1921, Ford continued to use the spurious document to substantiate his anti-Semitism until late in the decade. Everything wrong with modern American civilization, from the corruption of music to the corruption of baseball, was attributed to Jewish influence. Unable to admit that America as a whole might be blamed for its problems, unwilling to question the beneficence of time-honored ways, Ford searched for a scapegoat. He found it in the newcomers who, he believed, had no conception of or appreciation for American ideals.

The tension in Henry Ford's thought between old and new, between a belief in progress and a tendency to nostalgia, is dramatically illustrated in his attitude toward farming and farmers. On the one hand he believed farm life to be a ceaseless round of inefficient drudgery. Indeed, he had abundant personal evidence, remarking at one point, "I have traveled ten thousand miles behind a plow. I hated the grueling grind of farm work." With the incentive of sparing others this painful experience, Ford addressed himself to the problem of industrializing agriculture. The farmer, in Ford's opinion, should become a technician and a businessman. Tractors (Ford's, of course) should replace horses. Mechanization would make it possible to produce in twenty-five working days what formerly required an entire year. Fences would come down and vast economies of scale take place. Ford's modern farmer would not even need to live on his farm but instead could commute from a city home. To give substance to these ideals Ford bought and operated with astonishing success a nine-thousand-acre farm near Dearborn.

Still Ford, the "Father of Modern Agriculture," as he has been dubbed, was only part of the man. He also retained a strong streak of old-fashioned, horse-and-buggy agrarianism. Farming, from this stand-

point, was more than a challenge in production; it was a moral act. Constantly in the twenties, even while he was helping make it possible, Ford branded the modern city a "pestiferous growth." He delighted in contrasting the "unnatural," "twisted," and "cooped up" lives of city-dwellers with the "wholesome" life of "independence" and "sterling honesty" that the farm environment offered. In Ford's view the importance of cities in the nation's development had been greatly exaggerated. Early in the 1920s the *Dearborn Independent* editorialized: "when we all stand up and sing, 'My Country 'Tis of Thee,' we seldom think of the cities. Indeed, in that old national hymn there are no references to the city at all. It sings of rocks and rivers and hills — the great American Out-of-Doors. And that is really The Country. That is, the country is THE Country. The real United States lies outside the cities."

As such a manifesto suggests, a bias toward nature and rural conditions was an important element in Henry Ford's thought. "What children and adults need," he told one reporter, "is a chance to breathe God's fresh air and to stretch their legs and have a little garden in the soil." This ideal led Ford to choose small towns instead of cities as the sites of his factories. "Turning back to village industry," as Ford put it in 1926, would enable people to reestablish a sense of community — with nature and with men — that urbanization had destroyed. Ford believed that cities were doomed as Americans discovered the advantages of country life.

Ford's enthusiasm for nature did not stop with ruralism. From 1914 to 1924 he sought a more complete escape from civilization on a series of camping trips with Thomas A. Edison. John Burroughs, the naturalist, and Harvey Firestone, the tire king, also participated. Although the equipment these self-styled vagabonds took into the woods was far from primitive, they apparently shared a genuine love of the outdoors. In the words of Burroughs, they "cheerfully endured wet, cold, smoke, mosquitoes, black flies, and sleepless nights, just to touch naked reality once more." Ford had a special fondness for birds. With typical exuberance he had five hundred birdhouses built on his Michigan farm, including one with seventy-six apartments which he called, appropriately, a "bird hotel." There were also electric heaters and electric brooders for Ford's fortunate birds. The whole production mixed technology and nature in a way that symbolized Ford's ambivalence. When he could not camp or visit his aviary, Ford liked to read about the natural world. Indeed he preferred the works of Emerson, Thoreau, and Burroughs to the Bible. Ford so admired Burroughs' variety of natural history that even before becoming acquainted with him he sent him a new Ford car.

As for roads and automobiles, Ford saw them not as a threat to natural conditions but rather as a way for the average American to come into contact with nature. The machine and the garden were not incompatible. "I will build a motor car for the great multitude . . . ," Ford boasted, "so low in price that no man . . . will be unable to own one — and enjoy with his family the blessings of hours of pleasure in God's great open spaces." In *My Life and Work* of 1923 Ford again confronted the tension between nature and modern civilization. He declared that he did not agree with those who saw mechanization leading to a "cold, metallic sort of world in which great factories will drive away the trees, the flowers, the birds and the green fields." According to Ford, "unless we know more about machines and their use . . . we cannot have the time to enjoy the trees and the birds, and the flowers, and the green fields." Such reconciliations only partially covered Ford's nervousness about the mechanized, urbanized future. Contradictions persisted in his thinking. The same man who envisaged fenceless bonanza farms could say, "I love to walk across country and jump fences." The lover of trees could state in utmost seriousness, "better wood can be made than is grown."

Ford's attitude toward history has been subject to wide misunderstanding. The principal source of confusion is a statement Ford made in 1919 at the trial resulting from his libel suit against the *Chicago Tribune*. "History," he declared, "is more or less the bunk. It is tradition. We don't want tradition. We want to live in the present, and the only history that is worth a tinker's dam is the history we make today." On another occasion he admitted that he "wouldn't give a nickel for all the history in the world." Complementing this sentiment is Ford's reputation as a forward-looking inventor and revolutionary industrialist unsatisfied with the old processes. Here seems a man fully at home in the alleged new era of the 1920s. But in fact Ford idolized the past. His "history . . . is bunk" remark came in response to a question about ancient history and Napoleon Bonaparte and had reference to written history. For history itself — what actually happened in his nation's past and its tangible evidence — Ford had only praise.

The most obvious evidence of Ford's enthusiasm for history was his collector's instinct. He began with the bastion of his own youth, the McGuffey readers. Sending agents out to scour the countryside and putting aside considerations of cost, Ford owned by 1925 one of the few complete collections of the many McGuffey editions. Hoping to share his treasures with his contemporaries, Ford had five thousand copies of *Old Favorites from the McGuffey Readers* printed in 1926. The book contained such classic stories as "Try, Try Again" and "The Hare and the Tortoise." It dispensed an ideal of individualism and self-reliance at the same time that Ford's assembly lines were making men cogs in an impersonal machine.

From books Ford turned to things, and during the 1920s amassed a remarkable collection of American antiques. He bought so widely and so aggressively that he became a major factor in prices in the antique market. Everything was fair game. Lamps and dolls, bells and grandfather clocks made their way to Dearborn. Size was no problem. Ford gathered enough machines to show the evolution of the threshing operation from 1849 to the 1920s. Another exhibit traced the development of wagons in

America. Eventually the entire heterogeneous collection went into the Edison Museum at Dearborn, a pretentious building designed to resemble, simultaneously, Independence Hall, Congress Hall, and the old City Hall of Philadelphia. Ford delighted in showing visitors around the five-acre layout. Asked on one occasion why he collected, Ford replied, "so that they will not be lost to America." Later, on the same tour, Ford played a few bars on an antique organ and observed, "that takes me back to my boyhood days. They were beautiful days."

This sentiment undoubtedly figured in Ford's 1920 decision to restore his boyhood home. Everything had to be exactly as he remembered it. Furniture, china, and rugs were rehabilitated or reconstructed. Ford even used archaeological techniques to recover artifacts around the family homestead. The ground was dug to a depth of six feet and the silverware, wheels, and other equipment used by his parents in the 1860s were recovered. In 1922 Ford purchased the Wayside Inn at Sudbury, Massachusetts, to preserve it from destruction. Celebrated by the poet Henry Wadsworth Longfellow, the old inn appealed to Ford as a symbol of pioneer days. He opened it for the public's edification in 1924. But a new highway ran too near. Roaring cars disturbed the horse-and-buggy atmosphere. So, turning against the age he helped create, Ford had the state highway rerouted around the shrine at a cost of $250,000. He also bought and restored the schoolhouse in Sudbury alleged to be the site where Mary and her little lamb gamboled. Naturally the shop of the "Village Blacksmith," also in Sudbury, had to be included in Ford's antique empire.

Beginning in 1926 with the construction of Greenfield Village near Dearborn, Ford embarked on a career of large-scale historical restoration. This time not a building but a whole community was the object of his attention. Greenfield, named after the Michigan hamlet in which Ford's mother grew up, was a monument to his agrarianism as well as his reverence for the past. "I am trying in a small way," Ford explained with unwarranted modesty, "to help America take a step . . . toward the saner and sweeter idea of life that prevailed in pre-war days." Greenfield Village had gravel roads, gas street lamps, a grassy common, and an old-fashioned country store. The automobile mogul permitted only horse-drawn vehicles on the premises. The genius of assembly line mass production engaged a glass blower, blacksmith, and cobbler to practice their obsolete crafts in the traditional manner. Ford dispatched his agents to seek out, purchase, and transport to Greenfield the cottages of Walt Whitman, Noah Webster, and Patrick Henry. In time they even secured the crowning glory: the log cabin in which William Holmes McGuffey had been born and raised.

History, then, was not "bunk" to Henry Ford. The speed of change seemed to increase proportionately to his desire to retain contact with the past. As Ford declared in 1928, a year before completing Greenfield Village, "improvements have been coming so quickly that the past is being lost to the rising generation." To counter this tendency Ford labored to put history into a form "where it may be seen and felt." But values and attitudes were also on display. Ford looked back with nostalgia to the pioneer ethic. With it, he believed, the nation had been sound, wholesome, happy, and secure. "The Old Ways," as the *Dearborn Independent* declared, "Were Good."

Ford's opinion of the new morality of the jazz age was, not surprisingly, low. He deplored the use of tobacco and even went so far as to publish for mass circulation a tract, entitled *The Case Against the Little White Slaver,* which excoriated cigarettes. When Ford had the power he went beyond exhortation. "No one smokes in the Ford industries," their leader proclaimed in 1929. As for alcohol, Ford was equally unyielding. Twice he threatened to make his international labor force teetotalers at the risk of their jobs. In his American plants Ford enforced a policy of abstinence. Any workman detected drinking publicly or even keeping liquor at home was subject to dismissal. The prohibition policy of the 1920s, in Ford's estimation, was a great triumph. "There are a million boys growing up in the United States," he exulted in 1929, "who have never seen a saloon and who will never know the handicap of liquor." When confronted with evidence of widespread violation of the Eighteenth Amendment, Ford had a ready explanation. A Jewish conspiracy was to blame for illicit booze. The mass of real Americans, Ford believed, were, like himself, dry by moral conviction as well as by law.

Sex was too delicate a matter to be addressed directly, but Ford conveyed his opinions through a discussion of music and dancing. Few aspects of the American 1920s worried him more than the evils of jazz. The new music clashed squarely with his ruralism and Bible-belt morality. In 1921 Ford struck out in anger at "the waves upon waves of musical slush that invaded decent parlors and set the young people of this generation imitating the drivel of morons." Organized Jewry, once again, was blamed for the musical degeneracy. "The mush, the slush, the sly suggestion, the abandoned sensuousness of sliding notes," declared the Dearborn Independent, "are of Jewish origin." The problem, obviously, was not only musical but sexual as well. The loosening of morals in the 1920s appalled Ford. He expressed his feelings in reference to jazz: "monkey talk, jungle squeals, grunts and squeaks and gasps suggestive of cave love are camouflaged by a few feverish notes." What Ford could only bring himself to call "the thing" appeared also in song titles such as *In Room 202* and *Sugar Baby*. Pointing to the Jewish origin of these tunes (Irving Berlin was a frequent target of attacks), Ford called on his countrymen to crush the serpent in their midst.

The reform of dancing fitted nicely into Ford's campaign to elevate the nation's morals to old-time standards. His interest began with the collection of traditional folk dances. Not only the scores but the backwoods fiddlers themselves were invited to Dearborn to play *Old Zip Coon* and *Arkansas Traveler*. To

Ford's delight, here was something both wholesome and historical. He also manifested concern over social dancing, publishing in 1926 a guidebook entitled *"Good Morning": After a Sleep of Twenty-five Years Old-Fashioned Dancing is Being Revived by Mr. and Mrs. Henry Ford*. The book also endeavored to revive old-fashioned morality. It began by condemning as promiscuous the newer dances such as the Charleston and the whole flapper syndrome. "A gentleman," the book explained, "should be able to guide his partner through a dance without embracing her as if he were her lover." Proper deportment, according to Ford, minimized physical contact. "[The gentleman's] right hand should be placed at his partner's waist, thumb and forefinger alone touching her — that is, the hand being in the position of holding a pencil." There were also rules regarding gloves, handkerchiefs, and the way to request a partner for a dance. Ford's dance manual, in short, was a monument to the old conceptions of morality, decorum, and order, and the dances he and his wife hosted at Dearborn were implementations. Precisely at nine Ford's guests convened in evening dress in a lavish ballroom for a paean to Victorianism.

Ambivalence is the key to the mind of Henry Ford. He was both old and new; he looked both forward and backward. Confidently progressive as he was in some respects, he remained nervous about the new ways. The more conditions changed, the more the nostalgic Ford groped for the security of traditional values and institutions. He was not lost; on the contrary, he had too many gods, at least for consistency. Neither was he dissipated and roaring. And he hated jazz. But Ford was popular, indeed a national deity, in the twenties even if his senatorial and presidential bids fell short. As a plain, honest, old-fashioned billionaire, a technological genius who loved to camp out, he seemed to his contemporaries to resolve the moral dilemmas of the age. Like Charles A. Lindbergh, another god of the age, Ford testified to the nation's ability to move into the future without losing the values of the past.

QUESTIONS TO CONSIDER

1 Compare Henry Ford with "robber baron" Andrew Carnegie in selection 5. In what ways did each man symbolize the America of his age?

2 Analyze the sources of Ford's tremendous popularity in the 1920s. Was it true, as Nash argues, that despite the revolutionary social changes Ford's cars brought to American society, Ford's commitment to old-fashioned values comforted Americans who felt anxious about the effects of modernization?

3 Henry Ford was the symbol of the new industrial order of the 1920s, but he also reflected the urban-rural tensions of that decade, especially in his attitudes toward the "revolution in manners and morals" of the Jazz Age. Discuss Ford's attitudes toward alcohol, sex, music, and dancing and how they reflected the changes taking place in America in the 1920s.

4 In addition to being a technological genius, Ford was both an anti-Semite and a Victorian prude, but the American people loved him. How much of his appeal, do you think, was based on his ability to find simplistic solutions to the moral dilemmas of his age?

15

Why Suffrage for American Women Was Not Enough

ELISABETH PERRY

As we saw in selection 4, women first won the right to vote and hold office in Wyoming Territory, a triumph that attracted the attention of women's rights advocates all over the country. By 1900, as Elisabeth Perry says, American feminists had made the elective franchise "the focal point of the entire women's movement." In that year, the rival women's suffrage groups formed a joint organization called the National American Woman's Suffrage Association. To counter the accusation that they were out to destroy the home, the suffragists argued that the home was a microcosm of the nation. Politics, declared Francis Willard of the Women's Christian Temperance League, was "enlarged housekeeping." If women were to remain good mothers and gain the means to preserve their homes, they needed the right to vote. This ingenious argument, said one historian, broadened the appeal of the movement "and neutralized the opposition's charge that it sought to destroy the home."

At the same time, the suffragists successfully identified their movement with progressivism, contending that enfranchising women would help Progressive reformers improve the quality of American society. That argument won Woodrow Wilson, Theodore Roosevelt, and the entire nation to the cause. In 1920, some fifty years after Wyoming had enfranchised its female citizens, American women everywhere won the right to vote with the ratification of the Nineteenth Amendment.

Gaining the right to vote, however, scarcely made women equal partners with men in American political life. As Elisabeth Perry, a distinguished historian at Sarah Lawrence College, points out in the next selection, women still faced insurmountable prejudice and discrimination against them in American politics. There was no shortage of women with political experience, and some intrepid souls did run for political office in the twenties, only to find themselves without major party backing, running against incumbents, and losing. A "new office-seeking female leadership" should have emerged in the 1920s, Perry says, but none did so because men were determined to keep women in separate and subordinate political roles. Accommodating themselves to "a reality they could not control," veteran female leaders accepted the idea of operating politically within their own "gender sphere." Perry examines how that practice affected the careers of four famous suffragists, including Anna Eleanor Roosevelt. Although Perry does not say so, a group of militant feminists organized the Woman's party and not only advocated equal rights, but demanded an equal rights amendment to the Constitution. They were a small minority, however, and the male establishment ignored them. No equal rights amendment was passed then or since. In concluding her insightful essay, Perry reminds us of the difficulties American women still face in their efforts to "perform in an authoritative role."

GLOSSARY

NINETEENTH AMENDMENT (1920) Gave women age twenty-one and older the right to vote everywhere in America.

CLINTON, HILLARY RODHAM Wife of President Bill Clinton, she took an active part in her husband's first presidential campaign, in 1992, and headed a task force that addressed the need for a national system of health insurance.

SMITH, AL Governor of New York, 1918–1928. In 1928 he ran for president but lost to Republican candidate Herbert Hoover.

SUFFRAGE The legal right to vote in a political election.

SUFFRAGIST A woman or man who favored giving women the elective franchise.

PORTER, POLLY Lifelong companion of suffragist Mary Dewson.

As a result of the autumn elections in 1992, a year the American media billed as "The Year of the Woman," the numbers of women holding elective office in the United States rose to unprecedented heights. The percentage of women office holders at state level climbed to 22.2 percent for state-wide elected executives and 20.4 percent for legislators. At the national level, the number of female U.S. Senators tripled (from two to six), while the number in the House of Representatives rose from twenty-eight to forty-seven (there is a forty-eighth, who represents the District of Columbia, but she has no vote). Even with this impressive progress, however, women's share of elective office in the United States remains relatively small.

It is not hard to explain why. Deeply ingrained global traditions have long kept women out of public, authoritative roles. But why have these traditions remained so entrenched in the United States, ostensibly one of the most advanced, modernized countries of

From Elisabeth Perry, "Why Suffrage for American Women Was Not Enough," *History Today* (September 1993), pp. 36–41. Reprinted by permission.

the world? A close look at American women's political history in the immediate post-suffrage era might provide a few clues.

American women won the vote in 1920 with the ratification of the Nineteenth Amendment to the federal Constitution. Women had worked for this goal since 1848, when Elizabeth Cady Stanton, a reformer active in the campaigns to abolish slavery and also a temperance advocate, organized a public meeting in Seneca Falls, New York, to discuss women's rights. Many observers ridiculed her demand for the vote. By the turn of the century, this demand had become the focal point of the entire women's movement. Suffrage for women was eventually won in a number of the states, and then nationwide in August, 1920.

By the time this event occurred, women were no longer political novices. For decades they had been organizing conventions, giving public speeches, writing editorials, campaigning door-to-door, petitioning and marching. These activities gave them vast political expertise, as well as access to wide networks of other women activists and of male political leaders. This combination of expertise and contacts ought to have placed them at the center of American political life. It did not.

The winning of female suffrage did not mark the end of prejudice and discrimination against women in public life. Women still lacked equal access with men to those professions, especially the law, which provide the chief routes to political power. Further, when women ran for office—and many did in the immediate post-suffrage era—they often lacked major party backing, hard to come by for any newcomer but for women almost impossible unless she belonged to a prominent political family. Even if successful in winning backing, when women ran for office they usually had to oppose incumbents. When, as was often the case, they lost their first attempts, their reputation as "losers" made re-endorsement impossible.

American political parties did try to integrate women into their power structures after suffrage. They courted women's votes, especially in the early 1920s, when a "woman's voting bloc" seemed real. In addition, the parties formed "women's divisions" or created a committee system of equal numbers of committee women and committee men (with the latter usually choosing for the former). But when party leaders sought a candidate for preferment, they tended to look for "a good man," seldom imagining that a woman might qualify. In short, in the years immediately after suffrage most party leaders confined women to auxiliary, service roles. They expected women to help elect men but not seek office themselves. That party men in the early 1920s held to such an expectation is hardly surprising. That many of the most politically "savvy" American women went along with them is more difficult to understand.

In the post-suffrage United States, although there were many strong, executive-type women with considerable political expertise, none of them became the vanguard of a new, office-seeking female political leadership. Because of women's long exclusion from the vote and political parties, these women had worked for change only in a nonpartisan fashion from within their own gender sphere. After suffrage, in part because men kept them there, they accepted the notion that separate roles for women in politics ought to continue.

The reasons for this acceptance are complex, and probably differ from woman to woman. Some women felt most comfortable operating from within their own sphere. In single-sex groups, they made lifelong friendships with women who shared their interests and problems. In addition, in women's groups they did not have to compete with men for positions of authority. A deep suspicion of electoral politics was yet another important factor. Political women distrusted the world of electoral politics. It was a man's world, a world filled with "dirty games" that men had been trained to play, and indeed were forced to play, if they wanted to "get

Eleanor Roosevelt (second from the left in the second row from the front) with women of the press, 1933. Through groups like these, writes Elisabeth Perry, the First Lady "worked for legislation on a variety of important issues: public housing for low-income work- *ers, the dissemination of birth control information, the reorganization of the state government, and shorter hours and minimum wage for women workers." (Stock Montage, Inc.)*

ahead." For these women, it held few allures. Educated and middle-class, they had not been brought up to be career-oriented or personally ambitious. Rather, they had been taught that their proper role was to serve others and to work for idealistic causes. The winning of the vote did little to change this socialization.

These were some of the views of women's role in politics held by both men and women in the 1920s. The careers of four suffragists, all politically active in the post-suffrage era and all of whom could have held elective office had circumstances differed, serve to illustrate how these views affected individual lives. The four do not comprise a balanced "sample," for they were all based in New York City and were all active in the Democratic Party. They are exemplars, however, because they thrived in a hotbed of women's activism in the post-suffrage era. If any woman could have risen into electoral political prominence during that era, she would have been a New York City Democrat.

My first example is Belle Lindner Moskowitz (1877–1933). A shopkeeper's daughter born in Harlem, New York, she spent her early career as a social worker on the city's Lower East Side. After her marriage in 1903, while her children were growing up, she did volunteer work until, by the 1910s, she had developed a city-wide reputation as an effective social and industrial reformer. Although considering herself an independent Republican, in 1918, the first year New York State women voted, because of Democrat Alfred E. Smith's reputation as an advocate for labor, she supported him for governor.

After organizing the women's vote for him, Moskowitz proposed that Governor-elect Smith establish a "Reconstruction Commission" to identify and propose solutions for the state's administrative, social, and economic problems. Smith not only formed the Commission but appointed her its executive director. During the one year of its existence (1919–20), it outlined Smith's legislative program and launched Moskowitz's career as his closest political advisor. From 1923 on, she ran his state re-election campaigns and guided the legislative enactment of his policies, all the while preparing the ground for his nomination by the Democratic Party as presidential candidate in 1928. In that year, she directed national publicity for the campaign and served as the only woman on the national Democratic Party executive committee.

Al Smith lost that election to Herbert Hoover. But because Belle Moskowitz had played such a central role in his career throughout the 1920s, by the time of his presidential race she was a nationally known political figure. Still, her fame depended on his. Smith had offered her a number of government posts but she had refused them. She believed, and rightly so, that her work from behind the scenes would in the end give her more power than the holding of any bureaucratic, appointive office. Thanks to her, Smith, a man whose formal education had ended at the age of thirteen, was able to pursue his legislative program with enough success to become a viable presidential candidate. But because of her self-effacement, when Smith failed to win the presidency and then lost his party leadership

role to Franklin Delano Roosevelt, her career was eclipsed along with his. Future generations of political women would not see her example as an inspiration or model for their own careers.

More famous than Moskowitz, Anna Eleanor Roosevelt (1884–1962) became known worldwide for the role she played as the wife of Franklin Roosevelt, four-term president during the Great Depression and Second World War. Most portraits of Eleanor focus on her activities after 1933, when Franklin became president, until his death in 1945, when she became a United Nations delegate and moral force in world politics. What is less well known is that, before FDR became president, even before he became governor of New York, she had accumulated a vast amount of political experience and influence in her own right.

Unlike Moskowitz, Eleanor Roosevelt was born into wealth and privilege, but endured an unhappy childhood. A measure of fulfillment came to her through her education and volunteer social work. She married Franklin in 1905, bore him several children, and fostered her husband's promising political career. In 1920, this career reached its first culmination when he ran, unsuccessfully, for vice-president. By then their marriage was on shaky ground. Although in 1918 Eleanor had discovered Franklin's affair with Lucy Mercer, the couple had resolved to keep the marriage together. In 1921, Franklin was stricken with polio and withdrew from politics. Franklin's political manager and publicist, Louis Howe, convinced Eleanor to keep her husband's name alive by becoming active herself in women's organizations. Once involved in this work, Eleanor confirmed what she had discovered during her husband's earlier campaigns. She liked politics.

But primarily from within her own sphere. She took up volunteer work for four New York City women's groups: the League of Women Voters and Women's City Club, the Women's Trade Union League, and the Women's Division of the State

Democratic Party. For this latter group, from 1925 to 1928 she developed and edited a newspaper that, in bridging the gap between upstate and downstate Democrats, formed a critical base for Al Smith and her husband's future support. Through her other groups she worked for legislation on a variety of important issues: public housing for low-income workers; the dissemination of birth control information, the reorganization of the state government, and shorter hours and minimum wages for women workers.

To accomplish her goals, she gave talks on the radio and published articles. Journalists interviewed her. She traveled all around the state during and in between campaigns to keep local party leaders connected with one another. She ran the women's campaigns for the Democrats at the state level in 1924 and national level in 1928. As a result, she became a well known figure, almost as well known as her husband, at both state and national level. But when her husband won the governorship in 1928, she gave up all activity. She knew where her duty lay—to become Albany's First Lady, not to hold office herself.

By 1928, in the crucible of New York women's politics, Eleanor Roosevelt had forged for herself acute political skills. These would serve her well as she continued until her husband's death to support his political agendas and afterwards to pursue more directly her own. By 1928, however, she herself had become so prominent that had she wanted she could have run for office and probably won. It did not even occur to her to do so. That was not what women did, especially not women married to ambitious men.

The first woman in the United States to hold cabinet rank was Frances Perkins (1880–1965). Even though she held public office my argument holds true for her as well: her post was appointive, not elective, and she asserted to the end of her life that she had never been interested in a political career. Better educated than either Moskowitz or Roosevelt (she graduated from Mt. Holyoke College), Perkins had a background similar to theirs. After working as a teacher and in a social settlement, she became secretary of the New York Consumers' League, a group seeking labor legislation to improve factory safety and health conditions for all workers. Although always known as "Miss" Perkins, she was married and bore one child, but her husband suffered from mental illness and was later unable to earn a living. This circumstance gave her a keen interest in finding well paid jobs. Like Moskowitz, she came to admire Al Smith and in 1918 worked for his election as governor. Unlike Moskowitz, when Smith offered her a job as a State Industrial Commissioner, she accepted. This post became the launching pad from which she entered Roosevelt's cabinet in 1933.

Still, when she reflected on her career years later, she denied being a "career woman" with political ambitions. Doors had opened for her and she had gone through them. She had never dreamed of being Secretary of Labor or Industrial Commissioner, she said. A "series of circumstances" and her "own energies" had thrown her into "situations" where she had assumed responsibility and then was asked to assume more. Before she knew it she "had a career."

Here again is an accomplished, talented woman who had matured through social reform and suffrage politics in the 1910s and then moved into appointive office. As she plied her way, although she wanted and needed to work, ideas of personal advancement or career ambition were seldom at the forefront of her thinking. Convinced even at the moment of Roosevelt's elevation of her that she was probably unworthy, she accepted the offer as a "call to service." Once she attained office, fearful that men would resist answering to her, she took on the look, dress, and behavior of a schoolmarm so as to appear less threatening to them. Despite all of her accomplishments, the gender stereotypes and constraints of her time prevailed.

My last example from the period is Mary W. (Molly) Dewson (1874–1962). Like Perkins, Dewson was well educated. After graduating from Wellesley College and holding some research jobs, she became Superintendent of Probation at the nation's first reform school for girls and then executive secretary of the Massachusetts Commission on the Minimum Wage. Never married, she maintained a lifelong partnership with a friend, Polly Porter, with whom she farmed in Massachusetts and did suffrage and war work. Eventually, under the mentorship of Eleanor Roosevelt, Dewson moved into Democratic state and then national politics. Her personal ambitions remained severely limited, however.

When Dewson assessed women's political progress since suffrage, she confessed that their opportunities had barely expanded, [U]sually on the basis of their "looks, money," or a "late husband's service to the party," they had received only ceremonial party positions. In these circumstances, Dewson decided that the only way to build women's political strength was through separate women's divisions. As head of the Women's Division of the Democratic National Committee, she organized women workers for FDR's campaigns and co-ordinated support for his programs between elections. In so doing, she played roles essential to the success of the Democratic Party during the New Deal initiative. Like Perkins, Dewson followed a cautious philosophy in working with men: she took on a maternal or "aunty" pose and disclaimed any relationship to feminism. She also turned down posts when they threatened her partnership with Polly Porter. Only in her old age did she finally enter a political race in her own right. But the race she chose was in a solidly Republican district where she had no chance of winning.

Among the most politically adept of their generation, all four of these women pursued political goals in the 1920s but none as a man would have done. Moskowitz achieved an important advisory role but lost all her power at the fall of her mentor. Roosevelt sacrificed her own needs to those of her husband. Perkins reached high office but masked her strength and denied personal ambition. Dewson often put domestic happiness before career fulfillment and, like Perkins, downplayed her feminism.

Others of their generation who had been leaders in the suffrage struggle acted similarly.

When younger women growing up in the 1920s and 30s looked at their political forbears, Belle Moskowitz, Eleanor Roosevelt, Frances Perkins, and Molly Dewson were among the few successful ones they saw. But younger women wanted real careers, not roles as an amanuensis to a man or as a behind-the-scenes campaigner. But "real careers" were denied them. Either men discriminated against them and kept them out of central circles of power, or when they married they discovered that domestic life and a political career just did not mix.

The door was open to women in politics in the 1920s. But, as Molly Dewson once said, the battle was uphill and most women got quickly discouraged. By accommodating themselves to a reality they could not control, they participated in the perpetuation of a "separate spheres ideology" long after it had outlived its relevance. Looking back at them from the standpoint of 1993 we might judge these women as "old fashioned." But we ought not reject them as important role models. As smart, wily, and skilled political strategists, they have much to teach us. We must reject not them but the constraints that held them back.

Some of those constraints are still with us. Throughout the 1992 campaign, questions about women's appropriate roles in politics continued to surface. They dominated the controversies that swirled around Hillary Clinton, wife of Democratic presidential candidate, Bill Clinton. What role had she played in his years as governor of Arkansas? Why did she keep her maiden name when they were married? What was the quality of their married life together? Had she been a good mother or was she one of those career-orientated, ambitious feminists?

At its national convention in August, the Republican Party exploited popular doubts about Hillary Clinton's ability to operate in the traditional mode of the political wife. In an unprecedented move, convention organizers asked the wives of its candidates,

Barbara Bush and Marilyn Quayle, to speak. The shared theme of the women's speeches, "traditional" family values, sent out a clear message: political wives must adhere strictly to giving priority to their husbands' careers.

The Democratic Party response disturbed many feminists, but it was probably essential to victory. Hillary Clinton got a makeover. She baked cookies and, in response to rumors that she was childless, trotted out her daughter Chelsea at every possible occasion. Still, when Bill Clinton and his running mate, Albert Gore, Jr., made their victory speeches on election night, women heard some new words on national television. In describing their future government, for the first time in history both president and vice-president-elect included the category of "gender" as an important test of the diversity they envisioned.

Despite their personal openness to women in government, Hillary Clinton remained vulnerable to further attacks. As a lawyer with a distinguished record of accomplishment concerning the rights of children, she took active part in her husband's transition team discussions. Later, she received an appointment as unpaid head of a task force addressing one of the nation's most pressing problems, the lack of a national health insurance system. In response to a query by the press as to how reporters should refer to her, she asked them to use all three of her names, Hillary Rodham Clinton. The charges flew. Ambitious feminist. Power mad. Who is in charge here? In March 1993, on a flight over Washington, DC, an airline pilot joked over the loudspeaker, "Down below you can see the White House, where the president and her husband live."

If, on the brink of the twenty-first century, the wife of the President of the United States still cannot perform in an authoritative role without questions being raised about the appropriateness of her behavior how could the women of the 1920s have stood a chance? Today's "Hillary factor" shows just how far we have come and how far we have to go before women can at last take up citizenship roles equal to those of men.

QUESTIONS TO CONSIDER

1   What social and political obstacles tended to keep women out of political office in the twenties and thirties? How did the newly enfranchised women leaders adapt to these obstacles? Why does this country still not have an equal rights amendment to the Constitution? Does it need one?

2   Who was Belle Lindner Moskowitz and what was her political significance? Compare her background and political work to that of Anna Eleanor Roosevelt. The author says that by 1928 Roosevelt had become so famous that she could probably have won an elective political office, yet it never occurred to her to run. Why not?

3   One of the women profiled in this selection was the first woman ever to serve in a presidential cabinet. Who was she? What president did she work for? How successful was she?

4   What did Mary Dewson decide was the only way women could build political power? What did she do to build such power? What was her philosophy in working with men? Do you think that her lifelong partnership with Polly Porter hurt or helped her politically?

5   During the election of 1992, what did Republicans do to question Hillary Clinton's ability to function in "the traditional mode of the political wife"? What was the Democratic response? What is the "Hillary factor"?

VIII

LONG DARK NIGHT
OF THE DEPRESSION

16

Under Hoover, the Shame and Misery Deepened

T. H. WATKINS

By the beginning of 1929, the nation seemed to have reached a permanent state of prosperity. Business and foreign trade both were expanding, the stock market was rising at a phenomenal rate, and national leadership appeared to be in expert hands. Republican Herbert Hoover had won the presidency the previous November, having easily defeated his Democratic opponent. "For the first time in our history," wrote two economists, "we have a President who, by technical training, engineering achievement, cabinet experience, and grasp of economic fundamentals, is qualified for business leadership."

"We in America today," Hoover himself had said, "are nearer to the final triumph over poverty than ever before in the history of any land. The poorhouse is vanishing from among us." Hoover was equally optimistic in his inaugural address in March 1929: "I have no fears for the future of our country," he proclaimed. "It is bright with hope."

Eight months later, the country plummeted into the most severe and protracted economic depression in American history. It started with the stock market crash in October 1929 and deepened slowly and inexorably until the entire economy and perhaps even the nation itself approached total collapse. It was the worst disaster the United States had faced since the Civil War, and there were voices of doubt everywhere. How had it happened? What would become of the American dream? Would the nation disintegrate? And who was to blame—President Hoover, the Republican party, or capitalism itself?

We now know that several factors caused economic collapse—chief among them underconsumption and overproduction, as consumer buying power lagged behind the quantity of goods being turned out. As factories and other businesses found themselves overextended, they began laying off workers, which decreased consumer buying power, which in turn caused more layoffs and resulted in a vicious cycle. By 1932 some 12 million

Americans were unemployed. At the same time, factories and businesses themselves shuttered their windows and closed their doors, and banks, unable to call in their loans, began failing at an alarming rate, taking people's savings down with them. In 1930 and 1931, a total of 3,646 banks failed, representing more than $2.5 billion in deposits. Never, in all the previous depressions and "panics," had the country been confronted with such statistics.

The prosperity of the 1920s had turned into a nightmare. Unemployed men roamed the country in search of work, succumbing to feelings of guilt and worthlessness when they found nothing at all. In the following selection, excerpted from his prize-winning history of the Great Depression, a companion to the popular PBS series on that calamity, distinguished historian T. H. Watkins captures the human misery and the failure of early relief efforts through vignettes of common folk—whites, African Americans, and Mexican Americans. Watkins also offers an insightful discussion of President Hoover's approach to the crisis and why that failed.

As you read the next two selections, bear in mind that the Depression was a worldwide calamity that rocked industrial Europe and Japan as well as the United States. As historian John A. Garraty says, "While there were differences in its impact and in the way it was dealt with from one country to another, the course of events nearly everywhere ran something like this: By 1925 most countries had recovered from the economic disruptions caused by the Great War of 1914–18. There followed a few years of rapid growth, but in 1929 and 1930 the prosperity ended. Then came a precipitous plunge that lasted until early 1933. This dark period was followed by a gradual, if spotty, recovery. The revival, however, was aborted by the steep recession of 1937–38. It took a still more cataclysmic event, the outbreak of World War II, to end the Great Depression."

GLOSSARY

BLACK THURSDAY   The day the stock market crashed, October 24, 1929, causing a panic in the business world that presaged the Great Depression.

DEPRESSION   Called a "panic" in the nineteenth century, this was a severe downturn in the business cycle, characterized by low business activity, bank and business failures, high unemployment, and want in the midst of plenty.

HOOVER, HERBERT   President of the United States, 1929–1933, who was widely blamed for the stock-market crash and the onset of the Great Depression.

HOOVERVILLES   Derogatory name for shantytowns, made of box crates, loose timber, and whatever else could be found, which sprang up around many cities; unemployed families lived in them and called them Hoovervilles because they blamed a seemingly cold and remote president for their misery.

JIM CROW LAWS   State and local laws enacted in the South after Reconstruction, they denied African Americans the right to vote, hold political office, and sit on juries; relegated them to menial labor; restricted them to black sections of towns and cities; and excluded them from public accommodations. The laws took their name from a song, "Jim Crow," sung by Thomas Rice in a pre–Civil War black minstrel show.

MINEHAN, THOMAS   A sociologist who studied tramps and hoboes, roaming men and women who were unemployed.

RECONSTRUCTION FINANCE CORPORATION   Federal agency established by President Hoover, which in 1932 started handing out federal funds to support agriculture and industry; later it was a powerful agency of the New Deal.

RED CROSS   International philanthropic organization that provided relief in war; national disasters like floods, pestilence, fires, storms; and other calamities like the Great Depression.

UNIVERSAL FEAR

Gordon Parks was sixteen years old in 1929, a young black man trying to work his way through high school in St. Paul, Minnesota, as a bellboy at a downtown club for white businessmen. One Wednesday afternoon, a notice was tacked to the employee bulletin board: "Because of unforeseen circumstances, some personnel will be laid off the first of next month. Those directly affected will be notified in due time." This puzzled Parks until the next day, Thursday, October 24, when the evening papers broke the news of the crash. "I read everything I could get my hands on," he recalled,

gathering in the full meaning of such terms as Black Thursday, deflation and depression. I couldn't imagine such financial disaster touching my small world; it surely concerned only the rich. But by the first week of November I . . . knew differently; along with millions of others across the nation, I was without a job. . . . Finally, on the seventh of November I went to school and cleaned out my locker, knowing it was impossible to stay on. A piercing chill was in the air as I walked back to the rooming house. The hawk had come. I could already feel his wings shadowing me.

While only a small percentage of the public was directly affected by the collapse of the stock market in October, 1929, it was still a moment of history shared by nearly every American. Like the Japanese attack of Pearl Harbor or the assassinations of John F. Kennedy, Martin Luther King, Jr., and Robert

T. H. Watkins, "Under Hoover, the Shame and Misery Deepened," chapter originally titled, "The Shadow of the Hawk," in Watkins, *The Great Depression: America in the 1930s* (Boston and New York: Little, Brown, 1993), pp. 53–75. Copyright © 1993 by Blackside, Inc. By permission of Little, Brown and Company.

Unemployment reached staggering levels during the long dark night of the Depression. To raise a little money, this man is forced to sell apples on West Street in New York City, 1932. In back of him is a "Hooverville," a collection of wrecked and abandoned buildings that became "home" for unemployed New Yorkers and their families. (Culver Pictures)

Kennedy in our own time, the crash was a point of reference for those of that time. People took the measure of their era by using the crash as an emotional baseline, and it became the one event on which tens of millions could fix their worry as the full dimensions of the debacle slowly began to be discerned. Gordon Parks was not the only one who felt the shadow of the hawk.

President Herbert Clark Hoover, though, apparently remained oblivious to that shadow—or if he felt it, did not want to acknowledge it. Unemployment had grown from about 1.5 million to at least 3.2 million in the five months since the crash, but on March 7, 1930, Hoover gave the American public the results of his own analysis of the situation. "All the evidences," he said, "indicate that the worst effects of the crash upon unemployment will have passed during the next sixty days."

A more accurate measure could have been found in an unnamed southern city that Sherwood Anderson visited that same month. The writer spent some time standing outside a big basement soup kitchen, where on a single day he watched seven hundred people go inside to get fed. He was struck by the number of those who did not want him to know their hunger. The man, for example, who approached the soup kitchen three times before swallowing his pride and going down the steps. "I am not here for soup," he told Anderson, who had not said a word. "I came here to meet a friend." Or the young woman who asked him where the soup kitchen was. "I do not want any soup," she assured him when he obliged. She just wanted to say hello to some of the women who were serving the needy. "They are friends of mine."

"They were Americans, such people as you and I," Anderson wrote. "I stood watching them. I was ashamed of my warm overcoat, my stout shoes.

"I made men ashamed standing there."

Most of those who were still coming to the soup kitchen six months later, as the first anniversary of the crash approached, probably would have put little or no faith in anything Herbert Hoover said on the subject of what was now being called, openly and increasingly, a depression. Unemployment had not declined; it had risen, implacably, and in another six months would hit at least 7.5 million. And they would have found plainly incomprehensible the confidence of Rome C. Stephenson, vice president of the American Bankers' Association, if they had heard the pep talk he gave his fellow bankers in downtown Cleveland on September 30. The bankers should not worry, Stephenson said, because business was about to get better. The slump, he insisted, was largely a matter of misperception:

The depression of the stock market impressed the general public with the idea that it would depress general business. Because of a psychological consequence, it did, but it should not have. There are 120,000,000 persons in the country and at the maximum not more than 10,000,000 were involved in stock-market transactions. The remaining 110,000,000 persons suffered no loss.

The bulk of the American population may not have suffered the loss of stock investments, but there were plenty of other ways to calculate loss, and by the end of 1929, with unemployment rising, with

shops and factories suddenly ornamented by Closed or Out of Business signs, and, perhaps most terrifying of all, with scores of banks failing and taking with them millions of dollars in deposits (which were at that time uninsured), the "general public's" confidence in the financial health of the country and the wisdom of its leaders was shaky at best. Confidence fell even further when 256 banks failed in the single month of November, 1930, and further yet on December 11, when the United States Bank, with deposits of more than $200 million, went under. It was the largest single bank failure in American history up to that time, and contributed no little portion to an economic hangover in which, in the words of banker J. M. Barker, "cupidity turned into unreasoning, emotional, universal fear."

☆

FIGHTING FOR THE SCRAPS

There was reason enough for fear. The 1,352 banks that failed in 1930 represented more than $853 million in deposits. In 1931, 2,294 banks went under, with deposits of nearly $1.7 billion. In 1930, 26,355 businesses failed, and the rate of 122 failures per 10,000 was the highest ever recorded up to that time. Both numbers were surpassed in 1931 with 28,285 failures and a rate of 133. The 451,800 corporations still in business in 1932 had a combined deficit of $5.64 billion. The value of all farm property declined from $57.7 billion in 1929 (itself down from a high of $78.3 billion in 1920) to $51.8 billion in 1931. By the end of 1931 unemployment had climbed to 8 million and in a few months would be approaching 12 million.

There had never been such statistics in our history, and there have been none like them since. Their truest meaning, the effect they had on individual human lives, could be seen everywhere, as people struggled blindly and bravely to survive. Which is not to say that everyone was willing to see them for what they were. Like those who attempt to dismiss the homeless of our own day as aberrations, not indications, of the nation's economic condition, many of the pundits of the depression years spent a lot of time explaining away the presence of the poor and the hungry. These were temporary phenomena, it was said, transient indications of a momentary lapse in economic health. Many of the people were not even victims—they were just beggars too lazy or too ignorant to work. But the deprived of the depression years were even more difficult to ignore than the doorway sleepers and street-corner panhandlers of modern America. They could not be explained away, because they would not go away—and their numbers grew day by day, week by week. Like a plague, the disease of deprivation spread with such speed and across so many lines that there were few families in the United States who did not either experience or witness its pain. When neighbors you had known all your life were found one morning with all their furniture stacked on the sidewalk, nowhere to go, no hope in sight, it did not take much imagination to see yourself standing there with them.

You did not even have to be especially vulnerable to feel the power of deprivation. Daniel Willard, president of the Baltimore & Ohio Railroad and in no danger of having his furniture stacked on anybody's sidewalk, for instance, received an honorary doctorate at the University of Pennsylvania in June, 1931, but instead of mouthing the usual platitudes on this happy occasion, burst out with a jeremiad against the very economic system that had made him rich.

A system—call it what you will—under which it is possible for 5,000,000 or 6,000,000 of willing and able-bodied men to be out of work and unable to secure work for months at a time, and with no other source of income, cannot be said to be perfect or even satisfactory. . . . I would be less than candid if I did not say in such circumstances I would steal before I would starve.

"No one is going hungry and no one need go hungry or cold," President Hoover still insisted in the winter of 1931. Willard would have disagreed. So would Louise V. Armstrong. "We saw the city at its worst," she wrote in *We, Too, Are the People* (1941). "One vivid, gruesome moment of those dark days we shall never forget. We saw a crowd of some fifty men fighting over a barrel of garbage which had been set outside the back door of a restaurant. American citizens fighting for scraps of food like animals!"

"Why does Every Thing have exceptional Value Except the Human being," one destitute person wrote the president, "—why are we reduced to poverty and starving and anxiety and Sorrow So quickly under your administration as Chief Executor. Can you not find a quicker way of Executing us than to starve us to death."

On Chicago's South Side, wandering reporter Edmund Wilson took a look at the old Angelus Building, a tottering, stinking wreck of a place whose owner would have demolished it if he had found the money to do so. It was now stuffed with black people who could afford to live nowhere else. The place, Wilson said, was

seven stories, thick with dark windows, caged in a dingy mess of fire-escapes like mattress-springs on a junk-heap, hunched up, hunchback-proportioned, jam-crammed in its dumbness and darkness with miserable wriggling life. . . . There is darkness in the hundred cells: the tenants cannot pay for light; and cold: the heating system no longer works. . . . And now, since it is no good for anything else, its owner had turned it over to the Negroes, who flock into the tight-packed apartments and get along there as best they can.

In an Appalachian Mountains school, a child who looked sick was told by her teacher to go home and get something to eat. "I can't," the girl replied. "It's my sister's turn to eat."

The city fathers over in Muncie, Indiana, did not like to think of people being that hungry in their all-American town. Muncie, after all, was the "Middle-town" of the famous 1929 study of Robert S. and Helen Merrell Lynd, and was generally proud of it, too. But by the spring of 1932, the layer of confidence with which the city had consistently blanketed the depression began to grow a little tattered. That year, a Muncie businessman later told the Lynds, "people would go around saying in low tones, 'Have you heard that they're boarding up the so-and-so plant?' And a few days later, 'Have you heard that so-and-so-many trucks of machinery were moved out of town today? They say that half the floor at the plant is stripped already.' It got on our nerves as this went on!" The plant in question was a General Motors assembly plant, and by the end of the summer it had indeed stripped its floors of machinery, closed down, and left Muncie.

New Orleans did its best to keep reality from the door, too. Unemployment was greatly exaggerated, a writer to the letters column of the *Times-Picayune* said in February, 1930, a rumor spread by a "host of fly-speckers, calamity howlers and woe-be-tiders [who] are barnacles on prosperity," but a week later an estimated three to four hundred men showed up to answer a single classified advertisement for work available in Texas. When the advertisement turned out to be a fraud, the crowd started a small-scale riot and the police had to be brought in to put it down.

Out in Yavapai County, Arizona, depression was even harder to ignore for long. Hundreds of men who had been laid off from the copper mines in the southern part of the state wandered north to the vicinity of Prescott. During the summer of 1932, they spread "out into the hills and mountains in the hope of placer mining and getting a few cents a day out of the gravel-bars that were worked fifty years ago," Prescott poet Sharlot Hall wrote a friend in June. "Sometimes they really do pan out a few cents—or once in a while get a dollar or more—but the old diggings are very lean of gold. . . ." Others

were trying the same thing up in Nevada, where in one lonely canyon a reporter found a man shoveling dirt into a primitive riffle chute to wash out gold. "Me a minin' man?" he replied when asked. "Yes, I'm a miner—all of ten weeks now. Before that, I'd been a sailor all my life. Now it's a simple case of 'root, hog, or die, so I'm rootin'.'"

Hundreds of thousands of people were on the move by then. The Southern Pacific Railroad estimated that its "railroad bulls" had thrown as many as 683,000 transients off its boxcars in a single year. At least 200,000 of the transients were adolescents, most of them male but with no small number of females among them. In the summer of 1932 sociologist Thomas Minehan began a study that took him on the road with young tramps and hoboes. Most of them, he noted, traveled in gangs for safety, an especially important consideration for the young women among them. "Girls in box cars," he wrote, "are not entirely at the mercy of any man on the road whatever their relations with the boys may be. In event of loneliness or illness, the boys and girls have friends to comfort and care for them."

One of the tramps with whom he traveled for a time was a Pennsylvania Dutch boy nicknamed Blink—so named because he had lost an eye when a live cinder blew into his face while he was riding an open car on the Santa Fe railroad. "A bloody socket forms a small and ever-weeping cave on the left side of his face," Minehan wrote. "Tears streak his cheek, furrowing the dirt and coal soot, leaving a strange moist scar alongside his nose." The boy showed Minehan a diary he had been keeping since August, 1932, when he had run away from an abusive father. The entry for September 10 was eloquently typical:

Slept in paper box. Bummed swell breakfast three eggs and four pieces meat. Hit guy in big car in front of garage. Cop told me to scram. Rode freight to Roessville. Small burg, but got dinner. Walked Bronson. N. G. Couple a houses. Rode to Sidell. N. G. Hit homes for meals and turned down. Had to buy supper 20 cents. Raining.

Young and old, male and female, the transient army drifted in a dark caravan of desperation from hobo jungle to hobo jungle, city mission to city mission, begging for leftovers at the back doors of homes, panhandling for pennies on city sidewalks, stealing chickens where chickens could be found, cooking up "mulligan" stews out of whatever could be boiled into edibility, being seduced and raped, thrown into jail, beaten by yard bulls. Those homeless who did not drift—and there were thousands in every city of any size at all—slept in lice-ridden and rat-infested flophouses when they could afford the ten or fifteen cents for a urine-stained mattress on the floor, and on park benches, under park shrubbery and bridge abutments, in doorways, packing crates, concrete pipes, culverts, construction sites, and abandoned automobiles when they could not afford it. The more ambitious among them contrived fragile shelters from scraps of wood and cardboard, old beer signs and fence posts, anything they could find that would keep off the wind and rain of winter and the direct sun of summer. They built them anywhere they could, but most of the time on the outskirts of cities and towns big enough to have outskirts, where outlandish villages began to coalesce like ramshackle suburbs. Everyone called them Hoovervilles; it was not a term of endearment.

☆

THE LIMITS OF CHARITY

Like most of his contemporaries—and, indeed, most of the American middle class—if President Hoover believed in anything more profoundly than the virtues of self-reliance and individual initiative, it has not been recorded. This was, after all, the very ethos of a white, Protestant culture, the image that Hoover and his kind held up as the ideal of Americanism. Hard work, honesty, and independence, they believed utterly, had brought this country to the forefront of nations, had built a breed of men (and

women, too, some conceded, though not often) who had taken the institutions of the founding fathers and made them the wonder of the world. Anything that might weaken the strength of that tradition would weaken the very character of America and was, by definition, evil. Government charity, especially, by robbing people of initiative, would be the very embodiment of error. The national government should stay out of the personal lives of its citizens, even if they were in trouble. For Hoover and for the millions of Americans who shared his convictions, the idea that people would turn to Washington, D.C., to help them out of a bad spot was nearly unthinkable.

It was a hard theory, but part of the accepted wisdom of the time and difficult for Hoover to abandon even in the face of the present situation. Still, when the dimensions of the crisis reached proportions that simply could not be ignored, he did not, as is often supposed, coldheartedly refuse to do anything about it. What he did do, for the most part, was call upon the natural generosity of the American people and the paternalism of local governments. Throughout his term he held to the firm belief that direct aid to the individual was not the business of the federal government—unless there were no other course, in which case he made it clear he would act, though almost certainly in great fear of permanently crippling the national character. "This is not an issue as to whether people shall go hungry or cold in the United States," he said in a statement to the press in the winter of 1931.

It is solely a question of the best method by which hunger and cold shall be prevented. . . . I am willing to pledge myself that if the time should ever come that the voluntary agencies of the country, together with the local and State governments, are unable to find resources with which to prevent hunger and suffering in my country, I will ask the aid of every resource of the Federal Government. . . . I have faith in the American people that such a day will not come.

In the meantime, Hoover authorized the expenditure of about $700 million on various public works projects. He also set up the Reconstruction Finance Corporation, which in early 1932 began doling out the $2 billion that Congress had appropriated to stimulate and prop up industry and agriculture in their time of need. The RFC was one of the few such efforts that amounted to much (it would survive to become one of the most powerful agencies in New Deal Washington). The National Business Survey Conference, for instance, was designed to "market" an optimistic feeling in the business community and as part of this goal its members took a solemn vow not to cut wages. Defections were almost immediate. The National Credit Corporation, for another example, was designed to set up a system whereby healthy banks would assist unhealthy banks; few did, and the NCC virtually collapsed in two years. The Federal Farm Board, created before the depression, was designed to stabilize farm prices through the temporary purchase of surplus farm produce; it managed to lose some $345 million and satisfied no one. The President's Emergency Committee for Employment (PECE) and its successor, the President's Organization for Unemployment Relief (POUR), were largely designed to promote the belief that things were not as bad as they appeared to be and even if they were they would soon get better; neither managed to get the message across with any great success—though the POUR was useful in helping local agencies and private charities raise money by getting pro bono advertisements placed in newspapers and magazines.

It must be said that many Americans tried to sustain self-reliance, as Hoover advised. Probably the best-known examples were the apple sellers who for a time appeared on the sidewalks of nearly every major city. In the fall of 1930, the hard-pressed International Apple Shippers Association came up with the idea of selling apples to the unemployed on credit at $1.75 a crate. The apples would retail on the street at a nickel apiece and if a seller got rid of all the apples in his or her crate, the net could be as much as $1.85. By the end of November, 1930, there were six thousand apple sellers on the streets of New York City alone, crouching, in the words of newspaperman Gene Fowler, "like half-remembered sins sitting upon the conscience of the town." Down in New Orleans, the same device was tried with Louisiana oranges—"Health for You—Help for the Needy," the *Times-Picayune* declared. While people at first responded with sympathy to these peddlers, they were altogether too visible a reminder of the nation's troubles; sales fell off drastically in a few months—not aided in the slightest by Hoover's peculiar public assertion at one point that "many persons left their jobs for the more profitable one of selling apples."

Many people tried to "maintain the spirit of charity" and the dogma of self-reliance in other ways, and many local governments struggled valiantly to meet the crisis themselves, as Hoover so fervently wished. Nothing worked for very long, even in the most successful instances. In Seattle, for example, a few Socialists got together and formed the Unemployed Citizens' League in July, 1931. The organization swiftly grew to a membership of somewhere between forty and fifty thousand. The UCL organized numerous self-help projects—cutting wood on donated land, picking unwanted fruit crops, fishing in Puget Sound, setting up commissaries for the distribution of food and wood, negotiating with landlords to prevent evictions, and putting together a kind of barter economy in which members exchanged services and goods. In response, Seattle mayor Robert Harlin formed the Mayor's Commission on Improved Employment to work with the UCL, and when a million-dollar bond issue was raised to finance it, put the leaders of the UCL in charge of the District Relief Organization. The UCL remained the principal distributor of food and work to the city's estimated forty-five thousand unemployed until the money began to run out.

In Philadelphia, it was the rich who organized,

and for a time it seemed that the city would stand as the perfect model for Hoover's vision of private-public cooperation at the local level. On November 7, 1930, the Committee of One Hundred of the city's most influential people met for lunch at the Bellevue-Stratford Hotel and formed the Committee for Unemployment Relief, with Horatio Gates Lloyd, a partner in Drexel and Company, the Philadelphia branch of the House of Morgan, as its chairman. In order to "tide over the temporary distress" of the depression, the committee immediately raised $4 million, which Lloyd parceled out to various private charities. The committee also persuaded the Pennsylvania General Assembly to authorize the city to borrow $3 million for public relief. A municipal Bureau of Unemployment was established and Lloyd himself was put in charge of the distribution of its public funds. Like that of the Socialists in Seattle, the philanthropists' effort in Philadelphia was a great success—for as long as the money held out. The $7 million in private and public money was exhausted by November, 1931. A "United Campaign" raised another $10 million in cash and pledges; Lloyd's committee got $5 million of that, and in three months it, too, was gone, as was the remaining $5 million that had gone to other agencies. In April, 1932, the city got another $2.5 million in direct aid from the state; that was gone in two months. The Lloyd Committee, the *Philadelphia Record* reported on June 20, "is through. For fifty-seven thousand families to whom the Committee has meant life itself, it added, playing on the Hoover administration's assurances that "prosperity is just around the corner," "STARVATION is 'just around the corner.'"

Volunteerism had not worked in Philadelphia, and neither it nor self-reliance would be enough anywhere they were tried. They certainly were not enough in those states in which one of the worst droughts in history gave the overall economic calamity an almost biblical character. The hardest hit was Arkansas, which in July and August, 1930, received only 4.19 inches of rain—35 percent of what

it had gotten during the same two months the previous year—but rainfall in another twenty-two states in the Midwest, Great Plains, and South also dropped by an average of nearly 40 percent in those two months. "The families that are suffering now, or on the verge of it," the Red Cross representative for Arkansas wrote national headquarters in August,

are not singled out as by flood or tornado or fire, but are just in their homes, with gardens ruined, sweet potatoes not making a crop, the prospect of being in debt to the landlord when the pitiable cotton crop is gathered instead of having money with which to buy food and clothing for the winter.

Hoover immediately formed another committee—several committees, in fact. At a conference of governors from the affected states on August 14, he told them that they should establish local and state drought committees to handle the problem. For the most part, he insisted, local communities were going to have to carry the burden alone. Furthermore, he believed that the Red Cross should provide the lion's share of any help beyond that. During the terrible floods in the southern Mississippi River Valley in 1927, the Red Cross had stepped in and brought relief to hundreds of thousands of people whose homes and lives had been devastated. The organization had sheltered the homeless, fed the hungry, had helped thousands of people to survive the disaster. Surely, it could do so again.

But the drought of these years was not a single, isolated event like a flood; it had gone on for a long time already and would go on for some time to come, and its disruptive effect was magnified by the larger economic situation which the Red Cross would not have been in a position to do anything about in any event. The organization's institutional inadequacy to accomplish what Hoover expected of it was compounded by the philosophy of its leader, national chairman Judge John Barton Payne. Payne was a close friend of Hoover's and shared the president's reverence for self-reliance. He made it clear from the start that the local and state Red Cross chapters would depend on volunteers and money from the local and state regions, and only under the most extreme circumstances would the national organization step in to help.

The system thus established was more efficient at withholding aid than in furnishing it. The state and local Red Cross chapters, like the state and local drought committees, usually were headed up by the "best people" who had been part of the oppressive plantation system for generations, and were prepared to think the worst of those who sought direct help. Many people worried that if food were distributed, workers might refuse to pick cotton at the wages plantation farmers were willing to pay. "Some, you know," the Red Cross chairman for Monroe County, Arkansas, wrote in early September,

are ready to let the Red Cross do it all, we think after the cotton is out we can raise some money, and as the worst is to come in the cold winter months, we think it best to postpone doing only what is absolutely necessary at this time, knowing that a person can get along on very little during warm weather.

By November even the planters were calling for direct aid, because they could not feed the families of their workers. Still, most local chapters continued to tell the national headquarters what it wanted to hear and people at headquarters ignored the streams of letters from the desperate, like that from an African-American farmer in Jefferson County, Arkansas:

There is thousands of collard farmers in Jefferson and Lincoln counties that has not bread. They are Bairfooted and thin closed many has went to the County Judge and to the local Red Cross they Both say that they has no Funds We are planning on sending a Collard men to Washington to lay our Trubles more clearly before you.

Stubbornly holding to his principles, Hoover himself continued to insist that the burden of relief should be carried by the Red Cross, not the government, and he did not even support legislation that would have provided $60 million for feed and seed loans from the Department of Agriculture. And Judge John Barton Payne continued to hold back the distribution of funds from the national Red Cross. But by January the situation was so terrible that even the local chapters had abandoned the pretense that local and state resources could provide sufficient relief, and national headquarters finally responded with a fund-raising drive that began on January 10 and ultimately raised a little over $10 million. Between then and the end of the program in the spring, 2,765,000 people had been fed just enough to get them through the winter. It was pinch-penny charity at best, and no one will ever know how many suffered how much during all the months in which virtually nothing had been handed out. And since records were as carelessly managed as the relief program itself, no one will know how many died.

Some "relief" efforts did not even pretend to charity. Chief among these was the attempted deportation of Mexican Americans, which managed to combine racism with selfishness and desperation in one of the least edifying episodes in American history. By the beginning of the thirties, there was a Mexican-American, or Chicano, population in the United States of about 1.5 million, much of it the result of immigration—some legal, some not (slovenly kept records and conflicting estimates between Mexican and U.S. officials made it impossible to say how many belonged in either category). Thousands of the immigrants had gone north to work the sugar-beet fields of Michigan and the other Great Lakes states, while others had refused stoop labor as a career, moving to Chicago, East Chicago, Gary, and Detroit to look for work in steel mills, automobile plants, and other industries. By 1930 there were 19,362 Mexican Americans living in Chicago, some 9,000 in East Chicago and Gary, and another 8,000 in Detroit, where the allure of the Ford Motor Company had reached into the towns of northern Mexico to call young workers to the "wonderful city of the magic motor."

Most of the immigrants, however, had spilled into the sugar-beet and cotton fields of Texas, Colorado, and Arizona, or on into the huge agribusiness farms of the Imperial and San Joaquin valleys of California. Those who had not joined the stream of migrant labor had gravitated toward the growing Mexican-American settlements in the larger cities. The biggest of these settlements was in Los Angeles, where the Chicano population had increased from 33,644 in 1920 to 97,116 in 1930, making the city the "Mexican capital" of the United States, exhausting the bounds of the older Chicano settlements and spreading out into the neighborhoods of East Los Angeles, where it would remain the largest single segment of the city's minority population.

The bigotry exercised against these people rivaled that endured by African Americans, and when the weight of the depression began to fall upon cities with large Chicano populations, unabashed racism was buttressed by the theory that unemployment among Anglo workers could be blamed on the presence of a labor force willing to work cheap and under conditions that "real" American workers would not tolerate—the Mexican Americans. The answer, some concluded, was deportation—or repatriation, as it was described more benignly. In Gary, Detroit, and other industrial centers, open discrimination, physical threats, racist propaganda campaigns, and free transportation helped to persuade thousands of Chicanos to return to Mexico.

Nowhere was the movement more vigorous than in Los Angeles, however, where the first consignment of 6,024 *repatriados* (songwriter-activist Woody Guthrie would call them "deportees" in one of his most famous songs) left Union Station aboard the cars of the Southern Pacific Railroad in February, 1931. At $14.70 a head, it cost the city and county of Los Angeles $77,249.29 to ship them out, but the savings in relief payments for that year amounted to $347,468.41—a net gain of $270,219.12. "In the last analysis," historian Rudolfo Acuña writes, "President Coolidge's maxim—'the business of America is business'—was applicable, and repatriation proved profitable, at least in dollars and cents." Over the next three years, Los Angeles County would do a pretty good business, deporting 12,688 Chicanos back to Mexico—though Carey McWilliams, who had been on hand to watch the first trainload leave Los Angeles in February, 1931, later pointed out, "Repatriation was a tragicomic affair: tragic in the hardships occasioned; comic because most of the Mexicans eventually returned to Los Angeles, having had a trip to Mexico at the expense of the county."

Elsewhere, there was little comedy, even dark comedy, to be found. In New York City, the apple sellers had vanished by the end of 1931 and by April, 1932, 750,000 people were living on city relief efforts that averaged $8.20 a month per person—about one-fifth of what it took to keep one human being decently—while an estimated 160,000 more waited to get on the 'rolls as soon as the money became available. In 1930, $6 million had gone for relief in New York; in 1931, $25 million; in 1932, it was estimated, the cost would be closer to $75 million. In Atlanta, the cost of relief for only thirty weeks was estimated at $1.2 million, but by December, 1931, only $590,000 had been raised and no more was forthcoming; in June, 1932, 20,000 people in Atlanta and Fulton County were simply removed from the relief rolls, most of them African Americans. In St. Louis, relief agencies were going through a quarter of a million dollars a month, and in July, 1932, the city had to drop 13,000 families off the rolls. In Fort Wayne, Indiana, the Allen County Emergency Unemployment Committee, formed in December, 1930, managed to raise enough money in its first two years to stay more or less even with the relief load. But in 1932, fund-raising targets were not met and the city's own relief expenditures began to slide. Like those in many other regions, Fort Wayne and other Allen County cities began printing their own scrip and using that as currency for goods and services within their own confines.

In Detroit, the Ford Motor Company was forced to shut down production lines on its spectacularly successful Model A. Introduced to a clamorous public in December, 1927, the Model A had taken the lead in sales away from Chevrolet, and even in 1930 the company had sold 1.4 million cars. But by August, 1931, sales were running at rates only half those of 1930, and Ford simply stopped production. Up to then, Detroit had been carrying a welfare budget of $14 million; it now was cut to $7 million, while the number of those in need of relief swelled. Similarly, a $17 million public works program was slashed to $6 million. Michigan Senator James Couzens offered to start a private relief fund with a personal donation of $1 million if Detroit's other rich people would come up with an additional $9 million; no one appeared interested.

☆

A PRIVATE KIND OF SHAME

However desperate the measures taken against it by private and public agencies alike, nothing seemed powerful enough to lift the weight of the depression. For those in the middle class or those who might have hoped to work and save their way into the middle class, much of the weight was psychological. "What is surprising is the passive resignation with which the blow has been accepted," newsman Marquis Childs wrote, "this awful pretense that seeks to conceal the mortal wound, to carry on as though it were still the best possible of all possible worlds." Louis Adamic said of American workers, "I have a definite feeling that millions of them, now that they are unemployed, are licked," and many did seem to be finished, burdened

beyond the bearing of it by a terrible load of guilt. They had been taught all their lives that hard work and thrift and honesty would be rewarded with at least security, if not wealth. That hope had failed them, and the fault must be in themselves; millions, Studs Terkel remembered, "experienced a private kind of shame when the pink slip came."

The architecture of despair could be seen everywhere, even among those, like most African Americans, who had been at the bottom so long that it might have seemed that nothing could possibly get any worse. But the hopes and psychic toughness of many black people, too, were tried as they had never been tried before—in the black working-class ghetto of Detroit's "Inkster," for example, where Ford Motor Company worker Odie Stallings scratched to keep his family alive.

Stallings, whose story was told in *American Odyssey*, Robert Conot's history of Detroit, had come to Detroit from Virginia after serving in World War I, joining an internal migration that had changed the face of urban America. If World War I had offered the wheat farmer of the Midwest the dream of avarice, it had given the African American of the South the dream of escape. Wartime America had needed bodies, and blacks had responded. Half a million had departed the rural South between 1916 and 1919 alone, and another million or more had migrated during the twenties. Most had found the promised land close to home—in such cities as Birmingham, Alabama, where the black population had nearly doubled in twenty years; or Memphis, Tennessee, where it had more than doubled; or Houston, Texas, where it had nearly tripled. But many of those who joined the Great Migration also had found opportunity winking at them from the Northeast and Midwest. "I'm tired of this Jim Crow," they sang, "gonna leave this Jim Crow town,/Doggone my black soul, I'm sweet Chicago bound," then had boarded trains by the carloads and headed north for Chicago, Detroit, Pittsburgh, Philadelphia, New York. "I should have been here 20 years ago," one transplant had written from

Chicago to the folks back home in Hattiesburg, Mississippi.

I just begin to feel like a man. It's a great deal of pleasure in knowing that you got some privileges. My children are going to the same school with the whites and I don't have to umble to no one. I have registered—will vote the next election and there ain't any 'yes sir'—it's all yes and no and Sam and Bill.

Odie Stallings had been seduced by the same dream, settling in Inkster after finding work in the "black department" at the Ford Plant in River Rouge. He married, and he and his wife, Freda, soon produced two sons. She was pregnant with their third when Ford shut down operations in August, 1931. Shortly afterward, Freda gave birth to another boy. With no income, the Stallings family, like most of those in Inkster, lived on a diet that often was reduced to nothing but starches and water, and Odie dropped from 160 to 125 pounds. His wife was even more wasted, and her breasts were nearly dry; she fed the baby from a bottle filled with flour and water when she could not nurse him herself. Odie trudged the city streets and country roads all over Wayne County in search of any kind of work until his shoes were worn to less than shreds and he could no longer walk long distances. He patched his lightless and heatless shack with newspapers to keep out the cold, but when winter closed down on the ghetto like a fist, the children hacked and coughed incessantly, including the baby, who grew increasingly sick. The parents slept with the infant between them on a narrow bed to keep him warm, but nothing helped, and one morning when they woke he was dead. They put the tiny body in a cardboard box and walking close together under a gray morning sky the family carried their burden up the rutted muddy street and buried it in the makeshift cemetery next to the little community church.

So much, then, for belief in a system whose inherent strengths were supposed to prevent such misery

from ever taking place—or if it could not guarantee that, would at least move swiftly and purposefully to repair the damage that had been done. That faith had been tested and had failed—in Detroit, in New York, Chicago, Philadelphia, Seattle, in the farm fields of the Midwest, the cotton plantations of the South, everywhere, resoundingly. What was left, then? Despair, certainly, the bleak anguish of a psychological depression whose dimensions matched the somber statistical dirge of the economic slump. But in human terms, depression often is just another form of anger. And in the end it would be anger, not despair, that would question conventional wisdom, dismantle comfortable assumptions about American society, challenge the machinery of government itself, and bring the first light to the long darkness of the Great Depression.

People everywhere protested their lot. In Arkansas, angry farmers invaded the town of England and demanded food for their hungry families. With reassurances from the Red Cross that they would be reimbursed, merchants distributed bread and other food to the farmers. In Oklahoma City, a mob of hungry men and women invaded a grocery store and seized what they needed. Despite tear gas fired by police, hundreds of workers staged a hunger march on Ford Motor Company at Dearborn, Michigan. In 1932, 20,000 veterans of the Great War marched on Washington after Hoover withheld bonuses promised them for their service in that savage conflict. Hoover sent in the army and six tanks to disperse these "dangerous radicals." That same year an angry and fearful electorate voted Hoover out of office, replacing him with a patrician Democrat who assured Americans that they had "nothing to fear but fear itself."

QUESTIONS TO CONSIDER

1 What economic conditions characterized the crash and the beginning of the Great Depression? The author cites a set of harrowing statistics to illustrate the gravity of the crisis. To what did they refer?

209

2   How did the Depression affect ordinary Americans, both economically and psychologically? Give examples from the text. What happened to Mexican Americans? Who was Odie Stallings? What does his story illustrate?

3   What was President Hoover's approach to the crisis? What were the beliefs that guided him in his attempt to solve it? What did he tell Americans they must do? What agencies did he rely on to provide relief? Did his approach succeed or fail?

4   What role did the Red Cross play in the early years of the Depression? If charity and volunteerism failed to solve the crisis, what do you think was needed?

5   Given the poverty, frustration, anger, and disillusionment of millions of Americans during the Depression, how can you explain the relative lack of violence or popular demands for radical change?

17

FDR and the New Deal:
The Foundation of a New Political Tradition

ALONZO L. HAMBY

Franklin Roosevelt swept to power in 1932, carrying every state but six in the electoral college and gathering 23 million popular votes in contrast to Hoover's 16 million. It was a bitter defeat for the Republicans. But the election was even more disappointing for Norman Thomas and William Z. Foster, candidates for the Socialist and Communist parties, respectively. In this year of distress, with some 16 million people unemployed, Thomas collected 882,000 votes and Foster only 103,000.

Roosevelt was perhaps the most controversial president the United States ever had. For millions of Americans, he was a folk hero: a courageous statesman who saved a crippled nation from almost certain collapse and whose New Deal salvaged the best features of democratic capitalism while establishing unprecedented welfare programs for the nation. For others, he was a tyrant, a demagogue who used the Depression to consolidate his political power, whereupon he dragged the country zealously down the road to socialism. In spite of his immense popular appeal, Roosevelt became the hated enemy of much of the nation's business and political community. Conservatives denounced him as a Communist. Liberals said he was too conservative. Communists castigated him as a tool of Wall Street. And Socialists dismissed him as a reactionary. "He caught hell from all sides," recorded one observer, because few knew how to classify his political philosophy or his approach to reform. Where, after all, did he fit ideologically? Was he for capitalism or against it? Was his New Deal revolutionary or reactionary? Was it "creeping socialism" or a bulwark against socialism? Did it lift the country out of the Depression, or did it make the disaster worse?

In the next selection, Alonzo L. Hamby argues that the key to understanding Roosevelt is the Progressive tradition in which he grew up and participated. Roosevelt came to office, Hamby believes, with an ideological commitment to Progressive reform. Yet there were two brands of progressivism. The New Nationalism of Theodore Roosevelt and Herbert Croly, offered to the American electorate in 1912, had accepted business consolidation — monopolies and trusts — but had insisted that the federal government should regulate and control them. The New Freedom of Woodrow Wilson and Louis Brandeis, put forth in the same election, had held that competition must be preserved and that the best approach to monopolies was to destroy them by federal action (by his second year in office, however, Wilson had abandoned the New Freedom and embraced TR's New Nationalism). Both brands of progressivism had emerged in a period of overall prosperity in the United States; hence neither provided guidelines for dealing with an economic calamity such as the Great Depression. Franklin Roosevelt, says Hamby, preferred the ideas of the New Nationalism but found little in its doctrines to guide him in handling "the worst crisis of capitalism in American history." Therefore, flexible politician that he was, Roosevelt opted for a strategy of action: he borrowed what he could from Progressive doctrines, added some experimentation, tossed in some Keynesian economics (government spending to "prime" the stricken economy), and packaged his New Deal as a liberal reform program that appealed to many interest groups.

How successful was the New Deal? Hamby gives it a mixed score. Like many other scholars, he believes that it probably saved capitalism in America, although most corporate bosses hated Roosevelt with a passion. And while it provided relief for millions of Americans, protected the organization and bargaining rights of American labor, and saved the average farmer through a system of price supports and acreage allotments, the New Deal failed to end the Depression — World War II would finally do that. The problem lay with the inability of the New Dealers to devise a coherent strategy for dealing with the structure of the American economy and particularly with restoring consumer purchasing power — the key to successful recovery. Hamby attributes this to the influence of progressivism, which had "sought humanitarian social programs, advocated a more equitable distribution of American abundance for all social groups, decried unregulated corporate power, and possessed some impulses toward social engineering." The New Dealers tried to realize these old aspirations, but because none of them addressed an economic disaster, the efforts of the New Dealers often impeded recovery. Hamby also argues that Roosevelt's increasingly hostile rhetoric against the business elite, however understandable, "probably did more to prolong the Depression than to solve it."

Yet Hamby gives FDR high marks for balancing the conflicting groups of labor, agriculture, and business and for establishing big government as the arbiter. In the process, FDR created "a political economy of counter-veiling powers," which, with the institu-

tion of welfare measures, guarded against future depressions and helped maintain the prosperity of the postwar years. But Roosevelt's "final legacy" to the United States, Hamby believes, was his creation of a new political tradition, which defined American politics as pluralistic, liberal, and international and to which the majority of Americans subscribed.

GLOSSARY

AGRICULTURAL ADJUSTMENT ADMINISTRATION (AAA)   New Deal agency designed to relieve Depression-wracked farmers, who suffered from falling prices and mounting crop surpluses; the AAA, established in 1933, subsidized farm prices until they reached a point of "parity" and sought to reduce farm surpluses by telling farmers how much to plant (acreage allotments) and paying them for what they did not raise. Declared unconstitutional by the Supreme Court in 1935, the AAA was superseded by the Soil Conservation and Domestic Allotment Act, which authorized the federal government to pay farmers to reduce their crop production to prevent erosion and "preserve soil."

BRAINS TRUST   FDR's special group of advisers led by eminent political economists Raymond Moley, Rexford G. Tugwell, and Adolph A. Berle Jr.

HOPKINS, HARRY   FDR's close friend and adviser who headed the Civil Works Administration, 1933–1934, and the Works Progress Administration, 1935–1938; he was secretary of commerce, 1938–1940.

JOHNSON, HUGH   Director of the National Recovery Administration who devised voluntary codes of fair competition and used public relations and propaganda to persuade employers to adhere to them.

KEYNESIAN ECONOMICS   Propounded by British economist John Maynard Keynes and his followers, who advocated government programs for budgeting and for issuing currency in order to maintain employment.

McADOO, WILLIAM GIBBS   Wilson's secretary of the treasury who battled Alfred E. Smith for the Democratic presidential nomination in 1928; McAdoo's chief support came from the Democratic party's rural, prohibitionist wing.

MARXISM   Economic-political doctrine, espoused by Karl Marx and Friedrich Engels, that holds that the structural weaknesses and contradictions of capitalism doom it to failure, that ultimately the working class (proletariat) will revolt against the capitalist class and take control of the means of production, and that the result will be a classless society in which "rational economic cooperation" replaces "the coercive state."

NATIONAL RECOVERY ADMINISTRATION (NRA)   New Deal agency established in 1933 to promote industrial recovery and end unemployment by devising and promoting hundreds of "industrial fair practice codes"; in practice, it often impeded competition by sanctioning production quotas and price fixing; in 1935, the Supreme Court invalidated the act that had chartered the NRA.

PERKINS, FRANCES   The first woman to serve in a presidential cabinet, she was FDR's secretary of labor, 1933–1945; she mediated bitter labor disputes and helped write the Social Security Act of 1935, the National Labor Relations Act of 1935, and other important New Deal legislation.

RESETTLEMENT ADMINISTRATION (1935) AND FARM SECURITY ADMINISTRATION (1937)   Offered marginal farmers short- and long-term loans so that they could relocate on better land.

RURAL ELECTRIFICATION ADMINISTRATION (1935)   Established utility cooperatives that provided electrical power to farmers.

SMITH, ALFRED E.   Democratic nominee for president, 1928; the first Roman Catholic to be chosen as a party candidate for the presidency.

SOCIAL SECURITY ACT (1935)   Provided federal welfare assistance (up to $15 per month) for destitute elderly Americans and established a pension system for those working; the program, however, excluded domestic servants and agricultural workers, many of them women and African American.

TAMMANY HALL   New York's Irish-Catholic political machine; corrupt though it was, it did support welfare programs for the poor.

TENNESSEE VALLEY AUTHORITY (TVA)   Public corporation created by Congress in 1933 and "an unprecedented experiment in regional planning"; the TVA completed a dam at Muscle Shoals, Alabama, on the Tennessee River, and improved or built many others, which all but ended flooding in the region; the TVA also generated and sold inexpensive electricity to thousands of rural Americans who had never had it before.

WAGNER ACT (1935)   Guaranteed labor the right to organize and set up the National Labor Relations Board (NLRB), a policing agency with the power to coerce employers into recognizing and bargaining with bonafide unions.

WORKS PROGRESS ADMINISTRATION (WPA)   New Deal agency, established in 1935, that launched numerous improvement and building projects to furnish jobs for the unemployed; the agency's name was changed in 1939 to the Work Projects Administration.

Governor Roosevelt, wrote the eminent columnist Walter Lippmann in January 1932, was not to be taken seriously: "An amiable man with many philanthropic impulses, but . . . not the dangerous enemy of anything . . . no crusader . . . no tribune of the people . . . no enemy of entrenched privilege . . . a pleasant man who, without any important qualifications for the office, would very much like to be President." Lippmann's evaluation was to become the most frequently quoted example of the perils of punditry in the history of American journalism. But when it appeared it was just another expression of a widely held assessment of Franklin D. Roosevelt, written at a time when it was still possible to assume that his determined optimism and issue-straddling were the marks of a lightweight who by some accident had twice been elected governor of the nation's largest state.

By the time of FDR's death, four presidential election victories later, Lippmann's condescending dismissal was an object of ridicule. Roosevelt had become the focus of intense emotions, united in agreement only on his standing as a moving force in history. To his enemies, he represented evil incarnate — socialism and communism, dictatorship, war. To his admirers, he was an object of worship — the champion of the underprivileged, the symbol of the world struggle of democratic, humanist civilization against the darkness of fascism. Millions wept at his passing.

Roosevelt had in fact profoundly changed the nature of American politics. Although he failed to achieve many of his most important immediate objectives, although he was notoriously eclectic and nonsystematic in his approach to the enormous problems of his era, FDR was the founder of a distinctively new tradition which was to preempt the mainstream of American politics after his death.

Like all great departures in American politics, the Rooseveltian political tradition had deep roots in the past, specifically in the progressivism of Theodore Roosevelt and Woodrow Wilson, and generally in the optimism of a more innocent epoch. It was Roosevelt who achieved the actual implementation of what had been in many instances little more than abstract concepts formulated by earlier progressives, added to them — however unwittingly — Keynesian economics, and encased the whole package within a framework of "pluralist" or interest-group liberalism. And it was Roosevelt who fused the diplomatic realism of his cousin Theodore with the idealism of his old leader Woodrow Wilson in such a way that the American nation was irreversibly committed to active participation in a world it had largely shunned.

To all this, he added a new *style* of political leadership scarcely less important than the substantive changes he achieved. After Roosevelt, the most consistently successful American politicians were not those who relied upon the increasingly decrepit political machines or employed old-fashioned press

FDR at Warm Springs, Georgia, in December 1933. Roosevelt "added a new style of political leadership," writes Alonzo Hamby. "After Roosevelt, the most consistently successful American politicians ... were those who mastered mid-twentieth- *century mass communications to impart a sense of direct contact with the people." FDR " was great both because of what he did and how he did it." (UPI/Corbis-Bettmann)*

agentry. They were those who mastered mid-twentieth-century mass communications to impart a sense of direct contact with the people. Like many political leaders of the highest historical rank, Roosevelt was great both because of what he did and how he did it.

☆

THE MAN BEHIND THE MASKS

To be born and raised a Roosevelt in the penultimate decade of the nineteenth century was to discover the world in an environment of remarkable privilege and security. It was the quaint world of an American patrician aristocracy, a setting of Hudson River mansions, European vacations, private tutors, ponies, and loving, attentive parents. Moderately wealthy, possessing blood lines running back to the *Mayflower,* esteemed by the arbiters of society, still prominent in business and finance, the Roosevelts and the class they represented were on the whole free from the taints of greed, irresponsibility, vulgarity, and conspicuous consumption that the popular mind attributed to the *nouveaux riches* of the period.

Perhaps no other segment of American society so fully accepted and synthesized the dominant values and hopes of Western civilization at the high noon of the Victorian era. The young Franklin Roosevelt absorbed a climate of opinion characterized by belief in the near-inevitability of progress; the unquestioned superiority of Anglo-American liberalism; the imperative of duty to one's friends, family, church, and country; and the unimpeachable character of traditional moral standards. The Victorian world view imparted to those who accepted it an ebullient confidence and an unquenchable optimism.

The close, attentive world in which Roosevelt lived as a child provided little of the experience that one usually associates with the building of leadership. His vigorous, domineering mother both doted on him and attempted to make all his decisions up

through the early years of his marriage. From a very young age, however, he managed to establish his individuality in a smothering atmosphere. He developed a calculating other-directedness based on an understanding that he could secure his own autonomy and achieve his own objectives only by seeming to be the type of person that others — his mother, his schoolmates, his political associates — wanted him to be.

At the exclusive Groton preparatory school, at Harvard, and at Columbia Law School, he was never more than a respectable scholar. He preferred instead to concentrate on the nonacademic activities that he knew would win him the recognition of his peers. He stayed on as a nominal graduate student at Harvard only to be eligible to assume the editorship of the *Crimson* and never bothered to complete his M.A. A marginal law student, he dropped out of Columbia after passing the state bar examinations although he was but a few months away from his degree. His intelligence was keen and his interests wide-ranging, but he felt a certain amiable contempt for the world of academic scholarship and indeed for almost any sustained, disciplined intellectual effort. The appearance he presented to the world was that of a young man conventionally handsome, somewhat overeager for popularity, and determined to suppress the cerebral aspects of his personality. Girls who knew him as a college student called him "feather duster" and "the handkerchief-box young man." Many of his male acquaintances found him unimpressive. Indeed, Porcellian, the elite Harvard club of his father and of Theodore Roosevelt, rejected his candidacy for membership.

Largely because of his name and social position, young Roosevelt was taken into a prestigious Wall Street law firm. Establishing himself as a competent young attorney, he faced a secure, well-defined future in which he would move up from clerk to junior partner to senior partner, earning an increasingly lucrative income and spending his weekends as a country gentleman. Yet he possessed little interest in so confined and comfortable a life. In a rare moment of open introspection, he told some of his fellow clerks that he intended to go into politics and that he would follow precisely in the footsteps of his distant cousin, Theodore Roosevelt — from the state assembly to the assistant secretaryship of the navy to the governorship of New York to the presidency. It is hard to say how serious he was, and it is uncertain whether he actually had acquired the toughness and ambition that would eventually take him to the top. It is safe to say that he had been caught up in the idealism of early-twentieth-century reform.

The progressive movement that dominated American life in the first and second decades of the century was actually several reform movements representing different social groups, drawing upon diverse political philosophies, and pursuing divergent objectives. At its heart, however, was a rejection of the unfettered industrial capitalism of the late nineteenth century and a sense of concern for the victims of its abuses. As such, it had a special appeal to the somewhat displaced younger members of older socially prominent families such as the Roosevelts. Assuming that the American system would respond to pressures for gradual change, progressivism appealed to the Victorian optimism on which Roosevelt had been nurtured. . . .

FDR's early political career followed a progression along the lines he had projected to his fellow law clerks; it moved also from a shallow amateurism to a deep professionalism. Nominated for the state assembly in 1910 by a local Democratic organization that did not take him seriously, he campaigned intensively, frequently speaking to small groups from an open touring car. His nervousness and inexperience displayed themselves in awkward pauses as he tried to remember his lines or groped for something to say to the farmers who came to hear him. Roosevelt's district was strongly Republican, but he capitalized on a national surge of discontent with the inept administration of William Howard Taft. He had the advantage of the Roosevelt name, and he employed

incessant denunciations of "bossism" to identify himself with the GOP insurgent movement that looked to Theodore Roosevelt for inspiration. His victory was one of many Democratic upsets around the country.

In Albany, Roosevelt quickly made himself the leader of a small group of Democratic dissenters determined to block the election of a Tammany senatorial candidate. He held the quixotic movement together for two months, using his name and his already considerable talent for drawing attention to himself to garner national recognition. He made an ultimate defeat seem somehow a victory for political virtue, but he and his followers had exemplified only the shallow side of progressivism.

To many upper-middle-class Yankee reformers, Tammany Hall was simply a corrupt, Irish-Catholic political machine engaging in every manner of boodle and sustaining its power by buying the votes, one way or another, of illiterate immigrants. This attitude was true enough as far as it went, but incomplete and a shade bigoted. It showed little awareness of the social conditions to which the machine addressed itself through an informal but well-organized system of assistance to the poor and through increasing support of social welfare legislation. Moreover, Tammany produced men of substance (among them Roosevelt's legislative colleagues Robert F. Wagner and Alfred E. Smith) — honest, creative, and equipped by their own experience to understand the problems of the urban masses far more vividly than could an upstate neophyte. For the next two years, Roosevelt played the role of gadfly to Tammany, delighting his own district but needlessly making enemies of the powers within the Democratic party.

Had this been the sum of his politics, he doubtless would have gone the way of many a good government reformer of the time, enjoying a brief period of influence and attention followed by a long exile on the fringes of American public life. He was, however, capable of growth. Some of his "good government" causes, such as a bill to establish an honest, efficient state highway commission, were more soundly based. His progressivism gradually moved in other directions also: women's suffrage, conservation, public control of electrical power, workmen's compensation, and regulation of hours and working conditions in mines and factories. By the end of his second year in the legislature, Roosevelt had loosely identified himself with a style of progressivism that moved across the spectrum of reform causes. In doing so, he had paralleled the evolution of his revered kinsman, TR. Established as a noted, if not powerful, New York Democrat, he needed only the right bit of good fortune to move onto the national scene.

Remarkably, his advancement stemmed from the ostentatious insurgency that normally would have made him unelectable to any statewide office. Displaying sound instinct, he attached himself to a new national progressive figure destined to eclipse Theodore Roosevelt — Woodrow Wilson. Although he could deliver no votes, FDR served as an attractive spokesman for the New Jersey governor and became identified as one of his major New York supporters. Wilson's victory would bring the isolated young insurgent to Washington.

It was far from coincidental that he took the post of assistant secretary of the navy. He might have obtained other powerful positions — collector of the Port of New York or assistant secretary of the treasury, for example — but the navy position was yet another step along TR's old path. Moreover, it gave Roosevelt a chance to wield power and influence on a large scale. It was an extraordinary opportunity for a man who loved ships and the sea and who from his student days had been a disciple of the great advocate of naval power, Admiral Alfred Thayer Mahan.

As assistant secretary of the navy, young FDR functioned as the second-ranking official in the department and was primarily responsible for its day-to-day administration. Like his cousin before him, Roosevelt was the official who actually managed the navy: his chief, Josephus Daniels, was a small-town

North Carolina progressive chosen for his devotion to the ideals of the New Freedom and for his influence with Southern congressmen rather than for any knowledge of military matters.

In most respects, Roosevelt's performance was excellent. The coming of World War I made his office even more important than he could have anticipated, and he contributed significantly to the American military victory. Possessing more knowledge of technical naval matters and better read in the strategy of sea power than perhaps any other high civilian official in Washington, he was also a strong and effective administrator, audacious in the exercise of his authority, receptive to new ideas, daring in his own strategic concepts. He delighted in cutting red tape to facilitate one procurement operation after another; almost single-handedly, he overcame the opposition of both the entire British Admiralty and many of his own officers to secure the laying of a massive anti-submarine mine barrage across the North Sea.

He learned much, too. He established relationships with the ranking naval officials of the Allied powers, with important business executives, and with labor union leaders in the shipyards. He gained a sense of the contours of international diplomacy and developed the art of dealing with powerful interest groups. A key figure in a federal bureaucracy attempting to manage a national crisis, he received firsthand training in the use of governmental power to create a feeling of national purpose.

He also absorbed lessons of another sort. Still playing the role of insurgent, he had allowed his name to be entered in the 1914 New York Democratic senatorial primary as the anti-Tammany candidate. The machine had countered masterfully, backing President Wilson's widely respected ambassador to Germany, James W. Gerard, who won by a margin approaching 3 to 1. FDR quickly moved toward a rapprochement; by 1917, he was the featured speaker at the Tammany Fourth of July celebration, posing amiably with Boss Murphy for the photographers. Soon the organization indicated its willingness to accept him as a unity candidate for governor.

Instead, he was an attractive vice-presidential candidate in 1920 — young, able, nationally known, a resident of the largest state in the union. Among the Democratic rank and file, and especially among young intellectuals and activists, his nomination was popular. Handsome, vigorous, and by this time a skilled public speaker, he toured the country, delivering perhaps a thousand speeches. He attracted about as much attention as his running mate, James Cox, and made hundreds of personal contacts with the state and local leadership of the Democratic party from Massachusetts to California. When he and Cox went under in the Harding landslide, few would ever again tender Cox serious attention. But somehow Roosevelt seemed to speak for the future of the party. He alone had emerged from the debacle in a position of strength, possessing greater public recognition than ever and having obtained a first-hand knowledge of the structure of the Democratic party.

In such circumstances, it seemed especially tragic that in 1921, at the age of thirty-nine, he incurred a crippling attack of polio that promised to end his active political career. It is unquestionable that Roosevelt's suffering — both physical and psychological — was enormous. The ordeal may have deepened his character, giving him a greater sense of identification with the unfortunate of the world and strengthening his resolve. It was an existential challenge from which he emerged triumphant in spirit if not in body. Despite intensive physical therapy over a period of several years, he never regained the use of his legs. But he achieved a feat of self-definition against the will of his mother, who expected him to settle down under her wing to the life of an invalid country gentleman, and against that current of American political culture that expects political leaders to be specimens of perfect health. He quickly decided to stay in politics and to continue to pursue his ultimate goal, the presidency. From the perspective of that decision, his personal tragedy was political good fortune.

Polio removed Roosevelt from active political competition in an era in which the Democratic party was in a state of disintegration, effectively subdued by the economic successes of Republican normalcy and torn by bitter dissension between urban and rural factions led by Alfred E. Smith and William Gibbs McAdoo. Engaging instead in numerous charitable and civic activities, ostentatiously maintaining an interest in the future of his party, and carefully keeping lines open to both its wings, he remained a public figure and functioned, in Frank Freidel's phrase, as a "young elder statesman." The most elementary dictates of political loyalty required him to align himself with his fellow New Yorker Smith, but he did so in a way that could have antagonized only the most fanatical McAdoo supporter. His 1924 nominating speech for Smith was an attention-getting formal return to politics and the most universally praised event of an intensely bitter Democratic convention. He steadfastly avoided name-calling and, after the disastrous Democratic defeat in November, he sent out a letter to every convention delegate asking for suggestions on the regeneration of the party. In this and other ways, he reminded the rank and file of his probable eventual availability as the man who could unify them, and yet he could bide his time. . . .

[In 1928] Roosevelt benefited from another stroke of unlikely political luck — he was drafted for the Democratic gubernatorial nomination in what seemed certain to be a Republican year. Pressed into the race by the presidential candidate, Al Smith, who realized that Roosevelt's name on the ticket would be a great help in upstate New York, he eked out a narrow victory. Smith, nonetheless, lost the state badly to Hoover. Roosevelt had established himself as New York's senior Democrat, and his new office was generally considered in those days to be the best jumping-off position for a presidential nomination. At the end of his first year as governor, with the national economy dropping sharply downward, that jumping-off position began to look much more valuable than either he or Smith could have imagined in mid-1928.

Roosevelt was a strong and effective governor, although his tenure, inhibited by constant political warfare with a Republican legislature, was more important for what it attempted than for what it accomplished. Under the pressures of political responsibility and economic distress, Roosevelt's vague progressivism began to take on a more definite shape. He pushed strongly for conservation, public development of hydroelectric facilities on the St. Lawrence River, rural electrification, help for the hard-pressed farmer, and work relief projects for the unemployed. He surrounded himself with able, liberal-minded aides—Samuel I. Rosenman, Harry Hopkins, Frances Perkins. He developed his strongest grasp yet of public relations. Press releases and news handouts spewed from his office and got his viewpoint into many Republican papers. He took highly visible inspection trips that carried him around the state from one institution or project to another. Most importantly, he made superb use of the newest and most important medium of mass communication since the invention of the printing press—the radio. Undertaking a series of "fireside chats," he established himself as one of the few public figures of the era who instinctively knew how to project his personality over the airwaves. Roosevelt swept to a resounding reelection victory in 1930, establishing himself as the dominant contender for the Democratic presidential nomination in 1932.

The nomination was nonetheless a near thing. Facing the then hallowed rule of the Democratic party that a nominee required a two-thirds majority of the convention votes, he nearly fell to a "stop Roosevelt" alliance of candidates ranging from his former ally Smith to the one-time Wilsonian Newton D. Baker to the crusty old Southern conservative John Nance Garner of Texas. His opponents had only one thing in common: they all lacked the ideological flexibility to deal with the economic crisis America faced by 1932. Roosevelt went over the top, just as his support was on the verge of disintegration, by making a deal to give Garner the vice-presidency.

Victory in November was certain, and he took no chances in the campaign. He made it clear that his presidency would depart sharply from the policies of Herbert Hoover, that he had no respect for outmoded tradition, that he would, as he put it, give the nation "a New Deal." He ostentatiously put together a "Brains Trust" of advisers headed by three of the country's foremost political economists — Raymond Moley, Adolf A. Berle, Jr., and Rexford G. Tugwell. Still, he presented no coherent platform. His pronouncements hit both sides of some issues and approached others in the most general terms. Faced with two sharply opposing drafts of what was to be a major address on tariff policy, he was capable of telling his speechwriters to "weave the two together." He defeated Hoover by seven million votes.

☆

THE NEW DEALER

Like most politicians, Roosevelt had followed a path to success based upon an appealing style and a mastery of political techniques. Any effort to stake out a fixed, precise ideological position probably would have been politically counterproductive. But the American political and economic systems faced an unprecedented situation that seemed to demand rigorous analysis and reevaluation. The collapse of the economy during the Hoover years, the quantum increases in the unemployment rolls, the mortgage foreclosures that afflicted small-scale farmers and middle-class homeowners alike, the crops that went unharvested for lack of a market, the collapse of the banking system, the rapidly spreading misery and deprivation that attended the lack of any decent government aid for the unfortunate — all added up to the worst crisis of capitalism in American history.

Marxist solutions were unacceptable in America, even during the worst part of the Depression. The other reform alternative, the American progressive tradition to which Roosevelt loosely subscribed, had been forged during a time of general prosperity and was torn between conflicting economic visions of competition and concentration. Intellectually, progressives were almost as unprepared for the appalling disaster as Hoover had been. It is hardly surprising that Roosevelt and those around him met the challenge of depression with a curious blend of halfway measures, irrelevant reforms, and inconsistent attitudes.

Roosevelt sensed that the American people in 1933 wanted action above all, backed by displays of confidence and optimism. In his inaugural address, he exhorted America to fear nothing but fear itself. Invariably, he maintained a buoyant appearance, exemplified by his calculated cheerfulness or by the jaunty angle of his cigarette holder. Comparing himself to a quarterback who would call the next play only after the present one had been run, he made no pretense of working from a fixed design. Instead, he simply announced that his objectives would be relief, reform, and recovery. He pursued them with a bewildering cluster of programs that left no doubt of the government's concern for the plight of its citizens and of the administration's activism.

Relief was the easiest goal to pursue. By the time Roosevelt took office, poverty seemed on the way to becoming the normal condition of life for a majority of Americans. Facing a sea of human misery, untroubled by ideological inhibitions against federal aid to the needy, the Roosevelt administration swiftly instituted public works jobs, mortgage relief legislation, farm price supports, and federal insurance for bank deposits — programs aimed directly at the plight of the individual who had been hit in one way or another by the Depression.

By contemporary standards, it is true, these efforts were relatively modest. Moreover, Roosevelt fretted constantly about their cost, and, while accepting

them as a necessity, he never allowed them to be expanded sufficiently to provide jobs for the majority of the unemployed. All the same, most people who received some sort of help — a WPA job, a refinanced mortgage, an AAA acreage allotment check — were grateful in a direct personal way.

Reform posed a more difficult problem. In his own experience as an admirer of TR's New Nationalism and a participant in Wilson's New Freedom, Roosevelt embodied the two conflicting main lines of progressive thought, neither of which had been formulated to address the problem of recovery from an economic depression. The debate at bottom was between the TR–Herbert Croly vision of a political economy that accepted the dominance of the large corporation and sought to regulate it in the public interest and the Wilson–Louis Brandeis faith in an atomistic, intensely competitive economic society. The New Deal's resolution of the argument would in the end amount to little more than an evasion of choice.

The most permanent and successful items of the New Deal reform agenda were not specifically directed at Depression-created problems but had some of the appearance of relief acts. During the Progressive Era, reformers had reached a substantial consensus on the need for social legislation to provide ongoing protection to the working classes and the disadvantaged. The Social Security Act of 1935 established a national system of old-age insurance and committed the federal government to extensive subsidies for state welfare programs. The act marked a revolution in federal responsibility for the welfare of the needy. It quickly became politically unassailable, and over the next generation its coverage and benefits grew steadily.

Much the same process occurred with regard to agriculture. With the immediate objective of fighting the Depression, the New Deal introduced an extensive and quasi-permanent system of benefits and subsidies for rural America. For the cash-crop farmer and the agrarian middle class, the administration

Through the Works Progress Administration (later called the Work Projects Administration), the New Deal put unemployed men like these to work on a variety of projects, from building *bridges in the cities to blazing nature trails in the wilderness. These WPA workers are engaged in a street-widening project. (Corbis-Bettmann)*

produced a series of devices aimed at achieving profitable market prices (most important among them acreage allotments and federal purchase of surpluses). Roosevelt seems to have considered the price support program a temporary expedient, but his hopes that agriculture could become self-sufficient ran up against reality. By his second term, Secretary of Agriculture Henry A. Wallace was justifying long-term [government] buying of [farm] surpluses by proclaiming the goal of an "ever-normal granary."

Price supports were only the centerpiece of the New Deal agricultural program. Other aspects, such as rural electrification and soil conservation, were largely successful attempts to enhance the quality of

life on the land. Through the Resettlement Administration and the Farm Security Administration, the New Deal undertook the first important attack in American history on the structure of rural poverty. The agencies delivered assistance of one variety or another to the forgotten classes of the agricultural community — the impoverished dirt farmers, the sharecroppers, the migrant laborers. Their aid and rehabilitation programs sought to transform an agrarian *lumpenproletariat* [marginal underclass] into a self-sufficient yeomanry.

The results were mixed. Price support programs probably saved the average farmer from liquidation but failed to produce real prosperity; electrification and conservation brought firm gains to individuals and the land; the antipoverty efforts, underfunded stepchildren, were less successful. But in the guise of fighting the Depression, the New Deal had put the federal government into agriculture on a vast scale and a permanent basis.

The same was true of the labor programs. From the beginning, the New Deal endorsed the right of collective bargaining, and from 1933 on, union leaders told prospective recruits, "President Roosevelt wants you to join the union." Roosevelt actually had little personal enthusiasm for militant unionism. It was nonetheless a force that drew special sustenance from the New Deal's general endorsement of social change and fair play for the underdog. The Wagner Act of 1935 was not introduced at Roosevelt's behest, but it won his endorsement as it moved through Congress. The new law projected the federal government into labor-management relations in ways that would have been unimaginable just a few years earlier. It established procedures by which unions could win recognition from management, prohibited certain anti-union practices by employers, and set up a strong, permanent bureaucracy (the National Labor Relations Board) to provide continuing enforcement. For workers at the lowest, usually nonunionized levels of American business, the Fair Labor Standards Act of 1938 established nationwide wage and hour standards, prohibited child labor, and provided strict rules for the employment of teenagers.

In providing help to a blue-collar work force that had been hit hard by the Depression, the New Deal had effected long-term changes whose significance could barely be grasped as the thirties came to an end. Organized labor had emerged as a major force within the Democratic party, providing the campaign support Roosevelt and his followers needed to stay in power. The members of its unions would constitute the bulk of the additions to the post–World War II middle class.

Reform of the banking system, accompanied as it was by federal deposit insurance, was both relief for the "little people" who had lost their savings in bank failures and retribution against the bankers. Regulation of the securities markets, long overdue, was widely accepted as a form of discipline against the financiers who had encouraged irresponsible stock market practices during the twenties and thereby, it was widely (if erroneously) believed, brought on the Depression. An effort at establishing a more steeply graduated tax system, the so-called Wealth Tax Act of 1935, could achieve broad support as a way of striking at a class that had exhibited indifference to economic suffering.

The Tennessee Valley Authority [TVA], the most unique and in many ways the most radical of New Deal innovations, was an expression of Roosevelt's fullest progressive aspirations. Combining flood control, conservation, and public ownership of electrical power, it functioned in the short run as another work relief project but in the long run it was the most ambitious effort at regional economic planning ever undertaken in the United States. By almost any standard, the TVA was a resounding success. It tamed the destructive Tennessee River, encouraged sound land use practices, generated inexpensive power for homes and industries, and contributed greatly to the prosperity of the Tennessee Basin area. Yet it was never duplicated in any other region of the United States, nor did it become a model for the New Deal's approach to the American economy. These nonevents were indicative both of the American political system's resistance to sweeping change and of a split within the progressive mind over what may have been the central problem posed by the Great Depression — the organization of the American economy.

Roosevelt himself had always been primarily attracted to the New Nationalism of his kinsman, and the experience of World War I had reinforced this inclination. His natural impulse upon coming to power was to mobilize the nation in a great crusade against the Depression, much as the country had been mobilized against Germany in 1917. The economic corollary of such an effort was central management of the economy, and the New Deal's first mechanism for industrial recovery, the National Recovery Administration (NRA), was patterned closely upon the experience of the World War I War Industries Board. Quite in line with that experience, the NRA did much more than impose responsibilities upon the business community; it recognized business management as a legitimate and responsible sector of the American political economy and extended substantial benefits to it. NRA regulations, purposely mislabeled "codes of fair competition," actually stifled competition and in many instances sanctioned such cartel practices as production quotas, allocation of marketing territories, and price-fixing. The NRA represented in its way both the New Nationalism and a style of broker politics with which Roosevelt began his presidency. Had it been successful in overcoming the Depression, the words *New Deal* might today conjure up the image of a relatively moderate reform movement at war with no segment of American society.

The NRA failed for a host of reasons, some of them conceptual, some of them political. It failed to address what now appears to have been the central malady of the Depression, the liquidation of consumer spending power; in fact, its price-fixing approach actually made that problem worse. It was not sufficiently coordinated with the work relief programs, which could have injected much more money into the economy had they been managed less cautiously. It collapsed to some extent of its own weight as its frenetic head, Hugh Johnson, traveled about the country attempting to organize every mom-and-pop enterprise in sight and wildly overpromising what his agency could accomplish. By late 1934, Johnson had suffered a nervous breakdown, and the agency was washed up. Liberals decried its concessions to business; yet the business community displayed little support for it. In the spring of 1935, the Supreme Court ruled the NRA unconstitutional,

dredging up a seldom-invoked sanction against excessive delegation of legislative authority by the Congress and reverting to a hyper-restrictive interpretation of the government's authority to regulate interstate commerce. Economically, politically, and constitutionally, the NRA had reached a dead end — and so had the idea of central management of the economy.

Roosevelt and those who now became the dominant economic thinkers of his administration turned to the other ready-made alternative the progressive tradition had created for them — antitrustism. It was a natural move for an administration that had become bitter over persistent hostility from the business establishment. The Wheeler-Rayburn Public Utility Holding Company Act of 1935 struck an important blow at private consolidation in a key American industry. The Antitrust Division of the Department of Justice . . . became larger and more active than ever. In Congress, administration supporters secured the establishment of a special Temporary National Economic Committee (TNEC), which over several years undertook a massive study of the problem of consolidation and anticompetitive activities in the American economy.

Yet antitrustism, while it might be a valuable component of a program designed primarily to restore consumer purchasing power, did not directly address the urgent problem of the Depression. Moreover, it was not consistently applied. Here and there, in the railroad and coal industries, for example, centralized regulation continued dominant. And in order to protect small retailers, "fair trade laws" sanctioned price-fixing for many consumer items. The antitrust effort was directed more against specific abuses than against the fundamental structure of American big business. The TNEC became an academic enterprise that produced a shelf of scholarly monographs but no meaningful legislation. Far from resolving the conflict that existed in the progressive mind, the New Deal had simply acted it out. In part, this reflected Roosevelt's own uncertainty; but it also exemplified the mood of a nation that since the beginnings of modern American industrialism had feared the growth of the large corporation while lusting after its supposed economic benefits.

This ultimate inability to arrive at a coherent strategy for dealing with the structure of the American economy leads one finally to the most conspicuous failure of the New Deal — it never achieved a full economic recovery. It is easy today to pick out some of the reasons; any above-average undergraduate economics student can recite what might be called the Keynesian critique of Roosevelt's leadership. The fundamental task of the New Deal, so the argument runs, had to be the reconstruction of consumer purchasing power. The surest and most direct way of accomplishing this objective was through massive government spending. Because the unemployment problem was so horrendous, the amount of federal economic stimulus would have to be enormous and the federal budget deficits unprecedented. But once most Americans were back at work, paying off old debts and spending money on all manner of consumer goods, a prosperous economy would be able to maintain itself, federal tax revenues would roll in, and the budget deficits would become surpluses.

In addition to its economic merits, the Keynesian approach promised the political dividends that would accrue from even higher levels of relief spending. Yet Roosevelt disregarded the Keynesian argument. He did not fully understand it, and it was incompatible with his personality. "A Keynesian solution," James MacGregor Burns has written, "involved an almost absolute commitment, and Roosevelt was not one to commit himself absolutely to any political or economic method." The result was a halfway Keynesianism that failed to provide a full cure for a desperately sick economy and yet outraged conservative sentiment. And even this policy was inconsistent. In 1937, with economic recovery having reached at best an intermediate stage far short of prosperity, Roosevelt ordered cutbacks in government spending and attempted to balance the budget. A disastrous

recession ensued; there were months of hesitation, then a return to the old halfway spending levels. . . .

The failure to achieve economic recovery may be more fairly traced to the nature of the American progressive experience. Theodore Roosevelt and Woodrow Wilson had faced only sporadic economic difficulties. Roosevelt had coped with the panic of 1907 by cooperating fully with the financial establishment, led by J. P. Morgan; Wilson had all but ignored the economic problems arising from World War I. The older Populist tradition had grown out of economic distress, but its inflationary panaceas could hardly be taken seriously. (Some New Deal monetary tinkering — abandonment of the gold standard, devaluation of the dollar, a lavish silver purchase program — exhilarated populist-style politicians but failed utterly to have a positive effect on the economy.) The mainstream of American reformism, having come out of an era of prosperity, sought humanitarian social programs, advocated a more equitable distribution of American abundance for all social groups, decried unregulated corporate power, and possessed some impulses toward social engineering. Proceeding from this frame of reference, the New Deal seized upon an opportunity to realize old reformist aspirations, doing so at times with little regard for their impact upon the economy.

The Social Security Act, for example, financed by a system of payroll taxes on employers and employees, sucked millions of dollars out of the private economy and constituted a drag on the drive for recovery. While Roosevelt fully understood this, he nonetheless insisted upon payroll contributions, which he saw as a way of guaranteeing the program's fiscal integrity and providing political insurance for it. "With those taxes in there," he remarked privately, "no damn politician can ever scrap my social security program." The NRA likewise had great appeal to Roosevelt, representing as it did a culmination of the New Nationalism and something of a recreation of the World War I effort at industrial mobilization. In practice, however, it probably had a contractionist effect on the economy, by sanctioning cartel practices based on assumptions of oversupply and depressed consumer demand.

In general, moreover, Roosevelt's increasingly vehement antibusiness attitude after 1935 probably did more to prolong the Depression than to solve it. Business confidence can be a critical determinant in investment decisions if the economy is unprosperous, and it was terribly unprosperous even at the peak of the partial recovery the New Deal did achieve. During the recession of 1937–38, Roosevelt fumed that business was deliberately refusing to help recovery along by investing in new facilities. However, in an economic environment characterized by unemployment levels of around 15 percent, only a business community that had achieved a sense of identification with the New Deal could have seriously contemplated expansion. Instead, of course, the leaders of American corporate enterprise were overwhelmingly irrational and unenlightened in their attitudes toward Roosevelt and the New Deal. Discredited by the Depression, they had been psychologically declassed. Yet although they were hard to deal with, although it was easy and politically profitable to return their hostility in kind, there were no economic benefits in doing so.

Throughout Roosevelt's public rhetoric, beginning with his inaugural address, one finds a steadily increasing hostility toward the business elite. The money changers, he declared after taking the oath of office in 1933, had been driven at last from the temple of government. (In fact, as Arthur Schlesinger, Jr., has observed, they were helping the New Dealers draw up the Emergency Banking Act of 1933.) By 1936, he had declared open warfare, characterizing his opponents as "economic royalists" and delighting in inflammatory rhetoric. "We had to struggle with the old enemies of peace — business and financial monopoly, speculation, reckless banking, class antagonism, sectionalism, war profiteering," he declared in his final big campaign speech. "They are unanimous in their *hate* for *me* — *and I welcome their hatred.*"

Roosevelt was, of course, responding to a campaign of abuse that was equally bitter from his opposition. He suffered routine denunciation in the clubs and corporate boardrooms of America in the most irrational and scurrilous fashion — as a Communist, as a sinister tool of some imagined Jewish conspiracy (his "real name," so the story went, was Rosenfeld), as a syphilitic (the "actual cause" of his crippling paralysis). He derived emotional satisfaction from striking back, but he might have been better advised to do what many other great political leaders have done from time to time — to absorb criticism like a sponge and seek to coopt his enemies.

Nevertheless, Roosevelt was essentially correct in responding to conservative critics with a famous story in which he depicted himself as having rescued an aged and wealthy capitalist from drowning only to be attacked for having failed to retrieve the old man's silk hat. Roosevelt indeed probably had saved American capitalism, even if he was not appreciated by the capitalists. Although the New Deal never solved the Depression, it did bring forth some moderate reform legislation that strengthened the structure of the capitalist system. In particular, banking and securities legislation brought a new degree of responsibility and safety to the American financial world.

In a broad sense also, the New Deal strengthened American capitalism by changing its structure in a largely unplanned way. Throughout the 1930s, Roosevelt and his associates sought to balance conflicting groups within the American political economy. The New Deal farm programs had the effect of organizing agriculture; the Wagner Act permitted the self-organization of labor with federal encouragement; the once-dominant position of business was whittled down to some extent; and big government functioned as an arbiter between these forces. Half-consciously, Roosevelt created a political economy of countervailing powers.

Despite an economic record that might be charitably described as spotty, Roosevelt was remarkably successful in making himself the nation's dominant political figure and in rebuilding the structure of American politics. The intellectual and moral bankruptcy of his opposition obscured the shortcomings of the New Deal. His own charisma and his well-developed skills in the art of politics enabled him to take maximum advantage of his opportunities. Better than any other personality of his time, Roosevelt combined the two major techniques of democratic political leadership: the achievement of a sense of direct identification with the people and the construction of formidable organizational support. Neither objective required a total victory over the Depression, nor was it necessary to have a coherent vision of economic reorganization. (Here, Roosevelt's confusion may even have been politically profitable, reflecting as it did that of so many Americans.) What was required, and what Roosevelt delivered, was some progress combined with, above all, the *appearance* of caring about and attempting to alleviate the plight of the unfortunate.

Roosevelt provided the appearance with his expert use of the communications media. He regularly brought the White House reporters into the Oval Office twice a week for press conferences; a dramatic departure from past presidential aloofness, the practice won him the sympathy of most working journalists and assured his views a prominent place even in implacably Republican newspapers. His radio talks demonstrated a technical skill in the use of the medium, an ability to transmit a sense of warm concern over the airwaves, and a talent for explaining complex social-economic policies in simple but not condescending language. His entire demeanor, most fully captured by the newsreels (then shown in every movie house in America), was that of an optimistic, energetic chief executive with a sense of concern for the unfortunate.

To this, Roosevelt added the dispensing of real benefits of one sort or another to millions of people, who more often than not responded naturally enough with the feeling that he had given them a job or saved their homes or preserved their farms or secured their bank deposits. The New Deal relief programs were not evaluated by a populace employing today's expectations; rather, they were received by people who were desperate for any assistance and who could contrast FDR only with the seemingly cold and indifferent Herbert Hoover. Roosevelt encouraged the contrast and doubtless believed it valid. "Better the occasional faults of a Government that lives in a spirit of charity than the consistent omissions of a Government frozen in the ice of its own indifference," he declared in his acceptance speech at the 1936 Democratic convention. He won the uniquely personal allegiance of many individuals who had been helped in some way by the New Deal or who simply felt touched by his manifestations of sympathy with their difficulties.

At the same time, Roosevelt built organizational support broader and stronger than that of any previous Democratic leader. He was successful in bringing behind him both the traditional Democratic machines and the trade unions, the most natural representatives of the working classes and the underprivileged. He secured the support of key leaders of almost every ethnic or religious minority in the nation, ranging from such figures as Robert Vann, the most influential black newspaper editor in the country, to Joseph P. Kennedy, perhaps the wealthiest and most powerful layman in the Irish-Catholic community. The minorities were most likely to be among the underprivileged that the New Deal attempted to help, but the Roosevelt administration also took pains to give them symbolic recognition in the form of visible appointments to office.

Finally, as a fitting capstone to his coalition, Roosevelt preempted the progressive impulse for himself and his party like no Democrat before him. He actively sought and gained the backing of reformers who ran the gamut of American politics from heartland Republican mavericks to New York social democrats. Treating them almost as a minority group, he gave them important and prominent places in his administration. His secretary of the interior, Harold Ickes, and his secretary of agriculture, Henry A. Wallace, were eminent former progressive Republicans. Both embraced the Democratic party as well as the New Deal and in some respects became the rhetorical and ideological point men of the administration. . . .

Roosevelt's first reelection victory in 1936 was a landslide in which he won support from all groups. But from the beginning, his most fervent and devoted support came from the independent progressives and from those groups that might loosely be described as "working class" in the larger cities of America. (Roosevelt was not the first Democratic candidate to win over the urban working and lower classes — Alfred E. Smith had done so in 1928 — but his appeal was broader and deeper.) The liberals, the unionists, the ethnic-religious minorities, the blacks, and the urban lower classes would stay with FDR to the end.

Roosevelt and those around him interpreted the 1936 results as a mandate for an extension of the New Deal. In his second inaugural address, the President declared, "I see one third of a nation ill-housed, ill-clad, ill-nourished." He made it clear that more help for the underprivileged was his first priority. Armed with an overwhelming popular endorsement, given a Congress with Democratic majorities of 331–89 in the House of Representatives and 76–16 in the Senate, Roosevelt appeared all but invincible. Actually, his program faced serious institutional and popular obstacles. By the end of 1938, the New Deal was dead.

The immediate precipitant was Roosevelt's push for legislation to pack a Supreme Court that had demonstrated unqualified hostility to the New Deal. He handled the effort clumsily and somewhat dishonestly (he argued that he was simply trying to invigorate an excessively aged court), and he ran squarely up against popular reverence for the judicial system and the constitutional concept of separation of powers. Any chance of success evaporated when the two "swing justices," Charles Evans Hughes and

Owen Roberts, began to vote with the liberal bloc and thereby converted a pro–New Deal minority into a majority. The Court bill was killed in the Senate after a debate that split the Democratic party. Roosevelt bravely insisted that he had lost a battle but had won the war. Perhaps so, but he had sustained serious wounds. The demonstration that he could be beaten on an issue of vital importance encouraged many potential opponents who had been intimidated by his popularity.

Other events drained FDR's political strength. His identification with organized labor became something of a liability as militance increased during his second term, manifesting itself in sit-down strikes that outraged millions of property-owning Americans. The severe recession of 1937–38 graphically exposed the New Deal's failure to achieve economic recovery. Roosevelt attempted to "purge" several opponents within his own party in the 1938 Democratic primaries. Poorly conceived and executed, the purge was a near-total failure — and yet another exhibition of the limitations inherent in the President's ad hoc approach to public policy problems.

From the Court-packing battle on, Roosevelt faced an increasingly strong opposition bloc in Congress. Made up of Republicans and anti–New Deal Democrats, the conservative coalition was composed largely of congressmen who represented safe, rural constituencies. It subscribed to the individualistic ethic of an older America shocked by the changes the New Deal had inflicted upon the nation. It benefited also from a rather general congressional resentment against FDR's "dictatorial" tactics in his dealings with Capitol Hill. Heartened by Roosevelt's post-1936 setbacks, convinced by the failure of the purge that he could not oust them from office, augmented by sizable Republican gains in the 1938 elections, the congressional conservatives became the strongest political force in Washington. From 1939 on, it would be FDR who was on the defensive, unable to enlarge the New Deal and at times forced to accept cuts in some of its peripheral programs.

Thus ended a remarkable story of success and failure in domestic reform. Roosevelt had changed American life in many ways, but he had not overcome the Depression. He had drastically altered the pattern of American politics only to create a domestic stalemate that would endure long after his death. He had made the Democratic party the country's dominant political vehicle, yet he could not control it. The new shape of American politics included a reform-oriented presidential Democratic party able to control presidential nominations and a moderate-to-conservative congressional Democratic party. Seldom in tune with the White House on domestic issues, the congressional party represented local and regional interests, was generally removed from the pressures of close electoral competition, and often willing to cooperate with the Republicans. These contours would endure for a quarter-century — until reshaped by one of FDR's most devoted followers, Lyndon B. Johnson. . . .

☆

THE ACCOMPLISHMENT

Roosevelt left a deep imprint upon his era. At his death [in 1945], he was fiercely hated by his opponents and all but worshiped by his followers. As emotions subsided over the next generation, however, the most frequent criticism of him came from liberal and radical scholars in sympathy with his aims and disenchanted by his inability to achieve all of them. In some instances, they appeared to speak little more than a lament that the New Deal failed to establish some variety of democratic socialism or to resolve all the problems of American life. Others, evaluating him by the criteria of the seminar rather than the real world of the political leader, voiced unhappiness at his lack of a systematic social and political philosophy. Some leveled the charge that after 1937 he had failed as a party leader, and there could be no arguing that mass Democratic defections had made the conserva-

tive coalition possible. They have, however, been less convincing in demonstrating the means by which FDR or any president could have whipped well-entrenched congressmen and independent local party leaders into line. His undeniable tactical mistakes seem relatively insignificant when placed against such formidable constitutional barriers to presidential control as federalism and the separation of powers.

It is legitimate to observe that Roosevelt's New Deal failed to restore the prosperity of 1929. . . . But from almost any vantage point, the nation was stronger and more secure at his death than at the time he took office. If the New Deal did not restore prosperity, it did in a number of ways lay a strong groundwork for the maintenance of prosperity after World War II. By restructuring the American political economy into a system of countervailing powers, by establishing a minimal welfare state, the New Deal smoothed out the business cycle and laid the basis for a postwar political consensus based on a widely distributed affluence. Roosevelt's role in engineering the defeat of fascism removed the most serious challenge the nation had ever faced to its security. He brought America no utopia, but he took his country through difficult times and left it able to face the future with strength and confidence.

The way in which Roosevelt gained political power and support was in some respects as important as what he did. He won the backing of established organizations actively involved in the game of political power — the machines, the unions, the various organized interests — and he achieved a sense of direct communication and empathy with the ordinary people. He employed radio as a supplement to organizational support, not as a substitute for it, and by bringing the average American into direct involvement with his personality, he called forth the intensity with which his admirers loved him and his enemies hated him.

Roosevelt created a new era in the history of American politics. His moderate liberalism, fumbling though it might seem to later critics, and his charismatic optimism, whether realistic or not, drew millions to the Democratic party and made it a vehicle of majority sentiment for the first time since the Civil War. He created a new consensus to which that majority subscribed — one that defined the objectives of American politics as pluralist and liberal and the national interests of the United States as worldwide. FDR's final legacy to the nation was no less than a new political tradition.

Questions to Consider

1   How does Alonzo Hamby portray FDR's personality and cast of mind? Describe FDR's social background and its influence on him. What effect did his time as undersecretary of the navy have on FDR? His struggle with polio? His terms as governor of New York?

2   Why does Hamby say that reform was much harder to accomplish than relief during the Depression? What were the strengths and weaknesses of the Progressive tradition, and how did FDR deal with its ambiguities throughout the 1930s?

3   Describe FDR's relationship with big business during the Depression. Why does Hamby suggest that FDR saved capitalism in America? Do you agree?

4   Describe FDR as a politician. From whom did he get his principal support? How did ordinary Americans react to him? What effect did he have on the Democratic party? Why did he face a more determined and successful opposition after his 1936 reelection, and what did this say about the American people and their relationship to the administration and the Constitution?

5   What were some of the principal successes and failures of the New Deal? Why does Hamby think in the end it failed to bring about full economic recovery? Despite this, Hamby concludes that "FDR's legacy to the nation was no less than a new political tradition." Explain what he means. How in particular did the New Deal programs change the traditional relationship of the citizen to the federal government?

A WORLD AT WAR

18

Day of Infamy

OTTO FRIEDRICH

For years, detractors of Franklin Roosevelt have charged that he deliberately sent the United States Pacific Fleet to Pearl Harbor so that the Japanese could attack it and give him an excuse to involve the United States in the Second World War. There are those who still make this argument. But Gordon W. Prange's studies, At Dawn We Slept *(1981) and* Pearl Harbor: The Verdict of History *(1986), and the bulk of modern scholarship exonerate Roosevelt of such a monstrous accusation. In truth, the decisions and events that led to America's entry into the war were enormously complex, involving developments in Europe as well as Asia.*

When Nazi Germany invaded Poland in 1939 and plunged Europe into war, the United States, although theoretically neutral, was clearly sympathetic with the Allies, led by Britain and France. Indeed, Roosevelt was more preoccupied with the Nazi threat in Europe than with Japanese expansion in Asia. Time and again, he predicted that Hitler would eventually make war on the United States, and out of that belief flowed much of his European diplomacy: the destroyer-bases deal with Britain, Lend-Lease, and the Atlantic Charter. Still, through 1940 and 1941, as German planes bombed Britain and German armies swept into Russia, the Roosevelt administration often seemed adrift, as though the president and his advisers were confused, helplessly caught in a vortex of events over which they had no control.

Japanese intentions in the Pacific were especially perplexing. Since 1937, Japan had been laying waste to China, bombing its cities and capturing its coastal territory. Did Japan's aggressions against China constitute an immediate threat to United States secu-

rity? Was a showdown with Japan also inevitable, as United States military leaders in-sisted? While the United States watched Japanese movements in Asia, Congress de-clared economic war against Germany with the controversial Lend-Lease Program, which gave $7 billion in military aid to embattled Britain. Soon American convoys were carry-ing supplies across the Atlantic. When German U-boats torpedoed several American vessels, many observers contended that war with Hitler was only a matter of time.

Meanwhile, the Japanese question had become increasingly confusing. In Tokyo, a party led by General Hideki Tojo and the military demanded that the United States be driven from the Pacific so that Japan could establish an Asian empire free of Western influ-ence. But Prime Minister Fumimaro Konoye, a moderate, wanted to negotiate with the United States and directed his ambassador in America to present Washington with a set of proposals that might avoid war. At the same time, the war party proceeded with a top-secret plan to attack the United States Navy at Pearl Harbor if negotiations failed. By early December 1941, United States analysts knew that the Japanese were preparing to strike, but almost no one thought them capable of launching an air attack against distant Hawaii. When Japanese planes did exactly that, in a day that would "live in infamy," Americans from Pearl Harbor to Washington were caught completely by surprise.

Like the assassination of John F. Kennedy, Pearl Harbor was one of those crises that mark the people who experience them for the rest of their lives. As Otto Friedrich says, Americans of that period would recall exactly what they were doing when they first heard the news on that fateful Sunday. In this selection, Friedrich, a distinguished author, traces the dramatic events that led to the Pearl Harbor attack; he points out that if war between Japan and the United States was inevitable, it was perhaps inevitable from the time of the first contact between the two countries in 1853. Combining erudition with lucidity of expression, Friedrich describes the rise of modern, industrial Japan, the mili-taristic government that came to power there, and the Japanese conquest of China, which was prompted in part by the worldwide depression. From then on, Japan and the United States were on a collision course for supremacy in the Pacific. An example of narrative history at its best, Friedrich's article captures the mood, spirit, and rival perceptions of that momentous time; it shows how the interaction of people and events caused Japanese-American relations to deteriorate and finally convinced Japan to strike at Pearl Harbor, and it reconstructs in graphic detail the holocaust of destruction that virtually paralyzed American striking power in the Pacific and plunged the United States into a global con-flict. On Monday, December 8, 1941, the United States formally declared war on Japan. Three days later, Germany and Italy — Japan's Axis allies — declared war on the United States. Roosevelt and Congress reciprocated at once, thus placing America on the side of the Allied powers — Great Britain, the Soviet Union, and China.

GLOSSARY

BRATTON, COLONEL RUFUS   United States Army intelligence officer who guessed from the final Japanese note that Japan would strike somewhere on Sunday, December 7, 1941.

CHIANG KAI-SHEK   Commander of the Nationalist forces — the Kuomintang — in embattled China.

FUCHIDA, MITSUO   Operational commander of the Japanese air force that struck Pearl Harbor.

GENDA, MINORU   One of Yamamoto's trusted lieutenants who played a key role in planning the Pearl Harbor attack.

HIROHITO   Emperor of Japan and "a figurehead ruler."

HULL, CORDELL   FDR's secretary of state who had "a speech difficulty" and little knowledge of Japan.

KIMMEL, ADMIRAL HUSBAND   Commander of the Pacific Fleet, with headquarters at Pearl Harbor.

MacARTHUR, GENERAL DOUGLAS   Commander of all United States Army forces in the Far East, with headquarters in the Philippines.

MAO ZEDONG (MAO TSE-TUNG)   Head of the Chinese Communists and later (1949) founder and first chairman of the People's Republic of China.

MARSHALL, GENERAL GEORGE   United States chief of staff, stationed in Washington.

NOMURA, KICHISABURO   Japanese ambassador in Washington.

SHORT, LIEUTENANT GENERAL WALTER   Commander of United States Army forces in Hawaii.

STARK, ADMIRAL HAROLD   Chief of United States Naval Operations, stationed in Washington.

TOGO, ADMIRAL HEIHACHIRO   Japanese naval hero who annihilated the Russian fleet in the battle of Tsushima (1905) during the Russo-Japanese war; his victories established Japan's naval superiority.

TOJO, GENERAL HIDEKI   Dominated Japan's militarist government and succeeded Prince Konoye as Japanese prime minister in October 1941; he approved the Pearl Harbor attack.

YAMAMOTO, ADMIRAL ISOROKU   Harvard-educated commander of Japan's Combined Fleet who devised the Pearl Harbor attack plan with the help of trusted subordinates.

The brass band on the stern of the U.S.S. *Nevada* kept on playing *The Star-Spangled Banner* for the 8 a.m. flag raising even after a Japanese bomber roared overhead and fired a torpedo at the nearby *Arizona*. The torpedo missed, but the bomber sprayed machine-gun fire at the *Nevada's* band and tore up its ensign.

"This is the best goddam drill the Army Air Force has ever put on," remarked an *Arizona* sailor standing idly at the battleship's rail.

"Air raid, Pearl Harbor, this is no drill," said the radio message that went out at 7:58 a.m. from the U.S. Navy's Ford Island command center, relayed throughout Hawaii, to Manila, to Washington. But there was an even sharper sense of imminent disaster in the words someone shouted over the public address system on another docked battleship, the *Oklahoma:* "Man your battle stations! This is no shit!" Across the lapping waters of the harbor, church bells tolled, summoning the faithful to worship.

Almost alongside the *Oklahoma,* another torpedo hurtled through the air. After releasing it, recalled Lieut. Jinichi Goto, commander of the Japanese torpedo bombers, "I saw that I was even lower than the crow's nest of the great battleship. My observer reported a huge waterspout springing up ... '*Atari-mashita!* [It hit!]' he cried."

"I felt a very heavy shock and heard a loud explosion," said the *Oklahoma's* executive officer, Commander Jesse Kenworthy Jr., "and the ship immediately began to list to port. As I attempted to get to the conning tower over decks slippery with oil and water, I felt the shock of another very heavy explosion." Kenworthy gave the order to abandon ship. He barely made it over the rising starboard side as the giant battleship began to keel over, trapping more than 400 crewmen below decks.

"Day of Infamy" by Otto Friedrich. From *Time,* December 2, 1991. Copyright 1991 Time Inc. Reprinted by permission.

Just as the *Oklahoma* capsized, a tremendous explosion tore open the *Arizona*. "A spurt of flame came out of the guns in No. 2 turret, followed by an explosion of the forward magazine," said a mechanic on the nearby tanker *Ramapo*. "The foremast leaned forward, and the whole forward part of the ship was enveloped in flame and smoke and continued to burn fiercely."

In Commander Mitsuo Fuchida's bomber circling overhead, antiaircraft fire knocked a hole in the fuselage and damaged the steering gear, but Fuchida couldn't take his eyes off the fiery death throes of the *Arizona*. "A huge column of dark red smoke rose to 1,000 ft., and a stiff shock wave rocked the plane," he recalled years later, when he had become a Presbyterian missionary. "It was a hateful, mean-looking red flame, the kind that powder produces, and I knew at once that a big magazine had exploded. Terrible indeed."

As operational commander of the Japanese attackers, Fuchida watched and controlled everything. It was Fuchida who had given, exactly at 7:49 a.m. on Dec. 7, 1941, the order to attack the strongest naval base in the world: "*To!* [the first syllable of *totsug-ekiseyo*, meaning: Charge!] *To! To! To!*" It was Fuchida who sent back to Tokyo the triumphant signal that the attack had caught the Americans by surprise: "*Tora!* [Tiger!] *Tora! Tora!*"

Now Fuchida led the attack on the *Maryland*, another of the eight battleships berthed at the U.S. Navy's Pacific Fleet headquarters. He saw four bombs hurtling toward their target. "In perfect pattern [they] plummeted like devils of doom. They became small as poppy seeds and finally disappeared just as tiny white flashes of smoke appeared on or near the ship."

Pearl Harbor is peaceful now, blue waves in the winter sunshine, an occasional toot of harbor traffic. A concrete canopy shrouds the rusted wreckage of the *Arizona,* the remains of more than 1,000 American servicemen entombed inside. Her flag is still

Mitsubishi Reisen "Zero" fighters prepare to launch from one of six Japanese carriers in the Pearl Harbor strike force. (U.S. Naval Institute Photo Collection, Annapolis, MD)

raised and lowered every day on the mast emerging out of the quiet water.

The [fiftieth] anniversary of the greatest U.S. military defeat, the day President Franklin D. Roosevelt called "a date which will live in infamy," remains a day of death and disgrace, an inglorious event, and the spirit of reconciliation still bows before gusts of rancor. When President Bush, a World War II fighter pilot, indicated that he would attend the Pearl Harbor anniversary ceremonies, White House spokesmen stiffly squelched any talk of Japanese officials' joining in. So did the Pearl Harbor Survivors Association. "We did not invite the Japanese 50 years ago, and we don't want them now," says the association's president, Gerald Glaubitz.

In American mythology, Pearl Harbor still represents, even after a half-century, a classic moment of treachery and betrayal. Certainly it was a moment of historic surprise, a moment when the impossible happened, when warfare suddenly spread, for the first and only time in history, to virtually the whole world. This was the moment that changed Americans from a nation of provincial innocents, not only ignorant of the great world but proud of their ignorance, into a nation that would often have to bear the burdens of rescuing that world. The same cataclysm also changed the Japanese from a people trying to find their place on the rim of the great world into a nation that would eventually redefine that world and place itself at the very center.

The surprise, when it first exploded over Pearl Harbor, was shattering, and everyone who experienced it can still remember what was going on when the news interrupted that quiet Sunday: the Washington Redskins playing the Philadelphia Eagles, Arthur Rubinstein as soloist in the New York Philharmonic broadcast, or just a visit with friends. Trying to explain the national sense of bewilderment, the TIME of that time reflected the kind of racism that implicitly underlay the basic American attitude. "Over the U.S. and its history," declared the weekly newsmagazine, "there was a great unanswered question: What would the people . . . say in the face of the mightiest event of their time? What they said — tens of thousands of them — was: 'Why, the yellow bastards!'"

As often happens in surprise attacks, however, the surprise of Pearl Harbor was largely a matter of national illusions. The leaders on both sides fully expected a war, indeed considered it inevitable, even to some extent desirable, but neither side really wanted to fight unless it had to. Up to the last minute, each antagonist thought the other was bluffing.

Japan's navy had already begun planning and training for the attack on Pearl Harbor when Emperor Hirohito startled his assembled advisers on Sept. 6 by asking an imperial question. In the midst of a fervent debate over when and how to go to war, the Emperor, who traditionally never spoke during such gatherings, suddenly pulled out and read in his high-pitched voice a poem by his revered grandfather Emperor Meiji:

> All the seas, in every quarter,
> are as brothers to one another.
> Why, then, do the winds and waves of strife
> rage so turbulently throughout the world?

Roosevelt, re-elected to a third term in 1940 after pledging that "your boys are not going to be sent to any foreign wars," knew that Hirohito was just a figurehead ruler over a militarist government domi-

nated by the flinty General Hideki Tojo. Still, Roosevelt staked his hopes for peace on a last-minute message to the Emperor. "Both of us," Roosevelt said, "have a sacred duty to restore traditional amity and prevent further death and destruction in the world."

Japanese military censors delayed that message for 10 hours, so it was almost midnight on Dec. 7 in Tokyo when U.S. Ambassador Joseph Grew sped with it to the Foreign Ministry. It was past 3 a.m. — and Fuchida's bombers were within sight of Pearl Harbor — when Foreign Minister Shigenori Togo, in full diplomatic regalia, reached the Imperial Palace. He found the Emperor listening to his short-wave radio. Togo read him the message and then the response that the government had already written for him. It said that peace was the Emperor's "cherished desire." This would "do well," Hirohito told Togo. The Foreign Minister bowed low.

If war between the U.S. and Japan was inevitable, it had probably been inevitable for a long time, perhaps as long ago as July 8, 1853. That was the day when Commodore Matthew Perry sailed his black-hulled steam frigate *Susquehanna* into Edo Bay (now Tokyo Bay) and "opened" Japan at gunpoint, after more than two centuries of self-imposed isolation, to American merchants and missionaries. Humiliated, the Japanese decided to modernize their feudal regime by imitating the barbarian invaders. They hired French officers to retrain their soldiers and British shipbuilders to create their navy. From the Germans they learned the secrets of modern science and from the Americans the secrets of modern commerce.

But as Japanese commerce and Japanese emigration increased, so did Western talk of a "yellow peril." In 1922 the Supreme Court ruled that Japanese immigrants were ineligible to become U.S. citizens. The following year it ruled that they could be barred from owning American land — Japanese farmers were then growing 10% of California's agricultural produce on 1% of its land. In 1924, when

Congress imposed national immigration quotas, the figure for Japanese was zero.

The deepest conflict between the U.S. and Japan, though, was over the future of China, which had been in turmoil ever since the collapse of the Manchu Empire in 1911. Though Generalissimo Chiang Kai-shek claimed that his Canton-based Kuomintang represented the entire republic, local warlords ruled much of the country, notably the huge northern territory of Manchuria. The Japanese, who had blocked a number of Russian incursions into Manchuria, were moving in to gain control of the region's plentiful coal and iron, which Japan sorely lacked.

The explosive force in the midst of this ferment was Japan's fractious Kwantung Army, originally sent to the Kwantung Peninsula just east of Beijing to protect Japanese rail and shipping interests in Manchuria. After ultranationalist Kwantung officers murdered the Chinese [overlord] of Manchuria, Tokyo installed a puppet regime in 1932 and proclaimed the independence of what it called Manchukuo. Despite calls for sanctions against Japan, outgoing President Herbert Hoover had no enthusiasm for a crisis, and the incoming President Roosevelt was preoccupied with the onrushing Great Depression.

That left Chiang and his Chinese Nationalists to fight on against the Japanese, the growing communist guerrilla forces of Mao Zedong and a clutch of surviving warlords. On the night of July 7, 1937, came the murky events that constituted the long-expected "incident." A Japanese soldier apparently wandered off to relieve himself near the Marco Polo Bridge, outside Beijing. His comrades, who later claimed they feared he had been kidnapped, got into a gunfight with a nearby Chinese Nationalist unit, and the fighting soon spread.

The worldwide depression, which partly inspired Japan's move into China, left most Americans unable to deal with anything beyond their own breadlines and Hoovervilles and, Brother, can you spare a dime? To the extent that they worried about foreign problems at all, they worried mainly about Adolf Hitler, who had seized Austria and the Czech Sudetenland in 1938, then demanded western Poland in 1939.

Americans did hear horror stories — of civilians massacred in Japanese air raids on undefended Shanghai and of the Rape of Nanking, a month of slaughter that cut down more than 200,000 civilians. Roosevelt talked of "quarantining" Japan, but American ships went on supplying Tokyo with American oil and steel. Times were hard, and business was business.

What came to dominate Japan's overall strategy was the impact of Hitler's stunning victories over the Western Allies in the spring of 1940. The Dutch army was crushed within a week, and Queen Wilhelmina fled to London, leaving the immense wealth of the Dutch East Indies (now Indonesia) in the charge of a few colonial bureaucrats. France collapsed in a month, and Marshal Pétain's feeble puppet regime, based in the French resort of Vichy, had other worries than French Indochina (Vietnam, Laos and Cambodia). Britain, threatened by a Nazi invasion, could devote little more than some Churchillian rhetoric to the defense of Singapore, Malaya, Hong Kong and Burma.

Japan's Prince Fumimaro Konoye, a serpentine conservative who had twice been Premier since 1937, realized the way was now clear "to include the British, French, Dutch and Portuguese islands of the Orient" in a Japanese commercial empire that Tokyo called the Greater East Asia Co-Prosperity Sphere. On Sept. 27, 1940, Konoye joined the Axis powers, Nazi Germany and Fascist Italy, in a formal alliance known as the Tripartite Pact. He demanded that Britain shut down the Burma Road, supply route for aid to Chiang, and that Vichy accept Japanese bases in Indochina for a southern attack on Chiang.

The U.S., the only Western power strong enough to retaliate, banned all iron and steel shipments to

Japan. "It seems inevitable," said *Asahi Shimbun,* then Japan's largest daily, "that a collision should occur between Japan, determined to establish a sphere of interest in East Asia ... and the United States, which is determined to meddle in affairs on the other side of a vast ocean." Added *Yomiuri,* another giant newspaper: "Asia is the territory of the Asiatics."

Impersonally though the tides of history may seem to flow, they now waited on one man, a remarkably squat and broad-shouldered man, no more than 5 ft. 3 in. tall. He had been born Isoroku Takano, the first name meaning 56, because that was the age at which his proud father had been presented with his sixth and last son. Later adopted, according to an old custom, into a richer family, he acquired a new name: Yamamoto.

Trained as a naval cadet, Yamamoto proudly bore the scars he got at 21, when he lost the second and third fingers on his left hand during Admiral Togo's great victory over the Russian navy at the Strait of Tsushima in 1905. Yamamoto had come to know the U.S. as a graduate student at Harvard and as naval attaché in Washington. And as executive officer of Japan's naval flight school, he had learned the new religion of air power. He loved poker, bridge and *shogi,* the Japanese version of chess. Said one of his top aides: "He had a gambler's heart."

Now 57, with a gray crew cut, Admiral Yamamoto commanded Japan's Combined Fleet, but he disliked the imperial navy's cautious strategy. In case of war, its plan was to fall back and try to lure the U.S. Pacific Fleet into the Inland Sea between the Japanese home islands of Honshu and Kyushu. But as early as spring 1940, Yamamoto remarked to one of his officers: "I wonder if an aerial attack can't be made on Pearl Harbor."

Others had suggested such a strategy but it had always been rejected as too dangerous. Pearl Harbor was too far away, too inaccessible, too well defended. Besides, the overall strategy of striking south toward Malaya and the Dutch East Indies now re-

quired all the navy's resources. Yamamoto nonetheless began in early 1941 to assemble some trusted lieutenants to make plans for Operation Hawaii, which he also named Operation *Z,* after Admiral Togo's historic banner at the battle of Tsushima.

One of Yamamoto's key planners was Commander Minoru Genda, still only 36, still a hot pilot at heart, first in his class at the Etajima naval academy, combat ace over China, leader of a daredevil stunt team called Genda's Flying Circus. Genda contributed several key ideas: that every available Japanese carrier should be assigned to the attack, that it should combine dive-bombing, high-level bombing and torpedoes, that the attackers should strike at dawn.

Not the least important of his ideas was to recruit a cadet classmate named Mitsuo Fuchida, who could train all of Yamamoto's pilots and lead them into battle. Fuchida, grandson of a famous samurai, was born in 1902, a Year of the Tiger ("Tora! Tora!"), so he was 39 when summoned to his mission. An ardent admirer of Hitler, he had grown a toothbrush mustache.

The techniques of dive-bombing and torpedo bombing were still relatively new, and aerial torpedoes were almost impossible to use in water as shallow as Pearl Harbor. Filching an idea from a recent British torpedo raid against the Italian naval base of Taranto, Genda had technicians create auxiliary wooden tail fins that would keep torpedoes closer to the surface; others converted armor-piercing shells into bombs. But drilling was Fuchida's main task, and all summer his planes staged trial runs over Kagoshima Bay in Kyushu, chosen for its physical resemblance to Pearl. Only in September did Genda tell him, "In case of war, Yamamoto plans to attack Pearl Harbor."

Ironically, Yamamoto didn't want to carry out his own plan. But if Japan was going to be forced to fight, he believed it should strike first and strike hard, in the hope that a demoralized U.S. would then accept a negotiated peace. If he was deluded in that hope, he was not deluded about U.S. power. "If I am told to fight regardless of the consequences, I shall run wild for the first six months or a year," he presciently told Prince Konoye in the fall of 1940, "but I have utterly no confidence for the second or third year."

By 1940 Japan had installed a pro-Japanese regime in Nanking, but U.S. aid enabled Chiang to fight on. Konoye began wondering about mediators to end the exasperating war that Tokyo insisted on calling the Chinese Incident. Where angels fear to tread, in rushed the missionary fathers of the Maryknoll Society, who guilelessly assured each side that the other seemed ready to talk. And so talks began in Washington in the spring of 1941.

Talks is hardly the word. Tokyo's goal was to negotiate a victory in China, Washington's goal to negotiate a Japanese withdrawal. U.S. Secretary of State Cordell Hull, nearly 70, a longtime power on Capitol Hill, was a log-cabin-born Tennessee mountaineer who knew little of the Japanese and disliked what he knew. He once referred to Tokyo's envoys as "pissants." Japan's ambassador, Kichisaburo Nomura, 64, a one-eyed retired admiral and former Foreign Minister, was considered a moderate and so was mistrusted in Tokyo. It did not help that Hull had a speech difficulty, while Nomura was partially deaf.

Hardly had the talks begun when the Japanese, having already seized a number of bases in northern Vietnam, suddenly occupied the south in July 1941. That threatened not only the back route to China but British control of Malaya and Burma (now Myanmar). Roosevelt retaliated by freezing all Japanese assets and placing an embargo on all trade in oil, steel, chemicals, machinery and other strategic goods. (The British and Dutch soon announced similar embargoes.) At the same time, he announced that General Douglas MacArthur, the retired Chief of Staff now luxuriating in the Philippines, was being recalled to active military duty and financed in mo-

bilizing 120,000 Filipino soldiers. (Roosevelt had made another significant move that spring, when he shifted the Pacific Fleet's headquarters from San Diego to Pearl Harbor.)

Roosevelt's embargo was a devastating blow, for Japan bought more than half its imports from the U.S. The Japanese military leaders were determined to fight. When they met with the Cabinet on Sept. 3, they insisted on an October deadline for Konoye's diplomatic efforts. The Prince asked for a meeting with Roosevelt, but Hull was opposed, and Roosevelt, preoccupied with the increasing likelihood of war with Hitler, never answered. Konoye resigned on Oct. 16. Tojo, a Kwantung Army veteran who was then War Minister, became Premier.

Though Japan's military leaders had decided on war, they had not yet agreed to a surprise attack on Pearl Harbor. Yamamoto was adamant: "Japan must deal the U.S. Navy a fatal blow at the outset of the war. It is the only way she can fight with any reasonable prospect of success." But war games suggested that an attacking fleet would be spotted and badly mauled. As late as October, Yamamoto learned that the staff admirals, determined to concentrate on the drive into Southeast Asia, wanted to take away two or three of his six carriers. The First Air Fleet's own commander, Vice Admiral Chuichi Nagumo, supported that decision. "The success of our surprise attack on Pearl Harbor," Nagumo predicted dolefully, "will prove to be the Waterloo of the war to follow." Yamamoto sent an aide to inform the navy's high command that if his Pearl Harbor plan was rejected, "he will have no alternative but to resign, and with him his entire staff." Yamamoto got his way.

The military set a new target date of Dec. 8 (Dec. 7 in Hawaii), and the Emperor and his military chiefs formally approved Yamamoto's attack plan on Nov. 3. But the Foreign Ministry instructed Ambassador Nomura and Special Envoy Saburo Kurusu to make "a final effort" in Washington.

On Nov. 17, Yamamoto visited his training base in Saeki Bay to bid his men farewell. "Japan has faced many worthy opponents in her glorious history — Mongols, Chinese, Russians," Yamamoto said, "but in this operation we will meet the strongest opponent of all. I expect this operation to be a success." Genda, Fuchida and other officers joined him in eating *surume* (dried cuttlefish) for happiness and *kachiguri* (walnuts) for victory. Near portable Shinto shrines, they toasted the Emperor with sake and shouted, "Banzai!"

It took Nagumo's fleet five days to reach the rendezvous point at Hitokappu Bay in the Kuriles just north of Japan's main islands. Fog swirled over the desolate outpost, and snow fell intermittently as the fleet steamed eastward at dawn on Nov. 26.

The armada boasted six carriers, led by Nagumo's flagship, the *Akagi,* 400 warplanes, two battleships, two cruisers, nine destroyers and a dozen other surface ships. At an average 13 knots, refueling daily, the attack fleet pursued a course 3,500 miles through the empty expanse of the North Pacific. Its orders provided that "in the event an agreement is reached in the negotiations with the United States, the task force will immediately return to Japan," but nobody expected that to happen.

The envoys made their "final effort" on Nov. 20, presenting to Hull an unyielding proposal on which Foreign Minister Togo said "no further concessions" could be made. Nomura noted that this was an inauspicious day — "They call it Thanksgiving" — but he dutifully delivered the message. It said the U.S. must restore trade to pre-embargo levels, provide oil from the Dutch East Indies and not interfere with Japan's "efforts for peace" in China.

Hull's answer, just as forceful, said the U.S. oil embargo would continue, and demanded that Japan "withdraw all military, naval, air and police forces from China and from Indochina." He handed it to the envoys on Nov. 26, the day Nagumo's fleet left Hitokappu Bay for Pearl Harbor. Hull did not know that, since the fleet was under total radio silence, but he did know from intercepted messages that another

Japanese war fleet had passed Formosa on its way toward Indochina or Malaya. "We must all prepare for real trouble, possibly soon," Roosevelt cabled Churchill.

The War Department then sent Hawaii and other outposts an important but significantly ambiguous "war warning." "Negotiations with Japan appear to be terminated to all practical purposes," said this Nov. 27 message over the signature of Chief of Staff George Marshall. "Japanese future action unpredictable but hostile action possible at any moment . . . You are directed to undertake such reconnaissance and other measures as you deem necessary, but these measures should be carried out so as not repeat not to alarm civil population or disclose intent. Report measures taken." Hawaii's commander, Lieut. General Walter Short, not a man of broad vision, reported back that he was taking measures to avert sabotage — parking his aircraft close together and keeping all ammunition safely locked up. Since Washington did not specify a threat to Pearl Harbor, Short felt he had done his duty, just as Marshall felt he had done his.

The Navy Department sent an even stronger message to its top commanders, specifically including the Pacific Fleet chief in Pearl Harbor, Admiral Husband Kimmel: "This dispatch is to be considered a war warning. Negotiations with Japan . . . have ceased, and an aggressive move by Japan is expected within the next few days." Kimmel, 60, a hard-driving disciplinarian who had held his command less than a year, took the warning as "no more than saying that Japan was going to attack someplace."

Kimmel and Short were only too aware that Washington was concentrating on Hitler's victories in Russia and his submarines' ravages of Atlantic shipping. Though Chief of Naval Operations Harold Stark acknowledged to Kimmel that his Pacific Fleet was weaker than the Japanese forces arrayed against it, he not only turned aside Kimmel's request for two new battleships but took away three he had, plus one of his four carriers, to help fight the Battle of the Atlantic.

United States battleships anchored at Pearl Harbor were sitting ducks. A torpedo has just struck the Oklahoma, *kicking up a towering geyser. Struck by four additional torpedoes, the great battleship quickly capsized. (U.S. Navy Photo)*

Roosevelt's assertive strategy against Japan was largely a bluff, backed by inadequate armed forces and inadequate funds. Washington theoreticians saw the Philippines as a check to any Japanese move southward. MacArthur overconfidently promised that he would soon have 200,000 Filipinos ready for combat, and the War Department began in the summer of 1941 to ship him the first of a promised 128 new B-17 Flying Fortresses. By April 1942, said Marshall, that would represent "the greatest concentration of heavy-bomber strength anywhere in the world," able to interdict any Japanese assault on Southeast Asia and mount "incendiary attacks to burn up the wood and paper structures of the densely populated Japanese cities."

Perhaps the greatest single cause of American complacency in the Pacific was the fact that the U.S. military's Operation Magic had deciphered Japan's sophisticated Purple diplomatic code in 1940. But that triumph had its drawbacks. U.S. intelligence officials had to sift through so much trivia that they failed to react to some important messages, such as a Tokyo request to its Hawaiian consulate for the exact location of all ships in Pearl Harbor. Also, the code breaking was kept secret even from some key officials. While the British were plugged into Magic, and MacArthur too, Kimmel and Short were not.

Ironically, the Nazis warned the Japanese that their codes might have been broken, but Tokyo refused to believe the Americans were smart enough for such a feat. Just as ironically, while U.S. code breakers knew of the Japanese warships heading for Southeast Asia, Nagumo's radio silence meant that his carriers heading for Pearl Harbor simply disappeared. On Dec. 2, Kimmel's intelligence officer confessed that nothing had been heard from the Japanese carriers for about two weeks.

"What!" said Kimmel. "You don't know where [they] are?"

"No, sir, I do not. I think they are in home waters, but I do not know where they are."

"Do you mean to say that they could be rounding Diamond Head, and you wouldn't know it?"

"I hope they would be sighted before now."

And the Americans could intercept but not understand a message Yamamoto sent his fleet on Dec. 2: "Climb Mount Niitaka." That meant "Proceed with the attack."

One thing that the code breaking did tell Washington was Tokyo's answer to Hull's last proposal. Before the original even reached the Japanese envoys, a messenger brought an intercepted version to Roosevelt in his White House study after dinner on Dec. 6. The President read it carefully for about 10 minutes, then said to his closest aide, Harry Hopkins, "This means war."

Roosevelt tried to call Admiral Stark, but he was at a revival of Sigmund Romberg's *Student Prince;* the President didn't want him paged at the theater lest that cause "undue alarm." When Roosevelt did finally reach him shortly before midnight, the Navy chief said, according to his later recollection, that the message was not "something that required action." After all, Stark testified, warnings had already gone out that Japan was "likely to attack at any time in any direction."

That same Saturday night was the standard party night in Pearl Harbor, not orgiastic but convivial. Hundreds of soldiers and sailors from Schofield Barracks and Hickam and Kaneohe converged as usual on Waikiki Beach to see what was going on at Bill Leader's bar, the Two Jacks or the Mint. *Tantalizing*

Tootsies was the name of the variety show at the Princess.

Kimmel attended a staid dinner party at the Halekulani Hotel and left early. He had a golf date the next morning with General Short, who went to a charity dance at the Schofield Barracks and also left early. As he rode along the coast highway, Short admired the lights of Pearl Harbor glowing below him. "Isn't that a beautiful sight?" he said. "And what a target it would make!"

Though the final Japanese note said nothing about war or Pearl Harbor, it was not quite complete — it contained 13 parts and said another would soon follow. The 14th and last part reached Washington the morning of Dec. 7. It notified the U.S. that "it is impossible to reach an agreement through further negotiations." An accompanying message instructed Nomura to deliver the note "at 1 p.m. on the 7th, your time."

Nobody in Washington knew Hirohito had asked that the warning be delivered before the attack — 1 p.m. in Washington was 7:30 a.m. in Hawaii — but an Army intelligence officer, Colonel Rufus Bratton, guessed as much. Bratton telephoned Marshall at his quarters at Fort Myers, Va., but he was out riding. More than an hour later, about 10:30 a.m., Marshall called back and said he was coming to his office shortly. About the same time, Hull was meeting with War Secretary Henry L. Stimson and Navy Secretary Frank Knox. "Hull is very certain that the Japs are planning some deviltry," Stimson recorded in his diary, "and we are all wondering when the blow will strike."

Fuchida woke at 5 a.m. As he told American military historian Gordon Prange, he put on red underwear and a red shirt so that if he was wounded, his men would not be distracted by the sight of his blood. At breakfast, one of his lieutenants said, "Honolulu sleeps."

"How do you know?" asked Fuchida.

"The Honolulu radio plays soft music. Everything is fine."

At 5:50 a.m. Nagumo's fleet reached the takeoff point, about 220 miles north of Pearl Harbor. The six carriers turned east into a brisk wind and increased speed to 24 knots. Nagumo's flagship was flying the celebrated *Z* pennant that Admiral Togo had flown at Tsushima in 1905. The flight decks tilted more than 10°, and the wind whipped spray over them.

"We could hear the waves splashing against the ship with a thunderous noise," Fuchida recalled later. "Under normal circumstances, no plane would be permitted to take off in such weather.... There were loud cheers as each plane rose into the air." Once up, the pilots circled overhead until all 183 planes assigned to the first wave were airborne. At 6:15 Fuchida gave a signal, then led the way south.

At almost that very hour — around 11:30 a.m. in Washington — Marshall arrived at his office and read the ominous words Bratton had brought him. He asked the officers assembled there what they thought it meant. All expected an imminent Japanese attack — somewhere. Marshall recalled that every major U.S. base had been warned of that more than a week earlier. Bratton and others urged a new warning. Marshall scrawled a message reporting the 1 p.m. meeting and added, "Just what significance the hour set may have we do not know, but be on alert accordingly."

Bratton rushed the message to the War Department signal center, where Marshall's scrawl had to be retyped for legibility. The message went to several points within a few minutes, but because of atmospheric difficulties, the copy for Hawaii went by commercial wireless. It reached Honolulu at 7:33 a.m. and ended in a pigeon hole, awaiting a motorcycle messenger to deliver it.

Fuchida's bombers had to fly blind over dense banks of clouds, so they homed on the Honolulu commercial radio station KGMB. Over his receiver, Fuchida heard soothing music, then a weather report: "Partly cloudy . . . over the mountains. Cloud base at 3,500 ft. Visibility good." Fuchida flew on.

To save money and fuel and manpower, the Pearl Harbor authorities had recently canceled weekend reconnaissance flights. But they had acquired some new radar equipment, though the National Park Service strongly objected to towers being installed on scenic mountaintops.

Two trainees operating a mobile radar unit at Opana, on Oahu's northern coast, were about to shut down when their watch ended at 7 a.m. Suddenly, Private Joseph Lockard noticed a large blip — "probably more than 50" planes — approaching southward from about 130 miles away. On the phone to Fort Shafter, Lockard reported to Lieut. Kermit Tyler "the largest [flight] I have ever seen on the equipment." The inexperienced Tyler figured that the planes must be a flight of the new B-17s expected from California. He told Lockard, "Don't worry about it."

As Fuchida's bombers neared Oahu, the defenders of Pearl Harbor got the last of their many warnings. Just outside the harbor, the U.S. destroyer *Ward* spotted an intruding submarine at 6:30 a.m. and opened fire from 50 yds. away. As the sub began diving, the *Ward* finished it off with depth charges. Lieut. William Outerbridge's report of his action was still ricocheting around headquarters when Fuchida arrived overhead.

"What a majestic sight," he said to himself as he counted the vessels lined up in Battleship Row in the dawn's early light. He pulled the trigger on his flare gun. That was supposed to signal the slow-moving torpedo bombers to take advantage of the surprise and strike first. But Fuchida's fighter pilots missed his signal to provide cover, so he fired again for the dive bombers to begin, and then the Japanese all attacked at once. Even when they made mistakes, it seemed that nothing could go wrong.

Within minutes, Pearl Harbor was pandemonium: explosions, screams, tearing steel, the rattle of machine guns, smoke, fire, bugles sounding, the whine of diving airplanes, more explosions, more screams. With Battleship Row afire, Fuchida's bombers circled over the maze of Pearl Harbor's docks and piers, striking again and again at the cruisers and destroyers and supply ships harbored there.

Other Japanese bombers swarmed over Hawaii's military airfields, Hickam and Wheeler, Kaneohe and Ewa. Dive-bombing and strafing the American planes neatly parked on the runways, they quickly won control of the sky. They wrecked hangars, warehouses, barracks — as well as the Hickam Field chapel and the enlisted men's new beer hall, the Snake Ranch. And in the midst of all this, a rainbow appeared over Ford Island.

To many of the Americans, the whole morning had a dreamlike unreality. Disbelief had been the overwhelming first reaction — this couldn't be happening, it was a trick, a drill, a silly rumor, a prank — disbelief and then pain and then anger, and still disbelief.

Admiral Kimmel was preparing for his golf game with General Short when an officer phoned him with the news that Japanese planes were attacking his fleet. The admiral was still buttoning his white uniform as he ran out of his house and onto the neighboring lawn of his chief of staff, Captain John Earle, which had a fine view of Battleship Row. Mrs. Earle said later that the admiral's face was "as white as the uniform he wore."

"The sky was full of the enemy," Kimmel recalled. He saw the *Arizona* "lift out of the water, then sink back down — way down." Mrs. Earle saw a battleship capsize.

"Looks like they've got the *Oklahoma*," she said.

"Yes, I can see they have," the admiral numbly responded.

General Short, who couldn't see the explosions, bumped into an intelligence officer and asked, "What's going on out there?"

"I'm not sure, general," said Lieut. Colonel George Bicknell, "but I just saw two battleships sunk."

"That's ridiculous!" said Short.

Down on Battleship Row, Fuchida's bombers kept pounding the helpless battlewagons. The *West Virginia* took six torpedoes, then two bombs. One large piece of shrapnel smashed into the starboard side of the bridge and tore open the stomach of the skipper, Captain Mervyn Bennion. A medic patched up the dying man's wound, and a husky black mess steward, Doris Miller, who had once boxed as the ship's heavyweight champion, helped move the stricken captain to a sheltered spot.

Fire and smoke swirled around the bridge. Bennion told his men to leave him; they ignored him. He asked them how the battle was going; they told him all was well. After Bennion died, an officer told Miller to feed ammunition into a nearby machine gun. Like other blacks in the Navy of 1941, Miller had not been trained for anything but domestic chores, but he soon took charge of the machine gun and started firing away. A young ensign recalled later that it was the first time he had seen Miller smile since he last fought in the ring.

Caught by surprise, and then often finding all ammunition neatly locked away, the defenders hacked away the locks and fought back with any weapons at hand — machine guns, rifles, pistols. This usually achieved nothing, but there were some surprises. At Kaneohe Naval Air Station on the east coast of Oahu, a flight of Mitsubishi Zeroes was strafing the hangars when a sailor named Sands darted out of an armory and fired a burst with a Browning automatic rifle.

"Hand me another BAR!" shouted Sands. "I swear I hit that yellow bastard!"

Japanese Lieut. Fusata Iida turned to strafe Sands, but the sailor fired another BAR clip, then ducked the bullets that pocked the armory's wall. As Iida's Zero climbed again, gasoline began streaming from his fuel tank. Before takeoff, Iida had said that any pilot whose engine failed should crash his plane into the enemy, so now he turned for a last attack. For one incredible minute, the two enemies faced and fired at each other, Iida from his crippled Zero, Sands with his BAR. Then the Zero nosed into a highway and smashed into pieces.

As Admiral Kimmel stood near a window, a spent machine-gun bullet smashed the glass and hit him lightly in the chest. Kimmel — who would soon, like General Short, be dismissed from his command — picked up the bullet. To an aide, he observed, "It would have been merciful had it killed me."

In Washington the disbelief was just as overwhelming. "My God, this can't be true, this must mean the Philippines," said Secretary Knox on hearing the news. "No, sir," said Admiral Stark, "this is Pearl."

Knox called Roosevelt, and Roosevelt called Hull, who was supposed to meet Nomura and Kurusu at 1 p.m. But the envoys had trouble getting the message from Tokyo decoded and retyped and asked for a delay, so it was 2:05 before they seated themselves, all unknowing, in Hull's antechamber. Hull, who had already read their message and knew about the raid on Pearl Harbor as well, made a pretense of reading the document, then lashed out at the luckless envoys. "In all my 50 years of public service," he declared, "I have never seen a document that was more crowded with infamous falsehoods and distortions." When Nomura tried to answer, Hull raised a hand to cut him off, then showed him to the door.

Fuchida's surprise attack lasted only about half an hour. Then, after a short lull, a second wave of 171 more planes roared in. By now the Americans were on the alert and firing at anything in sight. Twenty planes flying in from maneuvers with the *Enterprise* came under heavy American fire; two were shot down.

The battered *Nevada* (its band having finished *The Star-Spangled Banner*) managed to get up enough steam to proceed majestically out into the channel to the sea. Despite a gaping hole in its bow, its guns were firing, and its torn flag flew high. As it edged past the burning *Arizona,* three of that doomed ship's crewmen swam over, clambered aboard and manned a starboard gun.

"Ah, good!" the watching Fuchida said to himself as he saw the slow-moving *Nevada.* At his signal, all available bombers attacked in an effort to sink it and block the channel to the sea. Bombs ignited huge fires in the ship's bow. It escaped total destruction only by deliberately running aground.

More fortunate — indeed kissed by fortune — were Army pilots George Welch and Kenneth Taylor, who had gone from a dance at the Wheeler Officers' Club to an all-night poker game. They were still in formal dress at 8 a.m. when they saw the first Japanese planes open fire overhead. Under strafing fire, Taylor's car careened back to the P-40 fighters at Haleiwa Field. Taking off, the two went looking for Japanese planes and soon found them over Wheeler.

"I got in a string of six or eight planes," Taylor recalled. "I was on one's tail as we went over Waialua . . . and there was one following firing at me . . . Lieut. Welch, I think, shot the other man down." Welch's version: "We took off directly into them and shot some down. I shot down one right on Lieut. Taylor's tail."

Landing only for more fuel and ammunition, the two sleepless lieutenants set off for the Marine base at Barber's Point. "We went down and got in the traffic pattern and shot down several planes there," said Taylor, who suffered a severe arm wound. "I know for certain I shot down two planes or perhaps more; I don't know." Official records credited the two of them with downing seven planes, almost one-quarter of all Japanese losses.

The great attack was really fairly short. The first bombers returned to their carriers just after 10 a.m., scarcely two hours after they descended on Battleship Row. Fuchida lingered to observe and photograph the damage and was the last to return to Nagumo's fleet. It was still only noon.

Fuchida and Genda argued fiercely for renewing the attack. The oil-storage tanks had not been hit, and the raiders had not found any of Kimmel's three carriers (the *Lexington* and *Enterprise* were at sea, the *Saratoga* undergoing repairs). But Admiral Nagumo, who had mistrusted the plan from the start, felt he had accomplished his mission and saw no reason to risk his fleet any further. Back in Japan, Yamamoto strongly disapproved of Nagumo's decision to withdraw but accepted the tradition that such decisions are left to the combat commander on the scene.

Long after the Japanese had left, Pearl Harbor reverberated with reports of enemy invasions, parachute landings and other nightmares. Jittery defenders fired wildly at anything that moved. A fishing boat returning with the day's catch was shot to pieces.

On the capsized hull of the *Oklahoma,* Commander Kenworthy strode up and down for hours listening for raps and banging from the men trapped inside. Some survivors were finally pulled to safety through holes cut in the hull, but others drowned in the water rushing through the openings. Kenworthy wouldn't leave until the last of 32 survivors had been saved. By then it was Monday afternoon. Six sailors caught inside the *West Virginia* died just before Christmas — after two weeks of incarceration.

In terms of casualties and destruction, this was one of the most one-sided battles in history. The U.S. lost 2,433 killed (about half of them on the *Arizona*) and 1,178 wounded. The Japanese, who had expected to sacrifice as much as one-third of their force, lost 55 airmen, nine crewmen aboard five minisubs and approximately 65 on one sunken submarine. The U.S. lost 18 surface warships, sunk or seriously damaged; the Japanese none. The U.S. lost 188 planes destroyed and 159 damaged; the Japanese lost 29. Yet three of the five wrecked U.S. battleships (the *California, Nevada* and *West Virginia*) were eventually restored to service, and all the lost warplanes were eventually replaced — more than replaced — by the bombers that struck Tokyo and Hiroshima.

If Pearl Harbor seemed an American disaster, it proved a Japanese disaster as well. Churchill knew that when he gloated at the news: "So we had won after all!" So did Stimson, who felt "relief . . . that a crisis had come in a way which would unite all our people." So did Admiral Yamamoto, when he predicted that he would run wild for only a year. Pearl Harbor united Americans in rage and hatred, and thus united, powerful and determined, they would prove invincible.

QUESTIONS TO CONSIDER

1   In what ways was the attack on Pearl Harbor a surprise, and in what ways was it not? What does this say about American hopes, preparedness, and history?

2   Explain the main lines of the history of American-Japanese relations. What were the purpose and consequences of the manner in which they started? Describe the conflict over China. What were Japan's intentions in going into China? Why did the United States not react more? Can you see examples of racism in the reactions of both the United States and Japan?

3   Describe Admiral Yamamoto's background and personality, as well as his plan for Pearl Harbor and its purpose. How did the Japanese government react to this plan? What finally made Japanese officials adopt it?

4   How did the United States react to the possibility of an attack from Japan, and how did Hawaii respond in particular? Should or could the United States have been better prepared?

5   Why does Otto Friedrich conclude that "if Pearl Harbor seemed an American disaster, it proved a Japanese disaster as well"? Could Japan have done anything to avert this disaster? What were the longer-term effects on the positions of the United States and Japan in the world community?

19

D-Day: What It Meant

CHARLES CAWTHON

The author of this selection offers a brilliant and highly original discussion of the global significance of the American and British invasion of Normandy, in German-occupied France, on June 6, 1944. But his stunning thesis needs to be placed in the larger context of the Second World War, both at home in America and at the battlefronts. The war brought unprecedented unity at home, as Americans of all colors and conditions rallied behind a righteous crusade against Japanese, German, and Italian aggression. In the course of this terrible war, 16 million Americans, including 300,000 women and 960,000 African Americans, served in the armed forces. But compared with the destruction wrought in China, Japan, the Soviet Union, and Europe, where some 49 million people died and whole cities were flattened, the United States suffered relatively light casualties. There were no invasions of the American mainland, no bombing raids on American cities, no civilian massacres. Far fewer Americans died in the Second World War than in the Civil War. Total American military deaths came to 408,000. By contrast, 2.2 million Chinese and from 20 to 25 million Soviets — soldiers and civilians alike — perished in this, the largest and deadliest war in human history. Such figures do not include the 6 million Jews exterminated by the Germans in the holocaust.

Despite relatively light casualties, the United States underwent profound changes during the war. With the government pumping billions of dollars into war production, full employment returned and the Great Depression finally ended. Americans savored wartime prosperity — weekly earnings of industrial workers alone rose 70 percent between 1940 and 1945 — and they endured food rationing and shortages of cigarettes and nylon stockings. In addition to producing a surge of national unity, the war crushed powerful isolationist sentiment in Congress and centralized even more power in Wash-

ington, D.C., where multiplying war agencies issued directives, devised complicated forms and schedules, and produced veritable blizzards of paper.

The war was also a crucial event for American women. In a zealous display of patriotism, they joined the Red Cross, drove ambulances, worked for the civil defense, and enlisted in the armed services. Women were also recruited for their brains. The navy chose select graduates of seven East Coast women's colleges to participate in military operations that were highly classified; five such women, from Goucher College, were involved in top-secret "Operation ULTRA," which broke the Germans' U-boat code. Because of labor shortages, the government in 1942 urged women to join the wartime work force, and 4.5 million did so. They flocked to Washington, D.C., to work as secretaries and typists in the government's mushrooming bureaucracy. They also donned slacks, covered their hair, and went to work in the defense plants. There they did every kind of job from clerking in toolrooms to operating cranes, welding, and riveting — in short, they performed the kind of physically demanding work once reserved for men. "Rosie the Riveter" became a famous wartime image, one that symbolized the growing importance of the female industrial worker. The story of "Rosie the Riveter" is ably documented in a film by the same name.

In the Pacific theater, meanwhile, the United States lost the Philippines, Guam, and Wake Island to imperial Japanese forces, and faced an even more formidable enemy in Adolf Hitler's Germany. Although America was already in a condition of semimobilization in December 1941, it took a year before the country was ready to fight a total war on two fronts. What happened in the Pacific theater will be covered in the next section. As for Germany and Italy, the first American move against them took place in November 1942, when an American expeditionary army landed in North Africa and went on to help the British whip German and Italian forces there. After that, an Anglo-American force captured Sicily and invaded the Italian mainland.

Then on D-day, June 6, 1944, an Allied invasion force — the largest ever assembled — landed at Normandy in what turned out to be the beginning of the end of Hitler's so-called Third Reich. Thanks to German errors and Allied planning and execution under General Dwight D. Eisenhower, the invasion was a success. With a foothold in Normandy, American, British, and French armies drove a wedge into German defenses and poured inland. As the Western Allies pushed toward Germany from the west, Soviet armies drove in from the east. By May 1945 — less than a year after D-day — German resistance has collapsed and the once mighty Reich was a smoldering ruin.

This sets the stage for the following selection by Charles Cawthon, a veteran of the Second World War and an expert on the military side of the conflict. It is the thesis of his essay that D-day was one of those great battles that changed history, marking "the final, pivotal point" in America's often hesitant march to global power. He compares D-day to other pivotal battles, such as the Greek victory over the Persians at Marathon and the American vic-

tory over the British at Saratoga, and goes on to offer a brilliant discussion of how D-day was a turning point in the grand events leading up to the Second World War and in the rise of the United States as a superpower, "looked to by the rest of the world for leadership and resources to solve the humanitarian problems and disease and famine." For the imaginative, Cawthon even speculates on what might have happened had the Allies been defeated on the beaches and cliffs of Normandy. This is state-of-the art military history.

GLOSSARY

BRADLEY, GENERAL OMAR Commander of American ground forces on D-day.

CHURCHILL, WINSTON British prime minister during World War II who worked closely with Franklin Roosevelt in shaping the war policies of the Western Allies.

BALKANS Countries on the Balkan Peninsula in southern Europe, comprising Yugoslavia, Rumania, Bulgaria, Albania, Greece, and the European part of Turkey.

CREASY, SIR EDWARD British military historian whose text, *Fifteen Decisive Battles of the World* (1851), advanced the thesis that decisive battles shaped human civilization and history.

EASTERN FRONT The German-Soviet fighting front, which in June 1944 stretched from the tip of Greece northward to the tip of Finland.

OMAHA BEACH The heaviest fighting on D-day took place on this beach, one of four beaches on which American, British, and Canadian forces landed on D-day.

V-1 AND V-2 German ballistic missiles that came into use in 1944. These revolutionary, unmanned rockets enabled Germany to bomb Britain without the use of airplanes.

WESTERN FRONT The fighting front between Germany and the Western Allies in France.

A conjecture, worthy of a certainty, is that no American soldier on Omaha Beach at high noon, June 6, 1944, gave thought to being present at a turning point in world history. Any abstract thinking he may have done was more likely along the lines of being in a major debacle. The English Channel to his back, his weapons fouled by saltwater and sand, he was largely naked before an enemy firing down from trenches and massive concrete bunkers along high bluffs looming to his immediate front. Fortunately for his mission, if of no comfort to his person, his allies invading Europe by sea and air along some fifty miles of less forbidding Normandy coast were in better straits.

Their battle is popularly known as D-day. Their mission was to break through the German coastal defenses and secure a lodgment area in Normandy for the mustering of the armed might of the Western Allies, then assembled in England. This accomplished, they were to attack and destroy the German armies in Western Europe and, in concert with the forces of the Soviet Union, advancing from the east, invade Germany and destroy the Nazi regime that had held most of Europe in bondage and terror over the past five years.

Charles Cawthon, "D-day: The Beginning of America's March to Global Power," originally titled "D-Day: What It Meant," *American Heritage,* vol. 45, no. 3 (May/June 1994), pp. 49–50, 52, 54, 56, 58. Reprinted by permission of *American Heritage* magazine, a division of Forbes, Inc. Copyright © Forbes, Inc., 1995.

The American soldiers, having left their landing barge, had to wade ashore under fire to reach the Normandy coast. The goal of the D-Day invasion, writes Charles Cawthon, "was to break through the German coastal defenses and secure a lodgment area in Normandy for the mustering of the armed might of the Western allies." (Brown Brothers)

This generalized American soldier's lack of interest in history at the darkest moment of his travail is understandable. In the end, of course, he prevailed on Omaha and, with his allies, secured the lodgment. This done, the ultimate success of the mission became as much a given as war ever affords. Costly battles that followed in Normandy, at Arnhem, and in Ardennes delayed but could not halt the Allied armies that continued to grow in strength, while those in their foes steadily eroded without hope or recovery. By any sort of reasoning, the D-day victory was decisive to victory in Western Europe.

Now, fifty years later, a clearer perspective of this victory shows that it not only was decisive in a theater of operations of a long-ago war but can also be strongly argued as the decisive turning point in America's long, hesitant march to the peak of power in a world of vast change in its every human aspect: political, social, economic. This perspective is supported by an abundance of recorded history. The battle and the blind avalanche of events leading to it are exhaustively documented. The half-century since is also minutely recorded; for many it is within living memory. For the first time, much of it has been under the electronic eye of television. Unfortunately — as with the written word — this inherently impartial eye can be manipulated to blink selectively. In time, however, the decisive direction of history emerges from these encumbrances with distinct clarity. Just so, from the varied records of this century emerges the trace of America's sometimes reluctant march to global power, with June 6, 1944, as its final, pivotal point.

No such perspective is now available on America's tenure in power or on the uses it will make of it, for on time's long calendar it is a position just assumed. Apart from its effectiveness in serving American interests in the Gulf War and its limitations and dangers in serving European interests in the Balkans and in serving humanitarian interests in Somalia, the record is blank, as only the pages of history yet to be enacted can be blank. The sole certainty is that this history, when enacted, will bear the imprint of what the late Barbara Tuchman identified as the "Unknown Variable . . . namely man." Over time this variable has demonstrated a strong proclivity toward illogical and unpredictable behavior — a trait made more confusing by frequent infusions of acts of sense and conscience.

So, this future of America as the global superpower is best left to its uncharted devices. There is no existing tool for determining its course. There is a tool, however, for examining the voluminous record surrounding D-day as the pivotal point in this march to power. It is best to stipulate that this tool is not the computer. Its astounding capabilities are invaluable, but it cannot, of course, solve problems involving tumultuous human emotions. At present the human stuff, the pulse, of history can be ciphered only by us humans, using humanly conceived criteria against which to measure actions and events; an inexact tool, but our own.

The criteria by which I measure the place of D-day in the unending parade of world history were propounded by Sir Edward S. Creasy, a noted nineteenth-century historian and jurist, in his classic study *Fifteen Decisive Battles of the World*. This work, first published in 1851, was followed in quick succession by five more editions over the next three years and frequent reprints since. It has been studied by generations of historians and read for pleasure by even more history buffs. The criteria are as I extract them from the text of the preface of the first edition. Their prose style is of his period; their content has stood up remarkably well to the test of time and dissent; I know of none better:

"They [the fifteen battles] have for us an abiding and actual interest, both while we investigate the chain of causes and effects, by which they have helped to make us what we are; and also while we speculate on what we probably should have been, if any one of those battles had come to a different termination." Concerning battle causes and effects: "I speak of the obvious and important agency of one fact upon another, and not of remote and fancifully infinitesimal influences." He discards fatalism and inevitability as factors in history but recognizes "the design of the Designer" in human affairs. In something of an aside, he notes: "I need hardly remark that it is not the number of killed and wounded in a battle that determines its general historical importance."

Pursuant to his criteria and method, he named the victory of the Greeks over the Persians on the Plain of Marathon (490 B.C.) as the first truly decisive battle in world history, because it ensured that the "whole future progress of human civilization" would stem from Greece, not from Persia. Among the great armed conflicts of the era, he wrote, to Marathon alone can be traced the spirit that "secured for mankind the treasures of Athens, the growth of free institutions, the liberal enlightenment of the western world and the gradual ascendancy for many ages of the great principles of European civilization."

Continuing up to his own time, he judged only fourteen other battles of like decisiveness in shaping his nineteenth-century world, with which, with the

British Empire as its superpower, he seemed quite content.

Thirteenth on his list is the American Continental Army's defeat of the British at Saratoga (1777). In his opinion, this victory decided the outcome of the Revolution, making possible the founding of the American Republic. He observed, with some awe, that the American citizen had in two centuries and a half "acquired ampler dominion then the Roman gained in ten [centuries]." To Britain, France, and Russia — the great powers of his day — he added "the great commonwealth of the western continent, which now commands the admiration of mankind."

Sir Edward did not venture far into predictions on the future of this "great commonwealth." Perhaps his judicial experience made him wary of guessing at human directions. He did, however, quote at length the predictions of his noted contemporary Tocqueville, the brilliant firsthand French observer of the American phenomenon. Tocqueville's predictions were not modest. He was emphatic that nothing could halt America's growth and power. His predictions about the limits of America's territorial and population expansion were quickly overtaken and passed, but his basic premise has proven sound.

America's potential as a world power was first put to the test in World War I. Entry into the war ensured the Allies' victory and secured a voice in the political squabbling that followed. Disillusioned by the cost of a war that yielded such obviously dangerous and desolate results, popular American opinion forced the return to an aloof position in world affairs; frequent reference was made to President Washington's warning against foreign entanglements. Then, with no military threat from any quarter, the country reduced its formidable wartime forces to negligible size and, in the heady postwar boom, turned to creating domestic problems, principally the devastating economic depression of the 1930's.

The world war of the 1940's, which incidentally ended the Depression, was the most critical test of national character since the American Revolution and the Civil War. From the Revolution came the nation; from the Civil War, a firmly united nation; from World War II, a nation that was one of two dominant world powers. The almost immediate confrontation that followed with the Soviet Union, the other power, developed into the long and costly Cold War. (Veterans of Korea and Vietnam can rightly call this title an oxymoron.) America emerged from that grueling test, which included the period of raucous and violent dissent over Vietnam, as victor and undisputed king of World Power Mountain. This distinction seems to rouse no great outpouring of national pride, because, perhaps, the reality of it reveals responsibilities that are onerous, homage that is given grudgingly and usually along with demands, blame that exceeds glory, and costs that impinge upon serious domestic needs. A thick national skin and a cool, unblinking eye appear essential to the holder of global power.

To speculate on how Sir Edward Creasy might measure D-day against his criteria would be grossly presumptuous and might disturb his rest. I apply his criteria and method as I interpret them, nothing more.

I have noted that the "causes and effects" leading to D-day and afterward are extensively and variously recorded. From the generally agreed-upon hard facts in this record — not upon "remote and fancifully infinitesimal influences," which Sir Edward disdained — it stands out as the time when and place where American leadership of the Western Allies was unequivocally asserted. This was a mantle bestowed not as a generous gesture but for the preponderance of American manpower and matériel committed to the battle.

Equally significant, American industry in 1944 was not only arming and supplying its own forces around the world but also producing more than 25 percent of the armament of its Allies. This imbalance was to grow. Britain, after five years of total war effort, had reached the limits of its resources. From the invasion on, it would at best maintain its forces at their D-day levels while American forces in the theater grew until by the time victory was declared in Europe, U.S. ground forces were some three times greater than those of all its Western Allies combined.

This shift in the balance of power in the military structure of the Western Allies was drastic. In hindsight it represented the descent of Britain from, and the rise of America to, the top rank of world power. When the Western Alliance was first formed, after Pearl Harbor, Britain was the senior partner as far as forces in being were concerned. It was bearing alone the air battle over its isles and Germany, the ground war in North Africa, the submarine warfare in the Atlantic, and the war against Japan in the Pacific and Asia. All this while American forces and war industry were in the hectic stage of coming on stream.

This disparity in forces confronting the enemy was rapidly closed; by the eve of D-day, thirty months later, the American commitment of forces worldwide was predominant. Outwardly, Britain's equality in the partnership was maintained; actually, it had ceased to exist. In the war councils American insistence that the invasion be in 1944 overrode British reluctance to risk what its leadership knew would be the last great effort Britain could mount. (In justice, once committed to the invasion, Britain, under the drive of Prime Minister Churchill, held back nothing. It risked all.) As to the Supreme Command of the Allied invasion, no question arose: It would be American.

(A strong case has been made that there have been not two separate world wars in this century but one war interrupted by a twenty-year intermission for refurbishing armaments and antagonisms. With only a slight adjustment in thinking, the Cold War can be included as a third phase of this one war, making, overall, a conflict covering three-quarters of a century — in length somewhere between the Thirty Years' War of the seventeenth century and the Hundred Years' War of the fourteenth and fifteenth centuries, if that be a distinction to cherish.)

History never seems to repeat itself in any exact sense: The close of World War I found America facing no military threat; World War II ended with the immediate threat of a Soviet Union bound for world domination. The price of aloofness here was disaster; America had to continue leadership and support of what was now called the Free World.

The Soviet Union was unable to sustain this long conflict of sometimes open warfare and always of worldwide clandestine war. When the Communist political and economic structure collapsed in 1989, the Soviet Union dissolved into deeply troubled component parts; the mighty Soviet military machine, including its nuclear weapons, was left at dangerous loose ends.

The breakup of colonial empires into independent nations brought freedom for them to engage in tribal, ethnic, and religious wars conducted by a new raft of ruthless tyrants. America, as the superpower, is looked to by the rest of the world for leadership and resources to solve the humanitarian problems of disease and famine that are always the camp followers of such wars. Also in this correctional field is the United Nations, a cumbersome organization with a mixed record of effectiveness. There is an uncertain relationship between America's responsibilities, by reason of national strength, and those of the United Nations. Once again, great nations do not have small problems.

This troublesome picture has a brighter side that is often obscured by the hurly-burly of the everyday world: the century's two major tyrannies, Nazi Germany and Communist Soviet Union, have been broken, though their doctrines and practices continue to surface in various hate groups. And I find no credible denial that with American leadership, freedom has a better chance of surviving and growing in the world today than at any time in history. While this leadership is not *pro bono* in its purest form, it is a historic departure from the tradition that territorial acquisition and economic gain are legitimate spoils of power.

Sir Edward Creasy decreed that the historical

stature of a battle must be judged not only on the basis of victory that helped "make us what we are" but also on the basis of "what we probably should have been" had it been lost. He correctly tags this latter process as speculation, not always a productive exercise. "What if" and "if only" applied to history are something on the order of trying to prove a negative. This may be harmless, ego-stroking exercise when practiced privately, but an irritant when imposed upon others. Sir Edward therefore insisted that the speculation he considered necessary to his method be within the bounds of "human probabilities only," a porous restraint but helpful. In dealing with human affairs, one must use any tool available.

That D-day could have been an Allied defeat with far-reaching consequences was a decidedly human probability. The generalized American soldier who was left, at the start of this essay, caught in the shambles of death and destruction on Omaha Beach would have been justified in thinking that the battle there had been lost. This thought also plagued Gen. Omar Bradley, commanding the American ground forces. In his autobiography General Bradley wrote that from reports he received around midday of the carnage of Omaha, he had to believe that the assault there "had suffered an irreversible catastrophe." He wrote that at the time he privately considered shifting further landings to the American Utah Beach on the right and the British beaches on the left. Later in the afternoon, with reports of the attack moving inland, he gave no more thought to evacuating Omaha.

The "what ifs" of a lost Omaha are all ominous; an attempt to evacuate under fire would have been more costly in landing craft and casualties than the initial assault. Shifting the troops and equipment of the entire Army corps destined for Omaha to other beaches that were already crowded would have raised confusion to the level of chaos. A German counterattack, which never came, would have accomplished the same havoc as an ordered withdrawal. The loss of Omaha would have left a gap of some twenty miles between Utah and the British beaches.

The German high command was slow in identifying the June 6 assault as the Allies' main effort and in assembling the first-class panzer and infantry divisions that it had available to contain and repulse it. Even so, it is highly unlikely that the gap in the Allies' line would not have been quickly discovered and exploited to flank the adjoining beachheads. As it was, with Omaha Beach won, the situation of the Allies remained serious. Attacks beyond the beachheads were brought to a slow and bloody crawl by stiff resistance in the difficult hedgerow terrain. The British objective of taking the important communications center of Caen on the first day was not accomplished until six weeks later. General Bradley observed in his autobiography that had Hitler launched the forces he had available within the first week of the invasion, "he might well have overwhelmed us."

The "human probability" that D-day could have ended as a Dunkirk, or as did the amphibious assault on Gallipoli in the First World War, is too real to be disregarded. Had it happened, Pandora, that well-known packager and purveyor of disasters, would have had a memorable day. The immediate military ill would have been the reduction of Germany's three-front land war to two fronts. Then the major part of their sixty-one divisions, including eleven panzer, stationed in France and the Low Countries, could have been shifted with small risk to both the Eastern Front confronting the Soviet Union and Italy confronting the Western Allies.

The Eastern Front stretched at the time from the tip of Finland south to the tip of Greece, well away from Germany's eastern border. In Italy the Allies had taken Rome but were faced with continuing the slow, costly attacks up the mountainous spine of the Apennines.

Even with the major reinforcements made available by repulse of the invasion, it is unlikely that the German Army could have repeated its great offensives of the early war. But that it could have stalemated both fronts is a probability well within the human range.

Churchill, before the invasion, called it "much the greatest thing we have ever attempted." Defeat would have been crushing to Britain, in both military losses and morale. America would have made good its own losses but would have had to brace for a longer, more costly war, and largely alone. The effect on Germany, of course, would have been a revival of faith in Hitler. It would also have provided time to produce new weapons that would have had dramatic effect on the war right up to its final exclamation point: the atomic bomb. On D-day this bomb was some fourteen months away from its first appointment in Hiroshima.

Time is more of the essence in war than in any other destructive endeavor. Given fourteen months, Hitler's Germany would certainly have been into mass production of the jet plane, ballistic missiles capable of wreaking great damage on Britain, and ground-to-air missiles that could destroy bombers by tracking the heat from their engines

These were not really "secret" weapons. Allied intelligence knew of them and sought to destroy their development and production sites by heavy bombings, none of which was entirely successful. In Britain and in America the jet engine was in development, but not up to the German stage of production. Shortly after D-day the first rocket missiles, the V-1, were launched against England. Had their launching sites not been overrun by the invasion, the V-1 and the much more advanced V-2 would have done incalculable damage to British industry and morale. Forereach in weapons systems has changed the course of battles and of wars.

One of the more tragic consequences of a D-day defeat would have been the time given the Nazis to complete the Holocaust and to destroy the Resistance movement in occupied Europe. With the launching of the invasion, the Resistance was signaled to begin large-scale sabotage of German communications. With the Resistance so exposed, German retaliation would have been swift and brutal. To rebuild the movement would have been slow and difficult. The thousands of additional lives lost in an extended Holocaust can be calculated; the effect on the establishment of Israel cannot.

That the war could have been ended by the assassination of Hitler is a human probability supported by the prior attempts on his life. That in a stalemated war it could have been ended between Germany and Russia by an accommodation reached between Hitler and Stalin is supported only by the recognized obsession of each dictator with staying in power, regardless of what was required to do so. This, however, runs off the scale of human probabilities.

Then there was the atomic bomb.

The two bombs dropped on Japan in August 1945 ended the war in Asia and the Pacific. This was a war that Japan could not have won, but it could have exacted a terrible price had defeat required an invasion.

That Germany would also have been targeted for the bomb is a human probability of the highest order. (In terms of death and destruction, the conventional bombing of Dresden in February 1945 was on the scale of that visited on Hiroshima some six months later.) To speculate on the response of Hitler to a threat of the bomb requires probing an exceedingly dark mind. He might have seen this new order of flame, smoke, and concussion as a *Götterdämmerung* scene fitting for his departure. I speculate no further than that. One way or another, the bomb would have ended the war in Europe.

Again, these are projections of things that never happened, of situations that never developed. There is no certain knowledge of what course history would have taken had the Persians won at Marathon, the British at Saratoga, or Napoleon at Waterloo, other than that in each instance oppression would have had a further run. And there is no certainty of the aftermath of a Nazi German victory on D-day, other than that it would have been followed by at least fourteen months of dark and bloody deeds that would have left an even more terrible scar on what we call civilization.

If we set aside probabilities, these, in sum, are the recorded facts: that D-day was won by the Western Allies; that it was fought at American insistence, with an American as supreme commander; that the most critical and hard-fought sector of the battle — Omaha Beach — was won by Americans against heavy odds imposed by terrain and enemy strength; and that from this battle to the end of the war, American preponderance in men and matériel continued to grow, and with it grew American influence and leadership in the Western Alliance. This pattern continued throughout the Cold War, the demands of survival denying any discharge from it.

From all this there emerges one overriding result: World leadership now rests upon the shoulders of a free people, committed to democracy — this at a level not equaled since the time of the Athenians and Marathon. It is a decisive turn in history; D-day is the pivotal point upon which this turn was made.

At nightfall after the Battle of Valmy (1792), in which the French revolutionary forces turned back Prussian and Austrian invaders, the poet Goethe, who was there, was asked by some dejected Prussians what he concluded from the defeat. "From this place," he said, "and from this day forth commences a new era in the world's history; and you can say you were present at its birth."

It would not be amiss to address these words to all who fought the D-day battle on the coast of Normandy on June 6, 1944

QUESTIONS TO CONSIDER

1   What were Sir Edward Creasy's criteria for determining a great battle that changed history? Why does the author of this selection, Charles Cawthon, believe that D-day fits Creasy's criteria? What was the historical significance of D-day?

2   What does Cawthon mean by a shift in the balance of power among the Western Allies? What happened on Omaha Beach? Why was it vital to D-day's success? To what other decisive battles might D-day be compared?

3   Cawthon discusses a "what if" — the "human probability" of what might have happened had the Allies been defeated at Normandy. What, in his judgment, would have been the "far-reaching consequences" of an Allied defeat? What terrible new weapon might the Allies have dropped to end the war in Europe? Do you think that such conjectures on the basis of "human probability" are worthwhile?

4   Cawthon argues that an Allied defeat on D-day would have given Germany time to employ several decisive new weapons. What were these? What would they have accomplished?

5   What was the difference between the close of the First World War and the Second World War? What two major tyrannies of the twentieth century have been broken? What political system do most countries of the world want to emulate?

THE BOMB

20

The Biggest Decision: Why We Had to Drop the Atomic Bomb

ROBERT JAMES MADDOX

Perhaps the most controversial episode of the Second World War was the decision of the American civilian and military leadership to drop atomic bombs on Japan in order to win the Pacific war. To place the debate in proper context, let us review what had transpired in the Pacific theater. In November 1943, American forces moved from a holding action to an aggressive, two-pronged island-hopping campaign, with Admiral Chester Nimitz's forces attacking at Tarawa and Kwajalein and General Douglas MacArthur's command breaking through the Japanese barrier on the Bismarck Archipelago, islands in the South Pacific. Eventually, MacArthur recaptured the Philippines while Nimitz pushed toward Japan itself from the central Pacific.

Japan fought back desperately, sending out kamikaze planes to slow the American advance with suicidal dives against United States warships. The kamikazes took a terrible toll: 34 American ships sunk and 288 damaged. But the "Divine Wind" vengeance that the kamikazes represented also cost the Japanese heavily: their losses were estimated at 1,288 to 4,000 planes and pilots. Moreover, they could not stop American army and naval forces, which moved on relentlessly, capturing Iwo Jima and then Okinawa, located just south of the Japanese home islands.

From Okinawa, the United States planned to launch an all-out invasion of the Japanese home islands, to begin sometime in November 1945. Army and naval leaders thought initial casualties would run from 31,000 to 50,000. But ultimately the losses could be staggering if it took a year to break Japanese resistance, as some experts predicted.

The invasion, however, never took place, because the United States soon had an awesome and terrible alternative. On July 16, 1945, after three years of top-secret development and production, American scientists successfully detonated an atomic bomb in the New Mexico desert. Some scientists involved in the project urged privately that a demonstration bomb be dropped on an uninhabited island. But an advisory committee of scientists opposed any such demonstration and recommended that the bomb be used against Japan at once. Secretary of War Henry L. Stimson emphatically agreed: while the bomb would kill thousands of civilians, he said, it would shock Japan into surrendering and save thousands of American lives. Had the soldiers and marines in America's Pacific forces known about the bomb, they would have agreed, emphatically.

The final decision lay with Harry Truman, who became president after Roosevelt had died of a brain hemorrhage in April 1945. "I regarded the bomb as a military weapon and never had any doubt that it should be used," Truman later wrote. "The top military advisers to the president recommended its use, and when I talked to [British Prime Minister Winston] Churchill he unhesitatingly told me that he favored the use of the atomic bomb if it might aid to end the war." On July 25, Truman ordered that atomic bombs be dropped on or about August 3, unless Japan surrendered before that date. Then the United States, Great Britain, and China sent the Japanese an ultimatum that demanded unconditional surrender. The Japanese made an ambiguous reply. When August 3 passed and Japan fought on, Truman's orders went into effect, and American B-29s unleashed two of the "superhuman fireballs of destruction" — the first on Hiroshima, the other on Nagasaki — that forced Japan to surrender. Thus, the Pacific war ended as it had begun — with a devastating air raid. You may find it profitable to compare the Pearl Harbor air raid, a sneak attack against military targets (described in selection 18) with the nuclear blast at Hiroshima (covered in the next selection), which annihilated an entire city, including civilians and military installations.

Ever since, the use of the bomb has generated extraordinarily heated debate. Those against the bomb argue passionately that the monstrous weapon was not the only alternative open to Truman and his advisors in July and August. They point out that the invasion of Japan was not scheduled until November, so Truman had plenty of time "to seek and use alternatives." He could have sought a Russian declaration of war against Japan, or he could have ignored the advisory committee of scientists and dropped a demonstration bomb to show Japan what an apocalyptic weapon it was. He had another bomb to drop if the Japanese remained unimpressed. But Truman, in a remarkable display of "moral insensitivity," used the bomb because it was there to be used, and he never questioned his decision. To these critics, it is almost unthinkable that Truman and his advisors should ignore the entire moral question of dropping the bombs on civilians and ushering in a frightening and unpredictable atomic age. To this day, they point out with despair, America remains the only nation that has ever dropped an atomic bomb on another.

Other critics contend that Truman employed the bomb with an eye toward postwar politics. In their view, the president wanted to end the war in a hurry, before the Soviet Union could enter the conflict against Japan, seize territory, and threaten America's role in the postwar balance of power. Still others argue that the United States could have offered the Japanese conditional surrender, or found other ways to demonstrate the bomb, and so could have ended the war before the Soviets entered it.

Many analysts, however, defend Truman as passionately as his critics denounce him. Those for the bomb insist that his decision was a wise one that avoided a protracted land invasion in which hundreds of thousands of soldiers and civilians would have died. Sure, the bomb killed civilians, these critics say; it was unavoidable because the Japanese established military installations in residential areas of Hiroshima and Nagasaki. Besides, the Japanese could not complain: in their aggressions in Asia, the Japanese military had left 8 million civilians dead. "Did we have to drop the bomb?" asked a physicist who helped develop it. "You bet your life we did." He referred to a recent demonstration in the United States in memory of Hiroshima. "No one seems to realize," he said, "that without Pearl Harbor there wouldn't have been a Hiroshima."

In the following selection, historian Robert James Maddox of Pennsylvania State University presents the case for the bomb. Drawing on all available facts, he demolishes the "myths" of the antibomb school, one of which holds that several leading military advisers beseeched Truman not to use the bomb. As Maddox says, there is no evidence that a single one of them did so. After the war, Truman and others maintained that half a million American soldiers would have fallen if the United States had been forced to invade the Japanese home islands. Truman's critics have dismissed such claims as "gross exaggerations designed to forestall scrutiny of Truman's real motives." They point out that a war-plans committee estimated "only" 193,500 casualties. Maddox lampoons "the notion that 193,500 anticipated casualties were too insignificant to have caused Truman to resort to atomic bombs" and concludes that they were indeed necessary to end the war: the Japanese army, which ran the country, was preparing to fight to the last man, and the bomb was the only way to bring Japanese leaders to their senses and force them to surrender.

GLOSSARY

BOCK'S CAR   Nickname of the B-29 that dropped a second atomic bomb, called Fat Man, on Nagasaki.

ENOLA GAY   Nickname of the B-29 that dropped the first atomic bomb, called Little Boy, on Hiroshima.

GREW, JOSEPH   Truman's undersecretary of state; he had spent ten years in Japan as an ambassador and believed that the Japanese in the summer of 1945 were not even close to surrendering. Their "peace feelers," he claimed, were "familiar weapons of psychological warfare" whose purpose was to "divide the Allies."

HIROHITO   Emperor of Japan; the Japanese believed that the very soul of their nation resided in him.

JOINT WAR PLANS COMMITTEE (JWPC)   A report from this committee estimated that an American invasion of the Japanese home islands of Kyushu and Honshu would result in 193,500 total casualties in dead, wounded, and missing.

KAMIKAZES   Nickname for the Japanese pilots who flew suicide missions against United States naval forces toward the end of the Pacific war; the objective of the kamikazes was to crash their bomb-laden planes into American warships. The term *kamikaze* means "divine wind" in Japanese.

KONOYE, PRINCE FUMINARO   Sent to Moscow as a personal envoy of Emperor Hirohito. Prince Konoye sought to open negotiations that would lead to an end to the Pacific war.

MacARTHUR, GENERAL DOUGLAS   Commander of the army's half of the island-hopping campaign in the Pacific; it ran through the Carolinas and Solomons to the Philippines.

MARSHALL, GENERAL GEORGE C.   Army chief of staff during the Second World War and a close adviser to both Roosevelt and Truman. Warning that it was difficult to estimate battle casualties in advance, Marshall nevertheless thought that initial American losses from an invasion of Japan would be around 31,000 men. A subsequent medical report estimated that "total battle and non-battle casualties might run as high as 394,859" for the invasion of the southernmost Japanese island alone. Marshall not only supported Truman's decision to drop the atomic bomb on Japan, but considered using such bombs as tactical weapons during the land invasion.

NIMITZ, ADMIRAL CHESTER W.   Commander of the Pacific Ocean area; he headed the United States Navy's island-hopping campaign that led to the costly Battle of Okinawa; he believed that an invasion of Kyushu, the southernmost Japanese home island, ought to follow the operation at Okinawa.

OLYMPIC   Code name for the first phase of an American invasion of Japan, to commence at Kyushu, the southernmost home island, on November 1, 1945.

OPERATION CORNET   Code name for the United States invasion of Honshu, the main Japanese home island, on March 1, 1946.

SATO, NAOTAKI   Japanese ambassador to the Soviet Union in 1945.

TOGO, SHIGENORI   Japanese foreign minister in 1945; he made an overture to the Soviets asking that they initiate peace talks between Japan and the United States.

On the morning of August 6, 1945, the American B-29 *Enola Gay* dropped an atomic bomb on the Japanese city of Hiroshima. Three days later another B-29, *Bock's Car*, released one over Nagasaki. Both caused enormous casualties and physical destruction. These two cataclysmic events have preyed upon the American conscience ever since. The furor over the Smithsonian Institution's *Enola Gay* exhibit and over the mushroom-cloud postage stamp in the autumn of 1994 are merely the most obvious examples. Harry S. Truman and other officials claimed that the bombs caused Japan to surrender, thereby avoiding a bloody invasion. Critics have accused them of at best failing to explore alternatives, at worst of using the bombs primarily to make the Soviet Union "more manageable" rather than to defeat a Japan they knew already was on the verge of capitulation.

By any rational calculation Japan was a beaten nation by the summer of 1945. Conventional bombing had reduced many of its cities to rubble, blockade had strangled its importation of vitally needed materials, and its navy had sustained such heavy losses as to be powerless to interfere with the invasion everyone knew was coming. By late June advancing American forces had completed the conquest of Okinawa, which lay only 350 miles from the southernmost Japanese home island of Kyushu. They now stood poised for the final onslaught.

Rational calculations did not determine Japan's position. Although a peace faction within the government wished to end the war — provided certain conditions were met — militants were prepared to fight on regardless of consequences. They claim to welcome an invasion of the home islands, promising to inflict such hideous casualties that the United States would retreat from its announced policy of unconditional surrender. The militarists held effective power over the government and were capable of defying the emperor, as they had in the past, on the ground that his civilian advisers were misleading him.

Okinawa provided a preview of what invasion of the home islands would entail. Since April 1 the Japanese had fought with a ferocity that mocked any notion that their will to resist was eroding. They had inflicted nearly 50,000 casualties on the invaders, many resulting from the first large-scale use of kamikazes. They also had dispatched the superbattleship *Yamato* on a suicide mission to Okinawa, where, after attacking American ships offshore, it was to plunge ashore to become a huge, doomed steel fortress. *Yamato* was sunk shortly after leaving port, but its mission symbolized Japan's willingness to sacrifice everything in an apparently hopeless cause.

The Japanese could be expected to defend their sacred homeland with even greater fervor, and kamikazes flying at short range promised to be even more devastating than at Okinawa. The Japanese had more than 2,000,000 troops in the home islands, were training millions of irregulars, and for some time had been conserving aircraft that might have been used to protect Japanese cities against American bombers.

Reports from Tokyo indicated that Japan meant to fight the war to a finish. On June 8 an imperial conference adopted "The Fundamental Policy to Be Followed Henceforth in the Conduct of the War," which pledged to "prosecute the war to the bitter end in order to uphold the national polity, protect the imperial land, and accomplish the objectives for which we went to war." Truman had no reason to believe that the proclamation meant anything other than what it said.

Against this background, while fighting on Okinawa still continued, the President had his naval chief of staff, Adm. William D. Leahy, notify the Joint Chiefs of Staff (JCS) and the Secretaries of War and

Robert James Maddox, "Why We Had to Drop the Atomic Bomb," originally titled, "The Biggest Decision: Why We Had to Drop the Atomic Bomb," *American Heritage*, vol. 46, no. 3 (May/June 1995), pp. 71–74, 76–77. Reprinted by permission of *American Heritage* magazine, a division of Forbes, Inc. Copyright © Forbes, Inc., 1995.

A Japanese soldier surrendering on Okinawa in May, 1945. This was unusual. Most Japanese soldiers refused to surrender — it violated their sacred code of honor — and fought to the death. Robert James Maddox points out that "Okinawa provided a preview of what invasion of the [Japanese] home islands would en- *tail. Since April 1 the Japanese had fought with a ferocity that mocked any notion that their will to resist was erroding. . . . The Japanese could be expected to defend their sacred homeland with even greater fervor." (UPI/Corbis-Bettmann)*

Navy that a meeting would be held at the White House on June 18. The night before the conference Truman wrote in his diary that "I have to decide Japanese strategy — shall we invade Japan proper or shall we bomb and blockade? That is my hardest decision to date. But I'll make it when I have all the facts."

Truman met with the chiefs at three-thirty in the afternoon. Present were Army Chief of Staff Gen. George C. Marshall, Army Air Force's Gen. Ira C. Eaker (sitting in for the Army Air Force's chief of staff, Henry H. Arnold, who was on an inspection tour of installations in the Pacific), Navy Chief of Staff Adm. Ernest J. King, Leahy (also a member of the JCS), Secretary of the Navy James Forrestal, Secretary of War Henry L. Stimson, and Assistant Secretary of War John J. McCloy. Truman opened the meeting, then asked Marshall for his views. Marshall was the dominant figure on the JCS. He was Truman's most trusted military adviser, as he had been President Franklin D. Roosevelt's.

Marshall reported that the chiefs, supported by the Pacific commanders Gen. Douglas MacArthur and Adm. Chester W. Nimitz, agreed that an invasion of Kyushu "appears to be the least costly worth-while operation following Okinawa." Lodgment in Kyushu, he said, was necessary to make blockade and bombardment more effective and to serve as a staging area for the invasion of Japan's main island of Honshu. The chiefs recommended a target date of November 1 for the first phase, code-named Olympic, because delay would give the Japanese more time to prepare and because bad weather might postpone the invasion "and hence the end of the war" for up to six months. Marshall said that in his opinion, Olympic was "the only course to pursue." The chiefs also proposed that Operation Cornet be launched against Honshu on March 1, 1946.

Leahy's memorandum calling the meeting had asked for casualty projections which that invasion might be expected to produce. Marshall stated that campaigns in the Pacific had been so diverse "it is considered wrong" to make total estimates. All he would say was the casualties during the first thirty days on Kyushu should not exceed those sustained taking Luzon in the Philippines — 31,000 men killed, wounded, or missing in action. "It is a grim fact," Marshall said, "that there is not an easy, bloodless way to victory in war." Leahy estimated a higher casualty rate similar to Okinawa, and King guessed somewhere in between.

King and Eaker, speaking for the Navy and the Army Air Forces respectively, endorsed Marshall's proposals. King said that he had become convinced that Kyushu was "the key to success of any siege operations." He recommended that "we should do Kyushu now" and begin preparations for invading Honshu. Eaker "agreed completely" with Marshall. He said he had just received a message from Arnold also expressing "complete agreement." Air Force plans called for the use of forty groups of heavy bombers, which "could not be deployed without the use of airfields on Kyushu." Stimson and Forrestal concurred.

Truman summed up. He considered "the Kyushu plan all right from the military standpoint" and directed the chiefs to "go ahead with it." He said he "had hoped that there was a possibility of preventing an Okinawa from one end of Japan to the other," but "he was clear on the situation now" and was "quite sure" the chiefs should proceed with the plan. Just before the meeting adjourned, McCloy raised the possibility of avoiding an invasion by warning the Japanese that the United States would employ atomic weapons if there were no surrender. The ensuing discussion was inconclusive because the first test was a month away and no one could be sure the weapons would work.

In his memoirs Truman claimed that using atomic bombs prevented an invasion that would have cost 500,000 American lives. Other officials mentioned the same or even higher figures. Critics have assailed such statements as gross exaggerations designed to forestall scrutiny of Truman's real motives. They had given wide publicity to the report prepared by the Joint War Plans Committee (JWPC) for the chiefs' meeting with Truman. The committee estimated that the invasion of Kyushu, followed by that of Honshu, as the chiefs proposed, would cost approximately 40,000 dead, 150,000 wounded, and 3,500 missing in action for a total of 193,500 casualties.

That those responsible for a decision should exaggerate the consequences of alternatives is commonplace. Some who cite the JWPC report profess to see more sinister motives, insisting that such "low" casualty projections call into question the very idea that atomic bombs were used to avoid heavy losses. By discrediting that justification as a cover-up, they seek to bolster their contention that the bombs really were used to permit the employment of "atomic diplomacy" against the Soviet Union.

The notion that 193,500 anticipated casualties were too insignificant to have caused Truman to resort to atomic bombs might seem bizarre to anyone other than an academic, but let it pass. Those who have cited the JWPC report in countless op-ed pieces in newspapers and in magazine articles have created a myth by omitting key considerations: First, the report itself is studded with qualifications that casualties "are not subject to accurate estimate" and that the projection "is admittedly only an educated guess." Second, the figures never were conveyed to Truman. They were excised at high military echelons, which is why Marshall cited only estimates for the first thirty days on Kyushu. And indeed, subsequent Japanese troop buildups on Kyushu rendered the JWPC estimates totally irrelevant by the time the first atomic bomb was dropped.

Another myth that has attained wide attention is that at least several of Truman's top military advisers later informed him that using atomic bombs against Japan would be militarily unnecessary or immoral, or both. There is no persuasive evidence that any of them did so. None of the Joint Chiefs ever made such a claim, although one inventive author has tried to make it appear that Leahy did by braiding together several unrelated passages from the admiral's memoirs. Actually, two days after Hiroshima, Truman told aides that Leahy had "said up to the last that it wouldn't go off."

Neither MacArthur nor Nimitz ever communicated to Truman any change of mind about the need for invasion or expressed reservations about using the bombs. When first informed about their imminent use only days before Hiroshima, MacArthur responded with a lecture on the future of atomic warfare and even after Hiroshima strongly recommended that the invasion go forward. Nimitz, from whose jurisdiction the atomic strikes would be launched, was notified in early 1945. "This sounds fine," he told the courier, "but this is only February. Can't we get one sooner?" Nimitz later would join Air Force generals Carl D. Spaatz, Nathan Twining, and Curtis LeMay in recommending that a third bomb be dropped on Tokyo.

Only Dwight D. Eisenhower later claimed to have remonstrated against the use of the bomb. In his *Crusade in Europe*, published in 1948, he wrote

that when Secretary Stimson informed him during the Potsdam Conference of plans to use the bomb, he replied that he hoped "we would never have to use such a thing against any enemy," because he did not want the United States to be the first to use such a weapon. He added, "My views were merely personal and immediate reactions; they were not based on any analysis of the subject."

Eisenhower's recollections grew more colorful as the years went on. A later account of his meeting with Stimson had it taking place at Ike's headquarters in Frankfurt on the very day news arrived on the successful atomic test in New Mexico. "We'd had a nice evening at headquarters in Germany," he remembered. Then, after dinner, "Stimson got this cable saying that the bomb had been perfected and was ready to be dropped. The cable was in code . . . 'the lamb is born' or some damn thing like that." In this version Eisenhower claimed to have protested vehemently that "the Japanese were ready to surrender and it wasn't necessary to hit them with that awful thing." "Well," Eisenhower concluded, "the old gentleman got furious."

The best that can be said about Eisenhower's memory is that it had become flawed by the passage of time. Stimson was in Potsdam and Eisenhower in Frankfurt on July 16, when word came of the successful test. Aside from a brief conversation at a flag-raising ceremony in Berlin on July 20, the only other time they met was at Ike's headquarters on July 27. By then orders already had been sent to the Pacific to use the bombs if Japan had not yet surrendered. Notes made by one of Stimson's aides indicate that there was a discussion of atomic bombs, but there is no mention of any protest on Eisenhower's part. Even if there had been, two factors must be kept in mind. Eisenhower had commanded Allied forces in Europe, and his opinion on how close Japan was to surrender would have carried no special weight. More important, Stimson left for home immediately after the meeting and could not have personally conveyed Ike's sentiments to the President, who did not return to Washington until after Hiroshima.

On July 8 the Combined Intelligence Committee submitted to the American and British Combined Chiefs of Staff a report entitled "Estimate of the Enemy Situation." The committee predicted that as Japan's position continued to deteriorate, it might "make a serious effort to use the USSR [then a neutral] as a mediator in ending the war." Tokyo also would put out "intermittent peace feelers" to "weaken the determination of the United Nations to fight to the bitter end, or to create inter-allied dissension." While the Japanese people would be willing to make large concessions to end the war, "For a surrender to be acceptable to the Japanese army, it would be necessary for the military leaders to believe that it would not entail discrediting warrior tradition and that it would permit the ultimate resurgence of a military Japan."

Small wonder that American officials remained unimpressed when Japan proceeded to do exactly what the committee predicted. On July 12 Japanese Foreign Minister Shigenori Togo instructed Ambassador Naotaki Sato in Moscow to inform the Soviets that the emperor wished to send a personal envoy, Prince Fuminaro Konoye, in an attempt "to restore peace with all possible speed." Although he realized Konoye could not reach Moscow before the Soviet leader Joseph Stalin and Foreign Minister V. M. Molotov left to attend a Big Three meeting scheduled to begin in Potsdam on the fifteenth, Togo sought to have negotiations begin as soon as they returned.

American officials had long since been able to read Japanese diplomatic traffic through a process known as the MAGIC intercepts. Army intelligence (G-2) prepared for General Marshall its interpretation of Togo's message the next day. The report listed several possible constructions, the most probable being that the Japanese "governing clique" was making a coordinated effort to "stave off defeat" through So-

viet intervention and an "appeal to war weariness in the United States." The report added that Undersecretary of State Joseph C. Grew, who had spent ten years in Japan as ambassador, "agrees with these conclusions."

Some have claimed that Togo's overture to the Soviet Union, together with attempts by some minor Japanese officials in Switzerland and other neutral countries to get peace talks started through the Office of Strategic Services (OSS), constituted clear evidence that the Japanese were near surrender. Their sole prerequisite was retention of their sacred emperor, whose unique cultural/religious status within the Japanese polity they would not compromise. If only the United States had extended assurances about the emperor, according to this view, much bloodshed and the atomic bombs would have been unnecessary.

A careful reading of the MAGIC intercepts of subsequent exchanges between Togo and Sato provides no evidence that retention of the emperor was the sole obstacle to peace. What they show instead is that the Japanese Foreign Office was trying to cut a deal through the Soviet Union that would have permitted Japan to retain its political system and its prewar empire intact. Even the most lenient American official could not have countenanced such a settlement.

Togo on July 17 informed Sato that "we are not asking the Russians' mediation in *anything like unconditional surrender* [emphasis added]." During the following weeks Sato pleaded with his superiors to abandon hope of Soviet intercession and to approach the United States directly to find out what peace terms would be offered. "There is . . . no alternative but immediate unconditional surrender," he cabled on July 31, and he bluntly informed Togo that "your way of looking at things and the actual situation in the Eastern Area may be seen to be absolutely contradictory." The Foreign Ministry ignored his pleas and continued to seek Soviet help even after Hiroshima.

"Peace feelers" by Japanese officials abroad seemed no more promising from the American point of view. Although several of the consular personnel and military attachés engaged in these activities claimed important connections at home, none produced verification. Had the Japanese government sought only an assurance about the emperor, all it had to do was grant one of these men authority to begin talks through the OSS. Its failure to do so led American officials to assume that those involved were either well-meaning individuals acting alone or that they were being orchestrated by Tokyo. Grew characterized such "peace feelers" as "familiar weapons of psychological warfare" designed to "divide the Allies."

Some American officials, such as Stimson and Grew, nonetheless wanted to signal the Japanese that they might retain the emperorship in the form of a constitutional monarchy. Such an assurance might remove the last stumbling block to surrender, if not when it was issued, then later. Only an imperial rescript would bring about an orderly surrender, they argued, without which Japanese forces would fight to the last man regardless of what the government in Tokyo did. Besides, the emperor could serve as a stabilizing factor during the transition to peacetime.

There were many arguments against an American initiative. Some opposed retaining such an undemocratic institution on principle and because they feared it might later serve as a rallying point for future militarism. Should that happen, as one assistant Secretary of State put it, "those lives already spent will have been sacrificed in vain, and lives will be lost again in the future." Japanese hard-liners were certain to exploit an overture as evidence that losses sustained at Okinawa had weakened American resolve and to argue that continued resistance would bring further concessions. Stalin, who earlier had told an American envoy that he favored abolishing the emperorship because the ineffectual Hirohito might be succeeded by "an energetic and vigorous figure who could cause trouble," was just as certain to interpret it as a treacherous effort to end the war before the Soviets could share in the spoils.

There were domestic considerations as well. Roosevelt had announced the unconditional surrender policy in early 1943, and it since had become a slogan of the war. He also had advocated that peoples everywhere should have the right to choose their own form of government, and Truman had publicly pledged to carry out his predecessor's legacies. For him to have formally *guaranteed* continuance of the emperorship, as opposed to merely accepting it on American terms pending free elections, as he later did, would have constituted a blatant repudiation of his own promises.

Nor was that all. Regardless of the emperor's actual role in Japanese aggression, which is still debated, much wartime propaganda had encouraged Americans to regard Hirohito as no less a war criminal than Adolf Hitler or Benito Mussolini. Although Truman said on several occasions that he had no objection to retaining the emperor, he understandably refused to make the first move. The ultimatum he issued from Potsdam on July 26 did not refer specifically to the emperorship. All it said was that occupation forces would be removed after "a peaceful and responsible" government had been established according to the "freely expressed will of the Japanese people." When the Japanese rejected the ultimatum rather than at least inquire whether they might retain the emperor, Truman permitted the plans for using the bombs to go forward.

Reliance on MAGIC intercepts and the "peace feelers" to gauge how near Japan was to surrender is misleading in any case. The army, not the Foreign Office, controlled the situation. Intercepts of Japanese military communication, designated ULTRA, provided no reason to believe the army was even considering surrender. Japanese Imperial Headquarters had correctly guessed that the next operation after Okinawa would be Kyushu and was making every effort to bolster its defenses there.

General Marshall reported on July 24 that there were "approximately 500,000 troops in Kyushu" and that more were on the way. ULTRA identified new units arriving almost daily. MacArthur's G–2 reported on July 29 that "this threatening development, if not checked, may grow to a point where we attack on a ratio of one (1) to one (1) which is not the recipe for victory." By the time the first atomic bomb fell, ULTRA indicated that there were 560,000 troops in southern Kyushu (the actual figure was closer to 900,000), and projections for November 1 placed the number at 680,000. A report, for medical purposes, of July 31 estimated that total battle and nonbattle casualties might run as high as 394,859 *for the Kyushu operation alone.* This figure did not include those men expected to be killed outright, for obviously they would require no medical attention. Marshall regarded Japanese defenses as so formidable that even after Hiroshima he asked MacArthur to consider alternate landing sites and began contemplating the use of atomic bombs as tactical weapons to support the invasion.

The thirty-day casualty projection of 31,000 Marshall had given Truman at the June 18 strategy meeting had become meaningless. It had been based on the assumption that the Japanese had about 350,000 defenders in Kyushu and that naval and air interdiction would preclude significant reinforcement. But the Japanese buildup since that time meant that the defenders would have nearly twice the number of troops available by "X-day" than earlier assumed. The assertion that apprehensions about casualties are insufficient to explain Truman's use of the bombs, therefore, cannot be taken seriously. On the contrary, as Winston Churchill wrote after a conversation with him at Potsdam, Truman was tormented by "the terrible responsibilities that rested upon him in regard to the unlimited effusion of American blood."

Some historians have argued that while the first bomb *might* have been required to achieve Japanese surrender, dropping the second constituted a needless barbarism. The record shows otherwise. American officials believed more than one bomb would be necessary because they assumed Japanese hard-liners would minimize the first explosion or attempt to explain it away as some sort of natural catastrophe, precisely what they did. The Japanese minister of war, for instance, at first refused even to admit that the Hiroshima bomb was atomic. A few hours after Nagasaki he told the cabinet that "the Americans appeared to have one hundred atomic bombs . . . they could drop three per day. The next target might well be Tokyo."

Even after both bombs had fallen and Russia entered the war, Japanese militants insisted on such lenient peace terms that moderates knew there was no sense even transmitting them to the United States. Hirohito had to intervene personally on two occasions during the next few days to induce hard-liners to abandon their conditions and to accept the American stipulation that the emperor's authority "shall be subject to the Supreme Commander of the Allied Powers." That the militarists would have accepted such a settlement before the bombs is farfetched, to say the least.

Some writers have argued that the cumulative effects of battlefield defeats, conventional bombing, and naval blockade already had defeated Japan. Even without extending assurances about the emperor, all the United States had to do was wait. The most frequently cited basis for this contention is the *United States Strategic Bombing Survey,* published in 1946, which stated that Japan would have surrendered by November 1 "even if the atomic bombs had not been dropped, even if Russia had not entered the war, and even if no invasion had been planned or contemplated." Recent scholarship by the historian Robert P. Newman and others has demonstrated that the survey was "cooked" by those who prepared it to arrive at such a conclusion. No matter. This or any other document based on information available only after the war ended is irrelevant with regard to what Truman could have known at the time.

What often goes unremarked is that when the bombs were dropped, fighting was still going on in the Philippines, China, and elsewhere. Every day that the war continued thousands of prisoners of war had to live and die in abysmal conditions, and there were rumors that the Japanese intended to slaughter them if the homeland was invaded. Truman was Commander in Chief of the American armed forces, and he had a duty to the men under his command not shared by those sitting in moral judgment decades later. Available evidence points to the conclusion that he acted for the reason he said he did: to end a bloody war that would have become far bloodier had invasion proved necessary. One can only imagine what would have happened if tens of thousands of American boys had died or been wounded on Japanese soil and then it had become known that Truman had chosen not to use weapons that might have ended the war months sooner.

QUESTIONS TO CONSIDER

1   What do you feel about Truman's decision to drop the atomic bomb on Japan? Do you think it was the right choice under the circumstances, or do you think it was wrong? What alternatives did he have? Would any of them have convinced the Japanese to accept America's terms of "unconditional surrender"?

2   Why did Truman and his advisers demand "unconditional surrender" by the Japanese? Why did Japan's political and military leaders balk at accepting such terms? Why were they so determined to preserve the Emperor? What was the American view of him?

3   Much has been made of the estimated casualties the Americans would have suffered had they been forced to invade the Japanese homeland. To invade the first home island alone (this was Kyushu), Marshall came up with one casualty figure and Admiral Leahy with a somewhat higher figure for the first month of fighting. The Report of the Joint War Plans Committee estimated total loses from an invasion of the Japanese homeland at 193,500. After the war, Truman claimed that an invasion would have resulted in 500,000 American deaths. How do you explain such discrepancies? What does Professor Maddox say about them? Were Japanese forces on Kyushu and the main home island, Honshu, strong enough to inflict such losses? What is Maddox's opinion of critics who use the estimate of the War Plans Committee to condemn Truman?

4   Why did the Japanese look to Stalin's regime in hopes of securing favorable peace terms? Why did the Soviet Union refuse to intercede in Japan's behalf in an effort to end the Pacific war? Had the Soviets approached the United States, asking for terms for Japan other than unconditional surrender, how do you think Truman and his advisers would have reacted?

5   In selection 19, Charles Cawthon used "human probability" to draw conclusions as to what might have happened had D-day failed. What do you think might have happened had the Truman administration decided not to use its nuclear capacity against Japan?

21

Hiroshima: The Victims

FLETCHER KNEBEL AND CHARLES W. BAILEY II

One of my friends, who thinks that dropping the bomb was a necessity, believes never-theless that the horrors it visited on Hiroshima and Nagasaki ought never to be forgot-ten. Indeed, perhaps the best argument against the bomb is what it did to its victims, which is the subject of the following selection. It and the previous selection ought to gen-erate fiery discussions in every classroom in which Portrait of America *is read.*

For the people of Hiroshima and Nagasaki, the questions faced by Truman and his advisers did not matter. Nothing mattered to them but the searing flash of light that ulti-mately killed some 130,000 people in Hiroshima and 60,000 to 70,000 in Nagasaki and scarred and twisted thousands more. One scorched watch, found in the wreckage at Hiroshima, stopped at the exact moment of the atomic blast: 8:16 A.M. When the bomb exploded two thousand feet above the center of the city, thousands of people "were simply burned black and dead where they stood by the radiant heat that turned central Hiroshima into a gigantic oven." Some 60 percent of the city — roughly four square miles — was totally vaporized. "Beyond the zone of utter death and destruction," as one history puts it, "lightly built houses were knocked flat as far as three miles from ground zero, so that 80 percent of all buildings were destroyed and almost all the rest badly damaged." Nothing was left of Hiroshima but a smoking, radioactive rubble. After the second bomb wrought similar destruction on Nagasaki, Emperor Hirohito spoke to his people by radio — the first time he had ever communicated with them. "The enemy," he said, "who has recently made use of an inhuman bomb, is incessantly subjecting innocent people to grievous wounds and massacre. The devastation is taking on incalculable proportions. To con-tinue the war under these conditions would not only lead to the annihilation of Our Nation, but the destruction of human civilization as well."

Since then, a number of books have appeared about the atomic explosions at Hiroshima and Nagasaki. Among the best are John Hersey's Hiroshima *(1946), available in a new edition, and* No High Ground *(1960), by Fletcher Knebel and Charles W. Bailey II. The latter recounts the entire history of the first atomic bomb at Hiroshima, from Truman's decision to use it, to the flight of the* Enola Gay *(which dropped "Little Boy," as the bomb was called), up to the actual explosion and its cataclysmic results. In this selection, Knebel and Bailey describe that explosion with telling details, narrating the experiences of several people who somehow lived through that "fireball of destruction." Telling the personal side of Hiroshima is what makes this such a powerful account, with implicit lessons about the horror of nuclear war that have universal resonance. We can all identify with the people here, with Mr. Nukushina, Mrs. Susukida, and Dr. Imagawa, as the atomic blast swept over their city and changed the world forever.*

GLOSSARY

ENOLA GAY   Nickname of the B-29 that dropped the atomic bomb called "Little Boy" on Hiroshima.

HIRANO, MAJOR TOSAKU   Staff officer stationed in Hiroshima, he had gone up to Tokyo, and his decision to stay there a couple of extra nights saved his life; later, he persuaded Japan's leading nuclear scientist, who already suspected that the bomb dropped on Hiroshima was a nuclear weapon, to fly there and investigate.

DR. IMAGAWA   Visiting a patient's home when the bomb burst, he found himself "standing on top of a five-foot pile of rubble" with his clothes shredded; he made for his home in a suburb, helping the wounded along the way.

KINOSHITA, HIDEO   An officer at the monitoring station of the Japanese quasi-governmental news agency near Tokyo, he reported to his boss the news from America that an atomic bomb had been dropped on Hiroshima, and the boss relayed that report to the chief secretary of the Japanese cabinet.

NAKAMURA, BIN   Subchief of the Hiroshima bureau of Japan's news agency, he was eating breakfast when the explosion "lifted him off the straw mat on which he was sitting and sent a wave of 'immense' heat washing over his face"; miraculously unhurt, he spent the day interviewing survivors and got a story out on a suburban radio station.

NUKUSHINA, MICHIYOSHI   Fire-truck driver at the Hiroshima Army Ordnance Supply Depot, he had just returned home when the bomb exploded, flattening his home and blowing him into a corner where two safes prevented the falling roof from crushing him; he eventually found himself at an emergency aid station on Ninoshima Island.

OPPENHEIMER, J. ROBERT   Scientist and director of the top-secret project at Los Alamos, New Mexico, that built the first atomic bomb.

SAKAMOTO, CHINAYO   A mother who was mopping her kitchen floor when the *Enola Gay* droned by overhead, she and her family escaped "the blast and fire," because their home was situated behind a high protective hill.

SAKAMOTO, MIHO   Chinayo Sakamoto's daughter-in-law, who, after learning that her husband and his entire military unit had been wiped out, slit her throat with a razor in front of a little altar.

SUSUKIDA, HAYANO   Picking up salvaged roof tiles with other volunteers, she found herself suddenly slammed to the ground, her back severely burned, and her watch blown off; she made it to the emergency aid station on Ninoshima Island.

YAMAGUCHI, YUKO   She lived with her children in a rented farmhouse in a suburb and was just cleaning up after breakfast when the walls exploded in a black cloud of soot; unhurt, she went into the wrecked city and found her father and mother, both dying, in a Red Cross hospital; she never did find her husband's parents.

The sounding of the all-clear signal in Hiroshima at 7:13 A.M. on August 6 made little change in the tempo of the city. Most people had been too busy, or too lazy, to pay much attention to the alert. The departure of the single, high-flying B-29 caused no more stir than its arrival over the city twenty-two minutes earlier.

As the plane flew out over the sea, Michiyoshi Nukushina, a thirty-eight-year-old fire-truck driver at the Hiroshima Army Ordnance Supply Depot, climbed onto his bicycle and headed for home. He had received special permission to quit his post half an hour before his shift ended. Wearing an official-duty armband to clear himself through the depot gates, and carrying a new pair of wooden clogs and a bag of fresh tomatoes drawn from the depot commissary, he headed home through the narrow streets of Hiroshima.

Nukushina crossed two of the seven river channels that divided the city into fingerlike islands and finally arrived at his home in Kakomachi precinct a little more than half an hour after leaving the firehouse. Propping his bicycle by an entrance to his small combination home and wineshop he walked inside and called to his wife to go get the tomatoes.

At this same instant, in a comfortable house behind the high hill that made Hijiyama Park a welcome variation in the otherwise flat terrain of Hiroshima, a mother named Chinayo Sakamoto was mopping her kitchen floor after breakfast. Her son Tsuneo, an Army captain fortunately stationed right in his home town, had left for duty with his unit. His wife Miho had gone upstairs. Tsuneo's father lay on the straw mat in the living room, reading his morning paper.

Pages 175–201 from *No High Ground* by Fletcher Knebel and Charles W. Bailey II. Copyright © 1960 by Fletcher Knebel and Charles W. Bailey II. Renewed © 1988 by Fletcher Knebel and Charles W. Bailey III. Reprinted by permission of HarperCollins, Publishers, Inc.

Off to the east and south of the city, a few men in air defense posts were watching the morning sky or listening to their sound-detection equipment. At the Matsunaga lookout station, in the hills east of Hiroshima, a watcher filed two reports with the air defense center. At 8:06, he sighted and reported two planes, headed northwest. At 8:09, he saw another, following some miles behind them, and corrected his report to include it.

At 8:14, the telephone talker at the Nakano searchlight battery also made a report. His sound equipment had picked up the noise of aircraft engines. Unidentified planes were coming from Saijo, about fifteen miles east of Hiroshima, and were heading toward the city.

The anti-aircraft gunners on Mukay-Shima Island in Hiroshima harbor could now see two planes, approaching the eastern edge of the city at very high altitude. As they watched, at precisely seventeen seconds after 8:15, the planes suddenly separated. The leading aircraft made a tight, diving turn to the right. The second plane performed an identical maneuver to the left, and from it fell three parachutes which opened and floated slowly down toward the city.

The few people in Hiroshima who caught sight of the two planes saw the parachutes blossom as the aircraft turned away from the city. Some cheered when they saw them, thinking the enemy planes must be in trouble and the crews were starting to bail out.

For three quarters of a minute there was nothing in the clear sky over the city except the parachutes and the diminishing whine of airplane engines as the B-29's retreated into the lovely blue morning.

Then suddenly, without a sound, there was no sky left over Hiroshima.

For those who were there and who survived to recall the moment when man first turned on himself the elemental forces of his own universe, the first instant was pure light, blinding, intense light, but light of an awesome beauty and variety.

In the pause between detonation and impact, a pause that for some was so short it could not register on the senses, but which for others was long enough for shock to give way to fear and for fear in turn to yield to instinctive efforts at self-preservation, the sole impression was visual. If there was sound, no one heard it.

To Nukushina, just inside his house, and to Mrs. Sakamoto, washing her kitchen floor, it was simply sudden and complete blackness.

For Nukushina's wife, reaching for the bag of tomatoes on her husband's bicycle, it was a blue flash streaking across her eyes.

For Dr. Imagawa, at his patient's city home, it again was darkness. For his wife, in the suburban hills to the west, it was a "rainbow-colored object," whirling horizontally across the sky over the city.

To Yuko Yamaguchi, cleaning up after breakfast in the rented farmhouse where she and her in-laws now lived, it was a sudden choking black cloud as the accumulated soot and grime of decades seemed to leap from the old walls.

Hayano Susukida, bent over to pick up a salvaged roof tile so she could pass it down the line of "volunteer" workers, did not see anything. She was merely crushed to the ground as if by some monstrous supernatural hand. But her son Junichiro, lounging outside his dormitory at Otake, saw a flash that turned from white to pink and then to blue as it rose and blossomed. Others, also at a distance of some miles, seemed to see "five or six bright colors." Some saw merely "flashes of gold" in a white light that reminded them — this was perhaps the most common description — of a huge photographic flashbulb exploding over the city.

The duration of this curiously detached spectacle varied with the distance of the viewer from the point in mid-air where the two lumps of U-235 were driven together inside the bomb. It did not last more than a few seconds at the most.

For thousands in Hiroshima it did not last even that long, if in fact there was any moment of grace at all. They were simply burned black and dead where

This scorched watch, found in the rubble at Hiroshima, stopped at the exact moment of the atomic blast: 8:16 A.M. When the bomb exploded, thousands of people "were simply burned black and dead where they stood by the radiant heat that turned central Hiroshima into a gigantic oven." (John Launois/Black Star; Hiroshima: National Archives)

they stood by the radiant heat that turned central Hiroshima into a gigantic oven. For thousands of others there was perhaps a second or two, certainly not long enough for wonder or terror or even recognition of things seen but not believed, before they were shredded by the thousands of pieces of shattered window glass that flew before the blast waves or were crushed underneath walls, beams, bricks, or any other solid object that stood in the way of the explosion.

For everyone else in history's first atomic target, the initial assault on the visual sense was followed by an instinctive assumption that a very large bomb had scored a direct hit on or near the spot where they were standing.

Old Mr. Sakamoto, who a moment before had been lounging on the living-room floor with his newspaper, found himself standing barefoot in his back yard, the paper still in his hand. Then his wife staggered out of the house, and perhaps half a minute later, his daughter-in-law Miho, who had been upstairs, groped her way out also.

Dr. Imagawa had just reached for his medical satchel to begin the examination of his patient. When the blackness lifted from his senses, he found himself standing on top of a five-foot pile of rubble that had been the sickroom. With him, surprisingly, were both the sick man and the patient's young son.

Mrs. Susukida, flat on the ground amid the pile of old roof tiles, was left all but naked, stripped of every piece of outer clothing and now wearing only her underwear, which itself was badly torn.

Mrs. Nukushina had just time to throw her hands over her eyes after she saw the blue flash. Then she was knocked insensible. When she recovered consciousness, she lay in what seemed to her to be utter darkness. All around her there was only rubble where a moment earlier there had been her home and her husband's bicycle and the bag of fresh tomatoes. She too was now without clothing except for her underwear. Her body was rapidly becoming covered with her own blood from dozens of cuts. She groped around until she found her four-year-old daughter Ikuko. She saw no trace of her husband. Dazed and terrified, she took the child's hand and fled.

But Michiyoshi Nukushina was there, and was still alive, though buried unconscious inside the wreckage of his home. His life had been saved because the blast blew him into a corner where two big, old-fashioned office safes, used in the family wine business, took the weight of the roof when it fell and thus spared him from being crushed. As he came to, raised his head and looked around, everything seemed strangely reddened. He discovered later that blood from cuts on his head had gushed down over his eyelids, forming a sort of red filter over his eyes. His first conscious thought was that the emergency water tank kept on hand for fire-bombing protection was only one-third full. As his head cleared, he called for his wife and daughter. There was no reply. Getting painfully to his feet — his left leg was badly broken — he found a stick for a crutch and hobbled out of the rubble.

Hold out your left hand, palm down, fingers spread, and you have a rough outline of the shape of Hiroshima. The sea is beyond the fingertips. The back of the hand is where the Ota River comes down from the hills to the north. The spot where the bomb exploded is about where a wedding ring would be worn, just south of the main military headquarters and in the center of the residential-commercial districts of the city. Major Ferebee's aim was nearly perfect. Little Boy was detonated little more than two hundred yards from the aiming point on his target chart, despite the fact that it was released from a fast-moving aircraft over three miles to the east and nearly six miles up in the air.

Dropped with such precision, the bomb performed better than its makers had predicted. Several factors combined by chance to produce even more devastation than had been expected.

First was the time of the explosion. All over Hiroshima, thousands of the charcoal braziers that were the stoves in most households were still full of hot coals after being used for breakfast cooking. Almost every stove was knocked over by the massive blast wave that followed the explosion, and each became an incendiary torch to set fire to the wood-and-paper houses. In addition, where [J. Robert] Oppenheimer had estimated casualties on the assumption that most people would be inside their air-raid shelters, almost no one in Hiroshima was sheltered when the bomb actually fell. The recent all-clear, the fact that it was a time when most people were on their way to work, the mischance by which there had been no new alert when the *Enola Gay* approached the city, the fact that small formations of planes had flown over many times before without dropping bombs, all combined to leave people exposed. Thus

more than seventy thousand persons instead of Oppenheimer's estimate of twenty thousand were killed outright or so badly injured that they were dead in a matter of hours.

The initial flash spawned a succession of calamities.

First came heat. It lasted only an instant but was so intense that it melted roof tiles, fused the quartz crystals in granite blocks, charred the exposed sides of telephone poles for almost two miles, and incinerated nearby humans so thoroughly that nothing remained except their shadows, burned into asphalt pavements or stone walls. Of course the heat was most intense near the "ground zero" point, but for thousands of yards it had the power to burn deeply. Bare skin was burned up to two and a half miles away.

A printed page was exposed to the heat rays a mile and a half from the point of explosion, and the black letters were burned right out of the white paper. Hundreds of women learned a more personal lesson in the varying heat-absorption qualities of different colors when darker parts of their clothing burned out while lighter shades remained unscorched, leaving skin underneath etched in precise detail with the flower patterns of their kimonos. A dress with blue polka dots printed on white material came out of the heat with dark dots completely gone but the white background barely singed. A similar phenomenon occurred in men's shirts. Dark stripes were burned out while the alternate light stripes were undamaged. Another factor that affected injury was the thickness of clothing. Many people had their skin burned except where a double-thickness seam or a folded lapel had stood between them and the fireball. Men wearing caps emerged with sharp lines etched across their temples. Below the line, exposed skin was burned, while above it, under the cap, there was no injury. Laborers working in the open with only undershirts on had the looping pattern of shoulder straps and armholes printed on their chests. Sometimes clothing protected the wearer only if it hung loosely. One man standing with his arm bent, so that the sleeve was drawn tightly over his elbow, was burned only around that joint.

The heat struck only what stood in the direct path of its straight-line radiation from the fireball. A man sitting at his desk writing a letter had his hands deeply burned because the heat rays coming through his window fell directly on them, while his face, only eighteen inches away but outside the path of the rays, was unmarked. In countless cases the human body was burned or spared by the peculiarity of its position at the moment of flash. A walking man whose arm was swinging forward at the critical instant was burned all down the side of his torso. Another, whose moving arm happened to be next to his body, was left with an unburned streak where the limb had blocked out the radiation. In scores of cases people were burned on one side of the face but not on the other because they had been standing or sitting in profile to the explosion. A shirtless laborer was burned all across his back — except for a narrow strip where the slight hollow down his spine left the skin in a "shadow" where the heat rays could not fall.

Some measure of the heat's intensity can be gained from the experience of the mayor of Kabe, a village ten miles outside the city. He was standing in his garden and even at that distance distinctly felt the heat on his face when the bomb exploded.

After the heat came the blast, sweeping outward from the fireball with the force of a five-hundred mile-an-hour wind. Only those objects that offered a minimum of surface resistance — handrails on bridges, pipes, utility poles — remained standing. The walls of a few office buildings, specially built to resist earthquakes, remained standing, but they now enclosed nothing but wreckage, as their roofs were driven down to the ground, carrying everything inside down under them. Otherwise, in a giant circle more than two miles across, everything was reduced to rubble. The blast drove all before it. The stone

columns flanking the entrance to the Shima Surgical Hospital, directly underneath the explosion, were rammed straight down into the ground. Every hard object that was dislodged, every brick, every broken timber, every roof tile, became a potentially lethal missile. Every window in the city was suddenly a shower of sharp glass splinters, driven with such speed and force that in hundreds of buildings they were deeply imbedded in walls — or in people. Many people were picking tiny shards of glass from their eyes for weeks afterward as a result of the shattering of their spectacles, or trying to wash out bits of sand and grit driven under their eyelids. Even a blade of grass now became a weapon to injure the man who tended it. A group of boys working in an open field had their backs peppered with bits of grass and straw which hit them with such force that they were driven into the flesh.

Many were struck down by a combination of the heat and the blast. A group of schoolgirls was working on the roof of a building, removing tiles as the structure was being demolished for a firebreak. Thus completely exposed, they were doubly hurt, burned and then blown to the ground. So quickly did the blast follow the heat that for many they seemed to come together. One man, knocked sprawling when the blast blew in his window, looked up from the floor to see a wood-and-paper screen across the room burning briskly.

Heat and blast together started and fed fires in thousands of places within a few seconds, thus instantly rendering useless the painfully constructed firebreaks. In some spots the ground itself seemed to spout fire, so numerous were the flickering little jets of flame spontaneously ignited by the radiant heat. The city's fire stations were crushed or burned along with everything else, and two-thirds of Hiroshima's firemen were killed or wounded. Even if it had been left intact, the fire department could have done little or nothing to save the city. Not only were there too many fires, but the blast had broken open the city's

Their homes destroyed, city dwellers huddle on the Miyuki Bridge near the heart of Hiroshima. After the heat of the explosion came the "black rain," with drops as big as marbles, and then the "fire wind." Swept with conflagration, Hiroshima grew hotter and hot- *ter. Many refugees, attempting to escape the heat, drowned in the rivers, and the "crush of fleeing people overflowed the bridges, making fatal bottlenecks of the only escape routes." (Culver Pictures)*

water mains in seventy thousand places, so there was no pressure. Between them, blast and fire destroyed every single building within an area of almost five square miles around the zero point. Although the walls of thirty structures still stood, they were no more than empty shells.

After heat, blast, and fire, the people of Hiroshima had still other ordeals ahead of them. A few minutes after the explosion, a strange rain began to fall. The raindrops were as big as marbles — and they were black. This frightening phenomenon resulted from the vaporization of moisture in the fireball and condensation in the cloud that spouted up from it. As the cloud, carrying water vapor and the pulverized dust of Hiroshima, reached colder air at higher altitudes, the moisture condensed and fell out as rain. There was not enough to put out the fires, but there was enough of this "black rain" to heighten the bewilderment and panic of people already unnerved by what had hit them.

After the rain came a wind — the great "fire wind" — which blew back in toward the center of the catastrophe, increasing in force as the air over Hiroshima grew hotter and hotter because of the great fires. The wind blew so hard that it uprooted huge trees in the parks where survivors were collecting. It whipped up high waves on the rivers of Hiroshima and drowned many who had gone into the water in an attempt to escape from the heat and flames around them. Some of those who drowned had been pushed into the rivers when the crush of fleeing people overflowed the bridges, making fatal bottle-necks of the only escape routes from the stricken islands. Thousands of people were simply fleeing, blindly and without an objective except to get out of the city. Some in the suburbs, seeing them come, thought at first they were Negroes, not Japanese, so blackened were their skins. The refugees could not explain what had burned them. "We saw the flash," they said, "and this is what happened."

One of those who struggled toward a bridge was Nukushina, the wine seller turned fireman whose life had been saved by the big office safes in his house just over a half mile from "zero," the point over which the bomb exploded. Leaning on his stick, he limped to the Sumiyoshi bridge a few hundred yards away, where, with unusual foresight, he kept a small boat tied up, loaded with fresh water and a little food, ready for any possible emergency.

"I found my boat intact," he recalled later, "but it was already filled with other desperate victims. As I stood on the bridge wondering what to do next, black drops of rain began to splatter down. The river itself and the river banks were teeming with horrible specimens of humans who had survived and come seeking safety to the river."

Fortunately for Nukushina, another boat came by, operated by a friend who offered to take him on board.

"With his assistance, I climbed into the boat. At that time, they pointed out to me that my intestines were dangling from my stomach but there was nothing I could do about it. My clothes, boots and everything were blown off my person, leaving me with only my loincloth. Survivors swimming in the river shouted for help, and as we leaned down to pull them aboard, the skin from their arms and hands literally peeled off into our hands.

"A fifteen- or sixteen-year-old girl suddenly popped up alongside our boat and as we offered her our hand to pull her on board, the front of her face suddenly dropped off as though it were a mask. The nose and other facial features suddenly dropped off with the mask, leaving only a pink, peachlike face front with holes where the eyes, nose and mouth used to be. As the head dropped under the surface, the girl's black hair left a swirling black eddy. . . ."

Here Nukushina mercifully lost consciousness. He came to five hours later as he was being transferred into a launch that carried him, with other wounded, to an emergency first-aid station set up on the island of Ninoshima in the harbor. There he found safety, but no medical care. Only twenty-eight doctors were left alive and able to work in a city of a quarter million people, fully half of whom were casualties.

When Hayano Susukida tried to get up off the ground onto which she and the other members of her tile-salvaging labor gang had been thrown, she thought she was going to die. Her whole back, bared by the blast, burned and stung when she moved. But the thought of her four-year-old daughter Kazuko, who had been evacuated from the city after Hayano's husband was sent overseas and the family home had been marked for destruction in the fire-break program, made her try again. This time she got to her feet and staggered home. The blast had not leveled her house, about a mile and a quarter from the zero point, and the fire had not yet reached it. Hurriedly she stuffed a few things — a bottle of vegetable oil, some mosquito netting, two quilts, a small radio — into an old baby carriage, and started wheeling it toward the nearest bomb shelter. After going a few feet, she had to carry the carriage, for the street was choked with debris. She reached the shelter and passed the oil around to those inside, using the last of it to salve her own burns, which had not blistered or peeled but were nevertheless strangely penetrating and painful. She wondered what time it was. Her wrist watch was gone, so she walked home again to get her alarm clock. It was still running; it showed a little after ten. Back at the shelter, she just sat and waited. At noon someone handed out a few rice balls. As the survivors ate, an Army truck miraculously appeared and carried them to the water front, just beyond the edge of the bomb's destruction. Then they were ferried over to the emergency hospital on Ninoshima Island.

Dr. Imagawa, a little further from the center of the blast, was not seriously injured, although he was cut by flying glass in a number of places. His first reaction was annoyance. His clothes were in tatters, and he wondered how he would find the new pair of shoes which he had left at his patient's front door. Helping the small boy down off the five-foot rubble pile that had been the sickroom, he asked the youngster to take him to the front door. Oddly enough, they could not even find where the front of the house had been. Imagawa, much to his disgust, was out a new pair of shoes. At an artesian well with a pump that was still operating, he washed as best he could and set out for suburban Furue where his wife and children should be. He stopped frequently in response to appeals for help from the injured. One was a woman who wandered aimlessly in the street holding her bare breast, which had been split open. She pleaded with him to tell her whether she would live. The doctor, although positive she could not survive, assured her that a mere breast injury would not be fatal. Later, he drew water for a score of wounded from another well pump. Down the street, a trolley car burned briskly. Finally he got clear of the city and climbed the hill to Furue, where he found his family safe and uninjured. The walls of the house had cracked, in some places fallen, but his wife and the two little children had escaped injury, while the oldest girl had walked home from school without a

scratch after the blast. The doctor ate, washed thoroughly, painted his cuts with iodine and worked till dark with his wife cleaning up their house. That evening the somewhat sybaritic physician sat down to dinner and then relaxed, as he had done the night before in Hiroshima — twenty-four hours and an age earlier — over a few cups of wine.

The doctor sipping his wine that night had one thing in common with Mrs. Susukida and Michiyoshi Nukushina, both lying injured and untended in the emergency hospital on Ninoshima Island. None of them knew what it was that had destroyed their city. Nor did they yet have either time or inclination to wonder.

But others, outside Hiroshima, were anxiously trying to find out what the *Enola Gay* had dropped on the city. The search for information was a frustrating one.

At first there had been no indication that anything unusual had happened in Hiroshima. A moment after 8:16 A.M., the Tokyo control operator of the Japanese Broadcasting Corporation noticed that his telephone line to the radio station in Hiroshima had gone dead. He tried to re-establish his connection, but found that he could not get a call through to the western city.

Twenty minutes later the men in the railroad signal center in Tokyo realized that the mainline telegraph had stopped working. The break seemed to be just north of Hiroshima. Reports began to come in from stations near Hiroshima that there had been some kind of an explosion in the city. The railroad signalmen forwarded the messages to Army General Headquarters.

It was almost ten o'clock when Ryugen Hosokawa, managing editor of the *Asahi* vernacular newspaper in Tokyo, received a telephone call at his home. It was the office, reporting that Hiroshima had "almost completely collapsed" as the result of bombing by enemy planes. Hosokawa hurried to the office and sifted through the reports collected by *Asahi*'s relay room. Every one of them sounded to him like something quite different from any previous bombing. This must have been caused, he thought to himself, by very unusual bombs.

At about the same time Major Tosaku Hirano, a staff officer of the II Army Corps, was in General Headquarters in Tokyo. He had come up from Hiroshima a week earlier to report on the status of military supplies in the port city, and had been scheduled to fly back on Sunday. But he put his departure off for a day or two and thus was still in the capital.

Now his telephone rang. It was a call from Central Command Headquarters in Osaka, an installation under the control of the II Army Corps in Hiroshima, reporting that its communications to Hiroshima and points west had failed.

Tokyo GHQ tried several times to raise the Hiroshima communications center, in the earth-and-concrete bunker next to the moat of the old castle, but could not get through. There was no explanation. The succession of reports from the radio network, from the railroad signal center, from *Asahi*'s newsroom and from Osaka indicated that something serious had happened, but no one could find out what it was.

Then, shortly after 1 P.M., General Headquarters finally heard from the II Army Corps. The message was short but stunning: "Hiroshima has been annihilated by one bomb and fires are spreading."

This flash came not from Corps Headquarters but from the Army shipping depot on the Hiroshima water front, which was outside the blast area and was not reached by the fire that followed. There was considerable damage at the shipping depot, something in the neighborhood of 30 per cent, but officers there were able to get a message out as far as Kure, where the naval station relayed it to Tokyo. There was no word at all from the II Army Corps Headquarters at the old castle in the northern part of town.

Reports continued to trickle in. By the middle of the afternoon, the Army knew that only three enemy planes had been over Hiroshima when the bomb exploded. It had been told that two of these did not drop any bombs. This information supported the startling assertion in the first flash that there had been only one bomb exploded. Something very big, and very frightening, had hit Hiroshima.

In mid-afternoon the managing editors of the five big Tokyo newspapers, plus their counterpart in the Domei news agency, were called to the office of the government Information and Intelligence Agency, which had charge of press and radio censorship. An Army press officer addressed the little group of newsmen:

"We believe that the bomb dropped on Hiroshima is different from an ordinary one. However, we have inadequate information now, and we intend to make some announcement when proper information has been obtained. Until we issue such an announcement, run the news in an obscure place in your papers and as one no different from one reporting an ordinary air raid on a city."

In other words, the lid was on. The Army already had a strong suspicion that the Hiroshima bomb might be an atomic weapon. Japanese Naval intelligence had reported U.S. work on the bomb in late 1944, noting the interest of the American government in buying up all available pitchblende (uranium ore). Thus, although the best scientists in Japan had agreed that there was no chance of the United States producing a fission bomb in less than three to five years, there was now immediate suspicion that an atomic bomb had fallen. But the Army, anxious to keep the war going so it could fight a showdown hand-to-hand battle with the Americans on Japanese soil, was determined to withhold the news from the Japanese people as long as it could.

The editors protested mildly, but the decision stood. At six o'clock that evening, the radio gave the people of Japan their first hint that Hiroshima had been chosen for a place in history as the spot where man first proved he could tear apart the basic structure of his world. A listener, however, would have been hard put to deduce the true story from the first news item as it was read:

A few B-29s hit Hiroshima city at 8:20 A.M. August 6, and fled after dropping incendiaries and bombs. The extent of the damage is now under survey.

This cryptic item was repeated several times between six and nine o'clock without further explanation. On the nine o'clock program in Osaka, the sound of the musical chime that signaled the switch from national to local news was followed by this item:

An announcement by the Osaka railway bureau in regard to changes in various transportation organs and changes in handling of passenger baggage:

First of all, the government lines. Regarding the down train, trains from Osaka will turn back from Mihara on the Sanyo line. From Mihara to Kaitichi, the trains will take the route around Kure. . . .

Mihara was about halfway from Osaka to Hiroshima. Kaitichi was on the southeastern edge of Hiroshima. Trains headed there from Osaka on the main line ordinarily ran through the Hiroshima yards and station before swinging back to the smaller community.

The morning *Asahi* in Tokyo on August 7 carried a long front-page story with a sizable headline reporting "Small and Medium Cities Attacked by 400 B-29s." At the end of this story, there was a four-line item tacked on. It read:

Hiroshima Attacked by Incendiary Bombs
Hiroshima was attacked August 6th by two B-29 planes, which dropped incendiary bombs.

The planes invaded the city around 7:50 A.M. It seems that some damage was caused to the city and its vicinity.

Those who survived in Hiroshima still did not know what it was that had struck them so viciously

the day before. They did not have much time for thinking about it. Merely keeping alive was a full-time job. Some thought, as they fled the burning city, that the Americans had deluged their homes with "Molotov flower baskets," as the unhappily familiar incendiary clusters were nicknamed. Others, sniffing the air and detecting a strong "electric smell," decided that some kind of poison gas had been dropped. Another explanation was that a magnesium powder had been sprayed on the city, exploding wherever it fell on trolley wires and other exposed electrical conductors.

The prefectural government did what it could to bring order in the city. Somehow almost two hundred policemen were found for duty on August 7. They set to work, with whatever help they could commandeer, to clear the streets of bodies and debris. Police stations became emergency food depots, doling out hastily gathered supplies of rice, salt, pickled radishes, matches, canned goods, candles, straw sandals, and toilet paper.

The governor of Hiroshima prefecture, Genshin Takano, issued a proclamation:

People of Hiroshima Prefecture: Although damage is great, we must remember that this is war. We must feel absolutely no fear. Already plans are being drawn up for relief and restoration measures. . . .

We must not rest a single day in our war effort. . . . We must bear in mind that the annihilation of the stubborn enemy is our road to revenge. We must subjugate all difficulties and pain, and go forward to battle for our Emperor.

But most people in Hiroshima, if they could overcome their pain on this second day of the atomic age, were more concerned with finding their loved ones than with battling for their Emperor.

Yuko Yamaguchi, waiting out the war in the rented suburban farmhouse while her husband served overseas in the Army, was unhurt. So were her three little children. But her father-in-law, who had driven into the city Sunday for the meeting of his gas company board of directors, and her mother-in-law, who had left early Monday morning to fetch more supplies from their requisitioned city house, had not been heard from since the bomb fell. Yuko had had no word, either, from her own parents.

So at 6:30 this Tuesday morning, she left her children and set out for the city, walking the whole way because the suburban rail lines were not running. It was a long walk. By the time she reached the Red Cross Hospital, where she thought her in-laws might have been taken, it was noon.

Yuko did not find her husband's parents there. But, by sheerest chance, she found her own father, lying untended on the floor with an ugly wound in the back of his head. He begged his grief-stricken daughter for some water. When she did her best and filled a broken cup with stagnant water from a nearby pond, the delirious eye specialist was furious, insisting that ice and a slice of lemon be added to make it more palatable. Somehow, she found both in the wrecked hospital kitchen and made him as comfortable as possible. Then she started through the littered, jammed wards and halls to search for her other relatives. Again she found no trace of her in-laws, but at five o'clock she came on her own mother, lying unconscious, her face smashed almost beyond recognition and her intestines bared by a savage stomach wound.

Daughter dragged mother through the corridors to her father's side so the two could at least be together. There was little enough time. Near dusk the mother died, and Yuko had to carry the body outside, build a crude pyre and cremate it herself. At about dawn her father also died. This time, there were enough other corpses on hand so the hospital arranged a makeshift mass cremation, and Yuko left. She spent the day searching again for her husband's parents, but there was no trace of them, and she finally walked home to the hills to join her children. It was to be more than a month before she found any trace of her in-laws. Then she got only the stub of a commutation ticket bearing her mother-in-law's name, recovered from the wreckage of the train she had been riding at 8:16 A.M. Monday. A few charred bones uncovered still later in the burned-out office of the gas company president were the only trace ever found of her father-in-law.

Some who survived seemed to accept with stoicism the death of their loved ones. Miho Sakamoto, who with her husband's parents had escaped the blast and fire because their home was protected by the city's only high hill, was told on August 7 that her husband's military unit had been completely wiped out. She shed no tears and showed no emotion. Four days later, she visited the ruins of the building in which he had died, found a bent ash tray which she recognized as his and brought it home. That night, she seemed in good spirits when she went upstairs to the room she had shared with her Tsuneo. The next morning she did not come down to breakfast. Her mother-in-law found her lying in front of a little altar, the ash tray in front of her beside a photograph of her dead husband, the razor with which she had cut her throat still clutched in her hand. She left a note of apology to "My Honorable Father and Mother":

What I am about to do, I do not do on sudden impulse; nor is it due to temporary agitation. It is a mutual vow exchanged with my husband while he still lived. This is the road to our greatest happiness and we proceed thereon. Like a bird which has lost one wing, we are crippled birds who cannot go through life without one another. There is no other way. Please, do not bewail my fate. Somewhere both of us will again be living happily together as we have in the past.... My honorable Tsuneo must be anxiously awaiting me and I must rush to his side.

Sixteen-year-old Junichiro Susukida, at his factory-school dormitory in Otake, sixteen miles west of Hiroshima, had seen the fireball and the great cloud that rose over the city Monday morning.

When the first refugees arrived with the news that the city had been badly hit, he was one of many students who demanded permission to go to their homes, and he was one of five finally allowed to go into the city to contact authorities at the main school building and seek news of the students' families.

By the time they reached Miya-jima, on the southwestern edge of the city, the students could see the fires still burning in the bright late afternoon. As they came closer, they began to realize the full extent of the calamity. It was dark before the boys reached their home neighborhood and began their search for relatives. Junichiro, though unable to find either his mother or younger brother, did at last encounter neighbors who told him his brother had survived, though wounded, and had been taken to the home of other relatives in Fuchu. He could learn nothing about his mother, however, and finally headed back to his dormitory in Otake. Dead tired when he arrived at 2 A.M., he was nevertheless too distraught to sleep. He sat in the school auditorium and incongruously played the piano until fatigue finally subdued his nerves just before dawn on Tuesday, August 7.

Junichiro was not the only one who did not sleep that night. In Tokyo, the truth about Hiroshima was beginning to be revealed in ways that made it clear that the facts could not be kept from the people of Japan much longer.

A little before midnight on the sixth, the Tokyo office of Domei, the quasi-governmental news agency that served the whole nation, much as the Associated Press or Reuters do in the West, received a bulletin from Okayama prefecture, just east of Hiroshima. It was followed by a longer dispatch: the first eye-witness account of the bombing by a professional newsman.

Bin Nakamura, subchief of Domei's Hiroshima bureau, had been eating breakfast in his suburban garden when the bomb's explosion lifted him off the straw mat on which he was sitting and sent a wave of "immense" heat washing over his face. Once Nakamura discovered that the concussion and heat had not been caused by the nearby explosion of a "blockbuster" — his first reaction had been the typical one — he went to work as a reporter. On his bicycle and on foot, he spent the day in the city and talking to the refugees who streamed through his suburb. Then, at 10 P.M., like the experienced press-association man he was, he found communications at the suburban Haramura radio station and dictated a story to Okayama, the only point he could reach. In his dispatch, he said there was no way to tell what kind of a bomb had caused such havoc.

But before the night was much older the editors of Domei, and the leaders of Japan, had a way of telling much more about the bomb. In Saitama prefecture outside Tokyo, Domei operated a big monitoring station where nearly fifty workers, many of them Nisei girls born in the United States, listened to broadcasts from American stations. About 1 A.M. on the 7th of August (noon on the 6th in Washington, D.C.), Hideo Kinoshita, chief of the monitoring room, was awakened by the Japanese youth who had charge of the operation that night. The boy reported that U.S. stations were all broadcasting a statement by President Truman, describing the weapon that had been dropped on Hiroshima as "an atomic bomb." Kinoshita listened to the account and the boy's explanation of what "atomic bomb" might mean. Then he quickly called his own superior, Saiji Hasegawa, Domei's foreign news chief. Hasegawa was asleep in his hotel. When he was told of an "atomic bomb," he had no idea what it was, but although he was irritated at being awakened he hustled to his office. When he saw the text transcripts that were beginning to come through from the Saitama monitors, he was glad he had come to work. He reached for his telephone and called Hisatsune Sakomizu, chief secretary of the cabinet.

Sakomizu sleepily answered his bedside telephone, then came suddenly wide awake as he listened to the

Domei executive. He already knew, from the first confused reports on the 6th, that the Americans had used some kind of new weapon. Now, learning that it was an atomic bomb, something the cabinet had discussed briefly almost a year earlier, he knew it meant just one thing: the war was over.

Sakomizu quickly called Prime Minister Suzuki, with whom he had been working in the effort to arrange a peace settlement by negotiation. They knew immediately, he said later,

... that if the announcement were true, no country could carry on a war. Without the atomic bomb it would be impossible for any country to defend itself against a nation which had the weapon. The chance had come to end the war. It was not necessary to blame the military side, the manufacturing people, or anyone else — just the atomic bomb. It was a good excuse.

The Army, however, was unwilling to accept this attitude, despite the urgings of the peace group that the bomb gave military leaders a chance to save face by blaming the "backwardness of scientific research" for Japan's inability to counter the new American bomb. The generals, sitting in an emergency cabinet meeting on the seventh, pointedly recalled an old Japanese legend about an Army commander who became a laughingstock because he mistook the fluttering of a flight of birds for the sound of the approaching enemy and fled. They argued that the bomb was not atomic but was merely a huge conventional projectile. They flatly refused Foreign Minister Togo's proposal to take up for immediate consideration the possibility of surrender on the terms of the Potsdam ultimatum, and insisted on keeping the Truman atomic statement from the Japanese people until the Army could conduct an "investigation" on the ground at Hiroshima.

The military had already started such a check. Major Hirano, the staff officer from the Hiroshima headquarters whose desire to spend a couple of extra nights in Tokyo had saved his life, called Yoshio Nishina, the nation's ranking nuclear scientist. He told him of the Truman claims and asked him to ride down to Hiroshima in his little liaison plane to investigate the matter. Nishina agreed to make the trip. The scientist was already pretty well convinced, on the basis of Hirano's report and further excerpts from the Truman statement given him a few minutes later by a reporter, that the bomb had indeed been the fission weapon which he and his colleagues had believed the United States could not manufacture so quickly. Truman's claim of a destructive power equal to twenty thousand tons of TNT coincided exactly with theoretical calculations made recently by one of Nishina's laboratory associates on the yield of an atomic bomb.

But the Army high command was keeping the lid on tight. When the Tokyo managing editors met again with the Information Agency censors that afternoon, they all had seen the text of Truman's statement. But they got nowhere with requests for permission to print it. The Army grudgingly allowed use of the phrase "a new-type bomb," but not the word "atomic." The editors argued hard this time, but to no avail. The end result of the wrangle was this communiqué from Imperial General Headquarters at 3:30 P.M. on Tuesday, August 7:

1   A considerable amount of damage was caused by a few B-29s which attacked Hiroshima August 6th.
2   It seems that the enemy used a new-type bomb in the raid. Investigation of the effects is under way.

By evening, the newsmen were stretching the Army embargo as far as they could. A home service broadcast at 7 P.M. amplified the cryptic communiqué by adding that "a considerable number of houses were reduced to ashes and fires broke out in various parts of the city ... investigations are now being made with regard to the effectiveness of the bomb, which should not be regarded as light." The broadcast went on to attack the Americans for "inhuman and atrocious conduct" and to urge the

Japanese not to be "misled" by "exaggerated propaganda" such as "an announcement regarding the use of a new-type bomb" by Truman.

One man who was not likely to be "misled" by any announcement that night was Major Hirano, who finally had started back to Hiroshima in his five-seater liaison plane late in the afternoon. He had arrived at the Tokyo airport with the hurriedly assembled team of investigators earlier in the day, but had been ordered to wait until afternoon to avoid the U.S. Navy fighter planes that were now operating over Japan daily. There was some top brass in the inspection group which apparently was not anxious to hasten the day of personal contact with American invaders. Thus it was almost seven in the evening when Hirano's plane came down over Hiroshima. It was still light, however, so he got the full picture with shocking suddenness:

Being a soldier, my eye had been inured to the effects of bombing by that time. But this was a different sight. *There were no roads in the wastes that spread below our eyes:* that was my first impression. In the case of a normal air raid, roads were still visible after it was over. But in Hiroshima, everything was flattened and all roads were undiscernibly covered with debris.

When Hirano stepped from his plane, the first person he saw was an Air Force officer who came out on the runway to meet the team from Tokyo. His face was marked by a sharp dividing line right down the middle. One side was smooth and unhurt. The other, the one that had been toward the explo

sion, was burned, blistered, blackened. The investigators picked their way through the city to the wreckage of II Army Corps headquarters. Nobody was there. They finally found what was left of the headquarters — a few officers holed up in a hillside cave. By the time they began their formal investigation the next morning, the men from Tokyo knew the truth anyway. Hirano, in fact, had known it the moment he caught sight of what was left of Hiroshima from his circling plane.

QUESTIONS TO CONSIDER

1   What chance factors at Hiroshima added to the inherent destructiveness of the atomic bomb and produced more deaths and devastation than American scientists had expected?

2   Describe the sequence of destruction caused by the bomb's explosion. What were the physical effects of the bomb on human beings?

3   What was the immediate reaction of the Japanese army and government to the news of what had happened at Hiroshima? Why was the true nature of the American attack kept from the Japanese people?

4   Discuss the responsibility of the Japanese high command for prolonging the war after the bombing of Hiroshima.

5   Given the present-day proliferation of atomic weapons, what lessons can we draw from the first-hand accounts of the Japanese who experienced the horrors at Hiroshima fifty years ago?

XI

FIGURES IN THE COLD WAR

22

Harry Truman:
"One Tough Son-of-a-Bitch of a Man"

DAVID MCCULLOUGH

When he learned that Roosevelt had died and that he was now president of the United States, Truman told a group of reporters: "Boys, if you ever pray, pray for me now. I don't know whether you fellows ever had a load of hay fall on you, but when they told me yesterday what had happened, I felt like the moon, the stars, and all the planets had fallen on me."

He did not want to be president, and he certainly did not look like one: though cheery and brisk and always dressed in a spotless suit "as if he had just stepped from a bandbox," as his wife said, he was short, slight, and plain looking, wore thick spectacles, spoke in a Missouri twang, and radiated ordinariness. But, as a friend said, behind that plain-looking facade was "one tough son-of-a-bitch." Though not privy to Roosevelt's war strategy and military secrets, Truman stepped into the job with alacrity and confidently made decisions that led the country to victory in the Second World War.

In the postwar world, he faced a vortex of difficulties that would have daunted a lesser man. At home, the United States had to demobilize its vast military forces and convert wartime industry back to peacetime production. Abroad, the Allied victory proved to be a victory without peace. For out of the muck and rubble of the Second World War emerged a Cold War between the Soviet Union and the West that threatened the very survival of humankind. The genesis of the Cold War, as Truman learned, went back to the early days of the Second World War and involved control of Eastern Europe. Russia and the Western Allies clashed over that area, and their rival strategies for the domina-

tion of Eastern Europe influenced most of the wartime conferences among the big three (the United States, Great Britain, and the Soviet Union). The West hoped to establish democratic regimes in Eastern Europe, but it proved an impossible program, for the massive Red Army overran Eastern Europe and Stalin vowed to maintain Russian supremacy there. He did so not to export world communism but to ensure Soviet security from the West — to make certain no Western army could ever sweep through Poland and invade Russia as the Germans had done. The Soviet Union had lost from 20 to 25 million people in the war against Germany; no other nation swept up in the war, not even Germany itself, had suffered such casualties. Dominating Eastern Europe, Soviet leaders hoped, would prevent such a catastrophe from ever happening again.

Once the Red Army occupied Eastern Europe, Roosevelt did the only thing he could do. At the Yalta Conference of February 1945, he acknowledged Soviet hegemony in the region but pressed Stalin to hold free elections in the countries he controlled. Mainly to hold the wartime alliance together, Stalin promised free elections for Eastern Europe. But obsessed as he was with Russian security, the Soviet boss never kept his promise, instead setting up Soviet puppet states from the Baltic to the Adriatic.

The West felt betrayed. By the time Truman came to power, the United States and many of its allies increasingly saw Stalin as a mad and devious Marxist dictator out to spread communism across the globe. In the United States especially, a profound suspicion of the Soviets and world communism swept over Washington and the Truman White House. Unlike Roosevelt, who had tried to conciliate the Russians, Truman in 1947 adopted a get-tough containment policy designed to block Soviet expansion and save the "free world" from communism. The purpose of containment was not to overthrow the Soviet regime or invade the Soviet sphere but to prevent the Soviets from expanding the influence of communism. To do that, Washington poured billions of dollars in aid into Greece, Turkey, and Western Europe and extended American military power around the globe. American aid to Western Europe, called the Marshall Plan, rebuilt its war-torn countries and neutralized communist parties there.

From 1947 on, containment formed the basis of United States foreign policy. When in 1948 the Soviets blockaded Allied-controlled West Berlin (Berlin was located in the Russian sector of occupied Germany), Truman ordered a massive airlift by B-29s that prevented West Berlin from falling to the Soviets. His containment policy dictated that the United States get tough with China, too, after the Communists took over there in 1949 and drove Chiang Kai-shek's Nationalist Chinese into exile on Formosa (now known as Taiwan). The fall of China whipped up a storm of outrage and fears of communism in the United States. In this sinister turn of events, Americans once again saw the evil hand of Joseph Stalin. At home, a terrible Red scare swept the land, as Americans saw communists everywhere, from Hollywood to Washington, D.C., plotting to overthrow the government and hand the country over to the Soviets. Truman himself contributed to the scare, by instituting a sweeping loyalty oath program and beginning extensive security checks for federal employment.

The Red scare produced in 1950 a finger-pointing rabble-rouser named Joseph McCarthy, who claimed that the State Department itself was crawling with Reds. He even accused Truman and General George Marshall, secretary of state, of being Communists. His strident accusations, which the press published with relish under black headlines, destroyed the careers of many innocent Americans. Yet not once in his anti-Communist crusade did McCarthy expose a single bona fide Communist.

The year, 1950, brought another shock. China's neighbor, Korea, was divided at the 38th parallel between a Communist regime in the north and a pro-Western government in the south. That June, North Korean forces invaded South Korea in what Washington viewed as an act of naked Communist aggression instigated by the Kremlin. Under the auspices of the United Nations, Truman sent in American troops, who in a few months drove the North Koreans back across the 38th parallel. By September, however, Truman had changed the purpose of the war: instead of simply maintaining the integrity of South Korea, he resolved to invade North Korea and liberate it from Communist rule. When United Nations forces under General Douglas MacArthur drove to the Chinese borders, that was enough for the Red Chinese: 260,000 of them crossed the Yalu and inflicted on MacArthur one of the worst military defeats in American history, sending him in pell-mell retreat back toward the 38th parallel. With that, Truman again changed the purpose of the war: he gave up fighting to liberate North Korea and fell back on the original United States goal of simply ensuring the sovereignty of South Korea. At that point, the Korean War bogged down in stalemate. When a frustrated MacArthur issued public statements vehemently criticizing Truman's policies and went on to advocate an all-out war against China, the president relieved him of command, on the grounds that the general was trying to force his policies on his civilian commander in chief, which violated the constitutional provision of civilian control of the military.

In the following selection, David McCullough, Truman's foremost biographer and winner of the Pulitzer Prize, brings the tough little man from Missouri brilliantly alive in a warm and sympathetic portrait. McCullough shows us how Truman's personality and character — his no-nonsense bluntness, honesty, determination, courage, sense of history, and love of people — affected his postwar decisions and made him an extremely effective president despite his flaws and mistakes.

GLOSSARY

ACHESON, DEAN   Truman's third secretary of state (1949–1953); he was the principal force behind the creation of the North Atlantic Treaty Organization (NATO), which allied the Western democracies against the Soviet Union and its Eastern bloc. Acheson implemented Truman's decision to send United States troops to South Korea, which had been invaded by Communist North Korea. Though Acheson was diehard anti-Communist, Republicans accused him of being soft on communism and blamed him for the Communist takeover of China in 1949.

BYRNES, JIMMY   A conservative Democrat and "avowed segregationist," he was Truman's friend and adviser and served as his secretary of state from 1945 to 1947. He was one of the most vigorous advocates of dropping the atomic bomb on Japan. After the war, he tried to reconcile the United States and the Soviet Union but then became a harsh critic of Soviet designs.

CLIFFORD, CLARK   Truman's special adviser from 1945 to 1950, he helped to formulate Truman's policy of containment and to create the Department of Defense.

DEWEY, THOMAS E.   Republican nominee for president in 1948; he was universally expected to defeat Truman, so much so that before all the votes were counted, one newspaper ran a front-page headline: DEWEY DEFEATS TRUMAN. As it turned out, Truman won the election, defying the pollsters and the odds.

FORRESTAL, JAMES   Served as secretary of the navy from 1944 to 1947 and became the first secretary of defense when the Truman administration established the Department of Defense in 1947. He advocated a powerful military to contain Soviet aggression and persuaded the federal government to institute a peacetime draft.

HARRIMAN, W. AVERELL   American businessman turned statesman; he served as United States ambassador to the Soviet Union from 1943 to 1946 and as Truman's secretary of commerce from 1946 to 1948.

KENNAN, GEORGE   Historian and diplomat who helped formulate Truman's policy of containment toward the Soviet Union; he served as United States ambassador to Moscow until the Soviets demanded his removal.

LILIENTHAL, DAVID   A long-time director of the Tennessee Valley Authority, which provided hydroelectric power for the Tennessee Valley. In 1946, Truman appointed him to chair of the United States Atomic Energy Commission, which stressed "civilian control and government monopoly of atomic energy."

LOVETT, ROBERT   Influential undersecretary of state during Truman's presidency.

MARSHALL PLAN   Also known as the European Recovery Program, it was the brainchild of George C. Marshall, Truman's second secretary of state (1947–1949) and former army chief of staff. The program distributed $12 billion in American aid that helped rebuild war-ravaged Western Europe.

McCARTHY, JOSEPH   Republican senator from Wisconsin who earned his reputation by making fantastic accusations of Communist infiltration into the federal government, particularly the State Department. The cartoonist Herblock coined the term *McCarthyism* to describe the senator's Cold War witch-hunt to ferret out alleged Communists.

MUNICH, LESSON OF   In 1938, in Munich, Germany, the British and the French reached an accord with Adolf Hitler allowing Germany to possess an area of Czechoslovakia called the Sudentenland in exchange for Hitler's promise not to seize any more European territory. British Prime Minister Neville Chamberlain flew home to London, where he proclaimed that the Munich Pact had achieved "peace in our time." It had done nothing of the kind. A year later, Hitler's mighty mechanized army invaded Poland, thus setting off the Second World War. The "lesson of Munich" was that aggressors must never be appeased.

PENDERGAST, TOM   Boss of Missouri's Democratic political machine, through which Truman rose from judge of a county court to the United States Senate.

VAUGHAN, HARRY   Lifelong friend of Harry Truman's who furnished him "comic relief." He was "Truman's Falstaff" — Falstaff being the bawdy, brazen, good-natured rascal in Shakespeare's *Henry IV, Parts 1 and 2,* and *The Merry Wives of Windsor.*

arry Truman was President of the United States for not quite eight years. Looking back now we see him standing there in the presidential line, all of five foot nine, in a double-breasted suit, between two heroic figures of the century, Franklin Delano Roosevelt and Dwight D. Eisenhower. It's hard to convey today the feeling Americans had about General Eisenhower, the aura of the man, after World War II. He was charismatic, truly, if anyone ever was. Truman was not like that, not glamorous, not photogenic. And from the April afternoon when Truman took office, following the death of Franklin Roosevelt, he would feel the long shadow of Roosevelt, the most colossal figure in the White House in this century. He had none of Roosevelt's gifts — no beautiful speaking voice, no inherited wealth or social standing, no connections. He is the only president of our century who never went to college, and along with his clipped Missouri twang and eyeglasses thick as the bottom of a Coke bottle, he had a middlewestern plainness of manner, that, at first glance, made him seem "ordinary."

He had arrived first in Washington in the 1930s as a senator notable mainly for his background in the notorious Pendergast machine of Kansas City. He was of Scotch-Irish descent, and like many of Scotch-Irish descent — and I know something of this from my own background — he could be narrow, clannish, short-tempered, stubborn to a fault. But he could also be intensely loyal and courageous. And deeply patriotic. He was one of us, Americans said, just as they also said, "To err is Truman."

He was back in the news again after the Republican sweep in November 1994, the first such Republican triumph since 1946, and so naturally compar-

Originally titled, "Harry S. Truman: 1945-1953," in Robert A. Wilson (ed.), *Character Above All: Ten Presidents from FDR to George Bush* (New York: Simon & Schuster, 1995), pp. 39–59. Reprinted with the permission of Simon & Schuster from *Truman* by David McCullough. Copyright © 1992 by David McCullough.

President Harry Truman, the tough little man from Missouri who made the decision to use atomic bombs against Japan, put forth the Truman doctrine to contain the spread of Communism, and sent American troops into the Korean War. Gruff and direct though he was, Truman also had "a resilient sense of humor" and particularly enjoyed "the good stories of politics." (Stock Montage)

isons were drawn. Like Bill Clinton, Truman had been humiliated in his mid-term election of 1946, treated with open scorn and belittlement by Republicans, and seldom defended by his fellow Democrats. He was written off.

But how Truman responded is extremely interesting and bears directly on our subject, character in the presidency. It was as if he had been liberated from the shadow of Roosevelt. "I'm doing as I damn please for the next two years and to hell with all of them," he told his wife, Bess. And what's so remarkable and fascinating is that the next two years were the best of Truman's presidency. The years 1947 and

1948 contained most of the landmark achievements of his time in office: the first civil rights message ever sent to Congress, his executive order to end segregation in the armed forces, the Truman Doctrine, the recognition of Israel, the Berlin Airlift, and the Marshall Plan, which saved Western Europe from economic and political ruin and stands today as one of the great American achievements of the century.

He showed again and again that he understood the office, how the government works, and that he understood himself. He knew who he was, he liked who he was. He liked Harry Truman. He enjoyed being Harry Truman. He was grounded, as is said.

He stressed, "I tried never to forget who I was, where I came from, and where I would go back to." And again and again, as I hope I will be able to demonstrate, he could reach down inside himself and come up with something very good and strong. He is the seemingly ordinary American who when put to the test, rises to the occasion and does the extraordinary.

Now by saying he knew himself and understood himself and liked himself, I don't mean vanity or conceit. I'm talking about self-respect, self-understanding. To an exceptional degree, power never went to his head, nor did he ever grow cynical, for all the time he spent in Washington. He was never inclined to irony or to grappling with abstract thoughts. He read a great deal, enjoyed good bourbon — Wild Turkey preferably — he was a good listener. His physical, mental, and emotional stamina were phenomenal.... There's much to be seen about people in how they stand, how they walk. Look at the photographs of Harry Truman, the newsreels — backbone American.

In the spring of 1945, the new untested President of the United States sat in the Oval Office. Across the desk, in the visitor's chair, sat a grim-looking old friend, Sam Rayburn, the Speaker of the House. They were alone in the room, just the two of them, and they were, in many ways, two of a kind. Rayburn knew he could talk straight from the shoulder to Truman, who had been in office only a few days.

"You have got many great hazards and one of them is in this White House. I've been watching this thing a long time," Rayburn began. "I've seen people in the White House try to build a fence around the White House and keep the very people away from the president that he should see. That is one of your hazards, the special interests and the sycophants who will stand in the rain a week to see you and will treat you like a king. They'll come sliding in and tell you you're the greatest man alive. But you know, and I know, you ain't."

Truman knew he wasn't Hercules, he knew he wasn't a glamour boy, he knew he didn't have — and this is so important — the capacity to move the country with words, with eloquence. He had none of the inspirational magic of his predecessor. If Roosevelt was Prospero, Truman was Horatio.

. . . Character counts in the presidency more than any other single quality. It is more important than how much the President knows of foreign policy or economics, or even about politics. When the chips are down — and the chips are nearly always down in the presidency — how do you decide? Which way do you go? What kind of courage is called upon? Talking of his hero Andrew Jackson, Truman once said, it takes one kind of courage to face a duelist, but it's nothing like the courage it takes to tell a friend, no.

In making his decision to recognize Israel, Truman had to tell the man he admired above all others, no — but more on that shortly.

Truman had seen a lot of life long before he came to Washington. He was born in 1884. He was a full-grown, mature, nearly middle-aged man by the time of the Great War, as his generation called World War I, which was the real dividing line between the nineteenth and the twentieth centuries and the turning point in his life. Everything changed in the period after World War I, which in retrospect may be seen as the first, hideous installment of a two-part world catastrophe. Even the same characters — Hitler, Churchill, Roosevelt, Truman, MacArthur, Marshall — reappear in World War II. Growing up in Victorian middle America, Truman came to maturity with much of the outlook, good and bad, of that very different time.

At heart he remained a nineteenth-century man. He never liked air-conditioning, hated talking by telephone. (And thank goodness, for he wrote letters instead, thousands as time went on, and as a result it is possible to get inside his life, to know what he thought and felt, in a way rarely possible with public figures, and presidents in particular.) He disliked Daylight

Saving Time and time zones. (He liked wearing two watches, one set on Eastern Standard Time, the other on Missouri time "real time," as he called it.)

He was also a farmer, a real farmer let it be remembered, not a photo opportunity or a gentleman farmer like FDR or Tom Dewey. With his father, he *worked* on the farm, facing all the perils of bad weather, failing crops, insect plagues, and debt. Truman & Son, of Grandview, Missouri, were never out of debt. He was there for eleven years, until he went off to war in 1917, and as he used to say, "It takes a lot of pride to run a farm." Certainly on a family farm, you don't "do your own thing." Let down your end and the whole enterprise may fall. And every morning there's your father at the foot of the stairs at five-thirty, no matter the weather, no matter the season, telling you it's time to be up and at it.

There was no running water on the Truman farm, no electricity. When his mother had to have an emergency appendectomy, she was operated on by a country doctor on the kitchen table, and it was young Harry who stood beside her through all of it holding the lantern.

He was, as his pal Harry Vaughan, once said, "one tough son-of-a-bitch of a man.... And that," said Vaughan, "was part of the secret of understanding him." He could take it. He had been through so much. There's an old line, "Courage is having done it before."

It's been often said that Truman was poorly prepared for the presidency. He came to office not knowing any of the foreign policy establishment in Washington. He had no friends on Wall Street, no powerful financial backers, no intellectual "brain trust." When Winston Churchill came to Washington in the early 1940s and busied himself meeting everybody of known influence, no one suggested he look up the junior senator from Missouri.

But Truman had experienced as wide a range of American life as had any president, and in that sense he was well prepared. He had grown up in a small town when the small town was the essence of American life. He'd been on the farm all those years, and he'd gone to war. And the war was the crucible. Captain Harry Truman returned from France in 1919 having led an artillery battery through the horrific Battle of the Argonne and having discovered two vitally important things about himself. First, that he had courage, plain physical courage. Until then he had never been in a fight in his life. He was the little boy forbidden by his mother to play in rough-house games because of his glasses. He was a bookworm — a sissy, as he said himself later on, using the dreaded word. But in France he'd found he could more than hold his own in the face of the horrors of battle and, second, that he was good at leading people. He liked it and he had learned that courage is contagious. If the leader shows courage, others get the idea.

Often he was scared to death. One of the most endearing of his many letters to Bess was written after his first time under fire in France, to tell her how terrified he was. It happened at night in the rain in the Vosges Mountains. The Germans had opened fire with a withering artillery barrage. Truman and his green troops thought it could be the start of a gas attack and rushed about trying frantically not only to get their own gas masks on, but to get masks on the horses as well. And then they panicked, ran. Truman, thrown by his horse, had been nearly crushed when the horse fell on him. Out from under, seeing the others all running, he just stood there, locked in place, and called them back using every form of profanity he'd ever heard. And back they came. This was no Douglas MacArthur strutting the edge of a trench to inspire the troops. This was a man who carried extra eyeglasses in every pocket because without glasses he was nearly blind. He had memorized the eye chart in order to get into the Army. And there he was in the sudden hell of artillery shells exploding all around, shouting, shaming his men back to do what they were supposed to do.

Now flash forward to a night thirty years later, in 1948, at the Democratic National Convention in

Philadelphia, when Democrats on the left and Democrats on the right had been doing everything possible to get rid of President Harry Truman for another candidate. The Dixiecrats had marched out of the convention. The liberals, who had tried to draft General Eisenhower, were down in the dumps as never before, convinced, after Truman was nominated, that all was lost. Truman was kept waiting backstage hour after hour. It was not until nearly two in the morning that he came on stage to accept the nomination. That was the year when the conventions were covered by television for the first time and the huge lights made even worse the summer furnace of Philadelphia. The crowd was drenched in perspiration, exhausted. For all the speeches there had been, nobody had said a word about winning.

Truman, in a white linen suit, walked out into the floodlights and did just what he did in the Vosges Mountains. He gave them hell. He told them, in effect, to soldier up — and that they were going to win. It was astounding. He brought the whole hall to its feet. He brought them up cheering. Old-hand reporters, even the most diehard liberals who had so little hope for him, agreed it was one of the greatest moments they had ever witnessed in American politics.

So there we have it, courage, determination, call it as you will. Dean Acheson, his Secretary of State, much later, searching for a way to describe the effect Truman could have on those around him, and why they felt as they did about him, quoted the lines from Shakespeare's *Henry V*, when King Henry — King Harry — walks among the terrified, dispirited troops the night before the Battle of Agincourt:

> *. . . every wretch, pining and pale before,*
> *Beholding him, plucks comfort from his looks. . . .*
> *His liberal eye doth give to every one . . .*
> *A little touch of Harry in the night.*

Acheson was remembering one of the darkest times of the Truman years, when unexpectedly 260,000 Chinese Communist troops came storming into the Korean War. Through it all, as Acheson and others saw at close hand, Truman never lost confidence, never lost his essential good cheer, never lost his fundamental civility and decency toward those who worked with him. He was never known to dress down a subordinate. "Give 'em hell, Harry" never gave anybody hell behind the scenes, on the job.

His decision to go into Korea in June 1950 was the most difficult of his presidency, he said. And he felt it was the most important decision of his presidency — more difficult and important than the decision to use the atomic bomb, because he feared he might be taking the country into another still more horrible world war, a nuclear war. Yet at the time, it was a very popular decision, a point often forgotten. The country was waiting for the President to say we would go to the rescue of the South Koreans, who were being overrun by the Communist North Korean blitzkrieg. The lesson of Munich weighed heavily on everyone. In Congress, the President had strong support on both sides of the aisle, at the start at least. He was applauded by the press across the country. It was only later that summer of 1950 when the war went so sour that it became "Truman's War."

But you see, there was no corollary between popularity and the ease or difficulty of the decision. His most popular decision was, for him, his most difficult decision, while his least popular decision was, he said, not difficult at all. That was the firing of General Douglas MacArthur, by far the most unpopular, controversial act of his presidency. Attacked by all sides, torn to shreds in editorials and by radio commentators, a potent force then as today, Truman went on with his work as usual, just riding it out. He seemed to have a sort of inner gyroscope for such times. Those around him wondered how it was possible. He said he was sure that in the long run the country would judge him to have done the right thing. Besides, he had only done his duty. The Constitution stated clearly that there will be civilian control over the military and he had taken an oath to uphold the Constitution. "It wasn't difficult for me at all," he insisted.

Truman's profound sense of history was an important part of his makeup. He believed every president should know American history at the least, and world history, ideally. A president with a sense of history is less prone to hubris. He knows he is but one link in the long chain going all the way back to the first president and that presumably will extend far into the future. He knows he has only a limited time in office and that history will be the final judge of his performance. What he does must stand the test of time. If he is blasted by the press, if his polls are plummeting as Truman's did during the Korean War, these are not the first concerns. What matters — or ought to matter — is what's best for the country and the world in the long run.

Truman probably understood the history of the presidency as well as or better than any president of this century with the exception of Woodrow Wilson, and in his first years in the White House he felt acutely the presence of the predecessors. He was sure the White House was haunted. This was before restoration of the old place, when it creaked and groaned at night with the change of temperature. Sometimes doors would fly open on their own. Alone at night, his family back in Missouri, he would walk the upstairs halls, poke about in closets, wind the clocks. He imagined his predecessors arguing over how this fellow Truman was doing so far.

His reputation seems to grow and will, I believe, continue to grow for the reason that he not only faced difficult decisions and faced them squarely, if not always correctly, but that the decisions were so often unprecedented. There were no prior examples to go by. In his first months in office, he made more difficult and far-reaching decisions than any president in our history, including Franklin Roosevelt and Abraham Lincoln. This much belittled, supposed backwater political hack, who seemed to have none or certainly very few of the requisite qualities of high office, turned out to do an extremely good job. And it is quite mistaken to imagine that nobody saw this at the time. Many did, and the closer they were to him, the more clearly they saw. Churchill, Marshall, and especially, I would say, Acheson, who was about as different from Harry Truman in background and manner as anyone could be. Acheson once remarked that he had great respect for Franklin Roosevelt, but that he reserved his love for another president, meaning Harry Truman. Acheson didn't much like Roosevelt, I suspect, because Roosevelt was condescending toward him. I imagine that if Acheson were to tolerate condescension, it would have to be Acheson being condescending toward someone else.

In the course of more than one hundred interviews for my biography of Truman, I found no one who had worked with him, no one who was on the White House staff, or the White House domestic staff, or his Secret Service detail, who did not like him. He knew everybody by name on the White House staff and in the mansion itself. He knew all the Secret Service people by name. He knew all about their families — and this wasn't just a politician's trick. If he could have picked his own father, one former Secret Service man told me, it would have been Truman.

John Gunther, in a wonderful interview with Truman when Truman was Vice President, asked him what he was most interested in. "People," Truman said without hesitation.

He had a further quality, also greatly needed in the presidency: a healthy, resilient sense of humor. He loved especially the intrinsic humor of politics, the good stories of politics. Campaigning in Texas by train in 1948, he had nothing but blue skies and huge, warm crowds everywhere he stopped. It was the first time a Democratic candidate for President had ever come to Texas to campaign. That had never been necessary before. The reason now was his civil rights program, which was anything but popular in Texas.

There had been warnings even of serious trouble if ever he were to show his face in Texas. But his reception was good-natured and approving the whole way across the state and Truman loved every moment. It was probably his happiest time of the whole 1948 whistle-stop odyssey. On board the train were Sam Rayburn and young Lyndon Johnson, who was running for the Senate, as well as Governor Beaufort Jester, who had earlier called Truman's civil rights program a stab in the back.

But all that was forgotten in the warmth of the days and the warmth of the crowds, and at the last stop, Rayburn's home town of Bonham, Rayburn invited the President to come by his little house on the highway, outside of the town. When the motorcade arrived, hundreds of people were on the front lawn. Rayburn told them to form a line and he would see they met the President. The Secret Service immediately objected, saying they had no identifications for anyone. Rayburn was furious. He knew every man, woman, and child on that lawn, he said, and could vouch for each and every one. So the line started for the house where Governor Jester offered greetings at the door and the President, a surreptitious bourbon within reach, shook hands with "the customers," as he called them. All was going well until Rayburn, who never took his eye off the line, shouted, "Shut the door, Beaufort, they're coming through twice."

Yet for all that it is mistaken to picture Harry Truman as just a down-home politician of the old stamp. The Harry Truman of Merle Miller's *Plain Speaking*, or of the play *Give-em Hell, Harry,* is entertaining and picturesque, but that wasn't the man who was President of the United States. He wasn't just some kind of cosmic hick.

Now he did make mistakes. He was not without flaw. He could be intemperate, profane, touchy, too quick with simplistic answers. In private conversation, he could use racial and religious slurs, old habits of the mouth. In many ways his part of Missouri was more like the Old South than the Middle West, and he grew up among people who in so-called polite society commonly used words like "nigger" and "coon."

Yet here is the man who initiated the first civil rights message ever and ordered the armed services desegregated. And let's remember, that was in 1948, long before Martin Luther King, Jr., or *Brown* v. *Board of Education*, the landmark Supreme Court decision on the desegregation of schools, or the civil rights movement. When friends and advisers warned him that he was certain to lose the election in 1948 if he persisted with the civil rights program, he said if he lost for that, it would be for a good cause. Principle mattered more than his own political hide. His courage was the courage of his convictions.

Truman's greatest single mistake was the loyalty oath program, requiring a so-called loyalty check of every federal employee. It was uncalled for, expensive, it contributed substantially to the mounting bureaucracy of Washington and damaged the reputations and lives of numbers of people who should never have had any such thing happen to them. He did it on the advice that it was good politics. He let his better nature be overcome by that argument. It was thought such a move could head off the rising right-wing cry of Communists in government, the McCarthy craze then in its early stages. But it didn't work. It was shameful.

His Supreme Court appointments weren't particularly distinguished. His seizure of the steel industry during the Korean War to avert a nationwide strike was high-handed and rightly judged unconstitutional, though his motives were understandable. We were at war and a prolonged shutdown of production of steel threatened the very lives of our fighting forces in Korea.

He himself thought one of his worst mistakes was to have allowed the pell-mell demobilization that followed World War II. Almost overnight American military might had all but vanished. When we intervened in Korea, we had little to fight with, except for the atomic bomb. That Truman refused to use the atomic bomb in Korea, despite tremendous pressure from General MacArthur and others, stands as one of his most important decisions and one for which he has been given little credit.

The idea that Harry Truman made the decision to use the bomb against Japan and then went upstairs and went to sleep is an unfortunate myth for which he is largely accountable. I think he gave that impression because he came from a time and place in America where you were not supposed to talk about your troubles. "How are you?" "I'm fine." You might be dying of some terrible disease — "I'm fine. And you?" He refused ever to talk of the weight of the decision except to say that he made it and that it was his responsibility. . . .

With the return of peace, Truman's political troubles began. The year 1946 was particularly rough. He seemed hopelessly ineffectual. He seemed to be trying to please everybody at once, willing to say to almost anybody whatever they most wanted to hear. He wasn't at all like the Harry Truman I've been describing. He had never wanted the job and for some time appeared willing to give it up as soon as possible. He tried twice to get General Eisenhower to agree to run as a Democrat in the next election, saying he would gladly step aside. According to one account, he even offered to run as Vice President with Ike at the head of the ticket. But then after the setback in the '46 congressional elections, he became a different man.

Fire-in-the-belly for presidential glory was never part of his nature. He wasn't in the job to enlarge his estimate of himself. He didn't need that. He didn't need the limelight or fawning people around him in order to feel good about being Harry Truman.

On that note, it is interesting to see whom he did choose to have around him, as a measure of his character. There were Omar Bradley and Matthew Ridgway at the Pentagon, Eisenhower at the head of NATO. George C. Marshall served as Secretary of State and later as Secretary of Defense. There were Dean Acheson, Averell Harriman, Robert Lovett, George Kennan, Chip Bohlen, David Lilienthal, James Forrestal, Sam Rosenman, Clark Clifford — the list is long and very impressive. That most of them had more distinguished backgrounds than he, if they were taller, handsomer, it seemed to bother him not at all. When it was suggested to him that General Marshall as Secretary of State might lead people to think Marshall would make a better president, Truman's response was that yes, of course, Marshall would make a better president, but that he, Harry Truman, was President and he wanted the best people possible around him.

As no president since Theodore Roosevelt, Truman had a way of saying things that was so much his own, and I would like to quote some of them:

"I wonder how far Moses would have gone, if he had taken a poll in Egypt."

"God doesn't give a damn about pomp and circumstance."

"There are more prima donnas in Washington than in all the opera companies."

He is also frequently quoted as having said, "If you want a friend in Washington, buy a dog," and, "If you want to live like a Republican, vote Democratic." I doubt he said the first, but the second does sound like him.

"The object and its accomplishment is my philosophy," he said. Let me say that again. "The object and its accomplishment is my philosophy." And no president ever worked harder in office. At times, a little discouraged, he would say, "All the President is, is a glorified public relations man who spends his time flattering, kissing and kicking people to get them to do what they are supposed to do anyway."

Where were his strengths and his weaknesses in conflict? In interviews with those who knew him, I would ask what they believed to have been the President's major flaw. Almost always they would say he was too loyal to too many people to whom he should not have been so loyal — not as President. They were thinking mainly of the cronies — people like Harry Vaughan. Or remembering when Boss Tom Pendergast died and Vice President Harry Truman commandeered an Air Force bomber and flew to Kansas City for the funeral. "You don't forget a friend," was Truman's answer to the press.

Tom Pendergast had made Truman, and the Pendergast machine, though colorful and not without redeeming virtues, was pretty unsavory altogether.

But Truman was also, let us understand, the product of the smoke-filled room in more than just the Kansas City way. He was picked at the 1944 Democratic Convention in Chicago in a room at the Blackstone Hotel thick with smoke. He was tapped as Roosevelt's running mate and almost certain successor by the party's big-city bosses, the professional pols, who didn't want Henry Wallace, then the Vice President, because Wallace was too left wing, an didn't want Jimmy Byrnes, another Roosevelt favorite, because Byrnes was too conservative, an avowed segregationist and a lapsed Roman Catholic. They wanted Harry Truman, so Truman it was. They knew their man. They knew what stuff he was made of. And remember, this was all in a tradition of long standing. Theodore Roosevelt had been picked by a Republican machine in New York, Woodrow Wilson by the Democratic machine in New Jersey. For Franklin Roosevelt, such "good friends" as Ed Kelly of Chicago, Boss Crump of Memphis, Ed Flynn of the Bronx were indispensable. And because a candidate had the endorsement of a machine, or as in Truman's case owed his rise in politics to a corrupt organization, it didn't necessarily follow that he himself was corrupt. John Hersey, who did one of the best of all pieces ever written about Harry Truman, for *The New Yorker,* said he found no trace of corruption in Truman's record. Nor did I. Nor did the FBI when it combed through Truman's past at the time Pendergast was convicted for an insurance fraud and sent to prison. Nor did all the Republicans

who ran against him in all the elections in his long political career.

I think he was almost honest to a fault. Still he understood, and felt acutely, the bargain he made with loyalty to the likes of Pendergast, and he understood why he was so often taken to task by the Republicans or the press or just ordinary citizens who didn't care for the kind of political company he kept.

Harry Vaughan was for comic relief, Truman's Falstaff. Among the delights of Truman as a biographical subject is that he enjoyed both Vaughan and Mozart. He loved a night of poker with "the boys," and he loved the National Symphony, which he attended as often as possible. If the program included Mozart or Chopin, he would frequently take the score with him.

This same Harry Truman, who adored classical music, who read Shakespeare and Cicero and *Don Quixote*, comes out of a political background about as steamy and raw as they get. And at times, this would get to him and he would escape to the privacy of a downtown Kansas City hotel room. There he would pour himself out on paper, an innermost anguish in long memoranda to himself, and these amazing documents survive in the files of the Truman Library in Independence, Missouri, along with thousands of his letters and private diaries.

Here is a striking example written when Truman was a county judge (a county commissioner really) and one of his fellow commissioners had made off with $10,000 from the county till:

This sweet associate of mine, my friend, who was supposed to back me, had already made a deal with a former crooked contractor, a friend of the Boss's . . . I had to compromise in order to get the voted road system carried out . . . I had to let a former saloonkeeper and murderer, a friend of the Boss's, steal about $10,000 from the general revenues of the county to satisfy my ideal associate and keep the crooks from getting a million or more out of the bond issue.

He is not exaggerating with the million-dollar figure. When the Pendergast organization collapsed and its ways of operation were revealed, a million dollars was found to be about standard. But then, importantly, Truman goes on:

Was I right or did I compound a felony? I don't know. . . . Anyway I've got the $6,500,000 worth of roads on the ground and at a figure that makes the crooks tear their hair. The hospital is up at less cost than any similar institution in spite of my drunken brother-in-law [Fred Wallace], whom I'd had to employ on the job to keep peace in the family. I've had to run the hospital job myself and pay him for it. . . . Am I an administrator or not? Or am I just a crook to compromise in order to get the job done? You judge it, I can't.

This is all very painful for him. He writes of being raised at his mother's knee to believe in honor, ethics, and "right living." Not only is he disgusted by the immorality he sees behind the scenes, he doesn't understand it.

But let me return to 1948, where I think we see Truman, the President, at his best. Consider first the crisis over Berlin. That spring the Russians had suddenly clamped a blockade around the city, which was then under Allied control though within the Russian zone of East Germany. Overnight, without warning, Berlin was cut off. Other than by air, there was no way to supply it. Two and a half million people were going to be without food, fuel, medical supplies. Clearly Stalin was attempting to drive the Allies out. The situation was extremely dangerous.

At an emergency meeting in the Oval Office, it was proposed that the Allies break through with an armored convoy. It looked as though World War III might be about to start. It was suggested that Berlin be abandoned. Nobody knew quite what to do. Truman said, "We stay in Berlin, period." He didn't know how that could be done any more than anyone else, but he said, "We stay in Berlin." Backbone.

An airlift had already begun as temporary measure. Truman ordered it stepped up to the maximum. It was said by experts, including the mayor of Berlin, that to supply the city by air would be impossible, given the size of the planes and the calculated number of landings possible per day. The whole world was on edge.

"We'll stay in Berlin," Truman said again, "come what may." The supposedly insoluble problem of the limit of the plane landings per day was nicely solved: they built another airport. The airlift worked. The Russians gave up the blockade. The crisis passed.

Among the most difficult and important concepts to convey in teaching or writing history is the simple fact that things never had to turn out as they did. Events past were never on a track. Nothing was foreordained any more then than now. Nobody knew at the start that the Berlin Airlift would work. It was a model, I think, of presidential decision making, and of presidential character proving decisive.

All this, I should also remind you, was taking place in an election year. Yet at no time did Truman include any of his political advisers in the discussions about Berlin. Nor did he ever play on the tension of the crisis for his own benefit in the speeches he made.

With the question of whether to recognize Israel, Truman faced an equally complex situation but one greatly compounded by emotion. Of particular difficulty for him, personally and politically, was the position of his then Secretary of State, George Marshall, who was gravely concerned about Middle Eastern oil supplies. If Arab anger over American support for a new Jewish state meant a cut-off of Arab oil, it would not only jeopardize the Marshall Plan and the recovery of Europe but could prove disastrous should the Berlin crisis indeed turn to war.

Marshall was thinking as a military man, determined to hold to a policy that was in the best interest of the United States. It was by no means a matter of anti-Semitism, as was sometimes charged, or any lack of sympathy for the idea of a Jewish homeland. But the fact that Marshall was against an immediate recognition put Truman in an extremely difficult position. No American of the time counted higher in Truman's estimate than Marshall. He saw Marshall as the modern-day equivalent of George Washington or Robert E. Lee and valued his judgment more than that of anyone in the cabinet. Further, Marshall was far and away the most widely respected member of the administration, and if Truman were to decide against him and Marshall were then to resign, it would almost certainly mean defeat for Truman in November. He could lose the respect of the man he most respected and lose the presidency.

Truman did recognize Israel — immediately, within minutes — and he never doubted he was doing the right thing. His interest in the history of the Middle East was long standing. He had been a strong supporter of a homeland for Jewish refugees from Europe from the time he had been in the Senate. But he also knew George Marshall and was sure Marshall would stand by him, as of course Marshall did.

I have spent a sizable part of my writing life trying to understand Harry Truman and his story. I don't think we can ever know enough about him. If his loyalty was a flaw, it was his great strength also, as shown by his steadfast loyalty to Dean Acheson when Joe McCarthy came after Acheson or the unflinching support he gave David Lilienthal when Lilienthal, Truman's choice to head the Atomic Energy Commission, was accused as a "pink," a Communist. Franklin Roosevelt had not been willing to stand up for Lilienthal. Truman did. And Lilienthal was approved by the Senate.

Perhaps Truman's greatest shortcoming was his unwillingness to let us know, to let the country know then, how much more there was to him than met the eye, how much more he was than just "Give 'em hell, Harry" — that he did have this love of books, this interest in history, his affection for

people, his kindness, his thoughtfulness to subordinates, the love of music, the knowledge of music, his deep and abiding love for his wife, his bedrock belief in education and learning. Though he had never gone beyond Independence High School, this was a president who enjoyed Cicero in the original Latin. We should have known that. It's good to know now, too.

A few words about the '48 campaign, which will always be part of our political lore. It's a great American metaphor, a great American story. The fellow who hasn't got a chance comes from behind and wins. Nobody in either party, not a professional politician, not a reporter, not even his own mother-in-law doubted that Tom Dewey would be the next president. The result of a *Newsweek* poll of fifty top political commentators nationwide who were asked to predict the outcome was Dewey 50, Truman 0.

No president had ever campaigned so hard or so far. Truman was sixty-four years old. Younger men who were with him through it all would describe the time on the train as one of the worst ordeals of their lives. The roadbed was rough and Truman would get the train up to 80 miles an hour at night. The food was awful, the work unrelenting. One of them told me, "It's one thing to work that hard and to stay the course when you think you're going to win, but it's quite another thing when you *know* you're going to lose." The only reason they were there, they all said, was Harry Truman.

For Truman, I think, it was an act of faith — a heroic, memorable American act of faith. The poll takers, the political reporters, the pundits, all the sundry prognosticators, and professional politicians — it didn't matter what they said, what they thought. Only the people decide, Truman was reminding the country. "Here I am, here's what I stand for — here's what I'm going to do if you keep me in the job. You decide."

Was he a great president? Yes. One of the best. And a very great American. Can we ever have another Harry Truman? Yes, I would say so. Who knows, maybe somewhere in Texas she's growing up right now.

1   Describe Truman's character. How did his character affect his political career, especially his presidency? How was Truman's "profound sense of history an important part of his makeup"? Compare him as a man to Franklin D. Roosevelt, the subject of selection 17.

2   What was the most difficult decision Truman had to make as president? What did he fear his decision might lead to? What was "the lesson of Munich"? What controversial move did Truman make in order to uphold his oath to the Constitution? Why did he insist that the move was "not difficult" for him?

3   What was Truman's "greatest single mistake" as president? Why did he make it? Why did David McCullough say it was "shameful"? According to McCullough, what were some of President Truman's other mistakes?

4   What crisis showed Truman, as president, at his best? How did his character affect his decision to stand firm in that crisis?

5   How did Truman make evident America's resolve to maintain the global status quo and yet avoid precipitating a third world war? When during his presidency did nuclear war seem probable?

23

The Ike Age

STEPHEN E. AMBROSE

Dwight David Eisenhower, the supreme commander of Allied forces in Europe during 1944 and 1945, was America's greatest hero in the postwar years. In 1952, the Republicans chose this balding, avuncular, mild-mannered soldier to win the White House back for the GOP after twenty straight years of Democratic chief executives. No Republican had occupied the White House since Herbert Hoover, whom much of the country had blamed for the crash and Depression. In the 1952 election, Eisenhower soundly defeated liberal Democrat Adlai E. Stevenson and went on to serve two terms in the White House. He left such a mark that the 1950s became popularly known as the Eisenhower years, or "the Ike Age."

For some contemporary critics, his mark was entirely negative, for they thought him an inept president who spent more time on the golf course than in tending to affairs of state. When he did attend to his job, such critics contended, his policies only worsened Cold War tensions. He ended up adopting Truman's containment policy and even announced "the domino theory," which held that if the West allowed the Communists to take over one country, they would seize its neighbors, then their neighbors, and so on until they had conquered the world. Other contemporary critics, however, regarded Ike as a masterful statesman who ended the Korean War, opposed military intervention in the internal struggles of other nations, and presided over a period of domestic prosperity.

In the years just after his presidency, historians tended to side with Eisenhower's hostile critics and rate him a poor chief executive. But more recently, with new evidence and new perspectives, scholars took another look at Eisenhower and liked what they saw. Their "revisionist" view has had a considerable influence on the current generation, so much so that a recent poll of historians and presidential scholars ranked Ike ninth on the list of presidents. In this selection, historian Stephen E. Ambrose, author of an authoritative two-volume biography of Eisenhower, evaluates the revisionist assessment of Ike and concludes that his record is indeed enviable. In the course of his discussion, Ambrose sheds light on the process of historical interpretation, the way historians use evidence to assess a figure and an era.

GLOSSARY

BROWN v. *BOARD OF EDUCATION OF TOPEKA* (1954)   Landmark case in which the United States Supreme Court outlawed segregated public schools (see selection 24).

COOK, BLANCHE WIESEN   Eisenhower scholar who maintains that Eisenhower was a "captive hero," an instrument of the multinational corporations "to fight for the world they wanted."

DULLES, JOHN FOSTER   Eisenhower's secretary of state (1953–1959) and a militant cold warrior who believed that threats of "massive nuclear retaliation" were the best way to deal with the Communist world.

HO CHI MINH   Leader of the Vietnamese nationalist–Communist forces, the Vietminh, that fought to liberate Vietnam from French colonial rule; Ho's forces defeated the French army at Dien Bien Phu (see selection 25).

POWERS, FRANCIS GARY   Pilot of a U-2 surveillance, or spy, plane who was shot down over the Soviet Union in 1960; furious at this invasion of Soviet air space, Nikita Khrushchev, Soviet premier and Communist party chief, canceled a scheduled summit meeting with the American president.

WARREN, EARL   Appointed chief justice of the Supreme Court by President Eisenhower in 1953, Warren wrote the opinion in the *Brown* v. *Board of Education of Topeka* decision and presided over the most activist Supreme Court in American history.

Since Andrew Jackson left the White House in 1837, 33 men have served as president of the United States. Of that number, only [five] have managed to serve eight consecutive years in the office — Ulysses Grant, Woodrow Wilson, Franklin Roosevelt, Dwight Eisenhower, [and Ronald Reagan]. Of these [five], only two were also world figures in a field outside politics — Grant and Eisenhower — and only two had a higher reputation and broader popularity when they left office than when they entered — Roosevelt and Eisenhower.

Given this record of success, and the relative failure of Ike's successors, it is no wonder that there is an Eisenhower revival going on. . . . Another major reason for the current Eisenhower boom is nostalgia for the 1950s — a decade of peace with prosperity, a 1.5 percent annual inflation rate, self-sufficiency in oil and other precious goods, balanced budgets, and domestic tranquility. Eisenhower "revisionism," now proceeding at full speed, gives Ike himself much of the credit for these accomplishments.

The reassessment of Eisenhower is based on a multitude of new sources, as well as new perspectives, which have become available only in the past few years. The most important of these is Ike's private diary, which he kept on a haphazard basis from the late 1930s to his death in 1969. Other sources

From Stephen E. Ambrose, "The Age of Ike," in "The Ike Age," *New Republic* (May 9, 1981). Reprinted by permission of the *New Republic,* © 1981, The New Republic, Inc.

include his extensive private correspondence with his old military and new big business friends, his telephone conversations (which he had taped or summarized by his secretary, who listened in surreptitiously), minutes of meetings of the cabinet and of the National Security Council, and the extensive diary of his press secretary, the late James Hagerty. Study of these documents has changed the predominant scholarly view of Eisenhower from, in the words of the leading revisionist, political scientist Fred Greenstein of Princeton, one of "an aging hero who reigned more than he ruled and who lacked the energy, motivation, and political skill to have a significant impact on events," to a view of Ike as "politically astute and informed, actively engaged in putting his personal stamp on public policy, [a man who] applied a carefully thought-out conception of leadership to the conduct of his presidency."

The revisionist portrait of Ike contains many new features. Far from being a "part-time" president who preferred the golf course to the Oval Office, he worked an exhausting schedule, reading more and carrying on a wider correspondence than appeared at the time. Instead of the "captive hero" who was a tool of the millionaires in his cabinet, Ike made a major effort to convince the Republican right wing to accept the New Deal reforms, an internationalist foreign policy, and the need to modernize and liberalize the Republican party. Rather than ducking the controversial issue of Joseph McCarthy, Eisenhower strove to discredit the senator. Ike's failure to issue a public endorsement of *Brown* v. *Topeka* was not based on any fundamental disagreement with the Warren Court's ruling [against segregated public schools], but rather on his understanding of the separation, the balance, of powers in the US government — he agreed with the decision, it turns out, and was a Warren supporter. Nor was Ike a tongue-tied general of terrible syntax; he was a careful speaker and an excellent writer who confused his audiences only when he wanted to do so.

Most of all, the revisionists give Eisenhower high marks for ending the Korean War, staying out of Vietnam, and keeping the peace elsewhere. They argue that these achievements were neither accidental nor lucky, but rather the result of carefully conceived policies and firm leadership at the top. The revisionists also praise Ike for holding down defense costs, a key factor in restraining inflation while maintaining prosperity.

Altogether, the "new" Ike is an appealing figure, not only for his famous grin and winning personality, but also because he wisely guided us through perilous times.

"The bland leading the bland." So the nightclub comics characterized the Eisenhower administration. Much of the blandness came from Ike's refusal to say, in public, anything negative about his fellow politicians. His lifelong rule was to refuse to discuss personalities. But in the privacy of his diary, . . . he could be sarcastic, slashing, and bitter.

In 1953, when Ike was president and his old colleague from the war, Winston Churchill, was prime minister, the two met in Bermuda. Churchill, according to Ike,

has developed an almost childlike faith that all of the answers to world problems are to be found merely in British-American partnership. . . . He is trying to relive the days of World War II. In those days he had the enjoyable feeling that he and our president were sitting on some rather Olympian platform . . . and directing world affairs. Even if this picture were an accurate one of those days, it would have no application to the present. But it was only partially true, even then, as many of us who . . . had to work out the solutions for nasty local problems are well aware.

That realistic sense of the importance of any one individual, even a Churchill or a Roosevelt, was basic to Eisenhower's thought. Back in 1942, with reference to MacArthur, Ike scribbled in his diary that in modern war, "no one person can be a Napoleon or a Caesar." What was required was teamwork and cooperation.

Although Lyndon Johnson, John F. Kennedy, Hubert Humphrey, and other Democratic senators of the 1950s catch hell from time to time in Ike's diary, he reserved his most heartfelt blasts for the Republicans (he never expected much from the Democrats anyway). Thus, Ike wrote of Senator William Knowland of California, "In his case there seems to be no final answer to the question 'How stupid can you get?'" In *Eisenhower the President . . .* William Bragg Ewald Jr., a former Eisenhower speechwriter, records that when Republicans urged Ike to convince [New York Governor] Nelson Rockefeller to take the second place on a 1960 ticket with Richard Nixon, Ike did so, rather half-heartedly, and then reported on Rockefeller: "He is no philosophical genius. It is pretty hard to get him in and tell him something of his duty. He has a personal ambition that is overwhelming." Eisenhower told Nixon that the only way to persuade Rockefeller to run for the vice presidency was for Nixon to promise to step aside in Rockefeller's favor in 1964.

Ike didn't like "politics," and he positively disliked "politicians." The behind-the-scenes compromises, the swapping of votes for pork-barrel purposes, the willingness to abandon conviction in order to be on the popular side all nearly drove him to distraction. His favorite constitutional reform was to limit congressional terms to two for the Senate and three or four for the House, in order to eliminate the professional politician from American life.

Nor did Ike much like the press. "The members of this group," he wrote in his diary, "are far from being as important as they themselves consider," but he did recognize that "they have a sufficient importance . . . in the eyes of the average Washington officeholder to insure that much government time is consumed in courting favor with them and in dressing up ideas and programs so that they look as saleable as possible." Reporters, Ike wrote, "have little sense of humor and, because of this, they deal in negative criticism rather than in any attempt toward constructive helpfulness." (Murray Kempton, in some ways the first Eisenhower revisionist, recalled how journalists had ridiculed Ike's amiability in the 1950s, while the president actually had intelligently confused and hoodwinked them. Kempton decided that Eisenhower was a cunning politician whose purpose was "never to be seen in what he did.")

The people Ike did like, aside from his millionaire friends, were those men who in his view rose above politics, including [his brother] Milton Eisenhower, Robert Anderson, and Earl Warren. Of Milton, Ike wrote in 1953, "I believe him to be the most knowledgeable and widely informed of all the people with whom I deal. . . . So far as I am concerned, he is at this moment the most highly qualified man in the United States to be president. This most emphatically makes no exception of me. . . ." Had he not shrunk from exposing Milton to a charge of benefiting from nepotism, Ike would have made his younger brother a member of his cabinet.

In 1966, during an interview in Eisenhower's Gettysburg office, I asked him who was the most intelligent man he had ever met, expecting a long pause while he ran such names as Marshall, Roosevelt, de Gaulle, Churchill, Truman, or Khrushchev through his mind. But Ike never hesitated: "Robert Anderson," he said emphatically. Anderson, a Texan and a Democrat, served Ike in various capacities, including secretary of the navy and secretary of the treasury. Now Ewald reveals for the first time that Eisenhower offered Anderson the second spot on the Republican ticket for 1956 and wanted Anderson to be his successor. Anderson turned down the President because he thought the offer was politically unrealistic.

Which inevitably brings up the subject of Richard Nixon. Eisenhower's relations with Nixon have long been a puzzle. Ike tried to get Nixon to resign during the 1952 campaign, but Nixon saved himself with the Checkers speech [in which he announced, "I'm not a quitter," and vowed to continue fighting "crooks and Communists"]. In 1956 Ike attempted to maneuver Nixon off the ticket by offering him a high-level cabinet post, but Nixon dug in his heels and used his connections with the right wing of the party to stay in place. And in 1960, Ike's campaign speeches for Nixon were distinctly unenthusiastic. Still, Eisenhower and Nixon never severed their ties. Ike stuck with Nixon throughout his life. He often remarked that Nixon's defeat by Kennedy was one of his greatest disappointments. And, of course, his grandson married one of Nixon's daughters. Sad to say, neither the diary nor the private correspondence offers any insights into Eisenhower's gut feelings toward Nixon. The relationship between the two men remains a puzzle.

Some writers used to say the same about the Eisenhower–Earl Warren relationship, but thanks to Ike's diary, Ewald's book, and the correspondence, we now have a better understanding of Eisenhower's feelings toward Warren personally, and toward his Court. In December 1955, Jim Hagerty suggested that if Ike could not run for a second term for reasons of health, Warren might make a good nominee. "Not a chance," Ike snapped back, "and I'll tell you why. I know that the Chief Justice is very happy right where he is. He wants to go down in history as a great Chief Justice, and he certainly is becoming one. He is dedicated to the Court and is getting the Court back on its feet and back in respectable standing again."

Eisenhower and Warren were never friends; as Ewald writes, "For more than seven years they sat, each on his eminence, at opposite ends of Pennsylvania Avenue, by far the two most towering figures in Washington, each playing out a noble role, in tragic inevitable estrangement." And he quotes Attorney General Herbert Brownell as saying, "Both Eisenhower and Warren were very reserved men. If you'd try to put your arm around either of them, he'd remember it for sixty days."

Ike had a great deal of difficulty with *Brown* v. *Topeka,* but more because of his temperament than for any racist reasons. He was always an evolutionist who wanted to move forward through agreement and compromise, not command and force. Ike much preferred consensus to conflict. Yet Ewald argues that he privately recognized the necessity and justice of *Brown* v. *Topeka.* Even had that not been so, he would have supported the Court, because — as he carefully explained to one of his oldest and closest friends, Sweed Hazlett, in a private letter — "I hold to the basic purpose. There must be respect for the Constitution — which means the Supreme Court's interpretation of the Constitution — or we shall have chaos. This I believe with all my heart — and shall always act accordingly."

Precisely because of that feeling, Eisenhower never made a public declaration of support for the *Brown* v. *Topeka* decision, despite the pleas of liberals, intellectuals, and many members of the White House staff that he do so. He felt that once the Supreme Court had spoken, the president had no right to second guess nor any duty to support the decision. The law was the law. That Ike was always ready to uphold the law, he demonstrated decisively when he sent the U.S. Army into Little Rock in 1957 to enforce court-ordered desegregation.

Despite his respect for Warren and the Court, when I asked Eisenhower in 1965 what was his biggest mistake, he replied heatedly, "The appointment of that S.O.B. Earl Warren." Shocked, I replied, "General, I always thought that was your best appointment." "Let's not talk about it," he responded, and we did not. Now that I have seen the flattering and thoughtful references to Warren in the diary, I can only conclude that Eisenhower's anger at Warren was the result of the criminal rights case of the early 1960s, not the desegregation decisions of the 1950s.*

. . . Ike also refused publicly to condemn Senator McCarthy, again despite the pleas of many of his own people, including his most trusted advisor, Milton. Ike told Milton, "I will not get into a pissing contest with that skunk."

The revisionists now tell us that the president was working behind the scenes, using the "hidden hand" to encourage peaceful desegregation and to censure McCarthy. He helped Attorney General Brownell prepare a brief from the Justice Department for the Court on *Brown* v. *Topeka* that attacked the constitutionality of segregation in the schools. As for McCarthy, Greenstein writes that Eisenhower,

working most closely with Press Secretary Hagerty, conducted a virtual day-to-day campaign via the media and congressional allies to end McCarthy's political effectiveness. The overall strategy was to avoid *direct mention* of McCarthy in the president's public statements, lest McCarthy win sympathy as a spunky David battling against the presidential Goliath. Instead Eisenhower systematically condemned the *types* of actions in which McCarthy engaged.

Eisenhower revisionism is full of nostalgia for the 1950s, and it is certainly true that if you were white, male, and middle class or better, it was the best decade of the century. The 1950s saw peace and prosperity, no riots, relatively high employment, a growing GNP, virtually no inflation, no arms race, no great reforms, no great changes, low taxes, little government regulation of industry or commerce, and a president who was trusted and admired. Politics were middle-of-the-road — Eisenhower was the

least partisan president of the century. In an essay entitled "Good-By to the 'Fifties — and Good Riddance," historian Eric Goldman called the Eisenhower years possibly "the dullest and dreariest in all our history." After the turmoil of the 1960s and 1970s — war, inflation, riots, higher taxes, an arms race, all accompanied by a startling growth in the size, cost, and scope of the federal government — many Americans may find the dullness and dreariness of the 1950s appealing.

Next to peace, the most appealing fact was the 1.5 percent inflation rate. The revisionists claim that Ike deserved much of the credit for that accomplishment because of his insistence on a balanced budget (which he actually achieved only twice, but he did hold down the deficits). Ike kept down the costs by refusing to expand the New Deal welfare services — to the disgruntlement of the Republican right wing, he was equally firm about refusing to dismantle the New Deal programs — and, far more important, by holding down defense spending.

This was, indeed, Ike's special triumph. He feared that an arms race with the Soviet Union would lead to uncontrollable inflation and eventually bankrupt the United States, without providing any additional security. In Ike's view, the more bombs and missiles we built, the less secure we would be, not just because of the economic impact, but because the more bombs we built, the more the Soviets would build. In short, Ike's fundamental strategy was based on his recognition that in nuclear warfare, there is no defense and can be no winner. In that situation, one did not need to be superior to the enemy in order to deter him.

The Democrats, led by Senator John F. Kennedy, criticized Ike for putting a balanced budget ahead of national defense. They accused him of allowing a "bomber gap" and, later, a "missile gap" to develop, and spoke of the need to "get America moving again." Nelson Rockefeller and Richard Nixon added to the hue and cry during the 1960 campaign, when they promised to expand defense spending.

---

*In a series of criminal rights decisions, most notably *Miranda* v. *Arizona* (1966), the Warren Court ruled that police had to advise suspects of their right to remain silent or to have an attorney present during interrogation, and that the state had to provide suspects with counsel at state expense, if they so requested.—Ed.

But as long as Eisenhower was president, there was no arms race. Neither the politicians nor the military-industrial complex could persuade Eisenhower to spend more money on the military. Inheriting a $50 billion defense budget from Truman, he reduced it to $40 billion and held it there for the eight years of his tenure.

Holding down defense costs was a longstanding theme of Ike's. As early as December 1945, just after he replaced George Marshall as army chief of staff, he jotted in his diary, "I'm astounded and appalled at the size and scope of plans the staff sees as necessary to maintain our security position now and in the future." And in 1951, before he became a candidate, he wrote in his diary that if the Congress and military could not be restrained about "this armament business, we will go broke and still have inefficient defenses."

President Eisenhower was unassailable on the subject. As one senator complained, "How in hell can I argue with Ike Eisenhower on a military matter?" But as Ike wrote in 1956 to his friend Hazlett, "Some day there is going to be a man sitting in my present chair who has not been raised in the military services and who will have little understanding of where slashes in their estimates can be made with little or no damage. If that should happen while we still have the state of tension that now exists in the world, I shudder to think of what could happen in this country."

One reason why Ike was able to reduce the military in a time of great tension was his intimate knowledge of the Soviet military situation. From 1956 on, he directed a series of flights by the U-2 spy plane over the Soviet Union. He had personally taken the lead in getting the U-2 program started, and he kept a tight personal control over the flights — he gave his approval to the individual flights only after a thorough briefing on where in the USSR the planes were going and what the CIA wanted to discover. Here too the revisionists have shown that the contemporary feeling, especially after Francis Gary Powers was shot

down in 1960, that Ike was not in charge and hardly knew what was going on inside his own government is altogether wrong. He was absolutely in charge, not only of broad policy on the use of the U-2, but of implementing details as well.

The major factor in Eisenhower's ability to restrain defense spending was keeping the peace. His record here is clear and impressive — he signed an armistice in Korea less than half a year after taking office, stayed out of Vietnam, and managed to avoid war despite such crisis situations as Hungary and the Suez, Quemoy and Matsu, Berlin and Cuba. The revisionists insist that the credit must go to Ike, and they equally insist that Eisenhower, not Secretary of State John Foster Dulles, was in command of American foreign policy in the 1950s. Dulles, says Greenstein, "was assigned the 'get tough' side of foreign-policy enunciation, thus placating the fervently anti-Communist wing of the Republican party." Ike, meanwhile, appeared to be above the battle, while actually directing it on a day-to-day basis.

"In essence, Eisenhower used Dulles." So writes Robert Divine, one of America's leading diplomatic historians, in his provocative new book, *Eisenhower and the Cold War.* . . . Divine concludes that "far from being the do-nothing President of legend, Ike was skillful and active in directing American foreign policy." All the revisionists agree that the contemporary idea that Dulles led Ike by the nose was a myth that Eisenhower himself did the most to encourage. Nevertheless, Eisenhower did have a high opinion of his secretary of state. Divine quotes Ike's comment to Emmet Hughes on Dulles: "There's only one man I know who has seen *more* of the world and talked with more people and *knows* more than he does — and that's me."

The quotation illustrates another often overlooked Eisenhower characteristic — his immense self-confidence. He had worked with some of the great men of the century — Churchill, Roosevelt, Stalin, de Gaulle, Montgomery, and many others — long before he became president. His diary entry for

President Eisenhower with his secretary of state, John Foster Dulles. Eisenhower was content to let Dulles take much of the credit for success in American foreign policy during the 1950s, but recent findings by historians and biographers strongly suggest that Eisenhower was really in charge. The firm, intelligent expression on Ike's face, the decisive gesture, and the energetic pose pictured here, tend to confirm the revisionist view. (UPI/Corbis-Bettmann)

the day after his inauguration speaks to the point: "My first day at the president's desk. Plenty of worries and difficult problems. But such has been my portion for a long time — the result is that this just seems (today) like a continuation of all I've been doing since July 1941 — even before that."

Ike's vast experience in war and peace made him confident in crises. People naturally looked to him for leadership. No matter how serious the crisis seemed to be, Ike rarely got flustered. During a war scare in the Formosa Straits in 1955, he wrote in his diary, "I have so often been through these periods of strain that I have become accustomed to the fact that most of the calamities that we anticipate really never occur."

Ike's self-confidence was so great that, Greenstein writes, he had "neither a need nor a desire" to capture headlines. "He's employed his skills to achieve his ends by inconspicuous means." In foreign policy, this meant he did not issue strident warnings, did not — in public — threaten Russia or China with specific reprisals for specific actions. Instead, he retained his room for maneuver by deliberately spreading confusion. He did not care if editorial writers criticized him for jumbled syntax; he wanted to keep possible opponents guessing, and he did. For example, when asked at a March 1955 press conference if he would use atomic bombs to defend [the islands of] Quemoy and Matsu [off the coast of Communist China], he replied:

Every war is going to astonish you in the way it occurred, and in the way it is carried out. So that for a man to predict, particularly if he has the responsibility for making the decision, to predict what he is going to use, how he is going to do it, would I think exhibit his ignorance of war; that is what I believe.

As he intended, the Chinese found such statements inscrutable, as they had in Korea two years earlier. When truce talks in Korea reached an impasse in mid-May 1953, Ike put the pressure on the Chinese, hinting to them that the United States might use atomic weapons if a truce could not be arranged, and backing this up by transferring atomic warheads to American bases in Okinawa. The Chinese then accepted a truce. As Divine writes, "Perhaps the best testimony to the shrewdness of the President's policy is the impossibility of telling even now whether or not he was bluffing."

Nearly all observers agree that one of Ike's greatest accomplishments was staying out of Vietnam in the face of intense pressure from his closest advisers to save the French position there or, after July 1954, to go in alone to defeat Ho Chi Minh. Ike was never tempted. As early as March 1951 he wrote in his diary, "I'm convinced that no military victory is possible in that kind of theater." And in a first draft of his memoirs, written in 1963 but not published until 1981 by Ewald, Ike wrote:

The jungles of Indochina would have swallowed up division after division of United States troops, who, unaccustomed to this kind of warfare, would have sustained heavy casualties until they had learned to live in a new environment. Furthermore, the presence of ever more numbers of white men in uniform probably would have aggravated rather than assuaged Asiatic resentments.

That was hardheaded military reasoning by General Eisenhower. But President Eisenhower stayed out of Vietnam as much for moral as for military reasons. When the Joint Chiefs suggested to him in 1954 that the United States use an atomic bomb against the Vietminh around Dien Bien Phu, the President said he would not be a party to using that "terrible thing" against Asians for the second time in less than a decade. And in another previously unpublished draft of his memoirs, he wrote:

The strongest reason of all for the United States refusal to [intervene] is that fact that among all the powerful nations of the world the United States is the only one with a tradition of anti-colonialism. . . . The standing of the United States as the most powerful of the anti-colonial powers is an asset of incalculable value to the Free World. . . . Thus it is that the moral position of the United States was more to be guarded than the Tonkin Delta, indeed than all of Indochina.

Ike's international outlook, already well known, is highlighted by the new documents. He believed that the bonds that tied Western Europe and the United States together were so tight that the fate of one was the fate of the other. In May 1947, one year before the Marshall Plan, he wrote in his diary, in reference to Western Europe:

I personally believe that the best thing we could now do would be to post 5 billion to the credit of the secretary of state and tell him to use it to support democratic movements wherever our vital interests indicate. Money should be used to promote possibilities of self-sustaining economies, not merely to prevent immediate starvation.

And, as Blanche Wiesen Cook, another of the new Eisenhower scholars (but no revisionist), points out in *The Declassified Eisenhower* . . . , Ike's vision of a peaceful world . . . "involved a determination to pursue political warfare, psychological warfare, and economic warfare everywhere and at all times." Under Ike's direction, she writes, the CIA and other branches of the government "ended all pretentions about territorial integrity, national sovereignty and international law. Covert operatives were everywhere, and they were active. From bribery to assassination, no activity was unacceptable short of nuclear war."

Cook does stress the importance of Eisenhower's stance against general war and his opposition to an arms race, but insists that these positions have to be placed in context, a context that includes the CIA-inspired and -led governmental overthrows in Iran and Guatemala, covert operations of all types in Vietnam and Eastern Europe, and assassination attempts against political leaders in the Congo and Cuba. Returning to an earlier view of Ike, Cook regards him as a "captive hero," the "chosen instrument" of the leaders of the great multinational corporations "to fight for the world they wanted."

One does not have to accept Cook's "captive hero" view to realize that . . . Ike had his shortcomings and he suffered serious setbacks. For all his openness to new ideas, he was rigid and dogmatic in his anti-communism. The darker side of Eisenhower's refusal to condemn McCarthy was that Ike himself agreed with the senator on the nature, if not the extent, of the problem, and he shared the senator's goals, if not his methods. After his first year in office, Ike made a list of his major accomplishments to date. Peace in Korea was first, the new defense policy second. Third on the list: "The highest security standards are being insisted upon for those employed in government service," a bland way of saying that under his direction, the Civil Service Commission had fired 2,611 "security risks" and reported that 4,315 other government workers had resigned when they learned they were under investigation. That was the true "hidden hand" at work, and the true difference between Ike and McCarthy — Ike got rid of Communists and fellow travelers (and many liberals) quietly and effectively, while McCarthy, for all his noise, accomplished nothing.

Thus, no matter how thoroughly the revisionists document Ike's opposition to McCarthy personally or his support for Warren, it remains true that his failure to speak out directly on McCarthy encouraged the witch hunters, just as his failure to speak out directly on the *Brown* v. *Topeka* decision encouraged the segregationists. The old general never admitted that it was impossible for him to be truly above the battle, never seemed to understand that the president is inevitably a part of the battle, so much so that his inaction can have as great an impact as his action.

With McCarthy and *Brown* v. *Topeka* in mind, there is a sad quality to the following Eisenhower diary passage, written in January 1954, about a number of Republican senators whom Ike was criticizing for being more inclined to trade votes than to provide clear leadership:

They do not seem to realize when there arrives that moment at which soft speaking should be abandoned and a fight to the end undertaken. Any man who hopes to exercise leadership must be ready to meet this requirement face to face when it arises; unless he is ready to fight when necessary, people will finally begin to ignore him.

One of Ike's greatest disappointments was his failure to liberalize and modernize the Republican party, in order to make it the majority party in the United States. "The Republican party must be known as a progressive organization or it is sunk," he wrote in his diary in November 1954. "I believe this so emphatically that far from appeasing or reasoning with the dyed-in-the-wool reactionary fringe, we should completely ignore it and when necessary, repudiate it." Responding to cries of "impeach Earl Warren," Ike wrote in his diary, "If the Republicans as a body should try to repudiate him, I shall leave the Republican Party and try to organize an intelligent group of independents, however small." He was always threatening to break with the Republican party, or at least rename it; in March 1954, he told Hagerty, "You know, what we ought to do is get a word to put ahead of Republican — something like 'new' or 'modern' or something. We just can't work with fellows like McCarthy, Bricker, Jenner and that bunch."

A favorite revisionist quotation, which is used to show Ike's political astuteness, comes from a 1954 letter to his brother Edgar:

Should any political party attempt to abolish social security and eliminate labor laws and farm programs, you would not hear of that party again in our political history. There is a tiny splinter group, of course, that believes that you can do these things. Among them are H. L. Hunt, a few other Texas oil millionaires, and an occasional politician and businessman from other areas. Their number is negligible and they are stupid.

Good enough, but a critic would be quick to point out that Ike's "tiny splinter group" managed to play a large role in the nominations of Barry

Goldwater, Richard Nixon, and Ronald Reagan. In short, although Ike saw great dangers to the right in the Republican party, he did little to counter the reactionary influence in his own organization. Franklin Roosevelt did a far better job of curbing the left wing in the Democratic party, and generally in building his party, than anything Ike did for the Republicans. . . .

Shortly after Ike left office, a group of leading American historians was asked to rate the presidents. Ike came in near the bottom of the poll. That result was primarily a reflection of how enamored the professors were with FDR and Harry Truman. Today, those same historians would compare Ike with his successors rather than his predecessors and place him in the top 10, if not the top five, of all our presidents. No matter how much one qualifies that record by pointing to this or that shortcoming or failure of the Eisenhower administration, it remains an enviable record. No wonder the people like Ike.

QUESTIONS TO CONSIDER

1 Describe the picture of Ike that dominated both historical and popular thinking in the twenty years following Eisenhower's second term of office. What kind of president did most people think he had been?

2 What led historians to reevaluate Eisenhower? In particular, what new sources came to light and what effect did they have on new scholarship?

3 Describe the "new" Ike discovered by revisionist historians in the 1970s and 1980s. Why do you think Ike's political and personal integrity, his energy, and his moderation are now seen as a deliberate policy rather than as products of apathy or lack of imagination? What motivated Eisenhower to keep his strong opinions about Chief Justice Warren, Senator McCarthy, and others to himself? Why did he allow people to think his foreign policy was being directed by Secretary of State John Foster Dulles? Why did Ike almost always work behind the scenes to achieve his aims? Why didn't he care if people thought he was a dull, golf-playing, do-nothing president?

4 Ambrose contends that Ike's major achievement was keeping the peace during the 1950s and resisting tremendous pressure from his critics and from his own party to increase military spending. Why did the old general understand the military as no one else could? Do you see a degree of prescience in Eisenhower's fears of the future effect of military spending on the American economy?

5 Were you surprised when Ambrose revised the revisionists in the last paragraphs of this selection? What does Ambrose see as Eisenhower's greatest disappointment? His most signal failures? Where would you rank Ike among all American presidents?

FROM THE CIVIL RIGHTS MOVEMENT TO VIETNAM

Trumpet of Conscience: Martin Luther King Jr.

STEPHEN B. OATES

For most African Americans, the Depression had been an unmitigated calamity. An im-poverished group to begin with, African Americans, especially southern sharecroppers, suffered worse than any other minority. World War II, however, offered African Ameri-cans relief, and they made considerable progress during the conflict. The war accelerated their exodus to the North, as southern blacks sought employment in war-related industry there. At first, white employers refused to hire African American workers, and the Roo-sevelt administration did little to stop such discrimination until A. Philip Randolph — the celebrated African American labor leader — threatened to lead a massive protest march. Roosevelt responded with an executive order that prohibited racial discrimination in defense plants and government agencies alike. By the close of 1944, 2 million African American men and women were working in shipyards, aircraft factories, steel mills, and other defense plants. At the same time, almost 1 million African Americans served in the United States armed forces — half of them overseas in segregated outfits. By war's end, however, some of the army bases at home were partly integrated, and African American sailors were serving on ships with whites.

Alas, African American soldiers and sailors who fought in a war against Nazi racists returned home to confront massive racial discrimination against them, especially in segre-gated Dixie. Many of those veterans joined the National Association for the Advance-ment of Colored People (NAACP), which now had chapters across the South, and be-came civil rights activists. In the postwar years, President Harry Truman proved to be sympathetic to the plight of African Americans and did much to help them: he estab-lished a special committee on civil rights, which worked out an agenda for attacking seg-regation that continued for two decades. Truman also issued an executive order that ended segregation in the armed forces. Ironically, the military would become the most integrated institution in the United States.

The NAACP, meanwhile, continued to battle segregation in case-by-case litigation in the federal courts and marked hard-earned victories against southern white primaries and segregated law schools in the border states. In May 1954, the NAACP Legal Defense Fund won its most spectacular triumph before the United States Supreme Court. In Brown *v*. Board of Education of Topeka, *the High Court outlawed segregation in public schools, thus reversing the doctrine of "separate but equal" that had prevailed since* Plessy *v*. Ferguson *fifty-eight years earlier. Said the Court: "Separate educational facilities are inherently unequal" and created "a feeling of inferiority" in African American students "that may affect their hearts and minds in a way unlikely ever to be undone." In one historic blow, the Supreme Court smashed the whole legal superstructure for the idea of racial separateness, knocking down a century and a half of devious rationalizations in defense of the doctrine that African Americans must be kept apart because they were inferior.*

But the white South obstructed the school decision at every turn. The Alabama legislature "nullified" the Court decision, vowing to preserve white supremacy come what may. Fiery crosses burned against Texas and Florida skies, and random Klan terrorism broke out against African Americans in many parts of Dixie. Faced with stiffening white resistance, the Supreme Court did not order immediate compliance with the Brown *decision and called instead for desegregation of public schools "with all deliberate speed." But the Court offered no guidelines and set no timetable. In 1956, more than one hundred southern members of Congress signed a "manifesto" that damned the Court decision and summoned the white South to defy it to the bitter end. Mustering its own legal forces, white officialdom promised to tie up the* Brown *decision in "a century of litigation."*

For African Americans, the road to freedom's land was elusive indeed. Most African Americans in the South languished in searing poverty and a rigid racial caste system that relegated them to the gutters of southern society and kept them away from the polls and out of politics.

How did African Americans feel about segregation? What did they say alone among themselves? "Lawd, man!" an elevator operator once told an African American writer. "Ef it wuzn't fer them polices n' them ol' lynch-mobs, there wouldn't be nothin' but uproar down here."

In 1955, African Americans in the South created an uproar despite the police and the lynchings. That was the year of the Montgomery bus boycott, an event that launched the nonviolent civil rights protest movement of the 1950s and 1960s. Many people rose to prominence in the movement, but Martin Luther King Jr. became its most popular and most eloquent spokesman. In this selection, you will walk with King from his birth in Atlanta and his intellectual odyssey in college to the great and impassioned days of the

319

civil rights movement in the 1960s. As you ponder King's life and significance, consider what writer-historian Garry Wills said of King in The Kennedy Imprisonment *(1982), "While Washington's 'best and brightest' worked us into Vietnam," Wills wrote, "an obscure army of virtue arose in the South and took the longer spiritual trip inside a public bathroom or toward the front of a bus. King rallied the strength of broken [men and women], transmuting an imposed squalor into the beauty of chosen suffering. No one did it for his followers. They did it for themselves. Yet, in helping them, he exercised real power, achieved changes that dwarf the moon shot as an American achievement. The 'Kennedy era' was really the age of Dr. King."*

GLOSSARY

BLACK POWER   In 1966, angry, disaffected young militants in the Student Nonviolent Coordinating Committee (SNCC) and the Congress of Racial Equality (CORE) turned away from nonviolence and racial integration; inspired by the earlier teachings of Malcolm X, a famous black Muslim, they started advocating Black Power — the need for African Americans to organize themselves and consolidate their economic and political resources — as well as black separatism and even violent resistance.

CIVIL RIGHTS ACT OF 1964   Outlawed segregated public accommodations — the goal of King's civil rights campaign in Birmingham.

CONGRESS OF RACIAL EQUALITY (CORE)   Founded in 1942, it staged sit-ins and applied Gandhian direct-action techniques to the American scene; in 1961, under the leadership of James Farmer, CORE sponsored the freedom rides to call attention to segregated busing facilities in the South, and the federal government responded by desegregating interstate bus stations.

CONNOR, EUGENE "BULL"   City police commissioner who gained worldwide notoriety when he turned firehoses and police dogs on King's followers during the Birmingham demonstrations in 1963.

GANDHI, MOHANDAS   The father of modern India whose teachings on nonviolent resistance and love for the oppressor profoundly influenced King.

MONTGOMERY BUS BOYCOTT (1955–1956)   King rose to prominence as leader of this protest demonstration against segregated seating on Montgomery city buses; the Supreme Court finally nullified the Alabama laws that enforced the practice.

RAY, JAMES EARL   King's assassin and a petty crook; subsequent evidence linked Ray to two white men in the St. Louis area who had offered "hit" money for King's life.

SOUTHERN CHRISTIAN LEADERSHIP CONFERENCE (SCLC)   King's civil rights organization, which worked through African American churches to effect social and political change.

STUDENT NONVIOLENT COORDINATING COMMITTEE (SNCC)   Established with King's help in 1960, SNCC organized sit-ins and voter-registration drives in segregated Dixie; many of its leaders were jealous of King, calling him "De Lawd."

VOTING RIGHTS ACT OF 1965   Passed in response to the Selma campaign, the measure outlawed barriers to voting by African Americans and authorized the attorney general to supervise federal elections in seven southern states where African Americans were kept off the voting rolls.

He was M.L. to his parents, Martin to his wife and friends, Doc to his aides, Reverend to his male parishioners, Little Lord Jesus to adoring churchwomen, De Lawd to his young critics in the Student Nonviolent Coordinating Committee, and Martin Luther King, Jr., to the world. At his pulpit or a public rostrum, he seemed too small for his incomparable oratory and international fame as a civil rights leader and spokesman for world peace. He stood only five feet seven, and had round cheeks, a trim mustache, and sad, glistening eyes — eyes that revealed both his inner strength and his vulnerability.

He was born in Atlanta on January 15, 1929, and grew up in the relative comfort of the black middle class. Thus he never suffered the want and privation that plagued the majority of American blacks of his time. His father, a gruff, self-made man, was pastor of Ebenezer Baptist Church and an outspoken member of Atlanta's black leadership. M.L. joined his father's church when he was five and came to regard it as his second home. The church defined his world, gave it order and balance, taught him how to "get along with people." Here M.L. knew who he was — "Reverend King's boy," somebody special.

At home, his parents and maternal grandmother reinforced his self-esteem, praising him for his precocious ways, telling him repeatedly that he was *somebody*. By age five, he spoke like an adult and had such a prodigious memory that he could recite whole Biblical passages and entire hymns without a mistake. He was acutely sensitive, too, so much so that he worried about all the blacks he saw in Atlanta's breadlines during the Depression, fearful that their children did not have enough to eat. When his maternal grandmother died, twelve-year-old M.L.

thought it was his fault. Without telling anyone, he had slipped away from home to watch a parade, only to find out when he returned that she had died. He was terrified that God had taken her away as punishment for his "sin." Guilt-stricken, he tried to kill himself by leaping out of his second-story window.

He had a great deal of anger in him. Growing up a black in segregated Atlanta, he felt the full range of southern racial discrimination. He discovered that he had to attend separate, inferior schools, which he sailed through with a modicum of effort, skipping grades as he went. He found out that he — a preacher's boy — could not sit at lunch counters in Atlanta's downtown stores. He had to drink from a "colored" water fountain, relieve himself in a rancid "colored" restroom, and ride a rickety "colored" elevator. If he rode a city bus, he had to sit in the back as though he were contaminated. If he wanted to see a movie in a downtown theater, he had to enter through a side door and sit in the "colored" section in the balcony. He discovered that whites referred to blacks as "boys" and "girls" regardless of age. He saw "WHITES ONLY" signs staring back at him in the windows of barber shops and all the good restaurants and hotels, at the YMCA, the city parks, golf courses, swimming pools, and in the waiting rooms of the train and bus stations. He learned that there were even white and black sections of the city and that he resided in "nigger town."

Segregation caused a tension in the boy, a tension between his parents' injunction ("Remember, you are *somebody*") and a system that constantly demeaned and insulted him. He struggled with the pain and rage he felt when a white woman in a downtown store slapped him and called him "a little nigger" . . . when a bus driver called him "a black son-of-a-bitch" and made him surrender his seat to a white . . . when he stood on the very spot in Atlanta where whites had lynched a black man . . . when he witnessed nightriding Klansmen beating blacks in the streets. How, he asked defiantly, could he heed the Christian injunction and love a race of people who

From "Trumpet of Conscience," by Stephen B. Oates. In *American History Illustrated* (April 1988), 18–27, 52. Reprinted through courtesy of Cowles Magazines, publisher of *American History Illustrated*.

hated him? In retaliation, he determined "to hate every white person."

Yes, he was angry. In sandlot games, he competed so fiercely that friends could not tell whether he was playing or fighting. He had his share of playground combat, too, and could outwrestle any of his peers. He even rebelled against his father, vowing never to become a preacher like him. Yet he liked the way Daddy King stood up to whites: he told them never to call him a boy and vowed to fight this system until he died.

Still, there was another side to M.L., a calmer, sensuous side. He played the violin, enjoyed opera, and relished soul food — fried chicken, cornbread, and collard greens with ham hocks and bacon drippings. By his mid-teens, his voice was the most memorable thing about him. It had changed into a rich and resonant baritone that commanded attention whenever he held forth. A natty dresser, nicknamed "Tweed" because of his fondness for tweed suits, he became a connoisseur of lovely young women. His little brother A.D. remembered how Martin "kept flitting from chick to chick" and was "just about the best jitterbug in town."

At age fifteen, he entered Morehouse College in Atlanta, wanting somehow to help his people. He thought about becoming a lawyer and even practiced giving trial speeches before a mirror in his room. But thanks largely to Morehouse President Benjamin Mays, who showed him that the ministry could be a respectable forum for ideas, even for social protest, King decided to become a Baptist preacher after all. By the time he was ordained in 1947, his resentment toward whites had softened some, thanks to positive contact with white students on an intercollegiate council. But he hated his segregated world more than ever.

Once he had his bachelor's degree, he went north to study at Crozer Seminary near Philadelphia. In this mostly white school, with its polished corridors and quiet solemnity, King continued to ponder the plight of blacks in America. How, by what method and means, were blacks to improve their lot in a white-dominated country? His study of history, especially of Nat Turner's slave insurrection, convinced him that it was suicidal for a minority to strike back against a heavily armed majority. For him, voluntary segregation was equally unacceptable, as was accommodation to the status quo. King shuddered at such negative approaches to the race problem. How indeed were blacks to combat discrimination in a country ruled by the white majority?

As some other blacks had done, he found his answer in the teachings of Mohandas Gandhi — for young King, the discovery had the force of a conversion experience. Nonviolent resistance, Gandhi taught, meant noncooperation with evil, an idea he got from Henry David Thoreau's essay "On Civil Disobedience." In India, Gandhi gave Thoreau's theory practical application in the form of strikes, boycotts, and protest marches, all conducted nonviolently and all predicated on love for the oppressor and a belief in divine justice. In gaining Indian independence, Gandhi sought not to defeat the British, but to redeem them through love, so as to avoid a legacy of bitterness. Gandhi's term for this — *Satyagraha* — reconciled love and force in a single, powerful concept.

As King discovered from his studies, Gandhi had embraced nonviolence in part to subdue his own violent nature. This was a profound revelation for King, who had felt much hatred in his life, especially toward whites. Now Gandhi showed him a means of harnessing his anger and channeling it into a positive and creative force for social change.

At this juncture, King found mostly theoretical satisfaction in Gandhian nonviolence; he had no plans to become a reformer in the segregated South. Indeed, he seemed destined to a life of the mind, not of social protest. In 1951, he graduated from Crozer and went on to earn a Ph.D. in theology from Boston University, where his adviser pronounced

A pensive King stands beside a portrait of Mohandas Gandhi, the Indian spiritual and political leader. "As King discovered from his studies, Gandhi had embraced nonviolence in part to subdue his own violent nature. This was a profound revelation for King, who had felt much hatred in his life, especially toward whites. Now Gandhi showed him a means of harnessing his anger and channeling it into a positive and creative force for social change." (Bob Fitch/Black Star)

him "a scholar's scholar" of great intellectual potential. By 1955, a year after the school desegregation decision, King had married comely Coretta Scott and assumed the pastorship of Dexter Avenue Baptist Church in Montgomery, Alabama. Immensely happy in the world of ideas, he hoped eventually to teach theology at a major university or seminary.

But, as King liked to say, the *Zeitgeist,* or spirit of the age, had other plans for him. In December 1955, Montgomery blacks launched a boycott of the city's segregated buses and chose the articulate twenty-six-year-old minister as their spokesman. As it turned out, he was unusually well prepared to assume the kind of leadership thrust on him. Drawing on Gandhi's teachings and example, plus the tenets of his own Christian faith, King directed a nonviolent boycott designed both to end an injustice and redeem his white adversaries through love. When he exhorted blacks to love their enemies, King did not mean to love them as friends or intimates. No, he said, he meant a disinterested love in all humankind, a love that saw the neighbor in everyone it met, a love that sought to restore the beloved community. Such love not only avoided the internal violence of the spirit, but severed the external chain of hatred that only produced more hatred in an endless spiral. If American blacks could break the chain of hatred, King said, true brotherhood could begin. Then posterity would have to say that there had lived a race of people, of black people, who "injected a new meaning into the veins of history and civilization."

During the boycott King imparted his philosophy at twice-weekly mass meetings in the black churches, where overflow crowds clapped and cried as his mellifluous voice swept over them. In these mass meetings King discovered his extraordinary power as an orator. His rich religious imagery reached deep into the black psyche, for religion had been the black people's main source of strength and survival since slavery days. His delivery was "like a narrative poem," said a woman journalist who heard him. His voice had such depths of sincerity and empathy that it could "charm your heart right out of your body." Because he appealed to the best in his people, articulating their deepest hurts and aspirations, black folk began to idolize him; he was their Gandhi.

Under his leadership, they stood up to white Montgomery in a remarkable display of solidarity. Pitted against an obdurate city government that blamed the boycott on Communist agitators and resorted to psychological and legal warfare to break it, the blacks stayed off the buses month after month, and walked or rode in a black-operated carpool.

When an elderly woman refused the offer of a ride, King asked her, "But don't your feet hurt?" "Yes," she replied, "my feet is tired but my soul is rested." For King, her irrepressible spirit was proof that "a new Negro" was emerging in the South, a Negro with "a new sense of dignity and destiny."

That "new Negro" menaced white supremacists, especially the Ku Klux Klan, and they persecuted King with a vengeance. They made obscene phone calls to his home, sent him abusive, sickening letters, and once even dynamited the front of his house. Nobody was hurt, but King, fearing a race war, had to dissuade angry blacks from violent retaliation. Finally, on November 13, 1956, the U.S. Supreme Court nullified the Alabama laws that enforced segregated buses, and handed King and his boycotters a resounding moral victory. Their protest had captured the imagination of progressive people all over the world and marked the beginning of a southern black movement that would shake the segregated South to its foundations. At the forefront of that movement was a new organization, the Southern Christian Leadership Conference (SCLC), which King and other black ministers formed in 1957, with King serving as its president and guiding spirit. Operating through the southern black church, SCLC sought to enlist the black masses in the freedom struggle by expanding "the Montgomery way" across the South.

The "Miracle of Montgomery" changed King's life, catapulting him into international prominence as an inspiring new moral voice for civil rights. Across the country, blacks and whites alike wrote him letters of encouragement; *Time* magazine pictured him on its cover; the National Association for the Advancement of Colored People (NAACP) and scores of church and civic organizations vied for his services as a speaker. "I am really disturbed how fast all this has happened to me," King told his wife. "People will expect me to perform miracles for the rest of my life."

But fame had its evil side, too. When King visited New York in 1958, a deranged black woman stabbed him in the chest with a letter opener. The weapon was lodged so close to King's aorta, the main artery from the heart, that he would have died had he sneezed. To extract the blade, an interracial surgical team had to remove a rib and part of his breastbone; in a burst of inspiration, the lead surgeon made the incision over King's heart in the shape of a cross.

That he had not died convinced King that God was preparing him for some larger work in the segregated South. To gain perspective on what was happening there, he made a pilgrimage to India to visit Gandhi's shrine and the sites of his "War for Independence." He returned home with an even deeper commitment to nonviolence and a vow to be more humble and ascetic like Gandhi. Yet he was a man of manifold contradictions, this American Gandhi. While renouncing material things and giving nearly all of his extensive honorariums to SCLC, he liked posh hotels and zesty meals with wine, and he was always immaculately dressed in a gray or black suit, white shirt, and tie. While caring passionately for the poor, the downtrodden, and the disinherited, he had a fascination with men of affluence and enjoyed the company of wealthy SCLC benefactors. While trumpeting the glories of nonviolence and redemptive love, he could feel the most terrible anger when whites murdered a black or bombed a black church; he could contemplate giving up, turning America over to the haters of both races, only to dedicate himself anew to his nonviolent faith and his determination to redeem his country.

In 1960, he moved his family to Atlanta so that he could devote himself fulltime to SCLC, which was trying to register black voters for the upcoming federal elections. That same year, southern black students launched the sit-in movement against segregated lunch counters, and King not only helped them form the Student Nonviolent Coordinating

Committee (SNCC) but raised money on their behalf. In October he even joined a sit-in protest at an Atlanta department store and went to jail with several students on a trespassing charge. Like Thoreau, King considered jail "a badge of honor." To redeem the nation and arouse the conscience of the opponent, King explained, you go to jail and stay there. "You have broken a law which is out of line with the moral law and you are willing to suffer the consequences by serving the time."

He did not reckon, however, on the tyranny of racist officials, who clamped him in a malevolent state penitentiary, in a cell for hardened criminals. But state authorities released him when Democratic presidential nominee John F. Kennedy and his brother Robert interceded on King's behalf. According to many analysts, the episode won critical black votes for Kennedy and gave him the election in November. For King, the election demonstrated what he had long said: that one of the most significant steps a black could take was the short walk to the voting booth.

The trouble was that most blacks in Dixie, especially in the Deep South, could not vote even if they so desired. For decades, state and local authorities had kept the mass of black folk off the voting rolls by a welter of devious obstacles and outright intimidation. Through 1961 and 1962, King exhorted President Kennedy to sponsor tough new civil rights legislation that would enfranchise southern blacks and end segregated public accommodations as well. When Kennedy shied away from a strong civil rights commitment, King and his lieutenants took matters into their own hands, orchestrating a series of southern demonstrations to show the world the brutality of segregation. At the same time, King stumped the country, drawing on all his powers of oratory to enlist the black masses and win white opinion to his cause.

Everywhere he went his message was the same. *The civil rights issue,* he said, *is an eternal moral issue that will determine the destiny of our nation and our world. As we seek our full rights, we hope to redeem the soul of our country. For it is our country, too, and we will win our freedom because the sacred heritage of America and the eternal will of God are embodied in our echoing demands. We do not intend to humiliate the white man, but to win him over through the strength of our love. Ultimately, we are trying to free all of us in America — Negroes from the bonds of segregation and shame, whites from the bonds of bigotry and fear.*

We stand today between two worlds — the dying old order and the emerging new. With men of ill-will greeting this change with cries of violence, of interposition and nullification, some of us may get beaten. Some of us may even get killed. But if you are cut down in a movement designed to save the soul of a nation, no other death could be more redemptive. We must realize that change does not roll in "on the wheels of inevitabilty," but comes through struggle. So "let us be those creative dissenters who will call our beloved nation to a higher destiny, to a new plateau of compassion, to a more noble expression of humaneness."

That message worked like magic among America's long-suffering blacks. Across the South, across America, they rose in unprecedented numbers to march and demonstrate with Martin Luther King. His singular achievement was that he brought the black masses into the freedom struggle for the first time. He rallied the strength of broken men and women, helping them overcome a lifetime of fear and feelings of inferiority. After segregation had taught them all their lives that they were *nobody,* King taught them that they were *somebody.* Because he made them believe in themselves and in "the beauty of chosen suffering," he taught them how to straighten their backs ("a man can't ride you unless your back is bent") and confront those who oppressed them. Through the technique of nonviolent resistance, he furnished them something no previous black leader had been able to provide. He showed them a way of controlling their pent-up anger, as he had controlled his own, and using it to bring about constructive change.

The mass demonstrations King and SCLC choreographed in the South produced the strongest civil rights legislation in American history. This was the goal of King's major southern campaigns from 1963 to 1965. He would single out some notoriously segregated city with white officials prone to violence, mobilize the local blacks with songs, scripture readings, and rousing oratory in black churches, and then lead them on protest marches conspicuous for their grace and moral purpose. Then he and his aides would escalate the marches, increase their demands, even fill up the jails, until they brought about a moment of "creative tension," when whites would either agree to negotiate or resort to violence. If they did the latter, King would thus expose the brutality inherent in segregation and ... stab the national conscience so [much] that the federal government would be forced to intervene with corrective measures.

The technique succeeded brilliantly in Birmingham, Alabama, in 1963. Here Police Commissioner Eugene "Bull" Connor, in full view of reporters and television cameras, turned firehoses and police dogs on the marching protesters. Revolted by such ghastly scenes, stricken by King's own searching eloquence and the bravery of his unarmed followers, Washington eventually produced the 1964 Civil Rights Act, which desegregated public facilities — the thing King had demanded all along from Birmingham. Across the South, the "WHITES ONLY" signs that had hurt and enraged him since boyhood now came down.

Although SNCC and others complained that King had a Messiah complex and was trying to monopolize the civil rights movement, his technique worked with equal success in Selma, Alabama, in 1965. Building on a local movement there, King and his staff launched a drive to gain southern blacks the unobstructed right to vote. The violence he exposed in Selma — the beating of black marchers by state

troopers and deputized possemen, the killing of a young black deacon and a white Unitarian minister — horrified the country. When King called for support, thousands of ministers, rabbis, priests, nuns, students, lay leaders, and ordinary people — black and white alike — rushed to Selma from all over the country and stood with King in the name of human liberty. Never in the history of the movement had so many people of all faiths and classes come to the southern battleground. The Selma campaign culminated in a dramatic march over the Jefferson Davis Highway to the state capital of Montgomery. Along the way, impoverished local blacks stared incredulously at the marching, singing, flag waving spectacle moving by. When the column reached one dusty crossroads, an elderly black woman ran out from a group of old folk, kissed King breathlessly, and ran back crying, "I done kissed him! The Martin Luther King! I done kissed the Martin Luther King!"

In Montgomery, first capital and much-heralded "cradle" of the Confederacy, King led an interracial throng of 25,000 — the largest civil rights demonstration the South had ever witnessed — up Dexter Avenue with banners waving overhead. The pageant was as ironic as it was extraordinary, for it was up Dexter Avenue that Jefferson Davis's first inaugural parade had marched, and [it was] in the portico of the capitol [that] Davis had taken his oath of office as president of the slave-based Confederacy. Now, in the spring of 1965, Alabama blacks — most of them descendants of slaves — stood massed at the same statehouse, singing a new rendition of "We Shall Overcome," the anthem of the civil rights movement. They sang, "Deep in my heart, I do believe, We have overcome — *today.*"

Then, watched by a cordon of state troopers and the statue of Jefferson Davis himself, King mounted a trailer. His vast audience listened, transfixed, as his words rolled and thundered over the loudspeaker: "My people, my people listen. The battle is in our hands. . . . We must come to see that the end we seek is a society at peace with itself, a society that can live with its conscience. That day will be a day not of the white man, not of the black man. That will be the day of man as man." And that day was not long in coming, King said, whereupon he launched into the immortal refrains of "The Battle Hymn of the Republic," crying out, "Our God is marching on! Glory, glory hallelujah!"

Aroused by the events in Alabama, Washington produced the 1965 Voting Rights Act, which outlawed impediments to black voting and empowered the attorney general to supervise federal elections in seven southern states where blacks were kept off the rolls. At the time, political analysts almost unanimously attributed the act to King's Selma campaign. Once federal examiners were supervising voter registration in all troublesome southern areas, blacks were able to get on the rolls and vote by the hundreds of thousands, permanently altering the pattern of southern and national politics.

In the end, the powerful civil rights legislation generated by King and his tramping legions wiped out statutory racism in America and realized at least the social and political promise of emancipation a century before. But King was under no illusion that legislation alone could bring on the brave new America he so ardently championed. Yes, he said, laws and their vigorous enforcement were necessary to regulate destructive habits and actions, and to protect blacks and their rights. But laws could not eliminate the "fears, prejudice, pride, and irrationality" that were barriers to a truly integrated society, to peaceful intergroup and interpersonal living. Such a society could be achieved only when people accepted that inner, invisible law that etched on their hearts the conviction "that all men are brothers and that love is mankind's most potent weapon for personal and social transformation. True integration will be achieved by true neighbors who are willingly obedient to unenforceable obligations."

Even so, the Selma campaign was the movement's finest hour, and the Voting Rights Act the high point of a broad civil rights coalition that included the federal government, various white groups, and all the other civil rights organizations in addition to SCLC. King himself had best expressed the spirit and aspirations of that coalition when, on August 28, 1963, standing before the Lincoln Memorial, he electrified an interracial crowd of 250,000 with perhaps his greatest speech, "I Have a Dream," in which he described in rhythmic, hypnotic cadences his vision of an integrated America. Because of his achievements and moral vision, he won the 1964 Nobel Peace Prize, at thirty-four the youngest recipient in Nobel history.

Still, King paid a high price for his fame and his cause. He suffered from stomachaches and insomnia, and even felt guilty about all the tributes he received, all the popularity he enjoyed. Born in relative material comfort and given a superior education, he did not think he had earned the right to lead the impoverished black masses. He complained, too, that he no longer had a personal self and that sometimes he did not recognize the Martin Luther King people talked about. Lonely, away from home for protracted periods, beset with temptation, he slept with other women, for some of whom he had real feeling. His sexual transgressions only added to his guilt, for he knew he was imperiling his cause and hurting himself and those he loved.

Alas for King, FBI Director J. Edgar Hoover found out about the black leader's infidelities. The director already abhorred King, certain that Communist spies influenced him and masterminded his demonstrations. Hoover did not think blacks capable of organizing such things, so Communists had to be behind them and King as well. As it turned out, a lawyer in King's inner circle and a man in SCLC's New York office did have Communist backgrounds, a fact that only reinforced Hoover's suspicions about King. Under Hoover's orders, FBI agents conducted a ruthless crusade to destroy King's reputation and drive him broken and humiliated from public life. Hoover's men tapped King's phones and bugged his hotel rooms; they compiled a prurient monograph about his private life and showed it to various editors, public officials, and religious and civic leaders; they spread the word, Hoover's word, that King was not only a reprobate but a dangerous subversive with Communist associations.

King was scandalized and frightened by the FBI's revelations of his extramarital affairs. Luckily for him, no editor, not even a racist one in the South, would touch the FBI's salacious materials. Public officials such as Robert Kennedy were shocked, but argued that King's personal life did not affect his probity as a civil rights leader. Many blacks, too, declared that what he did in private was his own business. Even so, King vowed to refrain from further affairs — only to succumb again to his own human frailties.

As for the Communist charge, King retorted that he did not need any Russians to tell him when someone was standing on his neck; he could figure that out by himself. To mollify his political friends, however, King did banish from SCLC the two men with Communist backgrounds (later he resumed his ties with the lawyer, a loyal friend, and let Hoover be damned). He also denounced Communism in no uncertain terms. It was, he believed, profoundly and fundamentally evil, an atheistic doctrine no true Christian could ever embrace. He hated the dictatorial Soviet state, too, whose "crippling totalitarianism" subordinated everything — religion, art, music, science, and the individual — to its terrible yoke. True, Communism started with men like Karl Marx who were "aflame with a passion for social justice." Yet King faulted Marx for rejecting God and the spiritual in human life. "The great weakness in Karl Marx is right here," King once told his staff, and he went on to describe his ideal Christian commonwealth in Hegelian terms: "Capitalism fails to realize that life is social. Marxism fails to realize that life is individual. Truth is found neither in the rugged individualism of capitalism nor in the impersonal collectivism of Communism. The kingdom of God is found in a synthesis that combines the truths of these two opposites. Now there is where I leave brother Marx and move on toward the kingdom."

But how to move on after Selma was a perplexing question King never successfully answered. After the devastating Watts riot in August 1965, he took his movement into the racially troubled urban North, seeking to help the suffering black poor in the ghettos. In 1966, over the fierce opposition of some of his own staff, he launched a campaign to end the black slums in Chicago and forestall rioting there. But the campaign foundered because King seemed unable to devise a coherent anti-slum strategy, because Mayor Richard Daley and his black acolytes opposed him bitterly, and because white America did not seem to care. King did lead open-housing marches into segregated neighborhoods in Chicago, only to encounter furious mobs who waved Nazi banners, threw bottles and bricks, and screamed, "We hate niggers!" "Kill the niggers!" "We want Martin Luther Coon!" King was shocked. "I've been in many demonstrations all across the South," he told reporters, "but I can say that I have never seen — even in Mississippi and Alabama — mobs as hostile and as hate-filled as I've seen in Chicago." Although King prevented a major riot there and wrung important concessions from City Hall, the slums remained, as wretched and seemingly unsolvable as ever.

That same year, angry young militants in SNCC and the Congress of Racial Equality (CORE) renounced King's teachings — they were sick and tired of "De Lawd" telling them to love white people and work for integration. Now they advocated "Black Power," black separatism, even violent resistance to liberate blacks in America. SNCC even banished whites from its ranks and went on to drop "nonviolent" from its name and to lobby against civil rights legislation.

Black Power repelled the older, more conservative black organizations such as the NAACP and the Urban League, and fragmented the civil rights movement beyond repair. King, too, argued that black separatism was chimerical, even suicidal, and that nonviolence remained the only workable way for black people. "Darkness cannot drive out darkness," he reasoned: "only light can do that. Hate cannot drive out hate: only love can do that." If every other black in America turned to violence, King warned, then he would still remain the lone voice preaching that it was wrong. Nor was SCLC going to reject whites as SNCC had done. "There have been too many hymns of hope," King said, "too many anthems of expectation, too many deaths, too many dark days of standing over graves of those who fought for integration for us to turn back now. We must still sing 'Black and White Together, We Shall Overcome.'"

In 1967, King himself broke with the older black organizations over the ever-widening war in Vietnam. He had first objected to American escalation in the summer of 1965, arguing that the Nobel Peace Prize and his role as a Christian minister compelled him to speak out for peace. Two years later, with almost a half-million Americans — a disproportionate number of them poor blacks — fighting in Vietnam, King devoted whole speeches to America's "immoral" war against a tiny country on the other side of the globe. His stance provoked a fusillade of criticism from all directions — from the NAACP, the Urban League, white and black political leaders, *Newsweek, Life, Time,* and the *New York Times,* all telling him to stick to civil rights. Such criticism hurt him deeply. When he read the *Times*'s editorial against him, he broke down and cried. But he did not back down. "I've fought too long and too hard now against segregated accommodations to end up segregating my moral concerns," he told his critics. "Injustice *any*where is a threat to justice everywhere."

That summer, with the ghettos ablaze with riots, King warned that American cities would explode if funds used for war purposes were not diverted to emergency antipoverty programs. By then, the Johnson administration, determined to gain a military victory in Vietnam, had written King off as an antiwar agitator, and was now cooperating with the FBI in its efforts to defame him.

The fall of 1967 was a terrible time for King, the lowest ebb in his civil rights career. Everybody seemed to be attacking him — young black militants for his stubborn adherence to nonviolence, moderate and conservative blacks, labor leaders, liberal white politicians, the White House, and the FBI for his stand on Vietnam. Two years had passed since King had produced a nonviolent victory, and contributions to SCLC had fallen off sharply. Black spokesman Adam Clayton Powell, who had once called King the greatest Negro in America, now derided him as Martin Loser King. The incessant attacks began to irritate him, creating such anxiety and depression that his friends worried about his emotional health.

Worse still, the country seemed dangerously polarized. On one side, backlashing whites argued that the ghetto explosions had "cremated" nonviolence and that white people had better arm themselves against black rioters. On the other side, angry blacks urged their people to "kill the Honkies" and burn the cities down. All around King, the country was coming apart in a cacophony of hate and reaction. Had America lost the will and moral power to save itself? he wondered. There was such rage in the ghetto and such bigotry among whites that he feared a race war was about to break out. He felt he had to do something to pull America back from the brink. He and his staff had to mount a new campaign that would halt the drift to violence in the black world and combat stiffening white resistance, a nonviolent action that would "transmute the deep rage of the ghetto into a constructive and creative force."

Out of his deliberations sprang a bold and daring project called the poor people's campaign. The master plan, worked out by February 1968, called for SCLC to bring an interracial army of poor people to Washington, D.C., to dramatize poverty before the federal government. For King, just turned thirty-nine, the time had come to employ civil disobedience against the national government itself. Ultimately, he was projecting a genuine class movement that he hoped would bring about meaningful changes in American society — changes that would redistribute economic and political power and end poverty, racism, "the madness of militarism," and war.

In the midst of his preparations, King went to Memphis, Tennessee, to help black sanitation workers there who were striking for the right to unionize. On the night of April 3, with a storm thundering outside, he told a black audience that he had been to the mountaintop and had seen what lay ahead. "I may not get there with you. But I want you to know tonight that we as a people *will* get to the promised land."

The next afternoon, when King stepped out on the balcony of the Lorraine Motel, an escaped white convict named James Earl Ray, stationed in a nearby building, took aim with a high-powered rifle and blasted King into eternity. Subsequent evidence linked Ray to white men in the St. Louis area who had offered "hit" money for King's life.

For weeks after the shooting, King's stricken country convulsed in grief, contrition, and rage. While there were those who cheered his death, the *New York Times* called it a disaster to the nation, the *London Times* an enormous loss to the world. In Tanzania, Reverend Trevor Huddleston, expelled from South Africa for standing against apartheid, declared King's death the greatest single tragedy since the assassination of Gandhi in 1948, and said it challenged the complacency of the Christian Church all over the globe.

On April 9, with 120 million Americans watching on television, thousands of mourners — black and white alike — gathered in Atlanta for the funeral of a man who had never given up his dream of creating a symphony of brotherhood on these shores. As a black man born and raised in segregation, he had had every reason to hate America and to grow up preaching cynicism and retaliation. Instead, he had loved the country passionately and had sung of her promise and glory more eloquently than anyone of his generation.

They buried him in Atlanta's South View Cemetery, then blooming with dogwood and fresh green boughs of spring. On his crypt, hewn into the marble, were the words of an old Negro spiritual he had often quoted: "Free at Last, Free at Last, Thank God Almighty I'm Free at Last."

QUESTIONS TO CONSIDER

1   Martin Luther King Jr. was an angry young man who hated the segregated world of the American South and the injustices he saw inflicted on African Americans all over the nation. In adulthood, he came to feel that anger offered no solution to the problems that he and other African Americans faced. What made him change his mind? What were the roots of the philosophy that he adopted and used to lead the civil rights movement of the 1950s and 1960s? How did King give African Americans a sense of self-worth and the tools to achieve their aims?

2   What were SNCC and SCLC? How did these organizations differ from each other? In what ways were they alike? What changes took place in SNCC after the mid-1960s? How did Black Power differ from the civil rights movement under King?

3   What were the two major accomplishments of the civil rights movement in the mid-1960s? What specific actions did King and his followers undertake to influence public opinion and effect legislative change, and at what cost?

4   Describe the internal and external difficulties that beset King and the civil rights movement in the late 1960s. How did King defuse charges that he was a Communist? How did he react to the FBI crusade against him? To white and black backlashes? To the attacks on his policies that seemed to come from all sides? What did his support of the anti–Vietnam War movement cost him?

5   Why do you think Americans were receptive to King's pacifist message and nonviolent approach in the 1960s? Do you think similar tactics would be effective against oppression in a country such as the People's Republic of China?

25

The Nightmare of Vietnam

GEORGE C. HERRING

The Vietnam War was one of the most controversial episodes in United States history. American involvement in that conflict began with Truman and persisted through Democratic and Republican administrations alike, although the largest escalation took place under Lyndon Johnson — the subject of this selection.

To place George Herring's account in proper context, let us review what had gone on in Vietnam before the Johnson escalation. For more than twenty years, war had racked that distant Asian land. Initially, Communist and nationalist forces under Ho Chi Minh had battled to liberate their homeland from French colonial rule. The United States was suspicious of Ho, who was an avowed Communist trained in Moscow. But Ho was also an intense nationalist: he was determined to create a united and independent Vietnam and never wavered from that goal. Suspicious of Ho because of his Communist connections, the United States sided with the French against Ho and the Vietnamese; by 1954, when Dwight D. Eisenhower was president, the United States was footing 70 percent of the French cost of prosecuting a war that was highly unpopular in France. When Vietnamese forces surrounded and besieged twelve thousand French troops in Dien Bien Phu, Eisenhower's closest personal advisers urged armed American intervention to save the French position. Admiral Arthur Radford, chairman of the Joint Chiefs, even recommended dropping the atomic bomb on the Vietnamese. As Stephen Ambrose points out in selection 23, Eisenhower would have none of it.

The Eisenhower administration, however, continued using American aid and influence to combat communism in Indochina. In 1955, after suffering a humiliating defeat at Dien Bien Phu, the French withdrew from Vietnam, whereupon the United States acted to prevent Ho Chi Minh from gaining complete control there. Eisenhower and his secretary of state, John Foster Dulles, ignored an international agreement in Geneva that called for free elections and helped install a repressive, anti-Communist regime in South Vietnam, supplying it with money, weapons, and military advisers. From the outset, American policymakers viewed Ho Chi Minh's government in North Vietnam as part of a world Communist conspiracy directed by Moscow and Beijing. If communism was not halted in Vietnam, they feared, then all Asia would ultimately succumb. Eisenhower himself repeated the analogy that it would be like a row of falling dominoes.

American intervention aroused Ho Chi Minh, who rushed help to nationalist guerrillas in South Vietnam and set out to unite all of Vietnam under his leadership. With civil war raging across South Vietnam, the Eisenhower administration stepped up the flow of American military aid to the government there, situated in the capital city of Saigon. Under President John F. Kennedy, an enthusiast for counterinsurgency (or counterguerrilla warfare), the number of American advisers rose from 650 to 23,000. But Kennedy became disillusioned with American involvement in Vietnam and devised a disengagement plan before he was assassinated in November 1963. Whether he would have implemented the plan cannot be stated with certainty. When Vice President Johnson succeeded Kennedy, he nullified the disengagement plan and (with the encouragement of Kennedy's own advisers) continued American assistance to South Vietnam. Then, in the Gulf of Tonkin Resolution in August 1964, Congress empowered the president to use armed force against "Communist aggression" in Vietnam. But Johnson repeatedly vowed, "We are not going to send American boys nine or ten thousand miles away from home to do what Asian boys ought to be doing for themselves."

Over the next winter, however, all that changed. In November and December 1964, South Vietnamese guerrillas of the National Liberation Front (or Vietcong) killed seven United States advisers and wounded more than a hundred others in mortar and bomb attacks. Johnson's blood was up: he wasn't going to let them "shoot our boys" out there, fire on "our flag." He talked obsessively about Communist "aggression" in Vietnam, about Munich and the lesson of appeasement, about how his enemies would call him "a coward," "an unmanly man," if he let Ho Chi Minh run through the streets of Saigon. He couldn't depend on the United Nations to act — "It couldn't pour piss out of a boot if the instructions were printed on the heel." In February 1965, the administration became convinced that the coup-plagued Saigon government was about to collapse and that the United States had to do something drastic or South Vietnam would be lost and American international prestige and influence severely damaged. Accordingly, Johnson and his advisers moved to Americanize the war, sending waves of United States warplanes roaring over North Vietnam and 3,200 marines into the South.

The Americanization of the war took place with such stealth that people at home were hardly aware of the change. As reporter David Halberstam later wrote, United States decision makers "inched across the Rubicon without even admitting it," and the task of their press secretaries was "to misinform the public." The biggest misinformers were

Johnson and his spokesmen, who lied about costs (which were staggering), casualties, victories, and build-ups. By June, more than 75,000 American soldiers were in Vietnam, and combat troops were fighting Vietcong and North Vietnamese regulars in an Asian land war that Johnson had sworn to avoid. Soon troops were pouring in, and the war reeled out of control as each American escalation stiffened Vietcong and North Vietnamese resistance, which in turn led to more American escalation. By 1968, more than 500,000 American troops were fighting in that fire-scarred land. In the eyes of the administration and the Pentagon, it was unthinkable that America's awesome military power could fail to crush tiny North Vietnam and the Vietcong.

This sets the background for "The Nightmare of Vietnam," the story of the Americanization of the war under Lyndon Johnson. Herring not only offers trenchant insight into that powerful and pungent man but also captures the inconsistencies, frustration, and horror of America's longest and costliest war. Because of the similarities between the Vietnam War and the Philippine insurrection of 1898–1902, readers might want to review Kohler and Wensyel's "America's First Southeast Asian War" (selection 9), which draws important parallels between the two conflicts. Why do you think that Johnson and his advisers did not draw on the lessons learned in the Philippine war?

GLOSSARY

ARMY OF THE REPUBLIC OF VIETNAM (ARVN)   The South Vietnamese army.

BALL, GEORGE   Undersecretary of state and one of a handful of dissenters within the Johnson administration, Ball opposed the bombing of North Vietnam and Johnson's entire policy of escalation and Americanization of the war.

DOVES   Those who opposed the war in Vietnam.

HAWKS   Those who supported the war in Vietnam.

HO CHI MINH TRAIL   Communist supply route from North Vietnam to Vietcong hideouts in South Vietnam.

McNAMARA, ROBERT   Johnson's secretary of defense who was so closely associated with escalation that the Vietnam conflict became known as "McNamara's war"; by 1967, however, he had changed his mind about escalation and now pressed

for a basic change in policy, even for some face-saving way out of Vietnam; he resigned when Johnson lost confidence in him.

NEW LEFT   Radical, upper-middle-class college students who opposed the war and saw it as a means to overthrow American capitalism itself.

OPERATION ROLLING THUNDER   The American bombing campaign against North Vietnam that began early in 1965 and was expanded during the next two years in a vain attempt to check North Vietnamese aid to the Vietcong and force Ho Chi Minh to negotiate for peace; the bombing would continue until 1972.

VIETCONG (NATIONAL LIBERATION FRONT)   Communist guerrillas of South Vietnam who fought with the North Vietnamese regular army to unify the country.

WESTMORELAND, GENERAL WILLIAM C. United States commander in Vietnam who employed an aggressive strategy of attrition against the Vietcong and North Vietnamese.

While visiting the aircraft carrier *Ranger* off the coast of Vietnam in 1965, Robert Shaplen overheard a fellow journalist remark: "They just ought to show this ship to the Vietcong — that would make them give up." From Lyndon Johnson in the White House to the GI in the field, the United States went to war in 1965 in much this frame of mind. The President had staked everything on the casual assumption that the enemy could be quickly brought to bay by the application of American military might. The first combat troops to enter Vietnam shared similar views. When "we marched into the rice paddies on that damp March afternoon," Marine Lieutenant Philip Caputo later wrote, "we carried, along with our packs and rifles, the implicit conviction that the Viet Cong would be quickly beaten." Although by no means unique to the Vietnam War, this optimism does much to explain the form taken by American participation in that struggle. The United States never developed a strategy appropriate for the war it was fighting, in part because it was assumed that the mere application of its vast military power would be sufficient. The failure of one level of force led quickly to the next and then the next, until the war attained a degree of destructiveness no one would have thought possible in 1965. Most important, the optimism with which the nation went to war more than anything else accounts for the great frustration that subsequently developed in and out of government. Failure never comes easily, but it comes especially hard when success is anticipated at little cost.

Within two years, the optimism of 1965 had given way to deep and painful frustration. By 1967, the United States had nearly a half million combat troops in Vietnam. It had dropped more bombs than in all theaters in World War II and was spending more than $2 billion per month on the war. Some

American officials persuaded themselves that progress had been made, but the undeniable fact was that the war continued. Lyndon Johnson thus faced an agonizing dilemma. Unable to end the war by military means and unwilling to make the concessions necessary to secure a negotiated settlement, he discovered belatedly what George Ball had warned in 1964: "once on the tiger's back we cannot be sure of picking the place to dismount."

American strategy in Vietnam was improvised rather than carefully designed and contained numerous inconsistencies. The United States went to war in 1965 to prevent the collapse of South Vietnam, but it was never able to relate its tremendous military power to the fundamental task of establishing a viable government in Saigon. The administration insisted that the war must be kept limited — the Soviet Union and China must not be provoked to intervene — but the President counted on a quick and relatively painless victory to avert unrest at home. That these goals might not be compatible apparently never occurred to Johnson and his civilian advisers. The United States injected its military power directly into the struggle to cripple the Vietcong and persuade North Vietnam to stop its "aggression." The administration vastly underestimated the enemy's capacity to resist, however, and did not confront the crucial question of what would be required to achieve its goals until it was bogged down in a bloody stalemate.

While the President and his civilian advisers set limits on the conduct of the war, they did not provide firm strategic guidelines for the use of American power. Left on its own to frame a strategy, the military fought the conventional war for which it was prepared without reference to the peculiar conditions in Vietnam. . . .

The United States relied heavily on airpower. Military doctrine taught that bombing could destroy an enemy's warmaking capacity, thereby forcing him to come to terms. The limited success of airpower as applied on a large scale in World War II and on a more restricted scale in Korea raised serious

From George C. Herring, *America's Longest War: The United States and Vietnam, 1950–1975* (2nd ed.), McGraw-Hill Inc. Reproduced with permission of The McGraw–Hill Companies.

questions about the validity of this assumption, and the conditions prevailing in Vietnam, a primitive country with few crucial targets, might have suggested even more. The Air Force and Navy advanced unrealistic expectations about what airpower might accomplish, however, and clung to them long after experience had proven them unjustified. The civilian leadership accepted the military's arguments, at least to a point, because the bombing was cheaper in lives lost and therefore more palatable at home, and because it seemed to offer a quick and comparatively easy solution to a complex problem. Initiated in early 1965 as much from the lack of alternatives as anything else, the bombing of North Vietnam was expanded over the next two years in the vain hope that it would check infiltration into the south and force North Vietnam to the conference table.

The air war gradually assumed massive proportions. The President firmly resisted the Joint Chiefs' proposal for a knockout blow, but as each phase of the bombing failed to produce results, he expanded the list of targets and the number of strikes. Sorties against North Vietnam increased from 25,000 in 1965 to 79,000 in 1966 and 108,000 in 1967; the tonnage of bombs dropped increased from 63,000 to 136,000 to 226,000. Throughout 1965, [Operation] ROLLING THUNDER concentrated on military bases, supply depots, and infiltration routes in the southern part of the country. From early 1966 on, air strikes were increasingly directed against the North Vietnamese industrial and transportation system and moved steadily northward. In the summer of 1966, Johnson authorized massive strikes against petroleum storage facilities and transportation networks. A year later, he permitted attacks on steel factories, power plants, and other approved targets around Hanoi and Haiphong, as well as on previously restricted areas along the Chinese border.

The bombing inflicted an estimated $600 million damage on a nation still struggling to develop a viable, modern economy. The air attacks crippled North Vietnam's industrial productivity and dis-rupted its agriculture. Some cities were virtually leveled, others severely damaged. Giant B–52s, carrying payloads of 58,000 pounds, relentlessly attacked the areas leading to the Ho Chi Minh Trail, leaving the countryside scarred with huge craters and littered with debris. The bombing was not directed against the civilian population, and the administration publicly maintained that civilian casualties were minimal. But the CIA estimated that in 1967 total casualties ran as high as 2,800 per month and admitted that these figures were heavily weighted with civilians; [Secretary of Defense Robert] McNamara privately conceded that civilian casualties were as high as 1,000 per month during periods of intensive bombing. . . .

The manner in which airpower was used in Vietnam virtually ensured that it would not achieve its objectives, however. Whether, as the Joint Chiefs argued, a massive, unrestricted air war would have worked remains much in doubt. In fact, the United States had destroyed many major targets by 1967 with no demonstrable effect on the war. Nevertheless, the administration's gradualist approach gave Hanoi time to construct an air defense system, protect its vital resources, and develop alternative modes of transportation. Gradualism probably encouraged the North Vietnamese to persist despite the damage inflicted upon them.

North Vietnam demonstrated great ingenuity and dogged perseverance in coping with the bombing. Civilians were evacuated from the cities and dispersed across the countryside; industries and storage facilities were scattered and in many cases concealed in caves and under the ground. The government claimed to have dug over 30,000 miles of tunnels, and in heavily bombed areas the people spent much of their lives underground. An estimated 90,000 North Vietnamese, many of them women and children, worked full-time keeping transportation routes open, and piles of gravel were kept along the major roadways, enabling "Youth Shock Brigades" to fill craters within hours after the bombs fell. Concrete and steel bridges were replaced by ferries and pontoon bridges made of bamboo stalks which were sunk during the day to avoid detection. Truck drivers covered their vehicles with palm fronds and banana leaves and traveled at night, without headlights, guided only by white markers along the roads. B-52s devastated the narrow roads through the Mu Gia Pass leading to the Ho Chi Minh Trail, but, to the amazement of the Americans, trucks moved back through the pass within several days. "Caucasians cannot really imagine what ant labor can do," one American remarked with a mixture of frustration and admiration.

Losses in military equipment, raw materials, and vehicles were more than offset by increased aid from the Soviet Union and China. Until 1965, Russia had remained detached from the conflict, but the new leaders who succeeded Khrushchev in October 1964 took much greater interest in the Vietnam conflict, and U.S. escalation presented opportunities and challenges they could not pass up. The bombing created a need for sophisticated military equipment only the Soviet Union could provide, giving Moscow a chance to wean North Vietnam away from China. At a time when the Chinese were loudly proclaiming Soviet indifference to the fate of revolutions across the world, the direct threat to a Communist state posed by the air strikes required the Russians to prove their credibility. American escalation did not force the two Communist rivals back together, as George Ball had predicted. Fearful of Soviet intrusion in Vietnam, the Chinese angrily rejected Moscow's call for "united action" (a phrase borrowed, perhaps consciously, from Dulles) and even obstructed Russian aid to North Vietnam. The increasingly heated Sino-Soviet rivalry over Vietnam did, however, enable Hanoi to play off one power against the other to get increased aid and prevent either from securing predominant influence. The Chinese continued to supply large quantities of rice, small arms and ammunition, and vehicles. Soviet aid increased dramatically after 1965, and included such

modern weaponry as fighter planes, surface-to-air missiles, and tanks. Total assistance from Russia and China has been estimated in excess of $2 billion between 1965 and 1968. . . .

By 1967, the United States was paying a heavy price for no more than marginal gains. The cost of a B-52 mission ran to $30,000 per sortie in bombs. The direct cost of the air war, including operation of the aircraft, munitions, and replacement of planes lost, was estimated at more than $1.7 billion during 1965 and 1966, a period when aircraft losses exceeded 500. Overall, the United States between 1965 and 1968 lost 950 aircraft costing roughly $6 billion. According to one estimate, for each $1 of damage inflicted on North Vietnam, the United States spent $9.60. The costs cannot be measured in dollars alone, however. Captured American airmen gave Hanoi hostages which would assume increasing importance in the stalemated war. The continued pounding of a small, backward country by the world's wealthiest and most advanced nation gave the North Vietnamese a propaganda advantage they exploited quite effectively. Opposition to the war at home increasingly focused on the bombing, which, in the eyes of many critics was at best inefficient, at worst immoral.

American ground operations in the south also escalated dramatically between 1965 and 1967. Even before he had significant numbers of combat forces at his disposal, [United States commander William C.] Westmoreland had formulated the strategy he would employ until early 1968. It was a strategy of attrition, the major objective of which was to locate and eliminate the Vietcong and North Vietnamese regular units. Westmoreland has vigorously denied that he was motivated by any "Napoleonic impulse to maneuver units and hark to the sound of cannon," but "search and destroy," as it came to be called, did reflect traditional U.S. Army doctrines of warfare. In Westmoreland's view, North Vietnam's decision to commit large units to the war left him no choice but to proceed along these lines. He did not have sufficient forces to police the entire country, nor was it enough simply to contain the enemy's main units. "They had to be pounded with artillery and bombs and eventually brought to battle on the ground if they were not forever to remain a threat." Once the enemy's regulars had been destroyed, Westmoreland reasoned, the South Vietnamese government would be able to stabilize its position and pacify the countryside, and the adversary would have no choice but to negotiate on terms acceptable to the United States.

Westmoreland's aggressive strategy required steadily increasing commitments of American manpower. Even before the 1965 buildup had been completed, the General requested sufficient additional forces to bring the total to 450,000 by the end of 1966. In contrast to the air war, over which it retained tight control, the administration gave Westmoreland broad discretion in developing and executing the ground strategy, and it saw no choice but to give him most of the troops he asked for. In June 1966, the President approved a force level of 431,000 to be reached by mid-1967. While these deployments were being approved, Westmoreland was developing requests for an increase to 542,000 troops by the end of 1967.

Furnished thousands of fresh American troops and a massive arsenal of modern weaponry, Westmoreland took the war to the enemy. He accomplished what has properly been called a "logistical miracle," constructing virtually overnight the facilities to handle huge numbers of U.S. troops and enormous volumes of equipment. The Americans who fought in Vietnam were the best fed, best clothed, and best equipped army the nation had ever sent to war. In what Westmoreland described as the "most sophisticated war in history," the United States attempted to exploit its technological superiority to cope with the peculiar problems of a guerrilla war. To locate an ever elusive enemy, the military used small, portable radar units and "people sniffers" which picked up the odor of human urine. IBM 1430 computers were pro-

grammed to predict likely times and places of enemy attacks. Herbicides were used on a wide scale and with devastating ecological consequences to deprive the Vietcong of natural cover. C–123 "RANCHHAND" crews, with the sardonic motto "Only You Can Prevent Forests," sprayed more than 100 million pounds of chemicals such as Agent Orange over millions of acres of forests, destroying an estimated one-half of South Vietnam's timberlands and leaving human costs yet to be determined. . . .

In a war without front lines and territorial objectives, where "attriting the enemy" was the major goal, the "body count" became the index of progress. Most authorities agree that the figures were notoriously unreliable. The sheer destructiveness of combat made it difficult to produce an accurate count of enemy killed in action. It was impossible to distinguish between Vietcong and noncombatants, and in the heat of battle American "statisticians" made little effort. "If it's dead and Vietnamese, it's VC, was a rule of thumb in the bush," Philip Caputo has recalled. Throughout the chain of command there was heavy pressure to produce favorable figures, and padding occurred at each level until by the time the numbers reached Washington they bore little resemblance to reality. Even with an inflated body count — and estimates of padding range as high as 30 percent — it is clear that the United States inflicted huge losses on the enemy. Official estimates placed the number as high as 220,000 by late 1967. Largely on the basis of these figures, the American military command insisted that the United States was "winning" the war.

As with the air war, the strategy of attrition had serious flaws. It assumed that the United States could inflict intolerable losses on the enemy while keeping its own losses within acceptable bounds, an assumption that flew in the face of past experience with land wars on the Asian continent and the realities in Vietnam. An estimated 200,000 North Vietnamese reached draft age each year, and Hanoi was able to replace its losses and match each American escala-

Soldiers evacuating the wounded during the Tet Offensive, mounted by the North Vietnamese in late January of 1968. By that time, more than a half million American men were fighting in Vietnam, and the war bogged down in a stalemate. At home protests mounted as the war became increasingly unpopular with ordinary Americans, and Lyndon Johnson, refusing to run for another term, ended his presidency in a cloud of adverse public opinion. (McCullin/Magnum Photos)

tion. Moreover, the conditions under which the war was fought permitted the enemy to control its losses. The North Vietnamese and Vietcong remained extraordinarily elusive and were generally able to avoid contact when it suited them. They fought at times and places of their own choosing and on ground favorable to them. If losses reached unacceptable levels, they could simply melt away into the jungle or retreat into sanctuaries in North Vietnam, Laos, and Cambodia.

Thus, the United States could gain no more than a stalemate. The North Vietnamese and Vietcong had been hurt, in some cases badly, but their main forces had not been destroyed. They retained the strategic initiative, and could strike sharply and quickly when and where they chose. Westmoreland did not have sufficient forces to wage war against the enemy's regulars and control the countryside. The Vietcong political structure thus remained largely untouched, and even in areas such as the Iron Triangle, when American forces moved on to fight elsewhere, the Vietcong quietly slipped back in. It all added up to a "state of irresolution," Robert Shaplen observed in 1967. . . .

Thus, despite the impressive body count figures, it was clear to many observers by mid-1967 that the hopes of a quick and relatively inexpensive military victory had been misplaced. Each American blow "was like a sledgehammer on a floating cork," the journalist Malcolm Browne observed. "Somehow the cork refused to stay down." . . .

. . . Americanization of the war created new and equally formidable problems. Among these, the most serious — and most tragic — was that of the refugees. The expansion of American and enemy military operations drove an estimated four million South Vietnamese, roughly 25 percent of the population, from their native villages. Some drifted into the already teeming cities; others were herded into shabby refugee camps. The United States furnished the government some $30 million a year for the care of the refugees, but much of the money never reached them. Resettlement programs were initiated from time to time, but the problem was so complex that it would have taxed the ingenuity of the most imaginative officials. In any event, nothing could have compensated the refugees for the loss of their homes and lands. A large portion of South Vietnam's population was left rootless and hostile, and the refugee camps became fertile breeding grounds for Vietcong fifth columns.

The sudden infusion of half a million American troops, hundreds of civilian advisers, and billions of dollars had a profoundly disruptive effect on a weak and divided nation. The buildup was so rapid and so vast that it threatened to overwhelm South Vietnam. Saigon's ports were congested with ships and goods, and vessels awaiting unloading were backed up far out to sea. The city itself became a "thorough-going boom town," Shaplen remarked, its streets clogged with traffic, its restaurants "bursting with boisterous soldiers," its bars "as crowded as New York subway cars in the rush hour." Signs of the American presence appeared everywhere. Long strips of seedy bars and brothels sprang up overnight around base areas. In a remote village near Danang, Caputo encoun-

tered houses made of discarded beer cans: "red and white Budweiser, gold Miller, cream and brown Schlitz, blue and gold Hamm's from the land of sky-blue waters."

American spending had a devastating effect on the vulnerable South Vietnamese economy. Prices increased by as much as 170 percent during the first two years of the buildup. The United States eventually controlled the rate of inflation by paying its own soldiers in scrip and by flooding the country with consumer goods, but the corrective measures themselves had harmful side effects. Instead of using American aid to promote economic development, South Vietnamese importers bought watches, transistor radios, and Hondas to sell to people employed by the United States. The vast influx of American goods destroyed South Vietnam's few native industries and made the economy even more dependent on continued outside aid. By 1967, much of the urban population was employed providing services to the Americans.

In the bonanza atmosphere, crime and corruption flourished. Corruption was not new to South Vietnam or unusual in a nation at war, but by 1966 it operated on an incredible scale. Government officials rented land to the United States at inflated prices, required bribes for driver's licenses, passports, visas, and work permits, extorted kickbacks for contracts to build and service facilities, and took part in the illicit importation of opium. The black market in scrip, dollars, and stolen American goods became a major enterprise. On Saigon's PX Alley, an open-air market covering two city blocks and comprised of more than 100 stalls, purchasers could buy everything from hand grenades to scotch whiskey at markups as high as 300 percent. Americans and Vietnamese reaped handsome profits from the illegal exchange of currencies. International swindlers and "monetary camp followers" quickly got into the act, and the currency-manipulation racket developed into a "massive financial international network" extending from Saigon to Wall Street with connections to Swiss banks and Arab sheikdoms. The pervasive corruption undermined the U.S. aid program and severely handicapped American efforts to stabilize the economy of South Vietnam.

American officials perceived the problem, but they could not find solutions. [Prime Minister Nguyen Cao] Ky candidly admitted that "most of the generals are corrupt. Most of the senior officials in the provinces are corrupt." But, he would add calmly, "corruption exists everywhere, and people can live with some of it. You live with it in Chicago and New York." The Embassy pressed the government to remove officials known to be corrupt, but with little result. "You fight like hell to get someone removed and most times you fail and you just make it worse," a frustrated American explained to David Halberstam. "And then on occasions you win, why hell, they give you someone just as bad." The United States found to its chagrin that as its commitment increased, its leverage diminished. Concern with corruption and inefficiency was always balanced by fear that tough action might alienate the government or bring about its collapse....

Tensions between Americans and South Vietnamese increased as the American presence grew. Because of chronic security leaks, the United States kept Vietnamese off its major bases, and Vietcong infiltration of the ARVN's top ranks compelled U.S. officers to keep from their Vietnamese counterparts the details of major military operations.... The seeming indifference of many Vietnamese, while Americans were dying in the field, provoked growing resentment and hatred. The unerring ability of the villagers to avoid mines and booby traps that killed and maimed GIs led to charges of collusion with the enemy.

The Vietnamese attitude toward the foreigner was at best ambivalent. The Vietnamese undoubtedly appreciated American generosity, but they came to resent American ways of doing things. They complained that American soldiers "acted despicably"

toward the villagers, tearing up roads and endangering the lives of noncombatants by reckless handling of vehicles and firearms. An ARVN major protested that Americans trusted only those Vietnamese who accepted without question their way of doing things and that they doled out their aid "in the same way as that given to beggars." The Vietnamese recognized their need for U.S. help, and some were probably quite content to let the United States assume complete responsibility for the war. On the other hand, many Vietnamese resented the domineering manner of the Americans and came to consider the U.S. "occupation" a "demoralizing scourge." Thoughtful Vietnamese recognized that Americans were not "colonialists," Shaplen observed. But, he added, "there has evolved here a colonial ambiance that can sometimes be worse than colonialism itself." ...

The steady expansion of the war spurred strong international and domestic pressures for negotiations, but the military stalemate produced an equally firm diplomatic impasse. American officials later tallied as many as 2,000 attempts to initiate peace talks between 1965 and 1967. Neither side could afford to appear indifferent to such efforts, but neither was willing to make the concessions necessary to make negotiations a reality. Although the North Vietnamese attempted to exploit the various peace initiatives for propaganda advantage, they counted on the American people to tire of the war and they remained certain that they could achieve their goals if they persisted. Hanoi adamantly refused to negotiate without first securing major concessions from the United States. Johnson and his advisers could not ignore the various proposals for negotiations, but they doubted that anything would come of them and suspected, not without reason, that Hanoi was expressing interest merely to get the bombing stopped. Despite any firm evidence of results, the President remained confident at least until 1967 that North Vietnam would eventually bend to American pressure, and he feared that if he were too conciliatory it would undercut his strategy. To defuse international and domestic criticism, Johnson repeatedly insisted that he was ready to negotiate, but he refused to make the concessions Hanoi demanded. As each side invested more in the struggle, the likelihood of serious negotiations diminished.

The positions of the two sides left little room for compromise. The North Vietnamese denounced American involvement in Vietnam as a blatant violation of the Geneva Accords, and as a precondition to negotiations, insisted that the United States withdraw its troops, dismantle its bases, and stop all acts of war against their country. Hanoi stressed that the internal affairs of South Vietnam must be resolved by the South Vietnamese themselves "in accordance with the program of the National Liberation Front." North Vietnam was apparently flexible in regard to the timing and mechanism for political change in the south, but on the fundamental issues it was adamant. The "puppet" Saigon regime must be replaced by a government representative of the "people" in which the front would play a prominent role. Hanoi made clear, moreover, that the "unity of our country is no more a matter for negotiations than our independence." . . .

By mid-1967, Johnson was snared in a trap he had unknowingly set for himself. His hopes of a quick and relatively painless victory had been frustrated. He was desperately anxious to end the war, but he had been unable to do so by force, and in the absence of a clearcut military advantage, or a stronger political position in South Vietnam, he could not do so by negotiations. As the conflict increased in cost, moreover, he found himself caught in the midst of an increasingly angry and divisive debate at home, a debate which by 1967 seemed capable of wrecking his presidency and tearing the country apart.

At one extreme were the "hawks," largely right-wing Republicans and conservative Democrats, who viewed the conflict in Vietnam as an essential element in the global struggle with Communism. Should the United States not hold the line, they ar-

gued, the Communists would be encouraged to further aggression, allies and neutrals would succumb to Communist pressures, and the United States would be left alone to face a powerful and merciless enemy. Strong nationalists, certain of America's invincibility, and deeply frustrated by the stalemate in Vietnam, the hawks bitterly protested the restraints imposed on the military and demanded that the administration do whatever was necessary to attain victory. . . .

At the other extreme were the "doves," a vast, sprawling, extremely heterogeneous and fractious group, which opposed the war with increasing bitterness and force. The antiwar movement grew almost in proportion to the escalation of the conflict. It included such diverse individuals as the pediatrician Dr. Benjamin Spock, heavyweight boxing champion Muhammad Ali, actress Jane Fonda, and author Norman Mailer, old-line pacifists such as A. J. Muste and new radicals such as Tom Hayden, the black civil rights leader Dr. Martin Luther King, Jr., and Arkansas Senator J. William Fulbright. The doves comprised only a small percentage of the population, but they were an unusually visible and articulate group. Their attack on American foreign policy was vicious and unrelenting. In time, their movement became inextricably linked with the cultural revolution that swept the United States in the late 1960s and challenged the most basic of American values and institutions.

Although it defies precise categorization, the antiwar movement tended to group along three principal lines. For pacifists such as Muste, who opposed all wars as immoral, Vietnam was but another phase of a lifelong crusade. For the burgeoning radical movement of the 1960s, opposition to the war extended beyond questions of morality. Spawned by the civil rights movement, drawing its largest following among upper-middle-class youths on college campuses, the "New Left" joined older leftist organizations in viewing the war as a classic example of the way the American ruling class exploited helpless people to sustain a decadent capitalist system. Antiwar liberals far exceeded in numbers the pacifists and radicals. Although they did not generally question "the system," they increasingly questioned the war on both moral and practical grounds. Many liberal internationalists who had supported World War II, Korea, and the Cold War found Vietnam morally repugnant. By backing a corrupt, authoritarian government, they contended, the United States was betraying its own principles. In the absence of any direct threat to American security, the devastation wreaked on North and South Vietnam was indefensible. Many more liberals questioned the war on practical grounds. It was essentially an internal struggle, they argued, whose connection with the Cold War was at best indirect. Liberals questioned the validity of the domino theory.... They agreed that Vietnam was of no more than marginal significance to the security of the United States. Indeed they insisted that the huge investment there was diverting attention from more urgent problems at home and abroad, damaging America's relations with its allies, and inhibiting the development of a more constructive relationship with the Soviet Union. The liberal critique quickly broadened into an indictment of American "globalism." The United States had fallen victim to the "arrogance of power," Fulbright claimed, and was showing "signs of that fatal presumption, that over-extension of power and mission, which brought ruin to ancient Athens, to Napoleonic France and to Nazi Germany.

... Most liberals stopped short of advocating withdrawal from Vietnam, much less domestic revolution, proposing merely an end to the bombing, gradual deescalation, and negotiations. Disagreement on methods was even sharper. Liberals generally preferred nonviolent protest and political action within the system and sought to exclude the Communists from demonstrations. Radicals and some pacifists increasingly pressed for a shift from protest to resistance, and some openly advocated the use of violence to bring down a system that was itself violent.

Opposition to the war took many different forms.

Fulbright conducted a series of nationally televised hearings, bringing before the viewing public critics of administration policies. There were hundreds of acts of individual defiance. The folk singer Joan Baez refused to pay that portion of her income tax that went to the defense budget. Muhammad Ali declared himself a conscientious objector and refused induction orders. Three army enlisted men — the Fort Hood Three — challenged the constitutionality of the conflict by refusing to fight in what they labeled an "unjust, immoral, and illegal war." Army Captain Howard Levy used the doctrine of individual responsibility set forth in the Nuremberg war crimes trials to justify his refusal to train combat teams for action in Vietnam. Thousands of young Americans exploited legal loopholes, even mutilated themselves, to evade the draft; others fled to Canada or served jail sentences rather than go to Vietnam. A handful of Americans adopted the method of protest of South Vietnam's Buddhists, publicly immolating themselves. Antiwar rallies and demonstrations drew larger crowds in 1966 and 1967, and the participants became more outspoken in their opposition. Protesters marched daily around the White House chanting "Hey, hey, LBJ, how many kids have you killed today?" and "Ho, Ho, Ho Chi Minh, NLF is going to win." Antiwar forces attempted "lie-ins" in front of troop trains, collected blood for the Vietcong, and tried to disrupt the work of draft boards, Army recruiters, and the Dow Chemical Company, one of the makers of the napalm used in Vietnam. The most dramatic single act of protest came on October 21, 1967, when as many as 100,000 foes of the war gathered in Washington and an estimated 35,000 demonstrated at the entrance to the Pentagon, the "nerve center of American militarism."

The impact of the antiwar protests remains one of the most controversial issues raised by the war. The obvious manifestations of dissent in the United States probably encouraged Hanoi's will to hold out for victory, although there is nothing to suggest that the

North Vietnamese would have been more compromising in the absence of the movement. Antiwar protest did not turn the American people against the war, as some critics have argued. The effectiveness of the movement was limited by the divisions within its own ranks. Public opinion polls make abundantly clear, moreover, that a majority of Americans found the antiwar movement, particularly its radical and "hippie" elements, more obnoxious than the war itself. In a perverse sort of way, the protest may even have strengthened support for a war that was not in itself popular. The impact of the movement was much more limited and subtle. It forced Vietnam onto the public consciousness and challenged the rationale of the war and indeed of a generation of Cold War foreign policies. It limited Johnson's military options and may have headed off any tendency toward more drastic escalation. Perhaps most important, the disturbances and divisions set off by the antiwar movement caused fatigue and anxiety among the policymakers and the public, and thus eventually encouraged efforts to find a way out of the war.

The majority of Americans appear to have rejected both the hawk and dove positions, but as the war dragged on and the debate became more divisive, public concern increased significantly. Expansion of the war in 1965 had been followed by a surge of popular support — the usual rally-round-the-flag phenomenon. But the failure of escalation to produce any discernible result and indications that more troops and higher taxes would be required to sustain a prolonged and perhaps inconclusive war combined to produce growing frustration and impatience. If any bird symbolized the growing public disenchantment with Vietnam, opinion analyst Samuel Lubell observed, it was the albatross, with many Americans sharing a "fervent desire to shake free of an unwanted burden." The public mood was probably best expressed by a housewife who told Lubell: "I want to get out but I don't want to give up."

Support for the war dropped sharply during 1967. By the summer of that year, draft calls exceeded 30,000 per month, and more than 13,000 Americans had died in Vietnam. In early August, the President recommended a 10 percent surtax to cover the steadily increasing costs of the war. Polls taken shortly after indicated that for the first time a majority of Americans felt that the United States had been mistaken in intervening in Vietnam, and a substantial majority concluded that despite a growing investment, the United States was not "doing any better." Public approval of Johnson's handling of the war plummeted to 28 percent by October. Waning public confidence was mirrored in the press and in Congress. A number of major metropolitan dailies shifted from support of the war to opposition in 1967, and the influential *Time-Life* publications, fervently hawkish at the outset, began to raise serious questions about the administration's policies. Members of Congress found it impossible to vote against funds for American forces in the field and hesitated to challenge the President directly, but many who had firmly backed him at first came out openly against him. Admitting that he had once been an "all-out hawk," Republican Senator Thruston B. Morton of Kentucky spoke for the converts when he complained that the United States had been "planted into a corner out there" and insisted that there would "have to be a change." White House aides nervously warned of further defections in Congress and major electoral setbacks in 1968 in the absence of dramatic changes in the war.

By late 1967, for many observers the war had become the most visible symbol of a malaise that had afflicted all of American society. Not all would have agreed with Fulbright's assertion that the Great Society was a "sick society," but many did feel that the United States was going through a kind of national nervous breakdown. The "credibility gap" — the difference between what the administration said and what it did — had produced a pervasive distrust of government. Rioting in the cities, a spiraling crime rate, and noisy demonstrations in the streets suggested that violence abroad had produced violence at home.

Increasingly divided against itself, the nation appeared on the verge of an internal crisis as severe as the Great Depression of the 1930s. Anxiety about the war had not translated into a firm consensus for either escalation or withdrawal, but the public mood — tired, angry, and frustrated — perhaps posed a more serious threat to the administration than the anti-war movement.

The public debate on Vietnam was paralleled by increasingly sharp divisions within the government. . . . The major proponent of change by the spring of 1967 was, ironically, the Secretary of Defense, a man who had been so closely associated with escalation that the war had for a time been called "McNamara's war." As early as the summer of 1966, McNamara began to fear that the vast expansion of the war was endangering the global security position he had labored so diligently to construct since taking office in 1961. He was troubled by the destructiveness of the war, particularly the civilian casualties, and by the growing domestic opposition, brought home to him time and again in public appearances when he had to shove his way through and shout down protesters. McNamara's reputation as a businessman and public servant had been based on his ability to attain maximum results at minimal cost. By early 1967, however, he was forced to admit that escalation of the war had not produced results in the major "end products — broken enemy morale and political effectiveness." The South Vietnamese government seemed no more stable than before; pacification had "if anything, gone backward." The air war had brought heavy costs but no results. "Ho Chi Minh is a tough old S.O.B.," McNamara conceded to his staff. "And he won't quit no matter how much bombing we do." Moreover, the Secretary of Defense admitted that the bombing had cost the United States heavily in terms of domestic and world opinion. "The picture of the world's greatest superpower killing or seriously injuring 1,000 non-combatants a week, while trying to pound a tiny, backward nation into submission on an issue whose merits are hotly disputed, is not a pretty one," he advised Johnson in early 1967. McNamara and his advisers were also disillusioned with the ground war in South Vietnam. Increases in U.S. troops had not produced correspondingly large enemy losses, and there was nothing to indicate that further expansion of the war would place any real strains on North Vietnamese manpower.

Throughout 1967, McNamara quietly and somewhat hesitantly pressed for basic changes in policy. Arguing that the major military targets in North Vietnam had already been destroyed, he proposed either an unconditional bombing halt or the restriction of the bombing to the area south of the twentieth parallel. Such a move, he added, would help to appease critics of the war at home and might lead to serious negotiations. The Secretary of Defense also advocated placing a ceiling on American troop levels, and shifting from search and destroy to a more limited ground strategy based on providing security for the population of South Vietnam. In somewhat ambiguous terms, he further proposed a scaling down of American political objectives. Inasmuch as the United States had gone to war to contain China, he argued, it had succeeded: the Communist defeat in Indonesia, as well as rampant political turmoil within China itself, suggested that trends in Asia were now running against China and in favor of the United States. The administration might therefore adopt a more flexible bargaining position. It could still hope for an independent, non-Communist South Vietnam, but it should not obligate itself to "guarantee and insist upon these conditions." Obliquely at least, McNamara appears to have been suggesting that the United States modify its military strategy and diplomatic stance in order to find a face-saving way out of its dilemma in Vietnam.

By the summer of 1967, Lyndon Johnson was a deeply troubled man, physically and emotionally exhausted, frustrated by his lack of success, torn between his advisers, uncertain which way to turn. He seems to have shared many of McNamara's reservations, and he flatly rejected the view of the military that the solution was expansion of the war. He was disenchanted by the Joint Chiefs. "Bomb, bomb, bomb, that's all you know," he is said to have complained on several occasions. He was worried by the implications of Westmoreland's ground strategy and his request for more troops. "When we add divisions, can't the enemy add divisions?" he asked the General pointedly in April. "If so, where does it all end?" He remained firmly opposed to mobilizing the reserves and expanding the war. Such measures would heighten the domestic opposition. They would not satisfy the military but would only lead to pressures for further escalation, perhaps even for the use of nuclear weapons. He continued to fear a confrontation with the Soviet Union or China. "I am not going to spit in China's face," he insisted.

Johnson could not accept McNamara's recommendations, however. He had gradually lost confidence in his Secretary of Defense, whose dovishness he incorrectly attributed to the pernicious influence of his arch-rival Robert Kennedy. The relationship between Johnson and McNamara had so soured by late 1967 that the Secretary gladly accepted an appointment to head the World Bank. Westmoreland continued to report steady progress, moreover, and the President was not ready to concede defeat. He would not consider a return to the enclave strategy — "We can't hunker down like a jackass in a hailstorm," he said — or even a ceiling on the troop level. Although he seems to have agreed that the bombing had accomplished nothing, he was not prepared to stop or even limit it. Denouncing McNamara's proposals as an "aerial Dienbienphu," the Joint Chiefs had threatened to resign en masse if Johnson approved them, and the hawkish Mississippi Senator John Stennis was planning an investigation into the conduct of the air war. The President was not prepared to risk a major confrontation with the hawks or a potentially explosive public debate on the bombing. . . .

[By the end of 1967, Vietnam was destroying Johnson's presidency.] The consensus which Johnson had so carefully woven in 1964 was in tatters, the nation more divided than at any time since the Civil War. Opposition in Congress, as well as inattention and mismanagement resulting at least partially from the administration's preoccupation with Vietnam, had brought his cherished Great Society programs to a standstill. The President himself was a man under siege in the White House, his popularity steadily waning, the target of vicious personal attacks. His top aides had to be brought surreptitiously into public forums to deliver speeches.

Johnson was alarmed by the position he found himself in, stung by his critics, and deeply hurt by the desertion of trusted aides such as McNamara. He angrily dismissed much of the criticism as unfair, and he repeatedly emphasized that his critics offered no alternatives. He had accomplished great things at home, he insisted. But the press could only whine "Veetnam, Veetnam, Veetnam, Veetnam," he would add, savagely mimicking a baby crying. The harsher the criticism became, the more Johnson chose to disregard it by discrediting the source. Fulbright was a "frustrated old woman" because he had never been appointed Secretary of State. The dissent of the young sprang from ignorance. They had not lived through World War II. They would not "know a Communist if they tripped over one." . . .

. . . Johnson did not reevaluate his essential goals in Vietnam. To take such a step would have been difficult for anyone as long as there was hope of eventual success. It would have been especially difficult for Lyndon Johnson. Enormously ambitious, he had set high goals for his presidency, and he was unwilling to abandon them even in the face of frustration and massive unrest at home. It was not a matter of courage, for by persisting in the face of declining popularity Johnson displayed courage as well as stubbornness. It was primarily a matter of pride. The President had not wanted the war in Vietnam, but once committed to it he had invested his personal prestige to a degree that made it impossible for him to back off. He chose to stay the course in 1967 for the same reasons he had gone to war in the first place — because he saw no alternative that did not require him to admit failure or defeat.

While quietly contemplating a change in strategy, the President publicly made clear his determination to see the war through to a successful conclusion. "We are not going to yield," he stated repeatedly. "We are not going to shimmy. We are going to wind up with a peace with honor which all Americans seek." At a White House dinner for the Prime Minister of Singapore, the President expressed his commitment in different terms. "Mr. Prime Minister," he said, "you have a phrase in your part of the world that puts our determination very well. You call it 'riding the tiger.' You rode the tiger. We shall!"

Although Johnson continued to boast that "the enemy had been defeated in battle after battle" and that America was winning the war, the Vietcong on the last day of January 1968 launched the massive Tet Offensive in South Vietnam, attacking thirty-six of forty-four provincial capitals, sixty-four district towns and countless villages, twelve United States bases, and even the American embassy in Saigon. This seemed undeniable proof that Johnson's military solution was a failure and that the claims of the President and his generals could not be believed.

In 1968, the war drove Johnson from office — he refused to seek another term — and helped bring Richard Nixon to the White House, because he promised to end the conflict. Yet Nixon seemed to take up where Johnson left off. Like his predecessors, Nixon worried about "American credibility," about what would happen to American prestige if the United States sold out its South Vietnamese ally, and in 1970 he sent American troops into contiguous Cambodia to exterminate Communist hideouts there. The Cambodian invasion brought antiwar protest to a tragic climax, as Ohio national guards troops opened fire on protesting students at Kent State University and killed four of them. With the campuses in turmoil and the country divided and adrift, Nixon gradually disengaged American

ground troops in Vietnam and sought détente with both Russia and China.

Although the Nixon administration continued to speak of "peace with honor" in Indochina, and although it continued to bomb Hanoi, it was clear nevertheless that American involvement in the Vietnamese civil war was a tragic and costly mistake. Indeed, the signs were unmistakable that the original premise for American intervention in Indochina was erroneous. The domino theory, based as it was on the assumption of a worldwide monolithic Communist conspiracy directed by Moscow, appeared more and more implausible. For one thing, China and Russia developed an intense and bitter ideological feud that sharply divided the Communist world, and they almost went to war over their disputed boundary. The Sino-Soviet split exploded the notion of a Communist monolith out for world dominion, and so did the fierce independence of North Vietnam itself. Although Hanoi continued to receive aid from both Russia and China, North Vietnam apparently never asked China to intervene in the struggle (and apparently China never offered to do so). The truth was that North Vietnam was fighting to unite the country under Hanoi's leadership rather than under Beijing's or Moscow's.

At last, in top-secret negotiations in Paris, United States Secretary of State Henry Kissinger and North Vietnam's Le Duc Tho worked out a peace agreement. Eventually, the United States removed its combat forces, and in 1975 South Vietnam's regime fell to the North Vietnamese and the National Liberation Front. After almost two decades of bitter civil war and the loss of more than 1 million lives, Vietnam was united under Hanoi's Communist government, something that would probably have happened without further violence had general elections been held in 1956, according to the Geneva agreements of two years before.

QUESTIONS TO CONSIDER

1   According to Herring, what were the major problems with American military strategy in Vietnam? Why were conditions in Vietnam unsuited for conventional warfare?

2   What important social and economic consequences did Americanization of the war have for
South Vietnam?

3   What repercussions did the war in Vietnam have
in American society? Would you agree with Senator
William Fulbright's assertion that the Great Society
was a sick society?

4   Compare the prowar and antiwar arguments of
American hawks and doves. How much influence
did the antiwar movement have in shaping public attitudes?

5   What trait in Lyndon Johnson's personality and
character made him unable to alter his course of action in Vietnam?

XIII

CULTURE SHOCK

26

Betty Friedan Destroys the Myth of the Happy Housewife

MARCIA COHEN

Previous selections have narrated women's long, hard struggle to gain the right to vote. That triumph, as we saw in selection 15, did not bring American women into the center of the nation's political life, and suffragists like Eleanor Roosevelt accepted a separate and subordinate "gender" role in their political work. During the Great Depression, as one feminist scholar has said, women "were partners in the struggle for survival." They also became involved in social and political activity; indeed, a "women's network" emerged within the New Deal and the Democratic party, allowing women for the first time to become a grassroots force. But women's achievements in the thirties proved to be short-lived, as Sara Evans has said, and women as a whole "were not empowered."

During the Second World War, women made significant economic advances as workers in America's defense plants. But after the war, as Marcia Cohen points out in this selection, the industrial establishment tended to push women back into the home because it recognized "the housewife's valuable role as the prime consumer of household products." At the same time, women's magazines such as Redbook *and* McCall's, *many of them published and edited by men, popularized the image of the happy housewife and stressed the old female virtues of passivity, marriage, and motherhood.*

The image of the happy homemaker and contented "auxiliary" troubled Betty Friedan, who in the mid-1950s was living in the suburb of Rockland County, New York, and trying to combine marriage and motherhood with freelance journalism. Back in the 1940s, she had been a brilliant student at Smith College and had done such out-

standing work in psychology that she won a fellowship from the University of California at Berkeley. There she studied with the famous analyst Erik Erikson and won an even more prestigious grant that would have carried her into a professional career. But for some incredible reason — perhaps because a young man she was dating complained about the fellowship — she turned it down. Almost at once she suffered a protracted attack of asthma. Wheezing, gasping for breath, she left academe and the young man and fled to New York, where she sought relief in psychoanalysis.

When she felt better, she secured an editorial position at a small labor newspaper, married an amusing, ambitious man named Carl Friedan, and started raising a family. When she became pregnant with her second child, her employer decided that one pregnancy leave was enough; the paper fired her, ignoring the stipulation in her contract that guaranteed her maternity leave. She protested, but the Newspaper Guild refused to support her. Meanwhile, her marriage to Carl was becoming stormy; when they argued, she said, books and sugar bowls seemed to fly. Racked again by asthma, she resumed psychoanalysis.

Now living in a suburban Victorian house, Friedan did occasional freelance writing for women's magazines. She was increasingly attracted to stories about women who wanted the same things she did — an integrated life that used all of a woman's talents. She noted that prosperity offered the American woman an education and a living standard her grandmother would have envied, but it brought frustration too. By the 1950s, the American woman had been educated as never before, but to what end? When Friedan sent out a questionnaire for an article she was writing for McCall's, she was astounded to learn that many women felt as unhappy as she did. Worse, their discontents were hidden behind the pervasive image of the happy housewife.

In 1963, after years of struggling, Friedan published a book that demolished that image, The Feminine Mystique; it galvanized millions of female readers, rocketed Friedan to national fame, and led to the modern feminist movement. Friedan's achievements were as important as many of the famous men we have studied thus far, and yet most of you would probably be hard pressed to identify her. You will get to know her well in the following selection, written by journalist Marcia Cohen, author of The Sisterhood (1988). Cohen recounts Friedan's extraordinary story, describing how she came to write The Feminine Mystique and to challenge a whole generation's assumptions and practices as far as women are concerned. An epilogue tells how Friedan initiated the "second wave" of ogranized feminism and founded and became first president of the National Organization for Women, the first mainstream women's organization and the most successful in history.

GLOSSARY

BROCKWAY, GEORGE   Editor at W. W. Norton who signed Friedan to write *The Feminine Mystique,* which grew out of her article "The Togetherness Woman."

BROWN, HELEN GURLEY   Author of *Sex and the Single Girl* (1962) and editor of *Cosmopolitan* who played a "pioneering role" in the sexual liberation of women in the 1960s and 1970s.

STEIN, BOB   Editor of *Redbook* who agreed to publish an article ("The Togetherness Woman") based on Friedan's Smith class questionnaire if she expanded it to include younger women; he rejected the completed article on the ground that it would appeal only to "the most neurotic housewife."

"THE TOGETHERNESS WOMAN"   An article Friedan wrote for *McCall's* magazine, the male editor of which refused to publish it; based on a questionnaire Friedan had sent to her Smith College classmates, the article attacked woman's "homemaking role" as dull and unrewarding.

WOMEN'S WORLD (1952)   Motion picture that stressed how much the home was a "woman's world" in which women buried their ambitions and subordinated themselves to their husbands.

It was a strange stirring, a sense of dissatisfaction, a yearning that women suffered in the middle of the twentieth century in the United States. Each suburban wife struggled with it alone. As she made the beds, shopped for groceries, matched slipcover material, ate peanut butter sandwiches with her children, chauffeured Cub Scouts and Brownies, lay beside her husband at night, she was afraid to ask even of herself the silent question — "Is this all?"

BETTY FRIEDAN, *The Feminine Mystique,* 1963

H er so-called "brilliant career"! Not much had come of that, Betty thought miserably as she trudged back to her beloved Smith College for her fifteenth reunion. The great promise her professors had seen — that eager, whirling intellectual energy — had come to nothing more than a couple of women's magazine articles. Hardly "brilliant." Hardly even worthy of the term "career"!

Betty — the class of 1942's hortatory, patriotic, tough tomato, always ready to take on an argument and, more often than not, *win* it. That same plump little girl who was so determined, way back in Peoria, to make her snooty contemporaries "respect her," who had set out, in her younger brother Harry's words, "to be somebody important . . ."

She was now, in 1957, returning to the alma mater that had been for her, such a glory, an affirmation, "that whole thing," as she would put it years later in her gruff, gravelly voice, "of the *passion* of the mind." And she was coming back not as the professional psychologist they must all have expected, but as, well, "just a housewife" with a few articles to her credit.

"It rankled me," she would remember, "because I hadn't lived up to my brilliant possibilities."

From "Shattering the Feminine Mystique" by Marcia Cohen, in Cohen's *The Sisterhood: The True Story of the Women Who Changed the World* (Simon and Schuster, 1988), 83–99. Copyright © 1988 by Marcia Cohen.

But the undergraduates on campus, she found, were not the slightest bit interested in such "possibilities," and she was shocked by their distracted answers to her questions. Questions about, naturally, their scholarly interests, what ideas or professors they were "passionately excited about."

"They looked at me," she would recall, "as if I were speaking a foreign language. 'We're not excited about things like that,' they said. 'All we want to do is to get married and have children and do things with them, like go ice skating . . .'"

But it was now, of course, the quiet Eisenhower era, the gritrock pit of what would be viewed in retrospect as the heavy-duty husband-hunting years. "I chased her until she caught me," was a standard husband's joke, though the truth probably lay as much in the male youth's intent on settling down as the female's. The house in the suburbs, the station wagon bursting with kids and collie dogs, the ability to provide for a family proved manhood as much as homemaking proved femininity, and testified as well to those most important virtues of the decade: "adjustment," "maturity."

By now psychology was a preoccupation. Freud's vaunted theory of "penis envy" and [Dr. Helene] Deutsch's interpretation of the achieving, intellectual woman as "masculinized . . . her warm, intuitive knowledge . . . [having] yielded to cold unproductive thinking," hinted of maladjustments to be avoided at all costs. The idea that woman's true nature, reflecting her anatomy, was passive and could be fulfilled only through renouncing her goals and "sublimating" to a male had taken firm root in the American ethic.

The women's magazines, growing ever more powerful as advertising pages and circulations mounted, had been pounding the message home for nearly a decade. Women, as [Ferdinand] Lundberg and [Dr. Marynia F.] Farnham had written [in *Modern Woman: The Lost Sex*], needed propaganda to keep them *in* traditional homemaking tasks, such as cooking or decorating, and *out* of those "fields belonging to the male area" — that is, "law, mathematics, physics, business, industry and technology." And indeed, the magazines invariably portrayed women as, above and beyond all else, housewives and mothers. If an interview subject happened to be an actress or dancer (two acceptably feminine undertakings), the editors quickly clarified: She was merely dabbling, taking a breather from her real work — and life — at home.

Nor was this notion purely the province of the popular press. Great citadels of learning were equally convinced and convincing. In most eastern women's schools, "gracious living" was the order of the day. This meant, on the whole, little more than learning to pour tea from a silver-plated samovar. But to carry out this future mission, give or take a samovar, you had to have a life of gentility, with, of course, a husband. Most college women, even those who never stood their turn at the tea kettle, knew beyond a shadow of a doubt that marriage — not a career — was their primary goal in life. Running a close second was the psychological health of their children, who were likely to erupt into neurotic misfits, psychologists warned, should Mother attempt any serious work outside the home.

Admittedly, the female's focus on marriage had an extra edge. The birth rate was soaring and given their dependent condition, women needed to be supported financially. The status gap of the thirties — between the gracious, respected matron, cared for by her breadwinner husband, and the lonely, forlorn working girl — was revived and slickly refurbished. Rare indeed was the college counselor who, by discussing the job market, would damn a female graduate to the latter state.

Some women left college without graduating. (Might as well get on with it. What's the point of waiting, anyhow?) Most collected a "Mrs." after or with their undergraduate degrees. You understood that you were marrying not just a husband but "a life," and this wholesale effort seemed at the time to blur class distinctions. Women cooked pot roast everywhere.

The idealized housewife from 1955, shown here on the cover of the Saturday Evening Post *for May 21, was well dressed and fashionably coiffed, even at home. Surrounded by modern appliances in her impeccable kitchen, she looks just as discontented as Betty Freidan found her a few years later — although the problem was a great deal more complex than runny chocolate icing. (The Saturday Evening Post)*

That there were, in fact, differences — in both class and interests — would eventually create knotty problems for feminists of the future. Many women, not only working-class women but also those with less defined intellectual appetites, very much enjoyed their roles as homemakers, household decision makers, disciplinarians, or managers, preferences that would eventually set them at odds with the revolutionaries of the sixties.

At the moment, though, like it or not, most women were preparing for the esteemed role of "auxiliary."

If, for instance, a woman was married to a doctor, she would join the hospital "auxiliary," have dinner ready when the doctor got home, and subscribe to a magazine called *Doctor's Wife.*

It was a given, in those days, that a young woman with a burning interest in the law should marry a lawyer. She would help him develop his practice and live the life of a lawyer's wife, mother of a lawyer's children. Or an engineer's, or a writer's, or a pharmacist's, or a retailer's — or especially a corporate executive's. That the deportment of an executive's wife had a major influence on her husband's advancement was a lesson clearly delivered, not just in an announcement from Radcliffe College of an Institute for Executive Wives, but in Jean Negulesco's popular film pointedly entitled *Women's World.*

In this 1952 movie, Lauren Bacall — no longer the sultry siren of the forties — played a devoted wife who, along with two others, June Allyson and Arlene Dahl, was summoned to corporate headquarters in New York, where their husbands were about to audition for top honcho.

"The best couple for the job," the company owner frankly informed the men, "will win. Your wife is under observation. She must never compete with the company. If there is a choice between wife and work, it must be work."

As the husbands in this "women's world" proceeded with their unmemorable politicking, the motivations (and "qualifications") of the wives were quickly established. June was frightfully anxious to rush home to her kids in the Midwest. Lauren fretted that the job might exacerbate her husband's ulcer. Arlene, on the other hand, was so delighted by the prospect of life in New York that she overreached by flirting with the owner, thus proving that she had missed not just one, but several commandments dosed out in the dialogue.

I.   "What's important to him is important to me."

II.   "You must convince him that you're perfectly happy even if you feel like screaming."

III.   "The man who gets the job must have a wife who loves him very much."

IV.   (the overriding theme): "A man is working for the children, and they're your children so it's a *woman's world.*"

And if, in the end, it's Arlene's man who does win the job, this plot twist occurs only after her restrained, expressionless husband has impressed the owner by dispensing with his "handicap": his ambitious, brazen, childless (and therefore dispensable) wife.

Though heavy-handed, the movie accurately reflected a large segment of the women's world of the fifties, where back in the suburbs wives quickly buried ambitions of the sort (vicarious or not) that plagued the unfortunate Arlene.

Few could imagine, in the expanding economy of the post–Korean War years, that among these selfless wives would be many who would find themselves, twenty and thirty years hence, in the wake of defunct marriages or financial belt-tightening, pounding the pavements, or training for jobs that could bring in much-needed cash or restore flagging self-esteem.

There were, of course, exceptions. A few remarkable college graduates *did* pursue professional careers. Among them, ironically — though barely noticed at the time — was an assertive, achieving Illinois woman who, in 1952, ran for Congress. Phyllis Schlafly, who would eventually stand forth as the new feminism's most vocal enemy, who would sound the alarm for women's return to the home, was among those who were not, at the moment, at home.

For even then, in spite of the social propaganda, many women, including those from middle-income families, were quietly moving into the workforce — so many, in fact, that they soon accounted for 60 percent of its growth in that decade. Among them

were many single women, including college graduates who, as they waited for Mr. Right, took jobs as "Gal Fridays" in ad agencies, or as researchers, "helping" a reporter on a news magazine. Many took speed-writing or shorthand courses so they could be secretaries and thus avoid the typing pool, jobs for which there was plenty of call under "Female" in the help-wanted columns. The men who ran America's industries knew better than to give their girls (as in "Call my girl, she'll make an appointment for you") dangerous notions about careers. "Gal Fridays," summa cum laude be damned, ran errands and made coffee. They were lucky, they were told, to be hired at all, since it was a given that they wouldn't be around for long. If they were "normal," they would soon drop out to get married, have babies.

And if they were "normal," they were known to be emotionally delicate as well, not cut out for the rough-and-tumble of the business world. . . .

If, for example, a wife was working outside the home, she retained her auxiliary, ladylike status by referring to her job as unimportant and transitory, a diversion, never a "career." She was helping out — just for the moment — with the family finances. She was subdued and modest. She strolled, seldom ran, let alone worked up a sweat. She knew better than to enter one of those rare girls' track meets, where young men guffawed to each other on the sidelines: "Nice tits" or "Some ass." She aspired, if not to June Allyson's saccharine self-sacrifice, to the controlled charm of Doris Day, the elfin poise of Audrey Hepburn, the serene aristocracy of Grace Kelly.

Any sign of ambition was disaster. What would be known in the seventies as "abrasive" in the fifties was a "castrating bitch."

Simone de Beauvoir's *The Second Sex,* a brilliant feminist polemic, was published in this country in 1953, but nobody in America talked about it much. The revolutionary Kinsey Report on *Sexual Behavior in the Human Female,* documenting the fact that women enjoyed sex both emotionally and physically pretty much the same way men did, went barely noticed in America's heartland. As the lure of television swept the country, people watched "Ozzie and Harriet" and "Father Knows Best," images of the perfect American family. Blacks appeared on the screen almost solely as servants; women, as wives and mothers. It was the age of "conformity," or, as probably suited best, the "silent generation."

And yet . . .

Anyone with an ear to the quiet, frozen lake of the mid-fifties might have heard the rumble, the growl and surge of a riptide beneath the ice. In the late forties, Holden Caulfield, J. D. Salinger's sensitive hero of *Catcher in the Rye,* inspired thousands of young fans by limning the hypocrisy he saw around him. (No one yet used the term "drop out," but Holden seemed destined to do it.) In 1954, the Supreme Court ordered desegregation in all public schools, an act that would not only change the paper-white face of the country, but may well have precipitated the enormous upheavals to come. In 1955, the sensitive, introspective James Dean struck a chord of disaffection in *Rebel Without a Cause.* Elvis Presley had begun to heat up and transform the soul of pop music. Writers Jack Kerouac in *On the Road* and Allen Ginsberg in "Howl" were giving voice to a strange youthful ennui, a rough-timbered, off-balance sense of disillusionment.

In 1953, *Playboy* magazine — with a nude calendar photo of Marilyn Monroe — was launched. Being the "party organ," as feminist writer Barbara Ehrenreich would one day call it, of the male, hedonistic rebellion, it had nothing good to say about collie dogs, station wagons, church picnics, or the family. It was billed as Hugh Hefner's answer to conformity, to "home, family and all that jazz," as he put it, and to "togetherness" — the resoundingly successful advertising slogan of *McCall's* magazine, the symbol of the happy, glorified home with Daddy at work, Mommy in the kitchen, and 2.5 children as total fulfillment.

"The Togetherness Woman" was, in fact, the title of the article Betty had promised *McCall's.* She had taken the assignment simply to justify the months and months she had spent on a questionnaire that Smith had asked her to prepare for her class reunion.

Betty had labored mightily over the thing, even brought a couple of her friends in to hash over the questions. She had worked so hard, in fact, that her classmates at the reunion had giggled about how *long* the form was. How involved, how detailed the questions.

"What difficulties have you found in working out your role as a woman?" "What are the chief satisfactions and frustrations of your life today?" "How do you feel about getting older?" Leave it to Betty, the psychology buff, they joked, to dream up all that stuff!

Yet all she had been trying to do was prove one little point, just a corollary to the women's home-is-all psychology of the day, a sort of reassurance to her classmates and herself.

"All I was trying to do with that questionnaire," Betty would remember, "was to show that an education wasn't *bad* for a woman, it didn't make her *maladjusted* in her role as wife and mother." That academic learning was not, in short — as so many psychologists were then implying — an actual hindrance to femininity.

"I didn't realize it at the time," she would recall, "but I was asking the questions that were beginning to concern me." For indeed, skilled as she was in social science, and guiltily restless, Betty had designed the sort of query that took dead aim at the secrets of the heart — including her own.

"How have you changed inside?" she asked. "What do you wish you had done differently?"

And when, finally, she sat down to analyze the results for *McCall's,* she discovered that the responses raised more questions than they answered. Why was it, for example, that those of her classmates who were not active outside their homes were not especially happy at all? That they seemed, in fact, just as restless as she was?

They had written about a strange sense of emptiness — how like her own! — or a gnawing guilt, or shame, an uncertainty about who, exactly, they were: Jim's wife? Sally's mother? Betty found turmoils of indecision among these stay-at-home moms, and ennui, feelings of failure, despair, depression — even, for some, alcohol and drugs. And, most striking of all, from those isolated posts in suburbia, the uneasy sense that, because they had these feelings, they were unquestionably "neurotic."

So clearly Betty was not, as she had once thought, alone with these feelings. She was not, as she had also thought, a "freak."

But was education the villain, as all the psychologists and anthropologists and social scientists and magazine writers were more or less subtly suggesting?

That was, quite simply, a premise that the intense, verbal, thirty-six year old sometime writer, with her longings for intellectual achievement, could not accept. And as Betty read and reread and searched and analyzed, she discovered yet another piece to the puzzle.

"I found," she would remember at a later, much calmer time of her life, "that the women who seemed the strongest were not quite living this complete image of the housewife and feminine fulfillment. And that education had made them not willing to settle. . . ."

She was on to something!

Slowly but passionately, she began to write. Words and sentences began to fill the pages, words that bore no resemblance to "Millionaire's Wife," or "Two Are an Island," or anything she had ever written before. No panaceas, no hopeful methods of adjusting to the status quo, of finding total fulfillment in the home, poured forth from her pen. Instead of praising the homemaking role, she attacked the endless, monotonous, unrewarding housework it demanded. Instead of soothing her potential readers into the "feminine role" prescribed by the magazine she was writing for, she blasted the notion of vicarious living through husband and children. Rather

than touting the "togetherness" so precious to *McCall's,* she indicted the slogan as a fraud.

She had to be kidding.

The male editor of *McCall's* summarily rejected "The Togetherness Woman."

A nasty shock for Betty Friedan. Never in her life had anything she had written been turned down. Quickly, she interviewed more women, then sent the piece to *Ladies' Home Journal.* There, sure enough, it was accepted, but . . .

"They rewrote it," she would remember years later, with the anger and dismay still in her voice, "to make the opposite point! That education *did* make women maladjusted in their role as women!"

Betty refused to allow the magazine to publish the article, retrieved it, and made one last try.

Bob Stein, then editor of *Redbook,* said he would indeed be interested in a piece based on Betty's Smith class questionnaire if it was greatly expanded to include younger women, and other, more extensive data.

Betty was already talking to younger married women and they weren't changing her view of the problem at all. In fact, she was beginning to think, the situation for women who graduated from college after 1942 seemed to be even worse than it was for her classmates. Given that domestic fantasy she had already seen among members of Smith's graduating class, even fewer women in their twenties and early thirties were active outside their homes; even *more* seemed vaguely unhappy.

She hadn't yet been paid for the article, of course, and she was violating that "enough-money-to-pay-the-maid" pact with herself. But still, since Bob Stein had asked — and since she was fascinated herself — she did more interviews. She rewrote the piece, integrating the new material, and shipped it off to the editor.

Who was, he would remember, stunned.

"I liked Betty a lot," Bob Stein would recall. "She was a solid, trustworthy writer, a bit argumentative maybe, but so were most writers worth their salt. I had been looking forward to 'The Togetherness Woman,' but when I read it, I could only wonder what in God's name had come over Betty Friedan. It was a very angry piece. I didn't think that our readers would identify with it at all."

The *Redbook* editor — like all successful editors of women's magazines — was fully aware of the link binding readers to *their* magazine, the great umbilical, as some called it, the trust which, if broken, could doom both magazine and its boss. And Betty was, Bob Stein would remember, "very sensitive about her writing.... Luckily, I'd never had to reject her work before." But this?

In years to come, Bob Stein would find himself on television and radio talk shows with Betty, defending her, if only because, as he would put it, "the opposition was so impossible," but admitting, too, that he hadn't realized "that the feelings dammed up out there were so strong." At the moment, though, he could only call Betty's agent and report regretfully: "Look, we can't print this. Only the most neurotic housewife would identify with this."

And that, perhaps, might have been the end of it.

Redbook had been Betty's last hope, and in the weeks that followed, she was very depressed. She wrote nothing and dropped out of an important writer's seminar because it met the same night of the week that she served as assistant den mother for her son's Cub Scout troop. She had already chastised herself, had an asthma attack, in fact, over missing some of those Scout meetings.

One night, though, just as a prop to her ego, just to make herself feel like a professional writer again, she made the trek in from Rockland County to hear the successful author Vance Packard talk about his book *The Hidden Persuaders,* an exposé of the sinister effects of advertising. Packard had written it, he said, after an article on the subject had been turned down by every major magazine.

And then — not long afterward, as Betty would remember it — she was riding the bus into Manhattan, taking the kids to the dentist, mulling it over . . . The juggernaut women's magazines, with their fingers on the commercial pulse, had been feeding the domestic palate to ever-rising profit margins . . .

"Damn it all," Betty suddenly realized, "I was right! Somehow what I was saying had gone against the grain of the women's magazines."

And now she knew she couldn't let it go.

In some deep place in the psyche of this impatient, demanding, worrisome, dedicated, prickly, volatile woman, a quiet vision was forming. Inside, as she would later write, she felt "this calm, strange sureness, as if in tune with something larger, more important than myself that had to be taken seriously."

It would be a book. Like *The Hidden Persuaders,* "The Togetherness Woman" could be a book. She would call that editor who had wanted her to expand "The Coming Ice Age," and this time she would tell him yes. Yes, she would write a book for W. W. Norton. But just as she had said before, it would not be about someone else's work. It would be hers. Her own research, her own social science, her own accomplishment in her field.

The Togetherness Woman.

And why not? said [Norton Editor] George Brockway, who immediately saw the potential.

The affluence of the fifties had permitted — even stimulated — critical examinations of contemporary life. *The Man in the Grey Flannel Suit, The Hucksters, Executive Suite, The View from the 40th Floor* had all been big sellers. *The Togetherness Woman,* the editor thought, would make a fine parallel to the latest sharp attack on the rage for conformity, William H. Whyte's *The Organization Man.*

And this woman had the fire in the belly.

"She was incredibly ambitious," Brockway would remember. "The most ambitious woman I had ever met. She said that she didn't know what to call the subject exactly, but that it had something to do with a lack of identity, that women weren't being told . . . they aren't being allowed . . ."

Betty talked on and on at that meeting, half her thoughts, as usual, dropping off mid-sentence, her mind going even faster than her tongue. She had been interviewing so many women. She didn't know quite how to put it, but . . .

There was *something* very wrong with the way women were feeling these days.

And, over the barrage, the furtive insights, the distress, George Brockway honed in.

"Ride it," he told Betty. "You've got the idea, now ride it, ride it!"

How long did she think it would take?

Well, she said, it took her about a month to do an article, so figure a chapter a month . . .

"A year," she said. "I'll have it done in a year." Oh, and yes, she supposed [an advance of] a thousand dollars now would be okay, with the rest of the $3,000 [advance] to come in installments.

It was years later — more research was required, a mysterious block arose — before Betty even *began* to write. She worked three days a week in the Frederick Lewis Allen Room of the New York Public Library and then, when her allotted time there ran out (and the maid quit), in her favorite spot at home, the beautiful dining room with windows on the garden.

"Neither my husband nor my publisher nor anyone else who knew about it thought I would ever finish it," she would write. "When the writing of it took me over completely . . . I wrote every day on the dining room table, while the children were in school, and after they went to bed at night. (It didn't do any good to have a desk of my own; they used it for their homework anyhow.)"

She worked against patronizing jokes about a "woman's book." Against guilt. Against fear. Given the resistance she had already encountered to her views, there must be *no* holes in her argument or her documentation, *no* room for attack.

But slowly, if not steadily, the chapters, scribbled on a legal pad, began to pile up in an old china cupboard in the corner of the dining room. In them, her thesis emerged.

At rock bottom, it was economics, if not to say greed. After World War II, women had been pushed back into the home as industrialists assessed the housewife's valuable role as the prime consumer of household products. The marketing of toasters, washing machines, cosmetics, and the like was the true purpose behind the hard sell of "femininity." Educators, sociologists, psychologists — and, of course, the women's magazines, with their hunger for the advertising dollar — followed suit.

One by one, Betty took them all on, both the current crop and their historical forebears.

Freud and his "sexual solipsism": "It is a Freudian idea . . . hardened into apparent fact, that has trapped so many American women today." Freud and his Victorian bias had perpetrated the greatest sin in psychotherapy; he had infantilized women, denied them their ability to grow, cut them off from "the zest that is characteristic of human health."

[Anthropologist] Margaret Mead: "The role of Margaret Mead as the professional spokesman of femininity would have been less important if American women had taken the example of her own life, instead of listening to what she said in her books."

Contemporary educators: They induced women into the superficial comfort of the home, thus depriving them of their function in society, consigning millions of women "to spend their days at work an eight-year-old could do."

As for the women's magazines, which offered that fraudulent home-as-religion editorial content: "I helped create this image. I have watched American women for fifteen years try to conform to it. But I can no longer deny its terrible implications. It is not a harmless image. There may be no psychological terms for the harm it is doing."

And, of course, "togetherness": "The big lie . . . the end of the road . . . where the woman has no independent self to hide even in guilt; she exists only for and through her husband and children."

It was this vicarious existence that caused educations to "fester," caused housewife's fatigue, ennui, depression. Not neurosis. It was society — not women — that was sick!

Like Lundberg and Farnham, Betty resurrected earlier feminists, but instead of damning them as sick souls, she sang their praises as heroines. Mary Wollstonecraft, Margaret Fuller, Elizabeth Cady Stanton, Lucy Stone, Susan B. Anthony. Anatomy, she agreed, with a somewhat cursory bow to Simone de Beauvoir's evocative phrasing in *The Second Sex,* is not destiny. Women were not simply their biology. They also had *minds.* And, "as if waking from a coma," they were beginning to ask, "Where am I? What am I doing here?"

She answered the hyperbole of Lundberg and Farnham with some of her own. The isolated suburban home, she wrote, was a "comfortable concentration camp," the women trapped within them cut off, like prisoners, from past adult interests and their own identities. It was a new neurosis, this modern ache, and you could read it in the hundreds of interviews and psychological tests she had accumulated — among them, one test that must have been reassuring, since it suggested that "the high-dominance woman was more psychologically free" than one who was "timid, shy, modest, neat, tactful, quiet, introverted, retiring, more feminine, more conventional." And perhaps, Betty herself speculated, only an "ugly duckling adolescence" or an unhappy marriage could fuel the ambition to resist the deadening, conformist pressure.

For "the problem lay buried, unspoken, for many years in the minds of American women." It was a problem, she wrote, "that had no name," a problem that was caused by the pervasive social pressure relegating women to the four walls of their homes, a pressure whose weapon was an image: "the feminine mystique."

Five years from the time Betty had signed the

contract, four years late, *The Feminine Mystique* was published.

It was February 1963, and the New York newspapers, including the *Times,* were on strike. With no review in the *Times,* the chances that a book — even this thunderous polemic — would reach a substantial public were practically nil. And there was plenty of competition. Morton Hunt had just published a gentle, affectionate paean to women's role *outside* as well as in the home. His book was called *Her Infinite Variety,* and it was moving off the bookstore shelves at a frighteningly rapid pace.

The photographer has captured Betty Friedan in a moment of profound weariness. In the years after the publication of The Feminine Mystique, *Friedan worked zealously for women's rights: she organized demonstrations, lobbied for antidiscrimination legislation, and struggled to hold the women's movement together in the face of internal dissension. "In truth, she paid a high personal price for her cause." (Michael Ginsburg/Magnum Photos)*

Betty was beside herself. And so, for that matter, was Carl. Never had the state of their marriage been worse, never stormier than during the last year she was writing, when, Carl would complain to friends, he would come home from work and "that bitch," instead of cooking dinner, was writing away at the dining-room table. Betty, friends would whisper, was writing out the problems of her marriage, writing a book instead of leaving Carl. His one-man advertising and public relations firm was far from a booming success, and now this. Who would even hear of *The Feminine Mystique,* let alone buy it? Where, after all these years, was the payoff?

"Betty would come in with ideas to promote the book," George Brockway would recall. "You could tell Carl was behind them, saying, 'Tell 'em to do this, tell 'em to do that.'

"One day she told me that Carl wanted to know what could be done to make *The Feminine Mystique* as big a seller as *Gifts from the Sea."* (This popular book was written by Anne Morrow Lindbergh, the wife of the heroic aviator.)

"'Tell Carl,' I told her, 'that he can fly the Atlantic solo.'"

Irascible Carl, George would call him — the low-key editor being far from charmed by what he regarded as Carl Friedan's "sharp and nasty" tongue.

But Betty thought her husband knew his business. She would always remember that it was Carl who had persuaded Norton to hire a publicist. Eventually, in fact, she would switch to another publishing house, leaving Brockway entirely.

"I remember him pleading with me," Betty would tell a reporter, "and I remember looking him right in the eye and saying, 'George, you made me feel Jewish for trying to sell that book. Go fuck yourself.'"

But, with the help of the publicist, excerpts from the book began to appear, and articles ran in major news magazines about Betty as an "angry battler for her sex." She began bouncing around the country for speaking engagements, crusaded enthusiastically on radio and that potent new vehicle, the television talk show.

After one of these appearances — outside Rockefeller Center — she met another author who had just taped a show herself. She was just about Betty's age, a former copywriter who had performed the remarkable feat of hitting the nonfiction best-seller list the year before.

The woman was Helen Gurley Brown, and her book, *Sex and the Single Girl,* aimed, obviously, at the burgeoning singles market, had actually set down in print the startling notion that it was perfectly all right to have "an affair." Even with a married man.

For those who would, in retrospect, regard the sexual revolution as either intrinsic to or actually the wellspring of the Golden Age of Feminism, it would be hard to ignore the pioneering role of Helen Brown. Most feminists, however, would manage to do just that.

It was a matter, in part, of philosophy. In even greater part, perhaps, of style.

Sex and the Single Girl was a typical how-to of the women's magazine genre. It offered advice on decorating your apartment, diet, clothes, and money — not, however, for the purpose of hooking a man into marriage, but for getting him into your bed.

Helen Brown didn't protest much of anything — least of all society's ills. She only wrote about, as she herself insisted, what was already going on anyhow. Single women having sex with men, married or not. She simply made them feel better about doing it. Like the women's magazines, and in a similarly blithe, not to say giddy style, she was reassuring and helpful. The major difference — the shocker — was that while the women's magazines were still righteously committed to the double standard, continually warning their readers of the dire consequences of sex without marriage, Helen Gurley Brown wrote that this was perfectly okay. "Nice single girls *do* have affairs and they don't necessarily die of them." *Sex and the Single Girl* — aimed, unlike underground erotica, at a mass audience — was undoubtedly something of a relief.

The single life the book touted was one of supreme independence, satisfying work, fashion and success and money — a life, in short, that most married women were bound to envy. The single woman was sexy, Helen had written, "because she lives by her wits." She was not "a parasite, a dependent, a scrounger, a sponger or a bum." And when, in 1965, Helen would take over the Hearst Corporation's ailing *Cosmopolitan,* the appeal of that view, and the skill of its pragmatic, meticulous editor, would eventually triple the magazine's circulation.

On television, Helen was, from the beginning, flirtatious, supremely tactful, frankly manipulative, an open disciple of male-flattering femininity. "Helen Gurley Girly," some viewers called her. She was a former secretary who had never gone to college and didn't plan to, a "girl" for whom *work* was the given, the man in one's life the pleasure to be sought. She had written her book at the suggestion of her husband, movie producer David Brown, and she had no hesitation about saying so.

And yet, in spite of Helen's flirtatiousness, and the focus on sex, which, Betty had written, was totally irrelevant, actually damaging to women's struggle for independence, the two women liked each other.

"We talked about business, promotion, all that," Helen would remember. "We became friends ... and we've been friends ever since." They differed, but, in spite of her passionate nature, Betty would often differ with someone and still remain a loyal friend.

Unlike Helen Brown, however, Betty wasn't "cool"; her personality was not tailor-made for television. Often, in impatient, enthusiastic pursuit of an idea, she would talk so fast that hardly anyone could understand her. Or leave sentences dangling. Or angrily demand time. Her publicist would remember her screaming at hostess Virginia Graham on "Girl Talk": "If you don't let me have my say, I'm going to say orgasm ten times."

But Betty had been provoked.

Virginia Graham, Betty would one day explain, had coaxed the camera: "Girls, how many of us really need bylines? What better thing can we do with our lives than to do the dishes for those we love?"

"Well, I knew that her agent fought for every foot of the size of her byline on the television screen, and I wondered when the last time was she'd done the dishes for someone she loved. I turned to the camera and said, 'Women, don't listen to her. She needs you out there doing the dishes, or she wouldn't have the captive audience for this television program, whose byline she evidently doesn't want you to compete for.'"

Betty never was, never would be, any talk show host's favorite guest. She was confrontational, often tactless, and not — by any standard — a TV beauty.

But neither was she a phony. And there was something about this woman, who looked like everyone's ... Aunt Minnie, something about what she proclaimed, in her hell-for-leather style, that made hundreds of viewers attend.

Scores of Americans, of course, including many women, were outraged. They could scarcely believe what they were hearing. A woman's career could be as important as a man's? A woman should go out in the world and compete with men? ...

One Smith alumna, writing in *Reader's Digest* about "the feminine *mistake,*" saluted the housewife's "small acts of domesticity" with the good Scout cheer: "Well, sure! That's what we signed up for!" And when the *New York Times* got around to reviewing the book — in a short blurb under "Digest" — Lucy Freeman, who had written a bestseller on her own conquest of mental illness, zapped it as "superficial. . . . The fault, dear Mrs. Friedan, is not in our culture, but in ourselves."

"Where," wailed a letter writer in *Commonweal* magazine, "are all these women to go, having fled their homes? And *what* are they to do?"

In the midst of it all, Betty brought Carl and the kids back to Peoria for her twenty-fifth high school reunion. There, instead of praise, she found herself sitting alone at the banquet table. She stayed with a friend, and the next morning found the tree outside her door festooned with toilet paper.

Yet the sales of *The Feminine Mystique* were beginning to climb, and there was no stopping Betty now. Especially since hundreds of letters, expressing enormous gratitude, were starting to pour in. Letters from women who said they had no idea, until they read her book, that anyone else had such strange feelings. They had felt, they wrote, like sexual freaks, or like "appliances," insecure in their dependence, unable, much longer, to keep up the "act" of selflessness. She had given them courage, they wrote, to go back to school, to begin careers.

For threaded through the social criticism of *The Feminine Mystique* was also a message of Emersonian self-reliance and responsibility. This message was not, at bottom, altogether unlike Helen Brown's, but it was one that would set Betty at odds with many women who might have been her allies. Since, as Betty wrote, the women she was addressing were not those beset by dire poverty or disease, they were not, therefore, *completely* at the mercy of an unjust society.

"In the last analysis," Betty had written, "millions of able women in this free land choose themselves not to use the door education could have opened for them. The choice — and the responsibility — for the race back [to the] home was finally their own."

The Feminine Mystique *reached women very much like Friedan herself: white, educated wives and mothers mainly of the middle class. "Inspired and validated by finding their own truth presented as truth," as writer Marilyn French has said, "many of them changed their lives, returning to school, entering the work force." The Feminine Mystique also aroused professional and single women, both white and African American, for it exposed the attitudes and practices that blocked their own advancement. Along with Helen Gurley Brown and Gloria Steinem, Friedan*

helped liberate younger women, too, especially on the college campuses. Had Friedan done nothing more than write her book, she would be historically significant.

But for her, The Feminine Mystique *was only the beginning. Thrust into national prominence as the voice of the new American woman, Friedan initiated the "second wave" of organized feminism, the first wave having ended with women's suffrage. In 1966, with the help of Dr. Kay Clarenbach, a Wisconsin women's leader, Friedan founded and became first president of the National Organization for Women (NOW), the first mainstream women's organization and the most successful in history. "It is a mystery," Betty would say later, "the whole thing — why it happened, how it started. What gave any of us the courage to make that leap?" Under NOW's banners, the new women's movement sought equality for women through political means, for the 1960s civil rights movement had shown Friedan and her colleagues how effective antidiscrimination legislation could be. Employing the civil rights methods of picket lines, marches, political pressure, and media exposure, NOW set out to gain full citizenship for women: it challenged federal guidelines that sanctioned discrimination against them in employment, initiated lawsuits against companies refusing to hire women in positions traditionally occupied by men, sought legal abortion, and campaigned for the Equal Rights Amendment (ERA), which had languished since 1923. NOW helped to bring about a body of laws and rulings that prohibited sexual discrimination in education and in hiring and promotion; NOW was also instrumental in gaining congressional approval of the Equal Rights Amendment. In the 1980s, however, the ERA went down to defeat when it failed to be ratified by three fourths of the states. Even so, NOW was strong enough by 1984 to pressure the Democratic presidential candidate into selecting a woman as his running mate.*

Meanwhile, the women's movement had splintered into various dissenting groups; one of them even advocated lesbianism as the ultimate expression of feminism and demanded that NOW affirm this by publicly avowing, "We are all lesbians." This shocked Friedan, who with other NOW leaders argued that such a stance would alienate men and would be a tactical blunder. Feminism, she said, regarded men not as eternal foes but also as victims of a repressive, dehumanizing society.

Struggling to hold the movement together wore Friedan out. In truth, she had paid a high personal price for her cause: she had lectured and traveled everywhere in its behalf, living out of suitcases in lonely motel rooms; she had missed her children fiercely and the warmth and intimacy of family life. Too, her marriage to Carl had failed — he had beaten her more than once. In 1970, divorced and exhausted, she resigned as NOW president and turned to writing, lecturing, and teaching. She remained faithful to feminism's larger vision, a vision of "human wholeness" that liberated men as well as women. It did so by repudiating the laws and customs that prevented men from expressing their own nurturing qualities and caused them to deny women their birthright as Americans — an equal opportunity to better themselves, to realize their full potential as their talent and industry allowed.

QUESTIONS TO CONSIDER

1   Describe the American cultural ideal of womanhood in the 1950s. What does Marcia Cohen think were some of the sources of our culture's "home-is-woman's-all" psychology? Explain the role that consumerism, the press, and the American educational system played in perpetuating prevailing assumptions about women. Was anyone rebelling against all this conformity?

2   Betty Friedan did not deliberately set out to start a feminist revolution. Describe the steps she took in raising her own consciousness and the series of revelations and reversals that led her to write *The Feminine Mystique.*

3   *The Feminine Mystique* was not a political book, but just a few years after its publication Friedan found herself at the head of a reform movement and president of NOW. At what point did the yearning for self-awareness and self-fulfillment that Friedan aroused in American women become transformed into political activity? Why did women feel they needed a political movement to achieve personal gains?

4   Discuss the basic thesis of *The Feminine Mystique.* Whose ideas did Betty Friedan attack? Specifically, how did she feel about Sigmund Freud and Margaret Mead? About "togetherness"? About suburbia? About women's magazines? How did Friedan's ideas differ from those of Helen Gurley Brown? What underlying message did the two writers have in common? Did Friedan feel the sexual revolution was compatible with the new feminism?

5   Friedan's book was addressed to educated, white, upper- and middle-class women. She herself was aware that she had not tackled the problems of uneducated or poor or African American or immigrant women. Is it possible to apply all or part of Friedan's analysis to this second group? What additional complications might issues of race and social class bring to women's lives?

6   What strides has feminism made since the publication of *The Feminine Mystique?* Has true equality been achieved? What do you see as the future of the historic "women's rights" movement as we enter the last years of the twentieth century?

Heyday of the Counterculture

ALLEN J. MATUSOW

The 1960s and early 1970s were times of profound change in fashion, music, and morals on both sides of the Atlantic. In the United States, a "counterculture" revolt against established values was part of a general rebellion against the unity and conformity that had characterized American life since the Second World War and the Eisenhower years. The civil rights movement was the first major postwar assault on the old American ways, and African Americans' struggle in turn inspired many other protest movements — by rebellious youth, the New Left, Chicanos, American Indians, feminists, and groups seeking to legitimize homosexuality and to legalize drugs and abortion.

The counterculture — or "hippie culture" — did not emerge suddenly in the 1960s. As Rice University historian Allen Matusow points out, it owed much to the beat generation of the 1950s, and its roots stretched back to the jazz era of the 1920s and the black hipster of the Depression era. Although Matusow does not say so, one could argue that the counterculture rebellion was comparable to the youth rebellion of the twenties. For the Charleston, the saxophone, jazz, bobbed hair, short skirts, and gin and cigarettes — weapons of revolt during the 1920s — were forerunners of the twist, the electric guitar, rock 'n' roll, long hair, miniskirts, and the drugs that characterized the counterculture revolt of the 1960s. Freudian psychology, which stimulated the youth rebellion of the twenties, also figured in the hippie counterculture in a reconstructed form. While Matusow does not hazard comparisons between the two decades, he describes the heroes and happenings of the counterculture in a spirited, insightful narrative, excerpted from his The Unraveling of America (1984), perhaps the best history of the sixties yet written. You will find a gallery of fascinating characters here, from Norman O. Brown, the intellectual prophet of the counterculture, and Timothy Leary, proselytizer of LSD and "the psychedelic revolution," to Allen Ginsberg, Ken Kesey and the Merry Pranksters, Bob Dylan, the Beatles, and the Hell's Angels, California's raunchy, violent motorcycle gang, which maintained "an uneasy alliance" with the counterculture rebels. Matusow concludes that while the hippie movement proved ephemeral, it was symptomatic of a culturewide revolt against the Protestant ethic, traditional institutions, and "the liberal values" that had long sustained American society.

Rebellious and outrageous though they often were, the youth of the 1960s were also passionately idealistic. This was the same younger generation that joined John F. Kennedy's Peace Corps and went off to live and work in countries from South America to the Far East. This was also the generation that responded to the eloquence of Martin Luther King Jr. and marched by the thousands in the civil rights movement; young people also filled up the ranks of the peace movement and helped persuade King himself to take a public stand against the war in Vietnam. Thus they contributed to the dismantling of segregation in the South and to the end of the divisive war in Asia. These facts should be kept in mind as you ride with Matusow on a rollicking trip through the counterculture scene.

GLOSSARY

BEATLES Irreverent British rock 'n' roll band that brought Beatlemania to America; initially, the Beatles mocked society, then, inspired by Bob Dylan, they started writing songs for "the cultural opposition."

BEATS Cultural rebels of the 1950s who were "profoundly alienated from dominant American values"; the "beat generation" included novelist Jack Kerouac (*On the Road*) and poet Allen Ginsberg ("Howl").

BROWN, NORMAN O. Classical scholar whose *Life Against Death* (1959) reconstructed Freud, arguing that there was no "instinctual dualism" — the sexual instinct versus the death instinct — inherent in human beings; people, he argued, could attain "eternal bodily pleasure," and he created "the Dionysian ego," which anticipated the counterculture impulse of the sixties — the search for bodily and mystic ecstasies through drugs, sex, and rock 'n' roll.

DIONYSIAN EGO The "new ego" created by Brown, "a body ego . . . overflowing with love, knowing no limits, affirming life, reuniting male and female, Self and Other, life and death."

DYLAN, BOB The greatest folk-rock composer of the sixties; he made rock 'n' roll an expression of "cultural radicalism"; after Dylan, rock both shaped and articulated the counterculture.

EROS Freud's term for the sexual instinct.

GRATEFUL DEAD, THE The "quintessential" hippie band of San Francisco, which played before packed houses of "hopelessly stoned" counterculture adherents.

HIPSTER The "hedonistic, sensual, and sexually uninhibited" young African American man of the 1930s; the hipster talked jive, wore a zoot suit, and showed open contempt for the white world; in 1945, a "white hipster" — Herbert Huncke — brought the "hip" underground to the rebel writers and intellectuals who would later constitute the beat generation.

KESEY, KEN   Novelist who created "the psychedelic style"; he and his Merry Pranksters established a drug commune near San Francisco, wore "weirdo" costumes and Day-Glo paint, and rode about in a hippie school bus rigged with a tape player and loudspeakers.

LEARY, TIMOTHY   Former Harvard psychologist who dropped out and spread "the psychedelic revolution," proclaiming the mystic and sensual ecstasies attainable through marijuana and LSD.

LSD   Lysergic acid diethylamide, first developed as a respiratory stimulant; although Congress outlawed it, this powerful hallucinogenic drug, nicknamed "acid," fueled the hippie revolution throughout the sixties.

PRESLEY, ELVIS   Led the rock 'n' roll revolution of the 1950s, which produced "a generation of cultural subversives"; although he was not the first rock 'n' roll singer, as Jimmy Guterman has noted, Presley "was the first performer to unite and then unleash all its sundry forces," earning him his legendary status as "the king of rock."

ROCK 'N' ROLL   A musical hybrid that fused black rhythm and blues with white country or hillbilly styles; "protest music" from the start, rock launched a musical revolution in the 1950s that profoundly altered American popular culture.

THANATOS   Freud's term for the death instinct.

☆

I

America discovered hippies at the world's first Human Be-In, Golden Gate Park, San Francisco, January 14, 1967. The occasion was something special, even in a Bay Area underground long accustomed to spectacle. Political activists from Berkeley mingled with dropouts from Haight-Ashbury, ending their feud and initiating a "new epoch" in the history of man. "In unity we shall shower the country with waves of ecstasy and purification," sponsors of the Be-In prophesied. "Fear will be washed away; ignorance will be exposed to sunlight; profits and empire will lie drying on deserted beaches." Preparations for the Be-In were casual but appropriate. A hippie newspaper called the *Oracle* invited everyone "to bring costumes, blankets, bells, flags, symbols, cymbals, drums, beads, feathers, flowers." A local painter named Michael Bowen arranged with his guru in Mexico to exchange weather for the day. The Hell's Angels motorcycle gang agreed to guard the electronic equipment of the rock bands, which would play this gig for free. And poets Allen Ginsberg and Gary Snyder arrived two hours early to perform a "purificatory circumambulation" of the field, a ritual they had observed in 1963 in Sarnath, India, to drive out demons.

By early afternoon a crowd estimated at twenty thousand gathered in the park to enjoy the unseasonably warm sun and commune with the hip notables on the makeshift stage. Timothy Leary was there, dressed in white and wearing flowers in his

Excerpts from "Rise and Fall of a Counterculture" from *The Unraveling of America: A History of Liberalism in the 1960's* by Allen J. Matusow. Copyright © 1984 by Allen J. Matusow. Reprinted by permission of HarperCollins Publishers, Inc. Fourteen lines from "Howl" from *Collected Poems 1947–1980* by Allen Ginsberg. Copyright © 1995 by Allen Ginsberg. Reprinted by permission of HarperCollins Publishers, Inc.

hair. "Turn on to the scene, tune in to what is happening, and drop out — of high school, college, grad school, junior executive — and follow me, the hard way," said Leary, reciting his famous commercial for the synthetic hallucinogen LSD. Ginsberg, in a white Khader suit and blue rubber sandals, chanted a Buddhist mantra as Snyder blew a conchshell he had obtained in Kyoto while studying Zen Buddhism. "We are primitives of an unknown culture . . ." Snyder had said on the eve of the Be-In, "with new ethics and new states of mind." Music for the occasion was acid rock, performed by Quicksilver Messenger Service, Jefferson Airplane, and the Grateful Dead. Already an underground legend, the Dead had played Ken Kesey's notorious "acid tests," which had done so much to spread LSD and the psyche-

delic style throughout California a year or so before. Representing the new left was Jerry Rubin, released that very morning from jail, but not yet hip enough for this occasion. "Tune-In — Drop-Out — Take-Over," Rubin had said at a press conference prior to the event. But few at the Be-In were in a mood (or condition) to take over anything.

The real show was the crowd. "The costumes were a designer's dream," wrote music critic Ralph Gleason in the San Francisco *Chronicle,* "a wild polyglot mixture of Mod, Palladin, Ringling Brothers, Cochise, and Hells Angels' Formal." Bells tinkled, balloons floated, people on the grass played harmonicas, guitars, recorders, flutes. Beautiful girls handed out sticks of incense. A young man in a paisley parachute drifted from the sky, though no plane was in

Hippies of the sixties, like those shown here, sought "a life of Dionysian ecstasy" in which to synchronize themselves with the *cosmos. (Henri Cartier-Bresson/Magnum)*

sight. An old man gave away his poems. A mysterious group called the Diggers had obtained seventy-five turkeys from a drug chemist named Owsley and supplied sandwiches, homemade bread, and oranges, free, to anyone who was hungry. When a sulfur bomb exploded under the stage, people on the grass thought it was a large cloud of yellow incense and broke into appreciative applause. Finally, after poets Michael McClure, Lenore Kandell, Snyder and Ginsberg read in the silent presence of Zen Master Suzuki Roshi who was seated on the stage, and the hours of tripping, dancing, and hugging had wound down, Ginsberg turned toward the setting sun, led a chant "om gri maitreya" (Salutations to Buddha of Futurity), and asked the people to practice "a little kitchen Yoga" by picking up their trash. Officials said that no gathering had left so little litter in the park in a generation.

Newsweek was on hand to photograph the Be-In in gorgeous color and report that "it was a love feast, a psychedelic picnic, a hippie happening." Images of hip quickly began to seep into the public consciousness, provoking intense curiosity and endless analysis in the straight world. Most of the pop sociology deserved the rebuke of Bob Dylan's "Ballad of a Thin Man": "Something is happening here but you don't know what it is. Do you, Mr. Jones?" Yet understanding was imperative, for the hippie impulse that was spreading through a generation of the young challenged the traditional values of bourgeois culture, values still underpinning the liberal movement of the 1960s — reason, progress, order, achievement, social responsibility. Hippies mocked liberal politicians, scorned efforts to repair the social order, and repudiated bourgeois society. In so doing, they became cultural radicals opposed to established authority. Among the movements arrayed against him toward the end of his tenure, none baffled Lyndon Johnson more than these hippies. Somehow, in the name of liberation, they rejected everything he stood for, including his strenuous efforts to liberate the poor and the black. Clearly, liberation meant something different to liberals like him from what it meant to radicals like them.

II

Few hippies read much, but those who did found their purpose strikingly described and anticipated in the strange books of Norman O. Brown. A classical scholar at Wesleyan University, whose underground explorations began in middle age and never strayed beyond the library, Brown published a book in 1959 called *Life Against Death*. A manifesto of cultural radicalism, this book established Brown as a prophet of the counterculture and its preeminent intellectual. Those seeking the meaning of the hippie movement could do no better than begin with him.

Brown was a Freudian who reshaped the ideas of the master to provide a happy ending; no mean feat, given Freud's pessimism. Man was unhappy, Freud argued, because his instincts were repressed. The realm of instinct was the id, wherein resided emotion, desire — above all, Eros, the sexual instinct, which sought bodily pleasure. But to accomplish the survival of the individual, Eros had to be controlled. Thus in childhood there emerged from the id the ego, which mediated between the individual and the outside world and attempted to repress the raging instincts. Eros could not be repressed entirely, however, and the ego was forced to admit it into consciousness — transformed, sublimated, desexualized. Sublimated Eros provided the energy for work, art, and culture. Hence the irony and tragedy of man: he can know happiness only in gratifying his instinctual need for bodily pleasure; but to preserve life and create civilization, that need must be denied. Freud had still other grounds for pessimism. In the id he had discovered, alongside Eros and warring against it, a second instinct, which he called the death instinct, or Thanatos. As civilization advances, Eros weakens, and the death instinct gains force. Directed outward,

Thanatos becomes aggression, threatening other men with harm and civilization with extinction. "Men have gained control over the forces of nature to such an extent," Freud concluded, "that with their help they would have no difficulty in exterminating one another to the last man."

Against Freud, Brown intended to show that man could achieve his infantile dream of eternal bodily pleasure. Brown began his reconstruction of Freud by denying that there existed an instinctual dualism — life and death, Eros *vs*. Thanatos — rooted in biology. The pre-Oedipal infant at his mother's breast experiences "union of the self with a whole world of love and pleasure." In this blissful state there are no dualism, no self and other, no subject-object, no life against death, only timeless experience of being one with the world, only instinctual fusion and undifferentiated unity. Bliss ends when the infant experiences separation from the mother, producing anxiety, a sense of loss, and fear of death. According to Brown's argument, it is the infant's attempt to flee death that initiates instinctual de-fusion. Eros emerges, seeking actively to reunite with the mother, the source of bodily pleasure; Thanatos emerges, seeking the peace known at her breast. The ensuing sublimations of the instincts produce the spiritual life of man and propel history, but they cannot make man happy. The flight from death, then, is the critical event in psychic life, condemning man to sickness and removing him from nature. Brown's prescription for health was simple: If man can accept death, he can accept life, achieve instinctual re-fusion, abolish repression, and find happiness through "the resurrection of the body."

There was much in *Life Against Death* that anticipated and expressed the hippie impulse. Like the hippies, Brown was resolutely nonpolitical. Man was the animal who repressed himself; his salvation lay not in social reorganization but in self-reconstruction. Like the hippies, Brown affirmed instinctual freedom against the rational, disciplined, puritanic life that had been the life of man in Western civiliza-

tion. Like the hippies, Brown was in revolt against civilized sex — exclusively genital, exclusively heterosexual, exclusively monogamous — affirming instead pan-sexualism, "polymorphous perversity," the union of many bodies: in short, erotic life based on the pre-Oedipal Eden. And finally Brown gave definition to the cultural project on which the hippies were soon to embark. Rejecting descent into the id as mere regression, Brown wished to make the unconscious conscious, incorporate the content of the id into the ego — to create, in other words, a new ego, a body ego, which Brown called the "Dionysian ego," overflowing with love, knowing no limits, affirming life. "Dionysus reunifies male and female, Self and Other, life and death," Brown wrote. The creation of the Dionysian ego, the ego in service of liberated Eros — this was a project millions of mothers would soon understand implicitly and fear with good reason. . . .

If Brown's books forecast the hippie projects — Dionysian ecstasies, bodily and mystic — the Human Be-In proclaimed the existence of a hippie culture, or counterculture, committed to realizing those projects through drugs, sex, and rock and roll. But just as Brown did not invent the projects, hippies did not invent their culture from scratch. Hip explorers in the realm of the Dionysian had spent a generation developing rituals and a life style from which hippies freely borrowed. Indeed, without pioneers to point the way, hippies might never have emerged to fascinate and outrage America.

☆

III

The history of hip began with the black hipsters of the 1930s. Black folk had always constituted something of a counterculture in America, representing, at least in the white imagination, pure id. Migrating into northern ghettos after World War I, young black men used their new freedom to improvise a new variation on black deviance — the hipster — who was not only hedonistic, sensual, and sexually uninhibited, but openly contemptuous of the white world that continued to exclude him. The language that hipsters invented on Harlem street corners was jive, an action language honed in verbal duels and inaccessible to most whites. Some jive words that became part of the permanent hip lexicon were *cat, solid, chick, Big Apple, square, tea, gas, dip, flip. Ofay,* the jive word for white, meant foe in pig Latin. The hipster costume was the zoot suit, designed, as hip garb always would be, to defy and outrage conventional taste. For kicks, the hipster smoked marijuana, which heightened his sense of immediacy and helped him soar above his mean surroundings. The only bigger kick was sex.

Vital to the hipster experience was the uninhibited black music called jazz. In 1922 a writer in the *Atlantic Monthly* described jazz as the result of "an unloosing of instincts that nature wisely has taught us to hold in check, but which, every now and then, for cryptic reasons, are allowed to break the bonds of civilization." Indeed, Louis Armstrong, playing his "hot," sensual, raunchy improvisations on trumpet, was the first hipster hero. As jazz changed, the hipster persona changed with it. In the early 1940s a group of rebel black jazzmen, hostile to the commercialization of the big bands, created bebop. Bebop relied on small groups and improvisation, as before, but the sound was cool, the rhythm variable, the volume low, and the technical virtuosity of its leading performers legend. The genius of bebop was Charlie "The Bird" Parker, who lived at "the level of total spontaneity," whether he was playing alto sax or getting kicks from booze, sex, or heroin. By the mid-1940s, partly because of heroin, hot was out and cool was in. Hipster dress had become more conservative; noise and brash behavior, a breach of taste; detachment, a required pose. By then, too, the hipster had ceased to be a type restricted to blacks only. In New York and other big cities, some disaffiliates among the white young found the hipster

persona so expressive of their own alienation that they adopted it as their own. Thus was born, in Norman Mailer's phrase, "the white Negro," living outside the law for sex, pot, jazz, kicks — in short, for Dionysian ecstasy.

Herbert Huncke was a white hipster who first heard the language and the music on Chicago's South Side in the thirties. Before moving to New York before World War II, he had become a junkie, a habitué of the underworld, and a petty criminal so notorious that the police would name him the Creep and bar him from Times Square. An experimenter with forbidden experience, Huncke took drugs to derange the senses and expand consciousness, and he provided rich source material for Dr. Alfred Kinsey's study of American sexual mores. When wearied of the streets, he sought refuge in a detachment so complete that he was beyond feeling. Huncke had a word to describe his weariness. He said he was "beat."

One day in 1945 Huncke encountered William Burroughs, not yet a famous writer, trying to get rid of a sawed-off shotgun and some morphine. Through Burroughs, Huncke met Allen Ginsberg, Jack Kerouac, John Clellon Holmes, and others in a circle of rebel writers and intellectuals who later became known as the beat generation. Living on the fringes of Columbia University as students or dropouts, the beats engaged in obscure resistance to the "Syndrome of Shutdown" (Ginsberg's later phrase) — the movement toward a totalitarian America based on mass consumption and mass acquiescence. They were rebels too against the official culture purveyed in academic classrooms and celebrated in the lifeless literary quarterlies. In reaction they created their literature from raw experience, which they consumed with reckless and undiscriminating abandon. When Herbert Huncke introduced the proto-beats to the hipster underground, its jive, jazz, drugs, and unconventional sex, they plunged right in. Ginsberg wrote, "As far as I know the ethos of what's charmingly Hip, and the first pronunciation of the word itself to my fellow ears first came

consciously from Huncke's lips; and the first information and ritual of the emergent hip subculture
passed through Huncke's person."

What the beats added to hip was the mystic quest.
In the summer of 1948, living alone in East Harlem
and grieving for his departed lover Neal Cassady,
Allen Ginsberg had the defining experience of his
life. As he lay in bed gazing at tenement roofs with a
book of William Blake's *Songs of Innocence* before
him, he heard the deep voice of the poet himself
reciting the "Sunflower," and knew it was the voice
of God. "Looking out the window, . . ." Ginsberg
remembered, "suddenly it seemed that I saw into the
depths of the universe, by looking simply into the
ancient sky." Ginsberg had auditory experience of
other poems that evening, and there were other visions in the days that followed, until, a week later,
standing in the athletic field at Columbia, Ginsberg
invoked the spirit and experienced the cosmos as
monster. "The sky was not a blue hand anymore but
like a hand of death coming down on me." It was
years before Ginsberg would seek that void again,
but in the meantime he did not forget those moments when the ego had overflowed the bounds of
the self and illumination had been his. A year later
Huncke moved in with Ginsberg, thoughtfully
stashing his stolen goods elsewhere. Arrested as an
accessory, Ginsberg was committed and stayed eight
months in the Columbia-affiliated New York Psychiatric Institute.

After graduating from Columbia in 1949, Ginsberg worked at straight jobs and tried to master his
real vocation, which was poetry. In 1954, forsaking
New York, he moved to San Francisco to visit Cassady. There a brilliant circle of poets had gathered
around Lawrence Ferlinghetti's City Lights Book
Store in a neighborhood called North Beach. North
Beach provided the cultural soil where the beat seed,
originally planted in New York, took root and flow-
ered. With its narrow streets, high walls, and cheap
houses overlooking the bay, North Beach reminded
Gary Snyder of "ancient terraced fertile crescent

pueblos." The beats were hipsters a decade later, explorers in the realm of the Dionysian, searching for
ecstasies, bodily and mystic.

For Ginsberg San Francisco was liberation. He
found a psychiatrist who told him to do what he
wanted, namely write poetry and love men; and he
met his "life long sex-soul union" in Peter Orlovsky.
Maturing rapidly, Ginsberg also found his authentic
voice as a poet. One weekend in 1955 he stayed in
his apartment and wrote a poem, with little revision,
which one part of him believed he could not publish
out of respect for his father and another part believed
would change America. In September, at an artists'
co-op called the Six Gallery, with his friend Jack
Kerouac there to pass around the jug and shout encouragement, Ginsberg read his astounding "Howl."
Taking as its subject the life of the poet and his beat
friends, "Howl" became a manifesto for the scattered
disaffiliates of fifties America.

> I saw the best minds of my generation destroyed
>   by madness, starving hysterical naked,
> dragging themselves through the negro streets at
>   dawn looking for an angry fix,
> angelheaded hipsters burning for the ancient
>   heavenly connection to the starry dynamo in the
>   machinery of night
> who poverty and tatters and hollow-eyed and high
>   sat up smoking in the supernatural darkness of
>   cold-water flats floating across the tops of cities
>   contemplating jazz
> who bared their brains to Heaven under the El and
>   saw Mohammedan angels staggering on tenement
>   roofs illuminated. . . .

When the authorities brought Ferlinghetti to trial for
publishing "Howl," on the grounds of obscenity, the
poem attained more than literary celebrity. "Howl"
sold 100,000 copies in ten years, making it perhaps
the most popular serious poem of the century. . . .

Jack Kerouac, the beat writer who shared so many
of Ginsberg's adventures, also shared his mystic

Beat poet Allen Ginsberg gives a poetry reading at Indiana University in 1966, while his "sex-soul" companion, Peter Orlovsky (wearing glasses), looks on. Ginsberg's poem "Howl" was the manifesto "for the scattered disaffiliates of fifties America" and a source of inspiration for hippies of the sixties. (AP/Wide World Photos)

quest. Kerouac had gone to Columbia to play football but rebelled against the discipline, deciding instead to write novels and probe the cultural underground. Recalling the 1940s, he wrote, "Anyway, the hipsters, whose music was bop, they looked like criminals but they kept talking about the same things I liked, long outlines of personal experience and vision, nightlong confessions full of hope that became illicit and repressed by War.... And so Huncke appeared to us and said, 'I'm beat' with radiant light shining out of his despairing eyes ... a word perhaps brought from some midwest carnival or junk cafeteria. It was a new language, actually spade (Negro) jargon but you soon learned it."

Kerouac made his artistic breakthrough when he decided to write a semi-fictional account of his road experiences with Neal Cassady. Some people might have regarded Cassady as a bum. Reared on the streets of Denver by his wino father, in and out of jails mostly for stealing cars, Cassady possessed so much energy and lived so completely in the moment that the beat circle could not resist him. In April

373

1951 Kerouac fed a roll of teletype paper into a typewriter and let tales of Cassady flow spontaneously from his mind, in one paragraph 120 feet long. It took three weeks to write *On the Road,* six years to get it published.

On the Road portrayed Kerouac, Cassady, Ginsberg, and their hipster friends speeding across the continent in the late forties, consuming pot, jazz, and sex, envying the Negro his spontaneity, his soul, his cool. Cassady (Dean Moriarty in the book) was the natural man, the Dionysian ego, joyfully slaking his unquenchable thirst for food, sex, and life. But Kerouac saw Cassady as more than a glutton. He was "a holy con-man," "the HOLY GOOF," "Angel Dean," questing for "IT," the moment "when you know all and everything is decided forever," — that moment in jazz, Dean explained, when the man making the music "rises to his fate and has to blow equal to it." In San Francisco, deserted by Cassady and delirious from hunger, Kerouac himself (Sal Paradise) had a mystic vision, reaching "the point of ecstasy that I always wanted to reach." Eventually, as Cassady became ensnared in complication, accusation, wounds of the body, he becomes, in Kerouac's view, "BEAT — the root, the soul of Beatific." A bestseller in 1957, *On the Road* became a literary inspiration for the restless young even then preparing to scale the walls of American suburbia in search of Dionysus....

By the late 1950s, a fully developed beat subculture had emerged not only in North Beach but also in Venice West (near Los Angeles), New York's Greenwich Village, and a few other hip resorts in between. The beats possessed deviant tastes in language, literature, music, drugs, and religion. Profoundly alienated from dominant American values, practicing voluntary poverty and spade cool, they rejected materialism, competition, the work ethic, hygiene, sexual repression, monogamy, and the Faustian quest to subdue nature. There were, to be sure, never more than a few thousand fulltime beats, but thanks to the scandalized media, images of beat penetrated and disconcerted the middle classes. Beats, like hula hoops, were a fad. Indeed, by the early 1960s the San Francisco poets had scattered, and cops and tourists had driven the rest of the beats from their old haunts in North Beach. A remnant survived, however, and found convenient shelter in another congenial San Francisco neighborhood. It was Haight-Ashbury, a racially integrated community, forty square blocks, bordering magnificent Golden Gate Park. There, beat old-timers kept alive the hip style and the Dionysian projects, until hippies moved in and appropriated both.

☆

IV

In the metamorphosis from beat to hippie, hallucinogenic drugs played an indispensable part. Indians had been using peyote and magic mushrooms for sacramental purposes since before the rise of the Aztec civilization. But in industrial civilizations, knowledge of mind-altering substances had virtually disappeared. In the 1920s chemists synthesized the active ingredient in peyote, calling it mescaline, and did the same thing in 1958 for the sacred mushrooms, producing psilocybin. Science even outdid nature in 1938 when Dr. Albert Hoffman of the Sandoz Chemical Works in Switzerland fabricated a compound many times more potent than anything imbibed by the most ecstatic Indian. Searching for a respiratory stimulant, Hoffman produced the diethylamide of lysergic acid, a colorless, odorless, apparently useless substance that he called LSD. Five years later, in the course of an experiment on animals, Hoffman accidentally ingested an "unmeasurable trace" of LSD and took the world's first acid trip. (It was, incidentally, a bummer.) Hoffman kept experimenting, and Sandoz began supplying LSD to psychiatric researchers trying to cure schizophrenia. By 1960 LSD was seeping out of the laboratory into the cultural underground.

The herald of the psychedelic revolution was the British author Aldous Huxley. Swallowing some mescaline in 1953, Huxley accidentally triggered a profound mystical experience, in which he watched "a slow dance of golden lights," discovered "Eternity in a flower" and even approached the "Pure Light of the Void," before fleeing in terror from "the burning brightness of unmitigated Reality." In *The Doors of Perception* (1954), which recounted his journey, Huxley lamented that the rich and highly educated white people of the earth were so wedded to words and reason that they had cut themselves off from mystic knowledge. Western man, he said, should accept the "gratuitous grace" of mind-expanding drugs, thus "to be shaken out of the ruts of ordinary perception, to be shown for a few timeless hours the outer and the inner world, not as they appear to an animal obsessed with survival or to a human being obsessed with words and notions, but as they are apprehended, directly and unconditionally, by Mind at Large."

The man who purveyed Huxley's holy message to the millions was Timothy Leary. Possessor of a Ph.D. in psychology, Leary quit his job as director of the Kaiser Foundation Hospital in Oakland, California, in 1958, convinced that conventional psychiatry did not work. Accepting a post at Harvard to pursue his unorthodox ideas, Leary was on his way to a productive scientific career until, one day in Mexico, he discovered the magic mushrooms.

Leary had retreated to a villa in Cuernavaca in the summer of 1960 to write a paper that he hoped would win him points in the academic game. He had never smoked marijuana and knew nothing about mind-altering drugs. But, when a friend procured the mushrooms from a local Indian, Leary thought it might be fun to try some. On a hot afternoon sitting around a pool, Leary and a few companions choked down a bowl of filthy, foul-tasting *crudos*. The game for Leary ended right there. "Five hours after eating the mushrooms it was all changed," he wrote. "The revelation had come. The veil had been pulled back. The classic vision. The

fullblown conversion experience. The prophetic call. The works. God had spoken."

Back at Harvard in the fall, Leary secured Huxley's help in designing a scientific experiment to investigate the behavioral effects of psilocybin (synthesized magic mushrooms). Soon Leary was turning on graduate students, ministers, convicts, and stray seekers showing up at his rented mansion in suburban Boston. In truth, Leary was using science to cloak his real purpose, which was to give away the keys to paradise. And he did grow in spiritual knowledge. He learned that drugs alone could not produce a state of blessedness, that they "had no specific effect on consciousness, except to expand it." God and the Devil resided together in the nervous system. Which of these was summoned depended on one's state of mind. Leary, therefore, emphasized the importance of proper "set and setting" (candles, incense, music, art, quiet) to help the seeker experience God.

In December 1960 Leary made the connection with the hip underground in the person of Allen Ginsberg. Having met him in New York, Ginsberg spent a week at Leary's home to enlist the professor in his own crusade for mind expansion. The two hit it off from the start. On Sunday, with dogs, children, and hangers-on scattered about, Leary gave Ginsberg and Peter Orlovsky the sacred mushrooms. The poets repaired to their room, stripped naked, and played Wagner on the record player. Lying in bed, Ginsberg began to succumb to hellish visions, until Leary came in, looked in his eyes, and pronounced him a great man. Ginsberg arose, and with Orlovsky padding behind, descended to the kitchen to proclaim himself the Messiah. We will go into the streets and call the people to peace and love, Leary reports him as saying. And we will get on the phone and hook up Burroughs, Kerouac, Mailer, Kennedy, and Khrushchev and "settle all this warfare shit." Hello operator, Ginsberg said. This is God. Get me Kerouac. And eventually she did. Sitting in the kitchen after the drug had worn off, Ginsberg plotted the psychedelic revolution. Everybody ought to have the mushrooms, he said, beginning with the influentials. They would not listen to him, a crazy beatnik poet, but they might listen to a Harvard professor. Leary must come to New York on weekends and turn on the likes of Kerouac, [poet] Robert Lowell, [author] LeRoi Jones, [jazz musician] Dizzy Gillespie, [jazz musician] Thelonious Monk, and other creative people in Ginsberg's personal telephone book. Leary was willing. "From this evening on," he wrote, "my energies were offered to the ancient underground society of alchemists, artists, mystics, alienated visionaries, dropouts and the disenchanted young, the sons arising."

Not until late 1961 did Leary try LSD — "the most shattering experience of my life." Taking him far beyond psilocybin, LSD enabled Leary to accomplish the projects of the counterculture — Dionysian ecstasies, mystic and bodily. He journeyed down the DNA ladder of evolution to the single cell at the beginning of life and then outward to the cosmic vibrations where he merged with pure energy, "the white light," nothingness. He also experienced the resurrection of the body. "Blow the mind and you are left with God and life — and life is sex," he said. Leary called LSD "a powerful aphrodisiac, probably the most powerful sexual releaser known to man. . . . The union was not just your body and her body but all of your racial and evolutionary entities with all of hers. It was mythic mating." *Playboy* asked Leary if it was true that women could have multiple orgasms under LSD. He replied with a straight face, "In a carefully prepared, loving LSD session, a woman can have several hundred orgasms."

Huxley had warned Leary that those in authority would oppose him. In April 1963, with LSD selling for a dollar a dose in Harvard Square, the university fired Leary, ostensibly because he cut classes, but really because his work had become an academic scandal. A month later, Richard Alpert, his colleague and collaborator, was fired too. After Mexico bounced the pair as well, a young millionaire came to Leary's rescue by renting him an estate in Millbrook, New York, complete with a musty sixty-four-room Victorian mansion and imitation Bavarian chalets. For the next two years Leary quit proselytizing and presided quietly over a religious commune based on drugs. . . .

Things began to go wrong for Leary in December 1965. On his way to Mexico with his family for a holiday, he was detained at the border and arrested with his daughter for possession of two ounces of marijuana. (Leary said he was probably the first person ever caught trying to smuggle pot *into* Mexico.) There followed more arrests, trials, convictions, appeals. The Millbrook idyll over, Leary again went public, playing to the hilt his role of unrepentant felon and high priest of the psychedelic movement. In 1966 he announced formation of a new religious organization called the League for Spiritual Discovery (LSD). That fall he conducted services in the Village Theatre in New York, where for three dollars a ticket observers could enjoy a multimedia show and a sermon by Leary. After a successful three-month run, Leary took his show on the college circuit, telling audiences to turn on, tune in, drop out. Few lines of the sixties wore so badly.

LSD was a big story in 1966. Congress outlawed it. *Newsweek, Life,* and the *Saturday Evening Post* all did cover stories on it. Sandoz stopped selling it. And the Food and Drug Administration sent a letter to two thousand colleges warning of its "widespread availability" and "profound effects on the mental processes." Years before, Leary had estimated that one million Americans would take LSD by 1967. According to *Life,* the nation had reached the million-dose mark in 1966. As for Leary himself, his reputation among heads declined rapidly after he went show biz. Many of them were already too young to know that he had once been a serious man and that at the dawn of the Aquarian Age Timothy Leary had been the Johnny Appleseed of acid.

If Leary spread the psychedelic revolution, Ken Kesey created the psychedelic style, West Coast version. In 1959, three years before publication of his modern classic *One Flew Over the Cuckoo's Nest,* Kesey took LSD as a subject in a medical experiment, and for him, then and there, the doors of perception blew wide open. In 1964, with a group of disciples called the Merry Pranksters, he established a drug commune in rural La Honda, an hour's drive from San Francisco. One of the Pranksters was Neal Cassady. On acid, Kesey and friends experienced the illusion of self, the All-in-One, the energy field of which we are all an extension. They tried to break down psychic barriers, attain intersubjectivity or group mind, and achieve synchronization with the Cosmos. And they committed themselves to a life of Dionysian ecstasy.

The Pranksters were hip, but in a new way. They were not beaten disaffiliates, warring against technology land, cursing their fate that they had not been born black. In *The Electric Kool-Aid Acid Test,* a history of Kesey in the underground, Tom Wolfe described this new hip generation, these hippies, as products of postwar affluence. Their teen years were spent driving big cars through the California suburbs, believing, like the superheroes in their Marvel comics, that anything was possible. No spade cool for them, no Zen detachment, none of Leary's "set and setting." The Pranksters used LSD to propel themselves out of their skulls toward the outer edge of Western experience. Their style was the wacko style: lurid costumes, Day-Glo paint, crazy trips in Kesey's 1939 multicolored International Harvester school bus, complete with speakers, tapes, and microphones. It was lots of kicks, of course, but it was more than kicks. For Kesey was a religious prophet whose ultimate goal was to turn America, as Michael Bowen put it, into an "electric Tibet."

Toward the end of 1965 Kesey conceived a ritual appropriate for spreading his version of cosmic consciousness. He called it the acid test. Hooking up with the rock group the Grateful Dead, he experimented with multimedia shows so noisy and frenzied that, by themselves, they menaced reason. To make sure that no one missed the point, lots of free LSD

was distributed, a legal act, since California did not get around to outlawing the drug until October 1966. The purpose of the acid test was to create an experience so Dionysian that revelers would overflow the bounds of ego and plug directly into the Cosmos. After Kesey tried out the acid tests in a dozen or so road shows on the West Coast, he headed for the big time.

On January 21–23, 1966, Kesey and the Merry Pranksters produced and directed the Trips Festival at Longshoremen's Hall, San Francisco. The timing was perfect. For more than a year teenage dropouts and disillusioned campus radicals had been drifting into the beat haven of Haight-Ashbury. They were on the verge of community, but not quite there, acid freaks in search of identity. At Kesey's festival the heads of the Bay Area discovered their numbers, came out in the open, and confirmed the wacko style. The estimated twenty thousand people who attended wore every variety of wild costume, including Victorian dresses, Civil War uniforms, four-inch eyelashes, serapes, Indian headbands. Live rock propelled dancers through an electronic chaos of strobe lights, movies, tape machines, and slide projectors. High above the hall, dressed in a silver space suit, directing the whole to get the parts into sync, was Kesey himself. A few days later he took off for Mexico rather than face the consequences of a second drug bust. But Kesey's place in the history of hip was secure, no one having done more to create the hippie style that he had now to leave behind.

☆

V

The Dionysian impulse in the hippie counterculture was made up in equal measures of drugs, sex, and music — not jazz music but rock and roll. When hippies moved in, the black jazz bars on Haight Street moved out. Spade jazz was now as irrelevant to hip as spade soul. Rock had once been black music too, but was so thoroughly appropriated by whites that many hip kids never knew its origins. Rock originated in the 1940s as "rhythm and blues," an urban-based blues music played with electric instruments, pounding beat, and raunchy lyrics — music by blacks for blacks. In 1952 the legendary Cleveland disc jockey Alan Freed hosted the first rhythm and blues record show for a white audience, calling the music "rock and roll." The music caught on among teenagers tired of sexless, sentimental ballads, and soon white performers fused pop and country styles with rhythm and blues to create white rock and roll. That's what Elvis Presley sang when he emerged in 1956 to become the biggest star in pop history. From the beginning, rock and roll was protest music, protest against Tin Pan Alley, protest against parental taste, protest against instinctual repression. Music of the id, fifties rock and roll helped create a generation of cultural subversives who would in time heed the siren song of hip.

In 1958, when Elvis went into the Army, rock entered a period of decline. Meanwhile, the black sound that had inspired it was being assimilated anew by other talented musicians, this time in England, and it would return to America, bigger than before, with the Beatles. During their long years of apprenticeship, playing lower-class clubs in Liverpool and Hamburg, John Lennon, Paul McCartney, and George Harrison explored the roots of rock and roll, even as they slowly fashioned a style of their own. By 1963 that style had fully matured. No longer just another scruffy group of Teddy Boys playing electronic guitars, they had become well-tailored professionals with a distinctive hair style (Eton long), immense stage presence, the best song-writing team in pop history (Lennon and McCartney), a fluid sound, contagious vitality, and, above all, the irrepressible beat of rock and roll. That beat helped propel the Beatles to stardom in Britain in 1963 and created Beatlemania.

Within days of its release in the United States in January 1964, "I Want to Hold Your Hand" climbed to the top of the charts, to be followed quickly by "She Loves You" and "Please, Please Me." In February the Beatles themselves arrived for a tour that began with a sensational TV performance on the *Ed Sullivan Show* and continued before hysterical teen mobs in New York, Washington, and Miami. In April all five top singles in the United States were Beatles songs and the two top albums were Beatles albums. In July the first Beatles movie, *A Hard Day's Night,* amazed critics and delighted audiences with its wit and verve. Meanwhile that year Beatles merchandise — everything from dolls to dishcloths — was grossing over $50 million. Nothing comparable to Beatlemania had ever happened in the history of pop culture.

Unlike Presley or their British rivals, the Rolling Stones, the Beatles did not menace society. They mocked it. Insouciant, irreverent, flip, they took seriously no institution or person, themselves included. "What do you think of Beethoven?" a reporter asked at the Beatles' first American press conference. "I love him," replied Ringo. "Especially his poems." Treating the adult world as absurd, they told their fans to kick off their shoes, heed their hormones, and have fun. However harmless initially, the Beatles phenomenon contained the possibility of danger. The frenzied loyalty they inspired endowed the Fab Four with immense potential power — power to alter life styles, change values, and create a new sensibility, a new way of perceiving the world. But in the early days, as they sang their songs of teen love, that power lay dormant. When Ken Kesey attended the 1965 Beatles concert in San Francisco, he was astonished by the "concentration and power" focused on the performers. He was just as astonished by their inability to exploit them. "They could have taken this roomful of kids and snapped them," said Kesey, "and they would have left that place enlightened, mature people that would never have been quite the same again. . . . They had the power to bring off this new consciousness to people, but they couldn't do it."

The artist who first seized the power of rock and used it to change consciousness was Bob Dylan. Born Robert Zimmerman, Dylan tried on every style of teen alienation available during the fifties in Hibbing, Minnesota. Though he wanted to be a rock and roll star, he discovered on enrolling at the University of Minnesota in 1959 that folk music was the rage on campus. In 1961 Dylan arrived in Greenwich Village, the folk capital of America, determined to become the biggest folkie of them all. A little over a year later, he was. Audiences responded to his vulnerability, the nasal whine with which he delivered his songs, and lyrics so riveting they transformed the folk art. Immersing himself in the left-liberal-civil-rights ethos permeating the Village in the early 1960s, Dylan wrote folk songs as protest. He did not compose from the headlines, as other protest singers did. He used figurative language and elusive imagery to distill the political mood of his time and place. Gambling that a poet could become a star, he won big. Two weeks after Peter, Paul, and Mary recorded his song "Blowin' in the Wind," it sold more than 300,000 copies. Songs like "A Hard Rain's Gonna Fall" were hailed as true art. And his "Times They Are A-Changin'" became a generational anthem. It was no less appropriate for Dylan to sing at the 1963 March on Washington than for Martin Luther King to deliver a sermon there.

Meanwhile, the Beatles arrived and Dylan was listening. "Everybody else thought they were for the teenyboppers, that they were gonna pass right away," Dylan said. "But it was obvious to me that they had staying power. I knew they were pointing the direction of where music had to go." In July 1965 Dylan outraged the folk world by appearing at the Newport Folk Festival, no longer the ragged waif with acoustic guitar, but as a rock and roll singer, outfitted in black leather jacket and backed by an electric band. That summer his rock single,

"Like a Rolling Stone," perhaps the greatest song he ever wrote, made it all the way to number one.

Dylan took rock and made it the medium for cultural statement — folk-rock, the critics quickly labeled it. As his music changed, so did the message. Moving with his generation, Dylan now abandoned liberal politics for cultural radicalism. The lyrics he sang in the mid-sixties were intensely personal and frequently obscure, but taken together, they formed a stunning mosaic of a corrupt and chaotic America. It is a fact of no small social consequence that in 1965 millions of radios and record players were daily pounding Dylan's message, subliminally or otherwise, into the skulls of a generation. There was, for example, "Highway 61," which depicted America as a junkyard road heading for war; "Maggie's Farm," a dropout's contemptuous farewell to the straight world; "Desolation Row," which portrayed an insane society, governed by insane men, teetering on the brink of apocalypse; "Ballad of a Thin Man," using homosexual imagery to describe an intellectual's confusion in a world bereft of reason; and "Gates of Eden," a mystical evocation of a realm beyond the senses, beyond ego, wherein resides the timeless Real. After Dylan, a host of other rock prophets arose to preach sex, love, peace, or revolution. After Dylan rock and roll became a music that both expressed the sixties counterculture and shaped it.

Among those acknowledging their debt to Dylan were the Beatles. After Dylan, they too began writing songs for the cultural opposition, to which they became increasingly committed. The Beatles induced mystic ecstasies with LSD, discovered the music and religion of the East, even took an abortive pilgrimage to India to study Transcendental Meditation with the Maharishi Mahesh Yogi. In June 1967 they released *Sergeant Pepper's Lonely Hearts Club Band,* a musically innovative album placing them at the head of the psychedelic parade. ("I'd love to turn you on," John Lennon sang on the record's best cut.) Timothy Leary, after *Sergeant Pepper,* proclaimed the Beatles "evolutionary agents sent by God, endowed with a mysterious power to create a new human species."

In the view of some, this new human species had already emerged with the San Francisco hippies, who played their own brand of rock and roll. Literally hundreds of bands had formed in the Bay Area by the mid-1960s, but because no major company recorded there, they developed in isolation from the commercial mainstream. Hippie musicians were freaks who played for freaks, having no other purpose than creation of Dionysian art. They were contemptuous of the star system, top forty stations, giant concerts for idolatrous audiences, Madison Avenue hype. They played their music live in dance halls where the musicians could jam as long as they wanted, and the dancers dressed like rock stars. The songs they wrote celebrated drugs and sex, and the music they played was music to trip on. One rock critic described the San Francisco Sound as "revelatory roaring, chills of ecstasy, hallucinated wandering, mysticopsychotic wonder."

San Francisco's dance-hall craze began in the fall of 1965 when local promoters rented seedy halls to feature hippie bands like the Jefferson Airplane, Big Brother and the Holding Company, Quicksilver Messenger Service, and the Grateful Dead. After Kesey's Trips Festival in January 1966, the acid tests merged with the dances, institutionalized at weekend freakouts at the Fillmore and the Avalon Ballroom. The quintessential San Francisco band was the Grateful Dead, who had been on Kesey's trip and never got over it. "It wasn't a *gig,* it was the Acid Tests where anything was OK," the Dead's Jerry Garcia recalled. "Thousands of people, man, all helplessly stoned, all finding themselves in a roomful of other thousands of people, none of whom any of them were afraid of. It was magic, far out, beautiful magic." In June 1966 the Dead moved into a house in Haight-Ashbury, where they lived together, jammed free for the people, got stoned, got busted, and continued to seek that magic moment in their

music when performers, audience, and Cosmos were One....

By summer [1967] the San Francisco Sound was making the city the new rock mecca and its performers the newest rock superstars. The big song on the top forty stations that season was the Airplane's "White Rabbit," psychedelic variations on a theme from *Alice in Wonderland,* ending with the command to "feed a head, feed a head." That summer, too, thousands of teenagers took literally Scott McKenzie's musical invitation, with its implicit promise of Dionysian revels, to come to "San Francisco (Be Sure to Wear Flowers in Your Hair)." Ralph Gleason, San Francisco's hip music critic, understood well the cultural significance of rock. "At no time in American history has youth possessed the strength it possesses now," he wrote. "Trained by music and linked by music, it has the power for good to change the world." Significantly, he added, "That power for good carries the reverse, the power for evil."

VI

By 1967 Haight-Ashbury had attained a population large enough to merit, at last, the designation "counterculture." The question was, where was this culture tending? A few days after the famous Human Be-In, the celebrities of the movement met on Alan Watts's houseboat off Sausalito to exchange visions of utopia. [A student of Zen] Watts summed up for the others the predicament of the West: rational, technological man had lost contact with himself and nature. Fortunately, Timothy Leary said, automation could now liberate man from work and enable him to live a simpler life. Feasting off technology, dropouts from megalopolis could form tribes and move back to the land. Yes, said poet Gary Snyder. Turn Chicago into a center for cybernetic technology and the rest of America into buffalo pasture. After a while, as life got simpler, "Chicago would rust away." Man's destruction of his natural environment would cease. Nuclear families would give way to communes or tribes, whose members would share food, work, and sex. Like the Comanche and the Sioux, members of these tribes would go off alone to have visions, and all who knew them would know them as men. Already in Big Sur, Snyder continued, kids were using A. L. Kroeber's *Handbook of the California Indians* to learn the art of primitive survival, to learn how to be Indians. Fine, countered Allen Ginsberg, "but where are the people going to buy their Uher tape recorder machines?" which were being used to record the conversation.

Ginsberg's was the authentic voice of Haight-Ashbury. Addicted to electronic amenities, hippies merely played at being Indians, satisfied to wear Navaho jewelry and feathers. They communed with nature by picking Golden Gate Park bare of flowers; their notion of tribal harmony was to let everyone "do their own thing." As love had supposedly done for the Hopi, so it would do for them: it would conquer all. Armed with "flower power," hippies would overwhelm their enemies and live a life of ecstasy on the asphalt pavements of urban America. Real Indians were not much impressed. In the spring of 1967, when Ginsberg and Richard Alpert met Hopi leaders in Santa Fe to propose a Be-In in the Grand Canyon, the tribal spokesman brushed them off, saying according to the *Berkeley Barb,* "No, because you mean well but you are foolish. . . . You are a tribe of strangers to yourselves." . . .

By summer of 1967 the Haight's bizarre cast of characters was performing for a national audience. This was the summer when *Time* described the neighborhood as "the vibrant epicenter of the hippie movement," hippies estimated their full-time population nationwide at 300,000, imitation Haight-Ashburys bloomed throughout urban America, acid rock dominated the music charts, prestigious museums exhibited psychedelic posters, and doing one's own thing became the national cliché. Once school ended, San Francisco expected one to two hundred

thousand kids to flood the city for the Summer of Love. But the real story that summer, unreported by the media, was that few of the thousands who did come stayed very long. Haight-Ashbury was already dying.

Its demise, so similar to the demise of hippie ghettos elsewhere, resulted from official repression, black hostility, and media hype. In San Francisco where city fathers panicked at the prospect of runaway hordes descending upon them, police began routinely roughing up hippies, health officials harassed their communes, and narcotics agents infiltrated the neighborhood. Meanwhile, black hoods from the nearby Fillmore district cruised the streets, threatening rape and violence. Blacks did not like LSD, white kids pretending to be poor, or the fact that Haight-Ashbury was, in the words of a leftover beatnik, "the first segregated Bohemia I've ever seen." Longtime residents began staying home after dark. Finally, the beguiling images of Haight-Ashbury marketed by the media attracted not only an invasion of gawking tourists, but a floating population of the unstable, the psychotic, and the criminal. By the end of the year, *reported* crime in Haight-Ashbury included 17 murders, 100 rapes, and nearly 3,000 burglaries.

In October 1967 community leaders staged a pageant called "Death of Hippie." . . . While a country fiddler made music, a parade carried an oversized coffin, filled with hippie litter, through "Hashbury." Halting at the panhandle, mourners set the coffin on fire and danced a Dionysian dance. . . . The vision of an acid utopia based on love and flowers was already ashes.

☆

VII

Though Haight-Ashbury died, the counterculture did not. If anything, in the last years of the decade the potent mix of drugs, sex, and rock and roll seduced an even larger proportion of the young. But few of these hip rebels called themselves hippies or talked of flower power any longer. Norman O. Brown had envisioned a cultural revolution in which a Dionysian ego would become the servant of Eros. But in the Freudian metaphor, Eros had to contend with Thanatos. The danger always existed that by liberating one, hip would liberate the other also. Brown himself had warned, "Not only does Dionysus without the Dionysian ego threaten us with dissolution of consciousness, he also threatens us with that 'genuine witches' brew,' 'that horrible mixture of sensuality and cruelty' (Nietzsche again), which is the result of the Dionysian against the Apollonian." After the fall from the Haight-Ashbury paradise, Thanatos, not Eros, prevailed in the counterculture. Confronted by hostile police, hysterical parents, and implacable draft boards, the freaks abandoned the rhetoric of love for the politics of rage. They became willing cannon fodder for the increasingly violent demonstrations of the new left. And they routinely threw rocks at police, rioted at rock concerts, and trashed stores. The nightmare of the Dionysian witches' brew, of Dionysus without the Dionysian ego, had become reality.

As the decade closed, it became clear that drugs, sex, and rock and roll lacked intrinsic moral content. The acid prophets had warned from the beginning that LSD did not inevitably produce the God experience. God and the Devil resided together in the nervous system, Leary had said. LSD could evoke either, depending on set and setting. The streets of Haight-Ashbury, even in the best days, had been littered with kids who deranged their senses on drugs — only to experience spiritual stupor. A fair number ended their trips in hospital emergency rooms, possessed of one or another demon. Satanic cults were not unknown in the Haight. One of them, the Process, apparently influenced Charles Manson, a hippie who lived in the neighborhood in 1967 and recruited confused young girls and a few men into his "family." Manson was an "acid fascist" who somehow found in the lyrics of the Beatles li-

cense to commit [the] ritual murder [of actress Sharon Tate and four acquaintances, whose bodies were heinously mutilated]. As violence in the counterculture mounted, LSD became chiefly a means to pierce the false rationality of the hated bourgeois world. The always tenuous link between drugs and love was broken.

Neither was sex itself necessarily the expression of Eros unalloyed with death. Sex in the counterculture did not imply love between two people, but merely gratification of the self — ecstasy through orgasm. Typical encounters in Haight-Ashbury were one-night stands. Rapists prospered, and carriers of venereal disease shared it generously. Janis Joplin, the greatest white blues singer who ever lived and the authentic voice of sexual ecstasy in Haight-Ashbury, sang Dionysian hymns to sexual climax. But for Janis the orgasm was the god that failed. How was your vacation on St. Thomas? a friend asked a year before Janis died of a heroin overdose. "It was just like anywhere else," she said. "I fucked a lot of strangers."

... Rock and roll was the principal art of the counterculture because of its demonstrable power to liberate the instincts. At the Woodstock Music Festival, held one weekend in August 1969 at Bethel, New York, Eros ran wild. An incredible 400,000 people gathered on a farm to hear the greatest line-up of rock talent ever assembled in one place. Overcoming conditions that could conventionally be described only as disastrous, the crowd created a loving community based on drugs, sex, and rock music. But four months later at the Altamont Raceway near San Francisco, rock revealed an equal affinity for death.

The occasion was a free concert conceived by the Rolling Stones as a fitting climax to their first American tour in three years and the documentary film that was recording it. Altamont was a calamity. Because of a last-minute cancellation elsewhere, concert promoters had only one day to ready the site for a crush of 300,000 kids. Sanitary facilities were inadequate; the sound system, terrible; the setting, cheerless. Lots of bad dope, including inferior acid spiked with speed, circulated through the crowd. Harried medics had to fly in an emergency supply of [the tranquilizer] Thorazine to treat the epidemic of bad trips and were kept busy administering first aid to victims of the random violence. The violence originated with the Hell's Angels. On the advice of the Grateful Dead, the Stones had hired the Angels to guard the stage for $500 worth of beer. Armed with loaded pool cues sawed off to the length of billy clubs, high on bad dope washed down with Red Mountain vin rose, Angels indiscriminately clubbed people for offenses real or imagined. Vibrations of fear and paranoia spread from them outward through the crowd. And yet, when the Jefferson Airplane did their set, they called the Angels on stage to pay them homage. Once a hippie band singing acid rock, the Airplane had moved with the times, expressing in their music the anarchic rage surging through the counterculture. The song they sang to the Angels was "We Can Be Together."

> We should be together.
> All your private property is target for your enemy
> And your enemy is me.
> We are forces of chaos and anarchy.
> Everything they say we are we are.
> And we are proud of ourselves.
> Up against the wall
> Up against the wall motherfucker.

Minutes later, when the Airplane's Marty Balin tried to stop an Angel from beating a fan, he himself was knocked cold.

At nightfall, after keeping the crowd waiting in the cold for more than an hour, the Rolling Stones came on stage. Many critics regarded the Stones as the greatest rock and roll band in the world. Ever since their emergence, they had carefully cultivated an outlaw image — lewd, sneering, surly — to differentiate themselves from their fellow Britons, the Beatles. Their most recent music, including, notably, "Street Fighting Man" and "Sympathy for the

Devil," reflected the growing violence of the culture of which they were superstars. Now at Altamont there was Mick Jagger, reveling in his image as rock's prince of evil, prancing on stage while the Angels flailed away with their pool cues below. It was too much even for him. Jagger stopped the music more than once to plead for order; but when the Angels ignored him, he had no choice except to sing on. Midway through "Sympathy for the Devil," only a few feet from the stage, an Angel knifed a black man named Meredith Hunter to death. The moment was captured by camera and made the highlight of the film *Gimme Shelter,* which as much as any counterculture document of the time revealed Thanatos unleashed.

☆

VIII

For a variety of reasons, after 1970 the counterculture faded. Economic recession signaled that affluence could no longer be assumed and induced a certain caution among the young. The Vietnam War, which did so much to discredit authority, rapidly deescalated. And its own revels brought the hippie movement into disrepute. Carried to the edge of sanity by their Dionysian revels, many of the once hip retreated, some to rural communes in New Mexico or Vermont, most all the way back to the straight world.

Not least among the reasons for the waning of the impulse was the ease with which the dominant culture absorbed it. Indeed, despite the generational warfare that marked the late 1960s, hippies were only a spectacular exaggeration of tendencies transforming the larger society. The root of these tendencies, to borrow a phrase from Daniel Bell, was a "cultural contradiction of capitalism." By solving the problems of want, industrial capitalism undermined the very virtues that made this triumph possible, virtues like hard work, self-denial, postponement of gratification, submission to social discipline, strong ego mechanisms to control the instincts. As early as the 1920s the system of mass production depended less on saving than consumption, not on denial but indulgence. Depression and war retarded the implications of these changes until the 1950s.

Unprecedented affluence after World War II created a generation of teenagers who could forgo work to stay in school. Inhabiting a gilded limbo between childhood and adult responsibility, these kids had money, leisure, and unprecedented opportunity to test taboos. For them the Protestant ethic had no relevance, except in the lingering parental effort to enforce it. When Elvis emerged from Memphis, hammering out his beat and exuding sexuality, the teen breakout from jailhouse America began. The next step in the process of liberation was hip.

But middle-class teenagers were not alone in kicking over the traces of Puritanism. Their parents too began reckoning with the cultural implications of affluence. Critics had attacked the hippies as hedonistic and narcissistic. By the 1970s social discipline was eroding so rapidly that fashion condemned the whole of middle-class culture as the "culture of narcissism." Parental discipline declined, sexual promiscuity rose along with the divorce rate, worker productivity fell, ghetto obscenity insinuated itself into standard speech, marijuana became almost commonplace, sexual perversions were no longer deemed so, and traditional institutions like the Army, the churches, and the government lost authority. At the same time, the impulse toward ecstasy found increasing expression in Oriental religion, the New Consciousness Movement, and charismatic Christianity. Dionysus had been absorbed into the dominant culture and domesticated, and in the process routed the Protestant ethic.

Cultural change had political implications. While liberals earnestly sought to purge capitalism of traditional problems like unemployment and poverty, a vocal minority of American youth regarded unemployment as a blessing and chose poverty as a way of life. In the short run, hippie scorn was one more problem complicating the life of [President] Lyndon Johnson, who never could understand whatever happened to earnest youth. In the long run, though it proved ephemeral, the hippie movement was profoundly significant, portending as it did the erosion of the liberal values that had [long] sustained bourgeois society. . . .

QUESTIONS TO CONSIDER

1   What are the historical origins of the counterculture, and how did it spread and change over time? What groups of people did it most affect? Describe the historical origins and development of counterculture music. How were the Beatles different from their predecessors and how were they similar? What does their career say about the counterculture and about the larger society at the time?

2   Compare the image that the hippies cultivated with the actual conditions of their lives and communities. How do you account for the differences? What do you think of the psychological explanation discussed by Matusow? Is it an objective explanation or a product of the same culture?

3   Do you see in the readings other examples of twentieth-century reactions against the traditional values of the culture?

4   Matusow suggests that the hippies were exaggerated products of the "cultural contradiction of capitalism." How do you evaluate his using affluence to explain rebelliousness? What do you think of the possibility that noneconomic factors, political or educational, for example, might explain the rebelliousness? Why was there such a great gulf between the counterculture and liberals?

5   What relationship does Matusow see between the hippies and cultural changes in society at large? Do you see consequences of this in today's social conditions? What implications might this have for the future?

XIV

THE SEVENTIES

28

"I Have Never Been a Quitter": A Portrait of Richard Nixon

OTTO FRIEDRICH

As his biographer Stephen Ambrose has said, Richard Nixon wanted to be one of the great presidents, even a modern-day Lincoln. But the flaws in Nixon's character prevented him from leaving that kind of legacy. He did accomplish many positive things during his tenure in the White House (1969–1973): though an ardent and dedicated anti-Communist during his entire political career, he effected a rapprochement with Communist China, established détente with the Soviet Union, and finally ended America's disastrous involvement in the Vietnam War. These were spectacular achievements for "the world's No. 1 anti-Communist," as Ambrose describes him. But Nixon above all was a pragmatist: his objective was to strengthen the United States in world affairs by playing the Soviets and Chinese off against one another through "triangular diplomacy."

At home, he reduced military spending and signed the measure that lowered the voting age to eighteen, but he was not much interested in getting legislation enacted on Capitol Hill. What occupied most of his time and energy was the antiwar movement and other enemies of his administration; he was obsessed with them and with what he perceived to be a liberal, anti-Nixon slant among the nation's major newspapers. Before long, a bunker mentality pervaded the Nixon White House: it viewed domestic politics as a desperate battlefield between "them" and "us," with the Nixon administration increasingly identifying "them" as traitors and "us" as the only patriots and true saviors of America. In the name of "national security," the Nixon administration flagrantly violated the law and the Constitution in its zeal to suppress dissent, defeat opponents, and uphold administration politics. *Nixon himself compiled a list of his "enemies" and not only had their phones tapped, but also ordered the Internal Revenue Service to audit them. Most frightening of all, Nixon's "campaign of subversion" produced the Watergate scandal. It began in June 1972, when five men associated with the Committee to Re-Elect the President (CREEP) broke into the Democratic National Committee headquarters in Washington, D.C., and were arrested on a charge of burglary. For a time, Nixon successfully covered up his complicity in the break-in and the abuse of executive power it represented. When reporters Carl Bernstein and Bob Woodward of the* Washington Post *exposed the Watergate scandal, it precipitated what one historian called "the greatest constitutional crisis the country had faced since the Civil War." The crisis shook Americans of every political persuasion and eventually brought down Nixon's presidency. In August 1973, he resigned his office — the first American President ever to do so — and flew back to California in disgrace.*

Some historians have linked Watergate to the growth of an "imperial presidency," which resulted in an imbalance of power, tilted to the executive branch. Lyndon Johnson had hastened the process by waging his undeclared war in Vietnam and pressuring Congress into endorsing and funding it. In the Watergate crisis, as historian William H. Chafe put it, the country rallied against the excesses of the imperial presidency, insisting on "a government of laws rather than personal whim."

Nixon's only crime was not, as many Americans still contend, that he simply got caught doing what other presidents have done. Historian C. Vann Woodward observes in Responses of the Presidents to Charges of Misconduct *(1974): "Heretofore, no president has been proved to be the chief coordinator of the crime and misdemeanor charged against his own administration. . . . Heretofore, no president has been held to be the chief personal beneficiary of misconduct in his administration or of measures taken to destroy or cover up evidence of it. Heretofore, the malfeasance and misdemeanor have had no confessed ideological purpose, no constitutionally subversive ends. Heretofore, no president has been accused of extensively subverting and secretly using established government agencies to defame or discredit political opponents and critics, to obstruct justice, to conceal misconduct and protect criminals, or to deprive citizens of their rights and liberties. Heretofore, no president has been accused of creating secret investigative units to engage in covert and unlawful activities against private citizens and their rights."*

In "a post-Watergate backlash," as one historian termed it, American voters in 1974 gave the Democrats the second-biggest congressional victory in their entire history. Two years later, they sent Democrat Jimmy Carter to the White House, ousting Republican Gerald Ford, whom Nixon had chosen as his successor.

In the following selection, Otto Friedrich, who authored the brilliant narrative about Pearl Harbor (selection 18), describes Nixon's painful and impoverished early years, which did so much to shape the angry, ambitious man he became. Though highly intelligent and gifted, as Friedrich shows, Nixon made his reputation by smearing political opponents, accusing them of being soft on communism. He rationalized such tactics on the grounds that he had to win. "Of course I knew Jerry Voorhis wasn't a communist," he said of one defeated opponent, "but I had to win. That's the thing you don't understand. The important thing is to win." Friedrich goes on to show how Nixon kept rising and falling, rising and falling, and finally rising again, in a political career that spanned more than a quarter of a century.

GLOSSARY

AGNEW, SPIRO Nixon's vice president (1969–1973); he resigned after being indicted for graft and corruption.

BROWN, PAT Incumbent governor of California who defeated Nixon in the gubernatorial election of 1962. Afterward Nixon held his "final press conference," in which he told reporters: "Think of what you've lost. You won't have Nixon to kick around anymore."

BREZHNEV, LEONID Soviet leader (first secretary of the Communist party) who with Nixon signed the 1972 SALT I treaty. In it, the United States and the Soviet Union agreed to limit antiballistic missiles and reached "an interim accord" on restricting offensive nuclear weapons.

CHECKERS SPEECH Nixon's maudlin speech on television during the presidential election of 1952; in that speech, Nixon sought to clear his name after news of his $18,000 slush fund donated by California businessmen had come to the surface. As he spoke, he told the story of the Nixon family dog, Checkers; hence the speech's name.

COX, ARCHIBALD Appointed special prosecutor in the Watergate case; he was fired during the "Saturday night massacre" for insisting that Nixon turn over the tapes he had made of his conversations in the Oval Office.

DEAN, JOHN Nixon's legal counsel; he was one of three top Nixon officials involved in the cover-up of the Watergate break-in. The other two officials were Attorney General John Mitchell and Mitchell's deputy, Jeb Stuart Magruder. Dean pleaded guilty when he was indicted for obstructing justice in the Watergate investigations.

DOUGLAS, HELEN GAHAGAN Nixon defeated this former movie actress in the 1950 election in California for a seat in the United States Senate. She gave him his pejorative nickname, "Tricky Dick." Nixon won this mud-slinging election by calling Douglas "the pink lady" — that is, a Communist — and insisting that she was "pink right down to her underwear."

EHRLICHMAN, JOHN Nixon's chief domestic adviser who was indicted by a grand jury for obstructing justice in the investigation of Watergate. He resigned his office, stood trial for his part in the Watergate scandal, and served time in a federal prison.

FORD, GERALD United States congressman and House minority leader from Michigan who in 1973 replaced Spiro Agnew as Nixon's vice president; Ford became president when Nixon resigned the office in 1974. One month later Ford pardoned Nixon for his crimes in the Watergate scandal.

HALDEMAN, H. R. Nixon's chief of staff. Like John Ehrlichman, Haldeman was indicted by a grand jury for obstructing justice in the Watergate investigations. He, too, resigned from the White House, stood trial for his role in the Watergate scandal, and was confined to a federal prison.

HISS, ALGER   Served in the State Department from 1936 to 1947; in that capacity he helped coordinate United States foreign policy. In 1948, Whittaker Chambers, an editor and confessed Communist courier, charged that Hiss had passed on confidential government documents to the Soviets. HUAC, led by Nixon, accused Hiss of espionage; he vigorously denied the charges and found himself indicted by a grand jury for perjury. He was later found guilty of that charge and sentenced to forty-four months in prison. He was never found guilty of espionage. The Hiss case "made Nixon a national figure."

HOOVER, J. EDGAR   Powerful head of the Federal Bureau of Investigation from 1924 to 1972. Hoover advised Nixon to order illegal wiretaps on his alleged enemies, as Lyndon Johnson had done.

HUAC   Acronym for the House Un-American Activities Committee (its official name was the House Committee on Un-American Activities), originally established in 1938 to uncover "malign foreign influences in the Unites States," was taken over by conservative Republicans who, in 1947, launched widely publicized investigations into the extent of Communist subversion in this country.

HUMPHREY, HUBERT   Lyndon Johnson's vice president (1965–1969) and Democratic nominee for president in the 1968 election; Nixon defeated him by a narrow margin.

KISSINGER, HENRY   Nixon's national security adviser and second secretary of state (1973–1974); he arranged Nixon's visit to Communist China in 1972 and negotiated with the North Vietnamese a cease-fire agreement in North Vietnam that called for an American withdrawal.

McGOVERN, GEORGE   Democratic nominee for president in 1972; Nixon soundly defeated him.

MITCHELL, JOHN   Nixon's attorney general (1969–1972) who was implicated in the cover-up of the Watergate break-in.

SALT I TREATY   See *Leonid Brezhnev.*

SATURDAY NIGHT MASSACRE   On the night of October 20, 1973, a Saturday, Nixon ordered Attorney General Elliot Richardson to fire special prosecutor Archibald Cox, who was investigating the Watergate case. Richardson refused Nixon's order and resigned; so did Deputy Attorney General William Ruckelshaus. General Alexander Haig, Nixon's new chief of staff, then persuaded Solicitor General Robert Bork to fire Cox. The "massacre" left the Nixon administration "a shambles."

STEVENSON, ADLAI   Democratic presidential nominee who lost to Eisenhower in the elections of 1952 and 1956. As Eisenhower's running mate, Nixon spent much of his time in the 1952 campaign accusing Stevenson of being soft on communism.

TEAPOT DOME SCANDAL   President Warren G. Harding (1921–1923), at the urging of Albert Fall, Secretary of the Interior, transferred control of the navy's oil reserves in Wyoming to Fall's Interior Department. Fall leased the oil reserves to a couple of wealthy businessmen in return for almost $500,000 in "loans." Tried and convicted of bribery, Fall served a year in prison.

VOORHIS, JERRY   The liberal Democrat Nixon defeated in the congressional election of 1946 in the Twelfth Congressional District east of Los Angeles.

Richard Nixon's first conscious memory was of falling—falling and then running. He was three years old, and his mother had taken him and his brother out riding in a horse-drawn buggy, and the horse turned a corner too fast on the way home. The boy fell out. A buggy wheel ran over his head and inflicted a deep cut. "I must have been in shock," Nixon recalled later, "but I managed to get up and run after the buggy while my mother tried to make the horse stop." The only aftereffect, Nixon said, was a scar, and that was why he combed his hair straight back instead of parting it on the side.

In a sense, Nixon spent his whole life falling and running and falling again. A symbol of the politics of anger, he was one of the most hated figures of his time, and yet he was also the only man in U.S. history ever to be elected twice as Vice President and twice as President. In the White House, he achieved many major goals: the U.S. withdrawal from Vietnam, restored relations with China, the first major arms agreement with the Soviet Union and much more. But he will always be remembered . . . as the chief perpetrator—and chief victim—of the Watergate scandal, the only President ever to resign in disgrace.

Despite all his gifts—his shrewd intelligence, his dedication and sense of public service, his mastery of political strategy—there was a quality of self-destructiveness that haunted Nixon. To an admiring aide he once acknowledged, "You continue to walk on the edge of the precipice because over the years you have become fascinated by how close to the edge you can walk without losing your balance."

He kept losing it, tumbling to great depths, then grimly climbing back. After being defeated in the presidential race of 1960 and then the California gu-

bernatorial race of 1962, he bitterly told reporters, "You won't have Nixon to kick around anymore." Six years later, he fought his way to another Republican presidential nomination, which he spoke of as "the culmination of an impossible dream." But at his last meeting with his Cabinet in August 1974, after what seemed like the final defeat in a lifetime devoted to the idea of winning, he burst into tears. "Always remember," he said, "others may hate you, but those who hate you don't win unless you hate them—and then you destroy yourself."

From anyone else, that might have served as a public farewell, but the disgraced Nixon spent more than a dozen years in climbing once more out of the abyss and re-creating himself as an elder statesman. He wrote his memoirs in 1978, then eight more books largely devoted to international strategy. He moved to the wealthy suburb of Saddle River, New Jersey (where he stayed until 1990, moving a mile away to Park Ridge), and began giving discreet dinners for movers and shakers. President Reagan called to ask his advice. So did President Bush. In November 1989, he became the first important American to make a public visit to Beijing after the massacre at Tiananmen Square.

The hallmark of Nixon's youth had been poverty—poverty and family illness and endless work. His father Frank, who had dropped out of school and run away from home after the fourth grade, was a combative and quarrelsome Ohioan. After running through a string of jobs, Frank moved to California in 1907, built a house in the desert-edge town of Yorba Linda and tried to grow lemons. There Frank's pious Quaker wife Hannah gave birth on Jan. 9, 1913, to a second son. She named him Richard, after the English King Richard the Lion-Hearted, plus Milhous, her own family name. The newborn baby, an attendant nurse later recalled, had a "powerful, ringing voice."

His mother sent him to school every day in a starched white shirt and a black bow tie, and he worked hard for his good grades. He liked to recite

Otto Friedrich, "I Have Never Been a Quitter," *Time* Magazine, vol. 143, no. 18 (May 2, 1994), pp. 43–51. Copyright © 1994 Time Inc. Reprinted by permission.

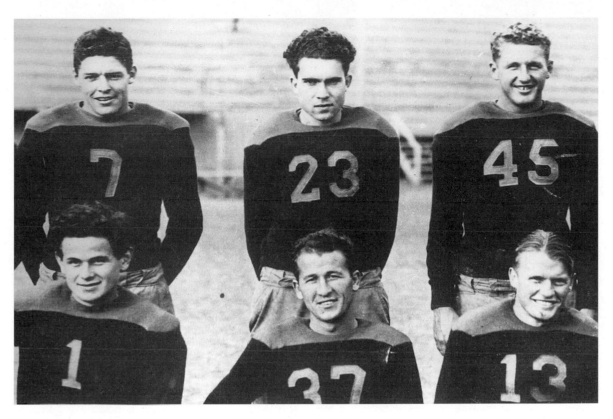

Richard Nixon (number 23), the second son of Frank and Hanna Nixon, was named after the English King Richard the Lion-Hearted. He attended Whittier College and wanted to play *football, but was "too small and slow to make the starting team," writes Otto Friedrich, so "he showed up every day for practice in the line." (UPI/Corbis-Bettmann)*

long poems and play the piano. One of his favorite forms of competition was debating, which he did well. Another was football. Too small and slow to make the starting team in Fullerton or Whittier High School or at Whittier College, he showed up every day for practice in the line. "We used Nixon as a punching bag," one of his coaches recalled. "What starts the process, really," Nixon later said of his life-long passion for winning, "are the laughs and slights and snubs when you are a kid. But if . . . your anger is deep enough and strong enough, you learn that you can change those attitudes by excellence, personal gut performance."

Nixon grew up in Whittier because his father had given up on citrus farming and found a new job there as an oil-field worker, then started a gas station, then expanded it into a general store. Hannah Nixon liked Whittier because it was largely a Quaker town where nobody drank or smoked or carried on. But life was not easy. All through high school, Nixon had to get up at 4 every morning and drive to the Seventh Street markets in Los Angeles to buy fresh vegetables for the family store.

When Dick Nixon was 12, his younger brother Arthur, the fourth of the five boys, complained of a headache; a month later he was dead of meningitis.

Nixon wrote later that he cried every day for weeks. When Harold, the eldest son, was stricken with tuberculosis, Hannah left the rest of the family to take him to the drier air in Prescott, Arizona. She could pay for this only by operating a clinic where other TB patients waited out their last weeks of life. In the summers Dick found jobs nearby as a janitor, a chicken plucker, a carnival barker. After five years, Harold died. "We all grew up rather fast in those years," Nixon recalled.

Harold's illness was also a great financial drain. Nixon had to turn down a scholarship offer from Harvard (Yale was also interested in him) and save money by attending tiny Whittier College. Duke University Law School was just starting when it offered Nixon one of the 25 scholarships available to a class of 44. At first he lived in a $5-a-month room. Later he shared a one-room shack that had no plumbing or electricity; he shaved in the men's room of the library. In three years at Duke, he never once went out on a date. He finished third in the class of 1937.

Nixon had shown an interest in politics since the age of six, when he began reading news of current events and talking about them with his father. When he was 11, the Teapot Dome scandal prompted him to announce to his mother, "I'll be a lawyer they can't bribe." The practice of law in Whittier was hardly so inspiring. Taken into the firm of a family friend, he spent his first day dusting the books in the office library, then bungled his first case, losing all his client's money in a real estate deal. But he persevered, began joining various clubs, making speeches. He even joined a local theater group, where he met a schoolteacher named Thelma ("Pat") Ryan.

Driving her home from the theater, he said, "I'd like to have a date with you."

"Oh, I'm too busy," she replied. An orphan, she was not only working but attending classes as well. The second time Nixon drove her home, he again asked for a date, again was shrugged off. The third time it happened, Nixon said, "Someday I'm going to marry you." It took two years of courtship before she agreed in 1940; she converted to the Quaker faith and used her own savings to buy the wedding ring.

Nixon probably would not have been content to stay in Whittier forever, but Pearl Harbor uprooted his whole generation. He knew that if he was ever to have a political career, he would have to join the armed forces. So despite the Quaker belief in pacifism, he won a commission in the Navy in June 1942. He served creditably as a supply officer in New Caledonia, then the Solomon Islands. His most remarkable activity, though, was to become a master at bluffing in stud poker. By the end of the war, he had won and saved a stake estimated at as much as $10,000. He invested half of it in the following year in launching his political career.

Jerry Voorhis, a popular liberal Democrat, had won five straight elections in the 12th Congressional District east of Los Angeles, but a group of local businessmen hoped to unseat him. Nixon promised them "an aggressive and vigorous campaign." He began working up to 20 hours a day, making speeches about his war experiences, denouncing the New Deal. When Pat gave birth to their first daughter Patricia (Tricia), Nixon was out campaigning. (Confident of re-election, he stayed home when Julie was born two years later.)

Nixon implied — falsely — that Voorhis was virtually a communist. "Remember," said one of Nixon's ads, "Voorhis is a former registered Socialist and his voting record in Congress is more socialistic and communistic than Democratic." This kind of smear was to become a Nixon trademark. To one of Voorhis' supporters, Nixon later offered a very personal rationale: "Of course I knew Jerry Voorhis wasn't a communist, but I had to win. That's the thing you don't understand. The important thing is to win."

Win he did, with 56% of the vote. This was part of the end-of-the-war landslide that gave the G.O.P. control of both houses for the first time since the election following the Great Crash of 1929. Nixon asked to be put on the Education and Labor Committee, which was going to rewrite the rules of labor relations through the Taft-Hartley Act. In return, he was asked to serve on an eccentric committee [the House Committee on Un-American Affairs] that devoted its time to noisy investigations of "un-American activities." It was to be the making of his career.

Nixon began looking for experts on communist influence in labor unions. This led him to a Maryknoll priest whose report on the subject included the fact that a TIME senior editor named Whittaker Chambers had told the FBI that he had belonged to a communist cell in Washington, and that it included Alger Hiss. It seemed incredible. A lawyer who had once clerked for Justice Oliver Wendell Holmes, Hiss had served as a State Department adviser at the Yalta conference, had helped organize the United Nations and was being touted as perhaps its first Secretary-General.

Hiss, then president of the Carnegie Endowment, denied ever having met anyone named Whittaker Chambers. Nixon had both men summoned before the committee to confront each other. Hiss finally admitted knowing Chambers slightly under a different name. Chambers insisted that they had been "close friends . . . caught in a tragedy of history." But nothing could be proved until Chambers produced the "pumpkin papers," microfilms of State Department documents that he said Hiss had given him for transmission to Moscow. Hiss was convicted of perjury in January 1950, served 44 months in prison and has spent the rest of his long life denying guilt.

The Hiss case made Nixon a national figure and launched him into a run for the Senate in 1950 against Helen Gahagan Douglas, a former actress who had served six years in the House as an ardent New Dealer. Since red hunting was a national mania in these Korean War days, Douglas foolishly tried to accuse Nixon of being soft on communism, and invented the name that haunted him for the rest of his life: Tricky Dick. But when it came to mudslinging,

she was up against a champion. He called her the "pink lady" and declared that she was "pink right down to her underwear." He won by the biggest plurality of any Senate candidate that year.

Nixon had hardly begun serving in the Senate before the Republican leadership started fighting over whether the 1952 presidential nomination should go to conservative Senator Robert Taft or to the immensely popular General Dwight Eisenhower. The convention was in danger of deadlocking, in which case it might turn to California Governor Earl Warren. That was certainly Warren's plan, and all the California delegates, including Nixon, were pledged to back him. In some complicated maneuvering, though, the Eisenhower forces put forward a resolution that would give them a number of disputed Southern delegations. Nixon, who had already been sounded out as a running mate for Eisenhower, persuaded the California delegates to back this resolution, and so Eisenhower won. Warren never forgave Nixon for what he considered a betrayal.

Once nominated as Vice President, Nixon was assigned to play hatchet man on "communism and corruption" while Eisenhower remained statesman-like. Nixon was all too eager to comply. He described Democratic nominee Adlai Stevenson as one who "holds a Ph.D. from [Secretary of State Dean] Acheson's College of Cowardly Communist Containment."

The Democrats got their revenge when the press discovered and trumpeted that Nixon had a secret slush fund of $18,000 provided by California businessmen to help finance his activities. Nixon insisted that the fund was perfectly legal and was used solely for routine political expenses, but the smell of scandal thickened. At Eisenhower's urging, Nixon went before a TV audience estimated at 58 million with an impassioned defense of his honesty. "Pat and I have the satisfaction that every dime we've got is honestly ours," he said. The only personal present he had received was "a little cocker spaniel dog in a crate. Black-and-white spotted. And our little girl — Tricia,

Nixon and Dwight Eisenhower. "Once nominated as Vice President," Friedrich points out, "Nixon was assigned to play hatchet man on 'communism and corruption' while Eisenhower"—the Republican nominee for President—"remained statesmanlike."

During the scandal over the secret slush fund provided for Nixon by California businessmen, Nixon gave his famous Checkers speech, after which Eisenhower proclaimed in public, "You're my boy!" (UPI/Corbis-Bettmann)

the six-year-old—named it Checkers. And you know, the kids love that dog." Hundreds of thousands of listeners cabled or wrote their support of Nixon, and Eisenhower settled his future by saying publicly, "You're my boy!"

Eisenhower won 55% of the vote, and the freshman Senator from California, still only 39, found himself the second youngest Vice President. He also found that a President and Vice President rarely like each other very much, because the latter's only real job is to wait for the former's death. Nixon faced the great test of this uneasy relationship when Eisenhower suffered a heart attack in September 1955. It

was up to Nixon to chair Cabinet meetings and generally run the White House machinery without ever seeming to covet the power that lay just beyond his fingertips. He did the job tactfully and skillfully throughout the weeks of Eisenhower's recovery.

One major function of modern Vice Presidents is to travel, and Nixon turned himself into a latter-day Marco Polo: nine trips to 61 countries. Everywhere he went, he conferred, orated, debated, press-conferenced. In Moscow to open a U.S trade exhibit in 1959, Nixon got into a finger-pointing argument on communism with Soviet Party Secretary Nikita

Khrushchev in the kitchen of an American model home.

To some extent, Vice Presidents' tasks are defined by their own skills and experiences. Nixon knew more about politics than almost anyone else in Eisenhower's Administration, so he became the G.O.P.'S chief campaigner. When Eisenhower's second term expired, Nixon was the inevitable successor; he was nominated to run against the Democrats' John F. Kennedy.

Eisenhower and others warned Nixon not to accept Kennedy's challenge to a televised debate — Nixon was the Vice President, after all, and far better known than the junior Senator from Massachusetts — but Nixon took pride in his long experience as a debater. He also ignored advice to rest up for the debate and went on campaigning strenuously until the last minute. So what a record 80 million Americans saw on their TV screens was a devastating contrast. Kennedy looked fresh, tanned, vibrant; Nixon looked unshaven, baggy-eyed, surly. The era of the politics of TV imagery had begun, and the debates were a major victory for Kennedy.

The vote was incredibly close, with Kennedy winning 50.4% of the popular vote and Nixon 49.6%. He accepted the bitter defeat and returned to California. Then Nixon's legendary political shrewdness abandoned him. He let himself be talked into running for Governor of California against the popular Edmund G. ("Pat") Brown, and tried to imply that Brown was a dangerous leftist. It was after his crushing defeat that Nixon blew up at reporters and announced that this was his "last press conference."

Still only 49, he decided to move to New York City and make some money by practicing corporate law. He joined a prosperous Wall Street firm, which thereupon became Nixon, Mudge, Rose, Guthrie and Alexander. But he never really retired from politics. He was just biding his time. He thought Jack Kennedy would be unbeatable in 1964, and Lyndon Johnson soon appeared almost as much so. Nixon played elder statesman, letting

Barry Goldwater and Nelson Rockefeller fight for the G.O.P. nomination. Nixon stumped loyally for Goldwater, and when that campaign ended in disaster, he became the logical man to reunite the splintered party in 1968.

Following the advice of a young advertising man named H. R. Haldeman, he finally learned how to make effective use of television: not in speeches or press conferences but answering questions from "typical voters" and then carefully editing the results. If that was artificial, so in a way was the whole 1968 campaign. Democratic candidate Hubert Humphrey dared not repudiate Johnson's doomed Vietnam policy and talked instead about "the politics of joy." Nixon, who had agreed with Johnson's escalation of the war and hoped to court segregationist votes in the South, spoke mainly in code words about "peace with honor" in Vietnam and "law and order" at home. In a year of assassinations and ghetto riots, Nixon sounded reassuring, or enough so to defeat Humphrey and the war-torn Democrats. But it was close: 43.4% for Nixon, 42.7% for Humphrey, 13.5% for George Wallace.

Nixon's first term included sweeping innovations, often surprisingly liberal. He was the first President in years to cut military spending; the first to tie Social Security increases to the cost of living. He instituted "revenue sharing" to funnel $6 billion a year in federal tax money back to the states and cities. He signed the act lowering the voting age to 18. And he benefited from Kennedy's decision to go to the moon. When Neil Armstrong landed there in 1969, Nixon somewhat vaingloriously declared that "this is the greatest week in the history of the world since the Creation."

His imaginative measures were shadowed, however, by Vietnam. Nixon, who had supported each previous escalation — and indeed repeatedly demanded more — had campaigned on a promise to end the war "with honor," meaning no surrender and no defeat. He called for a cease-fire and negotiations, but the communists showed no interest. And while U.S. casualties continued at a rate of about 400 a month, protests against the war grew in size and violence.

To quiet antiwar demonstrators, Nixon announced that he would gradually withdraw U.S. forces, starting with 25,000 in June 1969. From now on, the war would be increasingly fought by the Vietnamese themselves. When, from their sanctuaries in Cambodia, the North Vietnamese began harassing the retreating Americans in the spring of 1970, Nixon ordered bombing raids and made a temporary "incursion" into the country. The main effect of this expansion of the war was an explosion of new antiwar outcries on college campuses.

These were fiercely contentious times, and Nixon was partly to blame for that. He had always been the fighter rather than the conciliator, and though he had millions of supporters among what he liked to call "the Silent Majority" in "middle America," the increasing conflicts in American politics made it difficult to govern at all. Nixon, as the nation learned later when it heard the Watergate tapes, brought to the White House an extraordinarily permanent anger and resentment. His staff memos were filled with furious instructions to fire people, investigate leaks and "knock off this crap."

Together with this chronic anger, the mistrustful Nixon had a passion for secrecy. He repeatedly launched military operations without telling his own Defense Secretary, Melvin Laird, and major diplomatic initiatives without telling his Secretary of State, William Rogers. All major actions went through his White House staff members, particularly National Security Adviser Henry Kissinger and Nixon's two chief domestic aides, Bob Haldeman and John Ehrlichman.

Just as he loved secrecy, Nixon hated leaks to the press (though he himself was a dedicated leaker to favored reporters). And so when he first ordered an unannounced air raid against communist bases in Cambodia in April 1969, he was furious to read

about it in a Washington dispatch in the New York Times. FBI chief J. Edgar Hoover told the President that the only way to find the leaker was to start tapping phones. When Nixon entered the White House and dismantled the elaborate taping system that Johnson had installed, Hoover told him that the FBI, on Johnson's orders, had bugged Nixon's campaign plane. Now Nixon started down the same path, getting Attorney General John Mitchell to sign the orders for 17 taps.

When a series of secret Vietnam documents known as the Pentagon Papers began appearing in the New York Times in June 1971, Kissinger persuaded Nixon that the leaker, Daniel Ellsberg, "must be stopped at all costs." The FBI turned balky at extralegal activities, so Nixon told Ehrlichman, "Then by God, we'll do it ourselves. I want you to set up a little group right here in the White House."

Thus was born the team of "plumbers." Its only known job involving Ellsberg was to break into his psychiatrist's office that September in search of evidence against him. But once such a team is created, other uses for it tend to be found. The following June, seven plumbers (five of them wearing surgical rubber gloves) were arrested during a burglary of Democratic national headquarters in the Watergate office and apartment complex.

They admitted nothing, and nobody connected them with Nixon. The White House itself was already doing its best to block any FBI investigation, but it formally denied any involvement in what press secretary Ron Ziegler dismissed as "a third-rate burglary attempt." Nobody has ever disclosed exactly what the burglars were looking for or what they found, if anything.

The Watergate burglary quickly faded from the front pages. Nixon was campaigning hard for reelection, portraying himself as a global peacemaker. In February 1972 he had reversed nearly 30 years of American policy by flying to Beijing, ending restrictions on trade with China and supporting China's entry into the U.N. In May he had signed the first

On August 9, 1974, having resigned the Presidency in the wake of Watergate, Nixon bade good-bye to his staff and Cabinet in the East Room of the White House. To his right is his son-in-law, David Eisenhower. (Archives Photos)

arms-control agreement with Soviet leader Leonid Brezhnev, placing sharp restrictions on antiballistic missiles. And although Kissinger's protracted secret negotiations with the Vietnamese communists had not yet brought a truce agreement, Nixon pulled out the last U.S. combat troops in August.

Nixon trounced Senator George McGovern that fall, capturing nearly 61% of the vote. Then, after one last spasm of belligerence in the carpet bombing of Hanoi at Christmas, Nixon announced in January 1973, "We today have concluded an agreement to end the war and bring peace with honor to Vietnam."

But the Watergate mystery remained. In court, five of the burglars pleaded guilty in January 1973 (the other two were quickly convicted), but they still admitted nothing. Federal Judge John Sirica angrily sentenced them to long prison terms (up to 10 years) and indicated that he might reduce the punishment if they confessed more fully. One of the seven, James McCord, wrote Sirica on March 20 that "others involved in the Watergate operation were not identified during the trial." In two secret sessions with Watergate committee counsel Sam Dash, he later named three top Nixon officials: Attorney General Mitchell; Mitchell's deputy, Jeb Stuart Magruder; and White House counsel John Dean.

Caught lying — but still denying any wrongdoing — Nixon said he was ordering a new investigation of the situation. Two federal grand juries were also investigating. So was the press. Though a lot of this probing was only loosely connected to the burglary, the term Watergate began to apply to a whole series of misdeeds that seriously tainted Nixon's great election victory. Not only did more than $100,000 donated to Nixon's campaign end up in the bank account of one of the plumbers, but the entire fund-raising operation was marked by illegalities, irregularities and deceptions. Congress decided to investigate all this too. It chose a select committee to be headed by North Carolina's folksy Senator Sam Ervin.

Two and a half weeks before the committee was scheduled to open televised hearings in May 1973, Nixon made a stunning announcement: his two chief White House aides, Haldeman and Ehrlichman, were resigning, as were Attorney General Richard Kleindienst (who had succeeded Mitchell) and White House attorney Dean. "There can be no whitewash at the White House," Nixon said.

The Senate hearings soon showed otherwise. Magruder testified that Mitchell and Dean had been deeply involved. Then the dismissed Dean took the stand in June and testified that Nixon himself had been lying, that he had known about the White House cover-up attempts since at least September 1972. He also disclosed that the White House kept hundreds of names on an "enemies list" and used tax investigations and other methods to harass them. But how could anyone prove such charges? That question received an astonishing answer a month later when a former White House official named Alexander Butterfield almost offhandedly told the committee that Nixon had installed voice-activated recorders that secretly taped all his White House conversations.

When the senate committee promptly demanded the tapes, Nixon refused, claiming Executive privilege. The new Attorney General, Elliot Richardson, had appointed Harvard law professor Archibald Cox as a special prosecutor in the whole case, and Cox sent a subpoena for tapes he wanted to hear. Nixon refused him too. Judge Sirica upheld Cox's demand, so Nixon resisted him in the U.S. Court of Appeals, which backed Sirica.

Nixon then offered to produce an edited summary of the tapes. When Cox rejected that idea, Nixon on Oct. 20 angrily told Richardson to fire Cox. Richardson refused and resigned instead. Nixon told Deputy Attorney General William Ruckelshaus to fire Cox; he too refused and resigned. General Alexander Haig, Haldeman's successor as White House chief of staff, finally got Solicitor General Robert Bork to do the job, and so the "Saturday Night Massacre" ended, leaving the Nixon Administration a shambles. (In the midst of all this, it was almost incidental that Vice President Spiro Agnew resigned under fire for having taken graft and that he was replaced by Michigan Congressman Gerald Ford.)

The House began on Oct. 30 to look into the possibilities of impeachment. Inside the besieged White House, Nixon raged like a trapped animal. There were unconfirmed reports that he was drinking heavily, that he couldn't sleep, that he even wandered around late at night and spoke to the paintings on the walls. To a meeting of Associated Press editors, he piteously declared, "I am not a crook."

Special prosecutor Cox had by now been replaced by a conservative Texas attorney, Leon Jaworski, who appeared no less determined to get the tapes. Still resisting inch by inch, Nixon released 1,254 pages of edited transcript. They were a revelation of the inner workings of the Nixon White House, a sealed-off fortress where a character designated as P in the transcripts talked endlessly and obscenely about all his enemies. "I want the most comprehensive notes on all those who tried to do us in," P said to Haldeman at one point, for example. "We have not used . . . the Justice Department, but things are going to change now." The edited tapes still left uncertainties about Nixon's involvement in the Watergate cover-up, however, so Jaworski insisted on the unedited originals of 64 specific tapes, transcripts and other documents. Nixon refused. Jaworski filed suit. The Supreme Court ruled unanimously that a President cannot withhold evidence in a criminal case (Mitchell, Haldeman, Ehrlichman and others were by now under indictment, and Nixon himself had been named by the grand jury as an "unindicted co-conspirator").

During all this, the House Judiciary Committee, headed by New Jersey's Democratic Congressman Peter Rodino, had been conducting hearings on impeachment. It soon decided to impeach Nixon on three counts: obstruction of justice, abuse of presidential powers and defiance of the committee's subpoenas.

Nixon meanwhile sat out in his beach house in San Clemente, California, reading a biography of Napoleon and staring at the ocean. But he had also been listening to some of the disputed tapes, and he had found one — the "smoking gun" — that threatened to destroy his whole case. It was a talk with Haldeman on June 23, 1972, a time when Nixon had long pretended to know virtually nothing about the Watergate break-in just six days earlier. This tape recorded Nixon talking with Haldeman about Mitchell's involvement, ordering a cover-up, planning to use the FBI and CIA to protect himself. For good measure, the tape also included presidential slurs on Jews, women, homosexuals, Italians and the press. The reaction to the new tape, when Nixon finally released it, was disastrous. Even conservatives like Ronald Reagan and Barry Goldwater demanded Nixon's resignation, as did G.O.P. chairman George Bush. A congressional delegation told the President he had no more than 15 votes in the Senate, about the same in the House. Shortly after, Nixon told his family, "We're going back to California." His daughters burst into tears; his wife did not.

Two days later, on Aug. 8, 1974, Nixon made his last televised statement from the White House: "I have never been a quitter. To leave office before my term is completed is abhorrent to every instinct in my body. But as President I must put the interest of America first . . . Therefore, I shall resign the presidency effective at noon tomorrow." There remained then only a series of farewells. He spoke once again of winning and losing. "We think that when we suffer a defeat, that all is ended. Not true. It is only a beginning, always."

And so it was, once again, for Nixon. When he left Washington, there was a chance he might yet be prosecuted. Gerald Ford fixed that a month later by issuing a presidential pardon protecting Nixon from legal penalties for anything he had done in connection with Watergate. But Nixon's health was poor, his psychic shock obvious. An attack of phlebitis nearly killed him. He later told friends that he heard voices calling, "Richard, pull yourself back." And so he did.

His first public appearance came in 1978, and then the long, slow process of self-rehabilitation. Perhaps, in his last years, having regained a certain amount of public respect and even some grudging admiration, having acquired four grandchildren and all the comforts of leisurely wealth, Nixon finally found a little peace, finally got over that mysterious anger that had fueled his ambition throughout his long life. Perhaps.

QUESTIONS TO CONSIDER

1 What in Richard Nixon's background shaped him into the angry, ambitious man he became? How did his character traits affect his political career? What did he tell a supporter of Jerry Voorhis the most important thing was? What does this tell you about Nixon's character?

2 What was Nixon's favorite issue in his campaign against Jerry Voorhis for a seat in the national House and his campaign against Helen Douglas for a seat in the United States Senate? Describe the political atmosphere at the time that made that issue such a successful one for Nixon. What was Nixon's role on

HUAC? What famous case rocketed him to national prominence? .

3   What were Nixon's greatest successes as president? Why was he able to achieve momentous diplomatic breakthroughs with Communist China and the Soviet Union when nobody else could do so? We saw in selection 25 that Lyndon Johnson's policies trapped the United States in a stalemated war in Vietnam. How was Nixon able to end American involvement there? Why did he do so?

4   Discuss the Watergate scandal. How was the Nixon White House involved? Why did Nixon lie about his knowledge of the Watergate break-in and with the help of his aides try to cover it up? Why didn't Nixon simply tell the public the truth? What finally brought down the Nixon presidency, causing him to become the first American president ever to resign his office? Do you think that Gerald Ford should have pardoned Nixon?

5   Nixon's political career has been described as one of rising and falling, rising and falling, rising and falling, and rising again. How do you account for his resiliency? Do you think the nickname, Tricky Dick, was appropriate or inappropriate? How would you rate him as president compared with Roosevelt, Truman, and Eisenhower?

29

How the Seventies Changed America

NICHOLAS LEMANN

To many Americans, it was the "loser" decade, a ten-year hangover from the excesses of the sixties, a time of bitter disillusionment, what with Watergate and the withdrawal from Vietnam, the only war America ever lost. It was a plastic era, to use Norman Mailer's term, that featured polyester suits and disco music. Many Americans still regard the 1970s as a vague interim between the liberal idealism and social upheaval of the sixties and the conservative individualism of the eighties. But to journalist Nicholas Lemann, looking back from today's vantage point, the seventies can no longer be dismissed as "the runt decade" in which relatively nothing significant occurred. On the contrary, he finds profound importance in terms of several "sweeping historical trends" that began or were accelerated in the seventies and that went on to shape what American society has become in our time.

First, he says, it was the decade in which geopolitics started revolving less around ideology than around oil and religion. He cites the 1973–1974 oil embargo of the oil-producing Arab-Muslim states as the "epochal event" of the decade, one that dashed the 1960s assumption of endless economic growth and prosperity for all in the United States. The oil embargo spurred the growth of the Sun Belt, initiated a period of staggering inflation, and marked the end, maybe forever, of "the mass upward economic mobility of American society." And that in turn fragmented the country into squabbling interest groups that cared more about looking out for themselves than about sacrificing for the national good.

Second, the presidential electorate became conservative and Republican, a trend that would last throughout the eighties, ending, for the time being, in the election of Democrat Bill Clinton in 1992. In reaction to the seeming paralysis and weakness of Jimmy

Carter's liberal Democratic administration, 1977–1981, American voters sent Republican Ronald Reagan to the White House because he preached "pure strength" in foreign affairs and promised to reduce taxes at home (the Reagan presidency is treated in selection 30). Thus, Reagan capitalized on a third sweeping trend of the seventies — the middle-class tax revolt, which Lemann describes as "an aftershock" of the Arab oil embargo. For the first time, he says, the American middle class, once considered uniquely fortunate, perceived itself as an oppressed group, the victim of runaway inflation, and revolted against the use of federal funds to help the less privileged.

A reporter for the Washington Post *during the seventies, Lemann draws an arresting portrait of this oft-disparaged decade that invites comparison with Allen Matusow's discussion of the sixties (selection 27). Indeed, Lemann agrees with Matusow that the seventies witnessed "the working of the phenomena of the sixties into the mainstream of American life." Lemann contends that the sixties' obsession with self-discovery became "a mass phenomenon" in the seventies and that the ethic of individual freedom as the "highest good," converging with the end of the American economy as an "expanding pie," led Americans to look out mainly for themselves.*

GLOSSARY

DÉTENTE   Relaxing of international tensions.

EST (ERHARD SEMINARS TRAINING)
System of encounter groups designed to help people "get in touch with themselves."

ORGANIZATION OF PETROLEUM EXPORTING STATES (OPEC)   Bargaining unit for the oil-exporting states in the Middle East and Africa; OPEC's oil embargo of 1973 quadrupled the price of oil and caused soaring inflation.

PROPOSITION 13   Initiative on the California state ballot that called for a significant reduction in property taxes; it passed overwhelmingly and led to similar tax revolts across the country.

T hat's it," Daniel Patrick Moynihan, then U.S. ambassador to India, wrote to a colleague on the White House staff in 1973 on the subject of some issue of the moment. "Nothing will happen. But then nothing much is going to happen in the 1970s anyway."

Moynihan is a politician famous for his predictions, and this one seemed for a long time to be dead-on. The seventies, even while they were in progress, looked like an unimportant decade, a period of cooling down from the white-hot sixties. You had to go back to the teens to find another decade so lacking in crisp, epigrammatic definition. It only made matters worse for the seventies that the

From Nicholas Lemann, "How the Seventies Changed America," *American Heritage,* 42 (July/August 1991), 39–42, 44, 46, 48–49. Reprinted by permission of *American Heritage* magazine, a division of Forbes Inc. Copyright © Forbes Inc., 1991.

succeeding decade started with a bang. In 1980 the country elected the most conservative President in its history, and it was immediately clear that a new era had dawned. (In general the eighties, unlike the seventies, had a perfect dramatic arc. They peaked in the summer of 1984, with the Los Angeles Olympics and the Republican National Convention in Dallas, and began to peter out with the Iran-contra scandal in 1986 and the stock market crash in 1987.) It is nearly impossible to engage in magazine-writerly games like discovering "the day the seventies died" or "the spirit of the seventies"; and the style of the seventies — wide ties, sideburns, synthetic fabrics, white shoes, disco — is so far interesting largely as something to make fun of.

But somehow the seventies seem to be creeping out of the loser-decade category. Their claim to importance is in the realm of sweeping historical trends, rather than memorable events, though there were some of those too. In the United States today a few basic propositions shape everything: The presidential electorate is conservative and Republican. Geopolitics revolves around a commodity (oil) and a religion (Islam) more than around an ideology (Marxism-Leninism). The national economy is no longer one in which practically every class, region, and industry is upwardly mobile. American culture is essentially individualistic, rather than communitarian, which means that notions like deferred gratification, sacrifice, and sustained national effort are a very tough sell. Anyone seeking to understand the roots of this situation has to go back to the seventies.

The underestimation of the seventies' importance, especially during the early years of the decade, is easy to forgive because the character of the seventies was substantially shaped at first by spillover from the sixties. Such sixties events as the killings of student protesters at Kent State and Orangeburg, the original Earth Day, the invasion of Cambodia, and a large portion of the war in Vietnam took place in the seventies. Although sixties radicals (cultural and political) spent the early seventies loudly bemoaning the end of the revolution, what was in fact going on was the working of the phenomena of the sixties into the mainstream of American life. Thus the first Nixon administration, which was decried by liberals at the time for being nightmarishly right-wing, was actually more liberal than the Johnson administration in many ways — less hawkish in Vietnam, more free-spending on social programs. The reason wasn't that Richard Nixon was a liberal but that the country as a whole had continued to move steadily to the left throughout the late sixties and early seventies; the political climate of institutions like the U.S. Congress and the boards of directors of big corporations was probably more liberal in 1972 than in any year before or since, and the Democratic party nominated its most liberal presidential candidate ever. Nixon had to go along with the tide.

In New Orleans, my hometown, the hippie movement peaked in 1972 or 1973. Long hair, crash pads, head shops, psychedelic posters, underground newspapers, and other Summer of Love–inspired institutions had been unknown there during the real Summer of Love, which was in 1967. It took even longer, until the middle or late seventies, for those aspects of hippie life that have endured to catch on with the general public. All over the country the likelihood that an average citizen would wear longish hair, smoke marijuana, and openly live with a lover before marriage was probably greater in 1980 than it was in 1970. The sixties' preoccupation with self-discovery became a mass phenomenon only in the seventies, through home-brew psychological therapies like EST. In politics the impact of the black enfranchisement that took place in the 1960s barely began to be felt until the mid- to late 1970s. The tremendously influential feminist and gay-liberation movements were, at the dawn of the 1970s, barely under way in Manhattan, their headquarters, and

"*Steer clear of that one. Every day is always the first day of the rest of his life.*"

Charles Saxon's spirited sketch is good social history. In 1972 this is what a lot of Americans looked like. (Drawing by Charles

Saxon © 1972 from The New Yorker Collection. All rights reserved.)

certainly hadn't begun their spread across the whole country. The sixties took a long time for America to digest; the process went on throughout the seventies and even into the eighties.

The epochal event of the seventies as an era in its own right was the Organization of Petroleum Exporting Countries' oil embargo, which lasted for six months in the fall of 1973 and the spring of 1974. Everything that happened in the sixties was predicated on the assumption of economic prosperity and growth; concerns like personal fulfillment and social justice tend to emerge in the middle class only at times when people take it for granted that they'll be able to make a living. For thirty years — ever since

the effects of World War II on the economy had begun to kick in — the average American's standard of living had been rising, to a remarkable extent. As the economy grew, indices like home ownership, automobile ownership, and access to higher education got up to levels unknown anywhere else in the world, and the United States could plausibly claim to have provided a better life materially for its working class than any society ever had. That ended with the OPEC embargo.

While it was going on, the embargo didn't fully register in the national consciousness. The country was absorbed by a different story, the Watergate scandal, which was really another sixties spillover, the final series of battles in the long war between the antiwar liberals and the rough-playing anti-Communists. Richard Nixon, having engaged in dirty tricks against leftish politicians for his whole career, didn't stop doing so as President; he only found new targets, like Daniel Ellsberg and [Democratic Party chairman] Lawrence O'Brien. This time, however, he lost the Establishment, which was now far more kindly disposed to Nixon's enemies than it had been back in the 1950s. Therefore, the big-time press, the courts, and the Congress undertook the enthralling process of cranking up the deliberate, inexorable machinery of justice, and everybody was glued to the television for a year and a half. The embargo, on the other hand, was a non-video-friendly economic story and hence difficult to get hooked on. It pertained to two subcultures that were completely mysterious to most Americans — the oil industry and the Arab world — and it seemed at first to be merely an episode in the ongoing hostilities between Israel and its neighbors. But in retrospect it changed everything, much more than Watergate did.

By causing the price of oil to double, the embargo enriched — and therefore increased the wealth, power, and confidence of — oil-producing areas like Texas, while helping speed the decline of the automobile-producing upper Midwest; the rise of OPEC and the rise of the Sunbelt as a center of population and political influence went together. The embargo ushered in a long period of inflation, the reaction to which dominated the economics and politics of the rest of the decade. It demonstrated that America could now be "pushed around" by countries most of us had always thought of as minor powers.

Most important of all, the embargo now appears to have been the pivotal moment at which the mass upward economic mobility of American society ended, perhaps forever. Average weekly earnings, adjusted for inflation, peaked in 1973. Productivity — that is, economic output per man-hour — abruptly stopped growing. The nearly universal assumption in the post–World War II United States was that children would do better than their parents. Upward mobility wasn't just a characteristic of the national culture; it was the defining characteristic. As it slowly began to sink in that everybody wasn't going to be moving forward together anymore, the country became more fragmented, more internally rivalrous, and less sure of its mythology.

Richard Nixon resigned as President in August 1974, and the country settled into what appeared to be a quiet, folksy drama of national recuperation. In the White House good old Gerald Ford was succeeded by rural, sincere Jimmy Carter, who was the only President elevated to the office by the voters during the 1970s and so was the decade's emblematic political figure. In hindsight, though, it's impossible to miss a gathering conservative stridency in the politics of the late seventies. In 1976 Ronald Reagan, the retired governor of California, challenged Ford for the Republican presidential nomination. Reagan lost the opening primaries and seemed to be about to drop out of the race when, apparently to the surprise even of his own staff, he won the North Carolina primary in late March.

It is quite clear what caused the Reagan campaign to catch on: He had begun to attack Ford from the right on foreign policy matters. The night before the primary he bought a half-hour of statewide television time to press his case. Reagan's main substantive criticism was of the policy of détente with the Soviet Union, but his two most crowd-pleasing points were his promise, if elected, to fire Henry Kissinger as Secretary of State and his lusty denunciation of the elaborately negotiated treaty to turn nominal control of the Panama Canal over to the Panamanians. Less than a year earlier Communist forces had finally captured the South Vietnamese capital city of Saigon, as the staff of the American Embassy escaped in a wild scramble into helicopters. The oil embargo had ended, but the price of gasoline had not retreated. The United States appeared to have descended from the pinnacle of power

With fleeting success, Jimmy Carter brings moral pressure to bear on a troubled world in a 1977 cartoon by Edward Sorel. (Courtesy of Edward Sorel)

and respect it had occupied at the close of World War II to a small, hounded position, and Reagan had hit on a symbolic way of expressing rage over that change. Most journalistic and academic opinion at the time was fairly cheerful about the course of American foreign policy — we were finally out of Vietnam, and we were getting over our silly Cold War phobia about dealing with China and the Soviet Union — but in the general public obviously the rage Reagan expressed was widely shared.

A couple of years later a conservative political cause even more out of the blue than opposition to the Panama Canal Treaty appeared: the tax revolt. Howard Jarvis, a seventy-five-year-old retired businessman who had been attacking taxation in California pretty much continuously since 1962, got onto the state ballot in 1978 an initiative, Proposition 13, that would substantially cut property taxes. Despite bad press and the strong opposition of most politicians, it passed by a two to one margin.

Proposition 13 was to some extent another aftershock of the OPEC embargo. Inflation causes the value of hard assets to rise. The only substantial hard asset owned by most Americans is their home. As the prices of houses soared in the mid-seventies (causing people to dig deeper to buy housing, which sent the national savings rate plummeting and made real estate prices the great conversation starter in the social life of the middle class), so did property taxes, since they are based on the values of the houses. Hence, resentment over taxation became an issue in waiting.

The influence of Proposition 13 has been so great that it is now difficult to recall that taxes weren't a major concern in national politics before it. Conservative opposition to government focused on its activities, not on its revenue base, and this put conservatism at a disadvantage, because most government programs are popular. Even before Proposition 13, conservative economic writers like Jude Wanniski and Arthur Laffer were inventing supply-side economics, based on the idea that reducing taxes would bring prosperity. With Proposition 13 it was proved — as it has been proved over and over since — that tax cutting was one of the rare voguish policy ideas that turn out to be huge political winners. In switching from arguing against programs to arguing against taxes, conservatism had found another key element of its ascension to power.

The tax revolt wouldn't have worked if the middle class hadn't been receptive to the notion that it was oppressed. This was remarkable in itself, since it had been assumed for decades that the American middle class was, in a world-historical sense, almost uniquely lucky. The emergence of a self-pitying strain in the middle class was in a sense yet another sixties spillover. At the dawn of the sixties, the idea that *anybody* in the United States was oppressed might have seemed absurd. Then blacks, who really were oppressed, were able to make the country see the truth about their situation. But that opened Pan-

dora's box. The eloquent language of group rights that the civil rights movement had invented proved to be quite adaptable, and eventually it was used by college students, feminists, Native Americans, Chicanos, urban blue-collar "white ethnics," and, finally, suburban homeowners.

Meanwhile, the social programs started by Lyndon Johnson gave rise to another new, or long-quiescent, idea, which was that the government was wasting vast sums of money on harebrained schemes. In some ways the Great Society accomplished its goal of binding the country together, by making the federal government a nationwide provider of such favors as medical care and access to higher education; but in others it contributed to the seventies trend of each group's looking to government to provide it with benefits and being unconcerned with the general good. Especially after the economy turned sour, the middle class began to define its interests in terms of a rollback of government programs aimed at helping other groups.

As the country was becoming more fragmented, so was its essential social unit, the family. In 1965 only 14.9 percent of the population was single; by 1979 the figure had risen to 20 percent. The divorce rate went from 2.5 per thousand in 1965 to 5.3 per thousand in 1979. The percentage of births that were out of wedlock was 5.3 in 1960 and 16.3 in 1978. The likelihood that married women with young children would work doubled between the mid-sixties and the late seventies. These changes took place for a variety of reasons — feminism, improved birth control, the legalization of abortion, the spread across the country of the sixties youth culture's rejection of traditional mores — but what they added up to was that the nuclear family, consisting of a working husband and a nonworking wife, both in their first marriage, and their children, ceased to be the dominant type of American household during the seventies. Also, people became more likely to organize themselves into communities based on their family status, so that the unmarried often lived in singles apartment complexes and retirees in senior citizens' developments. The overall effect was one of much greater personal freedom, which meant, as it always does, less social cohesion. Tom Wolfe's moniker for the seventies, the Me Decade, caught on because it was probably true that the country had placed relatively more emphasis on individual happiness and relatively less on loyalty to family and nation.

Like a symphony, the seventies finally built up in a crescendo that pulled together all its main themes. This occurred during the second half of 1979. First OPEC engineered the "second oil shock," in which, by holding down production, it got the price for its crude oil (and the price of gasoline at American service stations) to rise by more than 50 percent during the first six months of that year. With the onset of the summer vacation season, the automotive equivalent of the Depression's bank runs began. Everybody considered the possibility of not being able to get gas, panicked, and went off to fill the tank; the result was hours-long lines at gas stations all over the country.

It was a small inconvenience compared with what people in the Communist world and Latin America live through all the time, but the psychological effect was enormous. The summer of 1979 was the only time I can remember when, at the level of ordinary life as opposed to public affairs, things seemed to be out of control. Inflation was well above 10 percent and rising, and suddenly what seemed like a quarter of every day was spent on getting gasoline or thinking about getting gasoline — a task that previously had been completely routine, as it is again now. Black markets sprang up; rumors flew about well-connected people who had secret sources. One day that summer, after an hour's desperate and fruitless search, I ran out of gas on the Central Expressway in Dallas. I left my car sitting primly in the right lane and walked away in the hundred-degree heat; the

people driving by looked at me without surprise, no doubt thinking, "Poor bastard, it could have happened to me just as easily."

In July President Carter scheduled a speech on the gas lines, then abruptly canceled it and repaired to Camp David to think deeply for ten days, which seemed like a pale substitute for somehow setting things aright. Aides, cabinet secretaries, intellectuals, religious leaders, tycoons, and other leading citizens were summoned to Carter's aerie to discuss with him what was wrong with the country's soul. On July 15 he made a television address to the nation, which has been enshrined in memory as the "malaise speech," although it didn't use that word. (Carter did, however, talk about "a crisis of confidence . . . that strikes at the very heart and soul and spirit of our national will.")

To reread the speech today is to be struck by its spectacular political ineptitude. Didn't Carter realize that Presidents are not supposed to express doubts publicly or to lecture the American people about their shortcomings? Why couldn't he have just temporarily imposed gas rationing, which would have ended the lines overnight, instead of outlining a vague and immediately forgotten six-point program to promote energy conservation?

His describing the country's loss of confidence did not cause the country to gain confidence, needless to say. And it didn't help matters that upon his return to Washington he demanded letters of resignation from all members of his cabinet and accepted five of them. Carter seemed to be anything but an FDR-like reassuring, ebullient presence; he communicated a sense of wild flailing about as he tried (unsuccessfully) to get the situation under control.

I remember being enormously impressed by Carter's speech at the time because it was a painfully honest and much thought-over attempt to grapple with the main problem of the decade. The American economy had ceased being an expanding pie, and by unfortunate coincidence this had happened just when an ethic of individual freedom as the highest good was spreading throughout the society, which meant people would respond to the changing economic conditions by looking out for themselves. Like most other members of the word-manipulating class whose leading figures had advised Carter at Camp David, I thought there *was* a malaise. What I didn't realize, and Carter obviously didn't either, was that there was a smarter way to play the situation politically. A President could maintain there was nothing wrong with America at all — that it hadn't become less powerful in the world, hadn't reached some kind of hard economic limit, and wasn't in crisis — and, instead of trying to reverse the powerful tide of individualism, ride along with it. At the same time, he could act more forcefully than Carter, especially against inflation, so that he didn't seem weak and ineffectual. All this is exactly what Carter's successor, Ronald Reagan, did.

Actually, Carter himself set in motion the process by which inflation was conquered a few months later, when he gave the chairmanship of the Federal Reserve Board to Paul Volcker, a man willing to put the economy into a severe recession to bring back price stability. But in November fate delivered the *coup de grâce* to Carter in the form of the taking hostage of the staff of the American Embassy in Teheran, as a protest against the United States' harboring of Iran's former shah.

As with the malaise speech, what is most difficult to convey today about the hostage crisis is why Carter made what now looks like a huge, obvious error: playing up the crisis so much that it became a national obsession for more than a year. The fundamental problem with hostage taking is that the one sure remedy — refusing to negotiate and thus allowing the hostages to be killed — is politically unacceptable in the democratic media society we live in, at least when the hostages are middle-class sympathetic figures, as they were in Iran.

There isn't any good solution to this problem, but

Carter's two successors in the White House demonstrated that it is possible at least to negotiate for the release of hostages in a low-profile way that will cause the press to lose interest and prevent the course of the hostage negotiations from completely defining the Presidency. During the last year of the Carter administration, by contrast, the hostage story absolutely dominated the television news (recall that the ABC show *Nightline* began as a half-hour five-times-a-week update on the hostage situation), and several of the hostages and their families became temporary celebrities. In Carter's defense, even among the many voices criticizing him for appearing weak and vacillating, there was none that I remember willing to say, "Just cut off negotiations and walk away." It was a situation that everyone regarded as terrible but in which there was a strong national consensus supporting the course Carter had chosen.

So ended the seventies. There was still enough of the sixties spillover phenomenon going on so that Carter, who is now regarded (with some affection) as having been too much the good-hearted liberal to maintain a hold on the presidential electorate, could be challenged for renomination by Ted Kennedy on the grounds that he was too conservative. Inflation was raging on; the consumer price index rose by 14.4 percent between May 1979 and May 1980. We were being humiliated by fanatically bitter, premodern Muslims whom we had expected to regard us with gratitude because we had helped ease out their dictator even though he was reliably pro–United States. The Soviet empire appeared (probably for the last time ever) to be on the march, having invaded Afghanistan to Carter's evident surprise and disillusionment. We had lost our most recent war. We couldn't pull together as a people. The puissant, unified, prospering America of the late 1940s seemed to be just a fading memory.

I was a reporter for the *Washington Post* during the 1980 presidential campaign, and even on the *Post*'s national desk, that legendary nerve center of politics,

Brian Basset saw Carter lying helpless while the 1980 election bore down; the polls never did let him loose. (Reprinted courtesy of Dennis Ryan)

the idea that the campaign might end with Reagan's being elected President seemed fantastic, right up to the weekend before the election. At first [Ted] Kennedy looked like a real threat to Carter; remember that up to that point no Kennedy had ever lost a campaign. While the Carter people were disposing of Kennedy, they were rooting for Reagan to win the Republican nomination because he would be such an easy mark.

He was too old, too unserious, and, most of all, too conservative. Look what had happened to Barry Goldwater (a sitting officeholder, at least) only six-

teen years earlier, and Reagan was so divisive that a moderate from his own party, John Anderson, was running for President as a third-party candidate. It was not at all clear how much the related issues of inflation and national helplessness were dominating the public's mind. Kennedy, Carter, and Anderson were all, in their own way, selling national healing, that great post-sixties obsession; Reagan, and only Reagan, was selling pure strength.

In a sense Reagan's election represents the country's rejection of the idea of a sixties-style solution to the great problems of the seventies — economic stagnation, social fragmentation, and the need for a new world order revolving around relations between the oil-producing Arab world and the West. The idea of a scaled-back America — husbanding its resources, living more modestly, renouncing its restless mobility, withdrawing from full engagement with the politics of every spot on the globe, focusing on issues of internal comity — evidently didn't appeal. Reagan, and the country, had in effect found a satisfying pose to strike in response to the problems of the seventies, but that's different from finding a solution.

Today some of the issues that dominated the seventies have faded away. Reagan and Volcker did beat inflation. The "crisis of confidence" now seems a long-ago memory. But it is striking how early we still seem to be in the process of working out the implications of the oil embargo. We have just fought and won [the Gulf War] against the twin evils of Middle East despotism and interruptions in the oil supply, which began to trouble us in the seventies. We still have not really even begun to figure out how to deal with the cessation of across-the-board income gains, and as a result our domestic politics are still dominated by squabbling over the proper distribution of government's benefits and burdens. During the seventies themselves the new issues that were arising seemed nowhere near as important as those sixties legacies, minority rights and Vietnam and Watergate. But the runt of decades has wound up casting a much longer shadow than anyone imagined.

QUESTIONS TO CONSIDER

1   What does Nicholas Lemann see as the long-term influence of the 1960s on American politics and culture? In what way were "the phenomena of the sixties" worked into the cultural mainstream? How does this view compare with Matusow's in selection 27?

2   Lemann sees the OPEC oil embargo of 1973–1974 as "the epochal event" of the 1970s. What were its economic and practical effects? What were the psychological effects on Americans' confidence in their country and their culture? How did the cultural trends of the 1970s make this reaction even more critical at the end of the decade?

3   According to Lemann, the 1970s were characterized by a "gathering conservative stridency." Discuss the events and developments in which this shows up. In what ways was it fed by trends from the 1960s, and in what ways was it a reaction against the sixties?

4   What is Lemann's judgment of Jimmy Carter and Ronald Reagan as men and as politicians? Does he find Reagan's presidency more successful than Carter's?

5   What does Lemann see as the long-term importance of the 1970s and their influence today? Do you see any signs of change, or do you think we are still working out the legacy of the 1970s?

XV

THE END OF THE COLD WAR

30

The Man Who Broke the Evil Empire

PETER SCHWEIZER

The collapse of the Soviet Union and the end of the Cold War came with such speed and surprise that the pace of events was almost too much to comprehend. It began in 1985 when Mikhail Gorbachev acceded to power as Soviet general secretary. To the utter astonishment of the West, he became "the most revolutionary figure in world politics in at least four decades," as one historian put it. Gorbachev not only launched glasnost, which ended many of the Soviet Union's most repressive practices, but started per-estroika, or the restructuring of the Soviet Union, in order to end decades of economic stagnation and backwardness under communism. Gorbachev sought to remake the Soviet economy by introducing such elements of capitalism as the profit motive and private ownership of property. Gorbachev's policies set the Soviet Union down the road toward a market economy; severely weakened the Soviet Communist party, which lost it monopoly of political power in 1990; brought about détente with the West and the pioneering Intermediate Nuclear Forces Treaty (INF) with the United States, which led the two countries to jettison their intermediate-range missiles.

In 1989, meanwhile, world communism itself appeared to collapse. Our television sets brought us the stunning spectacle of Eastern Europeans, subjected to decades of violent repression, demonstrating in the street in favor of individual freedom and democratic government. Every nation in the Eastern bloc — East Germany, Bulgaria, Romania, Hungary, Czechoslovakia, and Poland — overthrew its Communist regime or made that regime reform itself into a non-Communist government. Most dramatic of all was the dismantling of the Berlin Wall, long the preeminent symbol of Cold War between East and West, and the reunification of Germany itself. At long last, the troubled legacy of the Second World War appeared to be over, leaving our planet a safer place. For those of us who lived through

World War II and the entire length of the Cold War, the events of the late 1980s and early 1990s defied belief. Few thought we would ever live to see the downfall of the Soviet Communist state and the end of the Cold War at the same time.

But, as Peter Schweizer says, "a great geopolitical riddle remains." Did United States policy makers have anything to do with all this? Some analysts think not, contending that the Soviet Union fell apart because of "internal contradictions or pressures." But other analysts give a great deal of credit to Reagan himself. This former governor of California, one-time movie actor, and New Deal Democrat turned conservative Republican was an eloquent and dedicated foe of communism and made international headlines when he call the Soviet Union "the Evil Empire." Pro-Reagan critics argue that during his eight years as president (1981–1989), he made the Soviets spend so much on defense that their "Evil Empire" collapsed. He did this, as Professor Garry Wills has pointed out, by spending so much on America's military that the national debt more than doubled, to $2.3 trillion, the deficit almost tripled, and the trade deficit more than quadrupled. In addition to beefing up conventional weapons, Reagan embarked on the futuristic and inordinately expensive Strategic Defense Initiative (SDI), nicknamed Star Wars after George Lucas's phenomenally successful science-fiction movie. The Reagan people claimed that SDI, "through the use of lasers and satellites, would provide an impenetrable shield against incoming missiles and thus make nuclear war obsolete." The SDI program provoked something close to hysteria among Soviet leaders because the U.S.S.R. lacked the financial resources and the technical expertise to keep up with the United States in an escalation of the arms race into space. Perhaps this was a major reason why Gorbachev sought détente with the West, agreed to the Intermediate Nuclear Forces Treaty, and set about restructuring the Soviet system.

In the following selection, Peter Schweizer, the author of Victory (1994), argues that the Reagan administration did indeed trigger the fall of the U.S.S.R. Schweizer quotes a former Soviet official who freely admits that "programs such as the Strategic Defense Initiative accelerated the decline of the Soviet Union." In point of fact, says Schweizer, new evidence shows that as early as 1982 Reagan and a few close advisers began devising "a strategic offensive designed to attack the fundamental weaknesses of the Soviet system" and that it was remarkably successful. Reagan's huge defense buildup was part of the plan, for it capitalized on Soviet shortcomings in high technology. The Reagan administration also set out to roll back Soviet power in Eastern Europe by encouraging underground efforts to overthrow Communist rule there and by imposing economic sanctions on the U.S.S.R. itself. In these and other ways, Schweizer believes, the Reagan administration contributed to the fall of the Soviet Union, "the world's last great empire." Best-selling novelist Tom Clancy agrees. He dedicated his novel, Executive Orders (1996), "To Ronald Wilson Reagan, fortieth president of the United States: The man who won the war."

As you read Schweizer's essay, ask yourself if you buy his argument—if you think it is supported by persuasive evidence. If you disagree with Schweizer, who or what do you think brought down the Soviet Union and terminated the Cold War?

GLOSSARY

BESSMERTNYKH, ALEKSANDR Soviet foreign minister under Gorbachev; Bessmertnykh believes that United States military programs like the Strategic Defense Initiative (SDI) accelerated the fall of the U.S.S.R.

BUSH, GEORGE Reagan's vice president (1981–1989).

CASEY, BILL Head of the Central Intelligence Agency under Reagan; Casey was involved in many covert operations against the Soviet Union, such as funneling funds to Solidarity in Poland and stirring up resistance to the Soviets in Afghanistan.

CLARK, WILLIAM (BILL) Reagan's secretary of the interior (1983–1985).

DEFICIT The discrepancy between tax revenue and spending.

KING FAHD Saudi Arabia's ruler in the 1980s and 1990s who, thanks to Reagan's initiatives, became closely allied with the United States.

HAIG, ALEXANDER United States Army general and Reagan's first secretary of state (1981–1982).

MEESE, EDWARD Attorney general during Reagan's second term (1985–1989).

MUJAHEDIN In 1979, the Soviet Union invaded Afghanistan and established a pro-Soviet regime there with 100,000 Soviet troops supporting it. The *mujahedin* were Afghan resistance fighters who in 1985, with the help of the CIA, struck back at the Soviets and their puppet regime, finally forcing the Soviet government to withdraw its forces.

NATIONAL SECURITY COUNCIL (NSC) This comprised key members of an American president's staff and cabinet and the military joint chiefs of staff; the council usually met to discuss options in foreign policy.

NSDD-75 National Security Decision Directive No. 75. Issued by Reagan in 1983, it initiated a policy of rolling back, instead of containing, Soviet power in Eastern Europe.

OPEC Organization of Petroleum Exporting Countries; founded in 1960, it controlled the production and therefore the price of crude oil on the world market.

PIPES, RICHARD Harvard professor who served as a Reagan advisor and wrote early drafts of NSDD-75.

PSYOP Acronym for psychological operations, such as radio broadcasts to and the distribution of subversive literature in Soviet-controlled territory, in an effort to encourage pro-American revolution there.

SHAH OF IRAN Dynastic ruler of Iran whose full name was Mohammed Reza Shah Pahlev and who came to power in 1941 when his father abdicated in favor of him. The United States supported the shah's regime, but its increasingly repressive ways provoked such popular opposition that in 1979 the shah had to flee the country. The exiled Ayatolah Khomeini then returned to Iran and set up an Islamic republic.

SOLIDARITY Popular protest movement in Poland against Soviet domination and oppression.

STRATEGIC DEFENSE INITIATIVE (SDI, ALSO KNOWN AS STAR WARS) Reagan's program of lasers and satellites in space that, in theory, would provide the United States with a protective shield against nuclear missiles and "thus make nuclear war obsolete."

US-CENTCOM   United States Central Command, established in Saudi Arabia in the early 1980s. In 1991, US-CENTCOM set up Operation Desert Shield, which protected Saudi Arabia from an Iraqi invasion.

WEINBERGER, CASPAR   Reagan's secretary of defense (1981–1989).

Nine years have now passed since the Berlin Wall was breached, the first material sign of the Soviet empire's decline and fall. As the annals of current history continue to be written, a great geopolitical riddle remains: Did the Reagan Administration somehow trigger the collapse of the Evil Empire?

Shortly after the demise of the Soviet Union, Strobe Talbott, on the talk show *Inside Washington*, said: "The difference from the Kremlin standpoint . . . between a conservative Republican Administration and a liberal Democratic Administration was not that great. The Soviet Union collapsed, the Cold War ended almost overwhelmingly because of internal contradictions or pressures . . . And even if Jimmy Carter had been reelected and been followed by Walter Mondale, something like what we have now seen probably would have happened."

But a number of former Soviet officials don't see it that way. "American policy in the 1980s was a catalyst for the collapse of the Soviet Union," is the blunt assessment of former KGB General Oleg Kalugin. He adds, "Reagan and his views disturbed the Soviet government so much they bordered on hysteria. There were cables about an imminent crisis. He was seen as a very serious threat."

Yevgeny Novikov, who served on the senior staff of the Communist Party Central Committee, recalls, "There was a widespread concern and actual fear of Reagan on the Central Committee. He was the last thing they wanted to see in Washington."

Former Foreign Minister Aleksandr Bessmertnykh has said publicly that programs such as the Strategic Defense Initiative accelerated the decline of the Soviet Union.

Now there is new evidence that the Reagan Administration was far more active than had previously

President Reagan addressing the nation from the Oval Office in March 1983. He announced a profound shift in America's defensive strategy: the United States, he said, would develop a protective shield in space, consisting of lasers and satellites designed to interdict Soviet missiles and "make nuclear war obsolete." (UPI/ Corbis-Bettmann)

been believed. A paper trail of top-secret presidential directives indicates that in early 1982, President Reagan and a few key advisors began mapping out a strategic offensive designed to attack the fundamental weaknesses of the Soviet system.

Two canons of Reagan thinking drove the strategy. The first was the President's well-known anti-Communism, expressed in moral terms of good and evil. He did not believe that Communist regimes were "just another form of government," as George Kennan had once put it, but a monstrous aberration. When the words "evil empire" rolled from his lips,

Reagan meant it. But the other important ingredient in his thinking (often overlooked) was his belief in the profound weakness of the Soviet Union. Some of his public pronouncements seem rather prophetic in retrospect. "The years ahead will be great ones for our country, for the cause of freedom and the spread of civilization," he told students at Notre Dame in May 1981. "The West will not contain Communism, it will transcend Communism. We will not bother to denounce it, we'll dismiss it as a sad, bizarre chapter in human history whose last pages are even now being written." In June 1982 he told the

British Parliament: "In an ironic sense, Karl Marx was right. We are witnessing today a great revolutionary crisis — a crisis where the demands of the economic order are colliding directly with those of the political order. But the crisis is happening not in the free, non-Marxist West, but in the home of Marxism–Leninism, the Soviet Union." He said that Marxism–Leninism would be left on the "ash heap of history," and predicted that Eastern Europe and the Soviet Union itself would experience "repeated explosions against repression."

Reagan's view was not even within shouting distance of conventional wisdom. Distinguished Sovietologist Seweryn Bialer of Columbia University opined in *Foreign Affairs* (1982): "The Soviet Union is not now nor will it be during the next decade in the throes of a true systemic crisis, for it boasts enormous unused reserves of political and social stability . . ."

Nobel Laureate Paul Samuelson declared in his textbook *Economics* (1981): "It is a vulgar mistake to think that most people in Eastern Europe are miserable."

Historian Arthur Schlesinger Jr. declared after a 1982 visit to Moscow: "Those in the U.S. who think the Soviet Union is on the verge of collapse" are "only kidding themselves." "Wishful thinkers," he wrote, "always see other societies as more fragile than they are. Each superpower has economic troubles; neither is on the ropes."

In 1981 Strobe Talbott wrote: "Though some second-echelon hardliners in the Reagan Administration . . . espouse the early Fifties goal of rolling back Soviet domination of Eastern Europe, the U.S. simply does not have the military or political power to do that."

The direction of Reagan's Soviet strategy is most evident in National Security Decision Directive 75, signed by the President in early 1983. (An NSDD is a written order from the President directing his senior advisors on major foreign-policy matters.) The document was a break with the policy of containment, which had guided every previous postwar Administration. NSDD-75 declared instead a policy of rolling back Soviet power.

NSDD-75 changed the terms of the superpower relationship. According to Professor Richard Pipes of Harvard, who drafted early versions of the document while at the National Security Council (NSC): "It was the first document which said what mattered was not only Soviet behavior but the nature of the Soviet system. NSDD-75 said our goal was no longer to co-exist with the Soviet Union but to change the Soviet system. At its root was the belief that we had it in our power to alter the Soviet system."

☆

THE BIRTH OF ROLLBACK

The Reagan strategy of attacking Soviet vulnerabilities first emerged in early 1982, shortly after the hammer of martial law descended on Poland. Pipes recalls: "The President was absolutely livid. He said, 'Something must be done. We need to hit them hard.'"

In January 1982, he spoke with his closest advisors, in a meeting where much of the National Security Council was not included. "NSC meetings were not considered leak-proof; he didn't want to risk anything," recalls Pipes. Also present were George Bush, Alexander Haig, Caspar Weinberger, Bill Clark, Ed Meese, and Bill Casey. There was a general consensus that the U.S. had to send a strong message to Warsaw and Moscow. Economic sanctions were universally supported. But then someone raised the stakes: What about covertly funding Solidarity to ensure that the only above-ground anti-Communist organization in the Soviet bloc would survive the cold winter of martial law?

The specter of a risky covert operation haunted the room. After a few moments, Haig cut through the silence, calling the notion "crazy." Bush agreed, arguing that if the operation were discovered, it would only inflame Moscow. Pipes, Weinberger,

Casey, and Clark, however, voiced enthusiastic support for such an operation. But the President "didn't need any encouragement," according to Pipes. He immediately ordered Bill Casey to draw up a plan. Over the next several months Casey arranged for the CIA to provide advanced communication equipment and material assistance to the tune of approximately $8 million per year.

Next, the President asked Clark, his new National Security Advisor, to draw up a document redefining American goals in Eastern Europe. The directive that emerged was radical: the stated goal of U.S. policy would be to "neutralize efforts of the USSR" to maintain its hold on Eastern Europe. Reagan signed the directive in the spring of 1982. "In NSDD-32," recalls Bill Clark, "Ronald Reagan made clear that the United States was not resigned to the status quo of Soviet domination of Eastern Europe. We attempted to forge a multi-pronged strategy to weaken Soviet influence and strengthen indigenous forces for freedom in the region. Poland offered a unique opportunity relative to other states like Bulgaria, Rumania, and Czechoslovakia. This is not to say that we did not pursue activities — both overt and covert — in these other countries to loosen Moscow's grip." The activities included covert support for underground movements attempting to throw off Communist rule, and intensifying psychological operations (PSYOP), particularly broadcasts by Voice of America and Radio Free Europe.

In tandem with the geopolitical counteroffensive in Eastern Europe, the Administration fired the first volleys of what would become a secret economic war against the Kremlin. Using Poland as a justification, the Administration in 1982 imposed sanctions on Moscow, intended to cut off most of the technologies needed for a massive new natural-gas pipeline from Siberia, and for an energy program on the Sakhalin Islands being co-developed with Japan. The sanctions went to the heart of Soviet income: energy exports, which accounted for 80 percent of Soviet hard-currency earnings. U.S. sanctions, which Western Europe resisted, did not stop construction of the pipeline, but delayed it two years, and cut it back in size. The Kremlin was out $15 to $20 billion.

Meanwhile, the Administration realized that if international oil prices could be brought down, the U.S. economy, the world's largest importer of crude, would be the beneficiary, while the Kremlin, as a large exporter, could only be hurt.

The easiest means of bringing down prices was by raising world production, and the key to that was Saudi Arabia, the "swing producer" for the OPEC cartel. The Saudis had historically changed their production rates to ensure stable and high oil prices; they could just as easily change them to cause prices to drop.

☆

THE SAUDI OPERATION

To make the Saudis hospitable to Western interests, the Reagan Administration provided unprecedented security commitments to the Saudi royal family. There were of course arms sales (the AWACS deal in 1981 and the 1984 sale of Stinger missiles) in which the President used extraordinary powers to sidestep Congress. But the U.S. commitment went even deeper. Bill Casey's CIA helped modernize Saudi internal security to help protect the regime from its domestic opponents. And the U.S. flexed its military muscle by establishing in 1983 a U.S. Central Command (US-CENTCOM) for the Persian Gulf region, boasting an ability to mobilize 300,000 U.S. troops. In 1985 the U.S. began construction on "Peace Shield," a high-tech system manned by U.S. personnel to coordinate the defense of Saudi Arabia in case of attack. In addition, President Reagan himself expressed publicly (in 1981) and privately to King Fahd (in early 1985) his guarantee that so long as he was Commander-in-Chief, the royal family would not meet the same fate as the Shah of Iran.

Saudi Arabia, surrounded by multiple threats — South Yemen, Syria, the raging Iran-Iraq war — was clearly pleased, and the Administration hoped that this would lead to a change in Saudi oil-pricing policies. However, senior Administration officials insist that there was never any *quid pro quo* presented to the Saudis.

In the late summer of 1985, senior Saudi officials alerted the Administration that prices would soon drop. The Saudi decision to alert Washington to its production plans stands in stark contrast with the swings in Saudi policy that took America by surprise during the 1970s.

As production rose, prices plunged from $30 a barrel in November 1985 to $12 a barrel five months later. And it cost the Kremlin dearly. "The drop in oil prices was devastating, just devastating," says Yevgeny Novikov. "Tens of billions were wiped away." A secret May 1986 CIA report noted that for every dollar-per-barrel drop in the price of oil, the Kremlin would lose a half-billion to a billion dollars per year. The report concluded that the price drop "will substantially reduce the Soviets' ability to import Western equipment, agricultural goods, and industrial materials . . . [This] . . . comes at a time when Gorbachev probably is counting on increased inputs from the West to assist his program of economic revitalization."

Dozens of large projects were brought to an end for lack of funds. By July 1986 it took almost five times as much Soviet oil to purchase a given piece of West German machinery as it had taken a year earlier. Arms exports (the number-two Soviet export behind energy) also plunged, because most sales were to Middle Eastern countries no longer flush with petrodollars.

As the Soviets faced this catastrophic drop in their income, they also faced the prospect of spending more of their dwindling resources on an arms race. U.S. defense procurement budgets rose by 25 per-

cent in each of the early Reagan years. By the mid 1980s, U.S. military expenditures were exceeding those of the Soviet Union for the first time since the late 1960s.

More than anything else, the defense build-up — from SDI to conventional weapons — was predicated on high technology, a profound Soviet weakness. Computers and other advanced technologies were threatening to make old weapon systems obsolete — much as the tank had done to horse cavalry. As Marshal Nikolai Ogarkov put it: "The rapid development of science and technology in recent years creates real preconditions for the emergence . . . of even more destructive and previously unknown types of weapons based on new physical principles. Work on these new types of weapons is already in progress . . . most importantly the United States. Their development is a reality of the very near future, and it would be a serious mistake not to take account of this right now."

Gorbachev himself shared this view, noting: "The competition that has grown more acute under the impact of scientific and technological progress is affecting those who have dropped behind ever more mercilessly."

☆

IT IS NO ACCIDENT . . .

Documents reveal that the effect of the Reagan defense build-up on the Soviet economy was quite deliberate. A top-secret five-year planning directive for the Department of Defense, signed by Caspar Weinberger in early 1982, mentions the build-up could serve as a form of "economic and technical war" against Moscow. The Pentagon would push for "investment in weapon systems that render the accumulative Soviet equipment obsolete." SDI was part of this strategy. Yes, the President wanted a strategic defense system. But according to one NSDD from 1983, a measure of success for the program was the economic costs it would impose on Moscow.

And it worked. By 1984, General Secretary Konstantin Chernenko declared that "the complex international situation has forced us to divert a great deal of resources to strengthening the security of our country."

In 1985 General Secretary Gorbachev pushed for an 8 percent per year jump in defense spending. "The U.S. wants to exhaust the Soviet Union economically through a race in the most up-to-date and expensive weapons," he ominously warned.

By 1985, with a covert line of support running to Poland, a massive U.S. defense build-up, and the Kremlin facing a myriad of economic problems, the Reagan Administration dramatically expanded its commitment to rolling back Soviet power in Afghanistan. The program to aid the *mujahedin* began under Carter. When he first authorized covert support for the resistance in 1980, a top-secret finding declared that the U.S. goal was to "harass" Soviet forces.

By 1985, the Reagan Administration was far more ambitious. The President asked National Security Advisor Robert McFarlane to redefine and sharpen U.S. objectives in the region. The result was NSDD-166, signed by the President in March. The directive had several key elements, including a commitment to supply the resistance with more advanced weapons and better intelligence pulled from spy satellites. But most importantly, the long annex to NSDD-166 made the clear-cut goal in Afghanistan absolute victory. And an important ingredient in accomplishing that goal was a secret initiative to take the war into the Soviet Union itself.

Back in 1983, Bill Casey and Bill Clark had sat in the Oval Office mulling over the situation in Afghanistan. As Clark recalls, "The President and Bill Casey were determined that Moscow pay an ever greater price for its brutal campaign in Afghanistan." Bill Casey suggested a bold move: What about widening the war to include military operations on Soviet soil? The President liked the idea.

Casey, as Director of Central Intelligence, took the proposal to the Pakistanis in 1984, during one of his periodic secret trips to Islamabad. Fred Iklé, the undersecretary of defense at the time, recalls that Casey "simply told Zia [the Pakistani president] and Yaqub Khan [the foreign minister], 'This is something that should be done.'" Zia embraced the proposal and told Casey to raise it with General Abdul Akhtar and Brigadier Mohammad Yousaf of Pakistani intelligence (ISI), who were managing the war along the Afghan frontier.

In their regular meetings, Casey, Akhtar, and Yousaf covered a number of issues related to running a war. But this time, after dealing with the usual matters, Casey stood up and went to the wall map. The Soviet Union is vulnerable to ethnic tensions, he told his hosts. Soviet Central Asia is the soft underbelly of the Soviet Union. We should smuggle literature to stir up dissent. Then we should ship arms, to encourage local uprisings.

Casey was the first one to have openly pointed out this vulnerability, Yousaf recalls, "I can vividly remember that he used the phrase 'soft underbelly.'"

Taking the Administration's suggestion, the ISI began a program to subvert and launch strikes into Soviet Central Asia. In 1985, the resistance began by spreading subversive literature provided by the CIA. By early 1986, strikes were launched from Afghanistan's Jozjan and Badakshan provinces. The CIA outfitted these units with Chinese rocket launchers and special explosives, as well as rubber zodiac boats to cross the Amu River by night. Chinese 107mm rocket launchers with ranges of almost ten miles would be deployed at night along the south bank of the Amu River and fire a rain of explosives onto Soviet soil. Teams of specially trained *mujahedin* would make their way across the river to hit border posts, lay mines, and knock down power lines. An airfield north of the Soviet town of Pyandch was repeatedly hit by commandos. Once the *mujahedin* were on Soviet territory, locals would occasionally meet them and join in on operations. Only months after the attacks began, the Soviet

Politburo held the meeting in which it was decided to withdraw Soviet forces.

The Soviet edifice was brought down by a tempest whose causes we will never completely understand. But what is beginning to come into focus is the extent to which the Reagan Administration contributed to the decline of the world's last great empire.

Assume for a moment that the Administration's initiatives had not been taken — that Solidarity was strangled in its crib for lack of external support; that the *mujahedin* were given only enough weapons to lose more slowly; that the Kremlin was able to reap badly needed funds from world energy markets, and was relieved of its military burdens.

Events in history are rarely inevitable; they are created by human beings. Absent the aggressive policies of the Reagan Administration, a weakened Soviet Union might still be lumbering on the world stage.

QUESTIONS TO CONSIDER

1   What was NSDD-75? Why was it a landmark directive from an American president? how did it alter United States policy toward the Soviet Union?

2   Describe United States intervention in Poland and Afghanistan in the 1980s. How were the situations in the two countries similar? How were they different? Compare Soviet involvement in Afghanistan with American involvement in Vietnam. Do you think it is accurate to say that Afghanistan was the Soviets' Vietnam.

3   What, in your view, best accounts for the decline and fall of the Soviet Union and the end of the Cold War? Was it Reagan's "strategic offensive designed to attack the fundamental weaknesses of the Soviet system," as discussed in Schweizer's article? Or was it the internal problems and pressures within the U.S.S.R. and the bold reforms and initiatives of Soviet General Secretary Gorbachev discussed in the introduction?

4   Is the downfall of the Soviet Union and the end of the Cold War an appropriate reason to fasten the United States with a crippling deficit and national debt, as Reagan did? Has Reagan's costly victory in the Cold War created a domestic dilemma in the United States? If so, what areas of American life are endangered by the monstrous federal debt?

31

Some Lessons from the Cold War

Arthur M. Schlesinger Jr.

It is too soon to know what the demise of the Soviet Union and the end of the Cold War means for the future of humankind. But it is not too soon to reflect on some lessons of the Cold War, which on at least one occasion — the Cuban missile crisis of October 1962 — almost exploded into a nuclear holocaust and the end of the world as we know it. How did humankind survive the Cold War? What caused and sustained it? The experts do not agree. Some see the Cold War as fundamentally an ideological struggle between the forces of freedom and the forces of autocracy. Still others view the Cold War as a geopolitical and military contest that involved not just a Soviet–United States confrontation but a Western Europe–Soviet confrontation as well. While some specialists maintain that the Cold War strengthened hard-liners in the Soviet Union and sustained Communist rule there, others, such as Ronald Steel, believe that American policymakers exaggerated the military capacity of the Soviet Union throughout the Cold War, thus creating a bogus enemy that justified huge American defense build-ups.

In the selection that follows, Arthur M. Schlesinger Jr., one of our greatest historians, argues that it is irrelevant to allocate blame for the Cold War. It emerged, he says, from the efforts of the United States and the Soviet Union to fill the "power vacuum" left by World War II, and it developed into "a holy war" because of very real ideological differences between the two new superpowers and their allies. At bottom, Schlesinger believes, the Cold War was a "fundamental debate" between communism and liberalism, including democratic socialism, and that debate charged the Cold War with its religious intensity.

Now that the holy war is over, Schlesinger suggests six fallacies that helped make it so long, so dark, and so dangerous. These fallacies, Schlesinger suggests, resulted from the perception of events by both sides. Yes, the perception of reality is the crucial element in understanding the past. How people perceive events and the motives of an alleged enemy determine how they act, and how they act in turn affects the course of subsequent events. When it comes to the Cold War, human error, exaggeration, misunderstanding, over-interpretation — all played a key role in shaping and sustaining tensions between East and West. Schlesinger hopes that his six fallacies, or errors of perception, judgment, and action, will benefit future policymakers, so that the world can avoid another Cold War, another "intimate brush with collective suicide." In the end, he argues, "Democracy won the political argument between East and West" and "the market won the economic argument." Yet in retrospect, Schlesinger says, the Cold War can only remind us "of the ultimate interdependence of nations and of peoples."

GLOSSARY

QUISLING   Someone who betrays his country by helping enemy invaders and going on to serve in a puppet government; named after pro-Nazi Norwegian Vidkun Quisling (1887–1945).

STALIN, JOSEPH   Soviet dictator from the 1920s until his death in 1953, he ruled the Soviet Union with a brutal hand, resorting to massive purges in the 1930s and again in the post–World War II years; he viewed the West as a devious menace (several times in its history Russia had been invaded by Western European powers) and clamped an iron hand on Eastern Europe, using it as a bulwark against Western "aggression."

WALLACE, HENRY A.   FDR's vice president, 1941–1945, and Truman's secretary of commerce, 1945–1946; Wallace was forced to resign as commerce secretary after he publicly attacked Truman's "get tough" policy toward the Soviets; in 1948, Wallace made an unsuccessful bid for the presidency as the candidate of the Progressive party.

ZERO-SUM GAME   Cold War notion that "a gain for one side was by definition a defeat for the other."

In those faraway days when the Cold War was young, the English historian Sir Herbert Butterfield lectured at Notre Dame on "The Tragic Element in Modern International Conflict." Historians writing about modern wars, Butterfield said, characteristically start off with a "heroic" vision of things. They portray good men struggling against bad, virtue resisting evil. In this embattled mood, they see only the sins of the enemy and ignore the underlying structural dilemmas that so often provoke international clashes.

As time passes and emotions subside, history enters the "academic" phase. Now historians see "a terrible human predicament" at the heart of the story, "a certain situation that contains the element of conflict irrespective of any special wickedness in any of the parties concerned." Wickedness may deepen the predicament, but conflict would be there anyway. Perspective, Butterfield proposed, teaches us "to be a little more sorry for both parties than

From Arthur M. Schlesinger Jr., "Some Lessons from the Cold War," in Michael J. Hogan (ed.), *The End of the Cold War: Its Meaning and Implications* (Cambridge: Cambridge University Press, 1992), 53–62. Copyright © 1992 by Arthur M. Schlesinger Jr. Reprinted with permission of Cambridge University Press.

they knew how to be for one another." History moves on from melodrama to tragedy.

Butterfield made a pretty good forecast of the way Cold War historiography has evolved in the more than forty years since he spoke. In the United States the "heroic" phase took two forms: the orthodox in the 1940s and 1950s, with the Russians cast as the villains, and the revisionist in the 1960s, with the Americans as the villains. By the 1980s, American Cold War historians discerned what one of the best of them, John Lewis Gaddis, called an "emerging post-revisionist synthesis." History began to pass from a weapon in the battle into a more analytical effort to define structural dilemmas and to understand adversary concerns. *Glasnost* permitted comparable historiographical evolution in the former Soviet Union.

Quite right: The more one contemplates the Cold War, the more irrelevant the allocation of blame seems. The Second World War left the international order in acute derangement. With the Axis states vanquished, the Western European allies spent, the colonial empires in tumult and dissolution, great gaping holes appeared in the structure of world power. Only two nations — the United States and the Soviet Union — had the military strength, the ideological conviction, and the political will to fill these vacuums.

But why did this old-fashioned geopolitical rivalry billow up into a holy war so intense and obsessive as to threaten the very existence of human life on the planet? The two nations were constructed on opposite and profoundly antagonistic principles. They were divided by the most significant and fundamental disagreements over human rights, individual liberties, cultural freedom, the role of civil society, the direction of history, and the destiny of man. Each state saw the other as irrevocably hostile to its own essence. Given the ideological conflict on top of the geopolitical confrontation, no one should be surprised at what ensued. Conspiratorial explanations are hardly required. The real surprise would have been if there had been no Cold War.

And why has humanity survived the Cold War?

In late 1988, Gorbachev announced that he would reduce Soviet military presence in the Eastern bloc nations. Five months later, the first of the military units scheduled for withdrawal — thirty-one Soviet T.64 tanks — pulled out of Hungary and returned to the U.S.S.R. (Jean Gaumy/Magnum)

The reason that the Cold War never exploded into hot war was surely (and by providential irony) the invention of nuclear weapons. One is inclined to support the suggestion (Elspeth Rostow's, I think) that the Nobel Peace Prize should have gone to the atomic bomb.

At last this curious episode in modern history is over, and we must ask what lessons we may hope to learn from a long, costly, dark, dreary, and dangerous affair; what precautions humanity should take to prevent comparable episodes in the future. I would suggest half a dozen fallacies that the world might well forego in years to come.

The first might be called the fallacy of overinterpreting the enemy. In the glory days of the Cold War, each side attributed to the other a master plan for world domination joined with diabolical efficiency in executing the plan. Such melodramatic imagining of brilliant and demonic enemies was truer to, say, Sax Rohmer, the creator of Dr. Fu Manchu, than to shuffling historical reality.

No doubt Soviet leaders believed that the dialectic of history would one day bring about the victory of communism. No doubt Western leaders believed that the nature of man and markets would one day bring about the victory of free society. But such generalized hopes were far removed from operational master plans.

"The superpowers," as Henry Kissinger well put it,

often behave like two heavily armed blind men feeling their way around a room, each believing himself in mortal peril from the other whom he assumes to have perfect vision. Each side should know that frequently uncertainty, compromise, and incoherence are the essence of policy-making. Yet each tends to ascribe to the other a consistency, foresight, and coherence that its own experience belies. Of course, over time, even two blind men can do enormous damage to each other, not to speak of the room.

The room has happily survived. But the blind men meanwhile escalated the geopolitical/ideological confrontation into a compulsively interlocked heightening of tension, spurred on by authentic differences in principle, by real and supposed clashes of interest, and by a wide range of misperception, misunderstanding, and demagoguery. Each superpower undertook for what it honestly saw as defensive reasons actions that the other honestly saw as unacceptably threatening and requiring stern countermeasures. Each persevered in corroborating the fears of the other. Each succumbed to the propensity to perceive local conflicts in

global terms, political conflicts in moral terms, and relative differences in absolute terms. Together, in lockstep, they expanded the Cold War.

In overinterpreting the motives and actions of the other, each side forgot Emerson's invaluable precept: "In analysing history, do not be too profound, for often the causes are quite simple." Both superpowers should have known from their own experience that governments mostly live from day to day responding to events as they come, that decisions are more often the result of improvisation, ignorance, accident, fatigue, chance, blunder, and sometimes plain stupidity than of orchestrated master plans. One lesson to be drawn from the Cold War is that more things in life are to be explained by cock-up, to use the British term, than by conspiracy.

An accompanying phenomenon, at first a consequence and later a reinforcing cause of overinterpretation, was the embodiment of the Cold War in government institutions. Thus our second fallacy: The fallacy of overinstitutionalizing the policy. The Soviet Union, a police state committed to dogmas of class war and capitalist conspiracy and denied countervailing checks of free speech and press, had institutionalized the Cold War from the day Lenin arrived at the Finland Station. In later years the Cold War became for Stalin a convenient means of justifying his own arbitrary power and the awful sacrifices he demanded from the Soviet peoples. "Stalin needed the Cold War," observed Earl Browder, whom Stalin purged as chief of the American Communist party, "to keep up the sharp international tensions by which he alone could maintain such a regime in Russia."

In Washington by the 1950s the State Department, the Defense Department, the Central Intelligence Agency, the Federal Bureau of Investigation, and the National Security Council developed vested bureaucratic interests in the theory of a militarily expansionist Soviet Union. The Cold War conferred power, money, prestige, and public influence on these agencies and on the people who ran them. By the natural law of bureaucracies, their stake in the conflict steadily grew. Outside of government, arms manufacturers, politicians, professors, publicists, pontificators, and demagogues invested careers and fortunes in the Cold War.

In time, the adversary Cold War agencies evolved a sort of tacit collusion across the Iron Curtain. Probably the greatest racket in the Cold War was the charade periodically enacted by generals and admirals announcing the superiority of the other side in order to get bigger budgets for themselves. As President John F. Kennedy remarked to Norman Cousins, the editor of the *Saturday Review,* in the spring of 1963, "The hard-liners in the Soviet Union and the United States feed on one another."

Institutions, alas, do not fold their tents and silently steal away. Ideas crystallized in bureaucracies resist change. With the Cold War at last at an end, each side faces the problem of deconstructing entrenched Cold War agencies spawned and fortified by nearly half a century of mutually profitable competition. One has only to reflect on the forces behind the anti-Gorbachev conspiracy of August 1991 [which sought in vain to overthrow him].

A third fallacy may be called the fallacy of arrogant prediction. As a devotee of a cyclical approach to American political history, I would not wish to deny that history exhibits uniformities and recurrences. But it is essential to distinguish between those phenomena that are predictable and those that are not. Useful historical generalizations are mostly statements about broad, deep-running, long-term changes: the life-cycle of revolutions, for example, or the impact of industrialization and urbanization, or the influence of climate or sea power or the frontier. The short term, however, contains too many variables, depends too much on accident and fortuity and personality, to permit exact and specific forecasts.

We have been living through extraordinary changes in the former Soviet Union and in Eastern Europe, in South Africa and in the Middle East. What is equally extraordinary is that *no one foresaw these changes*. All the statesmen, all the sages, all the savants, all the professors, all the prophets, all those bearded chaps on "Nightline" — all were caught unaware and taken by surprise; all were befuddled and impotent before the perpetual astonishments of the future. History has an abiding capacity to outwit our certitudes.

Just a few years back some among us were so absolutely sure of the consequences if we did not smash the Reds at once that they called for preventive nuclear war. Had they been able to persuade the U.S. government to drop the bomb on the Soviet Union in the 1950s or on China in the 1960s ... but, thank heaven, they never did; and no one today, including those quondam preventive warriors themselves, regrets the American failure to do so.

The Almighty no doubt does know the future. But He has declined to confide such foresight to frail and erring mortals. In the early years of the Cold War, [theologian] Reinhold Niebuhr warned of "the depth of evil to which individuals and communities may sink ... when they try to play the role of God to history." Let us not fall for people who tell us that we must take drastic action today because of their conjectures as to what some other fellow or nation may do five or ten or twenty years from now.

Playing God to history is the dangerous consequence of our fourth fallacy — the fallacy of national self-righteousness. "No government or social system is so evil," President Kennedy said in his American University speech in 1963, "that its people must be condemned as lacking in virtue," and he called on Americans as well as Russians to reexamine attitudes toward the Cold War, "for our attitude is as essential as theirs." This thought came as rather a shock to those who assumed that the American side was so manifestly right that self-examination was unnecessary.

Kennedy liked to quote a maxim from the British military pundit Liddell Hart: "Never corner an opponent, and always assist him to save his face. Put yourself in his shoes — so as to see things through his eyes. Avoid self-righteousness like the devil — nothing is so self-blinding." Perhaps Kennedy did not always live up to those standards himself, but he did on great occasions, like the Cuban missile crisis, and he retained a capacity for ironical objectivity that is rare among political leaders.

Objectivity — seeing ourselves as others see us — is a valuable adjunct to statesmanship. Can we be so sure that our emotional judgments of the moment represent the last word and the final truth? The angry ideological conflicts that so recently obsessed us may not greatly interest our posterity. Our great-grandchildren may well wonder what in heaven's name those disagreements could have been that drove the Soviet Union and the United States to the brink of blowing up the planet.

Men and women a century from now will very likely find the Cold War as obscure and incomprehensible as we today find the Thirty Years War — the terrible conflict that devastated much of Europe not too long ago. Looking back at the twentieth century, our descendants will very likely be astonished at the disproportion between the causes of the Cold War, which may well seem trivial, and the consequences, which could have meant the veritable end of history.

Russians and Americans alike came to see the Cold War as a duel between two superpowers, a Soviet-American duopoly. But the reduction of the Cold War to a bilateral game played by the Soviet Union and the United States is a fifth fallacy. The nations of Europe were not spectators at someone else's match. They were players too.

Revisionist historians, determined to blame the Cold War on an American drive for world economic hegemony, have studiously ignored the role of Europe. Washington, they contend, was compelled to demand an "open door" for American trade and investment everywhere on the planet because American capitalism had to expand in order to survive. The Soviet Union was the main obstacle to a world market controlled by the United States. So,

by revisionist dogma, American leaders whipped up an unnecessary Cold War in order to save the capitalist system.

No matter that some fervent open door advocates, like Henry A. Wallace, were also fervent opponents of the Cold War. No matter that the republics of the former Soviet Union now want nothing more than American trade and investment and full integration into the world market. And no matter that most Western European nations in the 1940s had Socialist governments and that the democratic socialist leaders — Clement Attlee and Ernest Bevin in Britain, Leon Blum and Paul Ramadier in France, Paul-Henri Spaak in Belgium, Kurt Schumacher, Ernst Reuter, and Willy Brandt in West Germany — had powerful reasons of their own to fear the spread of Stalinist influence and Soviet power.

Such men could not have cared less about an open door for American capitalism. They cared deeply, however, about the future of democratic socialism. When I used to see Aneurin Bevan, the leader of the left wing of the British Labour party, in London in 1944, he doubted that the wartime alliance would last and saw the struggle for postwar Europe as between the democratic socialists and the Communists. "The Communist party," Bevan wrote in 1951, "is the sworn and inveterate enemy of the Socialist and Democratic parties. When it associates with them it does so as a preliminary to destroying them." Many in the Truman administration in the 1940s espoused this view and, dubbing themselves (in private) NCL, favored American support for the non-Communist Left.

The democratic socialists, moreover, were in advance of official Washington in organizing against the Stalinist threat. Despite his above-the-battle stance at Notre Dame, Herbert Butterfield himself wrote in 1969, "A new generation often does not know (and does not credit the fact when informed) that Western Europe once wondered whether the United States could ever be awakened to the danger from Russia." The subsequent opening of British

The Berlin Wall, a symbol of the Cold War for nearly three decades, separated Communist East Berlin from West Berlin. With the easing of Cold War tensions, "the wall" was torn down in 1989 and Germany itself was reunited under Western rule. (Guy Le Querrec/Magnum)

Foreign Office papers voluminously documents Sir Herbert's point.

Far from seeing President Truman in the revisionist mode as an anti-Soviet zealot hustling a reluctant Europe into a gratuitous Cold War, the Foreign Office saw him for a considerable period as an irresolute waffler distracted by the delusion that the United States could play mediator between Britain and the Soviet Union. Ernest Bevin, Britain's Socialist foreign secretary, thought Truman's policy was "to withdraw from Europe and in effect leave the British to get on with the Russians as best they could." A true history of the Cold War must add

European actors to the cast and broaden both research nets and analytical perspectives.

The theory of the Cold War as a Soviet-American duopoly is sometimes defended on the ground that, after all, the United States and the Soviet Union were in full command of their respective alliances. But nationalism, the most potent political emotion of the age, challenged the reign of the superpowers almost from the start: Tito [of Yugoslavia], Mao, and others vs. Moscow; De Gaulle, Eden and others vs. Washington. Experience has adequately demonstrated how limited superpowers are in their ability to order their allies around and even to control client governments wholly dependent on them for economic and military support. Far from clients being the prisoners of the superpower, superpowers often end as prisoners of their clients.

These are lessons Washington has painfully learned (or at least was painfully taught; has the government finally learned them?) in Vietnam, El Salvador, Israel, Saudi Arabia, Kuwait. As for the Soviet Union, its brutal interventions and wretched Quislings in Eastern Europe only produced bitterness and hatred. The impact of clients on principals is another part of the unwritten history of the Cold War. The Cold War was *not* a bilateral game.

Nor was it — our sixth and final fallacy — a zero-sum game. For many years, Cold War theology decreed that a gain for one side was by definition a defeat for the other. This notion led logically not to an interest in negotiation but to a demand for capitulation. In retrospect the Cold War, humanity's most intimate brush with collective suicide, can only remind us of the ultimate interdependence of nations and of peoples.

After President Kennedy and Premier Khrushchev stared down the nuclear abyss together in October 1962, they came away determined to move as fast as they could toward détente. Had Kennedy lived, Khrushchev might have held on to power a little longer, and together they would have further subdued the excesses of the Cold War. They rejected the zero-sum approach and understood that intelligent negotiation brings mutual benefit. I am not an unlimited admirer of Ronald Reagan, but he deserves his share of credit for taking Mikhail Gorbachev seriously, abandoning the zero-sum fallacy he had embraced for so long, and moving the Cold War toward its end.

And why indeed has it ended? If the ideological confrontation gave the geopolitical rivalry its religious intensity, so the collapse of the ideological debate took any apocalyptic point out of the Cold War. The proponents of liberal society were proven right. After seventy years of trial, communism turned out — by the confession of its own leaders — to be an economic, political, and moral disaster. Democracy won the political argument between East and West. The market won the economic argument. Difficulties lie ahead, but the fundamental debate that created the Cold War is finished.

Questions to Consider

1   What are the six fallacies of judgment and action that aggravated the tensions between East and West after World War II, according to Arthur Schlesinger, and why did the two sides fall into them? What are the overarching lessons Schlesinger would like nations and peoples to learn from the mistakes of the Cold War?

2   Schlesinger says that democracy and the market economy won the Cold War, but do we know for certain what the future holds for the former Soviet Union and for Eastern Europe? What do you think are the lasting effects of the Cold War on the United States and how might they affect our future?

3   What have been the general trends in Cold War historiography? How are historians influenced by the traditions from which they come and the times in which they live, and do you think they may in turn influence those times?

4   As you think about Schlesinger's selection and all the readings in this book, what do you think is the relative importance of general social and political factors and the actions of individuals on the course of history? Where have you seen examples of the influence of people's perceptions on subsequent events?

5   Arthur Schlesinger calls himself a "devotee of a cyclical approach to American political history." As you look back over the readings in this book and your general experience in American history, do you see certain recurring themes or trends or concerns in that story? What might these tell you about the basic principles and character of the American experience?